NERV

GOD'S IN HIS HEAVEN. ALL'S RIGHT WITH THE WORLD.

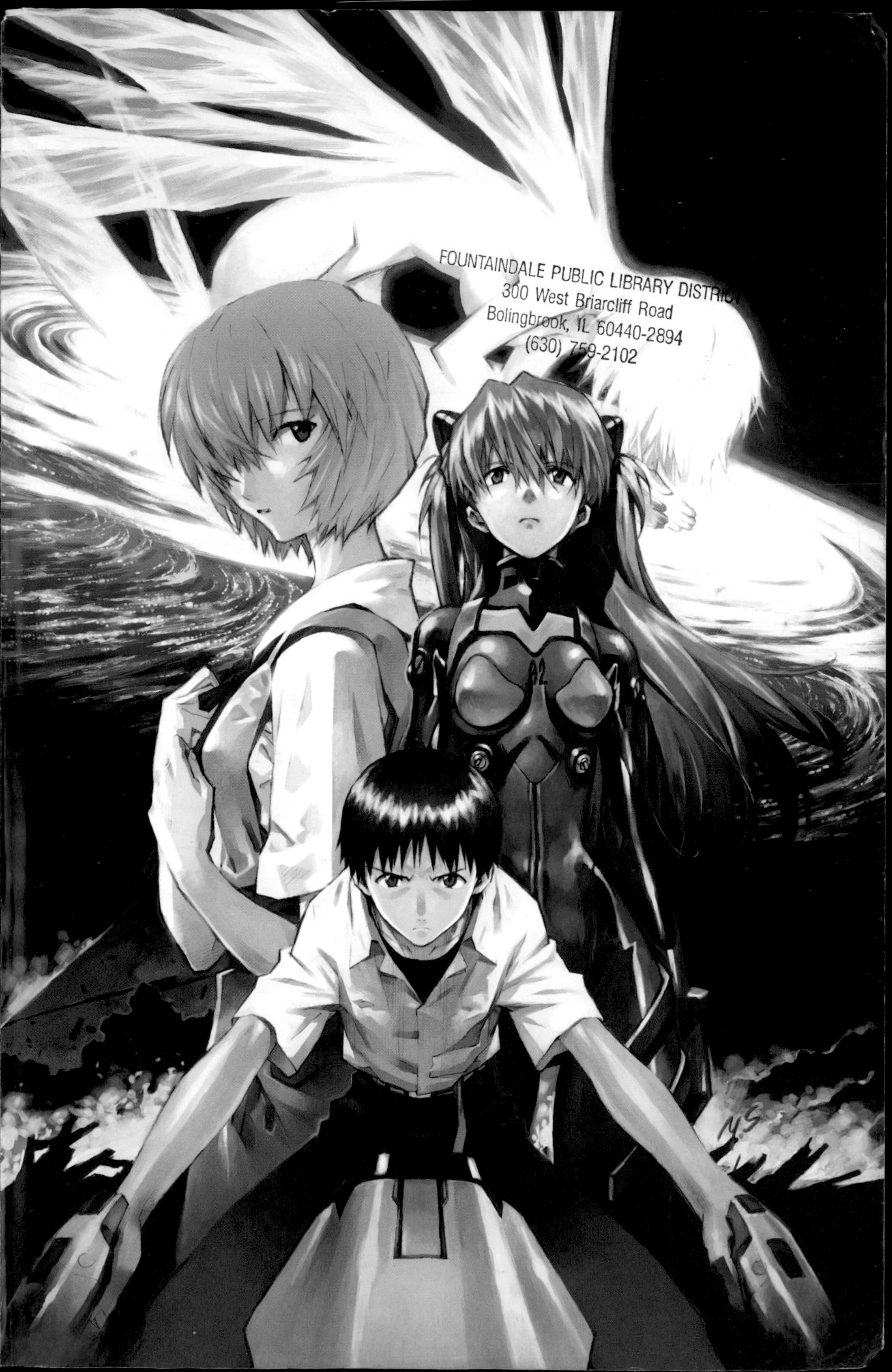

GOD'S IN HIS HEAVEN. ALL'S RIGHT WITH THE WORLD.

NEON GENESIS EVANGELION
2-in-1 Edition • Volume 5

STORY AND ART BY
YOSHIYUKI SADAMOTO

ORIGINAL CONCEPT BY
khara

TRANSLATION & ENGLISH ADAPTION // John Werry, Evan Galloway
TOUCH-UP ART & LETTERING // John Clark
GRAPHIC DESIGN // Fawn Lau
EDITOR // Mike Montesa

NEON GENESIS EVANGELION Volume 13 & 14
© khara
Edited by KADOKAWA SHOTEN
First published in Japan in 2012, 2014 by KADOKAWA CORPORATION, Tokyo.
English translation rights arranged with KADOKAWA CORPORATION, Tokyo.

Printed in China

Published by VIZ Media, LLC
P.O. Box 77010
San Francisco, CA 94107

10 9 8 7 6 5 4 3 2 1
First printing, June 2016

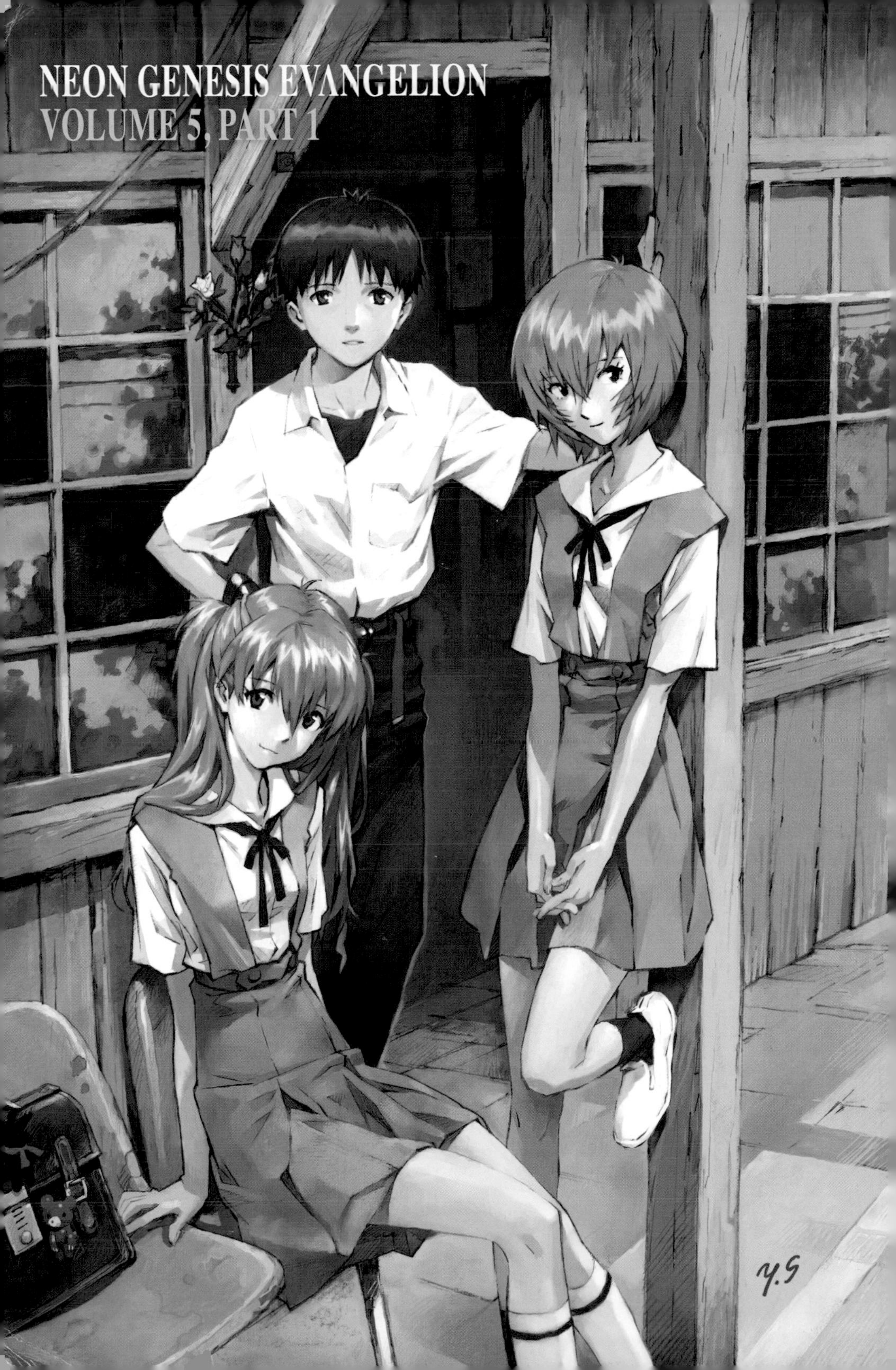
NEON GENESIS EVANGELION
VOLUME 5, PART 1
Y.S

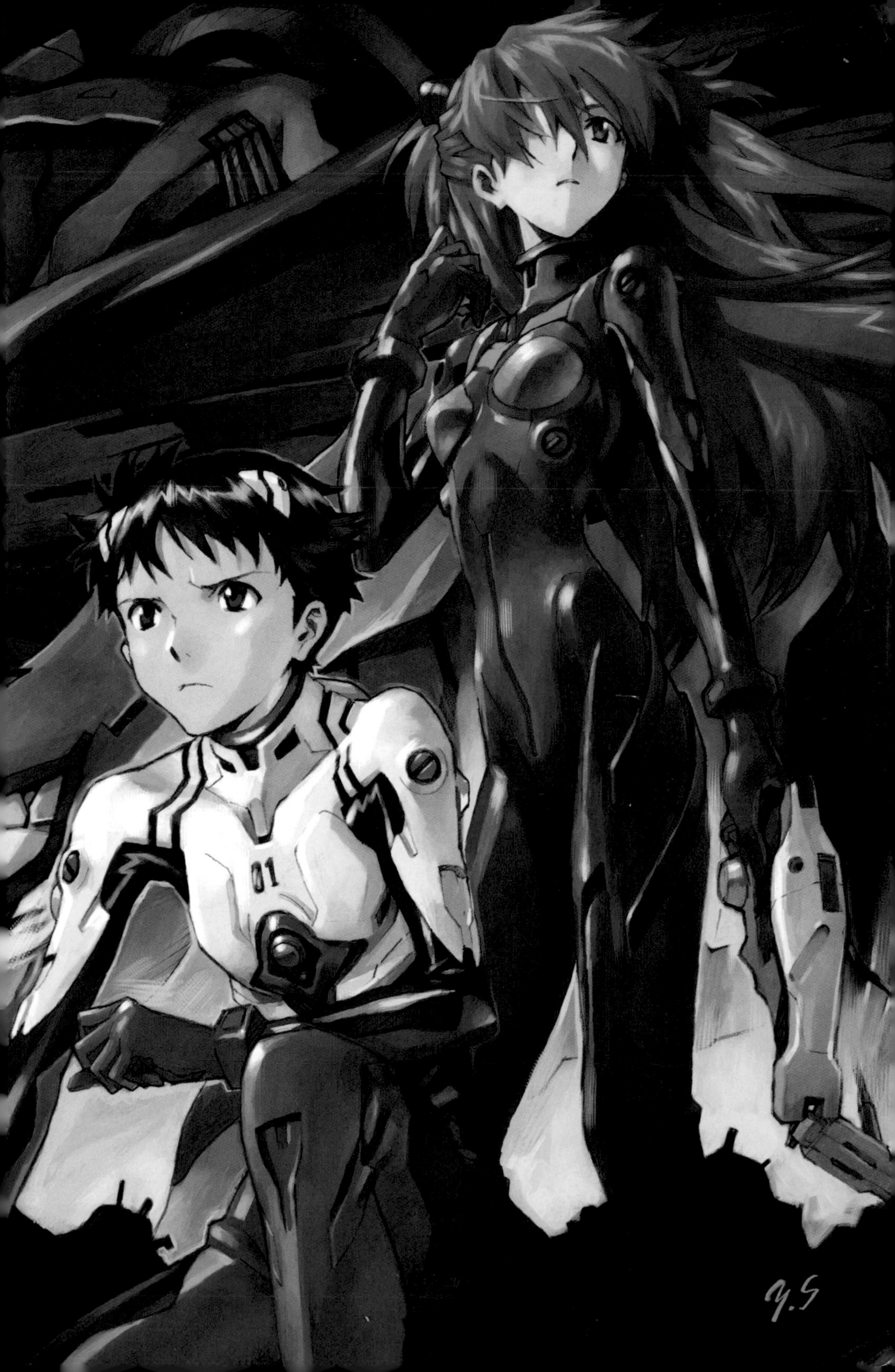
01
Y.S

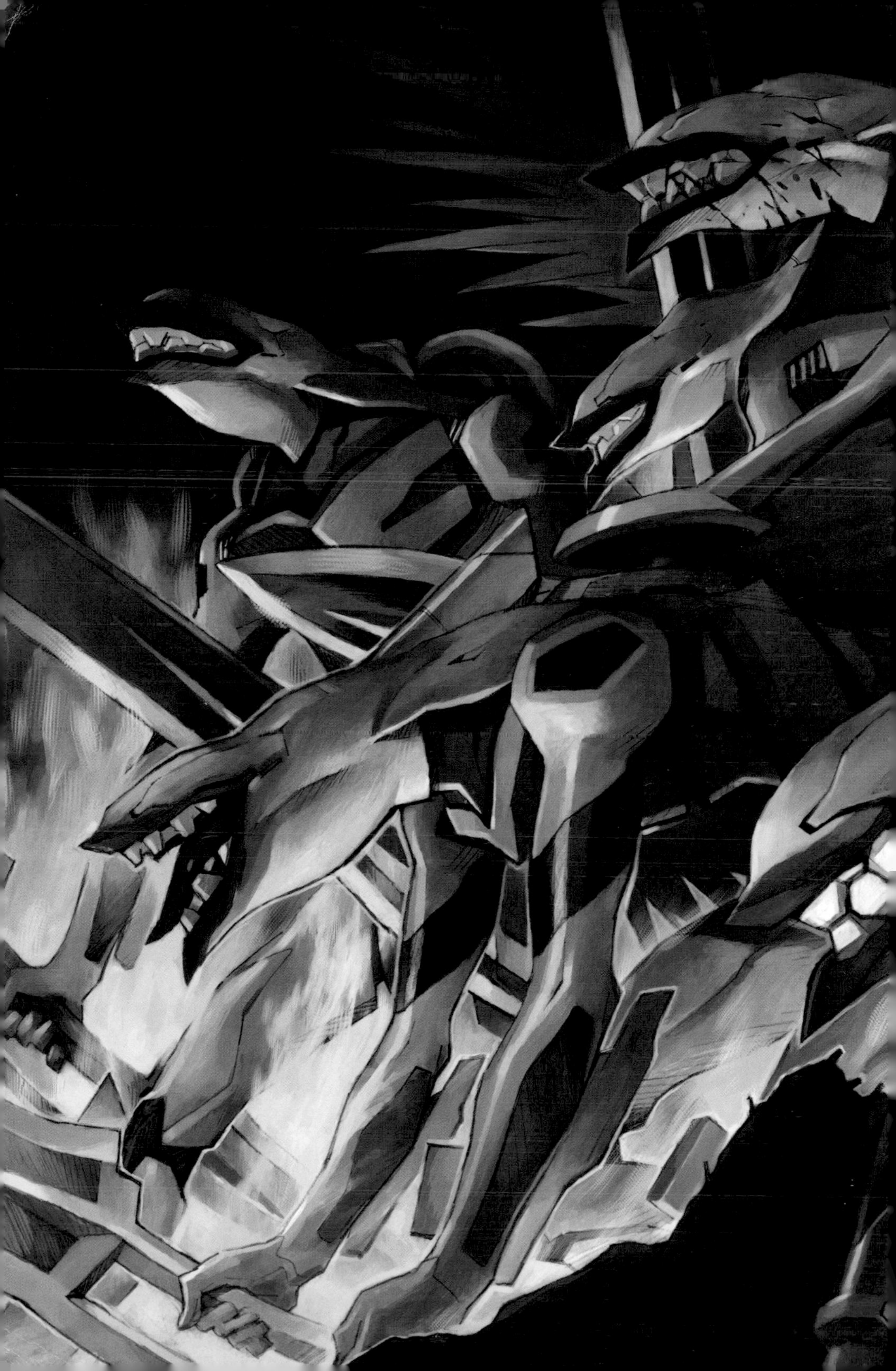

CONTENTS

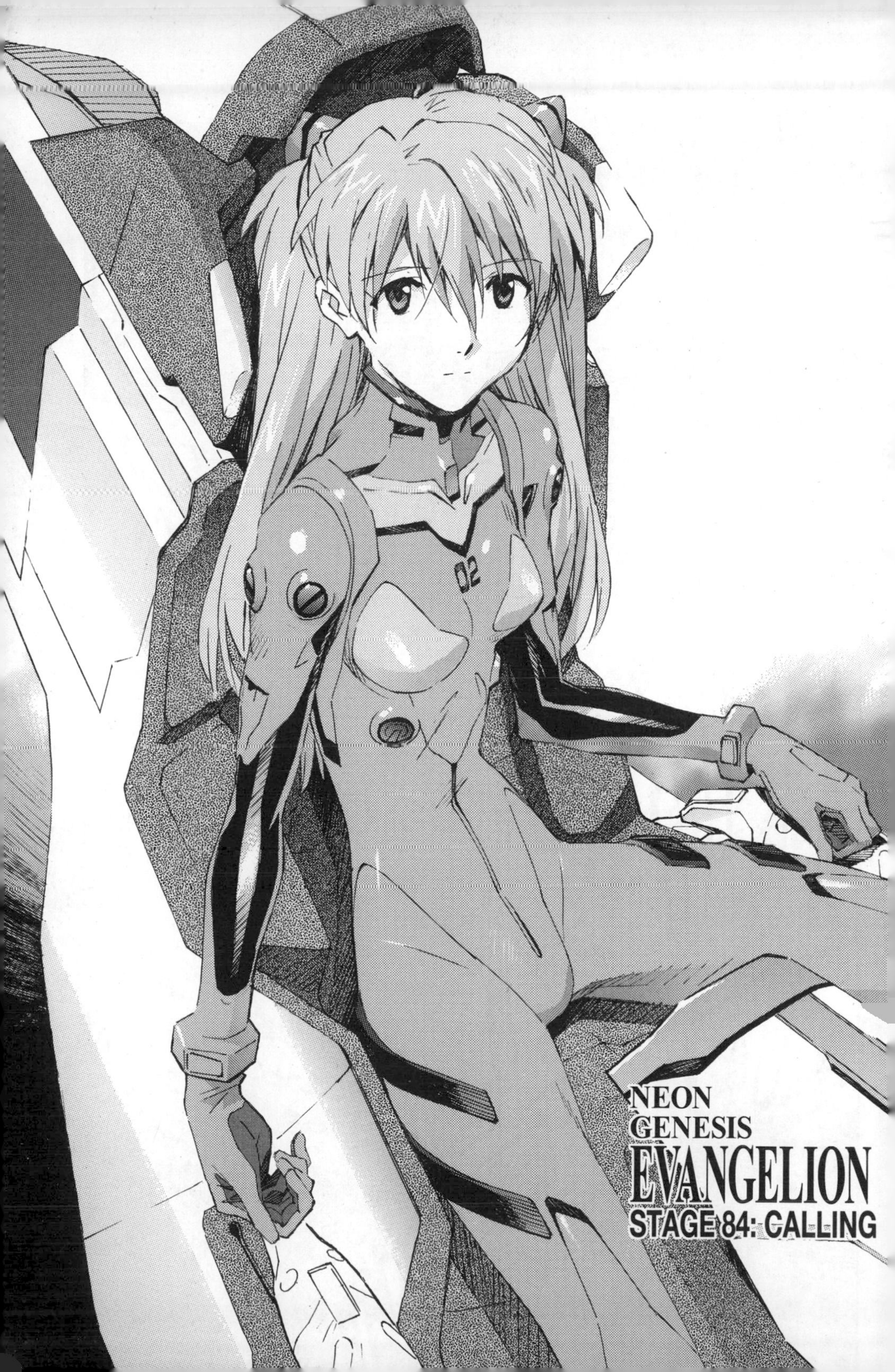
NEON
GENESIS
EVANGELION
STAGE 84: CALLING

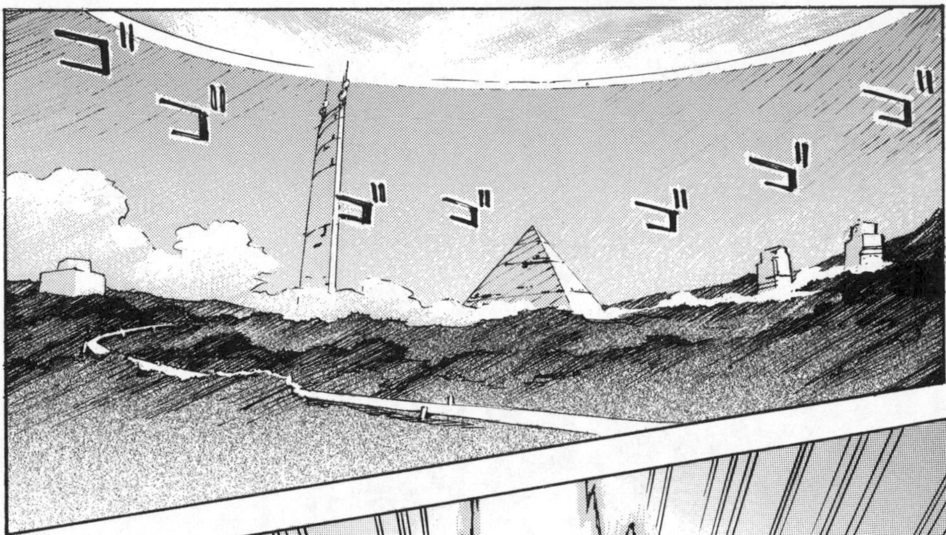
ゴゴゴゴ
ゴゴゴゴ

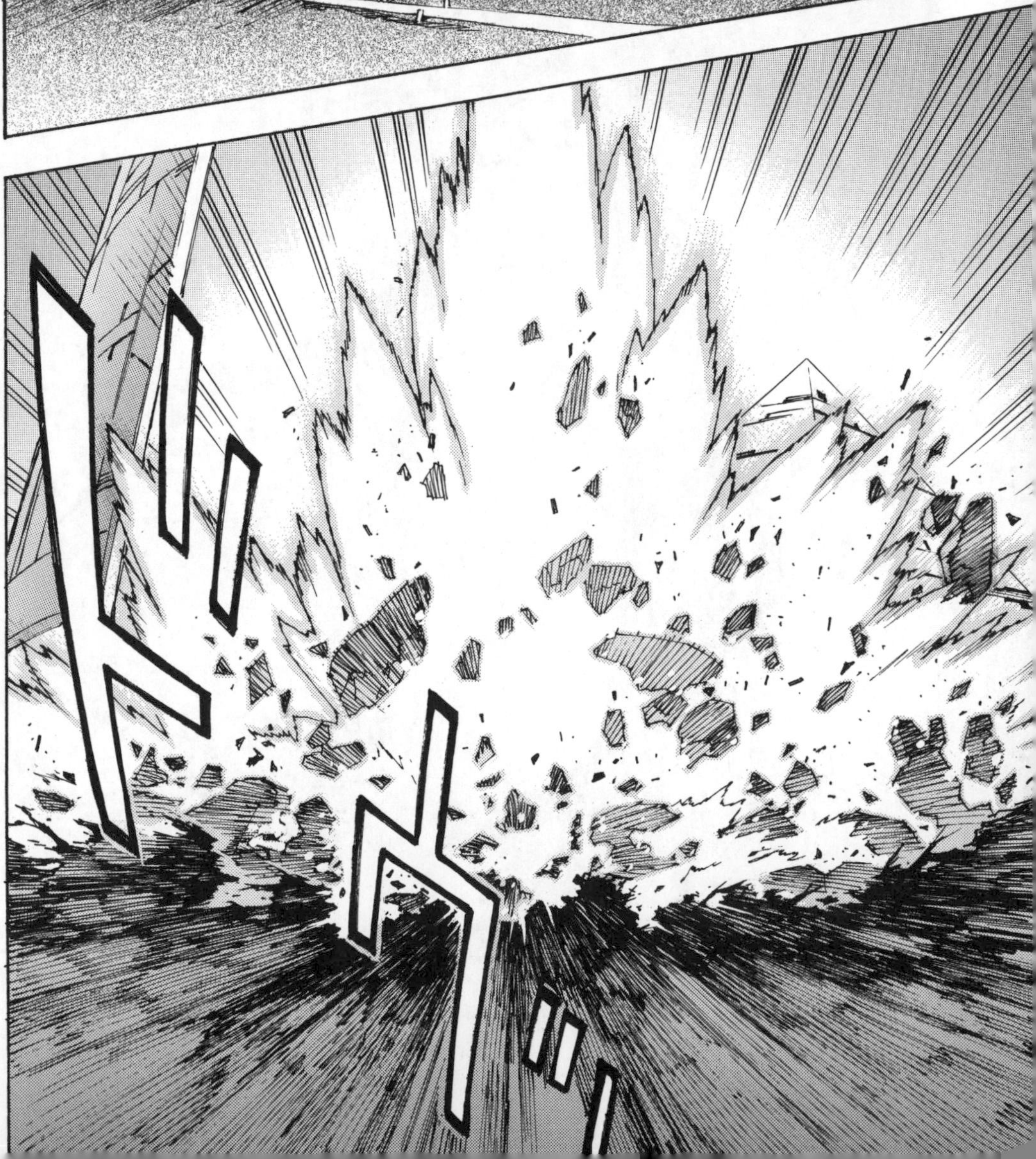

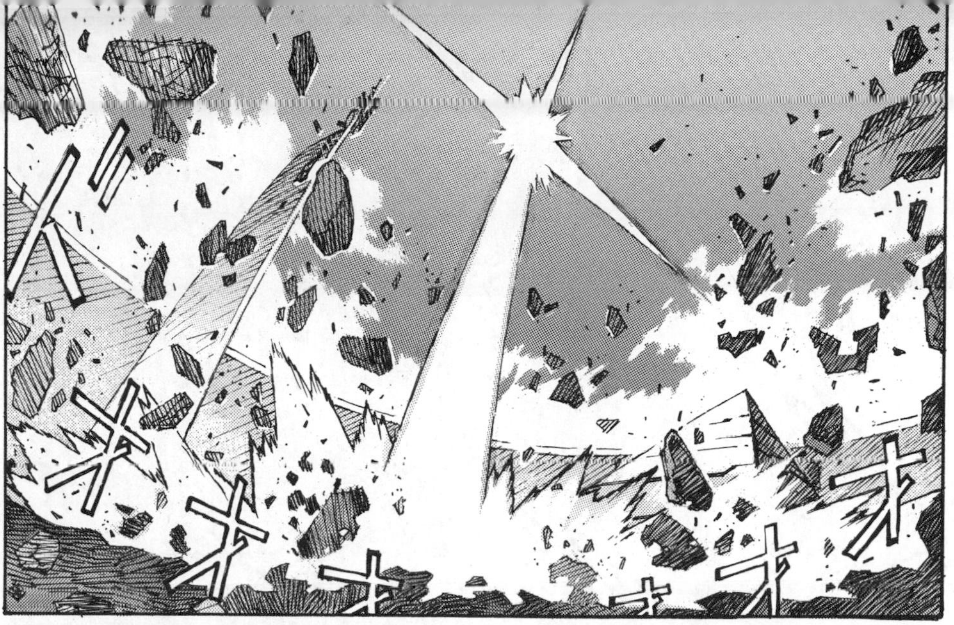

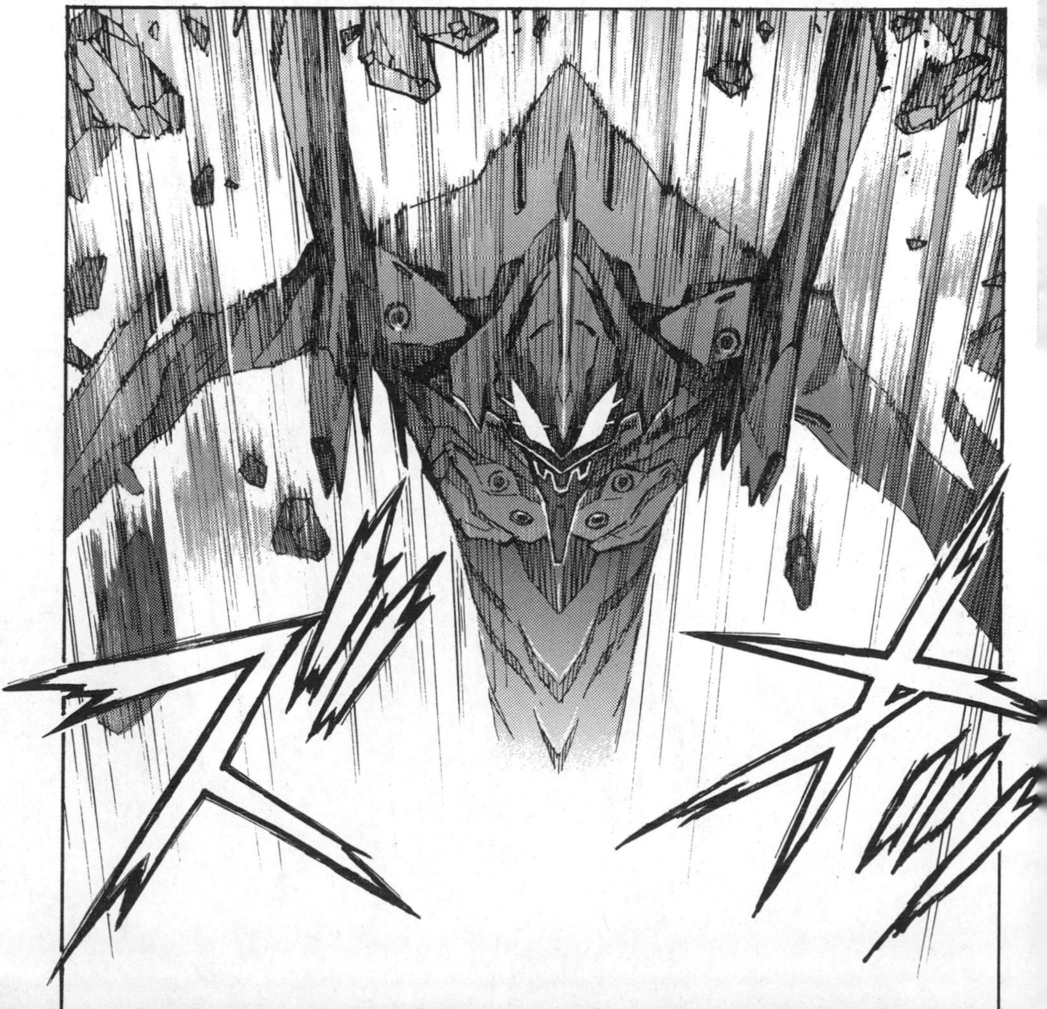

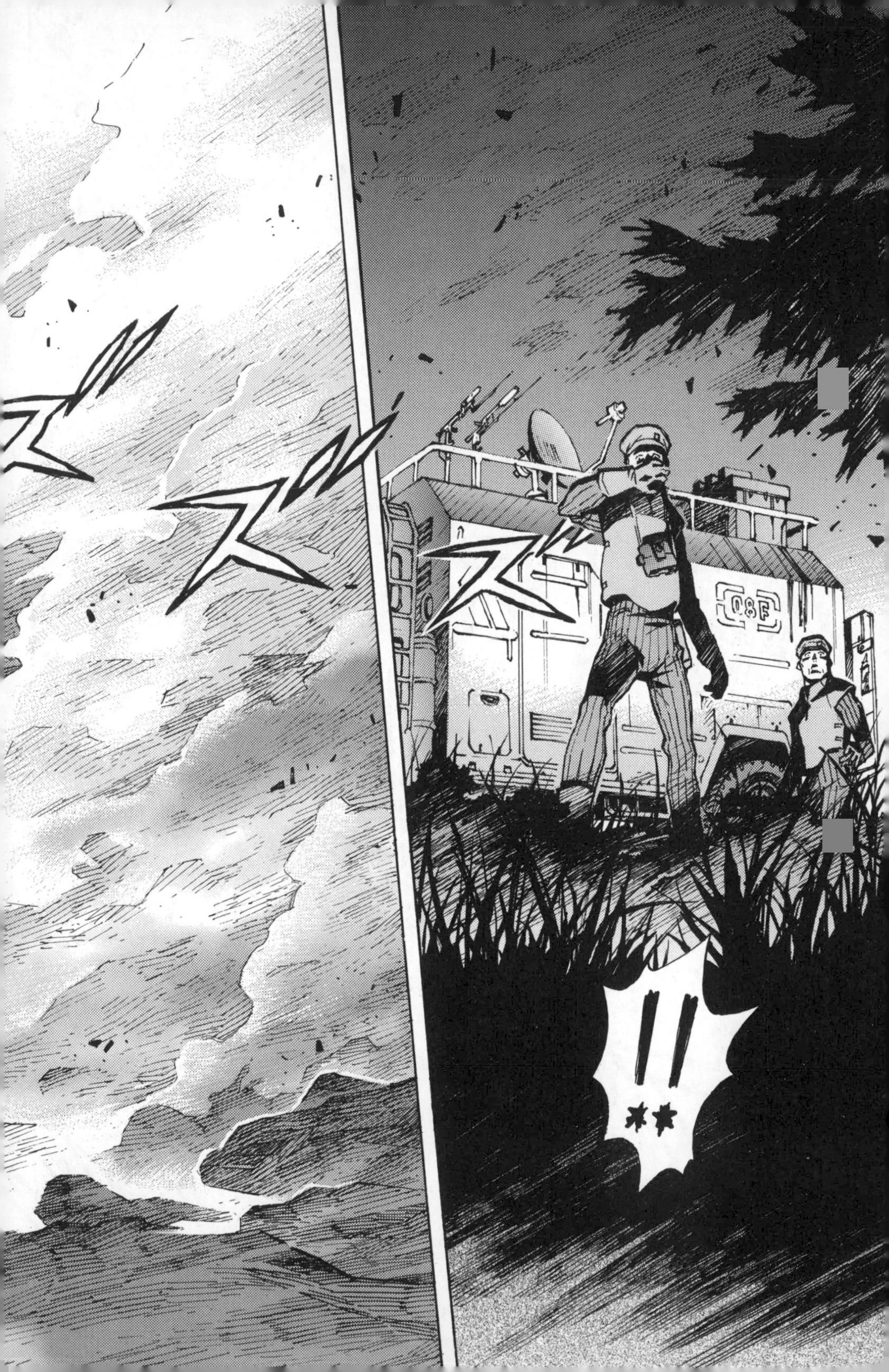
!!

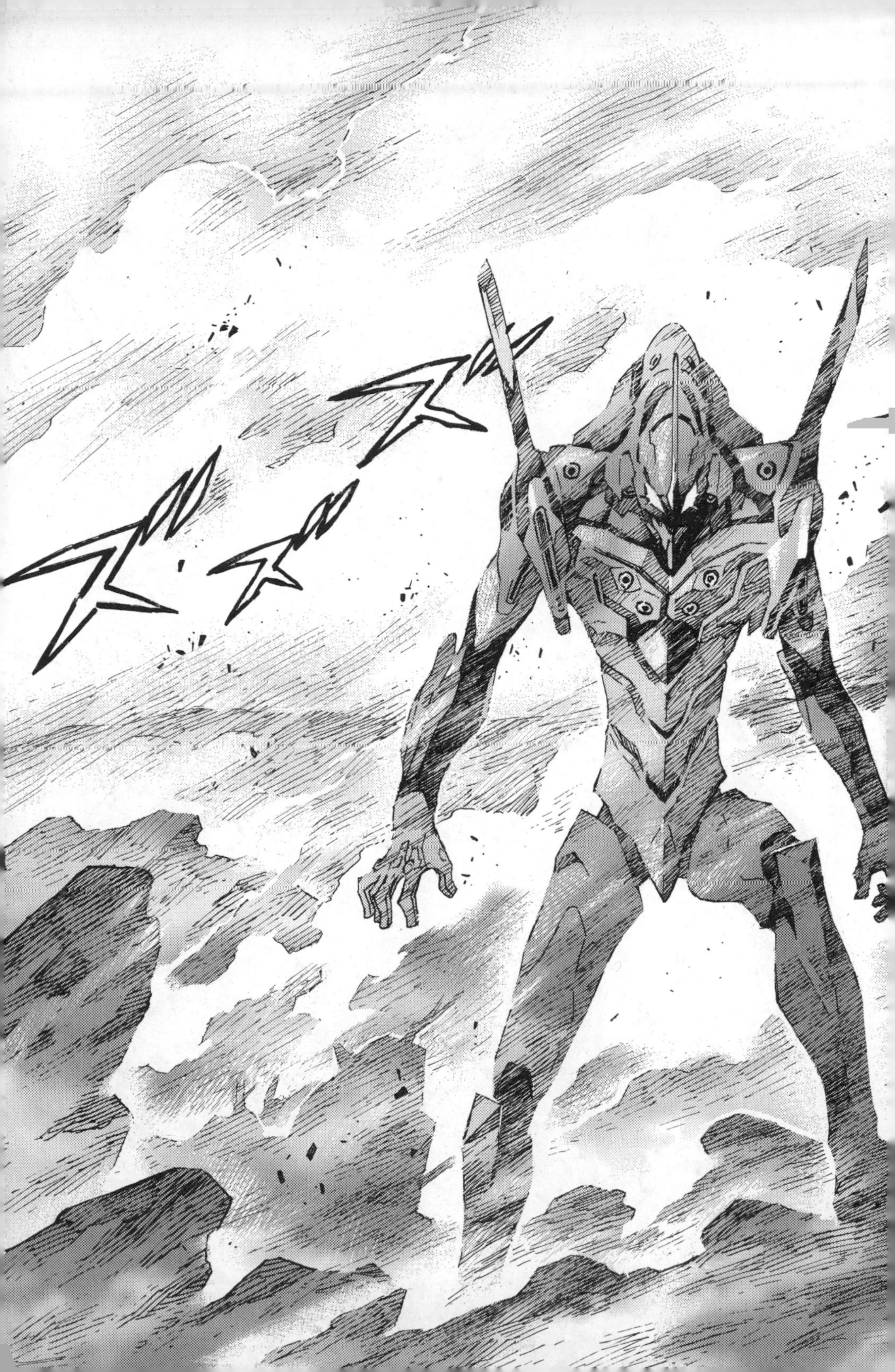
ズズズ

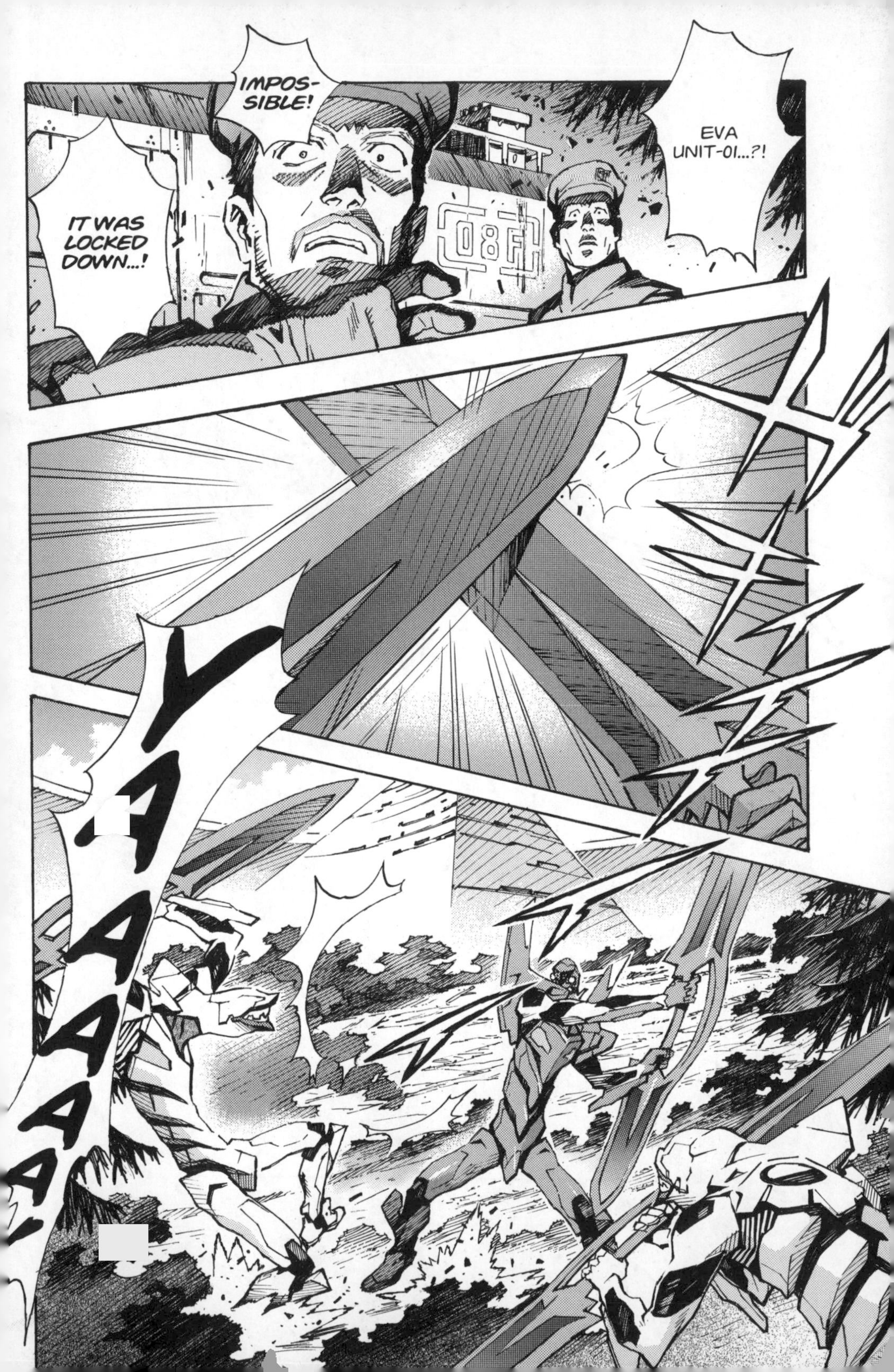
EVA UNIT-01...?!
IMPOSSIBLE!
IT WAS LOCKED DOWN...!
YAAAAAA

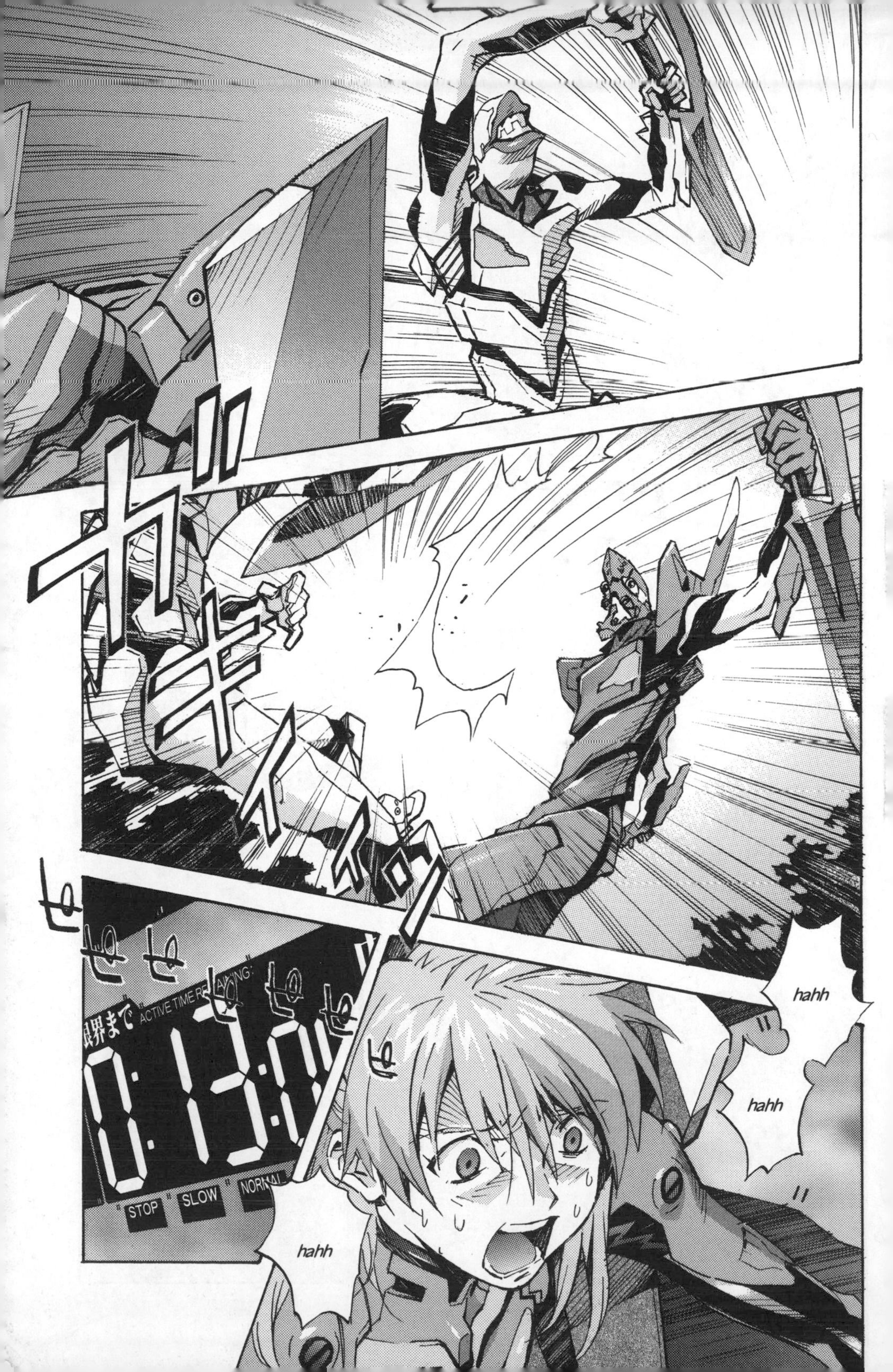
hahh
hahh
限界まで
STOP
SLOW
NORMAL
hahh

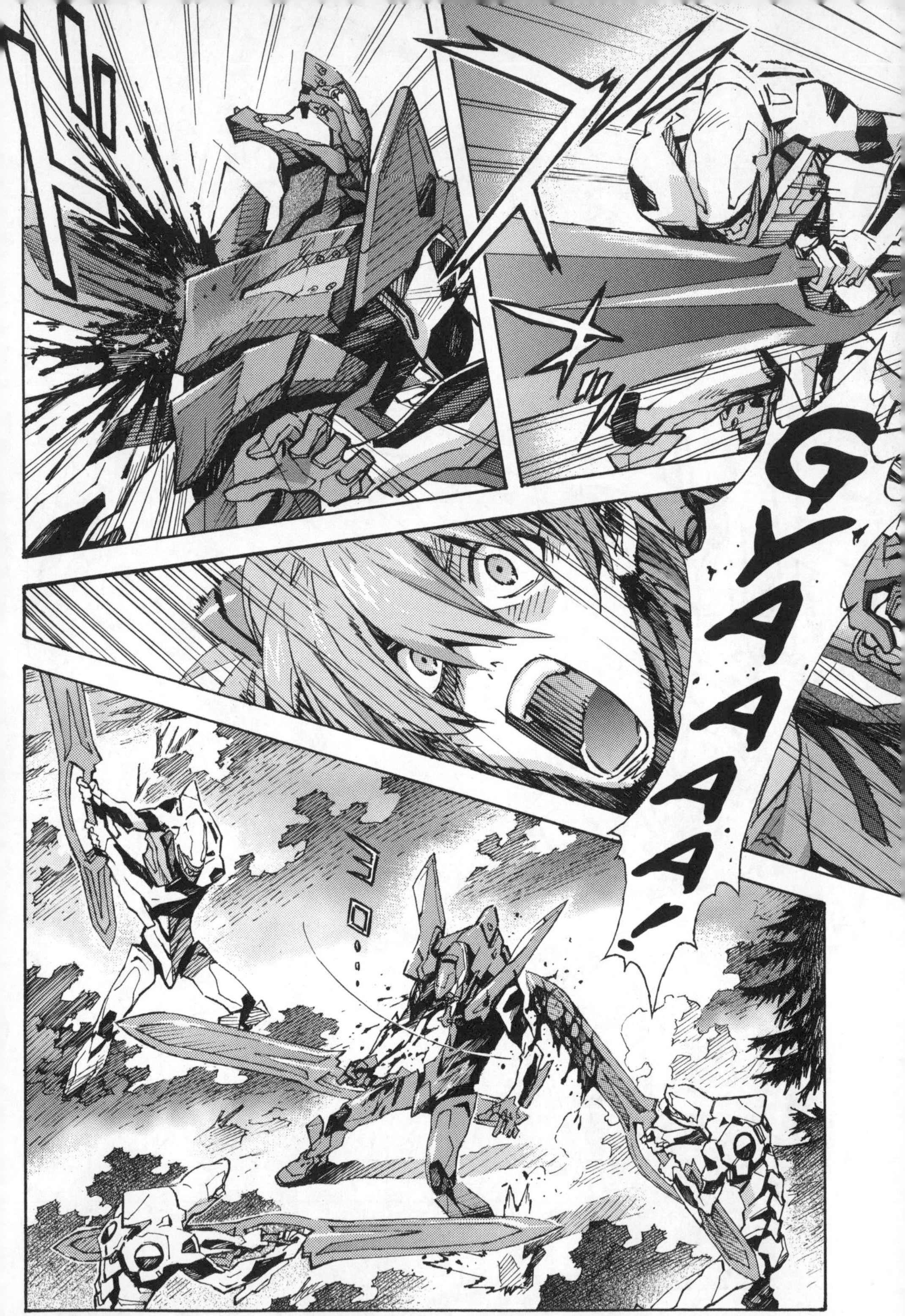
GYAAAA!

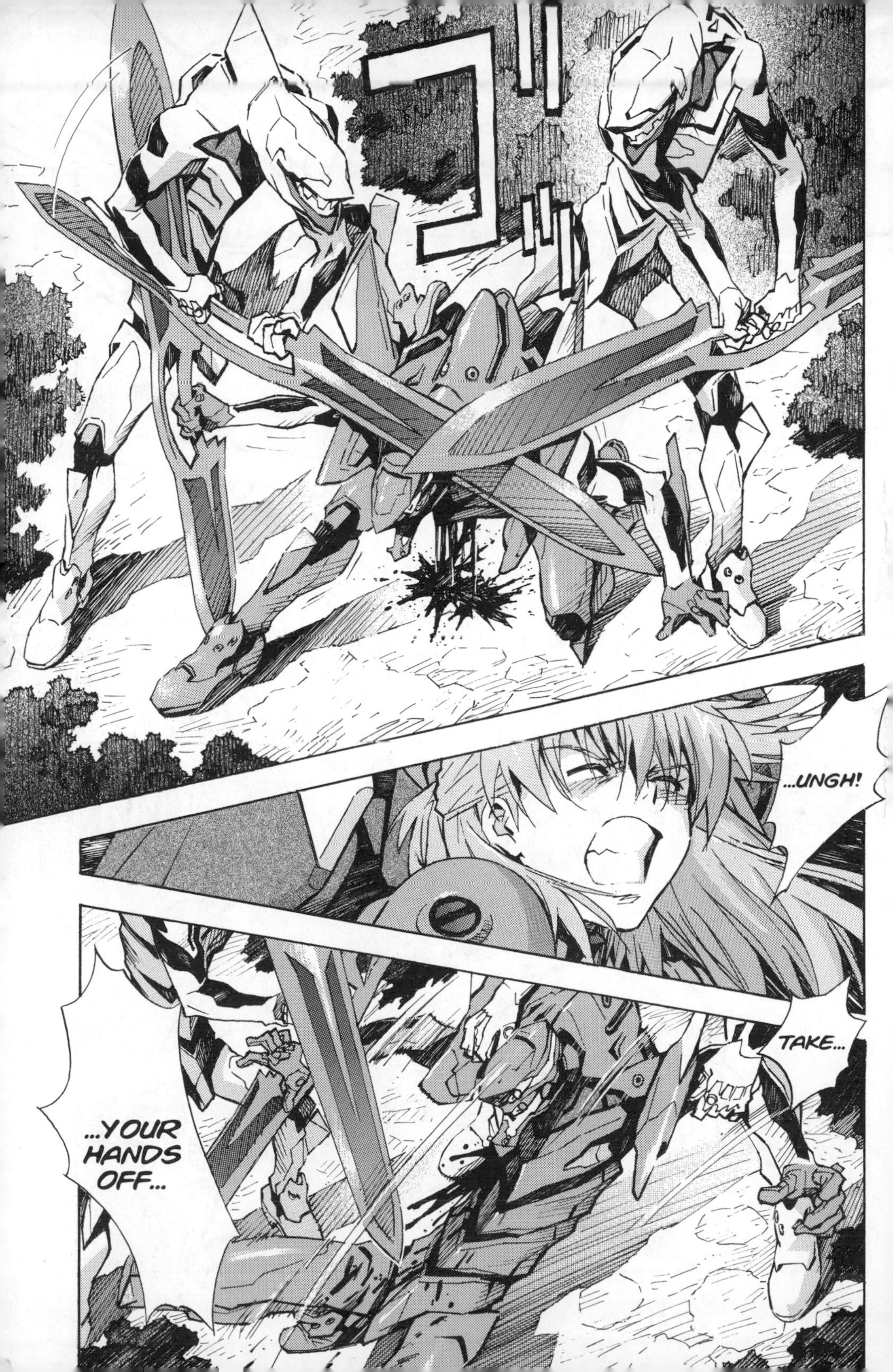
...UNGH!
TAKE...
...YOUR HANDS OFF...

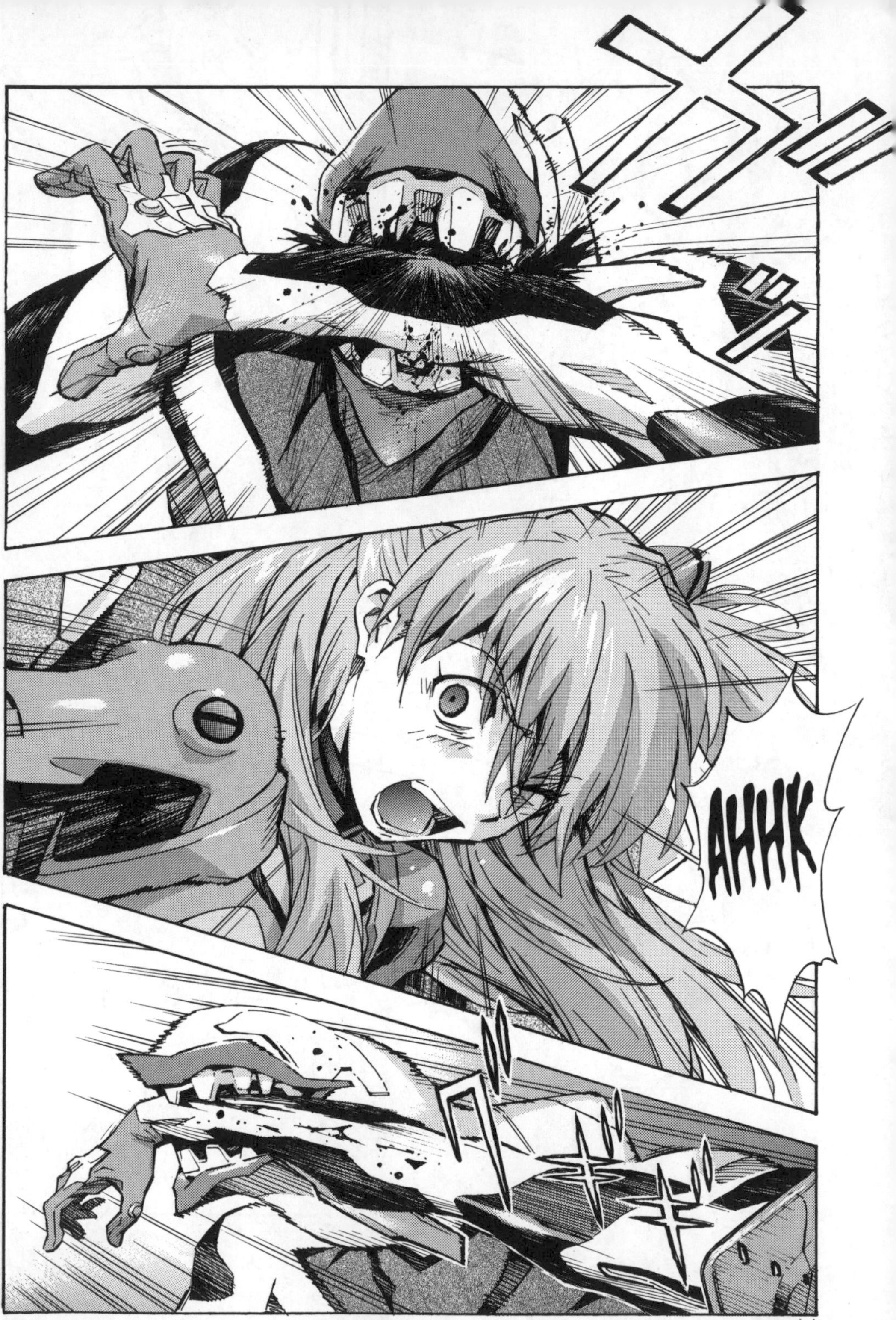
AHHK

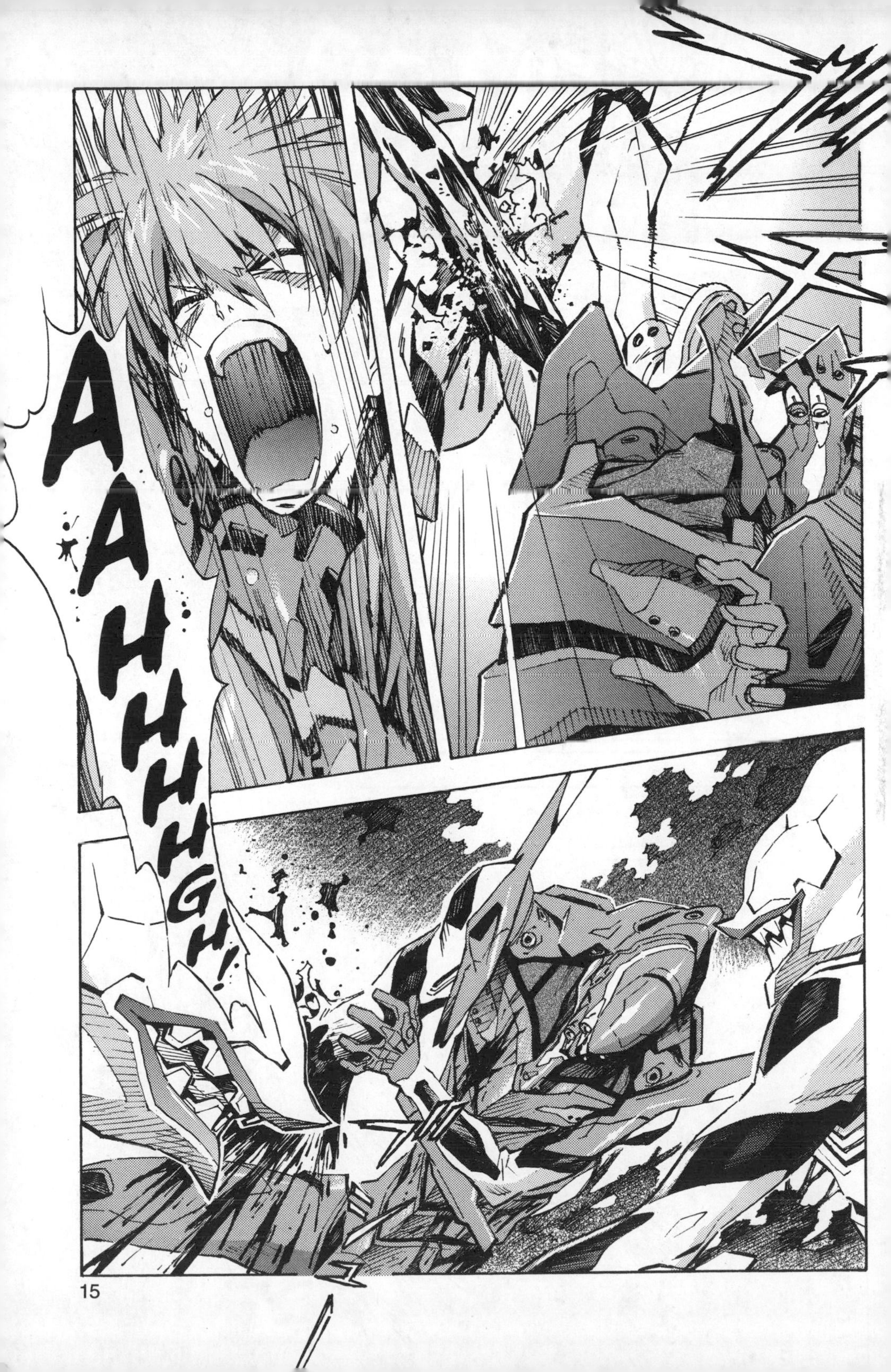
AAHHHHGH!

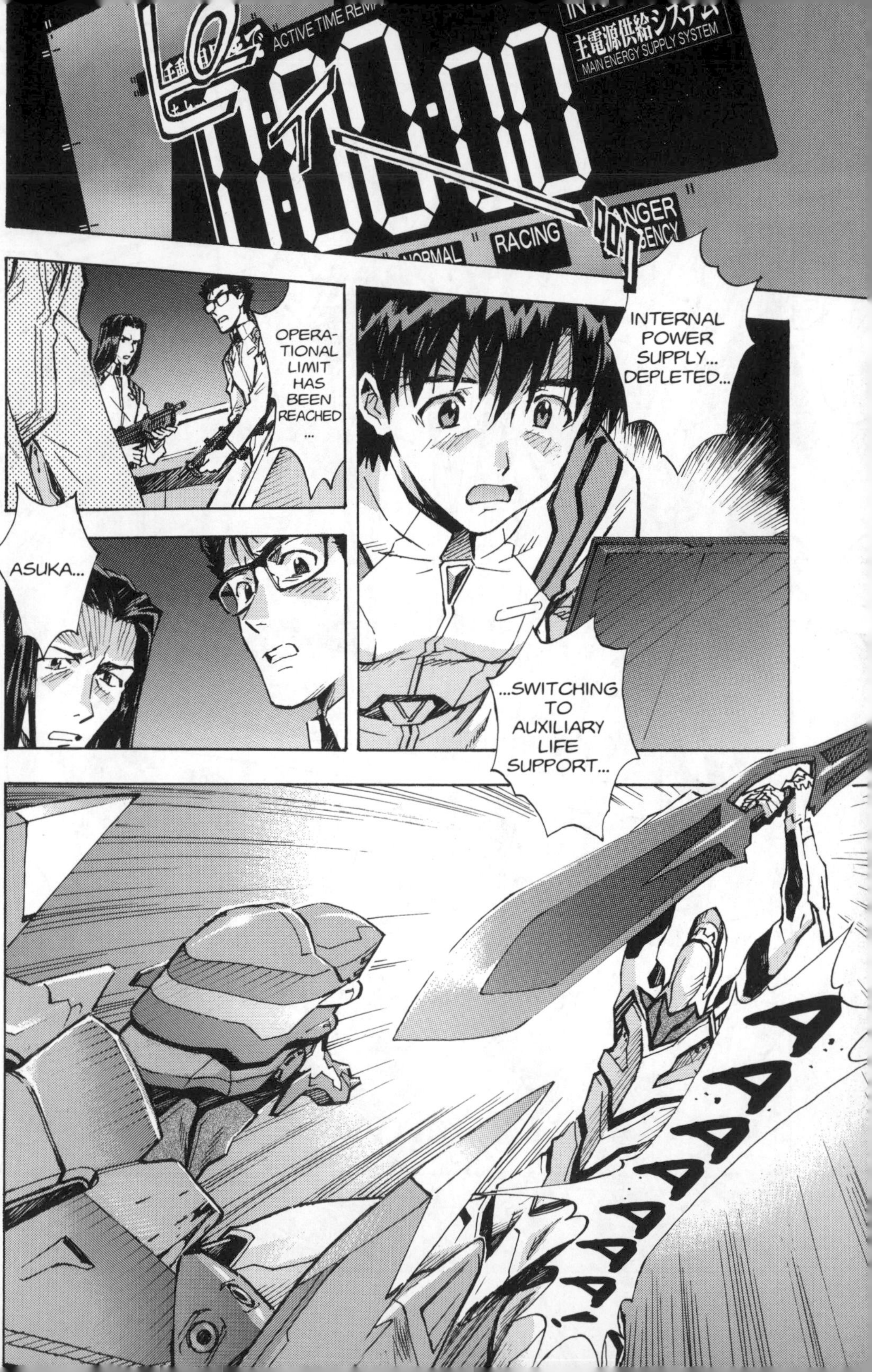
主電源供給システム
MAIN ENERGY SUPPLY SYSTEM
RACING
INTERNAL POWER SUPPLY... DEPLETED...
OPERATIONAL LIMIT HAS BEEN REACHED...
ASUKA...
...SWITCHING TO AUXILIARY LIFE SUPPORT...
AAAAAAAAA!

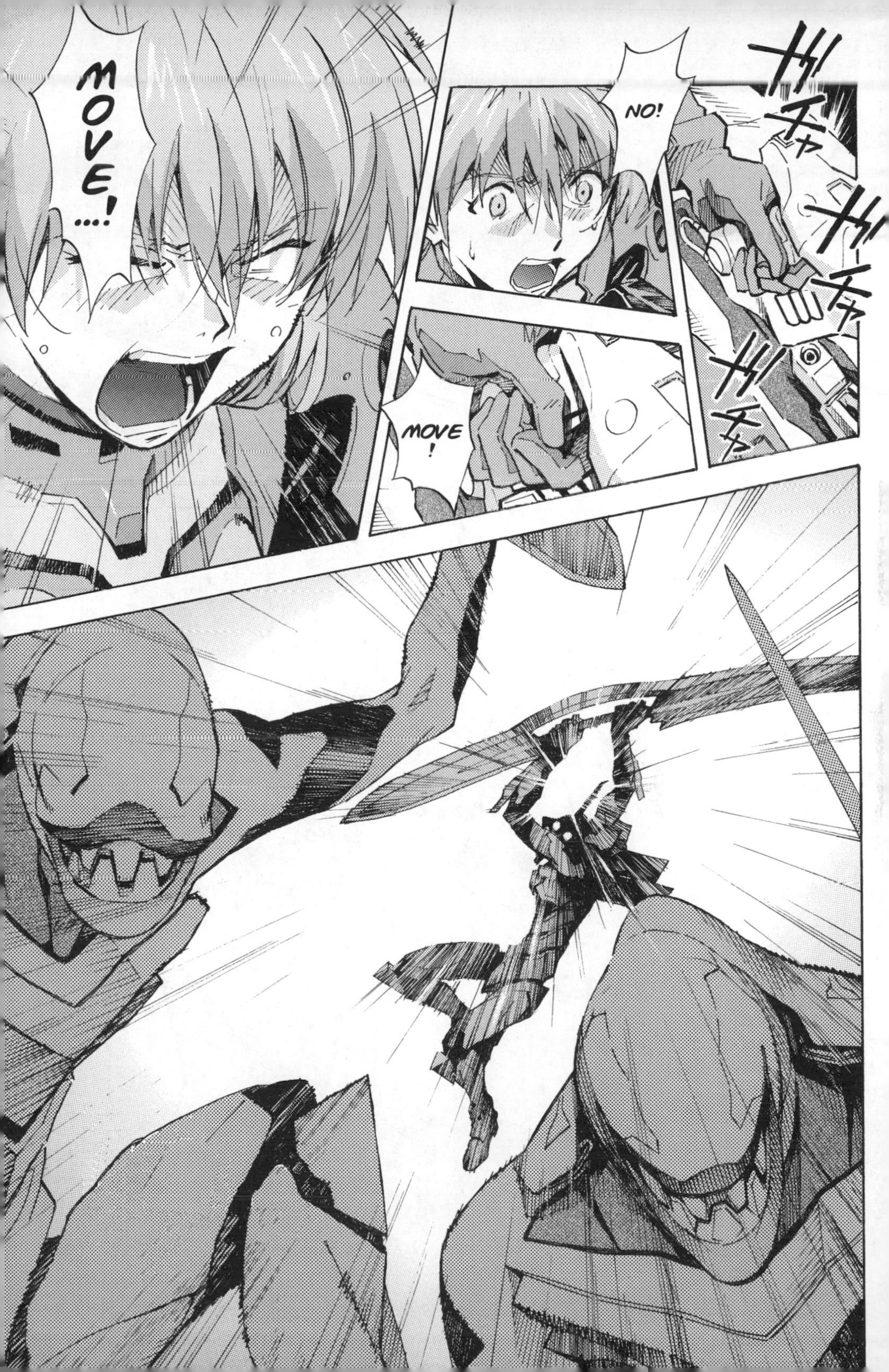
NO!
MOVE!
MOVE...!

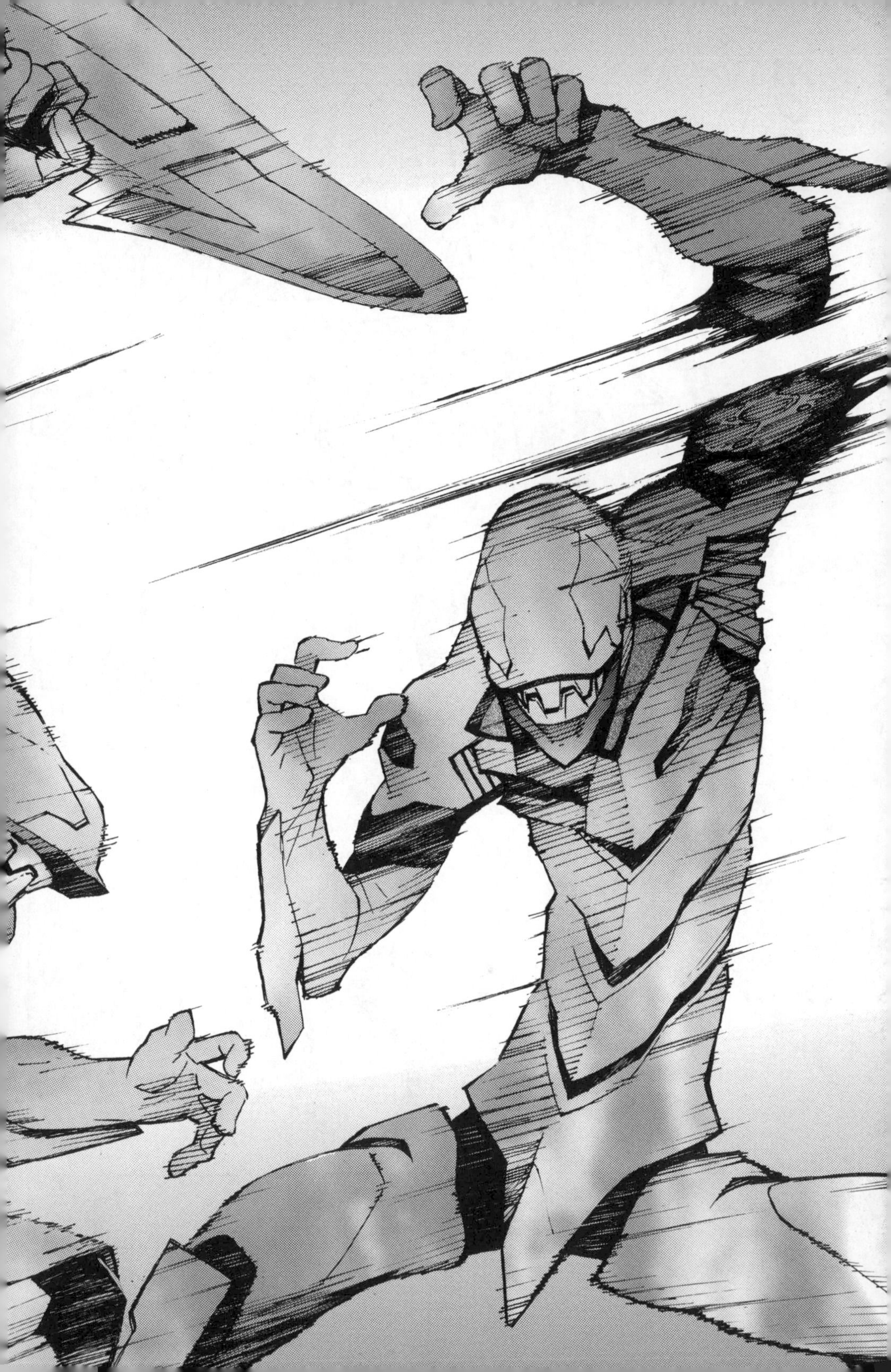

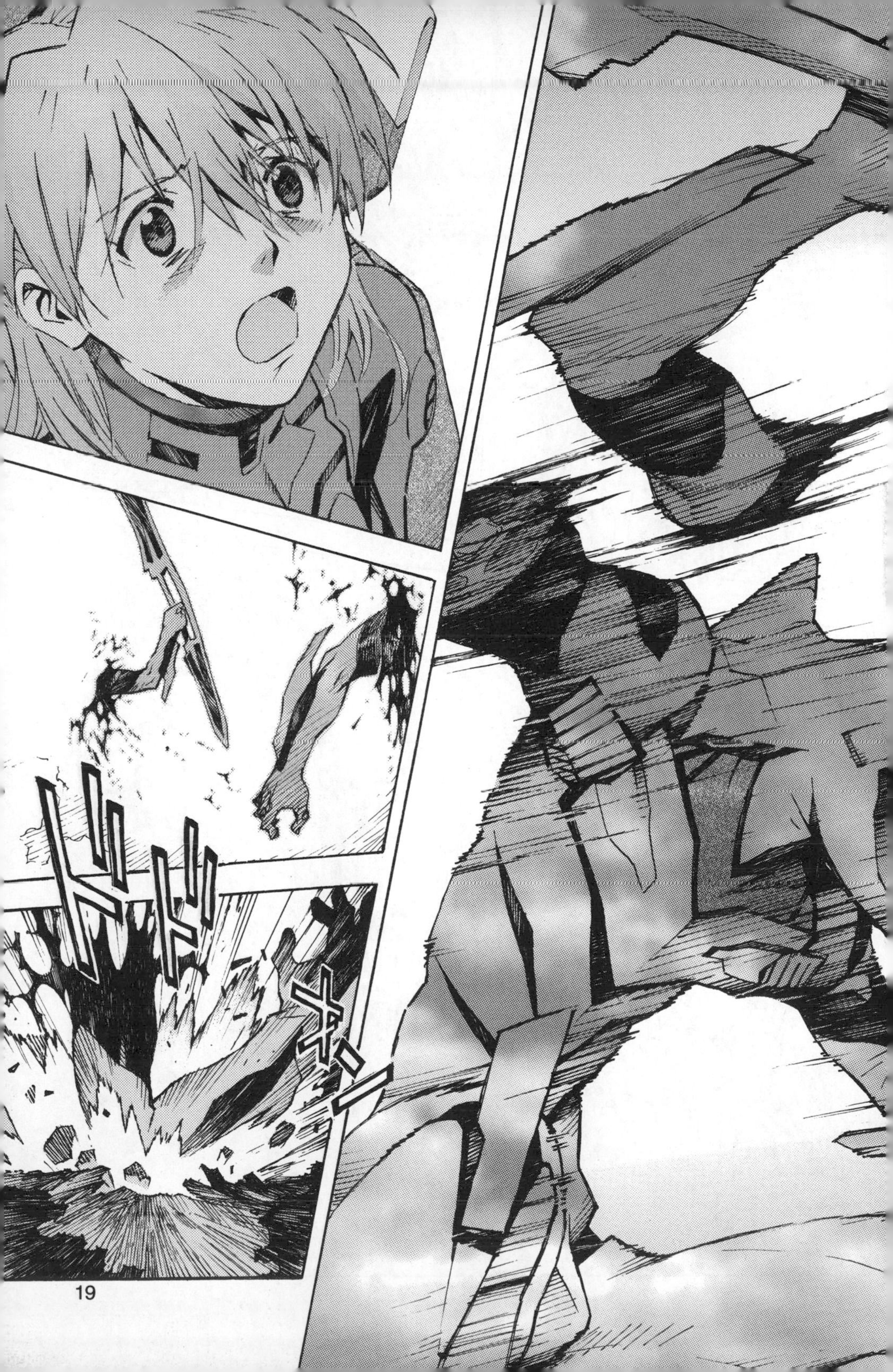
ドドーオッ!

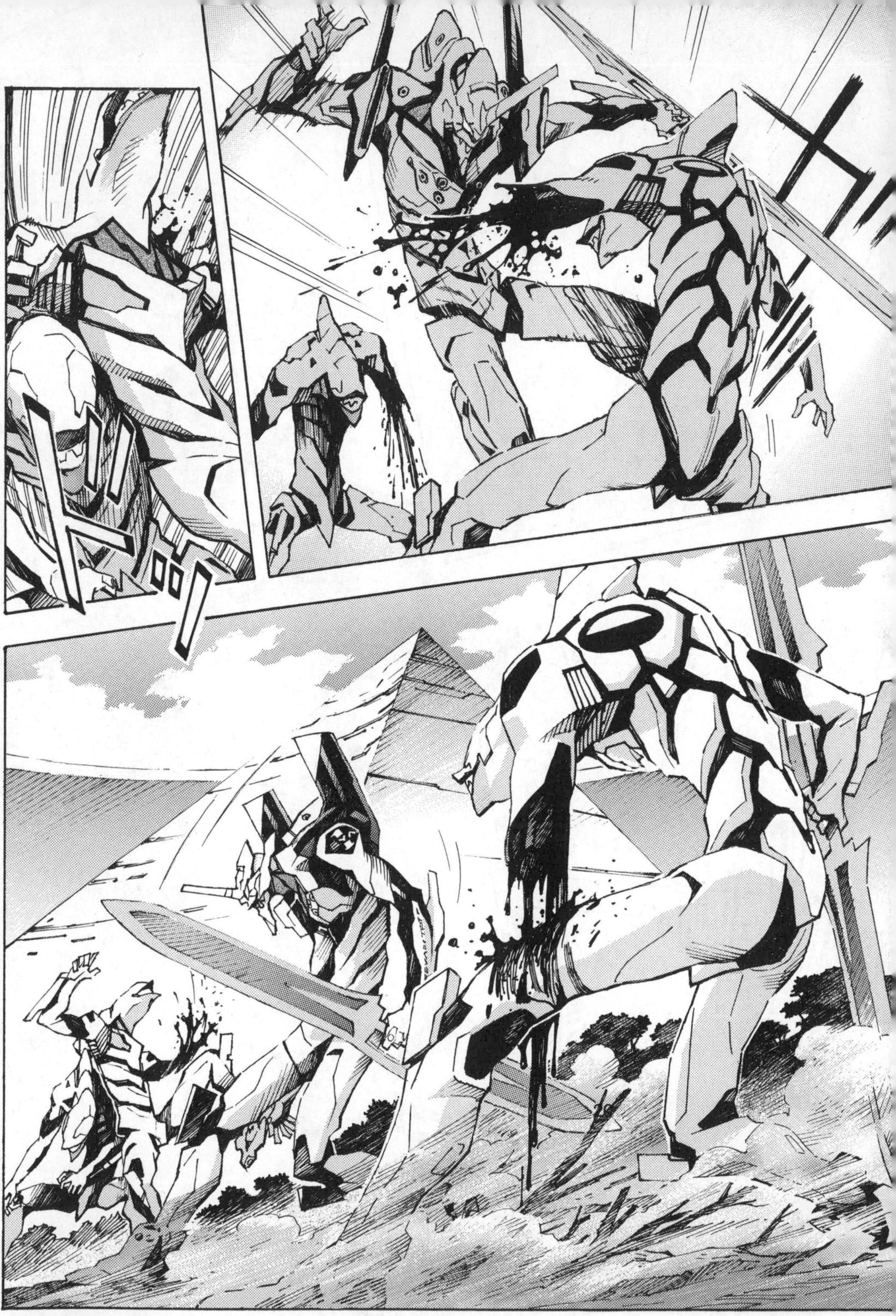

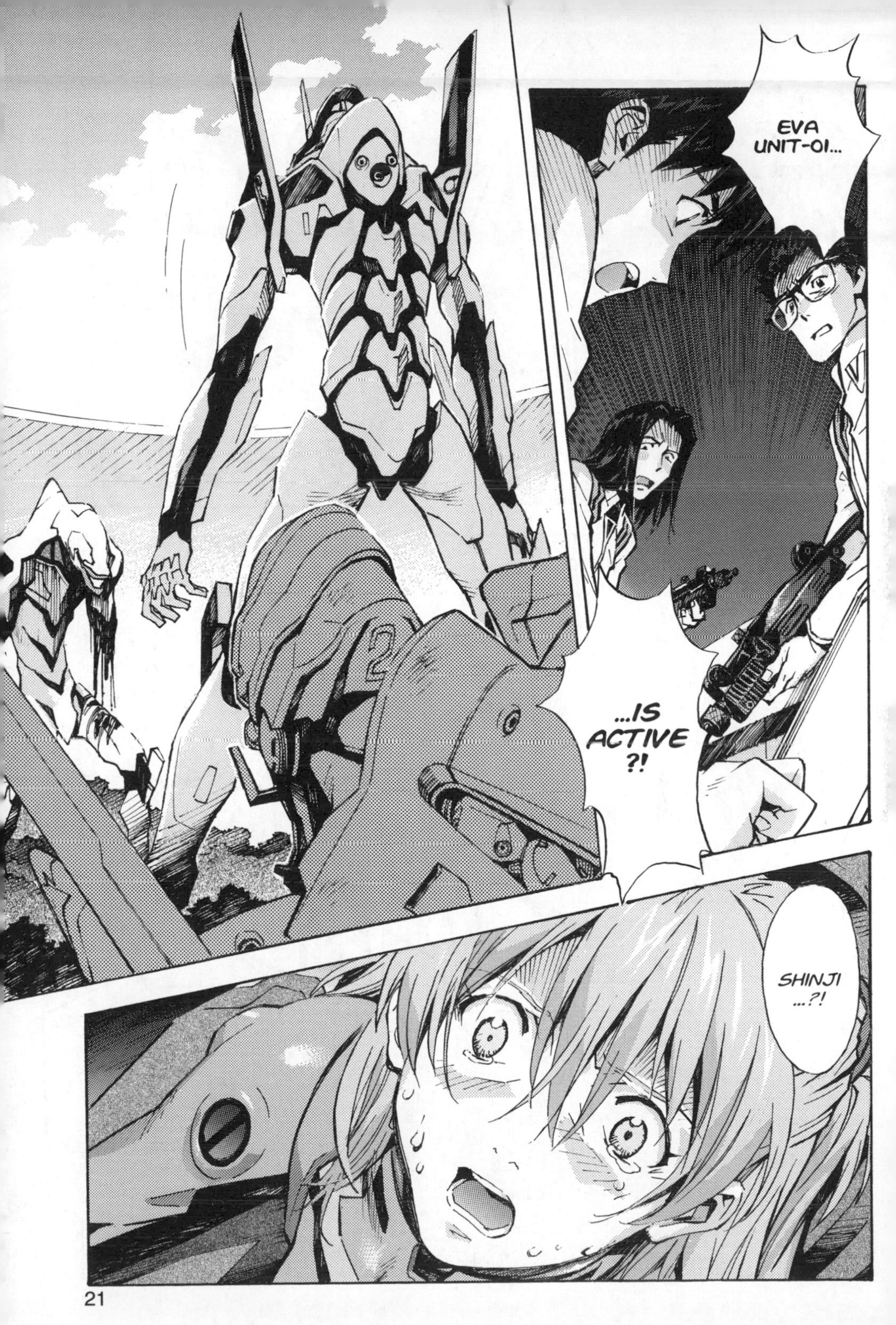
EVA UNIT-01...
...IS ACTIVE ?!
SHINJI ...?!

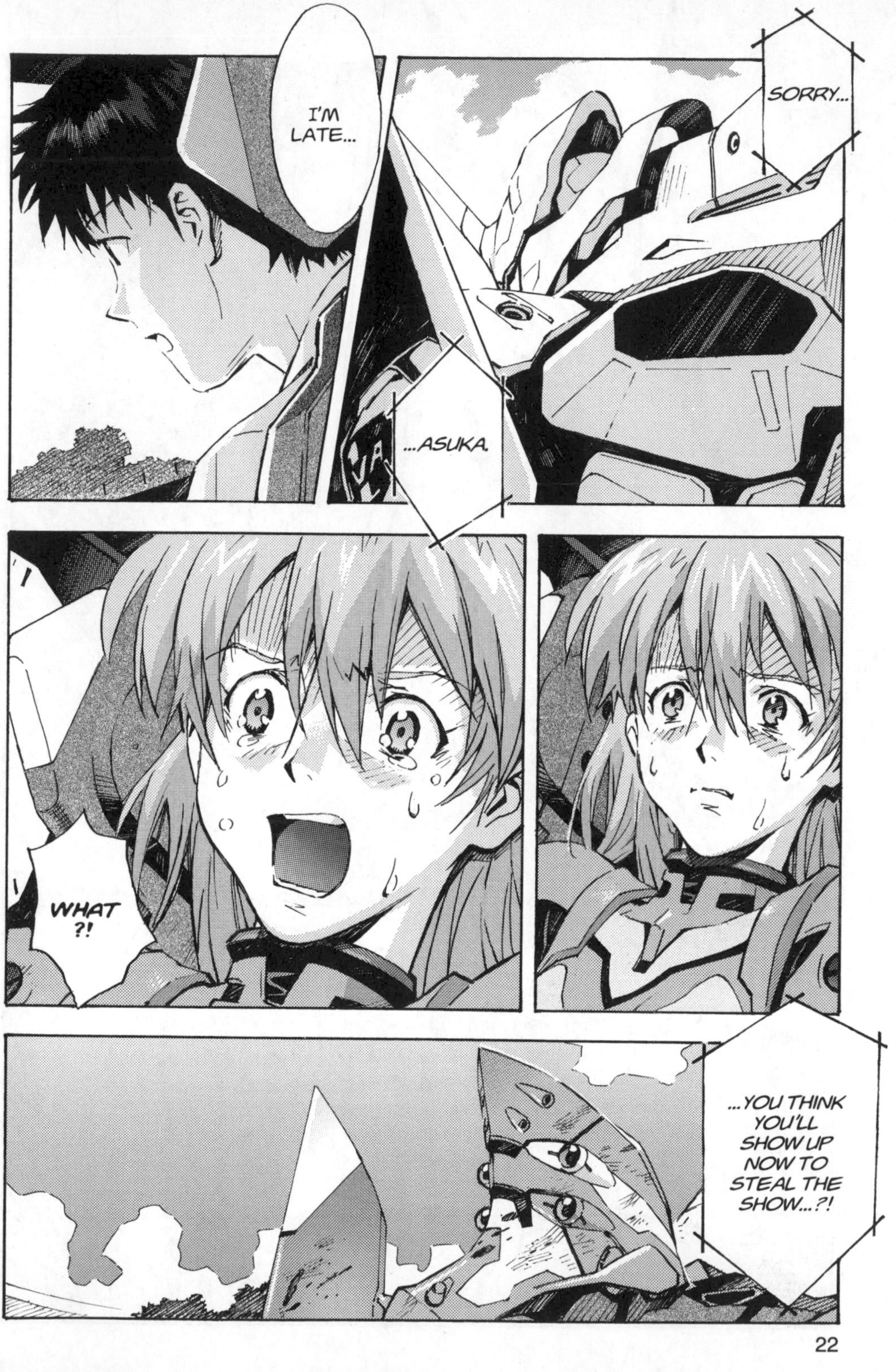
SORRY...
I'M LATE...
...ASUKA.
WHAT ?!
...YOU THINK YOU'LL SHOW UP NOW TO STEAL THE SHOW...?!

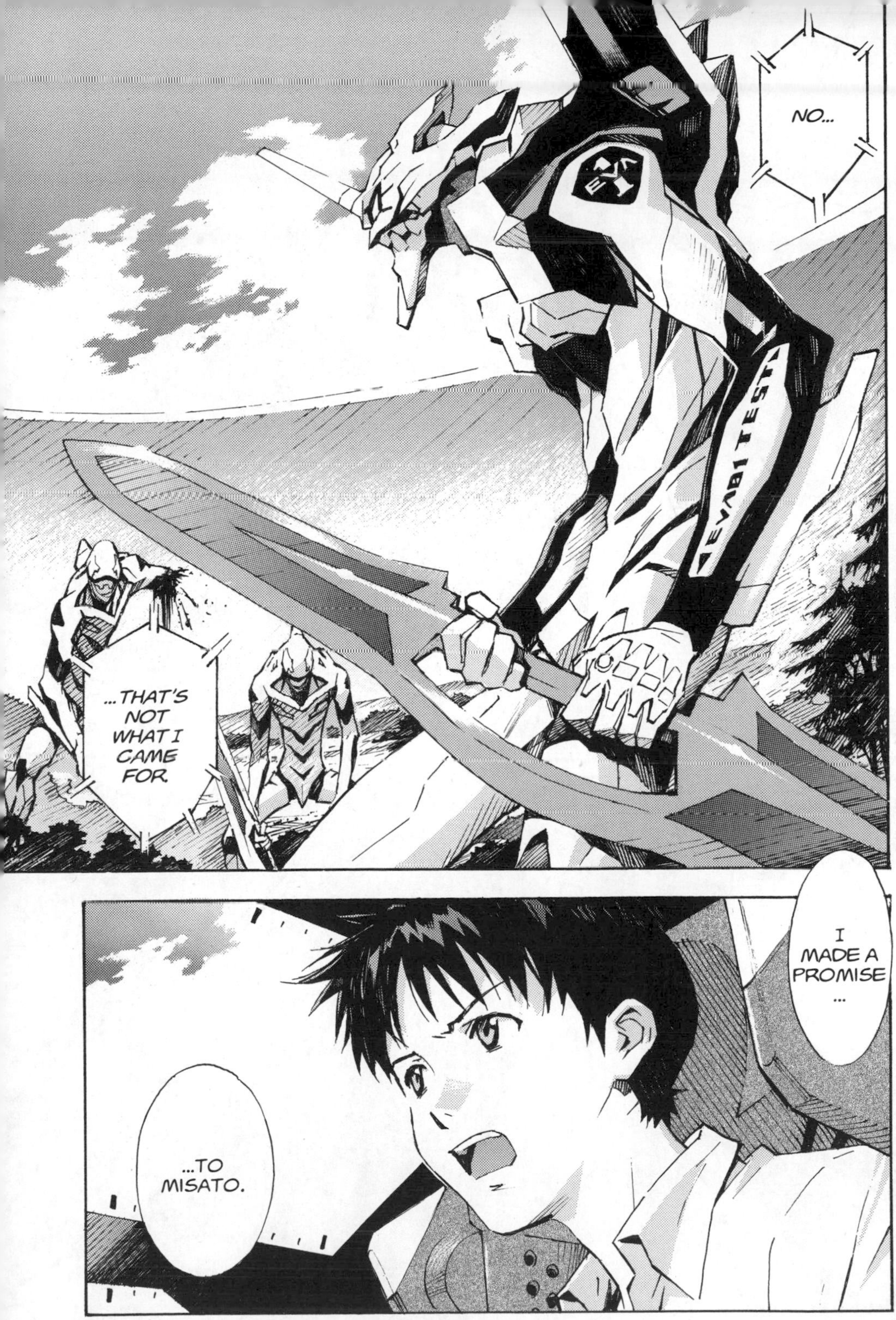
NO...
...THAT'S NOT WHAT I CAME FOR.
I MADE A PROMISE ...
...TO MISATO.

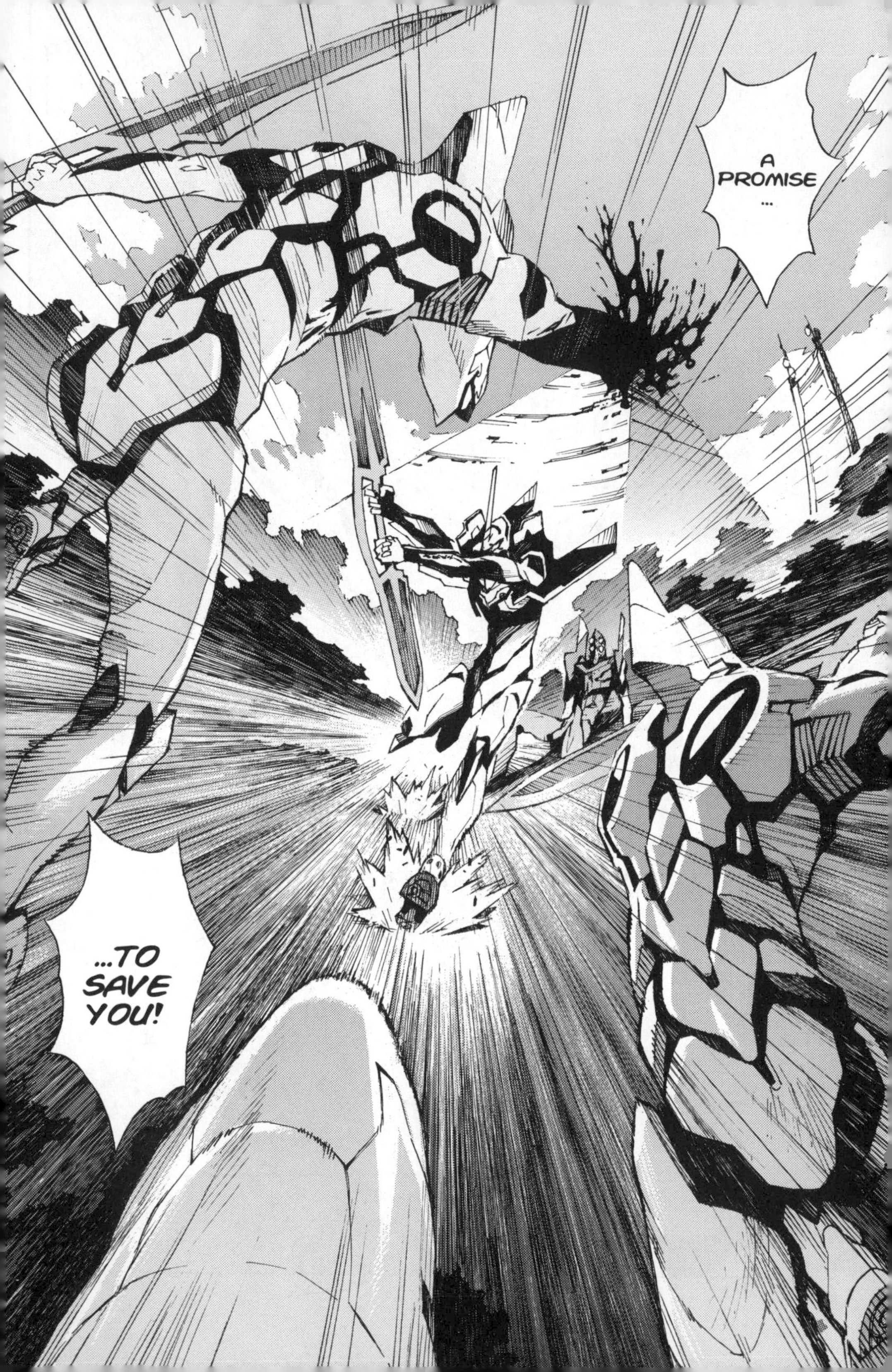
A PROMISE
...
...TO SAVE YOU!

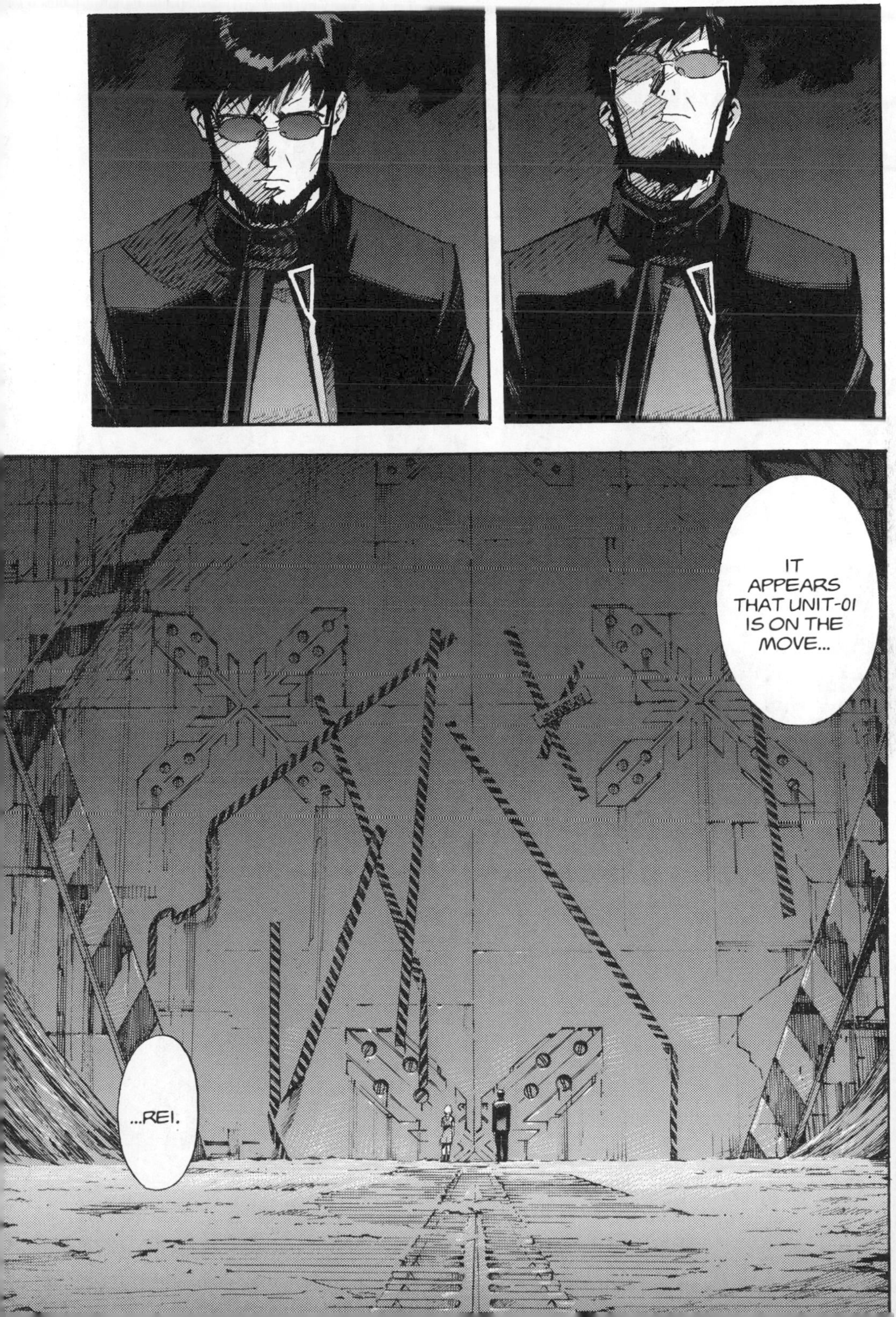
IT APPEARS THAT UNIT-01 IS ON THE MOVE...
...REI.

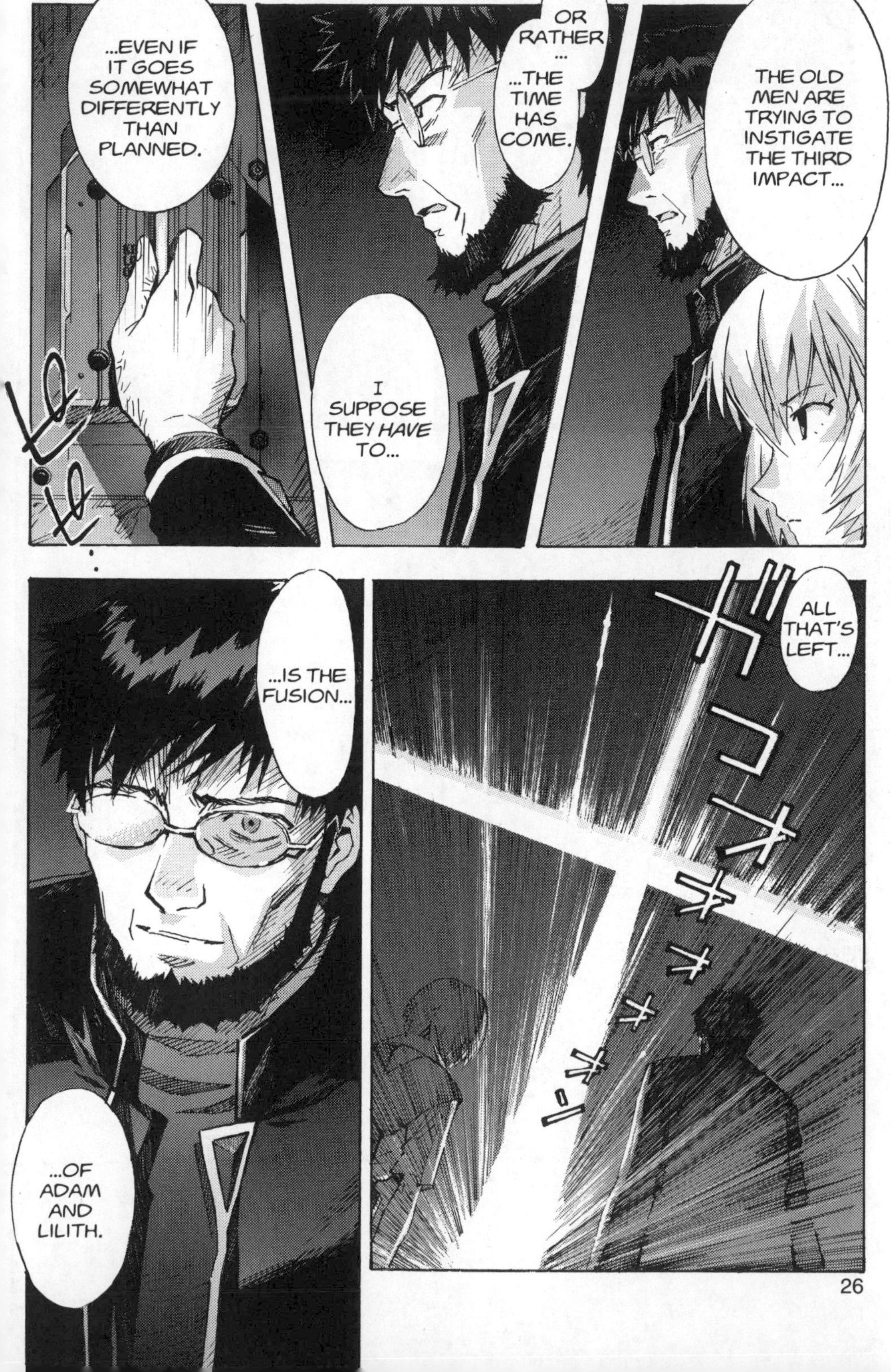
THE OLD MEN ARE TRYING TO INSTIGATE THE THIRD IMPACT...
OR RATHER ... ...THE TIME HAS COME.
I SUPPOSE THEY *HAVE* TO...
...EVEN IF IT GOES SOMEWHAT DIFFERENTLY THAN PLANNED.
ALL THAT'S LEFT...
...IS THE FUSION...
...OF ADAM AND LILITH.

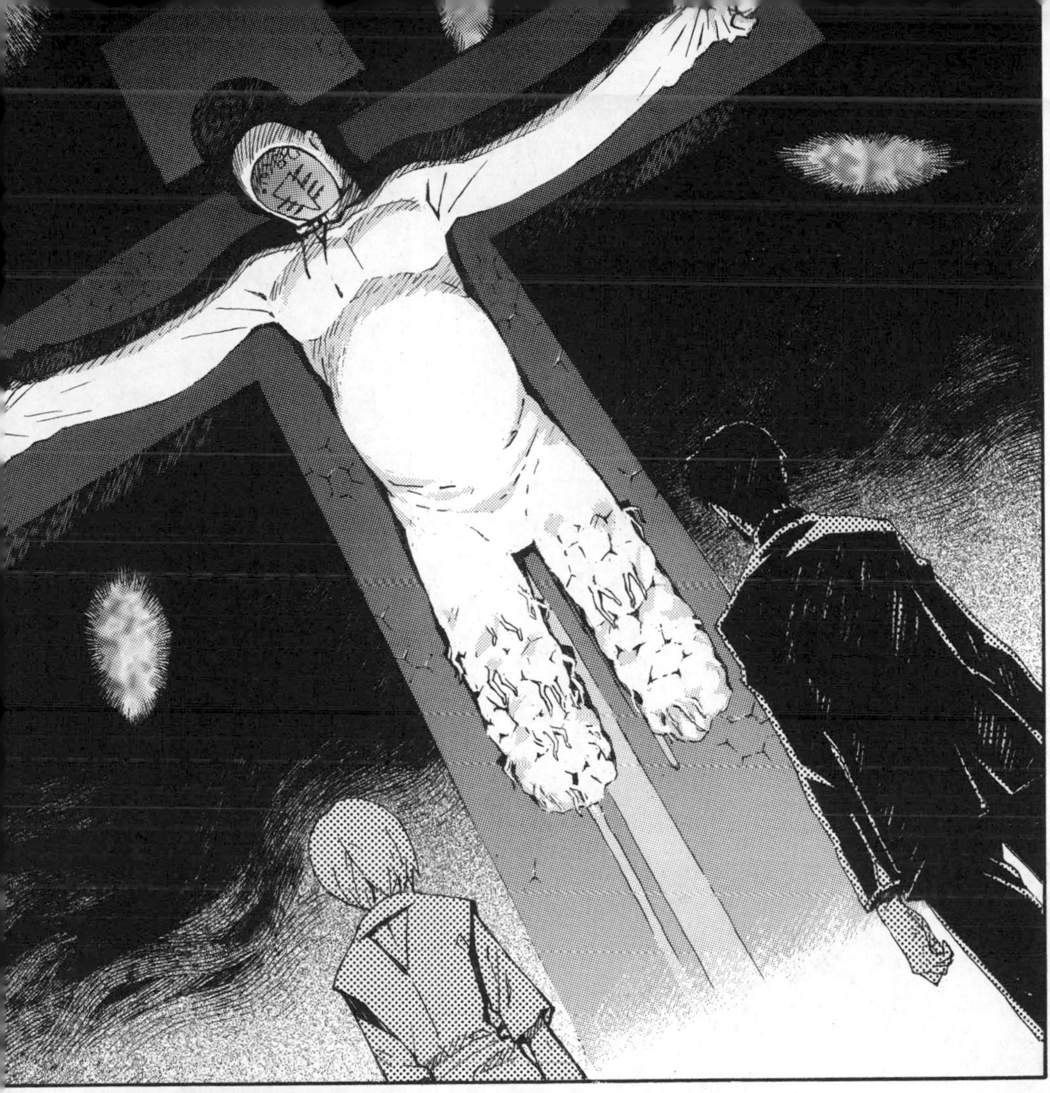
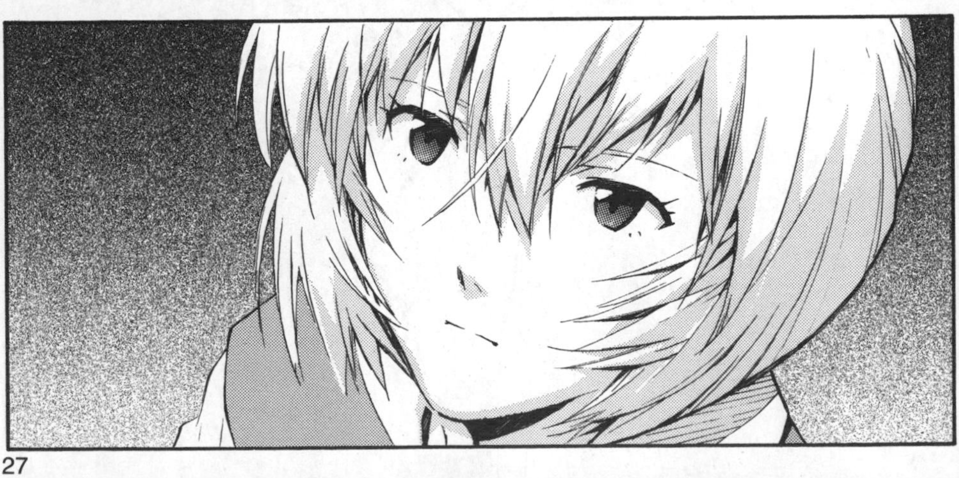

I'VE BEEN WAIT- ING...

...COM- MANDER IKARI.

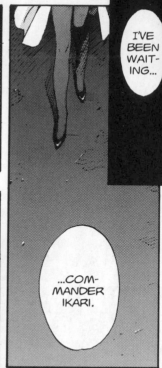

I WON'T LET THIS HAPPEN...

...THE WAY YOU WANT.

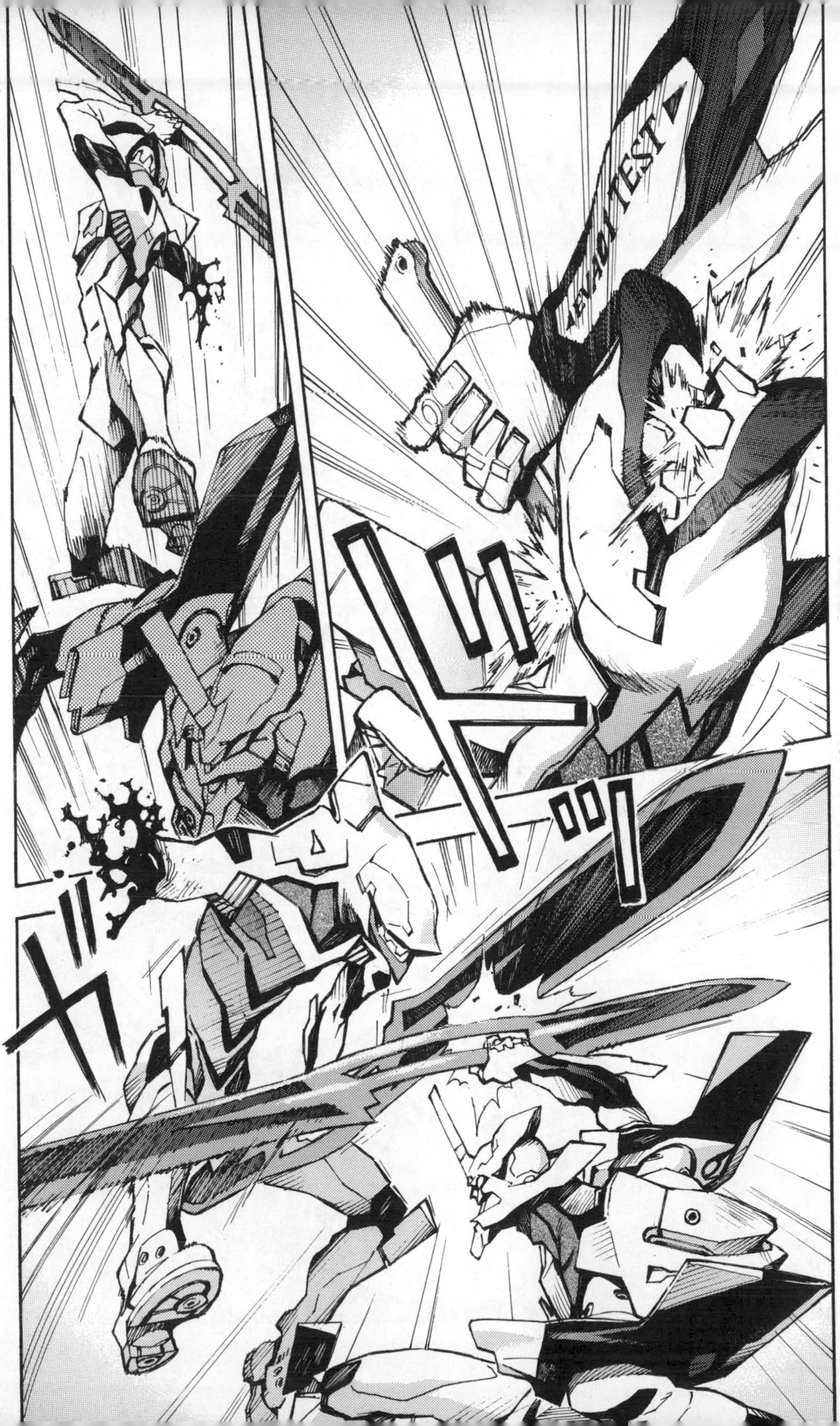
EVA01 TEST

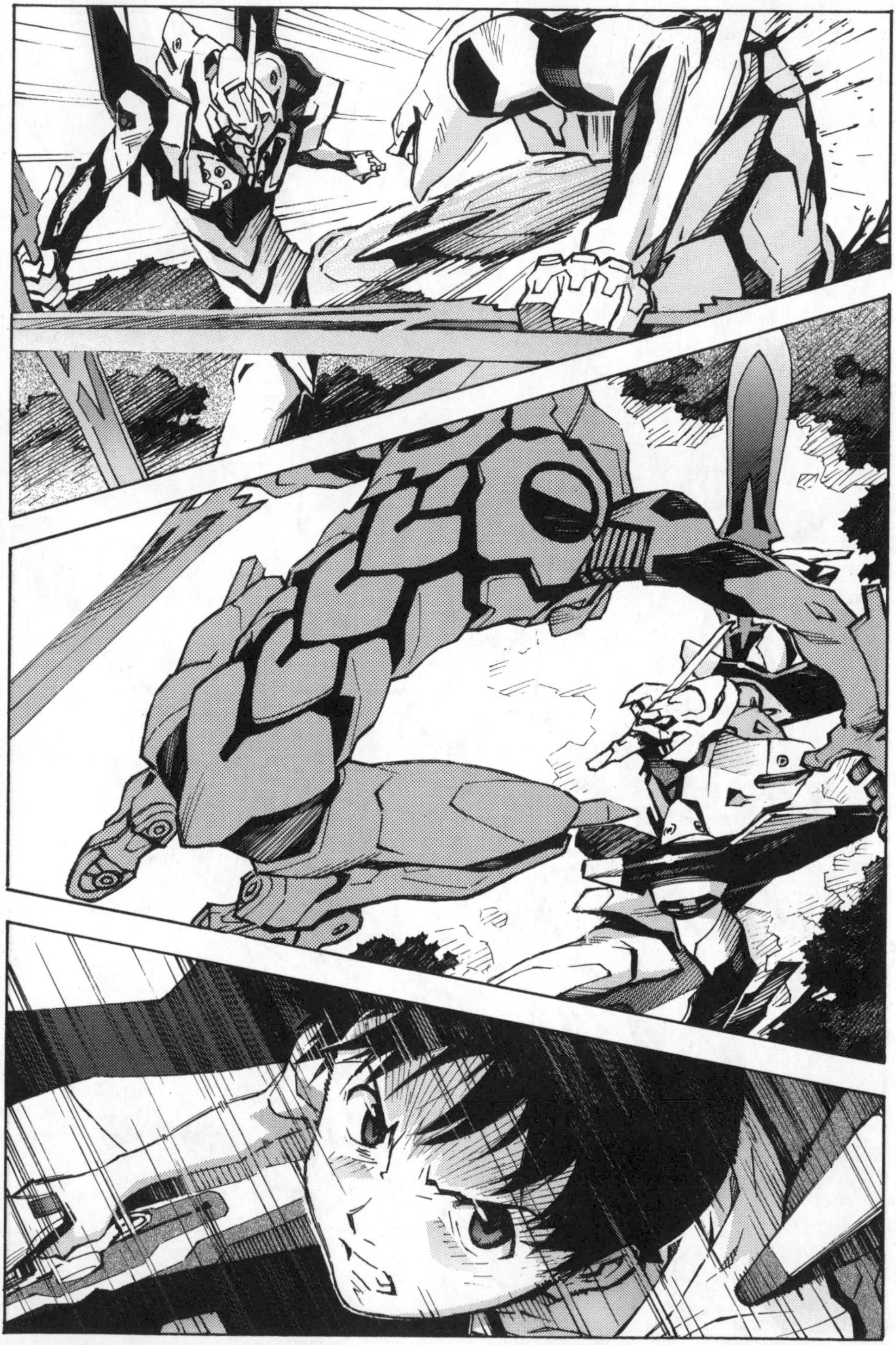

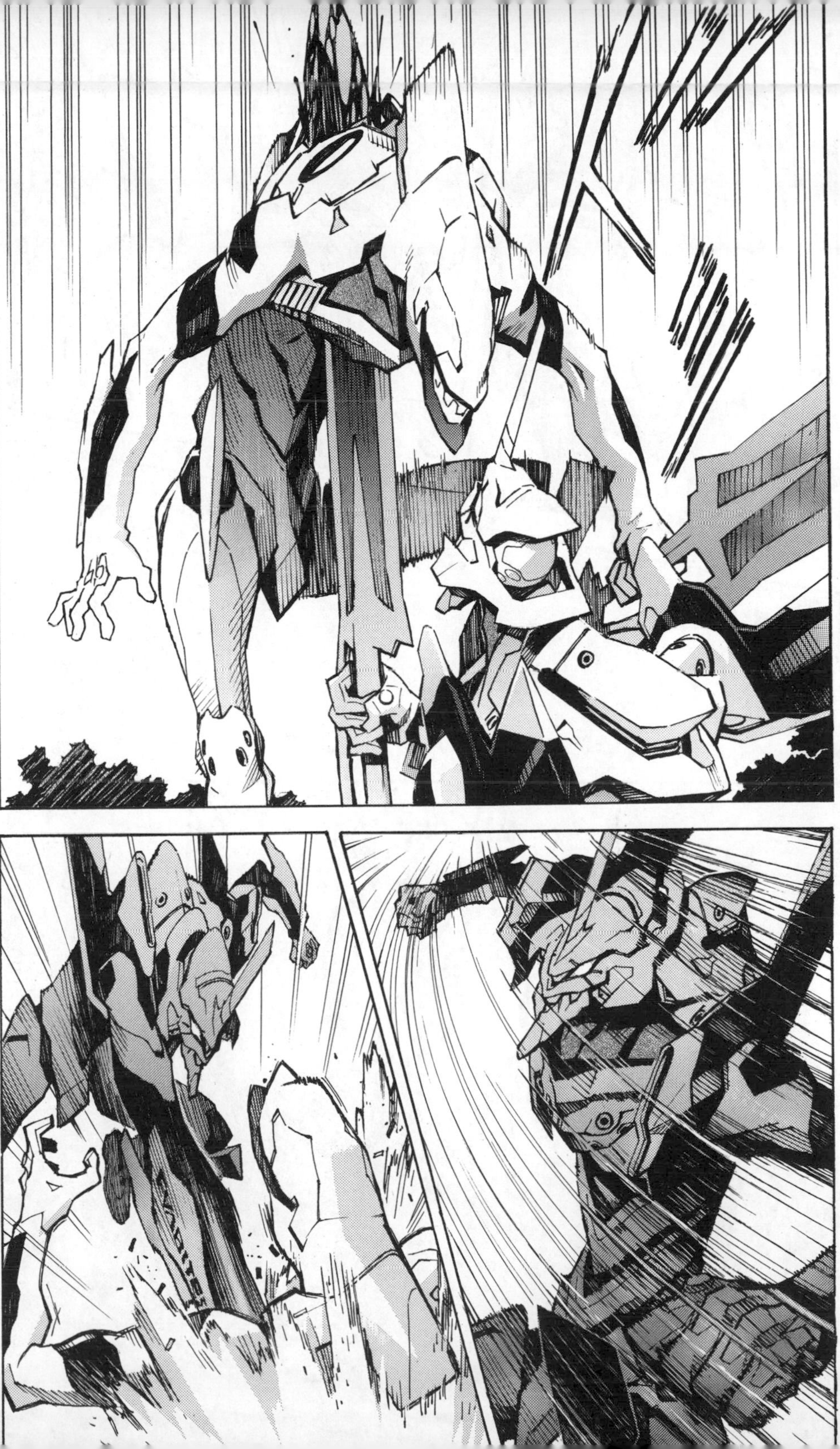

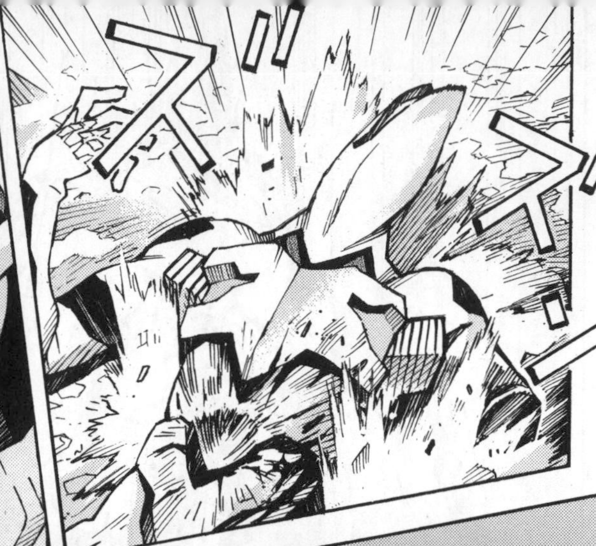
ズ
ズ
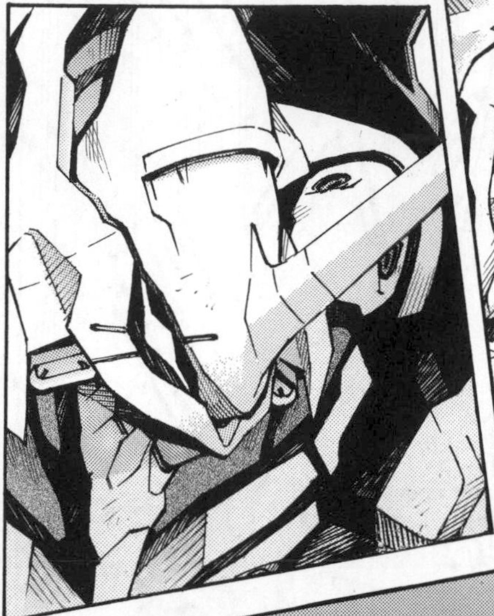
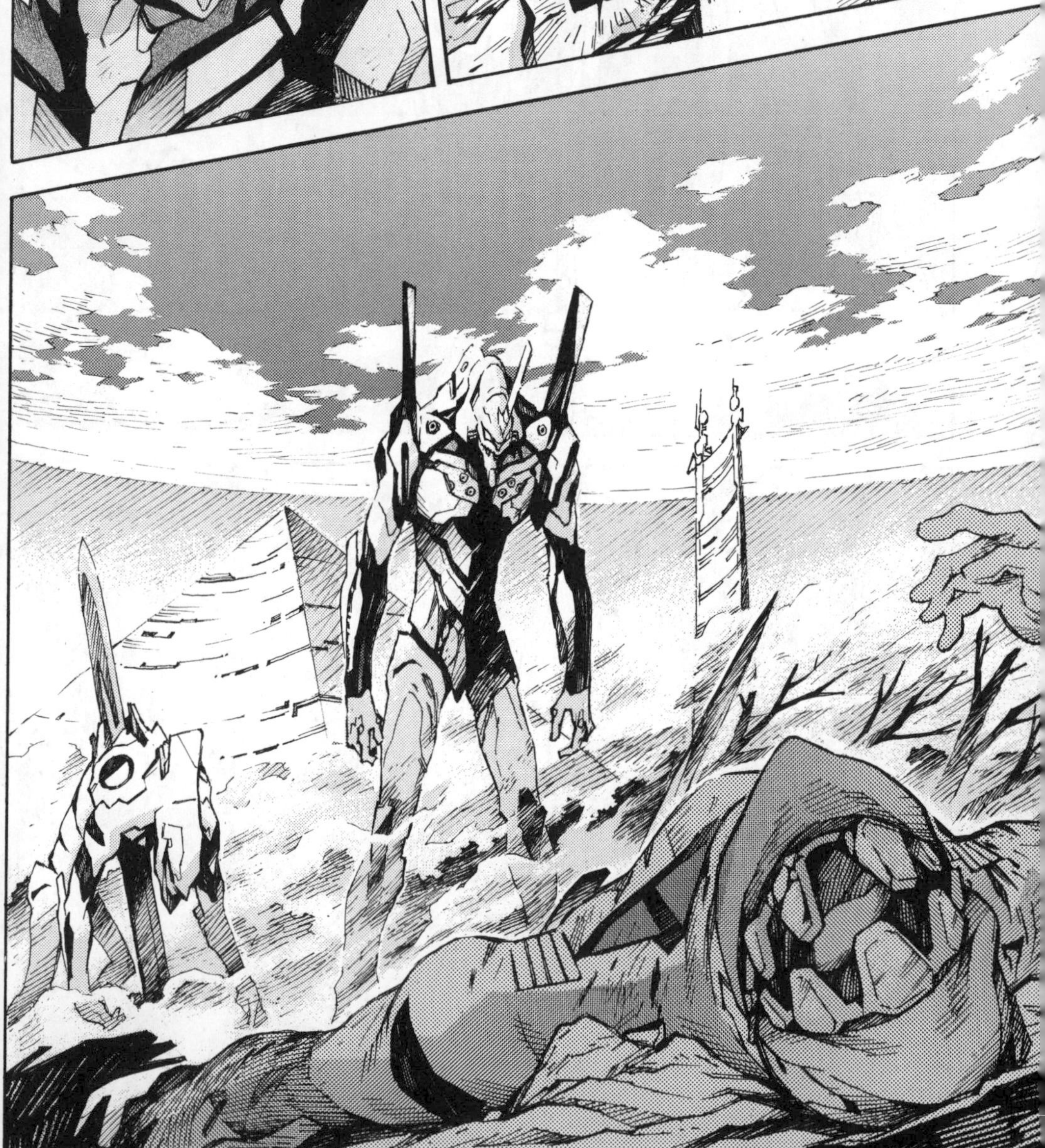

NEON GENESIS EVANGELION

STAGE 85: BETRAYAL

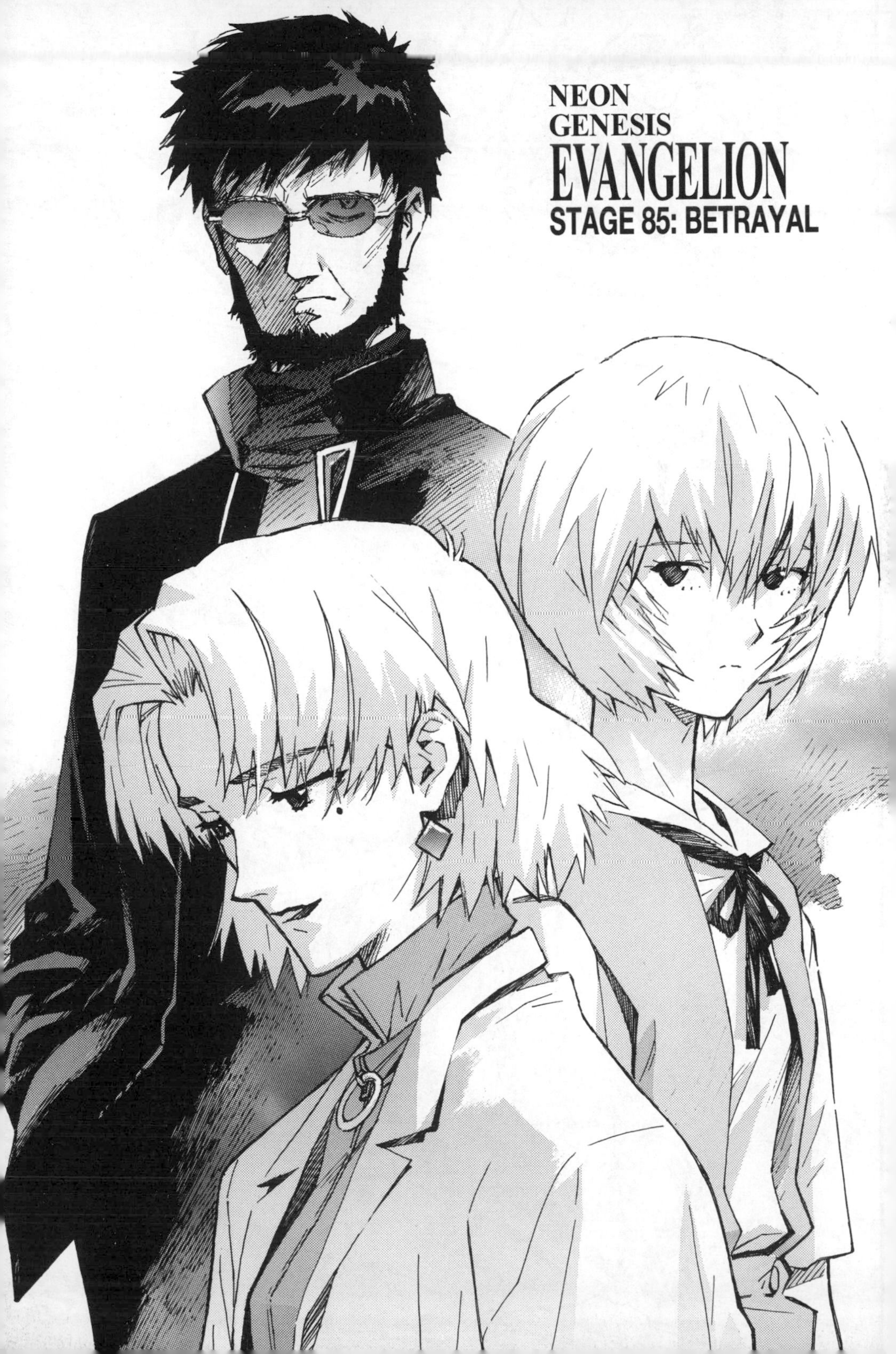

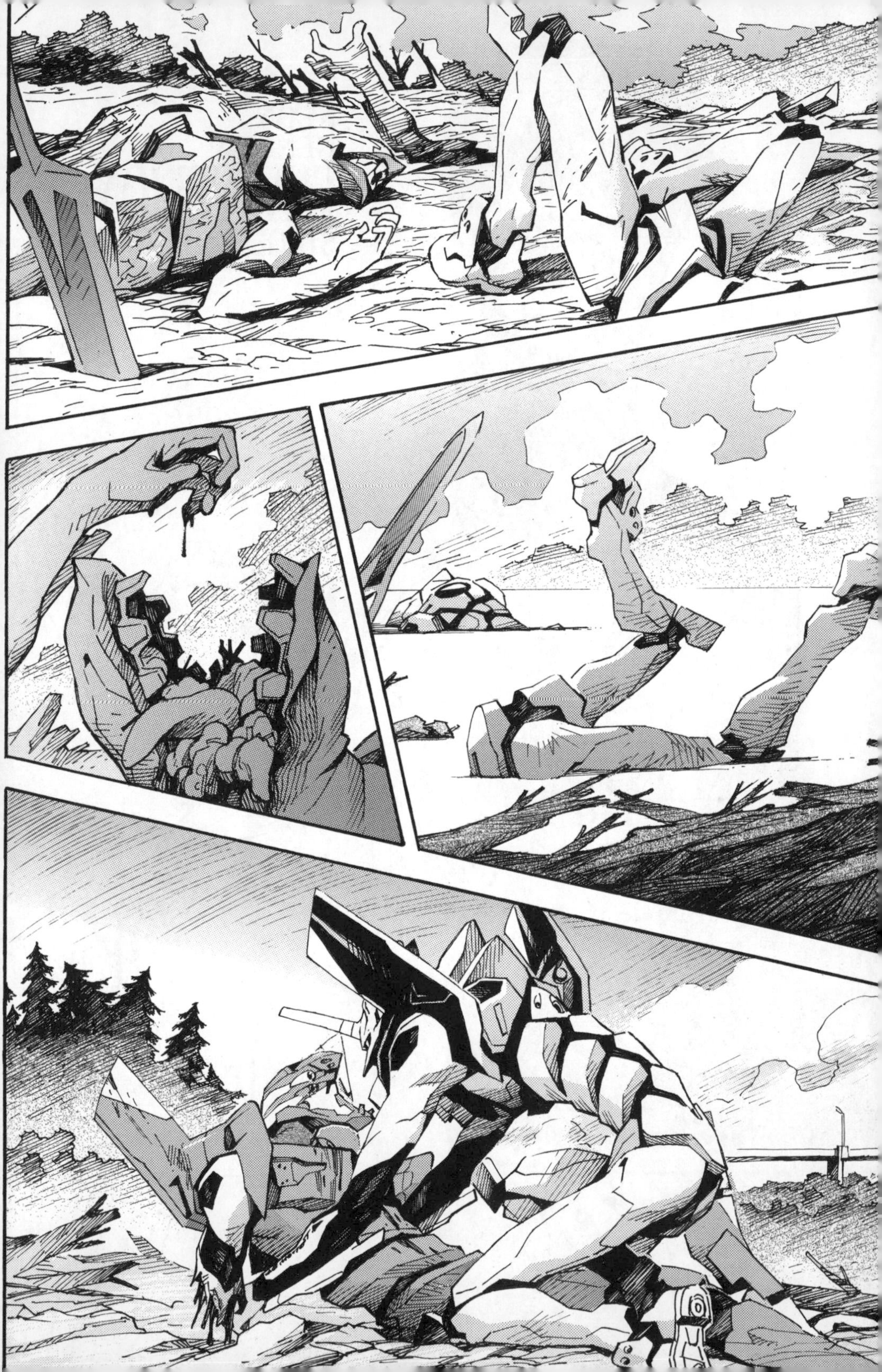

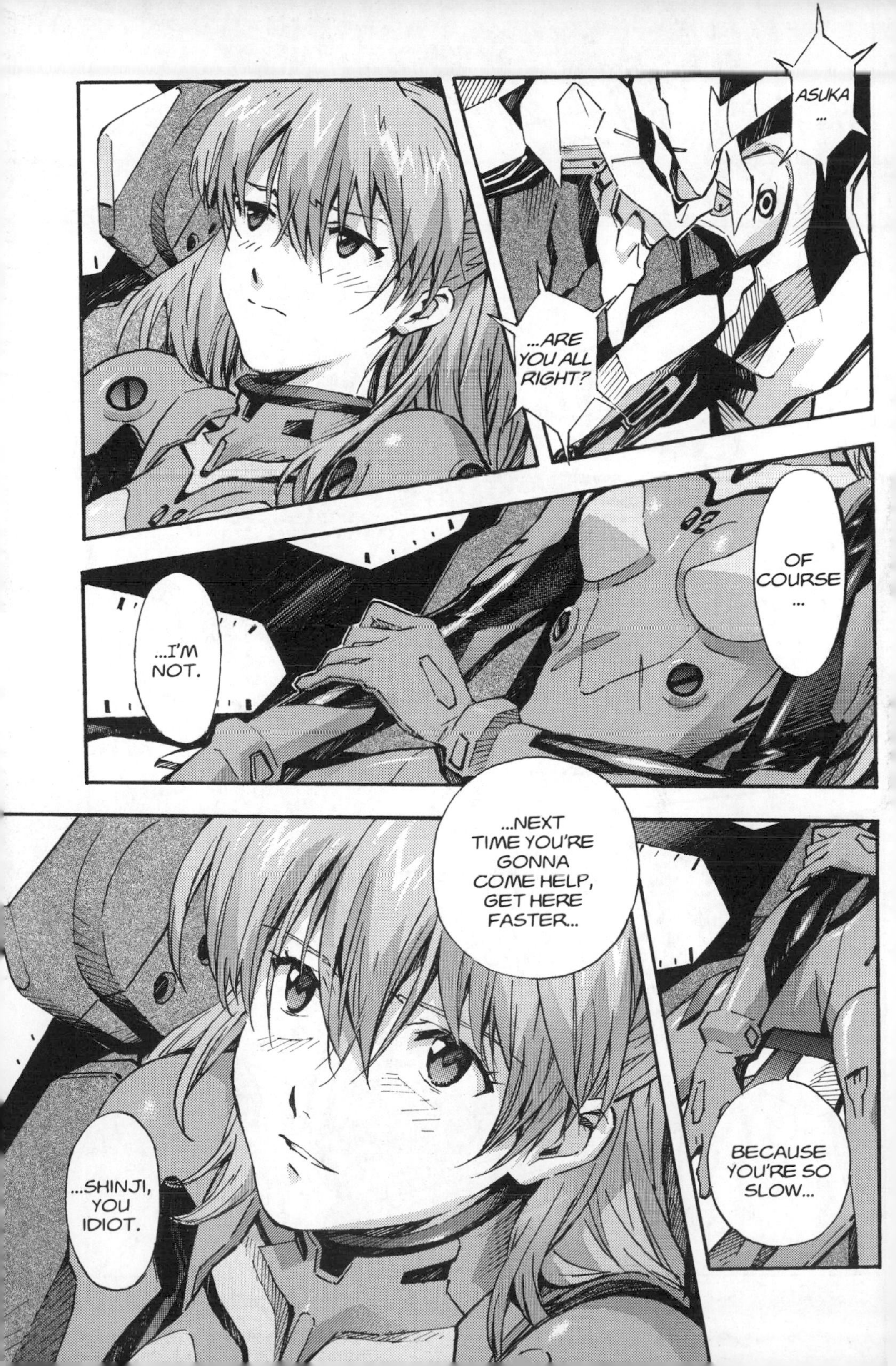
ASUKA ...
...ARE YOU ALL RIGHT?
OF COURSE ...
...I'M NOT.
...NEXT TIME YOU'RE GONNA COME HELP, GET HERE FASTER...
BECAUSE YOU'RE SO SLOW...
...SHINJI, YOU IDIOT.

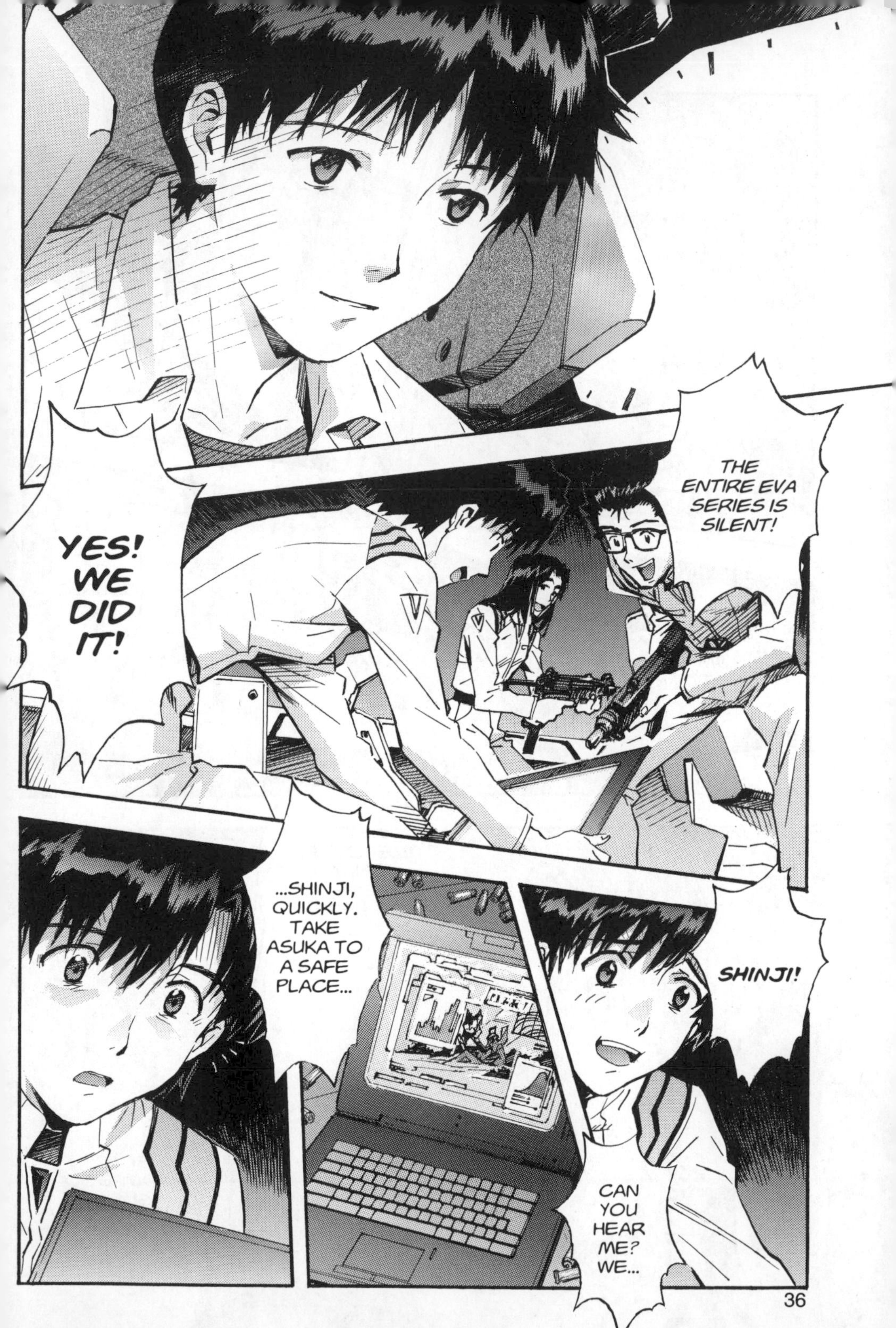
THE ENTIRE EVA SERIES IS SILENT!
YES! WE DID IT!
SHINJI!
CAN YOU HEAR ME? WE...
...SHINJI, QUICKLY. TAKE ASUKA TO A SAFE PLACE...

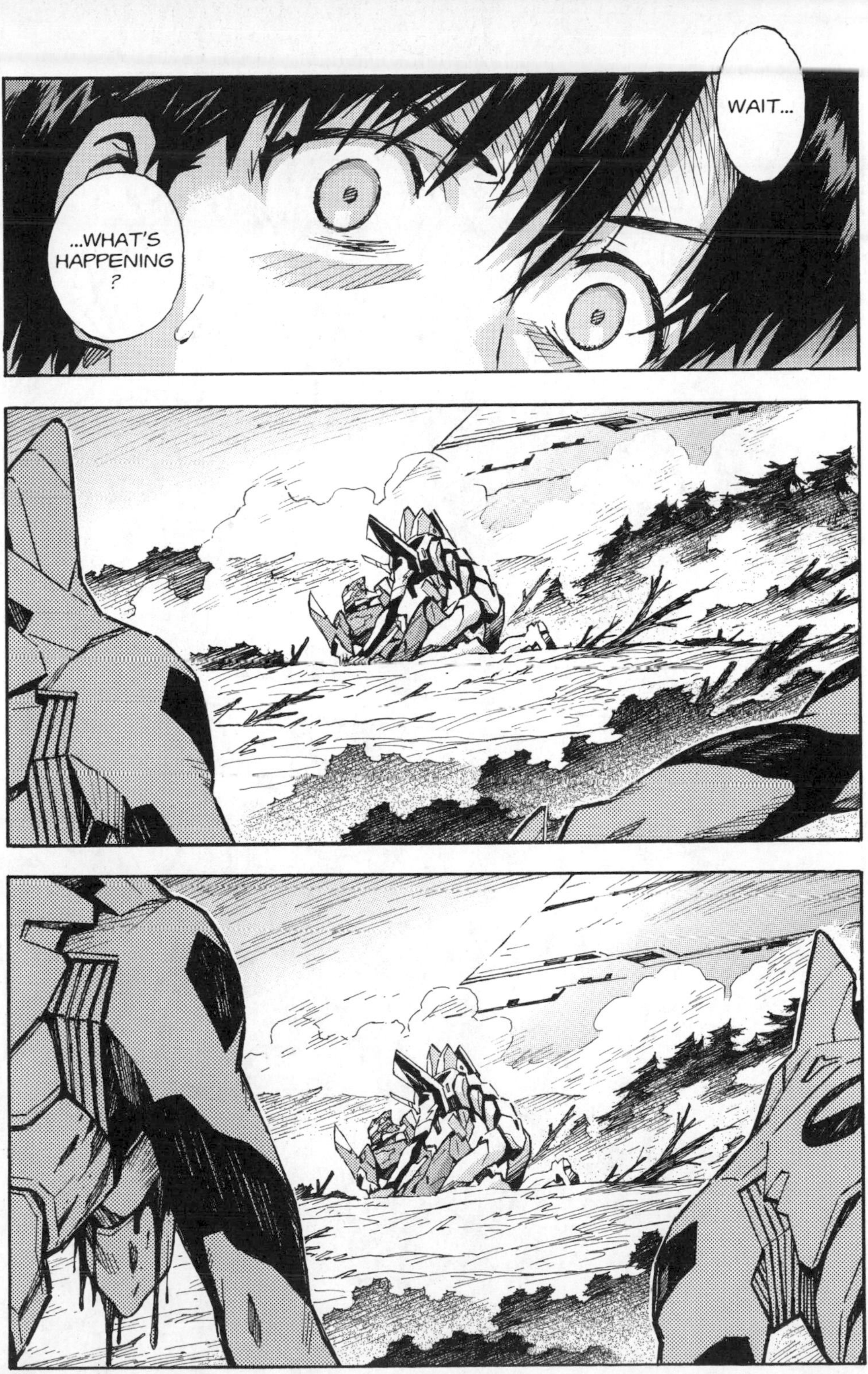
WAIT...
...WHAT'S HAPPENING ?

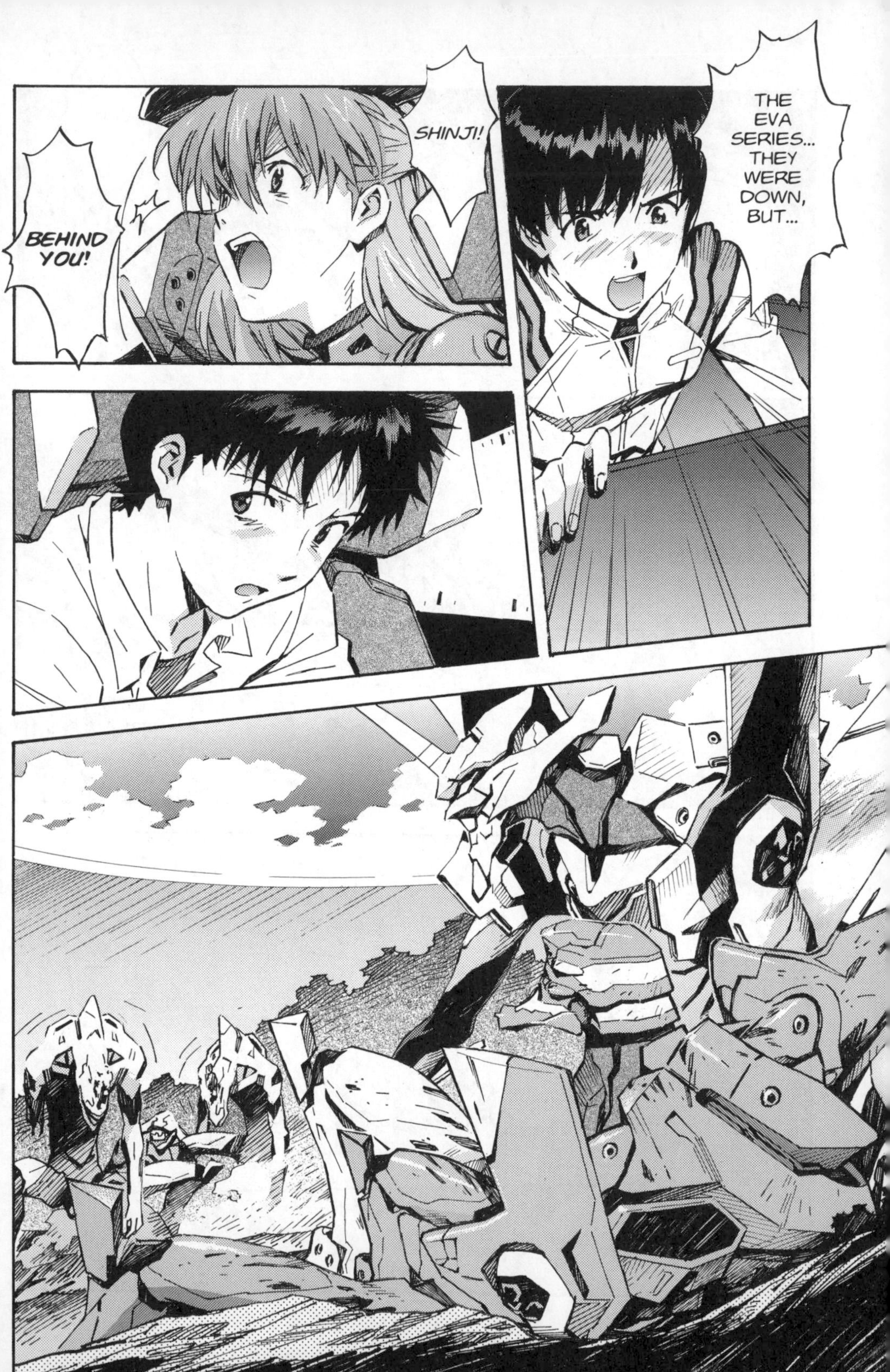
THE EVA SERIES... THEY WERE DOWN, BUT...
SHINJI!
BEHIND YOU!

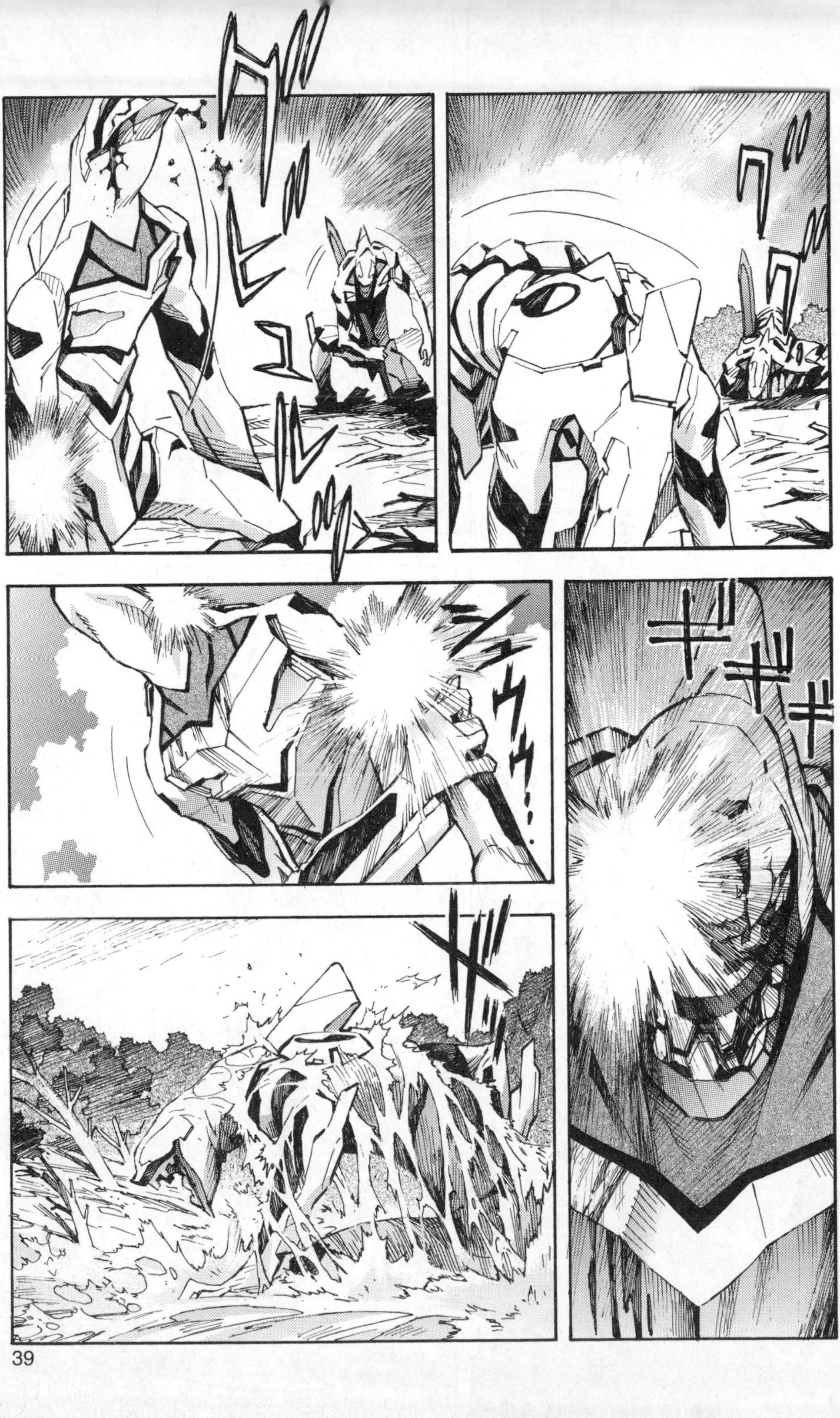
グググ
ギギギ

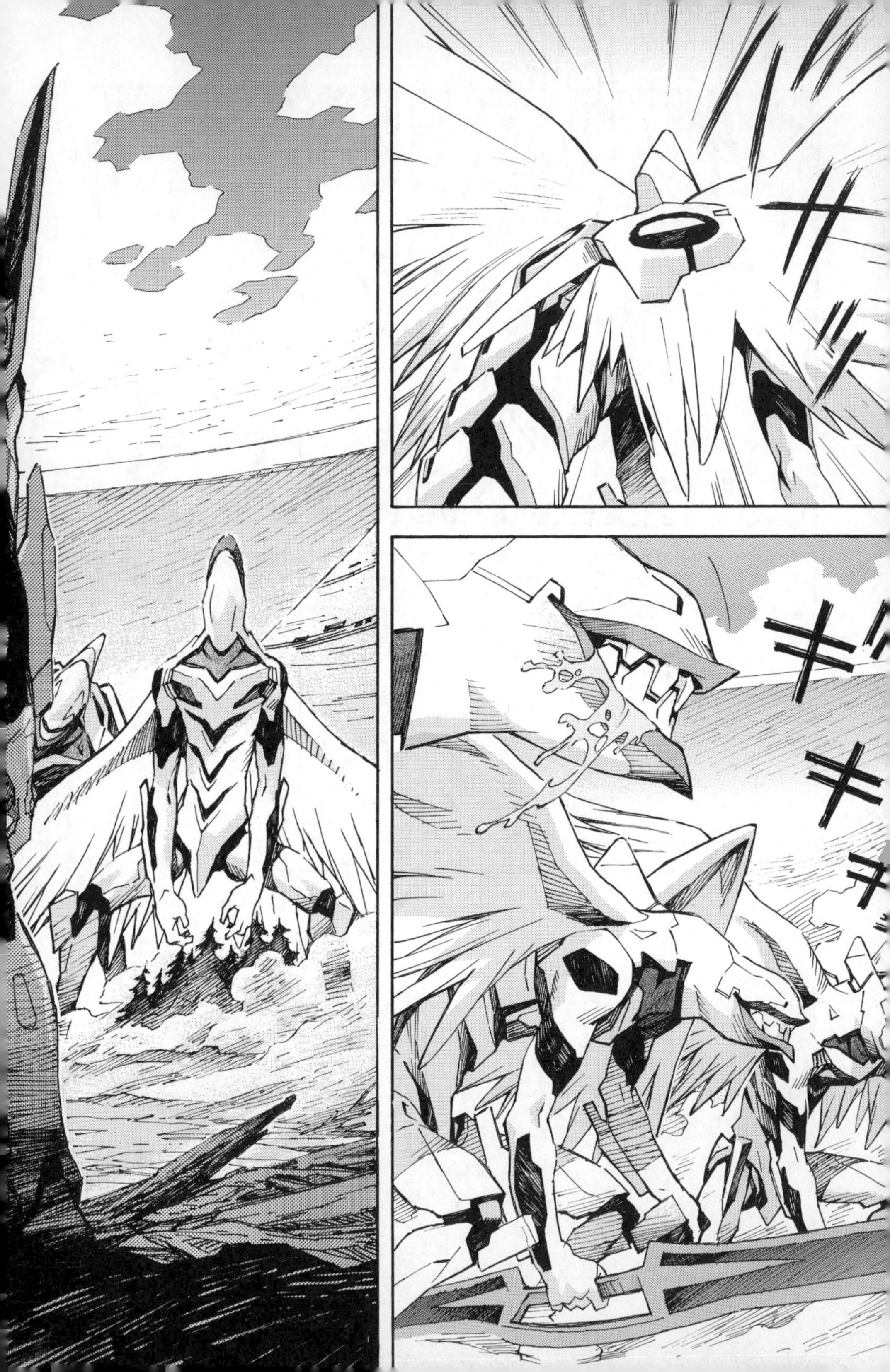

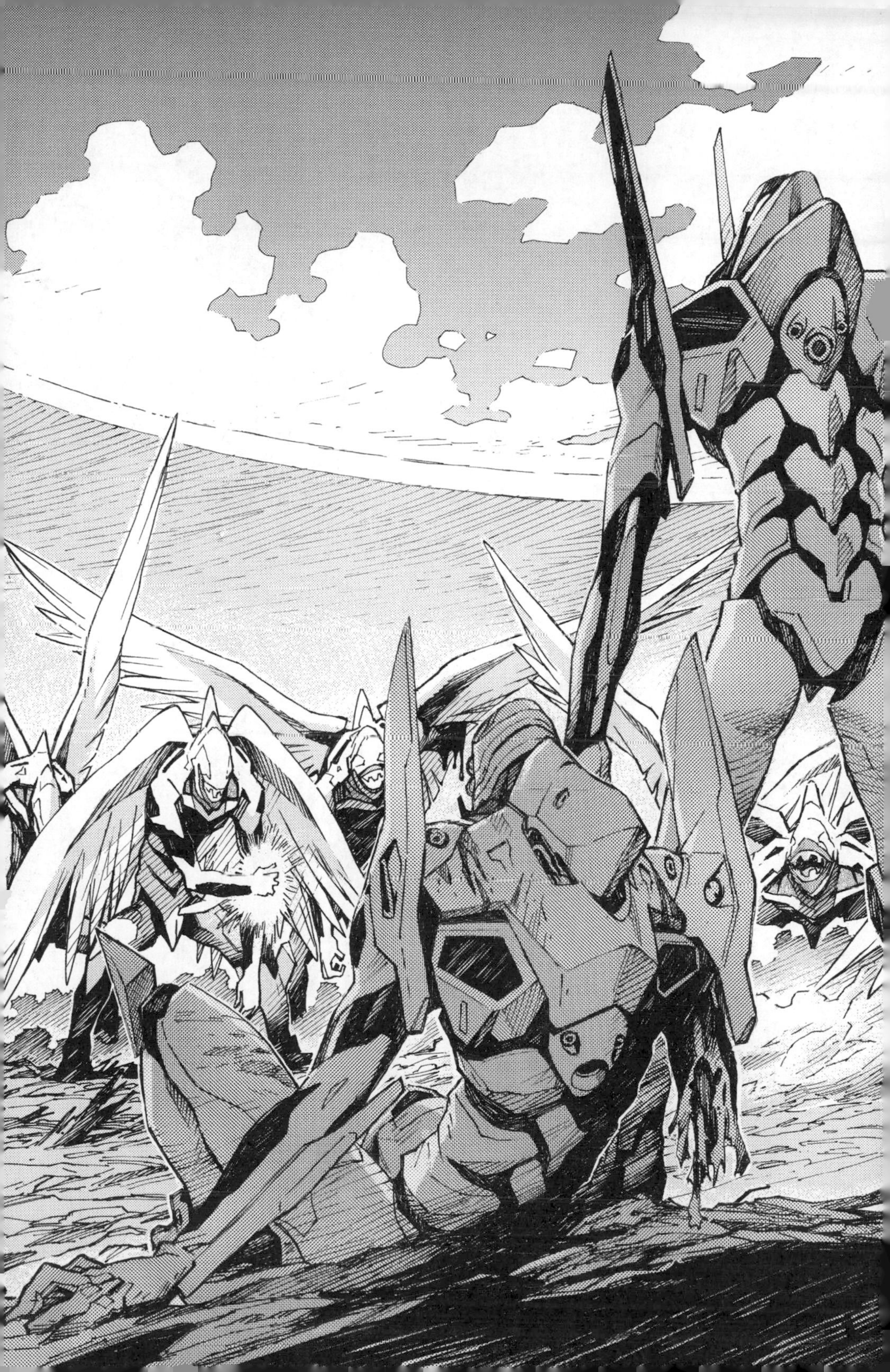

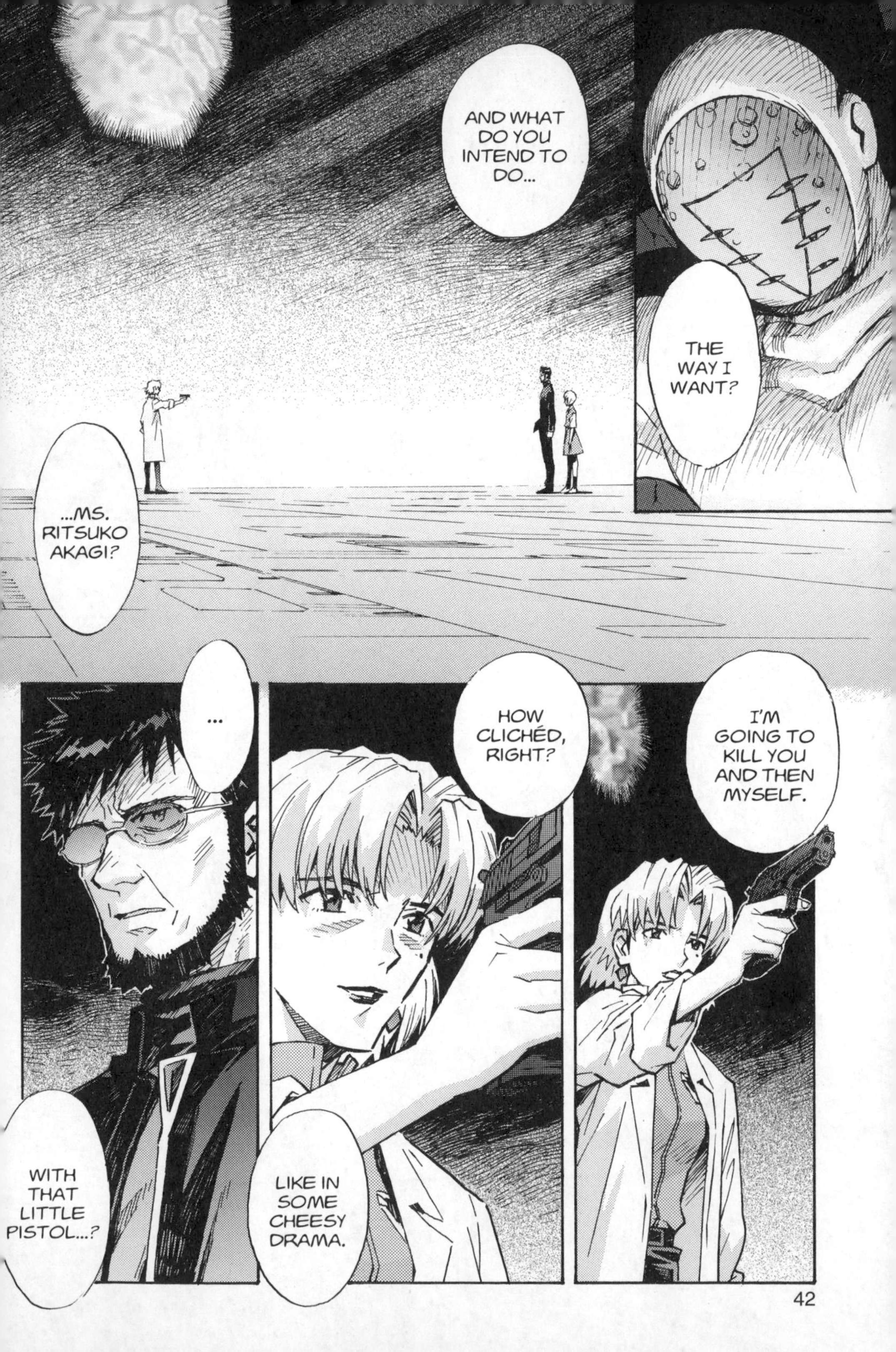
THE WAY I WANT?
AND WHAT DO YOU INTEND TO DO...
...MS. RITSUKO AKAGI?
I'M GOING TO KILL YOU AND THEN MYSELF.
HOW CLICHÉD, RIGHT?
LIKE IN SOME CHEESY DRAMA.
...
WITH THAT LITTLE PISTOL...?

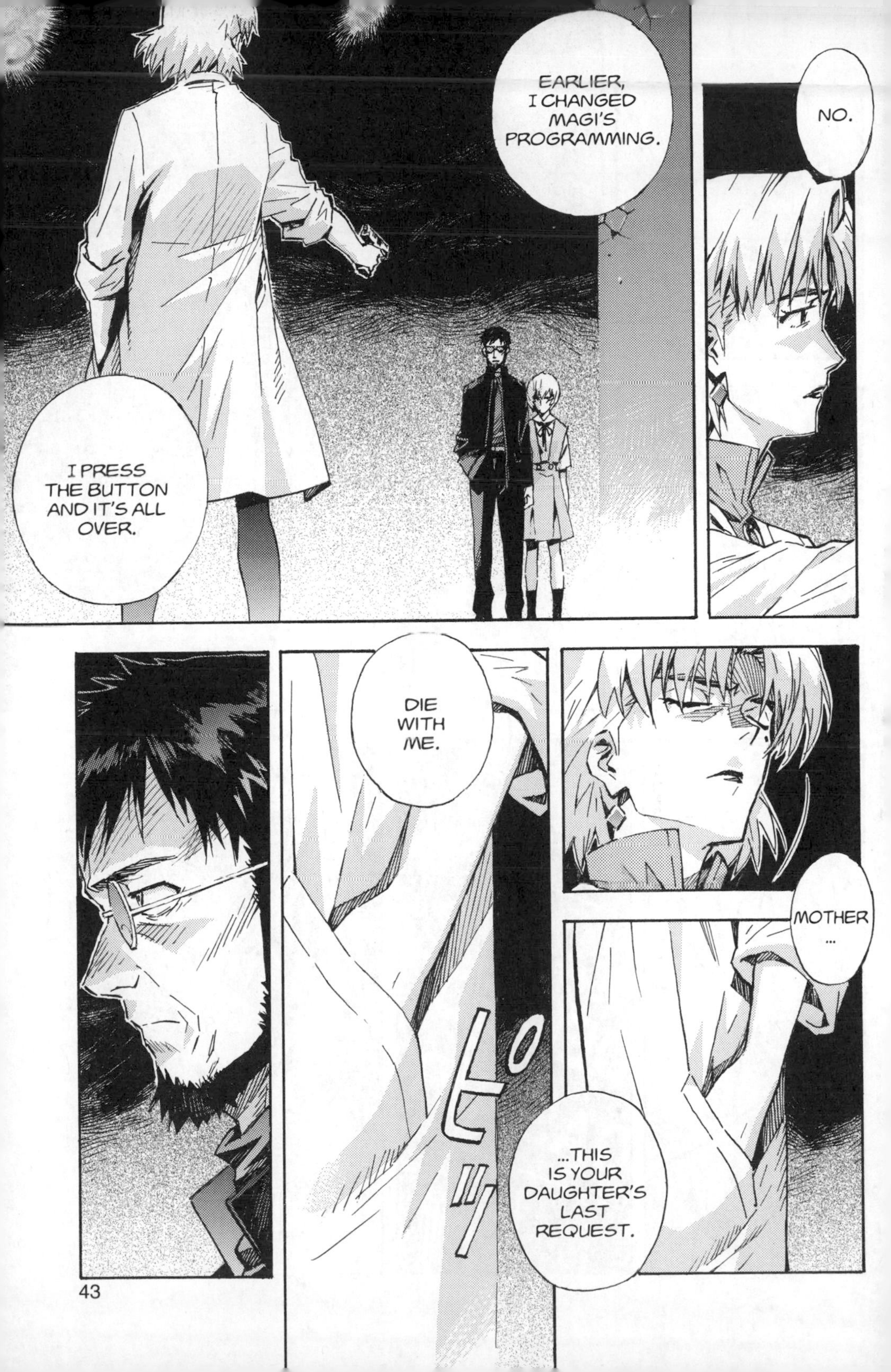
NO.
EARLIER, I CHANGED MAGI'S PROGRAMMING.
I PRESS THE BUTTON AND IT'S ALL OVER.
MOTHER ...
...THIS IS YOUR DAUGHTER'S LAST REQUEST.
DIE WITH ME.
ピッ

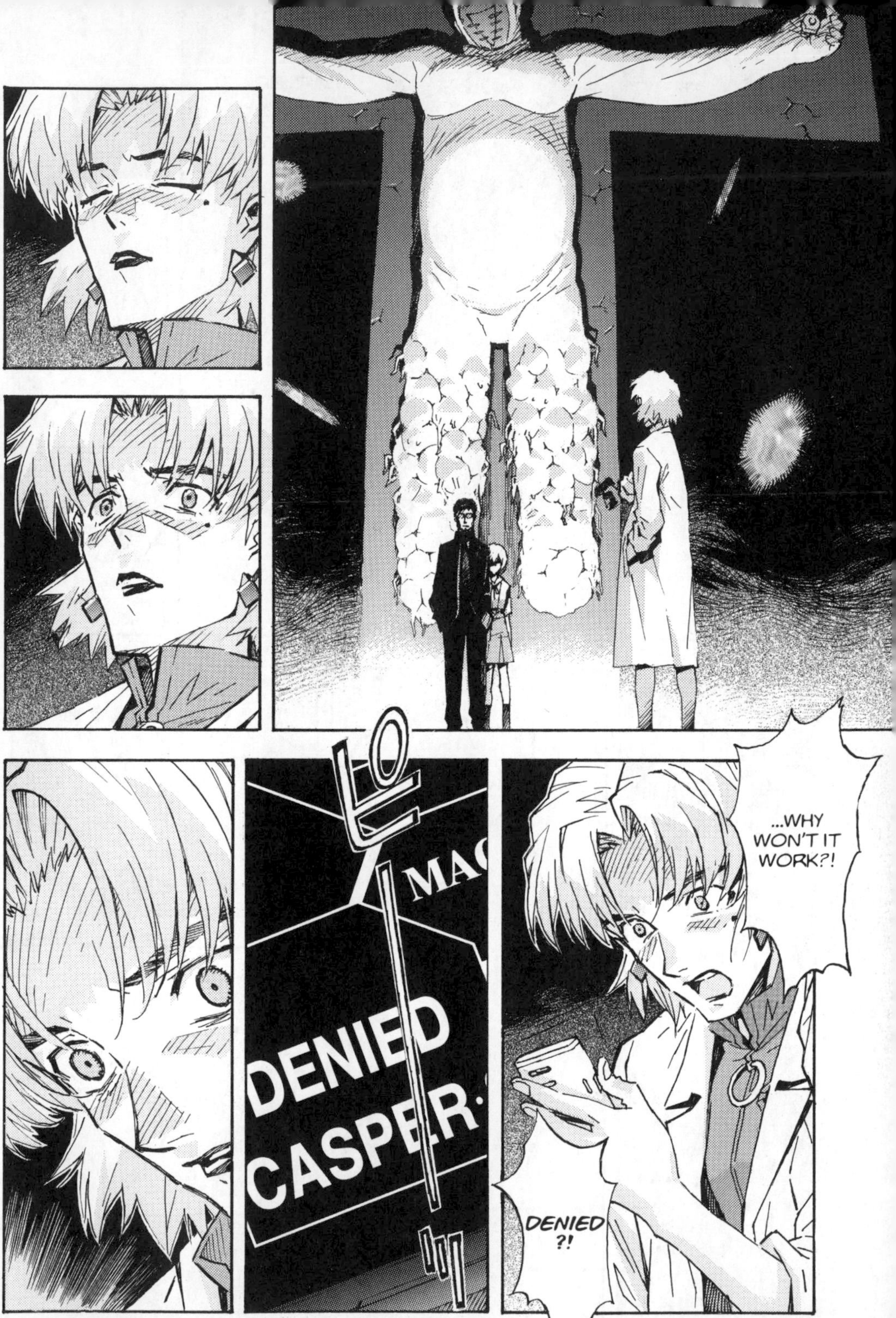
...WHY WON'T IT WORK?!
DENIED ?!
MAG
DENIED
CASPER·

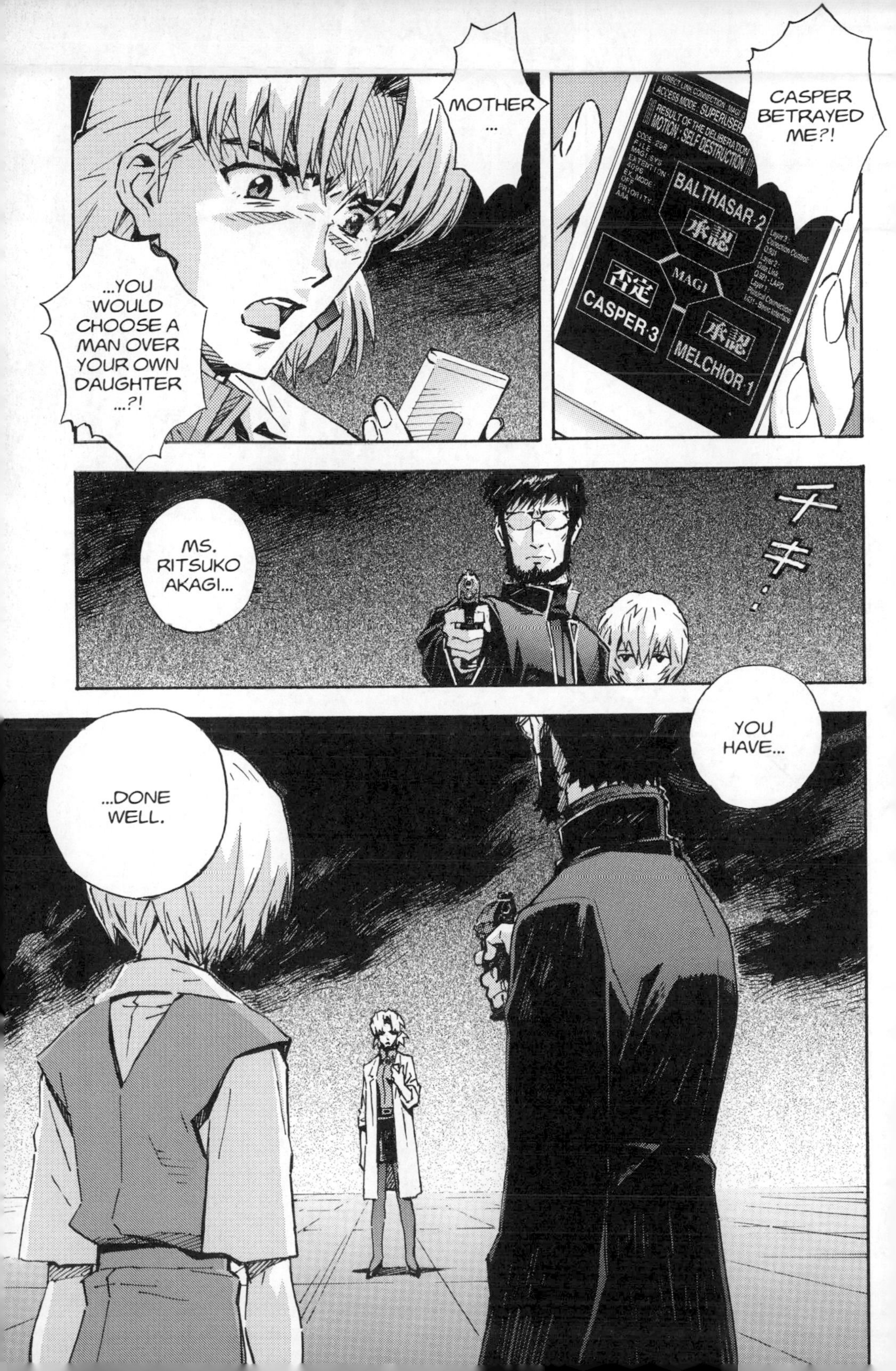
CASPER BETRAYED ME?!
ACCESS MODE : SUPERUSER
RESULT OF THE DELIBERATION
MOTION : SELF DESTRUCTION
BALTHASAR-2
承認
MAGI
否定
CASPER-3
承認
MELCHIOR-1
MOTHER ...
...YOU WOULD CHOOSE A MAN OVER YOUR OWN DAUGHTER ...?!
チキ...
MS. RITSUKO AKAGI...
YOU HAVE...
...DONE WELL.

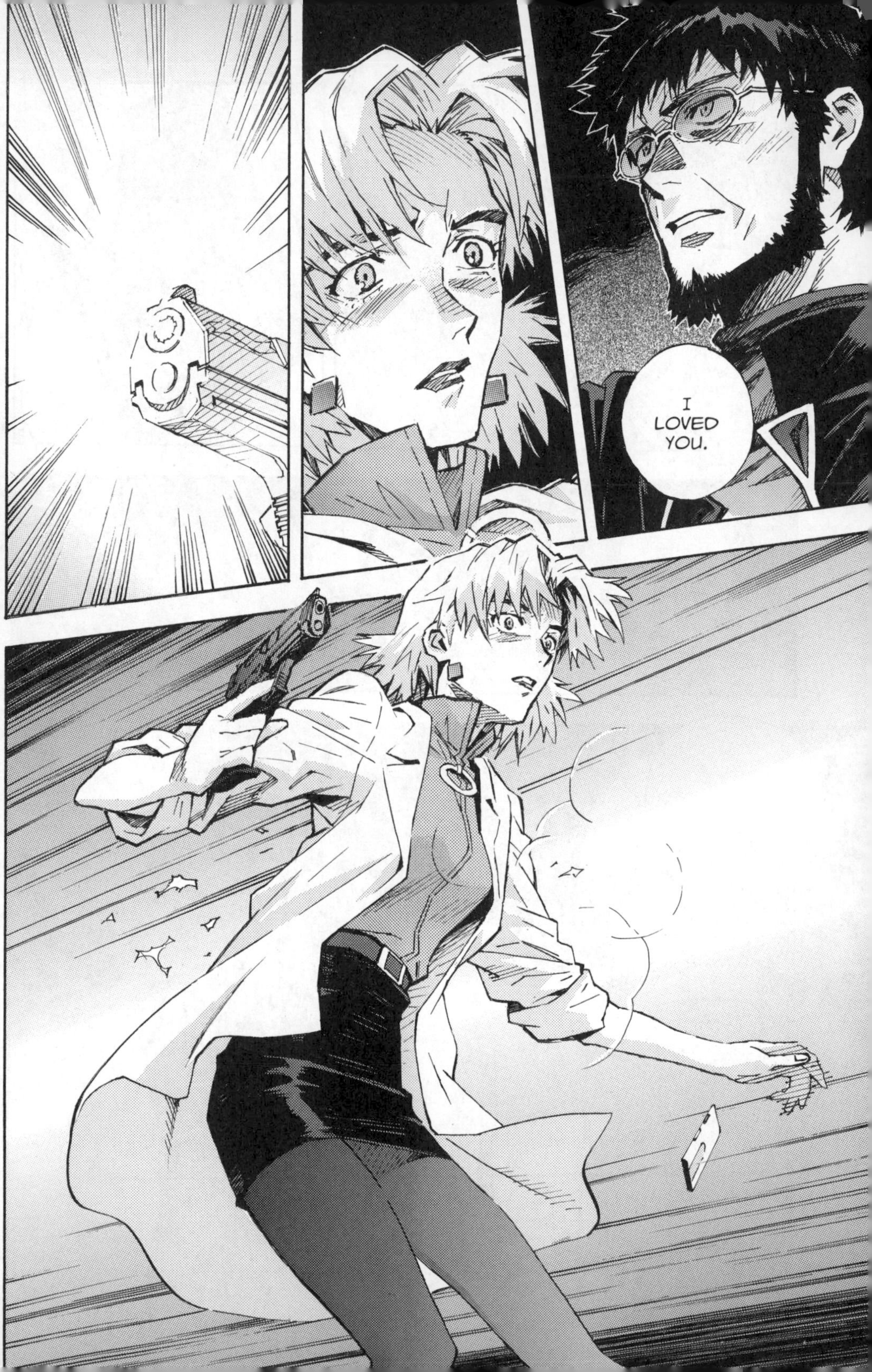
I LOVED YOU.

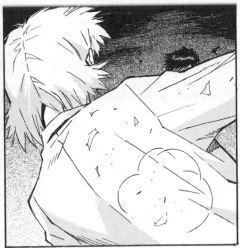

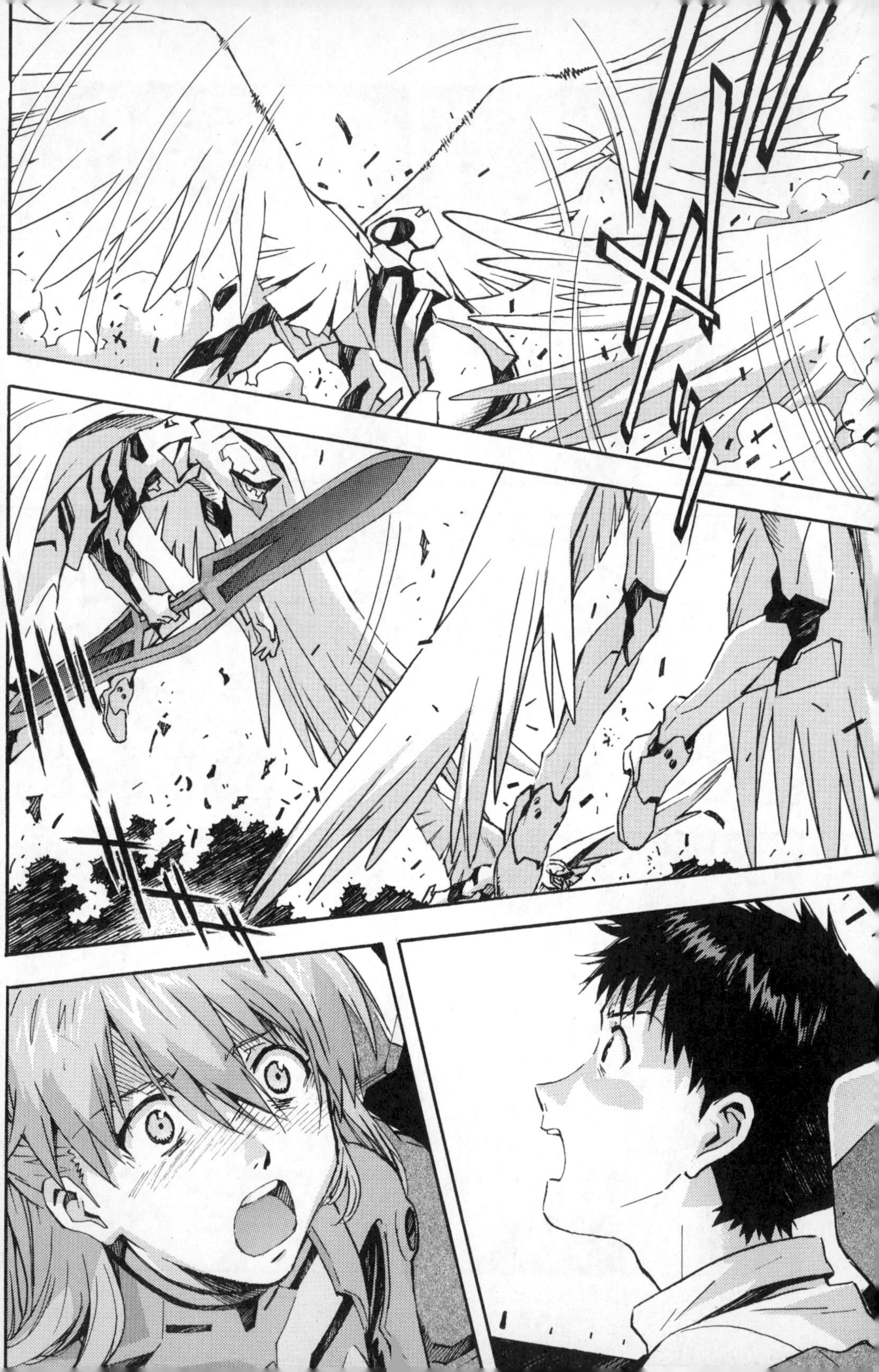

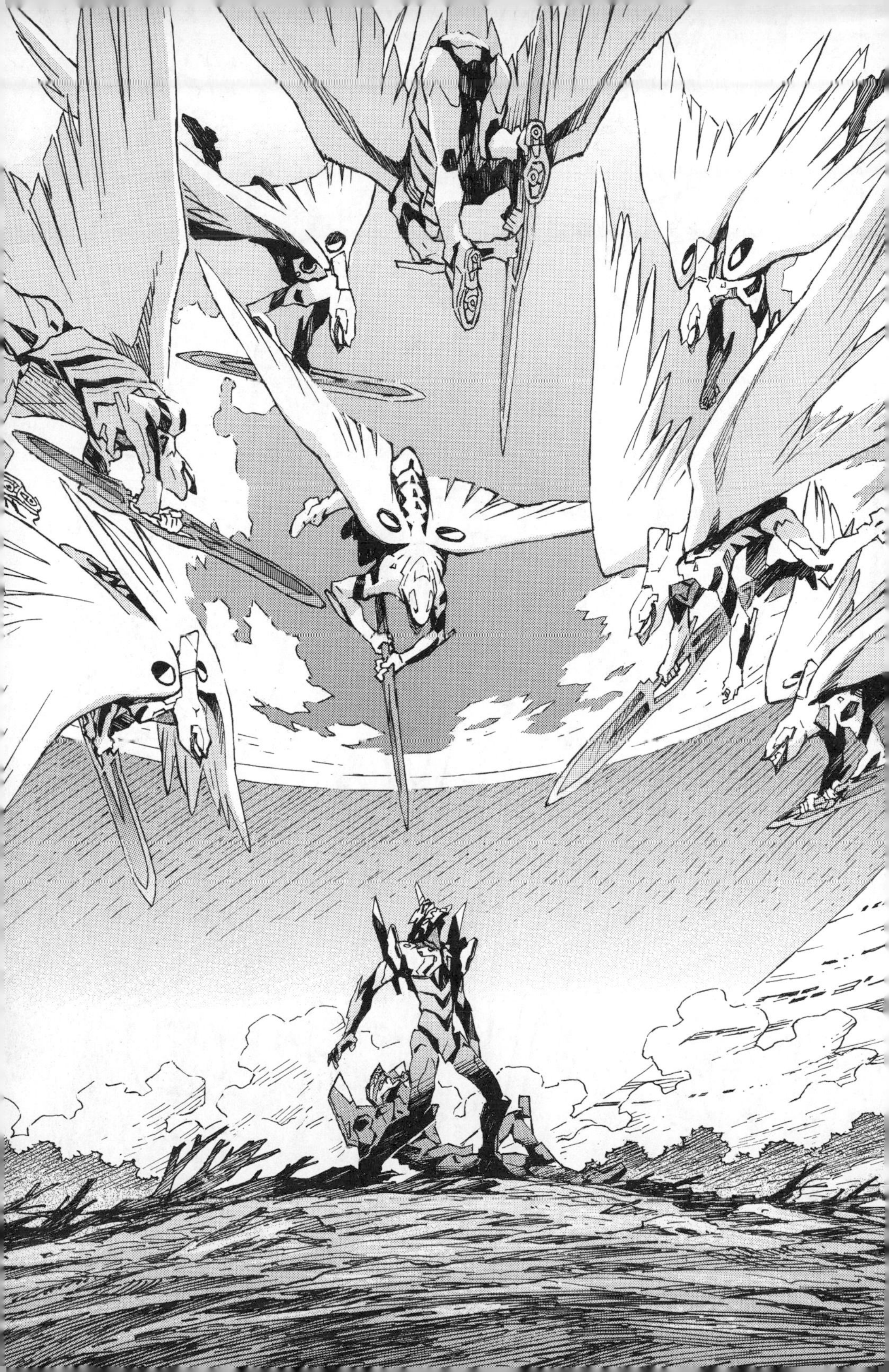

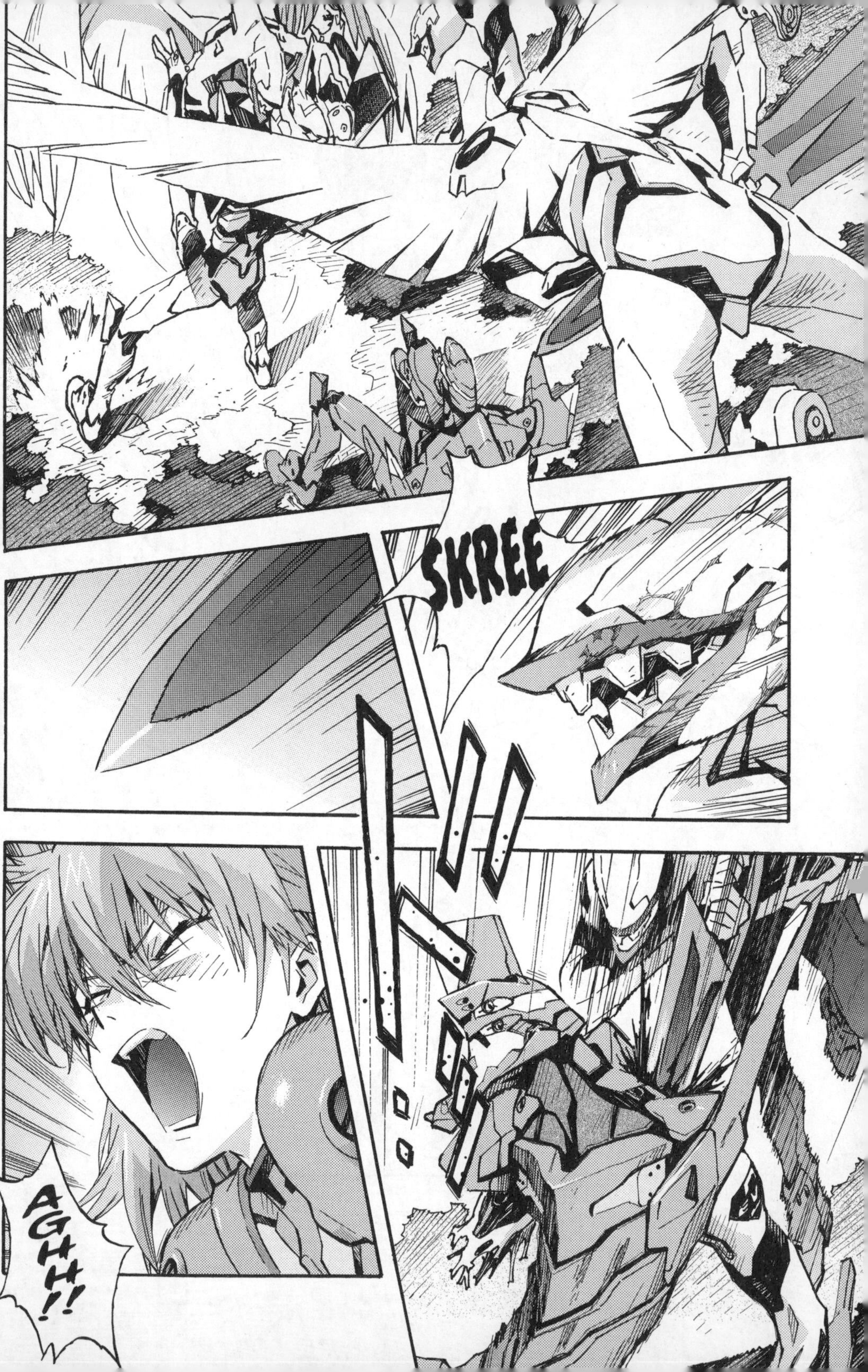
SKREE
AGHH!!

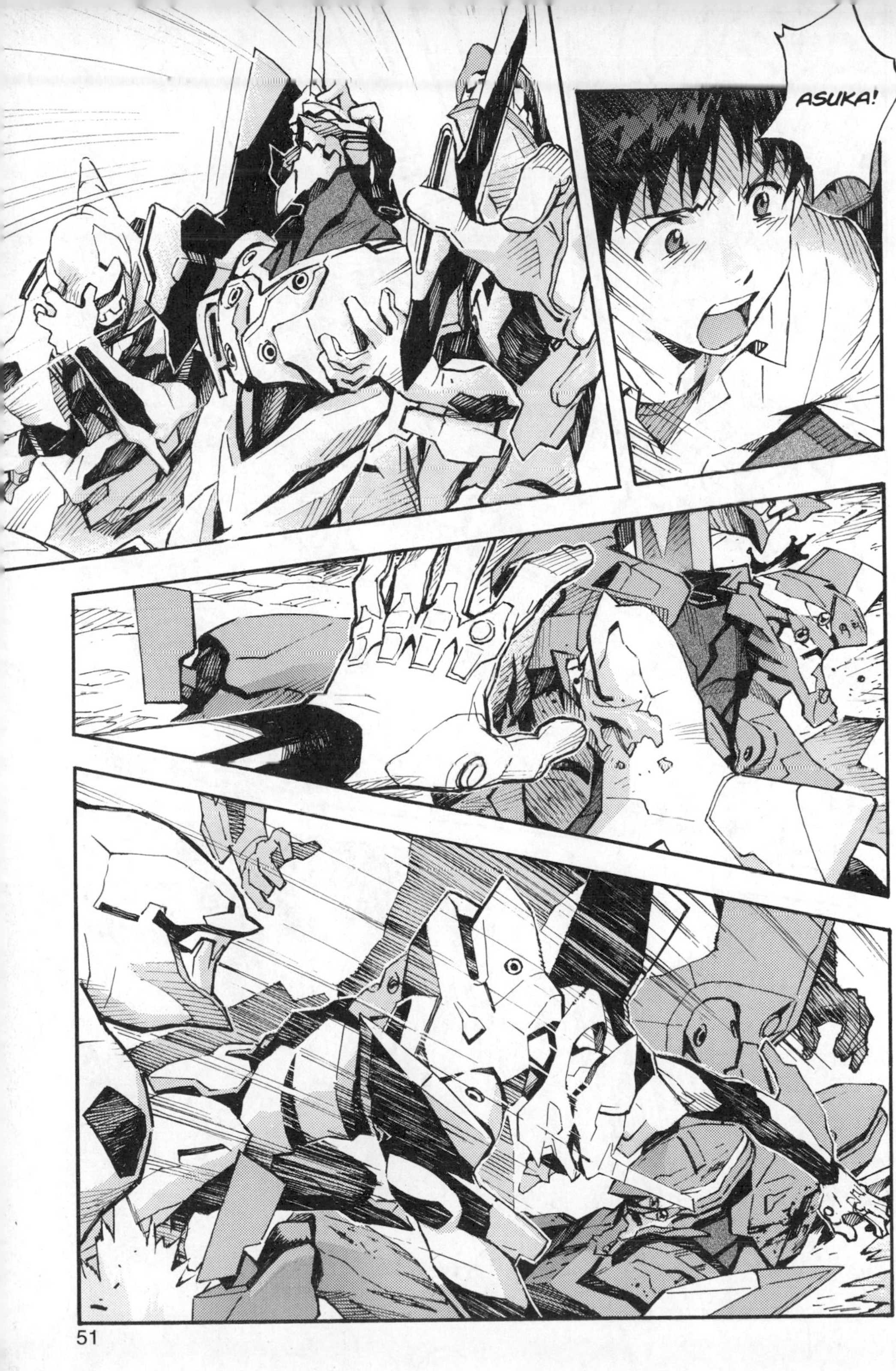
ASUKA!

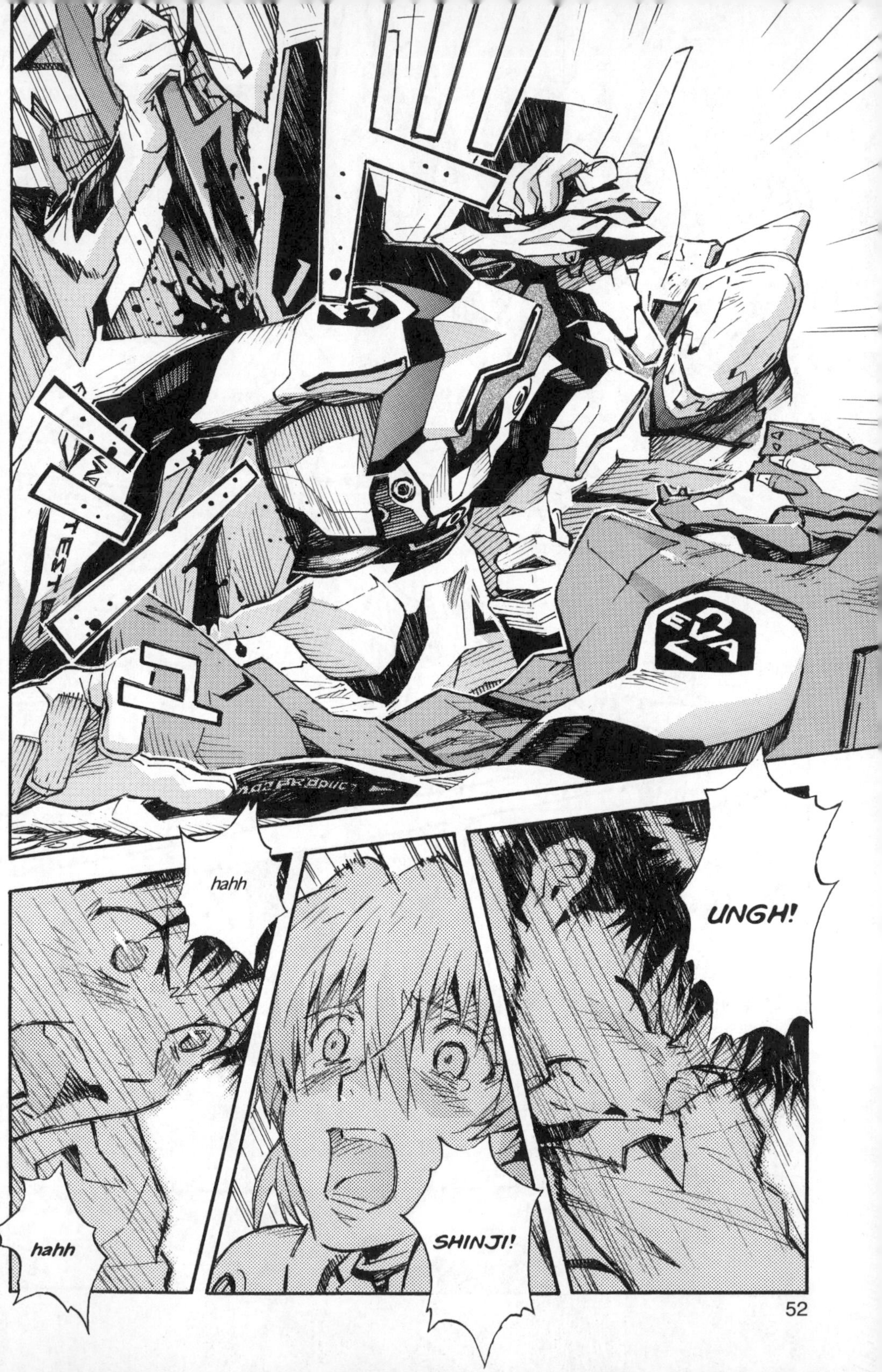
TEST
EVA
UNGH!
SHINJI!
hahh
hahh

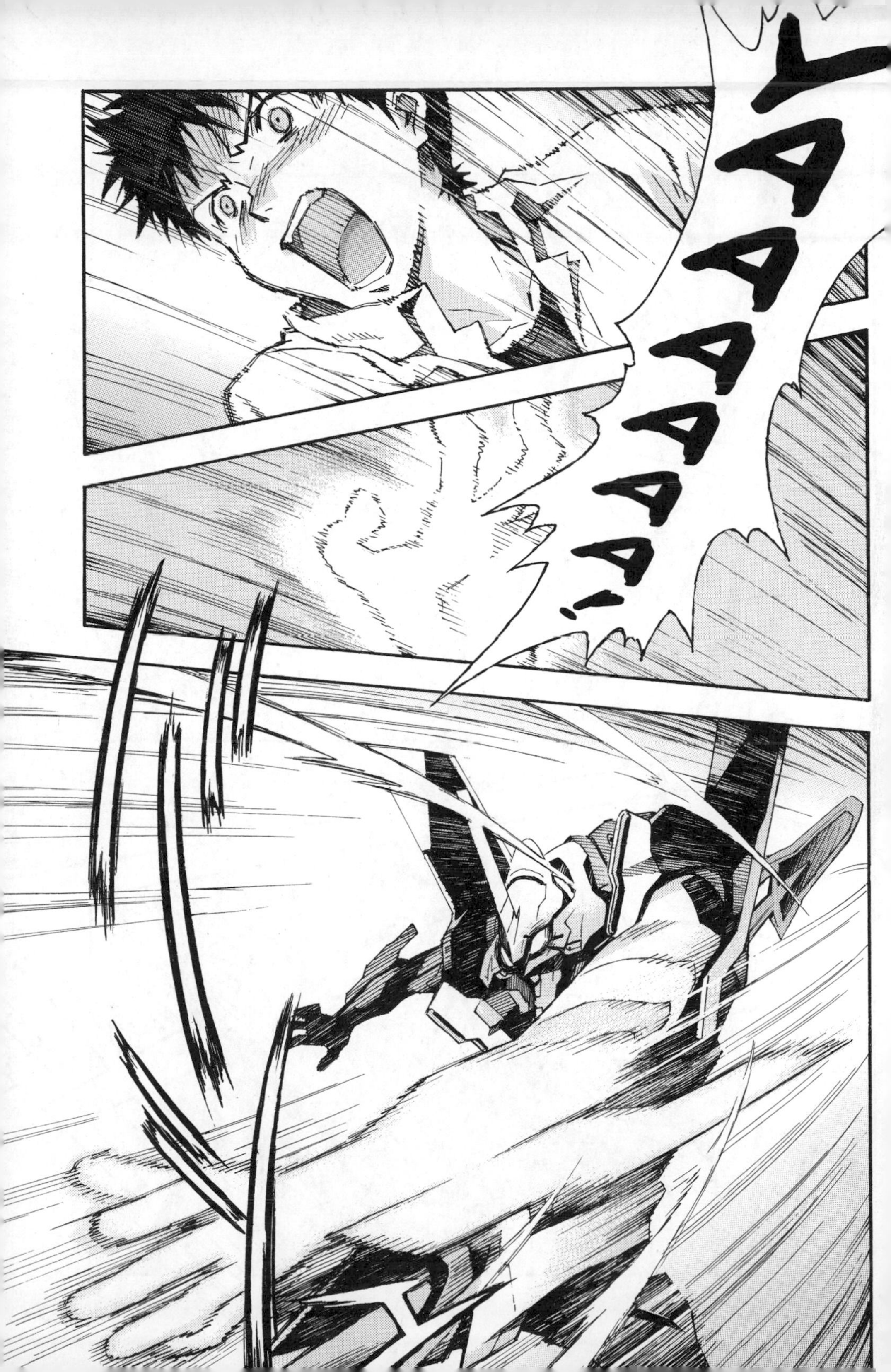
YAAAAAA!!

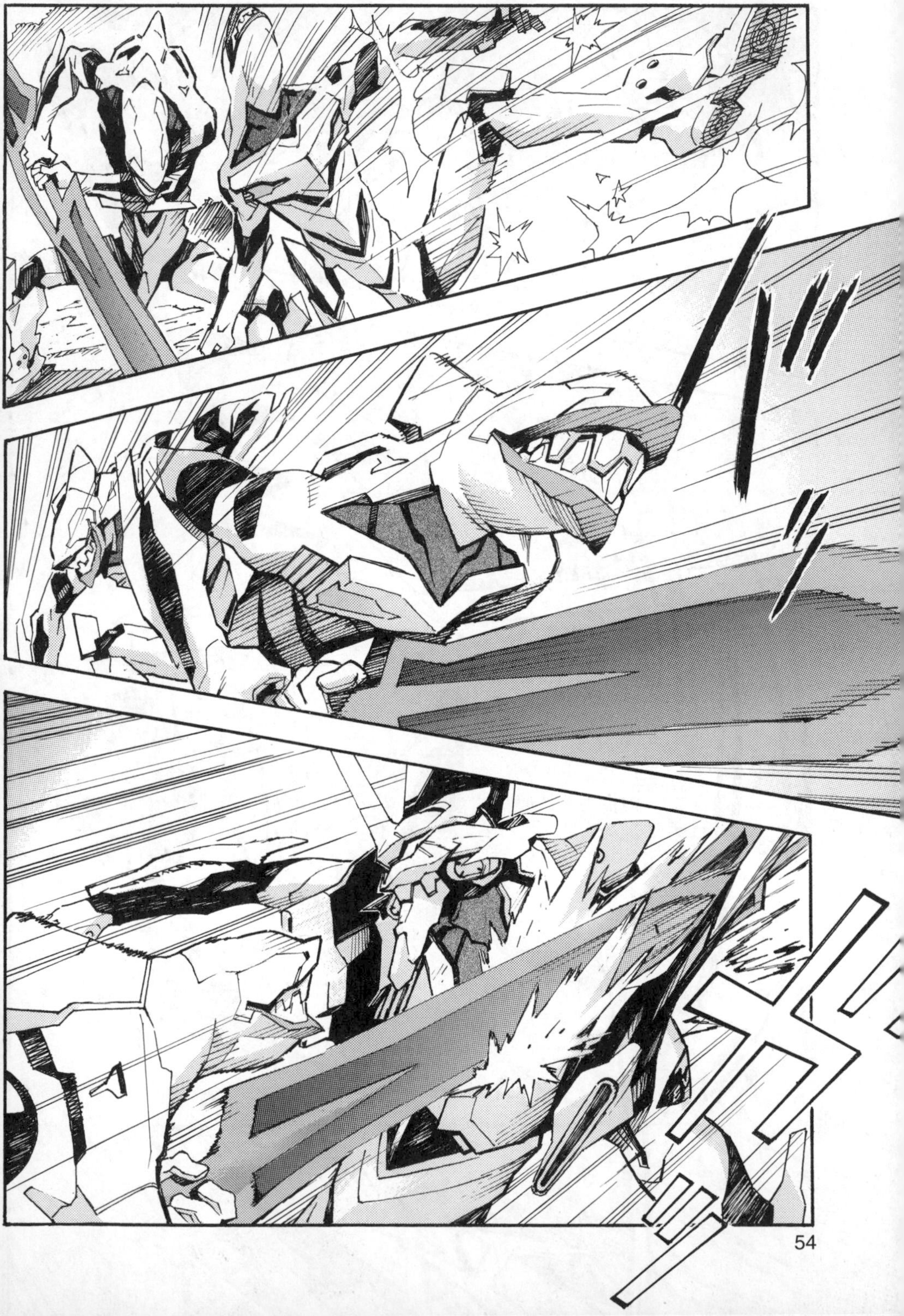

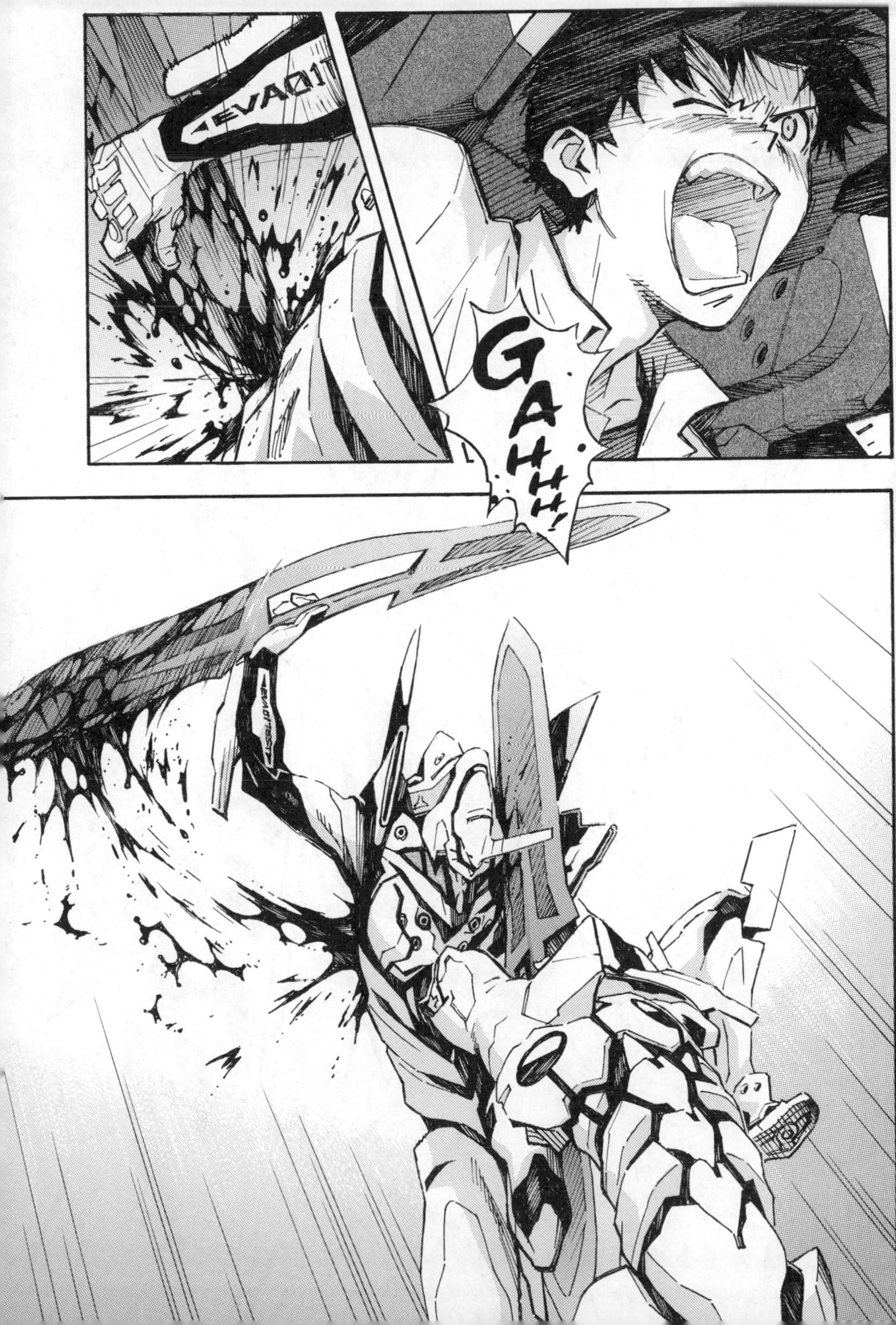
EVA01T
GAHHH!

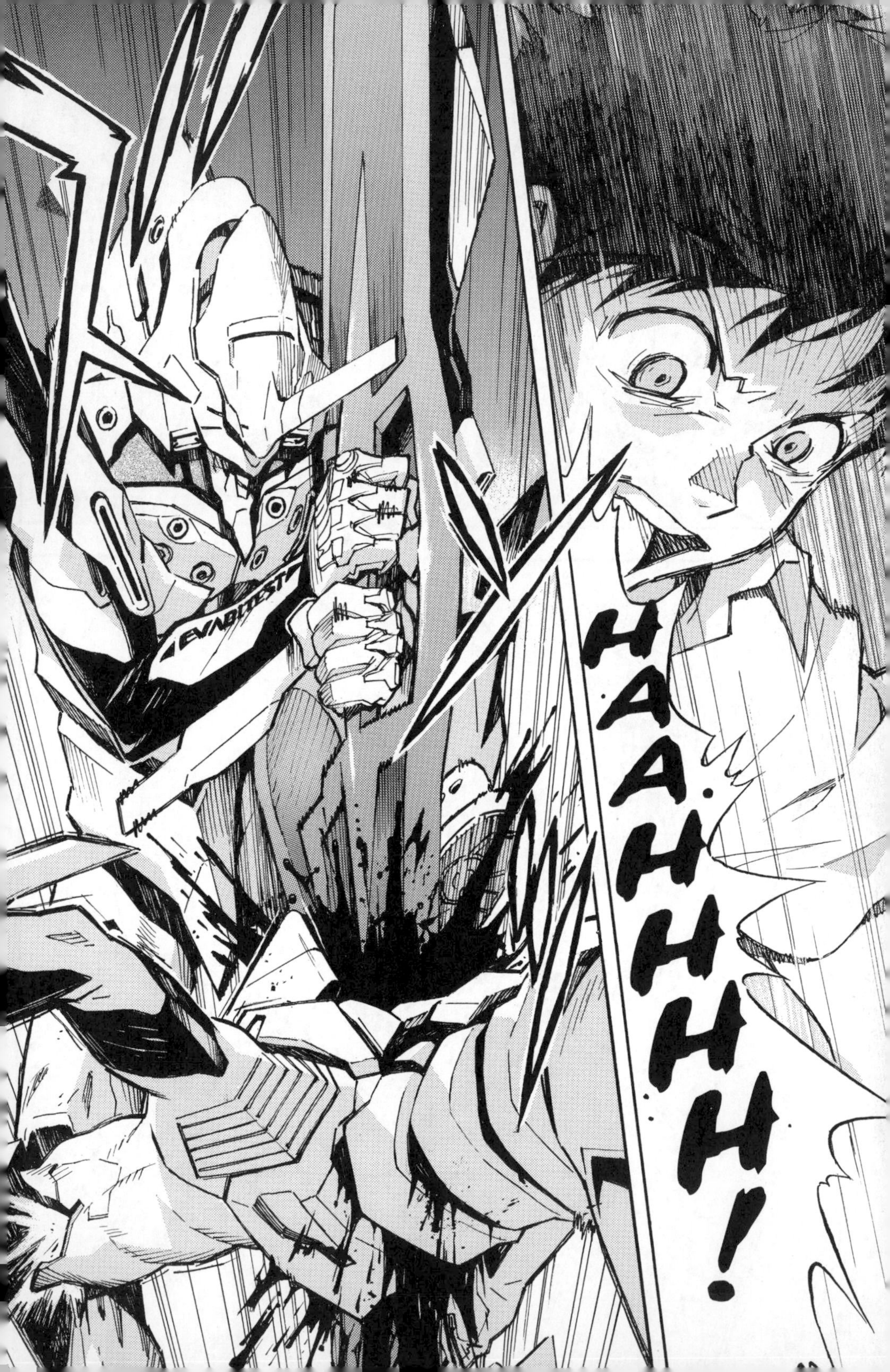
HAAHHHH!

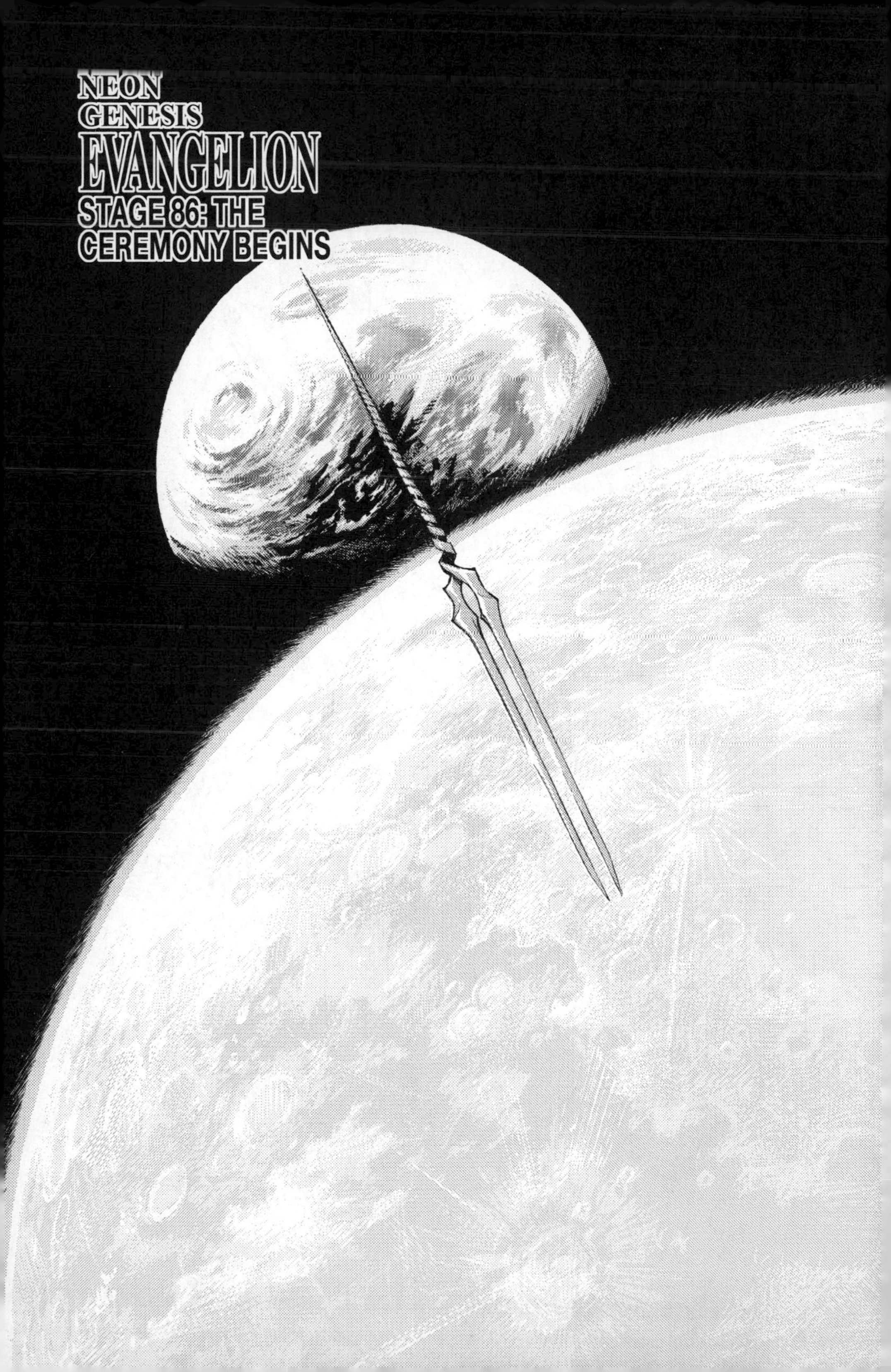
NEON GENESIS EVANGELION
STAGE 86: THE CEREMONY BEGINS

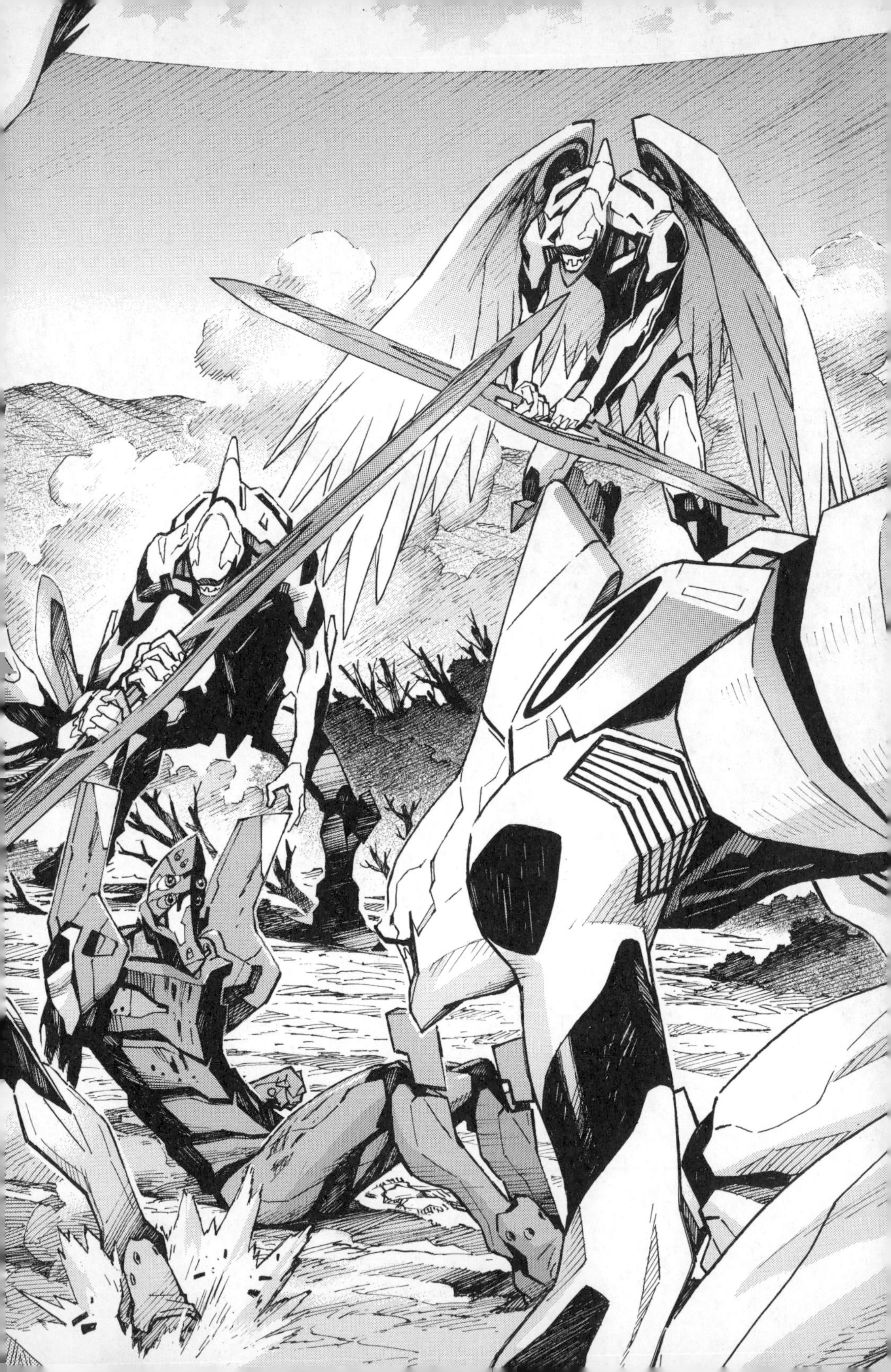

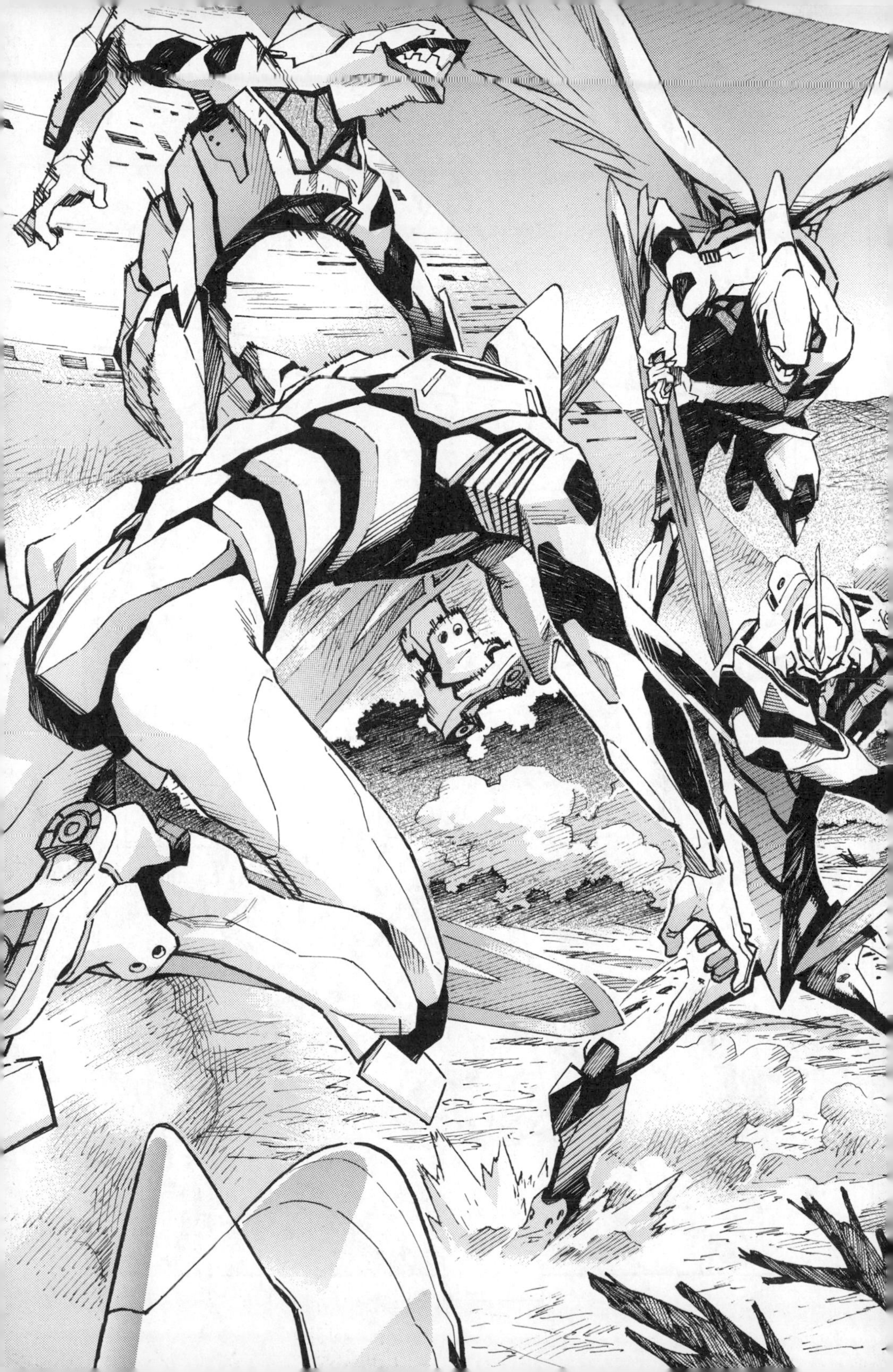

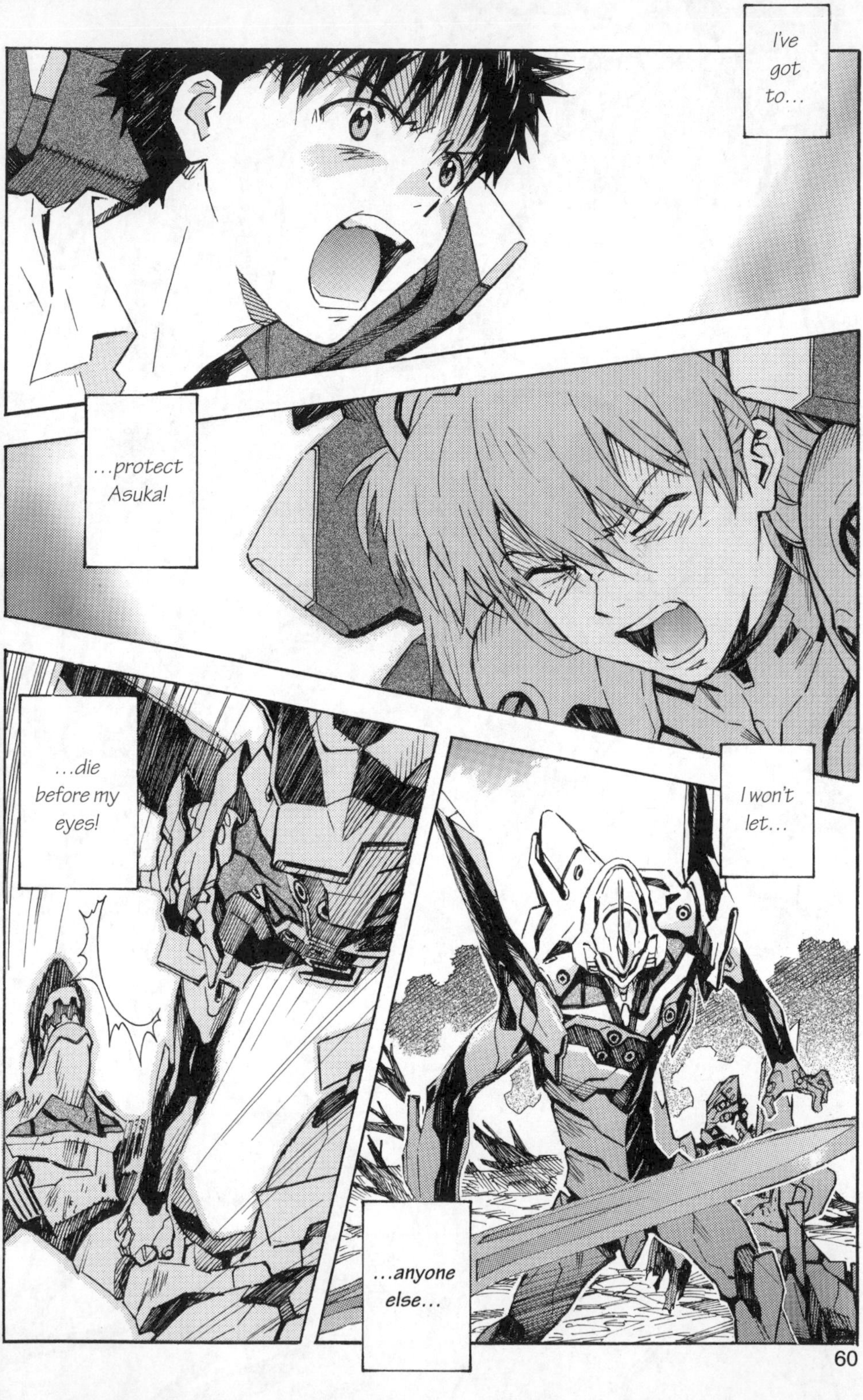
I've got to...
...protect Asuka!
I won't let...
...anyone else...
...die before my eyes!

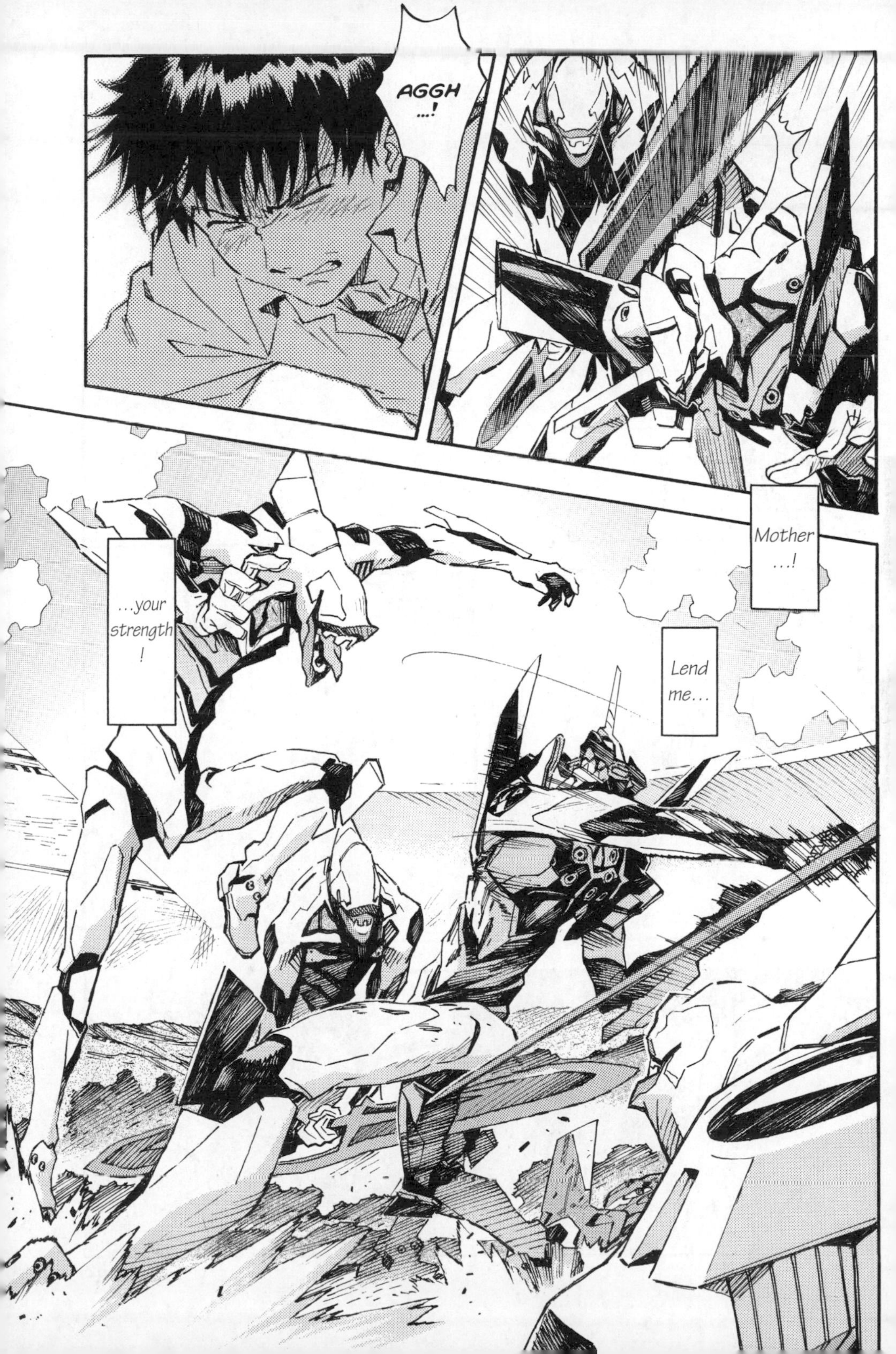
AGGH …!
Mother …!
Lend me…
…your strength !

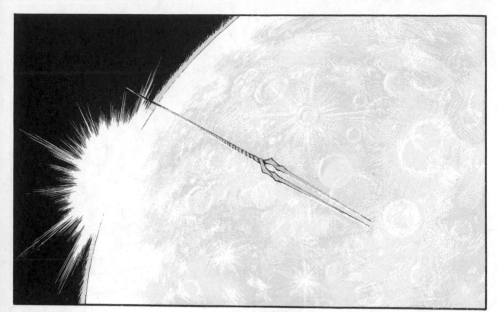

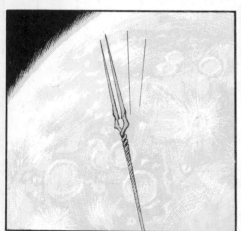

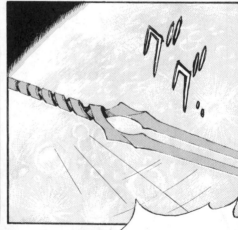

...UNIT-01'S SYNCHRO RATE HAS PASSED **250%**!

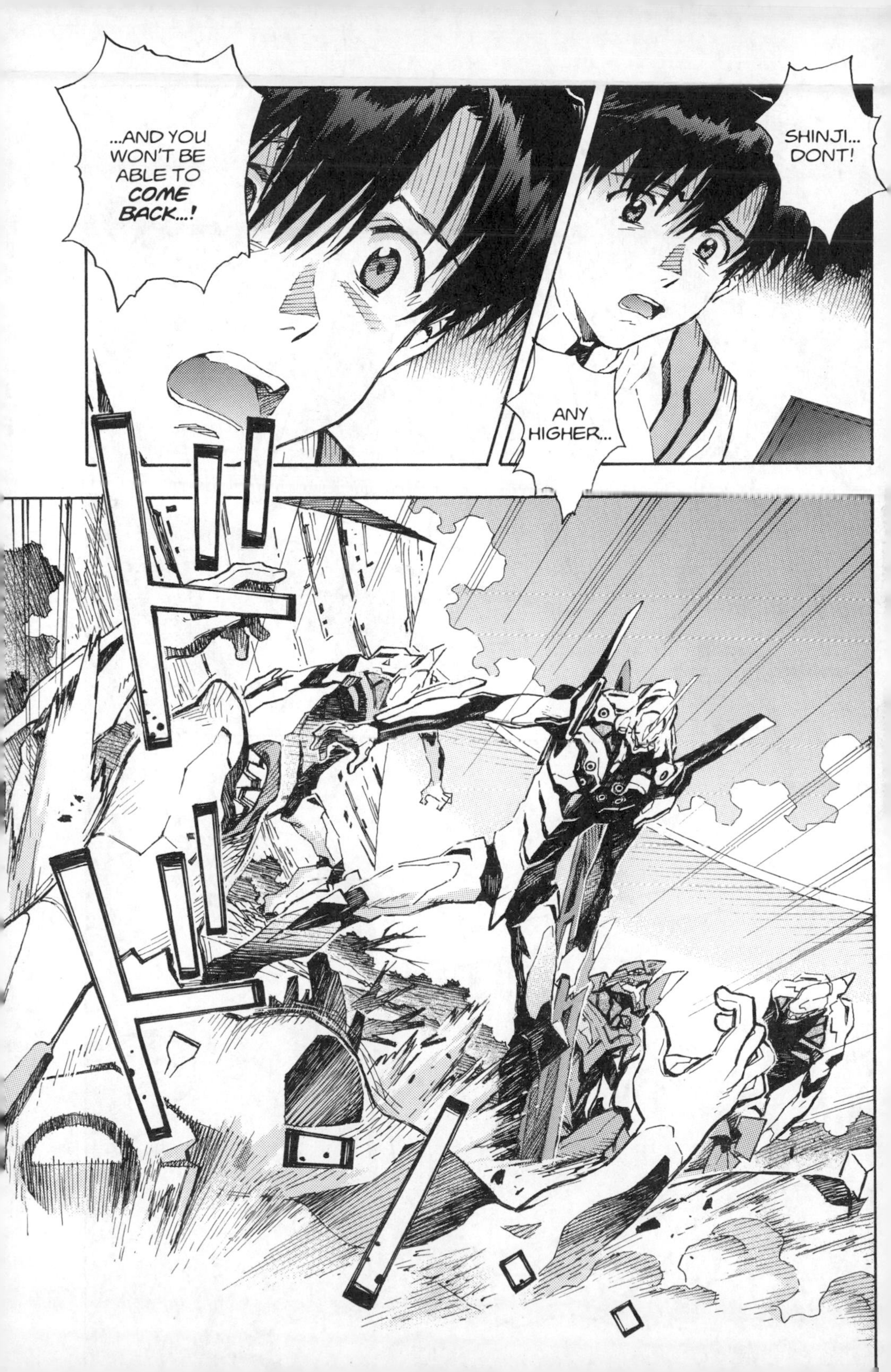
SHINJI... DONT!
ANY HIGHER...
...AND YOU WON'T BE ABLE TO COME BACK...!

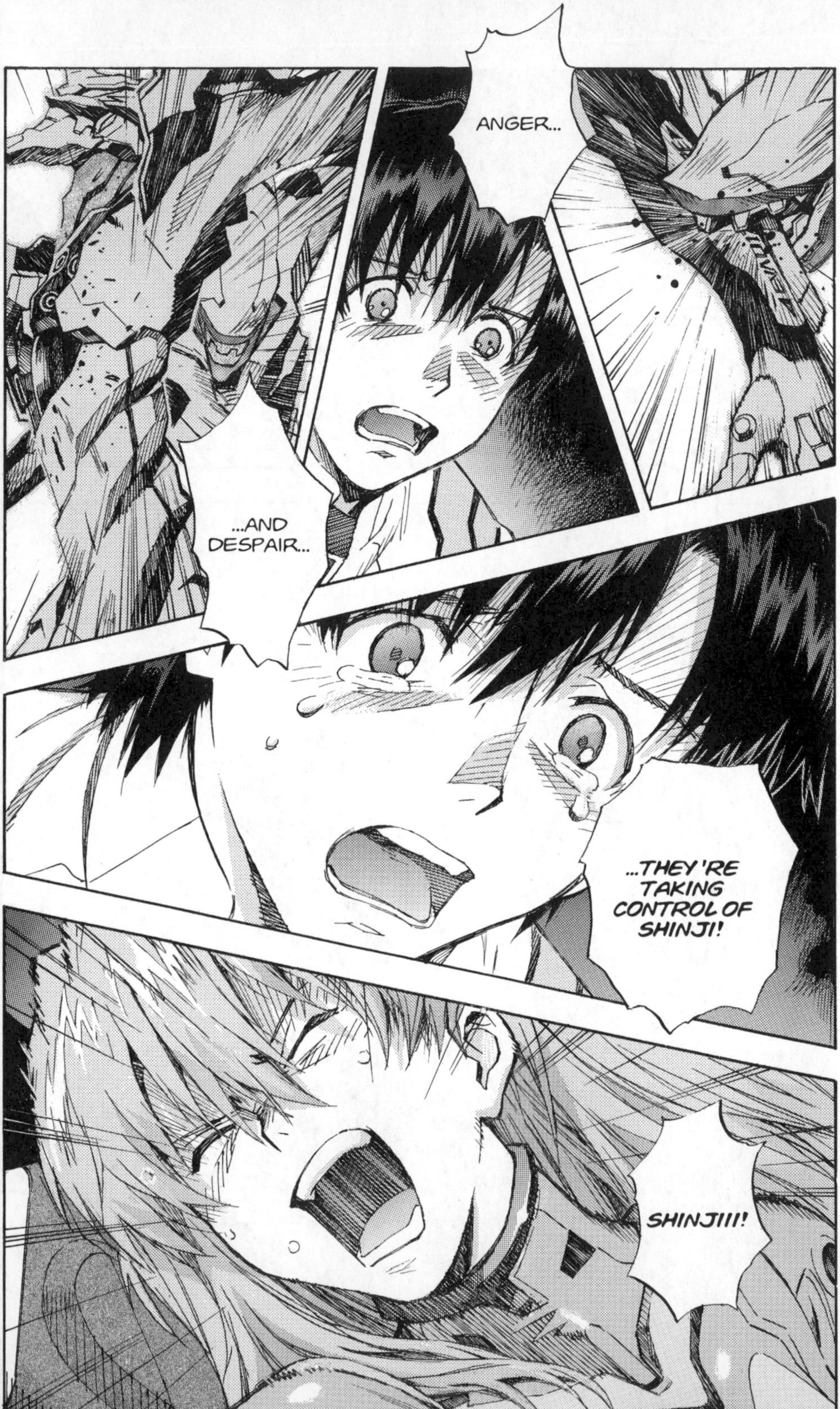
ANGER...
...AND DESPAIR...
...THEY'RE TAKING CONTROL OF SHINJI!
SHINJIII!

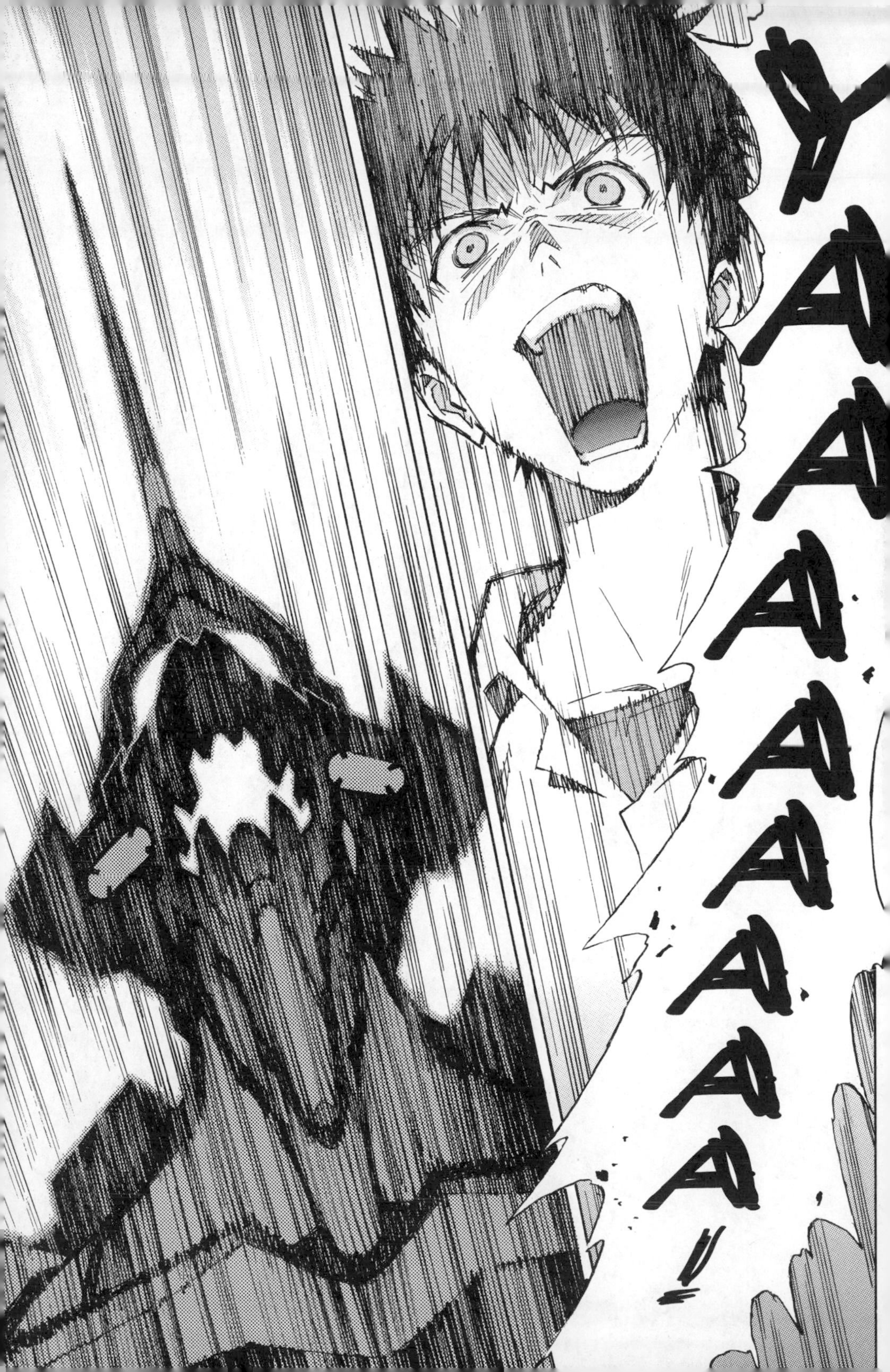
YAAAAAAAA!!

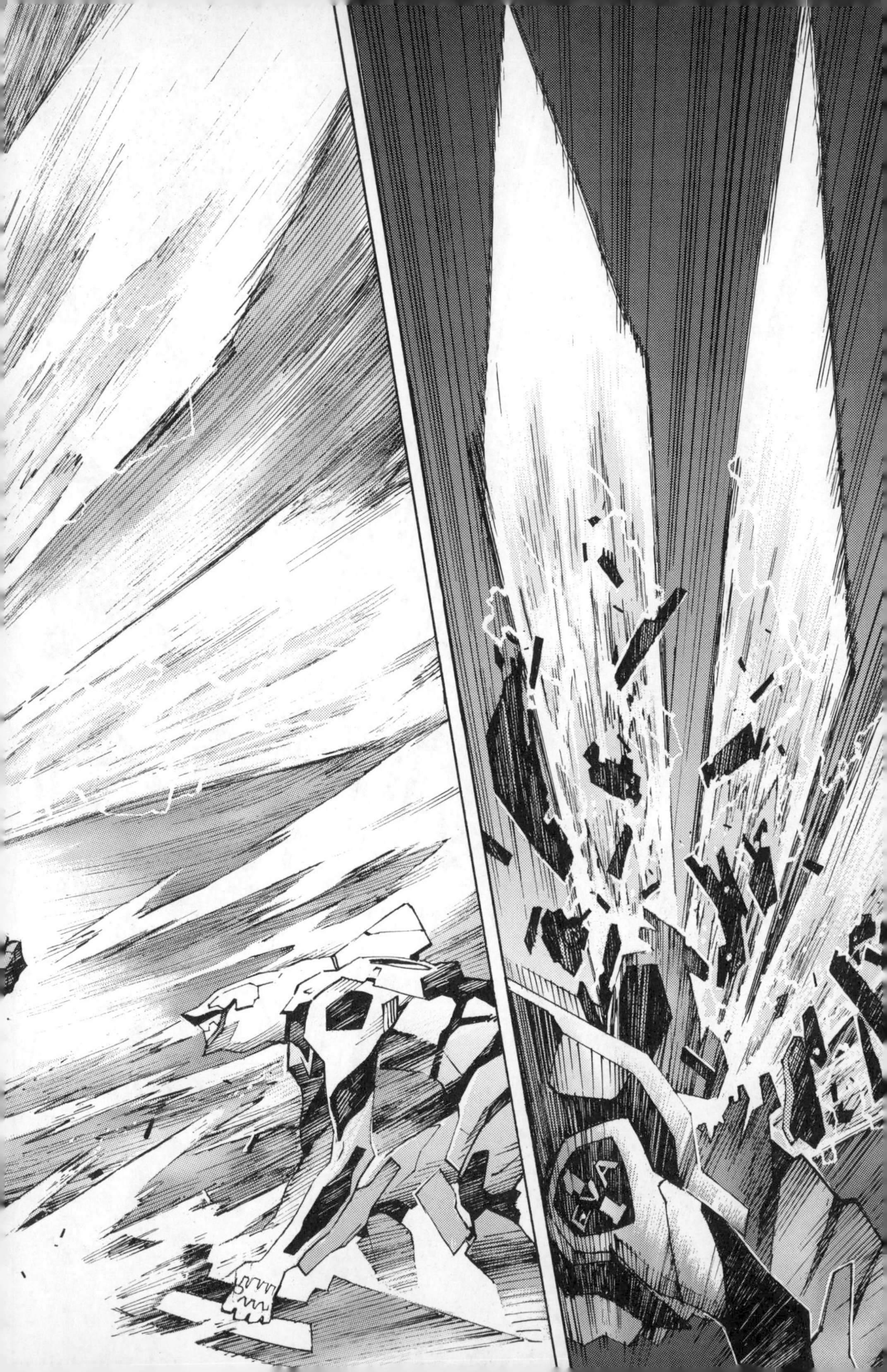

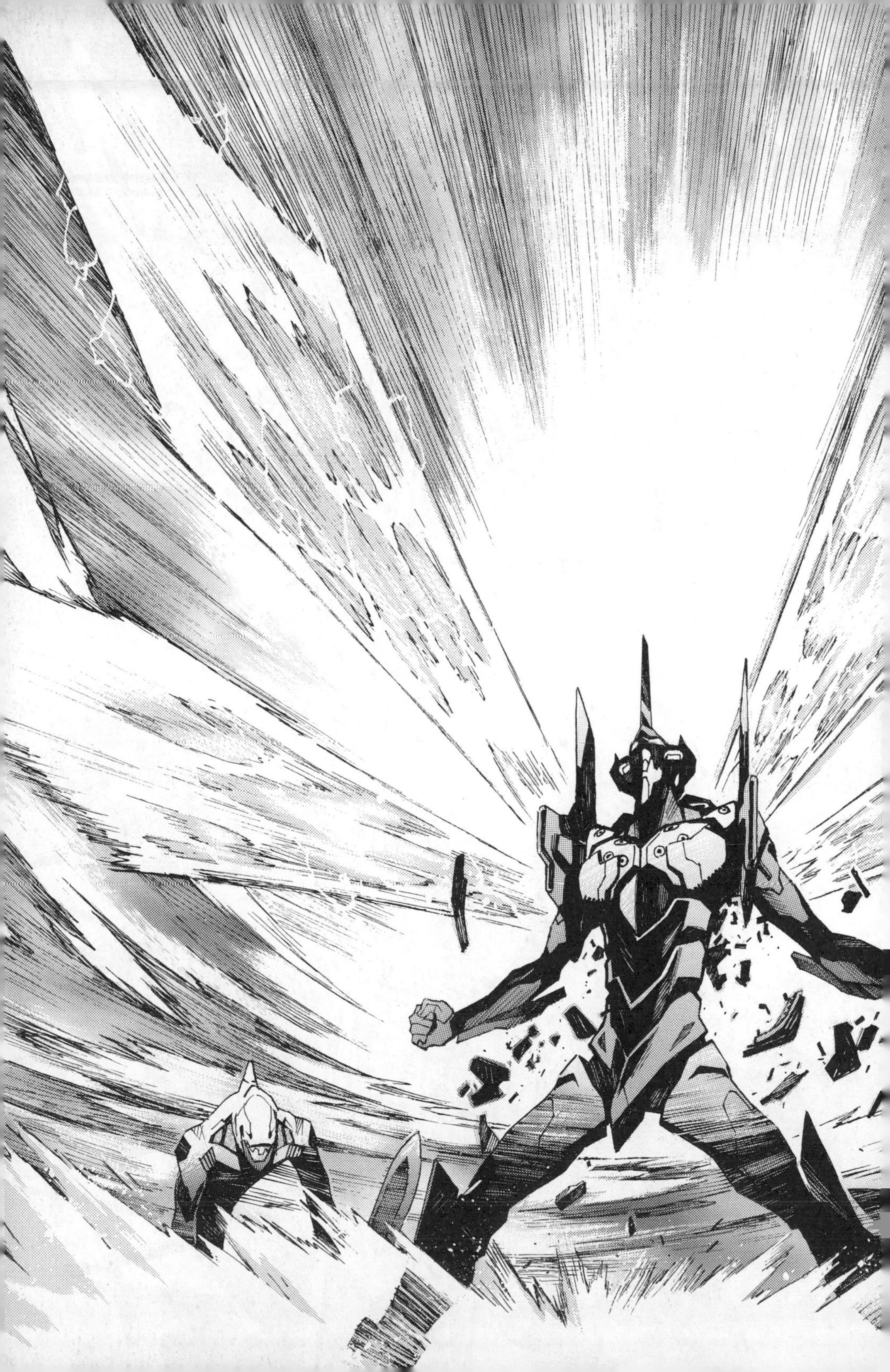

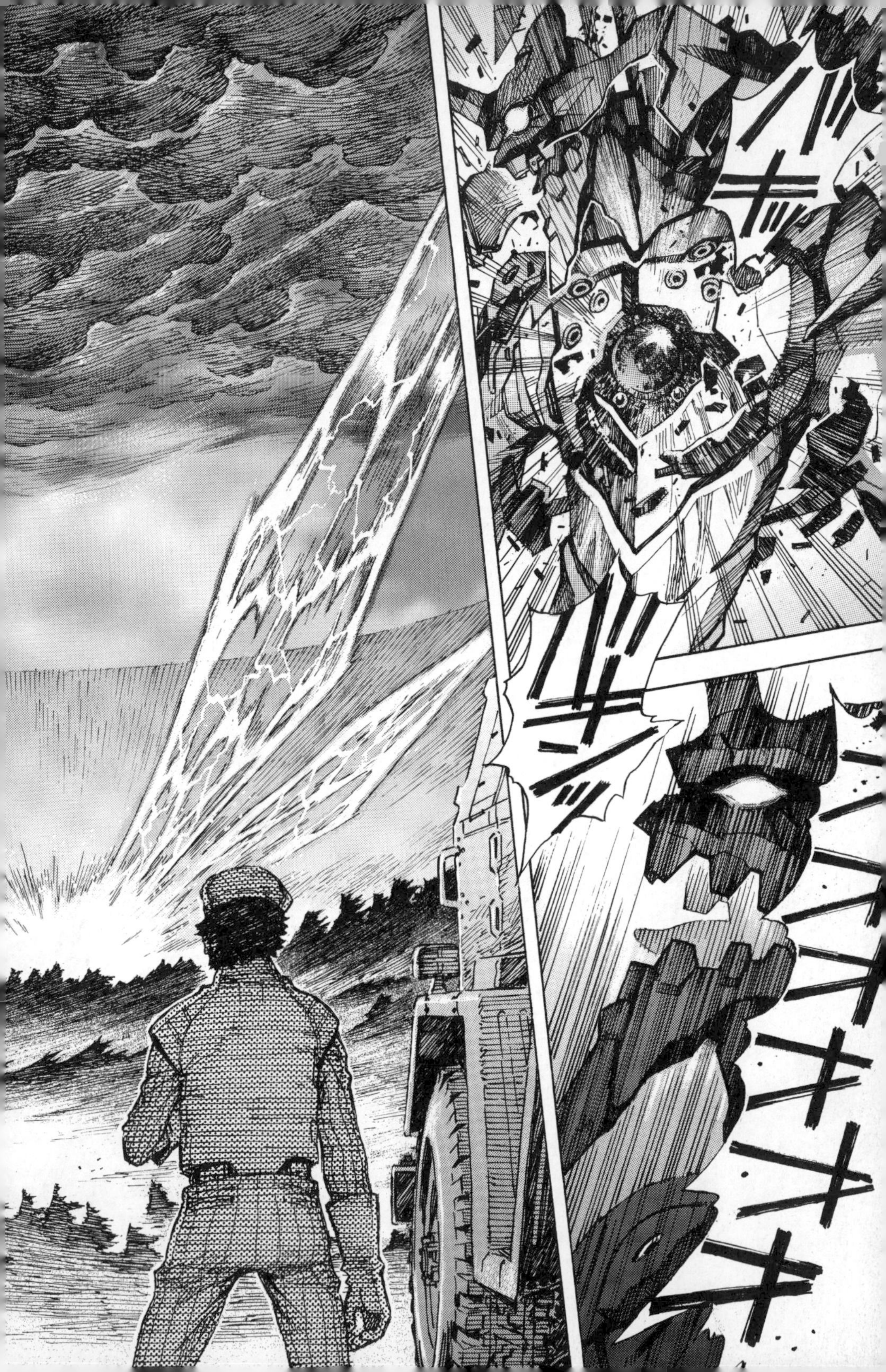

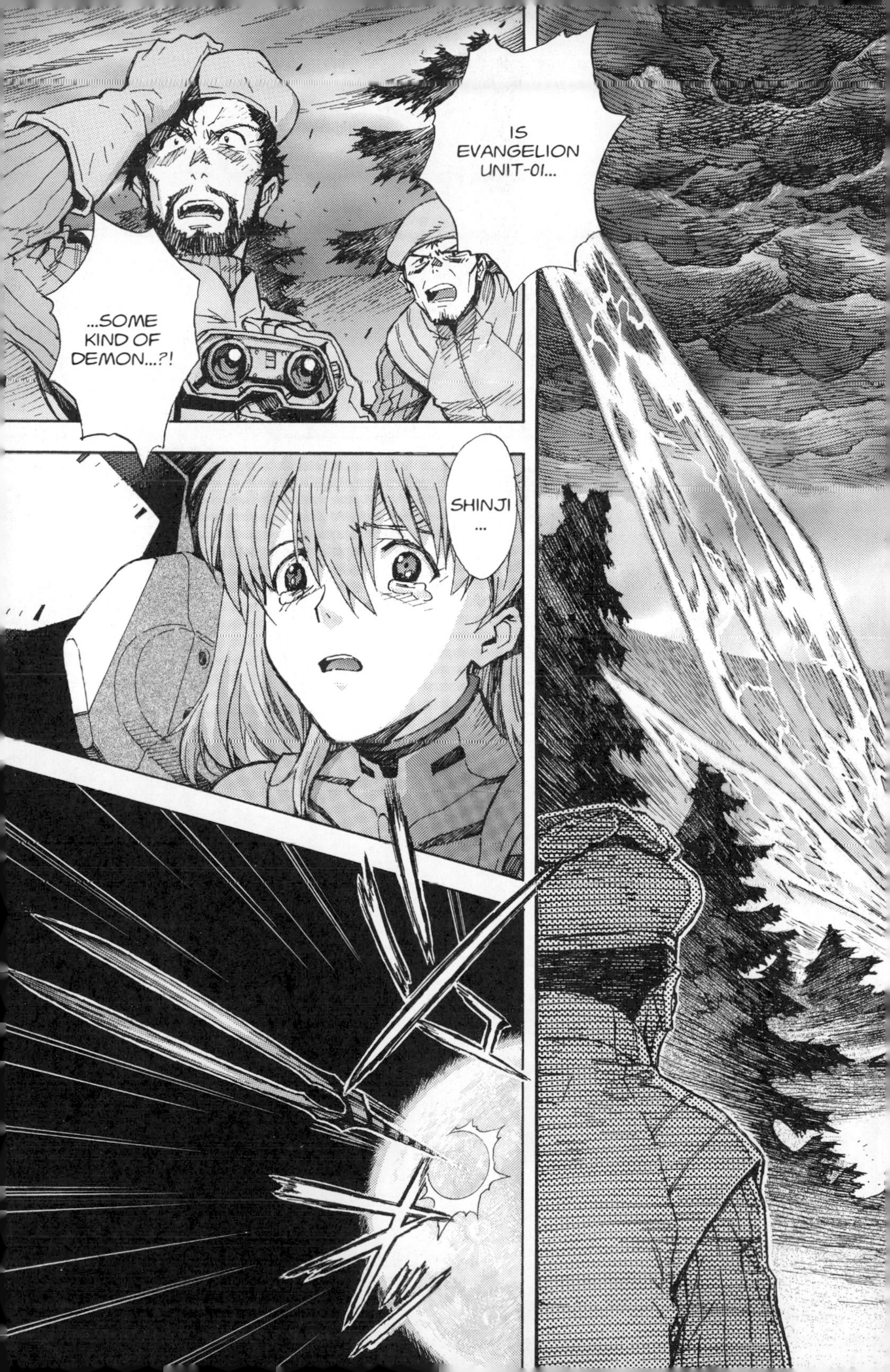
IS EVANGELION UNIT-01...
...SOME KIND OF DEMON...?!
SHINJI ...

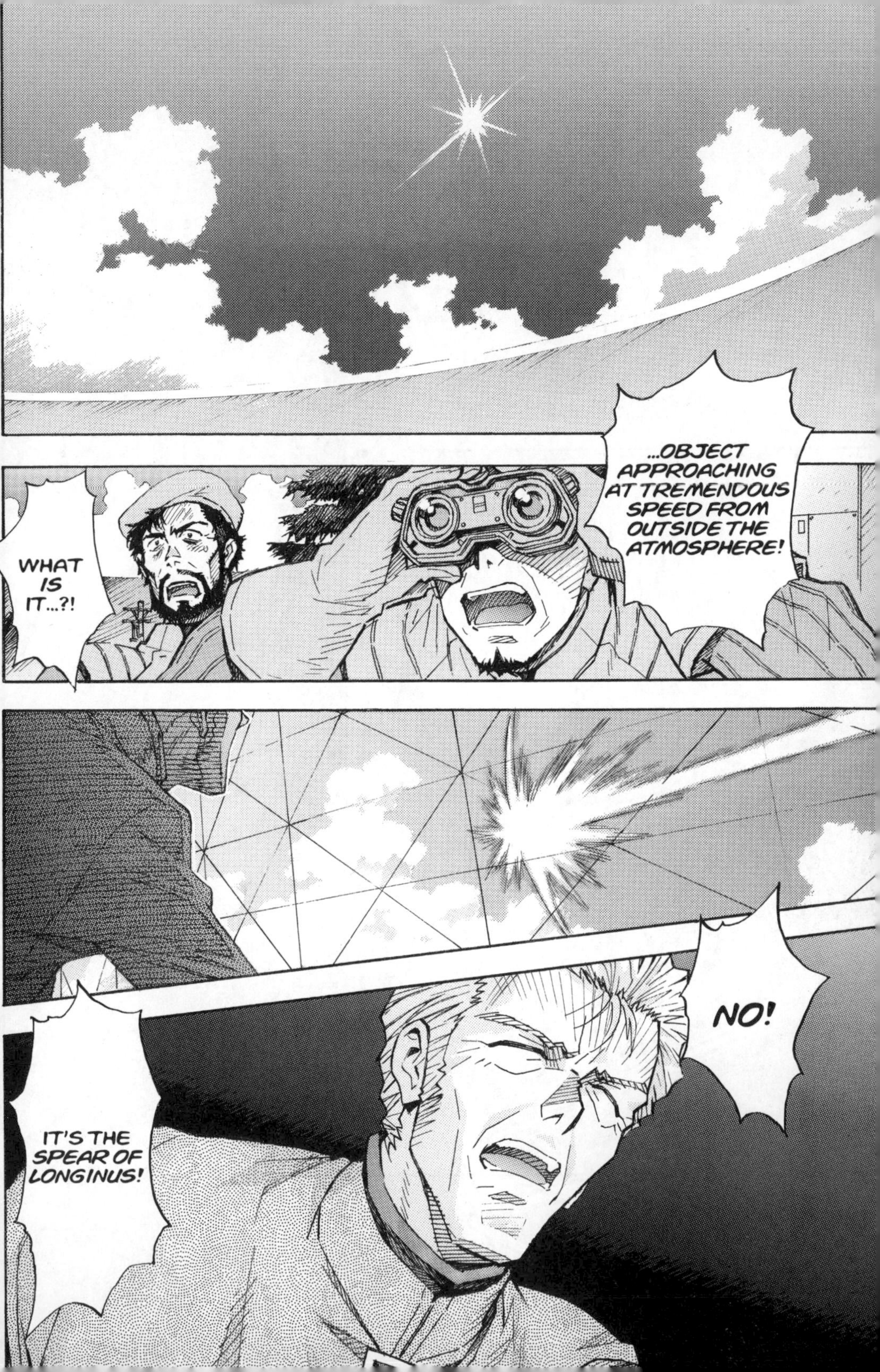
...OBJECT APPROACHING AT TREMENDOUS SPEED FROM OUTSIDE THE ATMOSPHERE!
WHAT IS IT...?!
NO!
IT'S THE SPEAR OF LONGINUS!

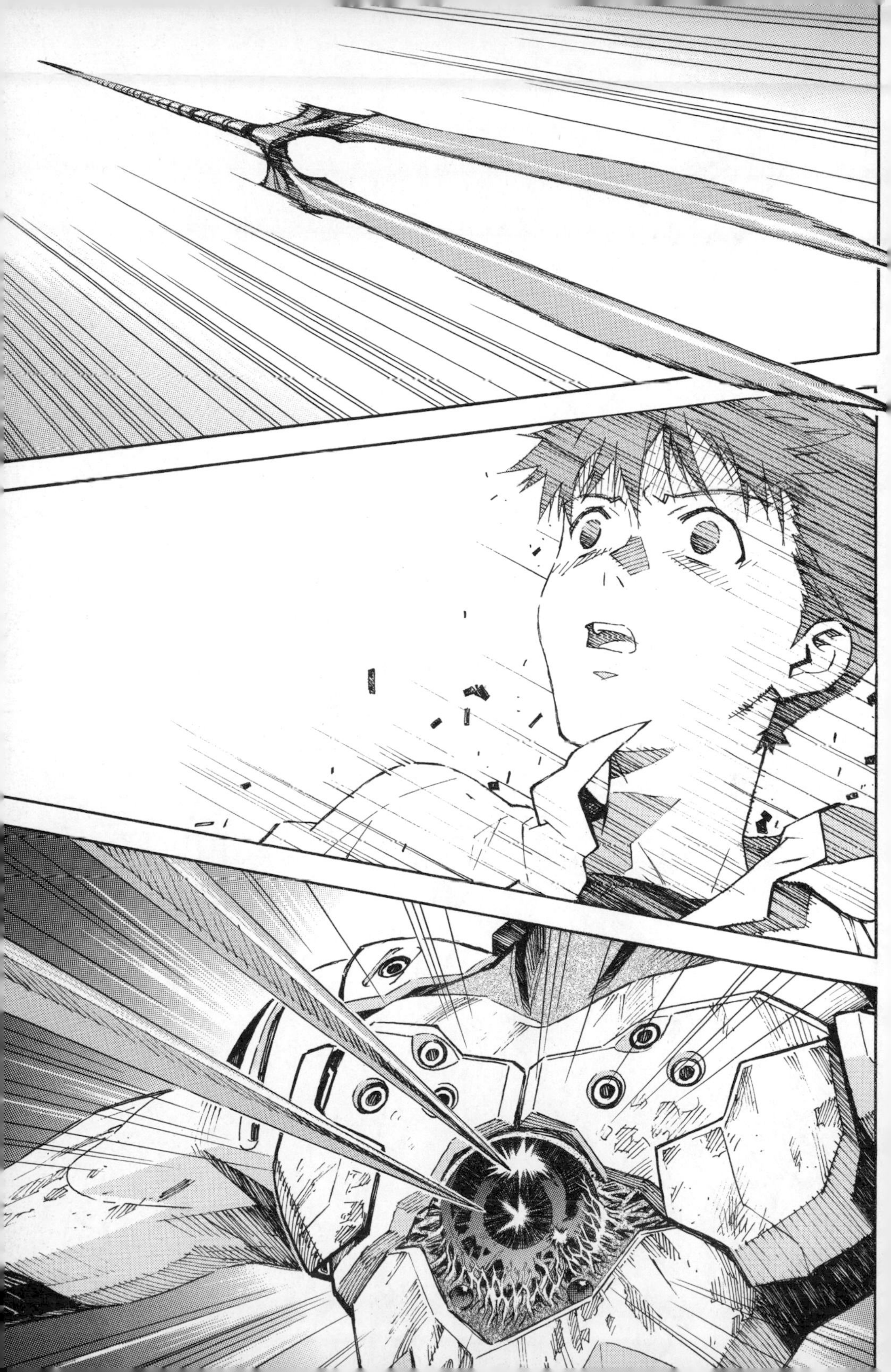

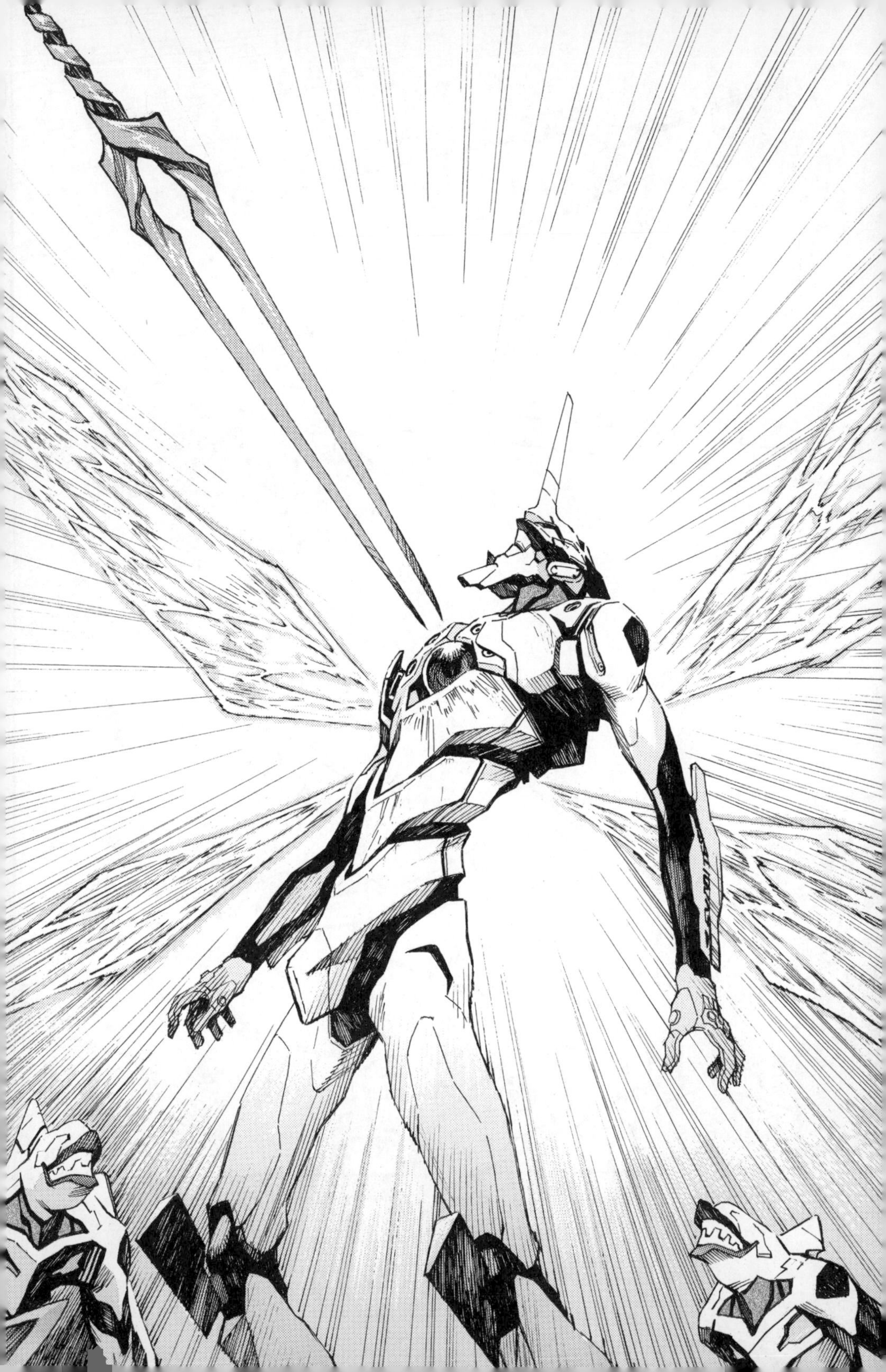

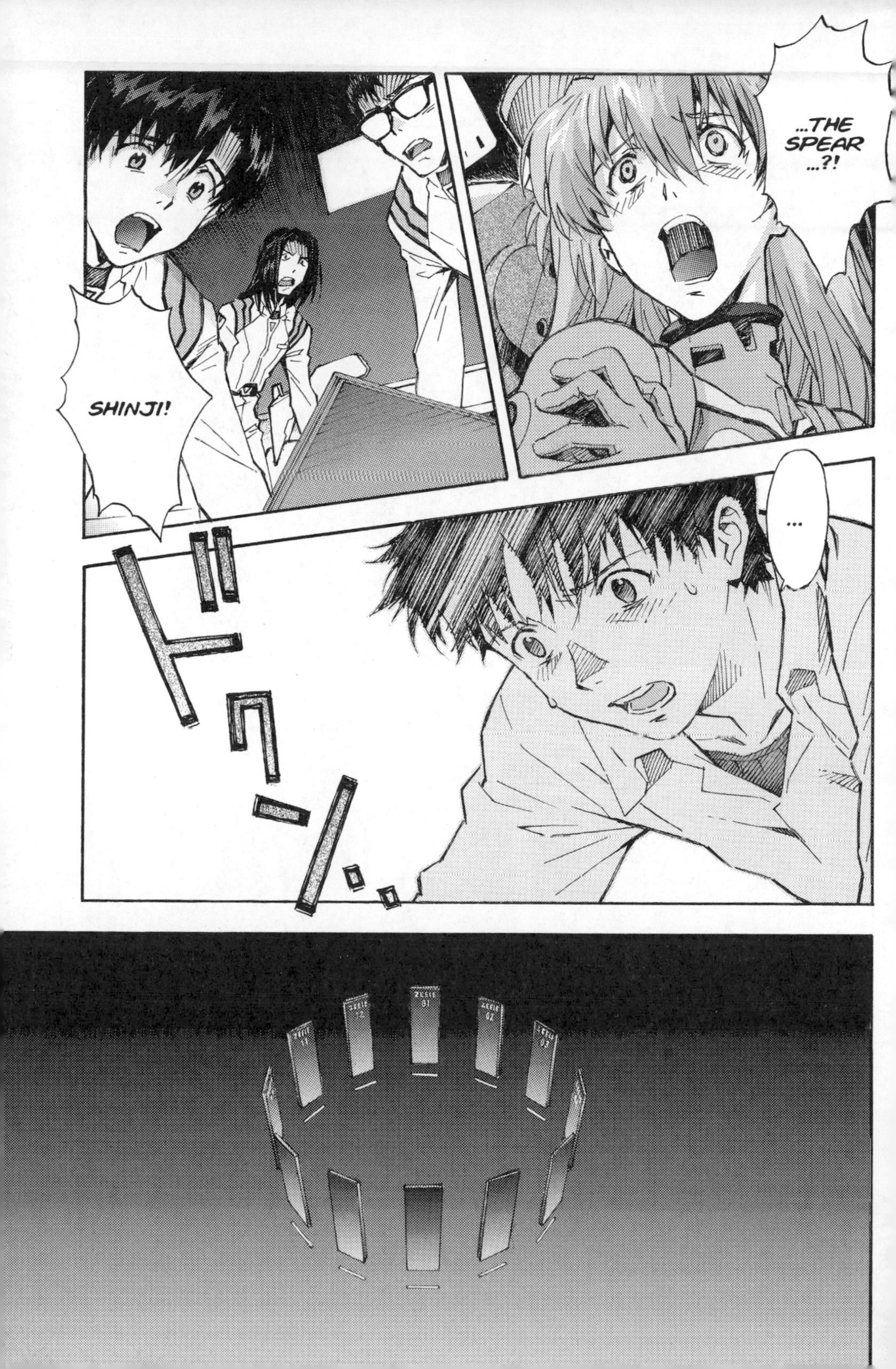
...THE SPEAR ...?!
SHINJI!
...
ドクン

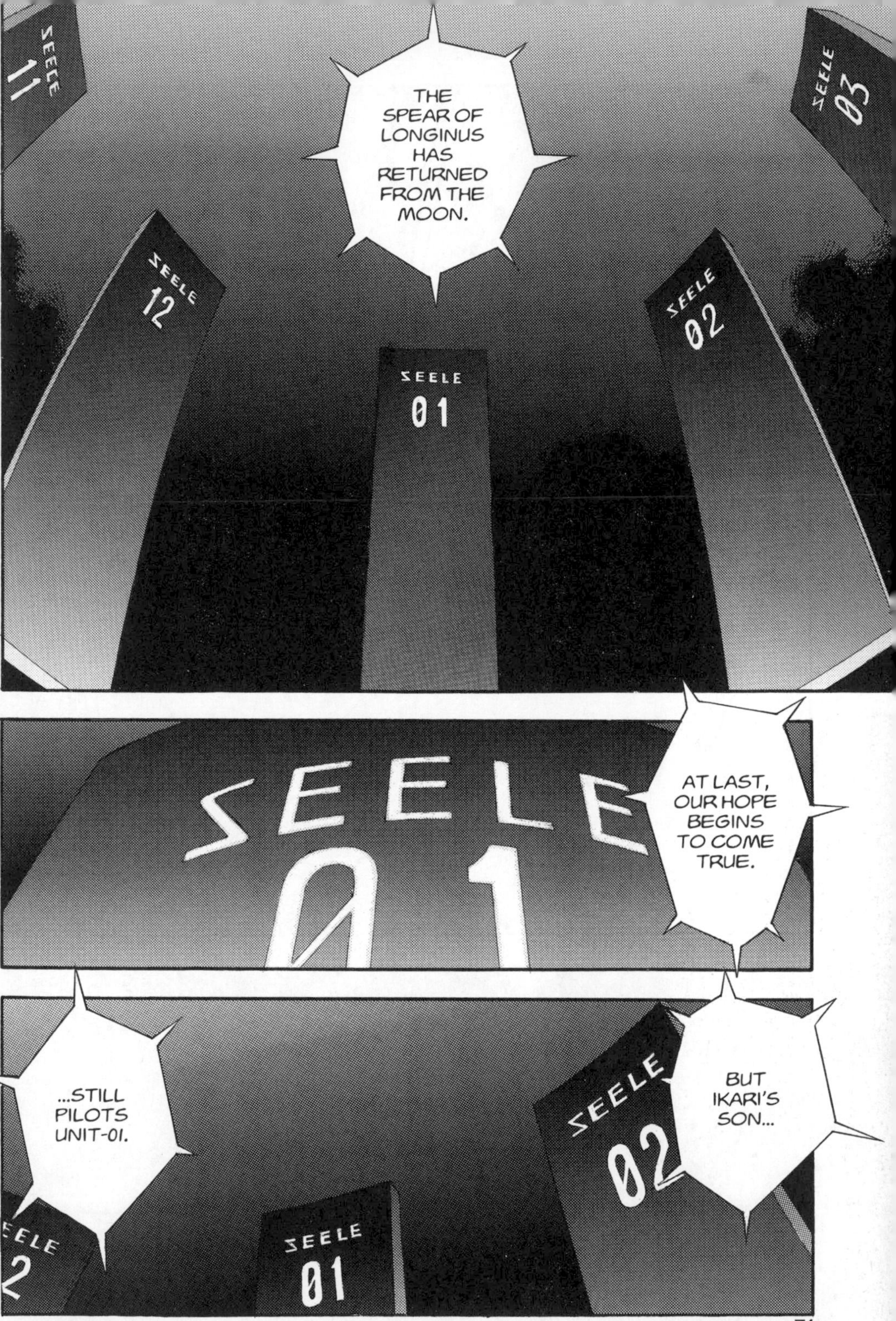
SEELE 11
SEELE 03
THE SPEAR OF LONGINUS HAS RETURNED FROM THE MOON.
SEELE 12
SEELE 02
SEELE 01
SEELE 01
AT LAST, OUR HOPE BEGINS TO COME TRUE.
BUT IKARI'S SON...
SEELE 02
...STILL PILOTS UNIT-01.
SEELE 01

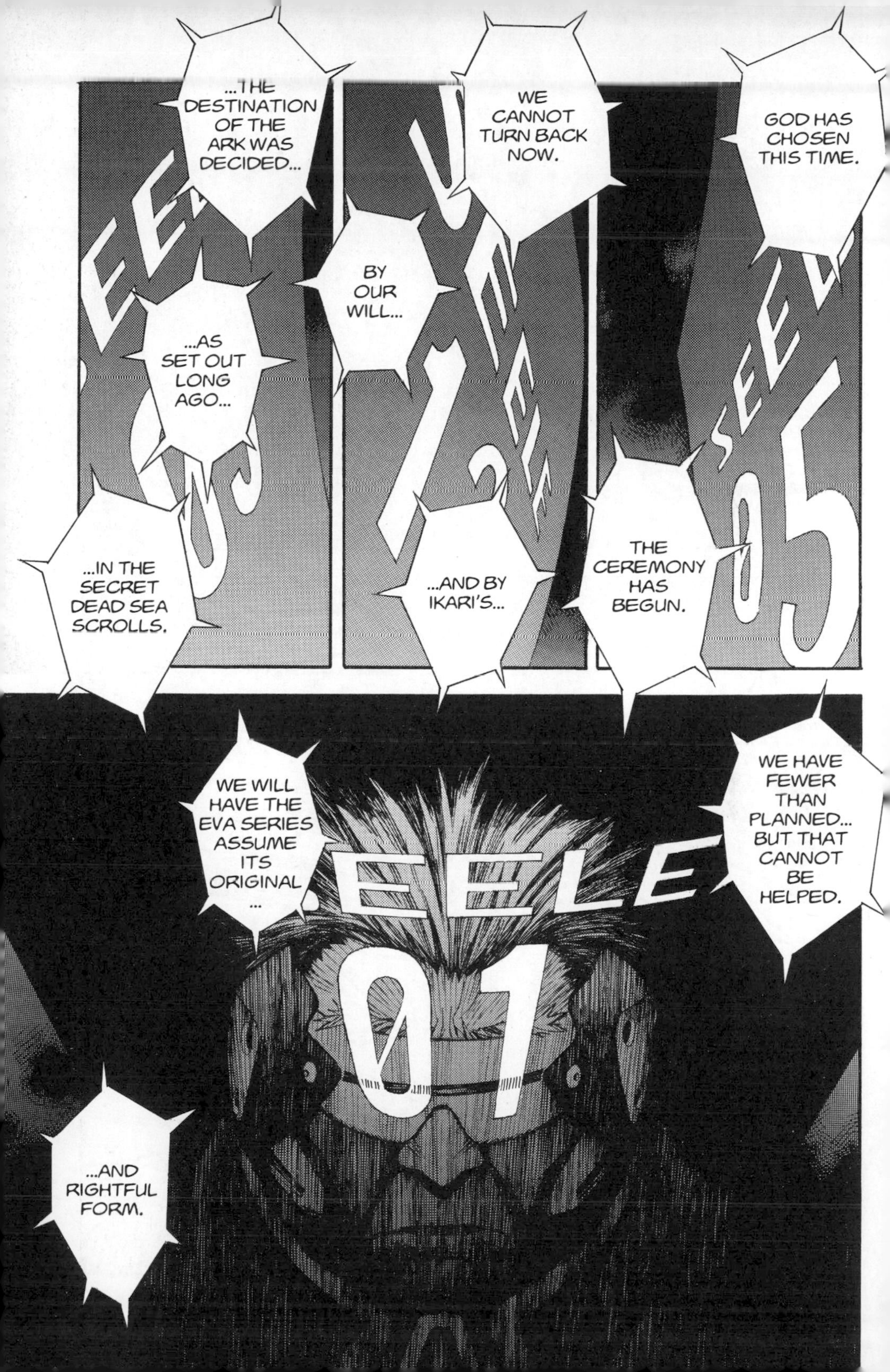
GOD HAS CHOSEN THIS TIME.
THE CEREMONY HAS BEGUN.
WE CANNOT TURN BACK NOW.
BY OUR WILL...
...AND BY IKARI'S...
...THE DESTINATION OF THE ARK WAS DECIDED...
...AS SET OUT LONG AGO...
...IN THE SECRET DEAD SEA SCROLLS.
WE HAVE FEWER THAN PLANNED... BUT THAT CANNOT BE HELPED.
WE WILL HAVE THE EVA SERIES ASSUME ITS ORIGINAL...
...AND RIGHTFUL FORM.

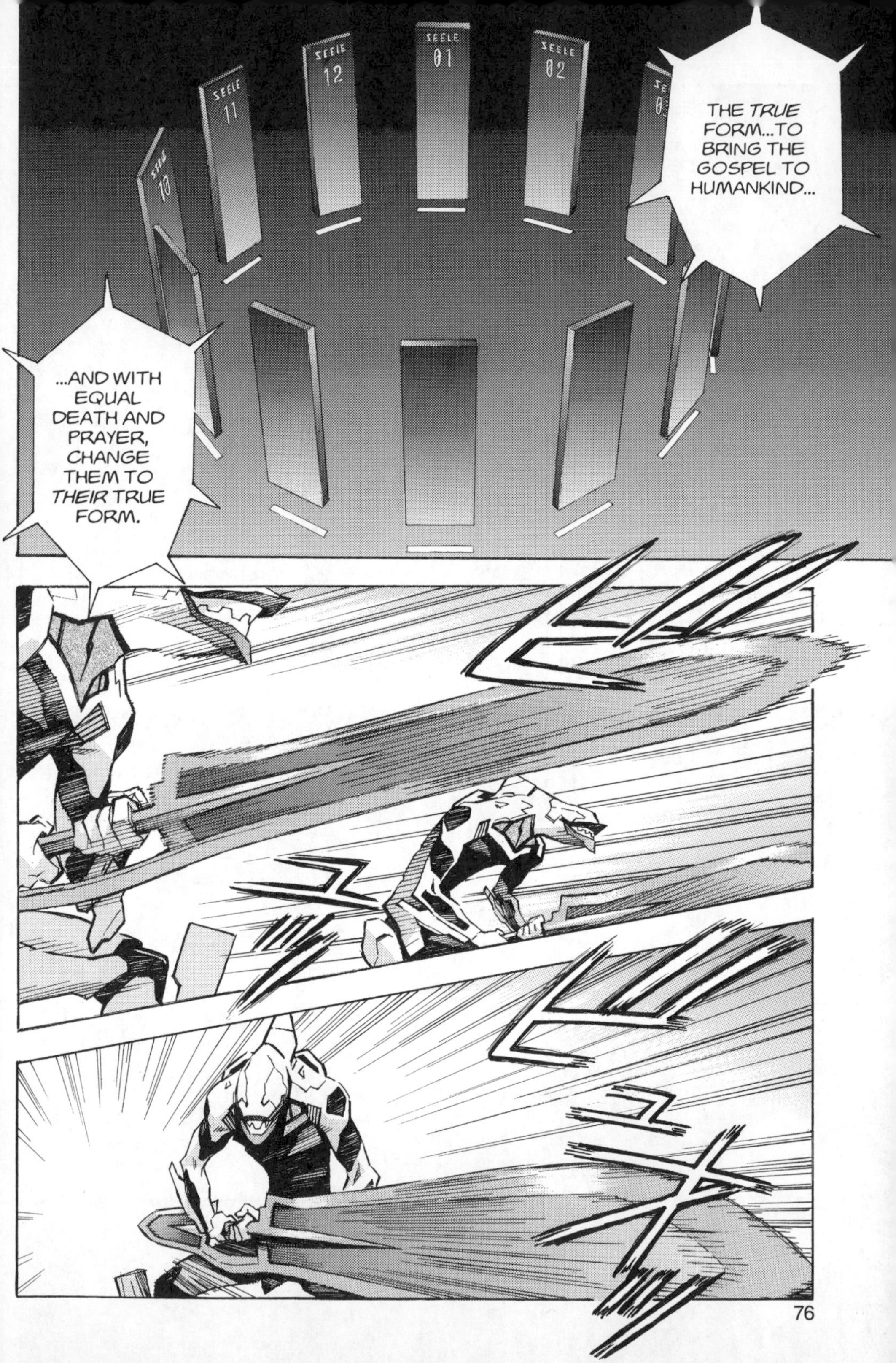
SEELE 11
SEELE 12
SEELE 01
SEELE 02
THE *TRUE* FORM...TO BRING THE GOSPEL TO HUMANKIND...
...AND WITH EQUAL DEATH AND PRAYER, CHANGE THEM TO *THEIR* TRUE FORM.

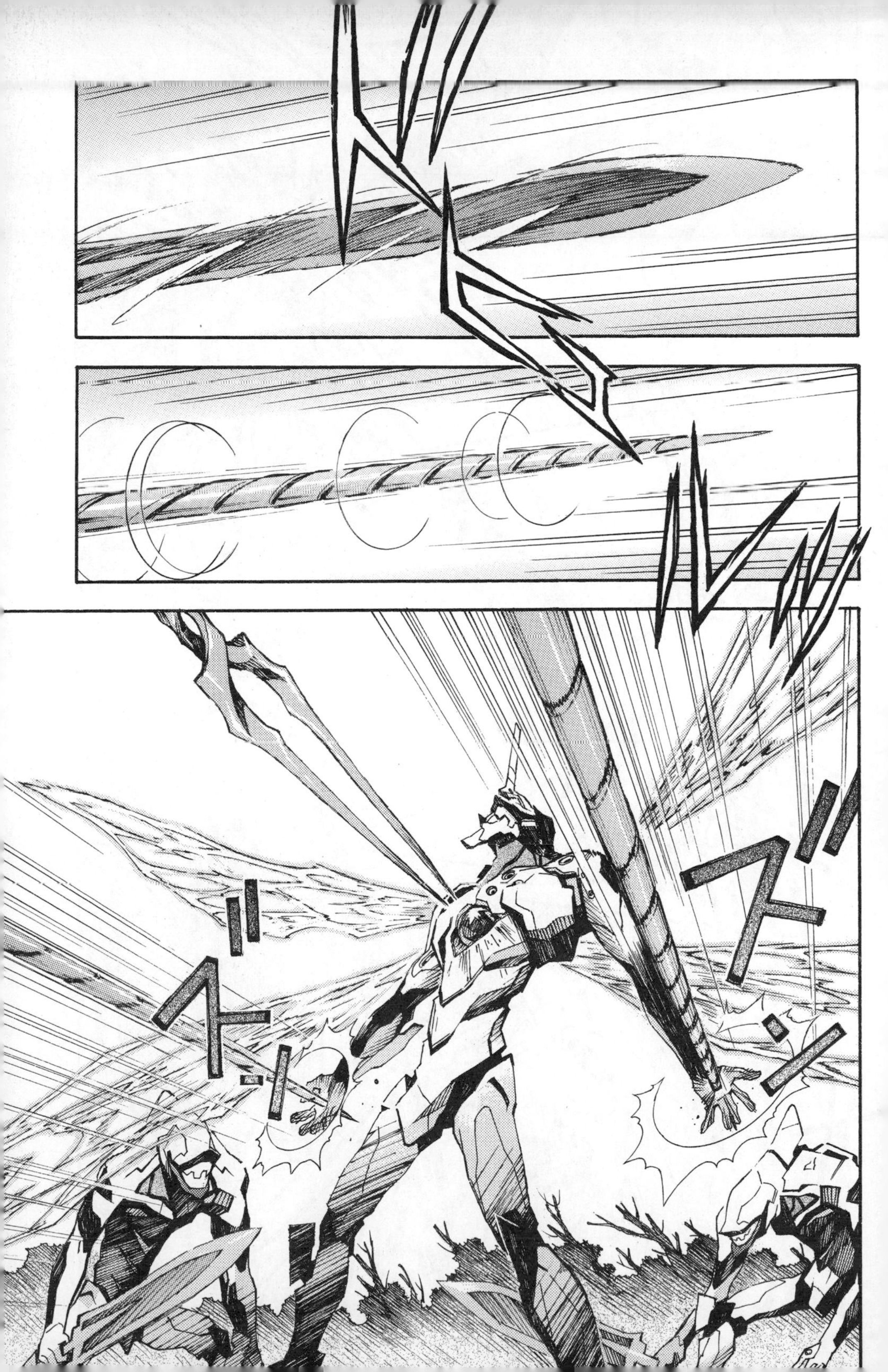

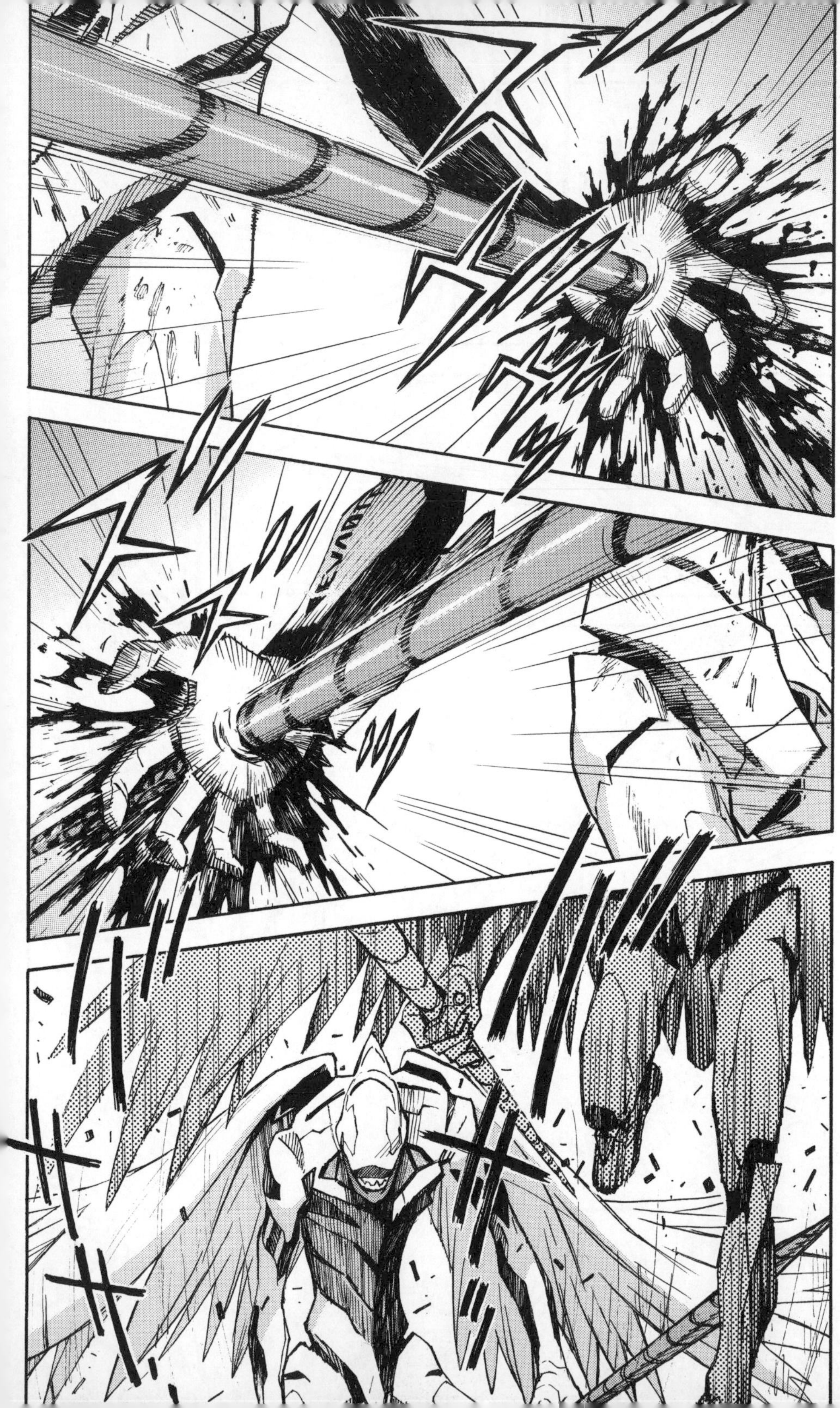

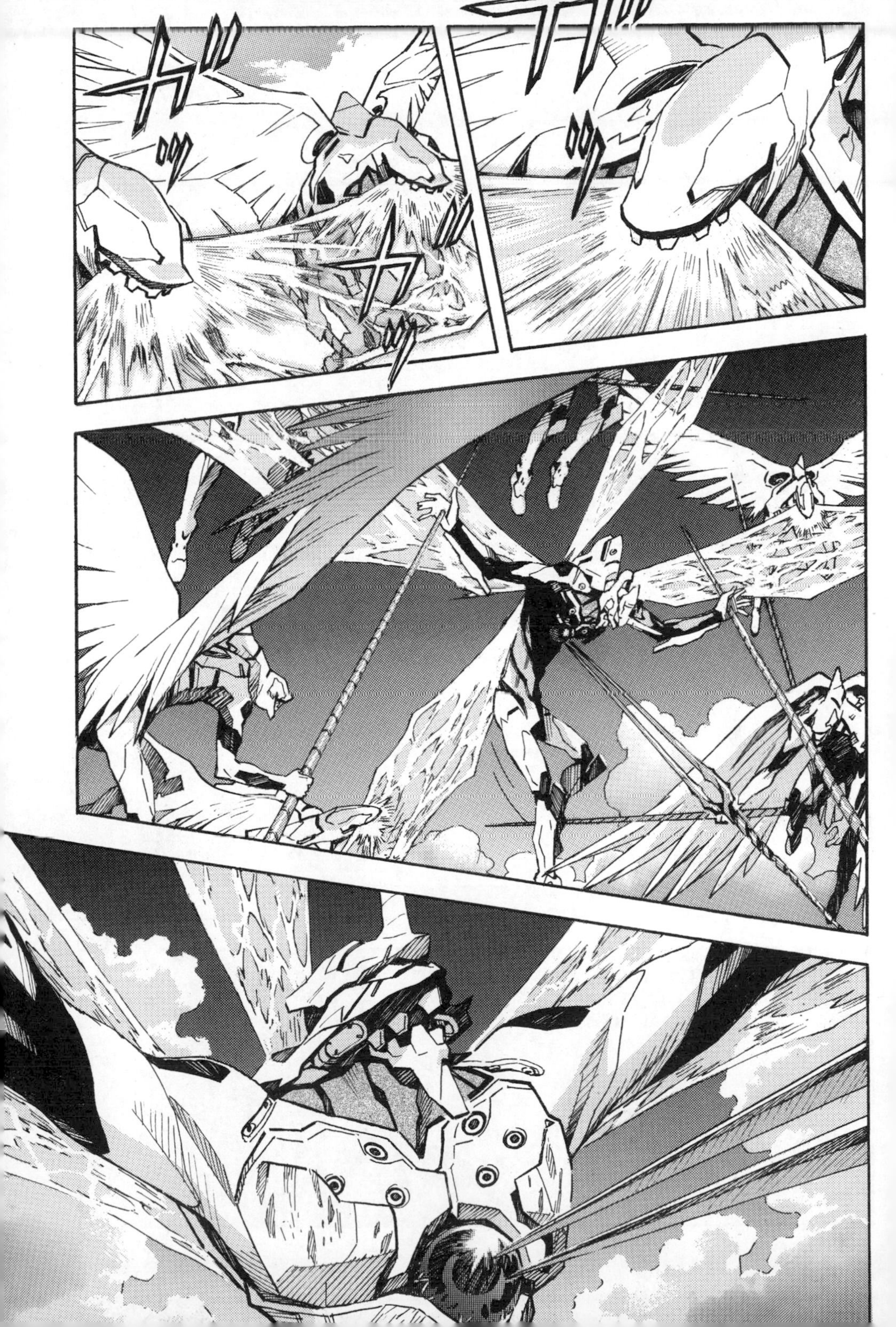
ガッ
ガッ
ガッ

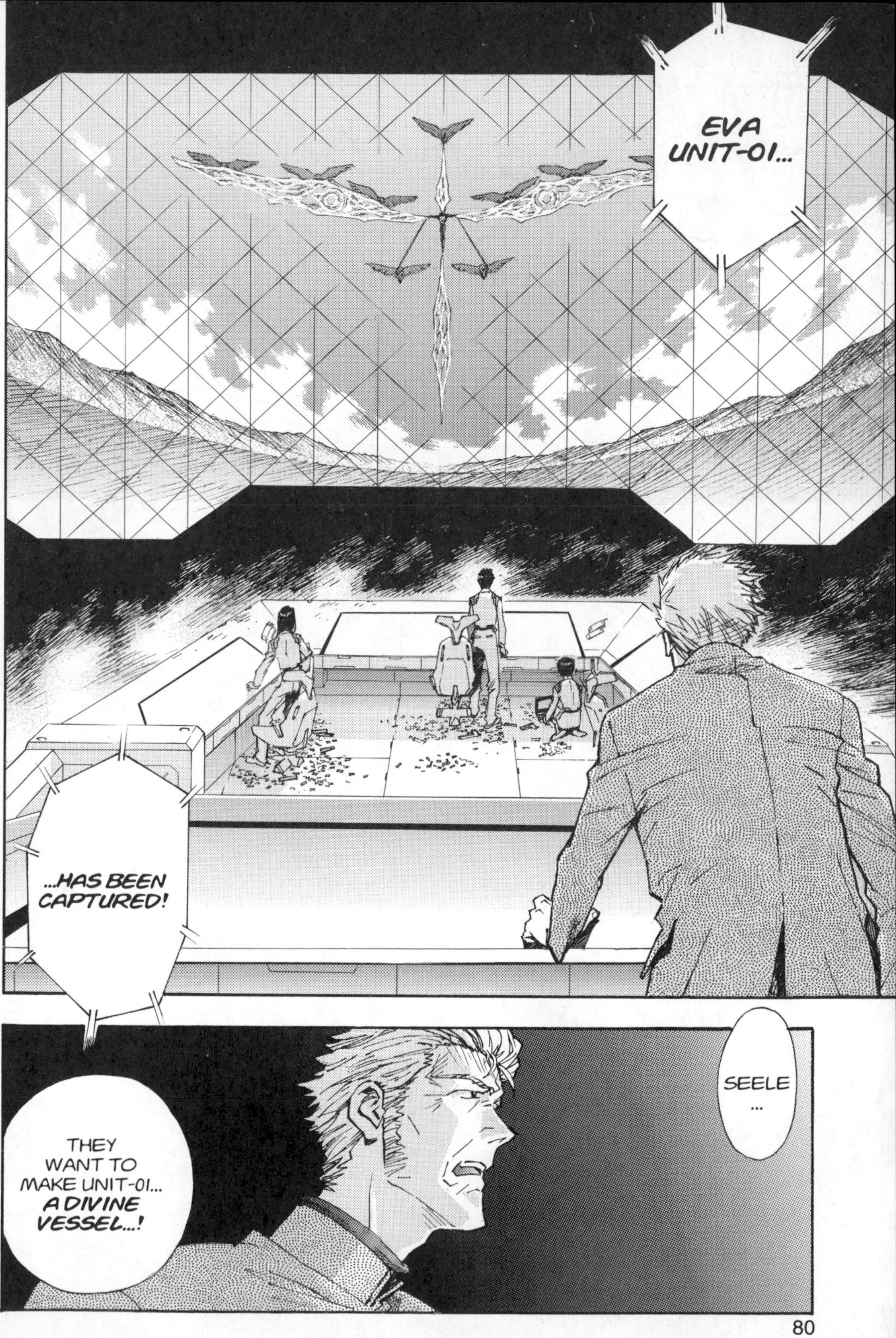
EVA UNIT-01...
...HAS BEEN CAPTURED!
SEELE ...
THEY WANT TO MAKE UNIT-01... A DIVINE VESSEL...!

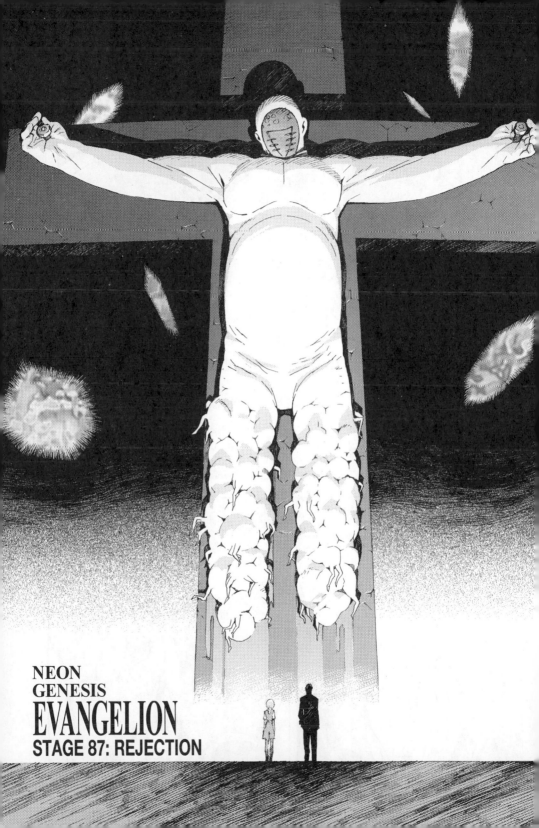

NEON
GENESIS
EVANGELION
STAGE 87: REJECTION

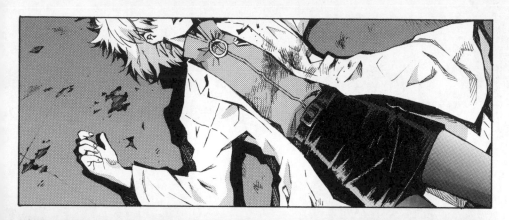

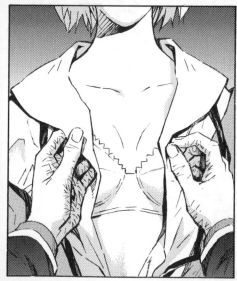

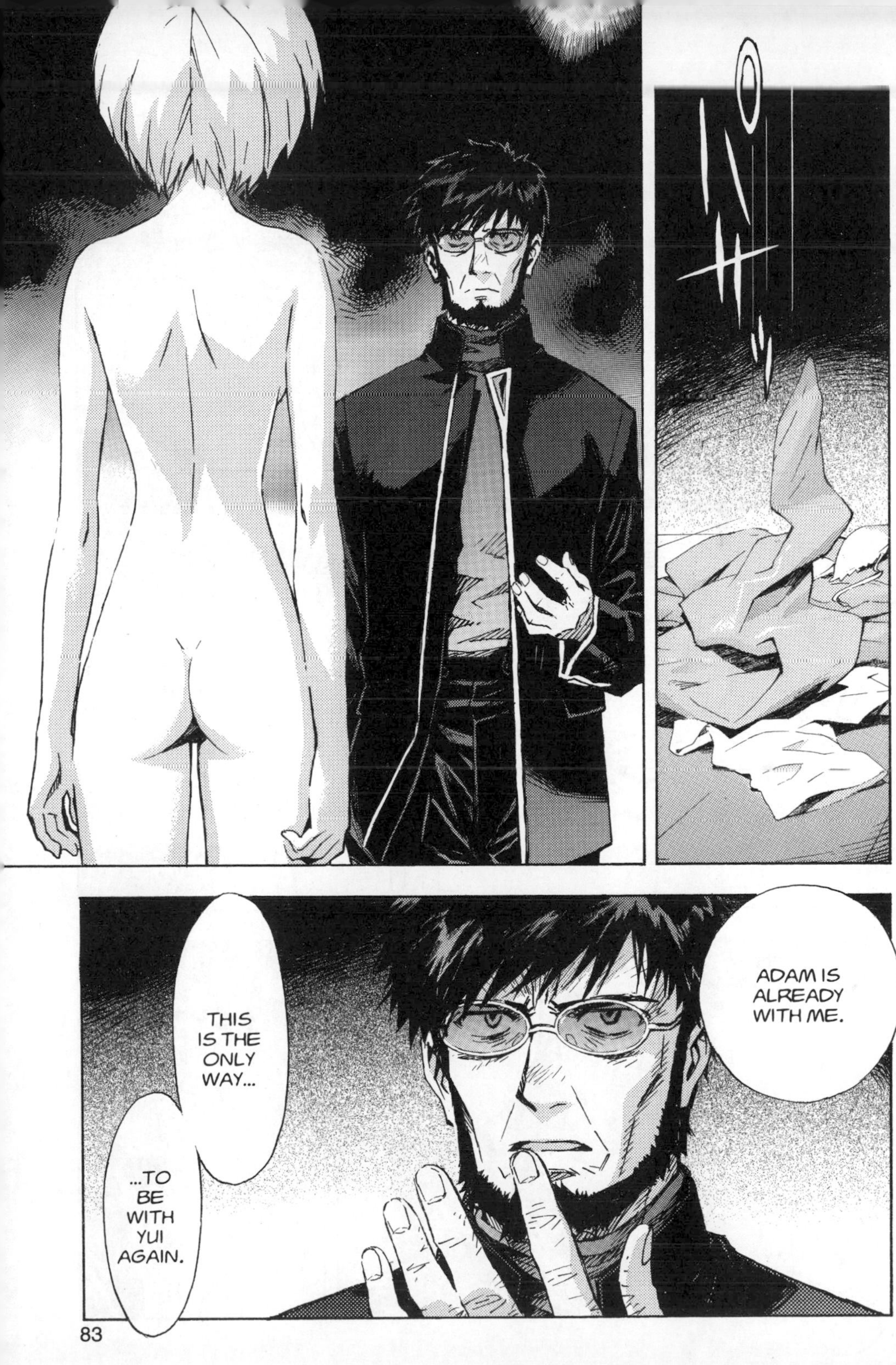
ADAM IS ALREADY WITH ME.
THIS IS THE ONLY WAY...
...TO BE WITH YUI AGAIN.

THE FORBIDDEN UNION...

...OF ADAM AND LILITH.

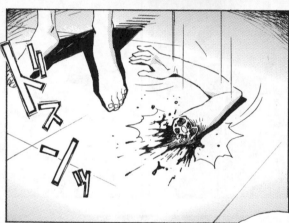

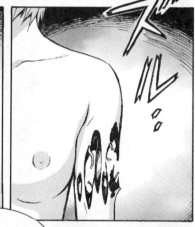

SOON THE A.T. FIELD WILL NOT BE ABLE TO HOLD YOUR FORM.

THERE IS NO TIME.

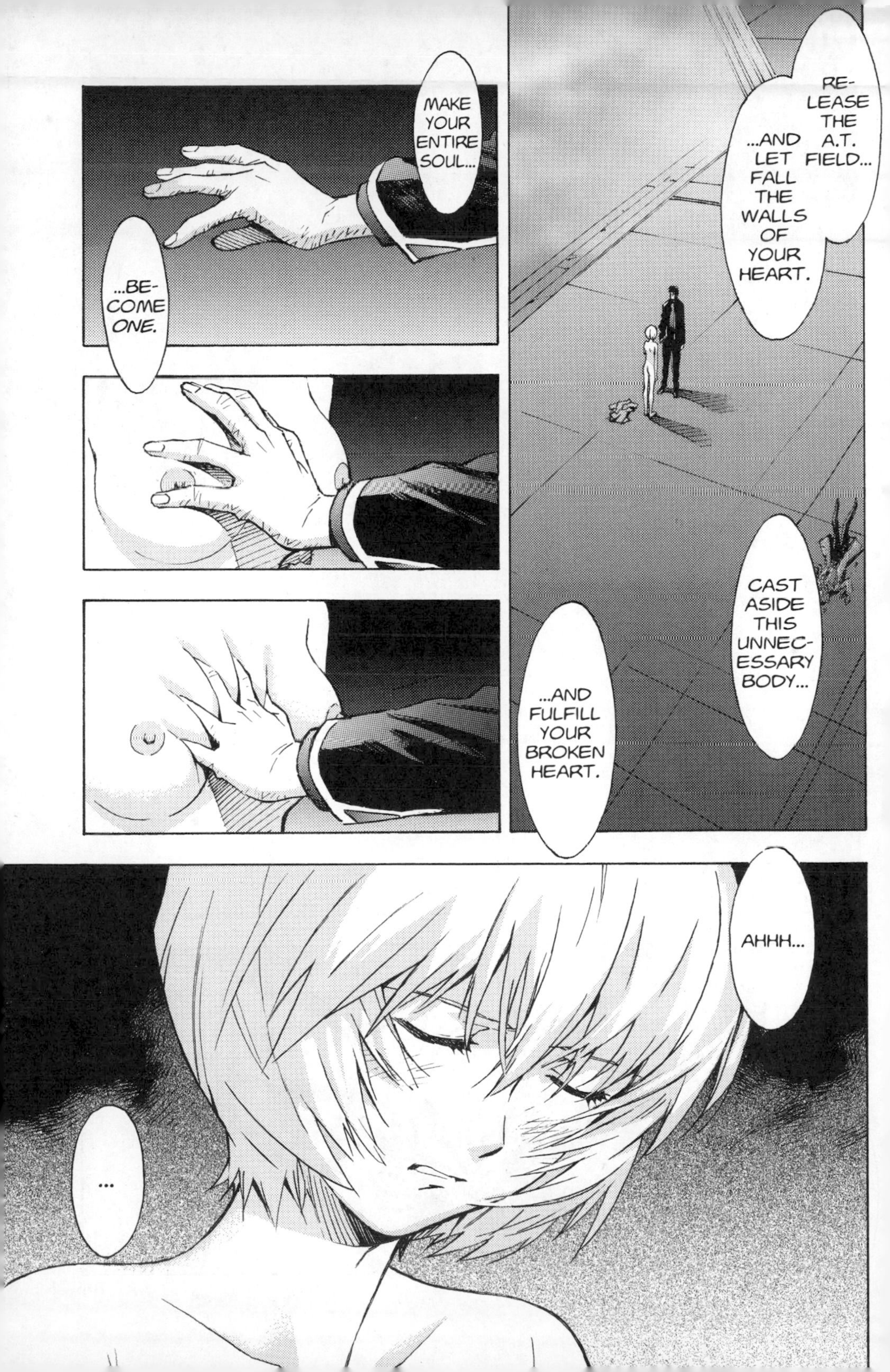
RE-LEASE THE A.T. FIELD...
...AND LET FALL THE WALLS OF YOUR HEART.
MAKE YOUR ENTIRE SOUL...
...BE-COME ONE.
CAST ASIDE THIS UNNEC-ESSARY BODY...
...AND FULFILL YOUR BROKEN HEART.
AHHH...
...

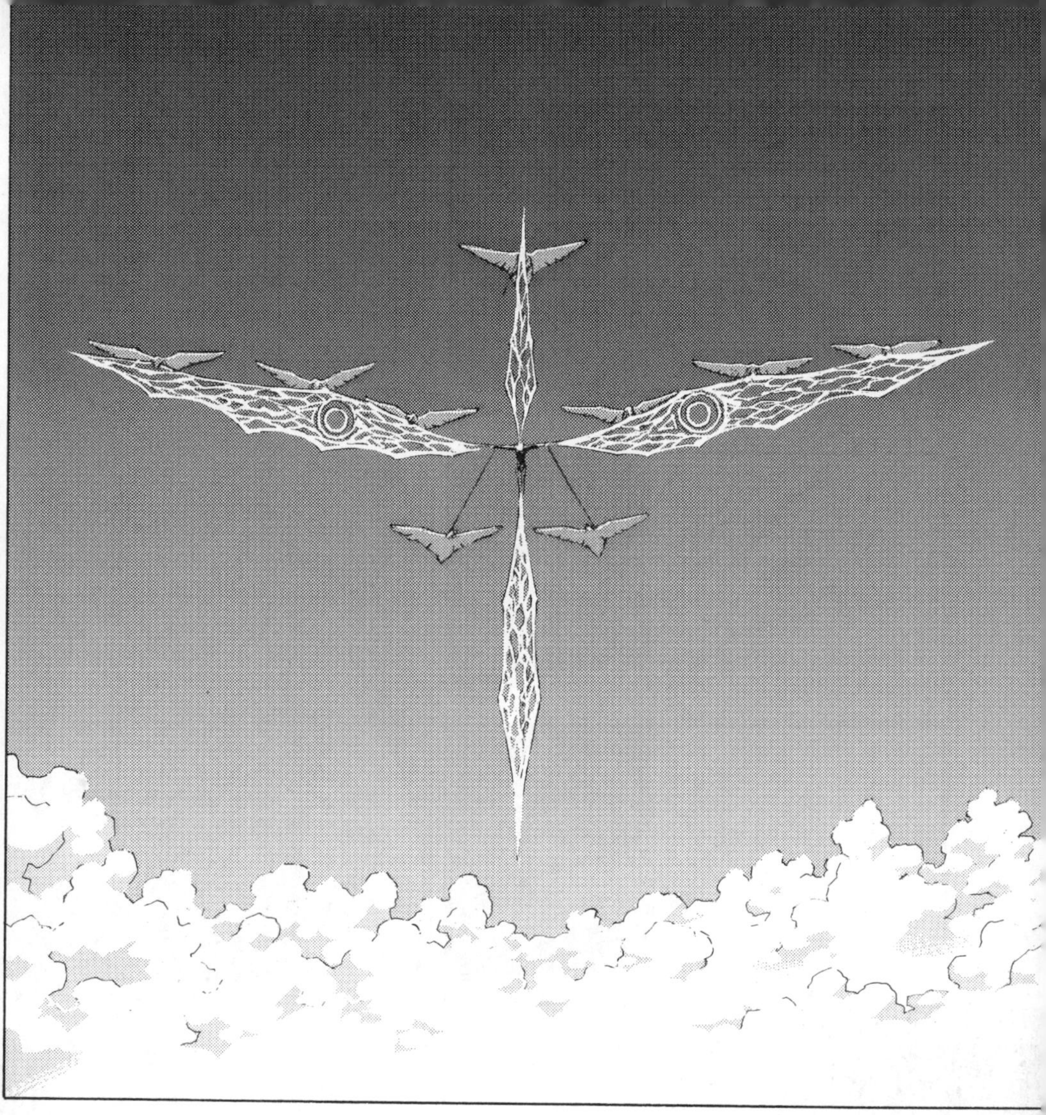

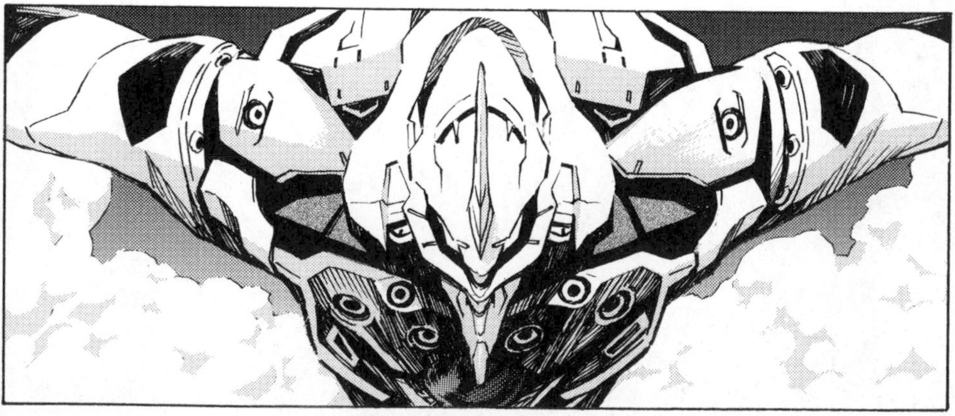

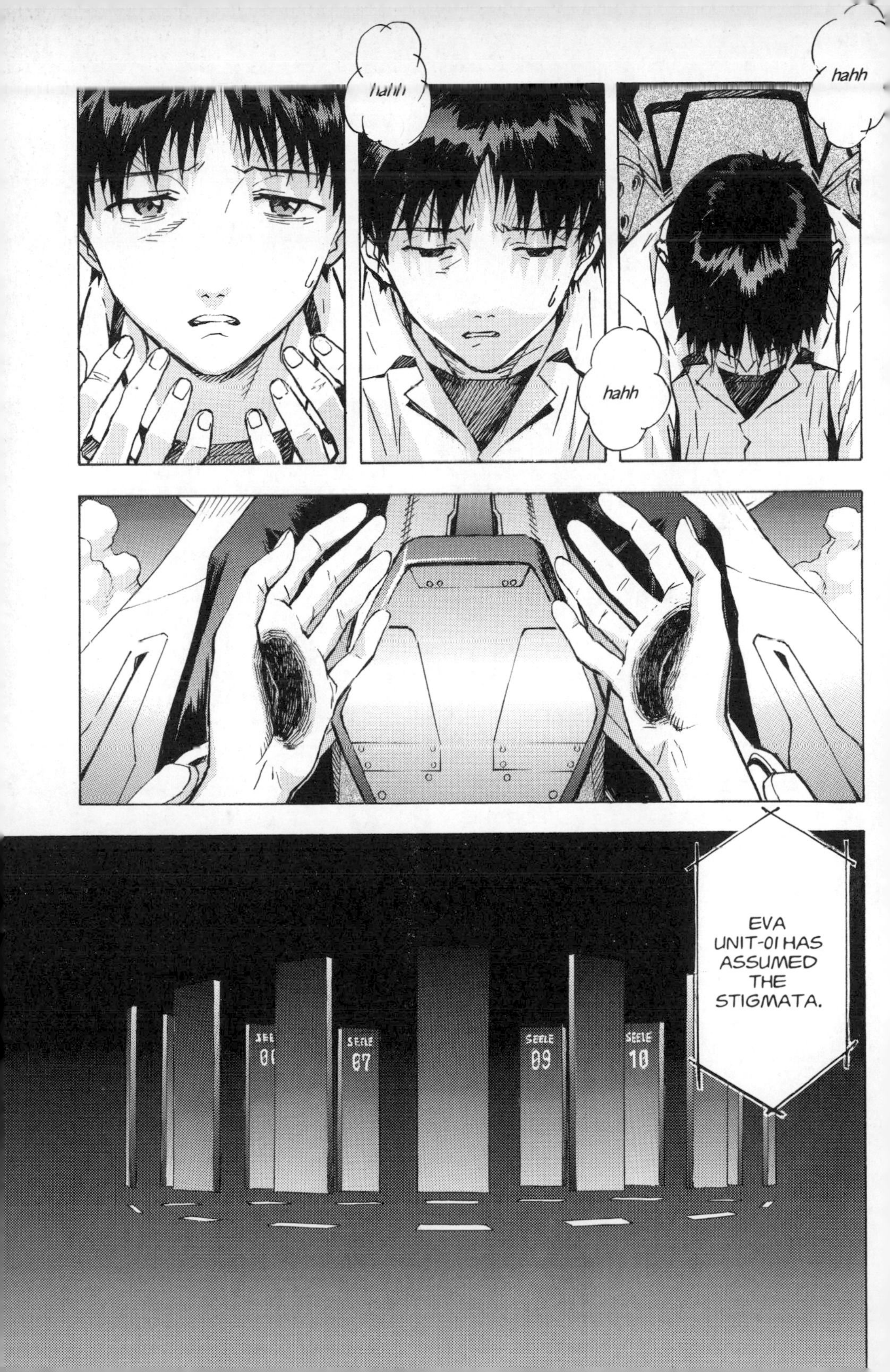
hahh
hahh
hahh
EVA UNIT-01 HAS ASSUMED THE STIGMATA.
SEELE 10
SEELE 09
SEELE 07

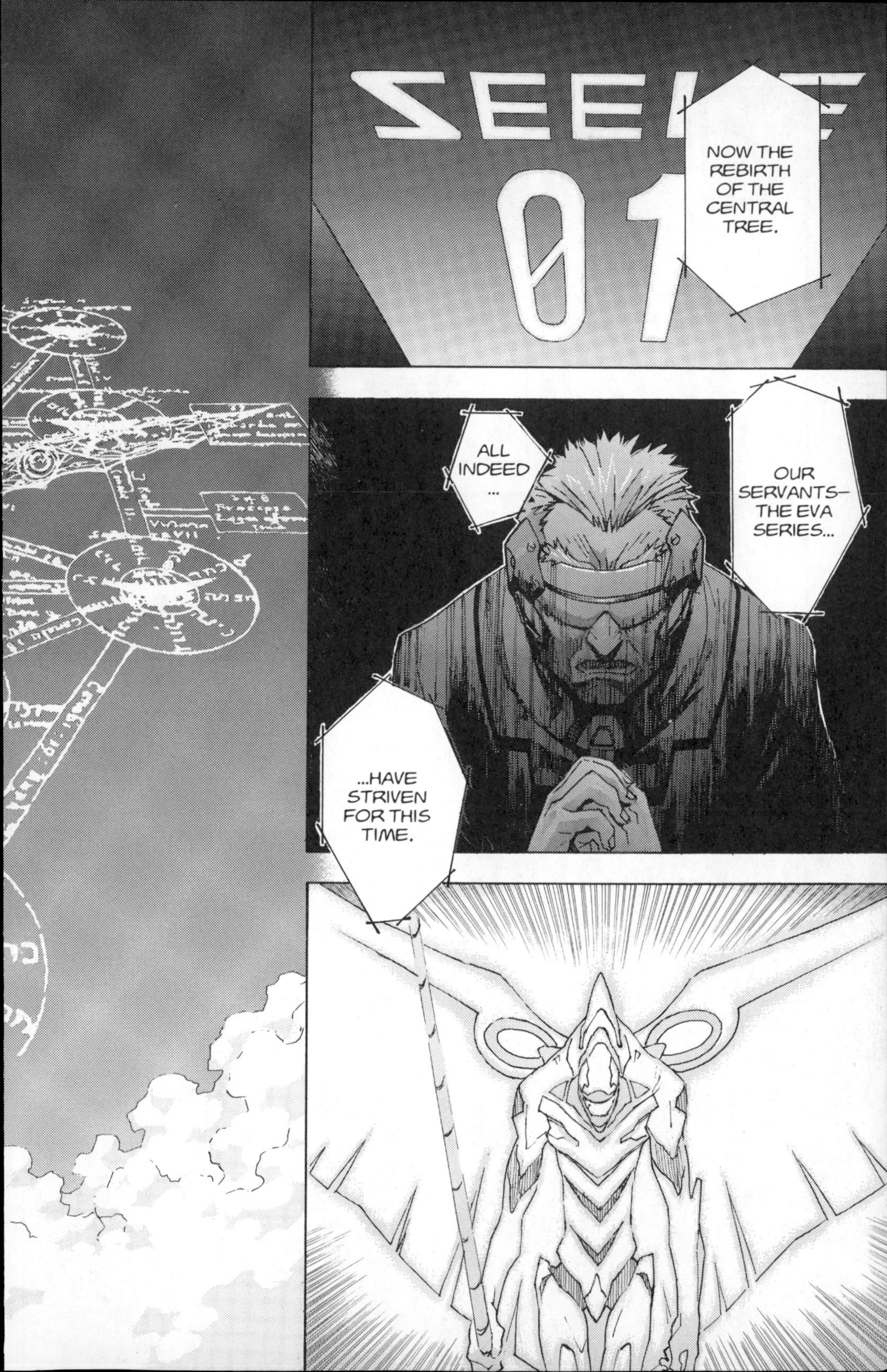
NOW THE REBIRTH OF THE CENTRAL TREE.
OUR SERVANTS— THE EVA SERIES...
ALL INDEED ...
...HAVE STRIVEN FOR THIS TIME.

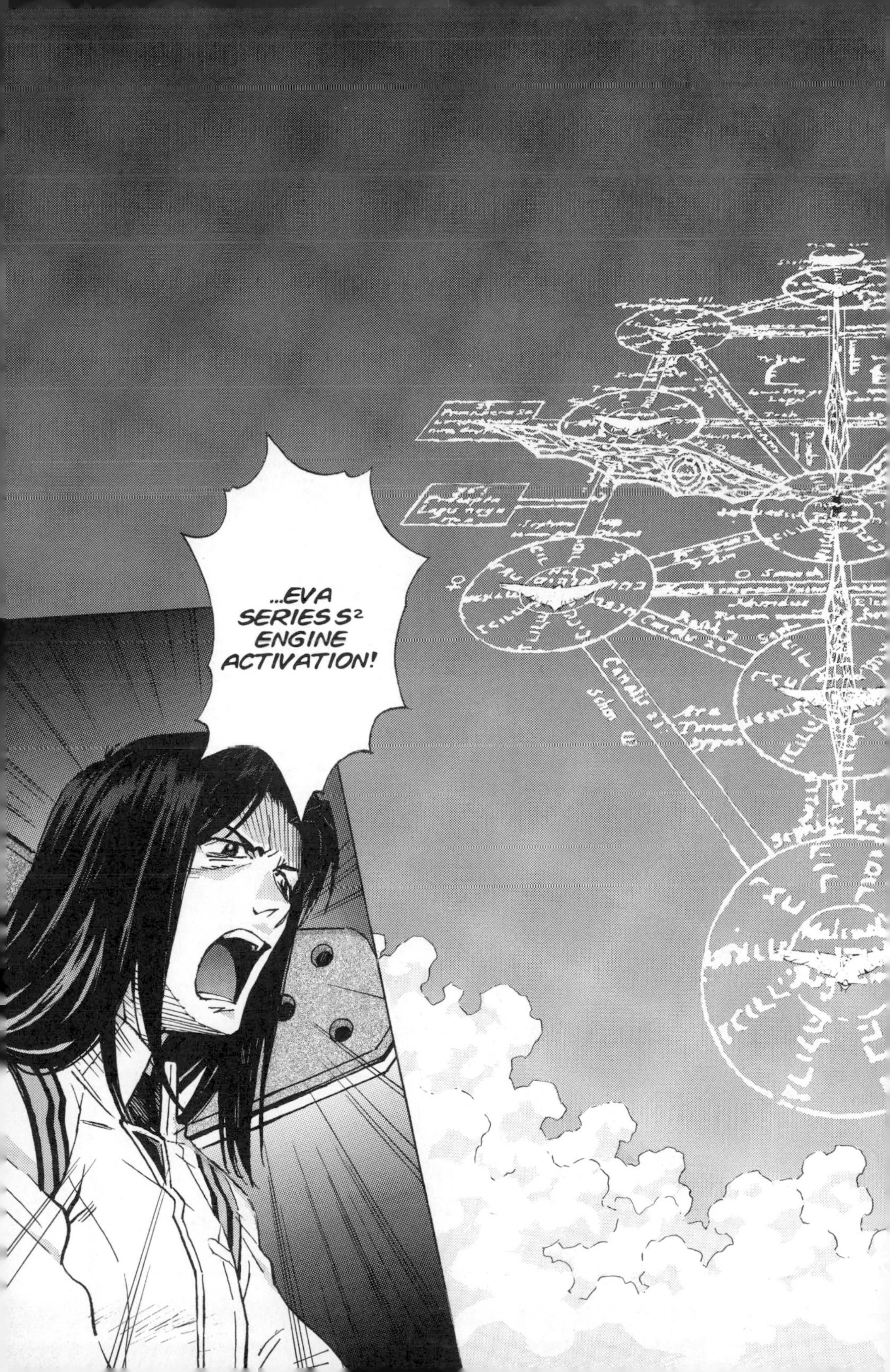
...EVA SERIES S^2 ENGINE ACTIVATION!

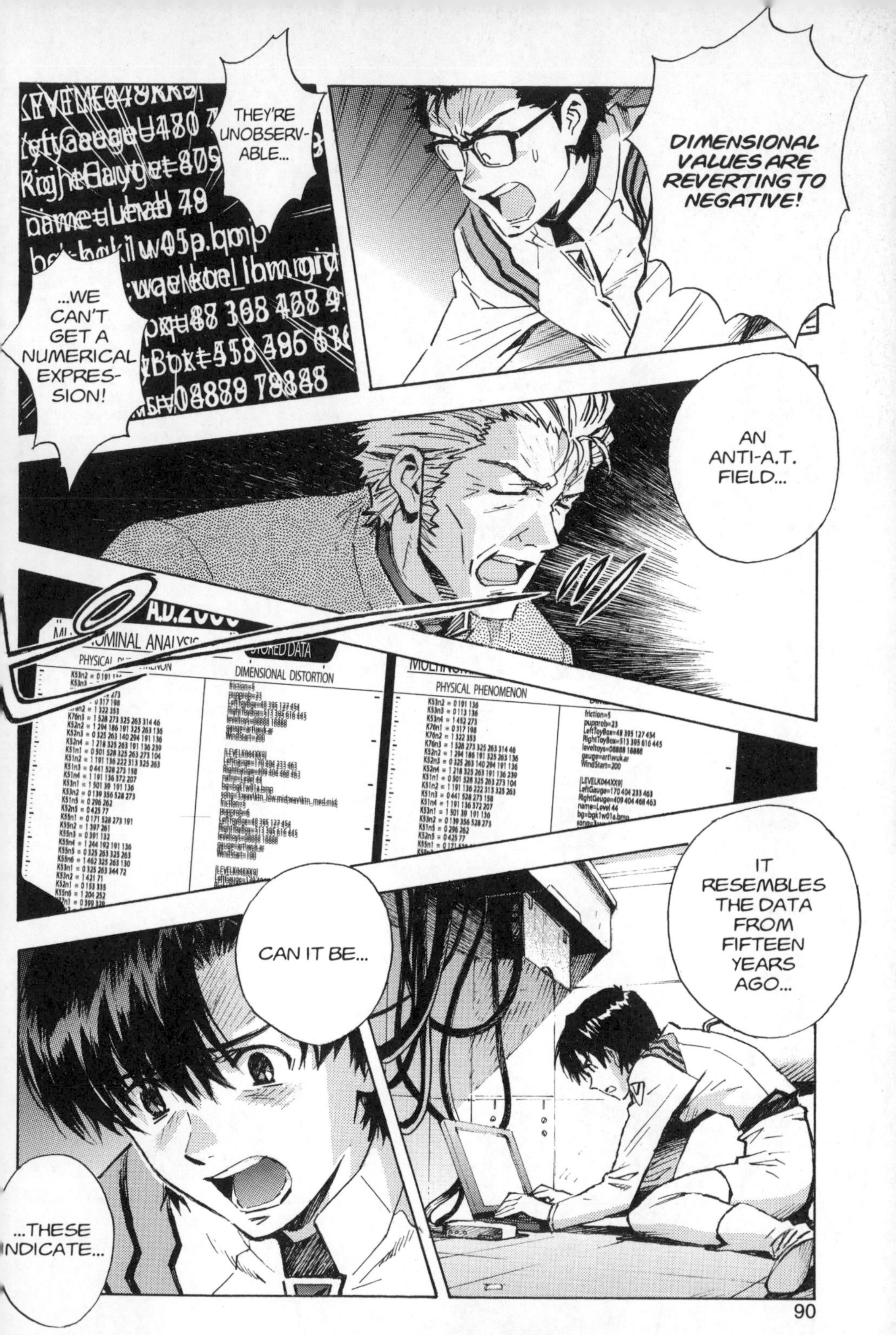
DIMENSIONAL VALUES ARE REVERTING TO NEGATIVE!
THEY'RE UNOBSERV-ABLE...
...WE CAN'T GET A NUMERICAL EXPRES-SION!
AN ANTI-A.T. FIELD...
DIMENSIONAL DISTORTION
PHYSICAL PHENOMENON
IT RESEMBLES THE DATA FROM FIFTEEN YEARS AGO...
CAN IT BE...
...THESE INDICATE...

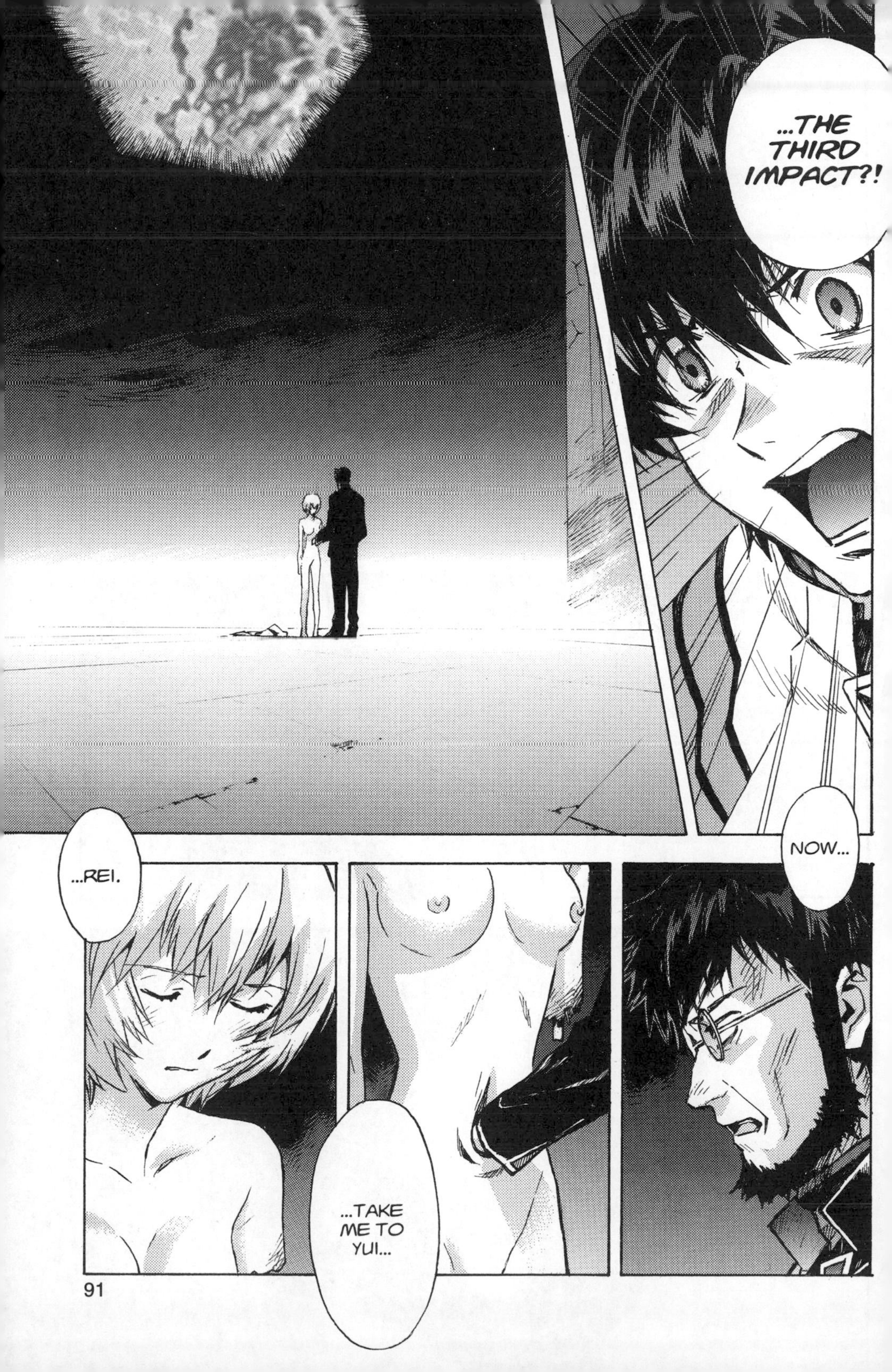
...THE THIRD IMPACT?!
NOW...
...TAKE ME TO YUI...
...REI.

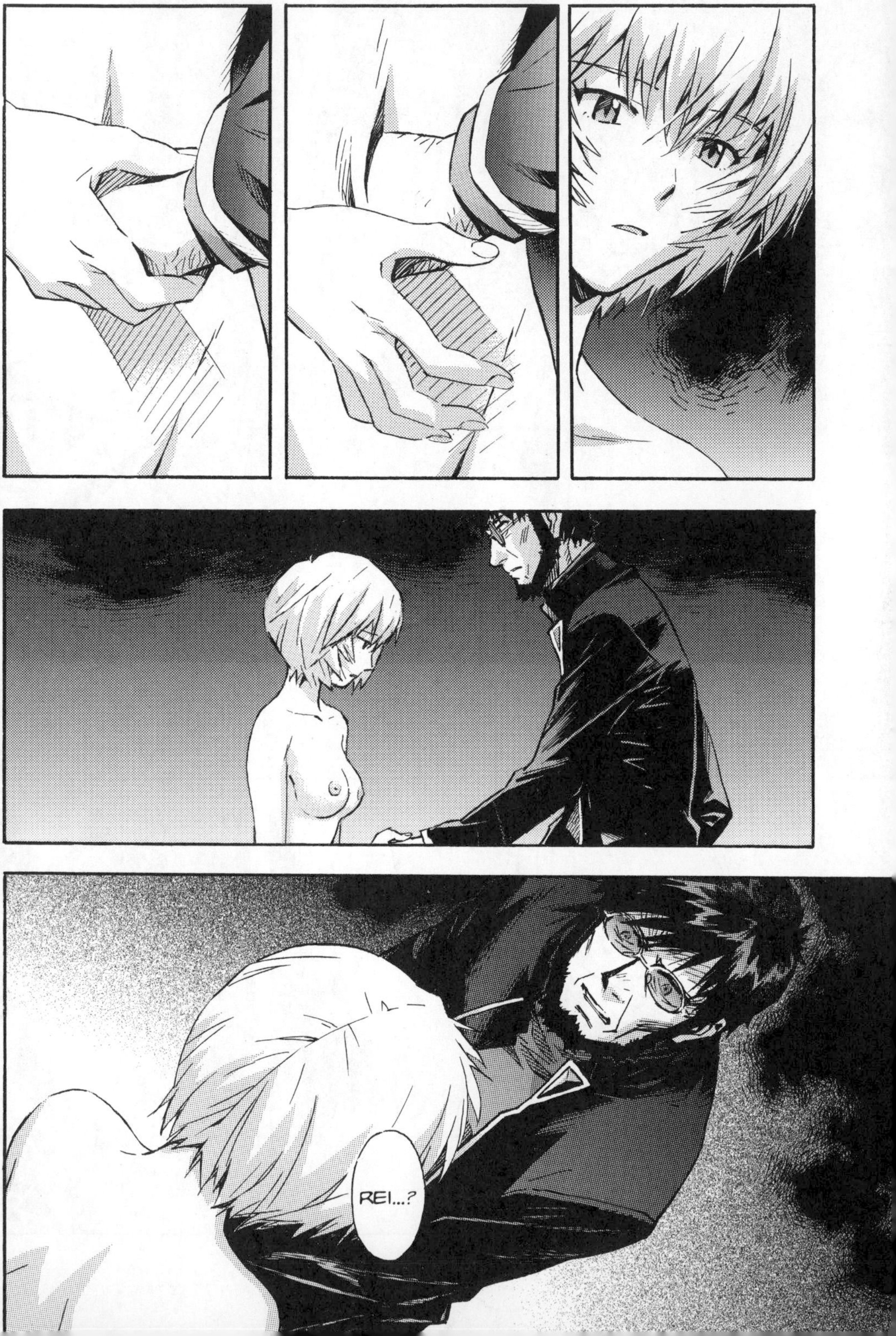
REI...?

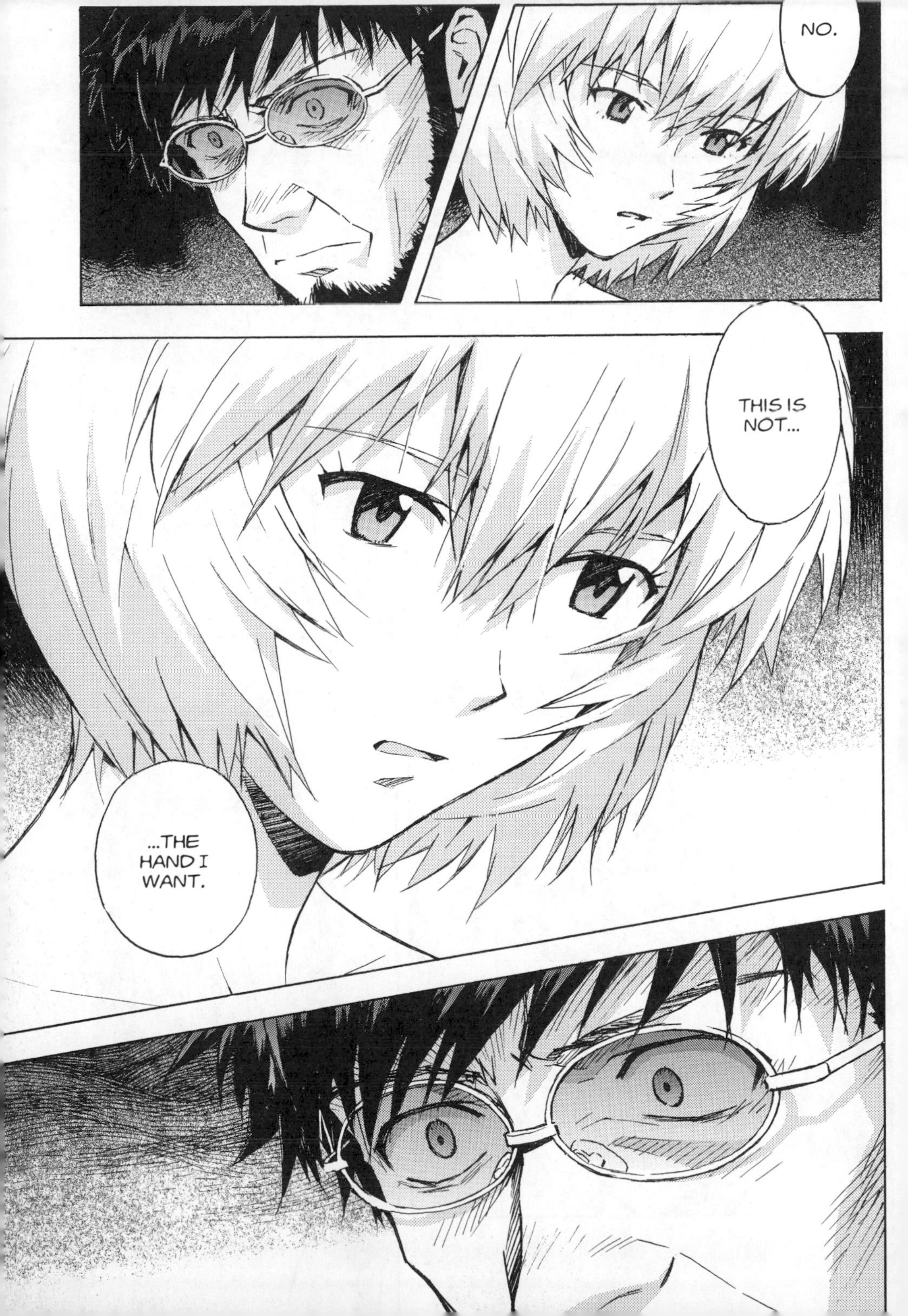
NO.
THIS IS NOT...
...THE HAND I WANT.

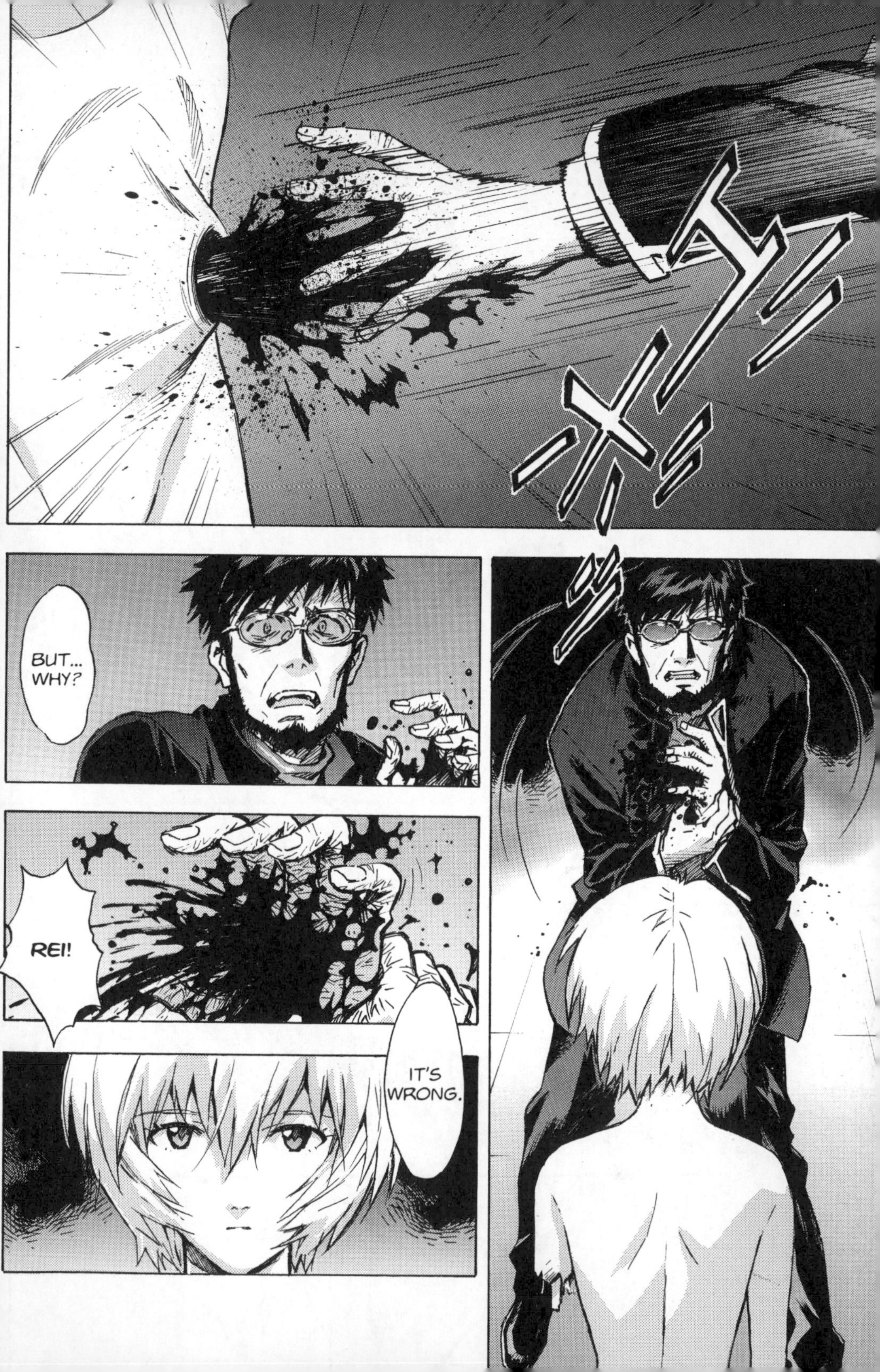
BUT... WHY?
REI!
IT'S WRONG.

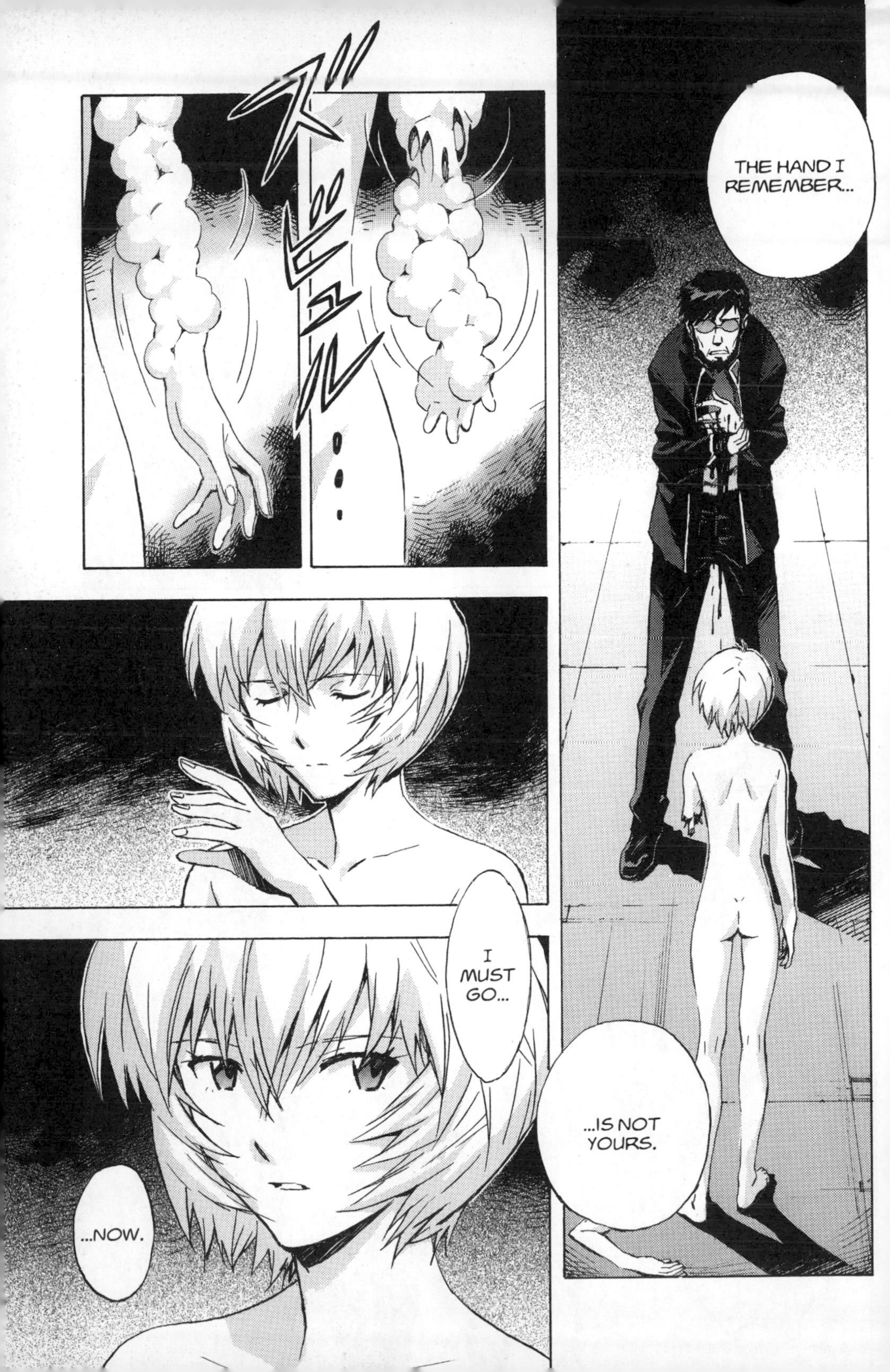
THE HAND I REMEMBER...
...IS NOT YOURS.
I MUST GO...
...NOW.

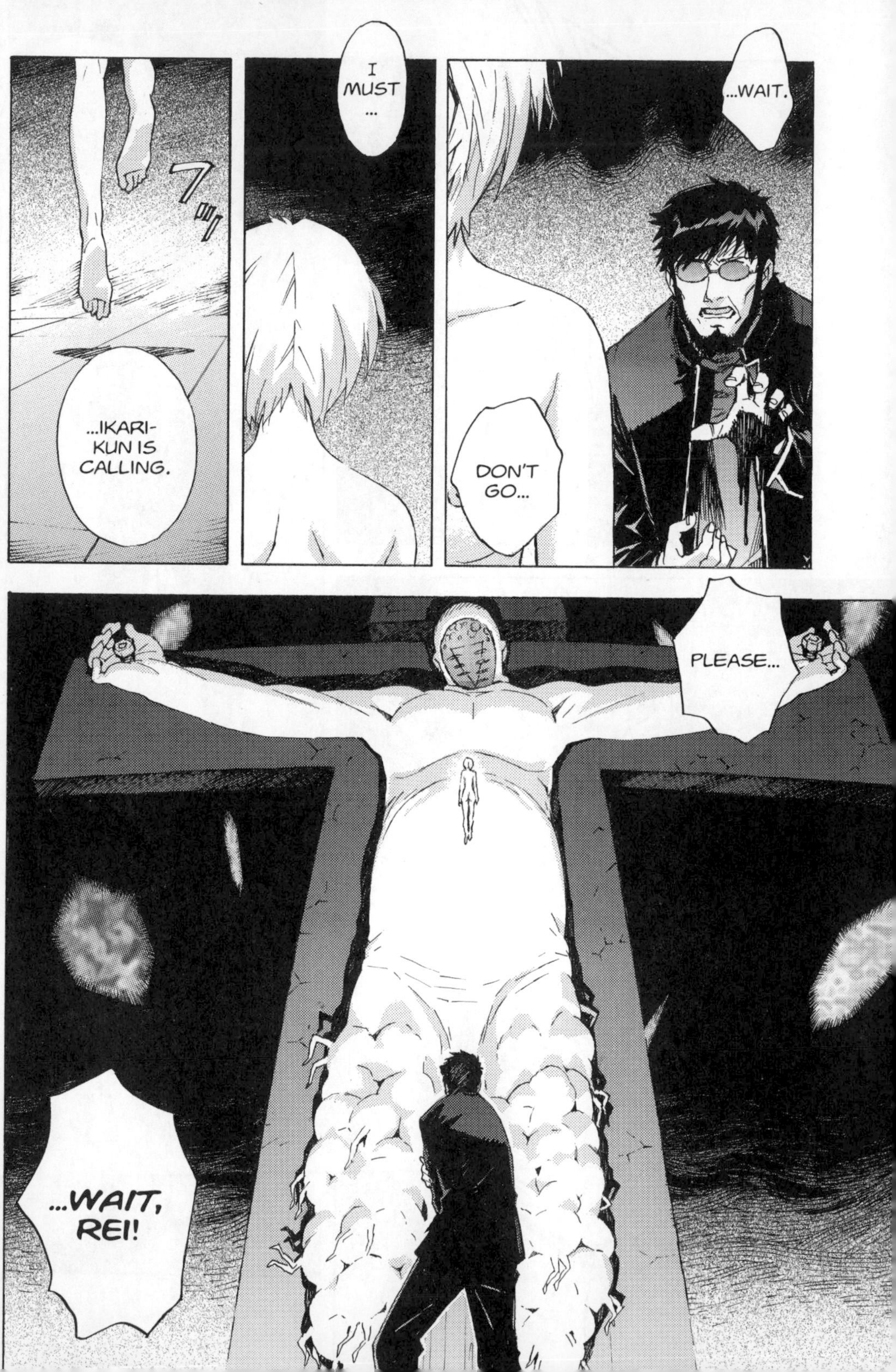
...WAIT.
DON'T GO...
I MUST ...
フッ
...IKARI-KUN IS CALLING.
PLEASE...
...WAIT, REI!

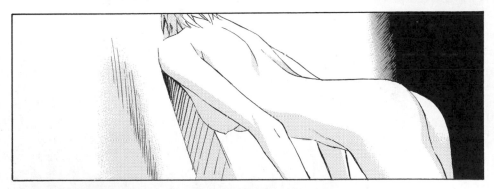

REI!

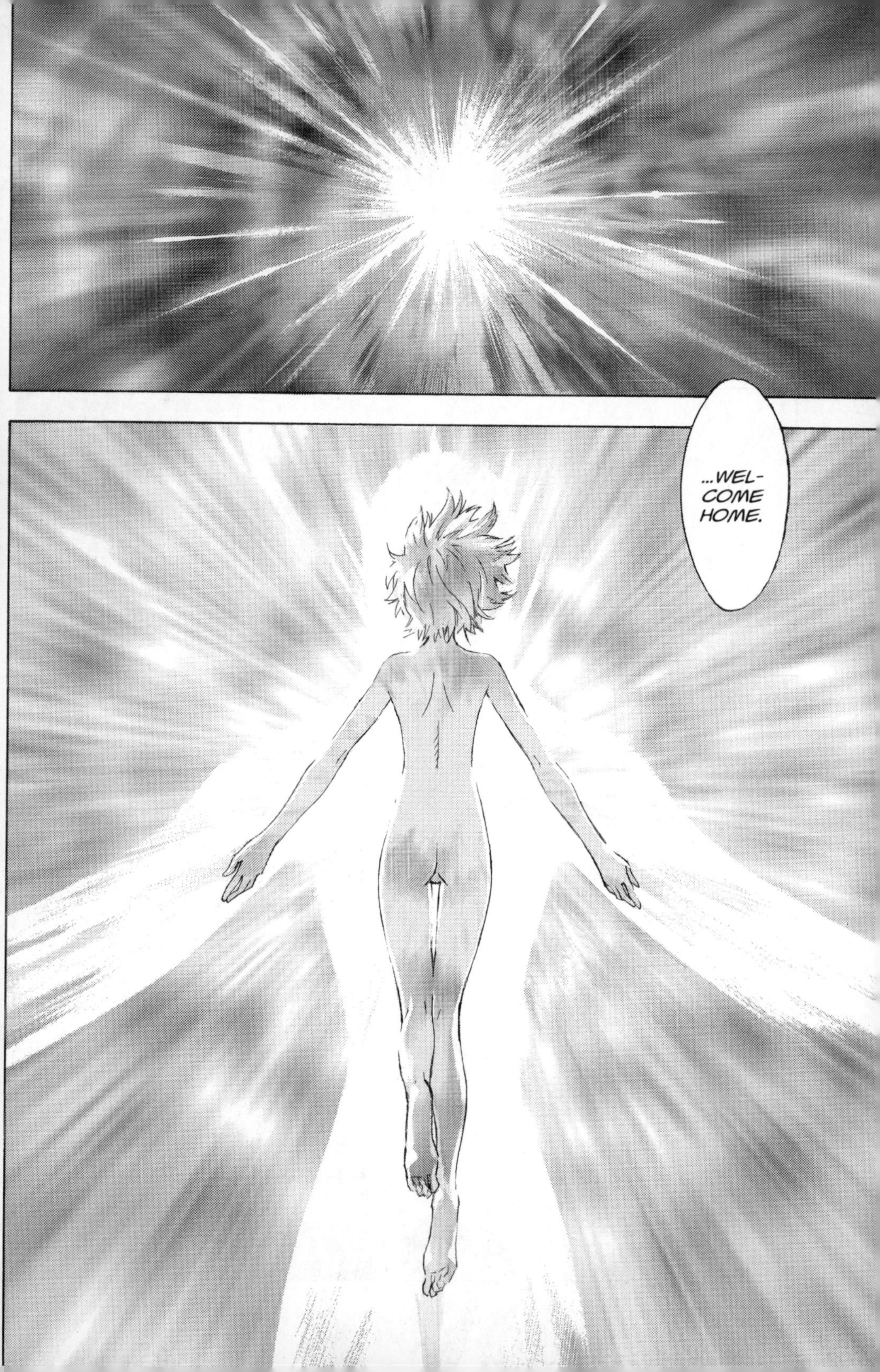
...WEL-
COME
HOME.

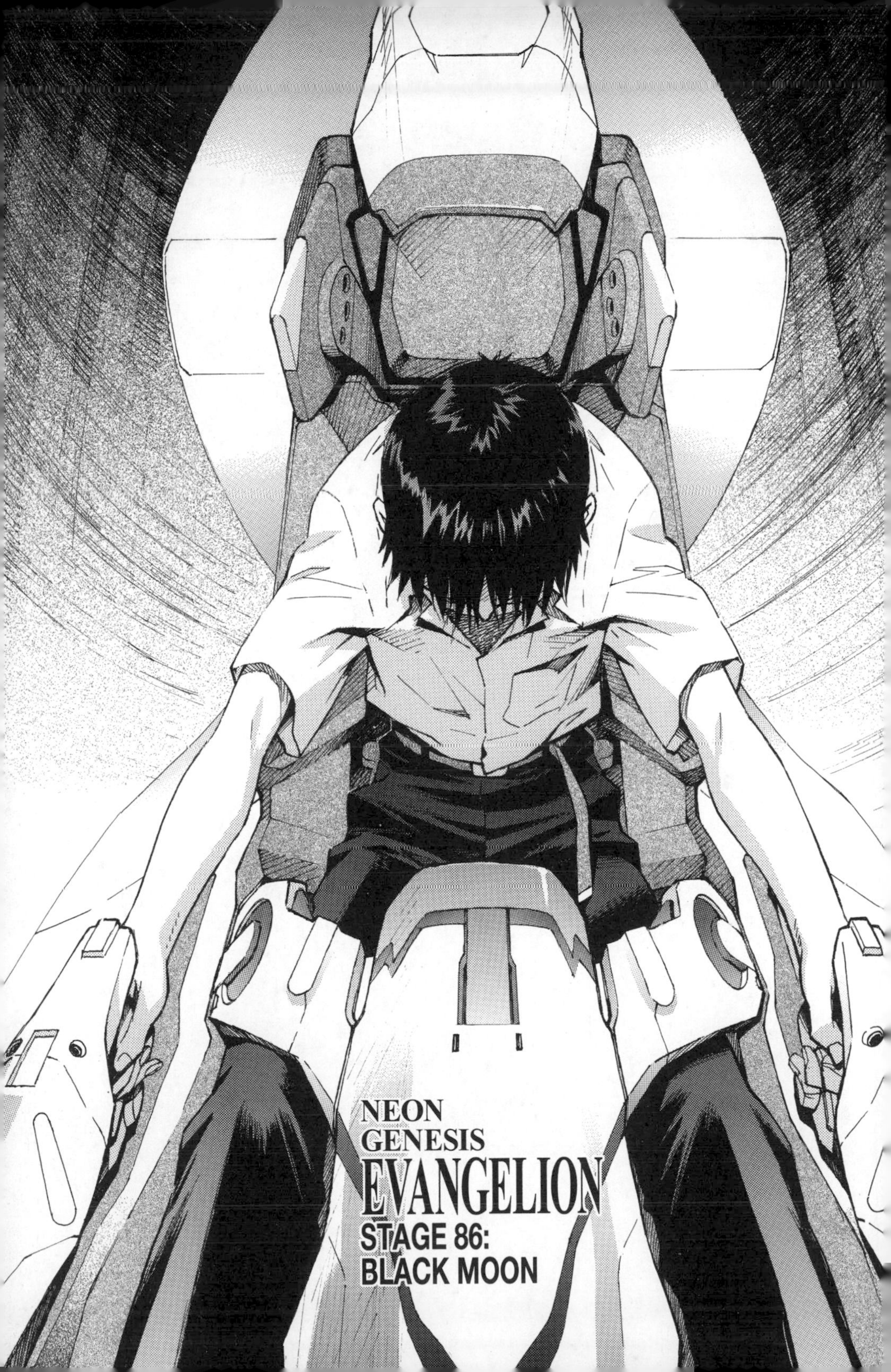
NEON
GENESIS
EVANGELION
STAGE 86:
BLACK MOON

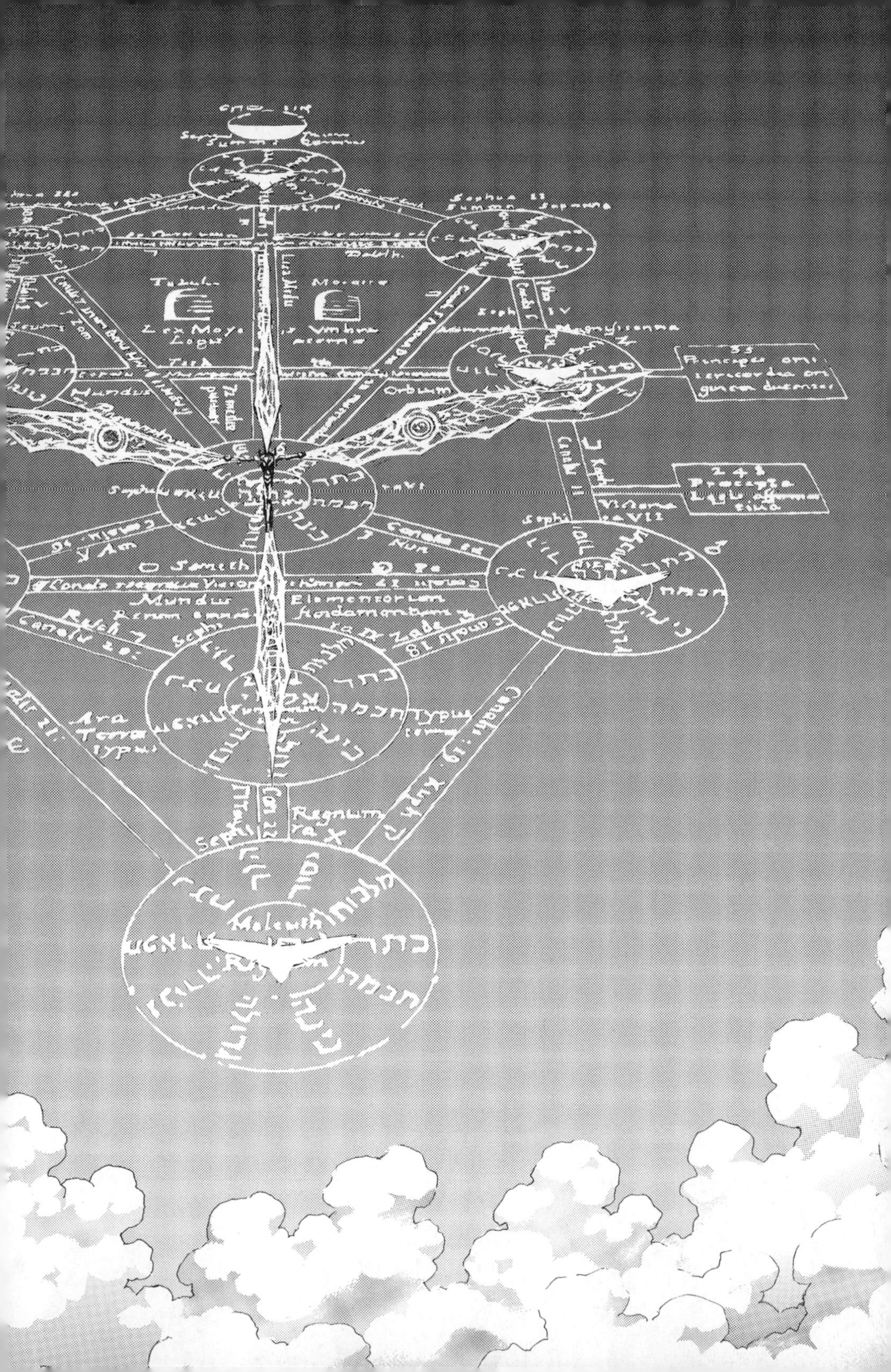
Mundus
Orbium
Elementorum
Ara
Terra
typus
Regnum

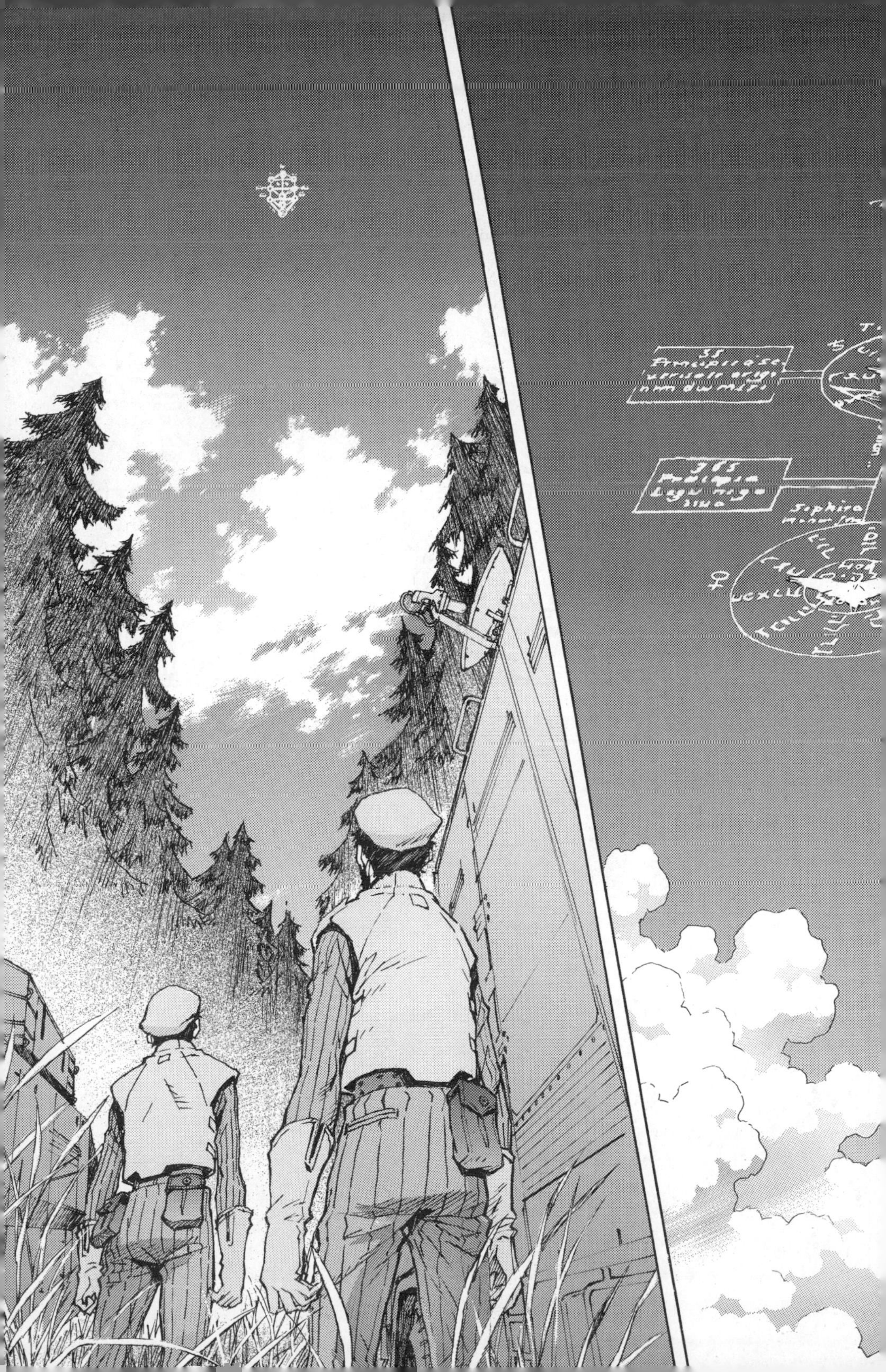

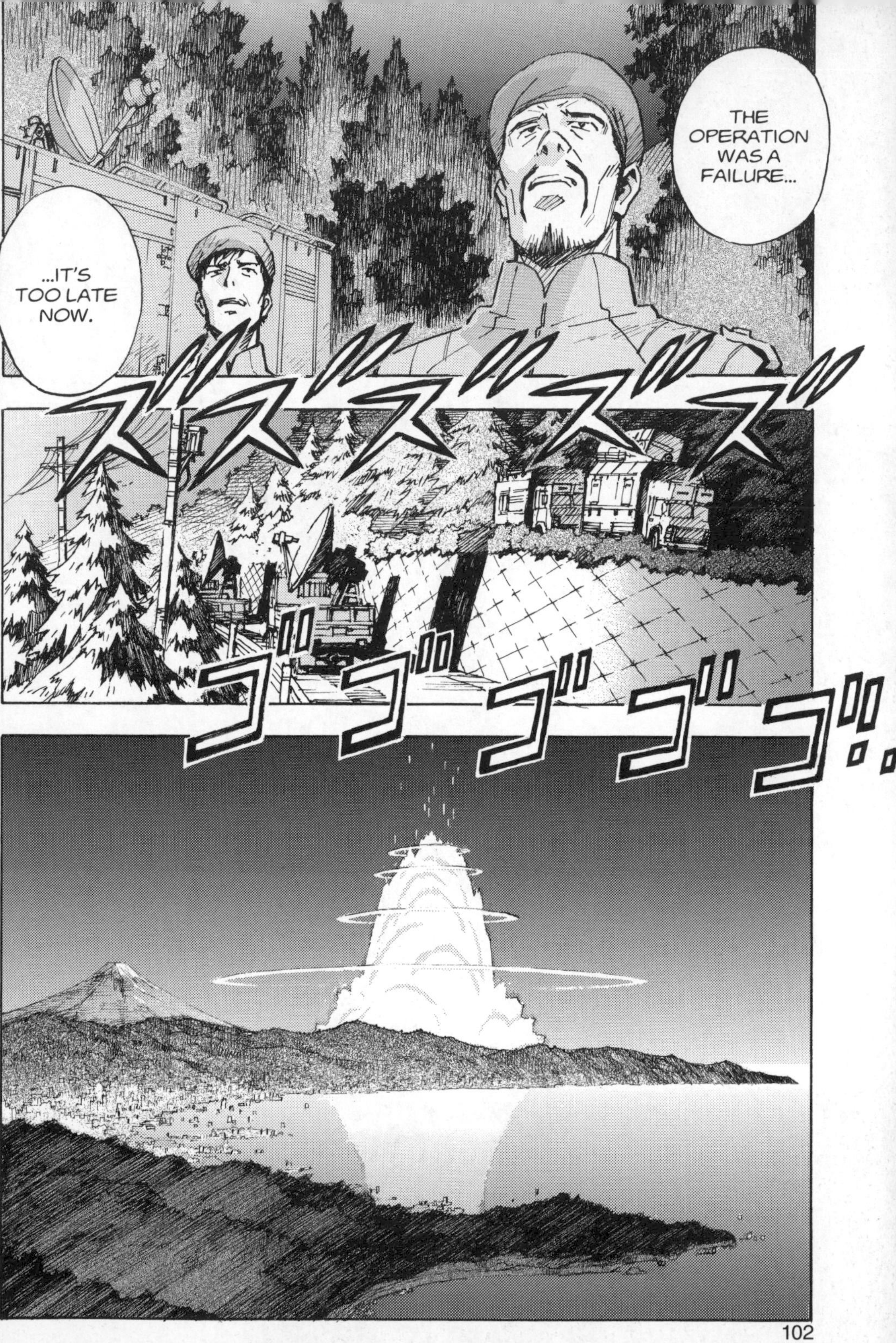
THE OPERATION WAS A FAILURE...
...IT'S TOO LATE NOW.
ズズズズズ
ゴゴゴゴゴ..

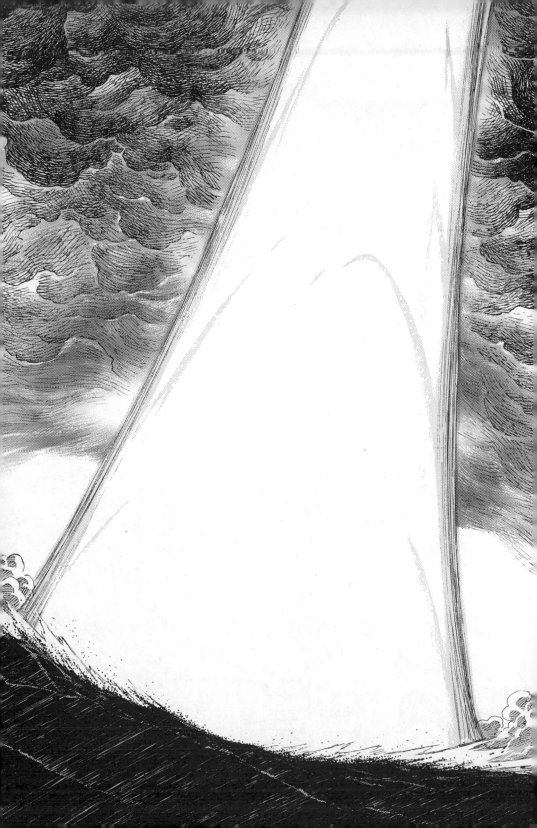

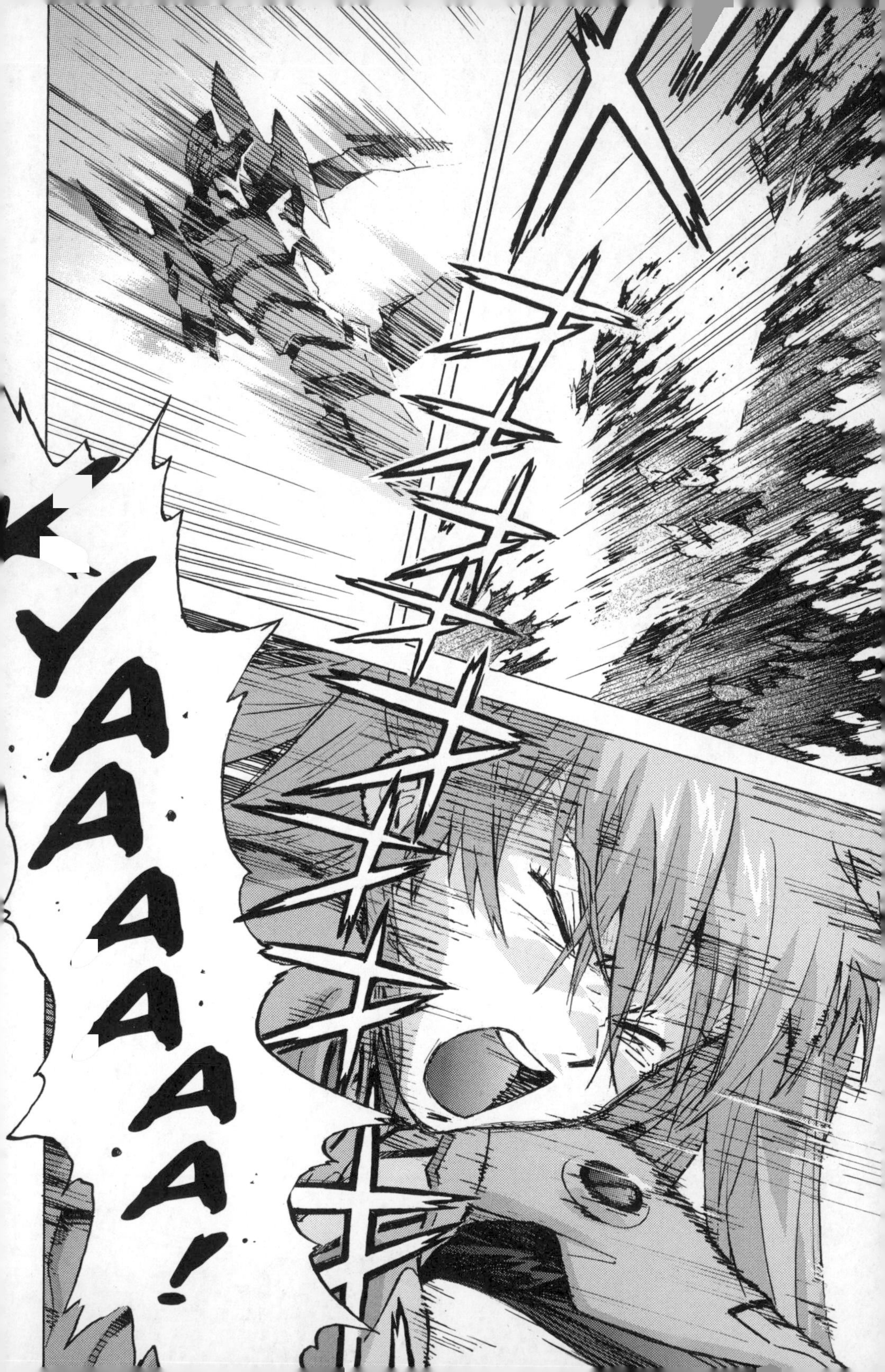
KYAAAAAA!

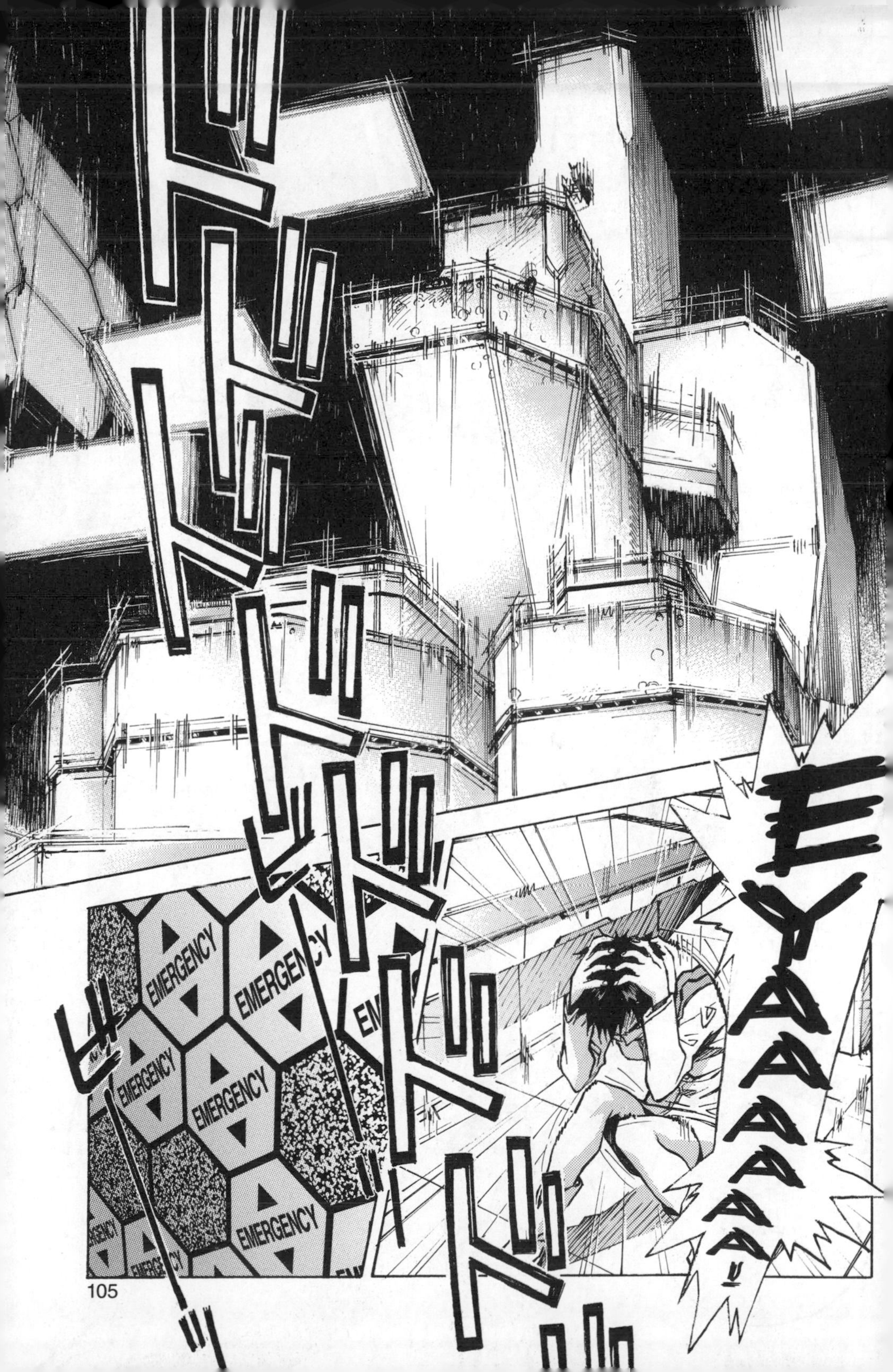
EYAAAAAAA!
EMERGENCY
EMERGENCY
EMERGENCY
EMERGENCY
EMERGENCY

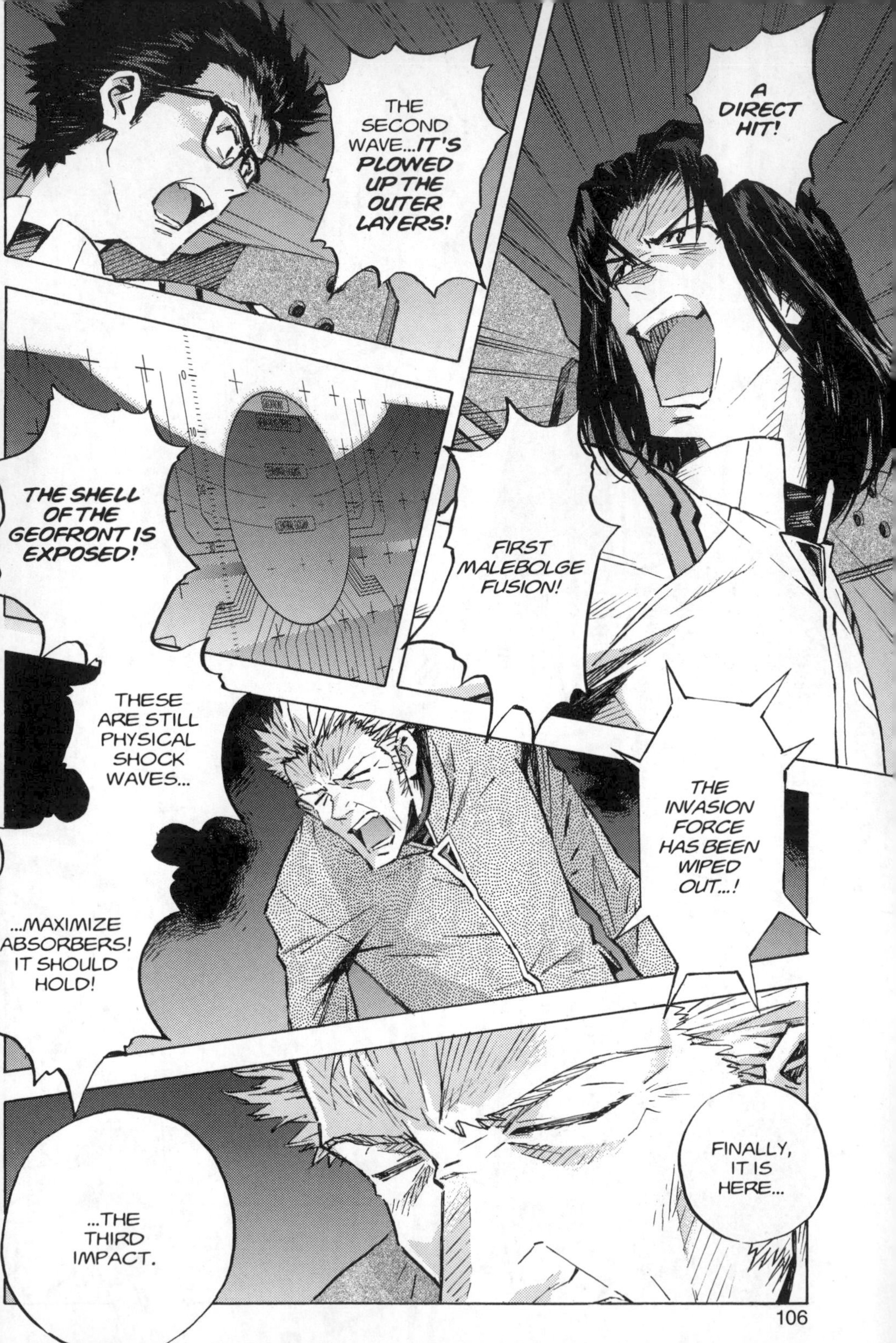
A DIRECT HIT!
FIRST MALEBOLGE FUSION!
THE SECOND WAVE...IT'S PLOWED UP THE OUTER LAYERS!
THE SHELL OF THE GEOFRONT IS EXPOSED!
THE INVASION FORCE HAS BEEN WIPED OUT...!
THESE ARE STILL PHYSICAL SHOCK WAVES...
...MAXIMIZE ABSORBERS! IT SHOULD HOLD!
FINALLY, IT IS HERE...
...THE THIRD IMPACT.

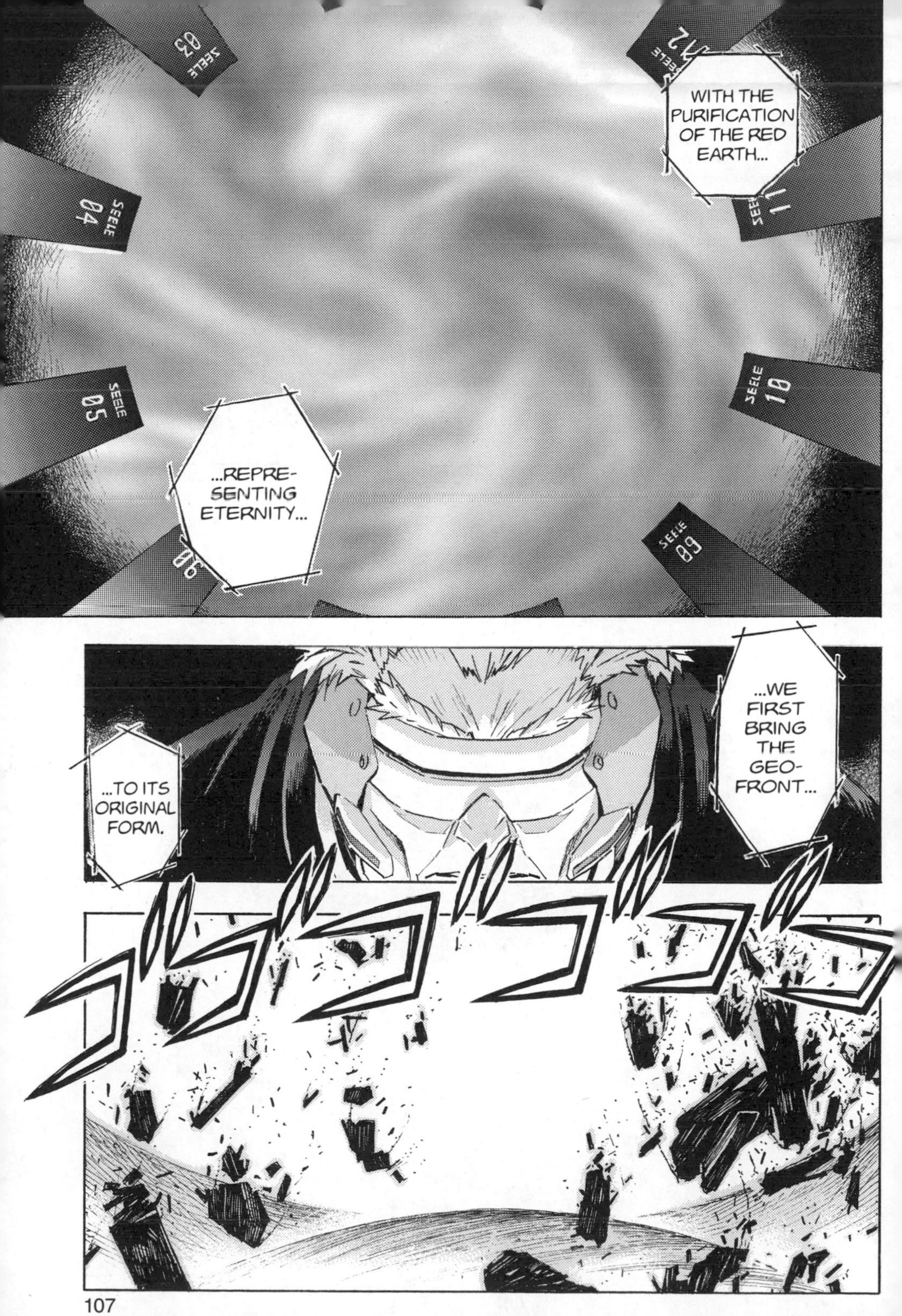
SEELE 12
SEELE 03
WITH THE PURIFICATION OF THE RED EARTH...
SEELE 11
SEELE 04
SEELE 10
SEELE 05
SEELE 09
...REPRESENTING ETERNITY...
...WE FIRST BRING THE GEO-FRONT...
...TO ITS ORIGINAL FORM.

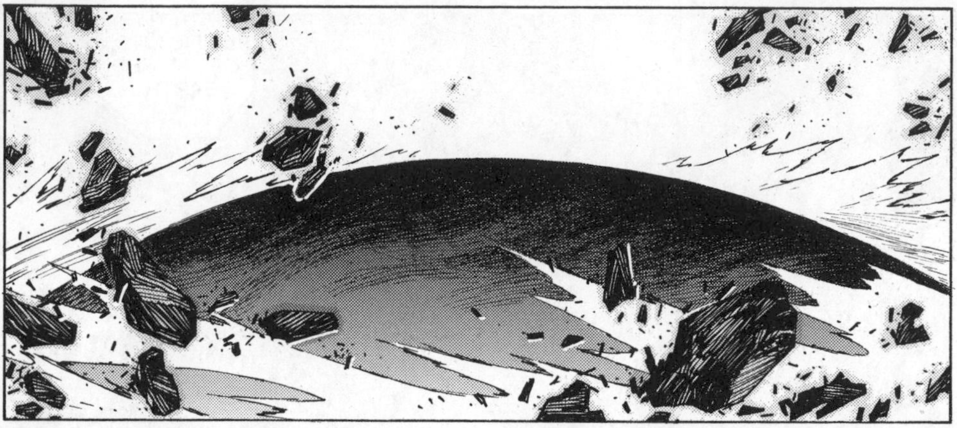
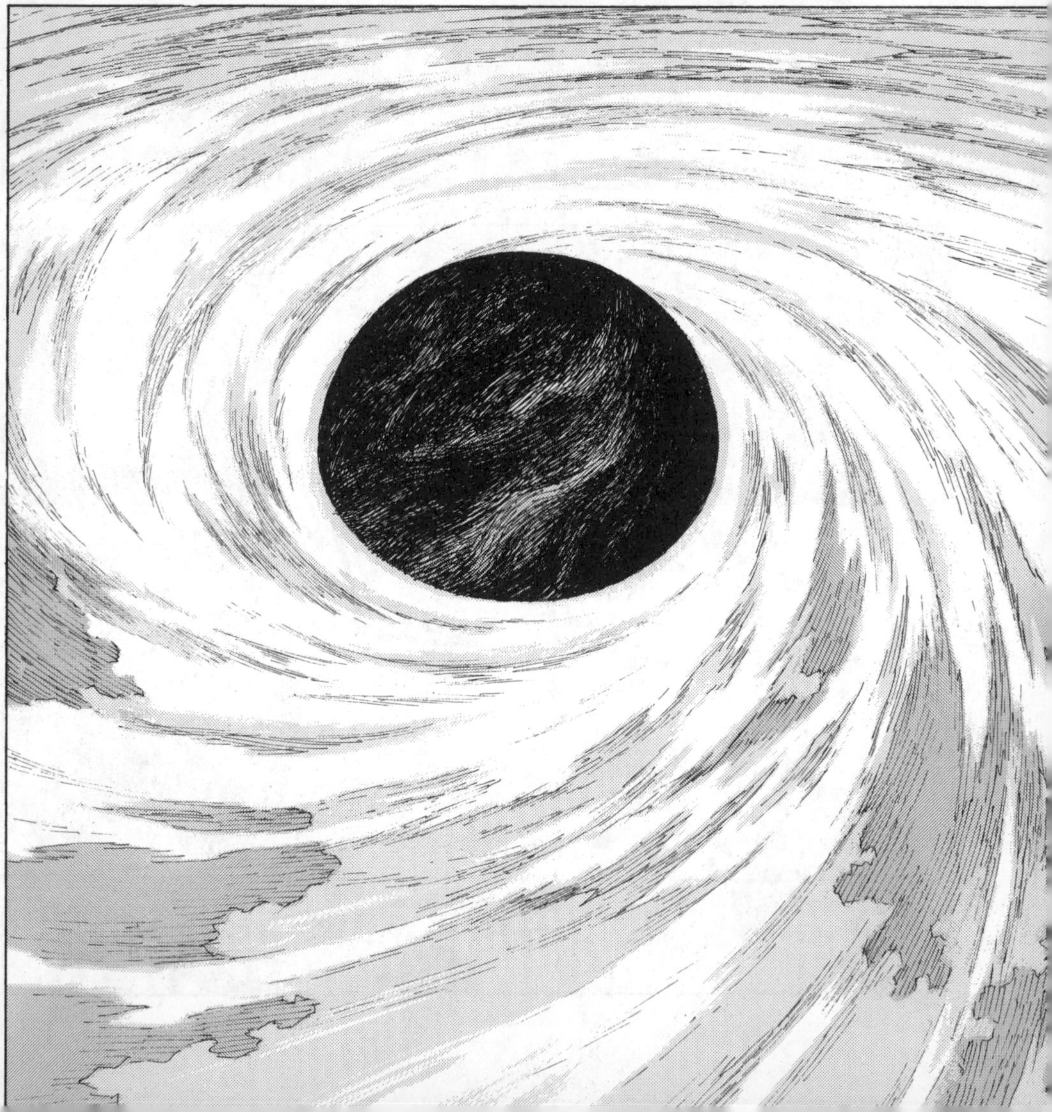

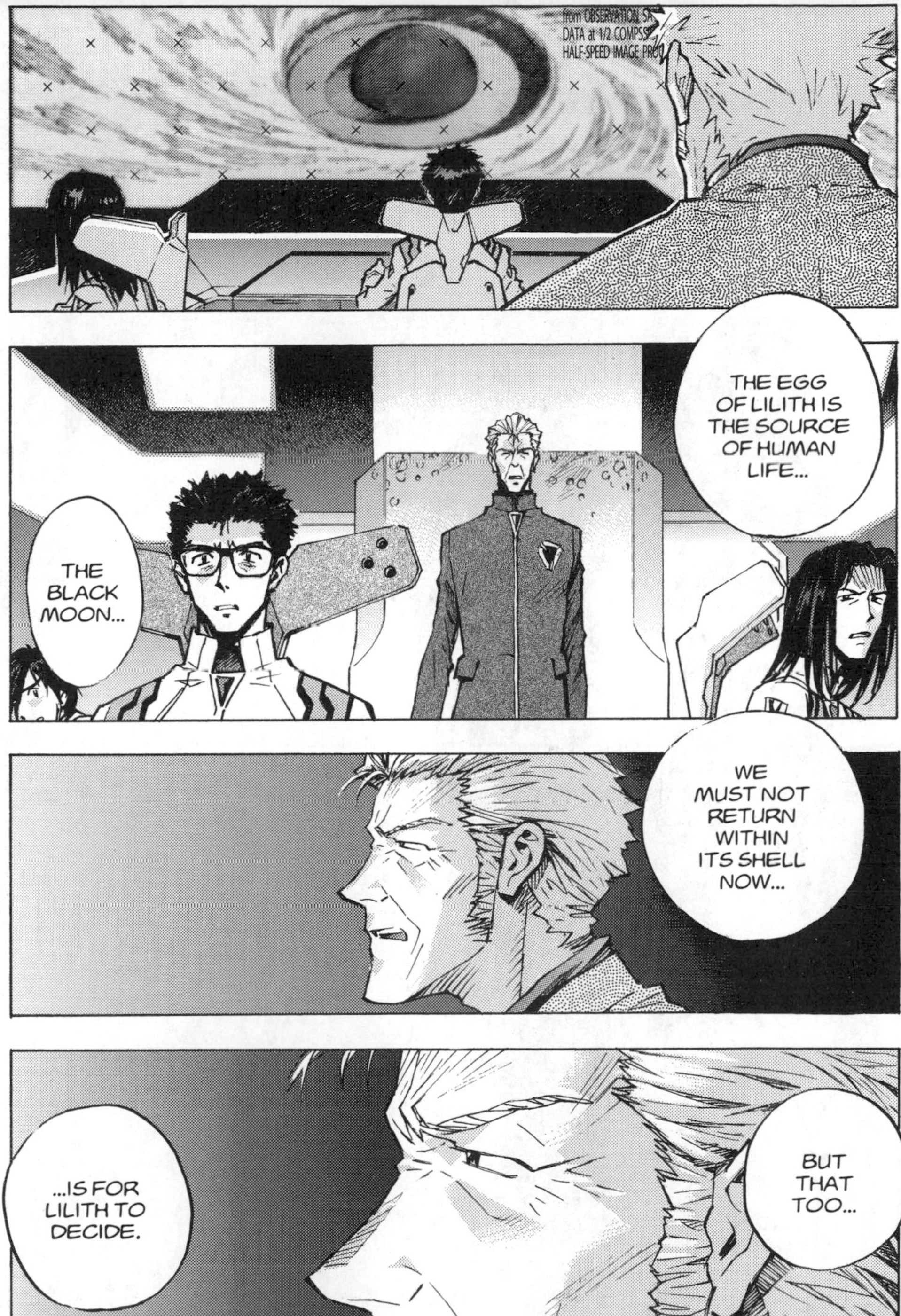
from OBSERVATION
DATA at 1/2
HALF-SPEED IMAGE
THE EGG OF LILITH IS THE SOURCE OF HUMAN LIFE...
THE BLACK MOON...
WE MUST NOT RETURN WITHIN ITS SHELL NOW...
BUT THAT TOO...
...IS FOR LILITH TO DECIDE.

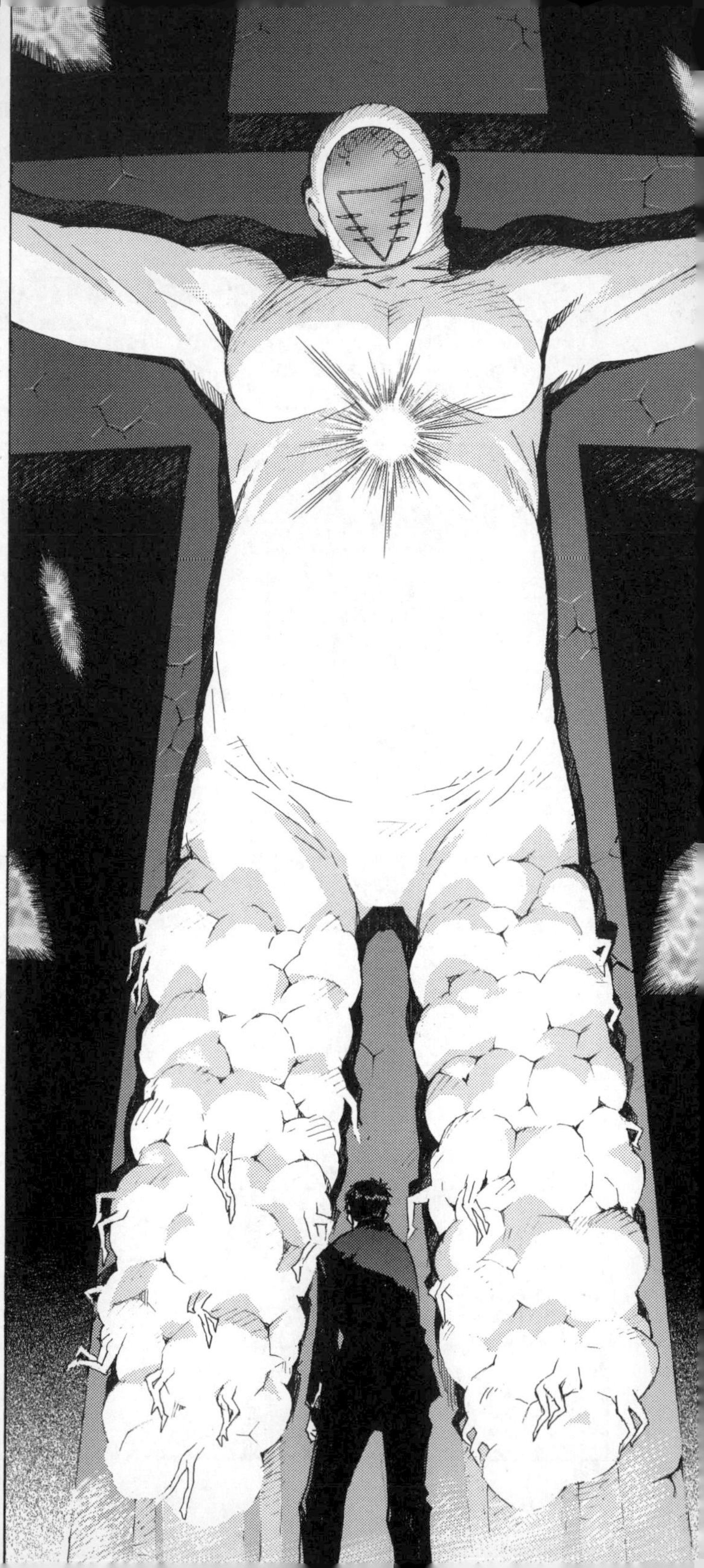
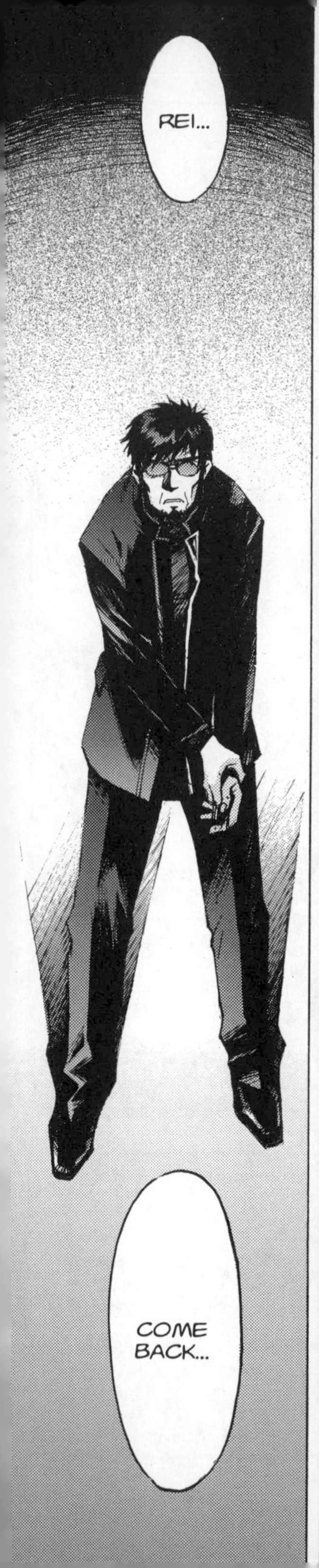
REI...
COME BACK...

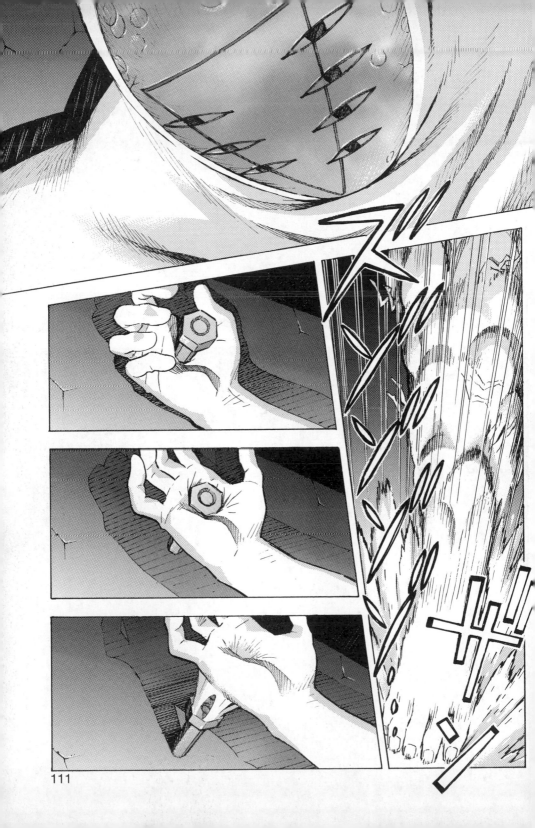

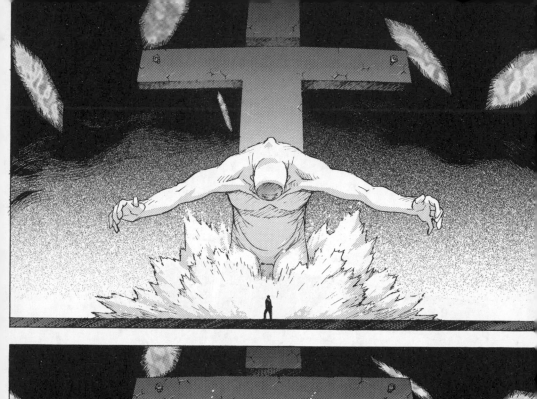
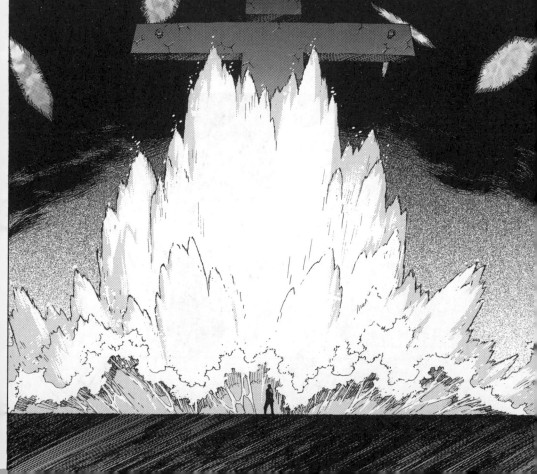

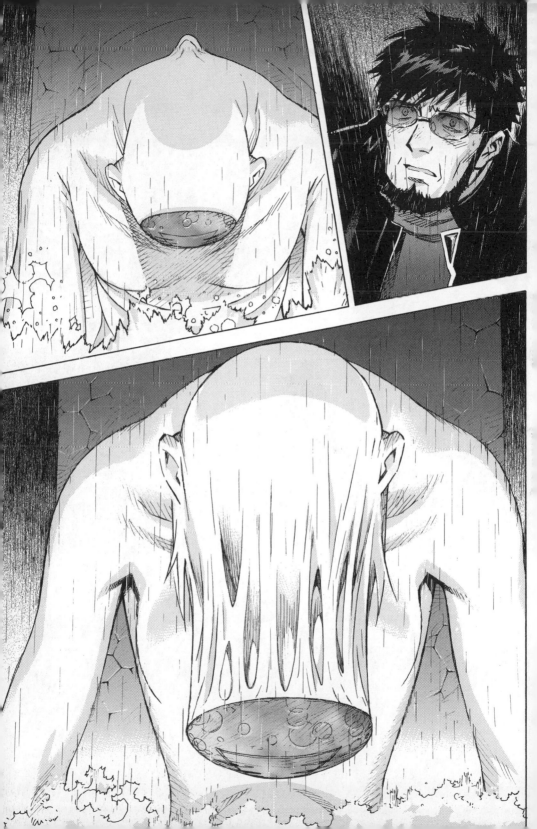

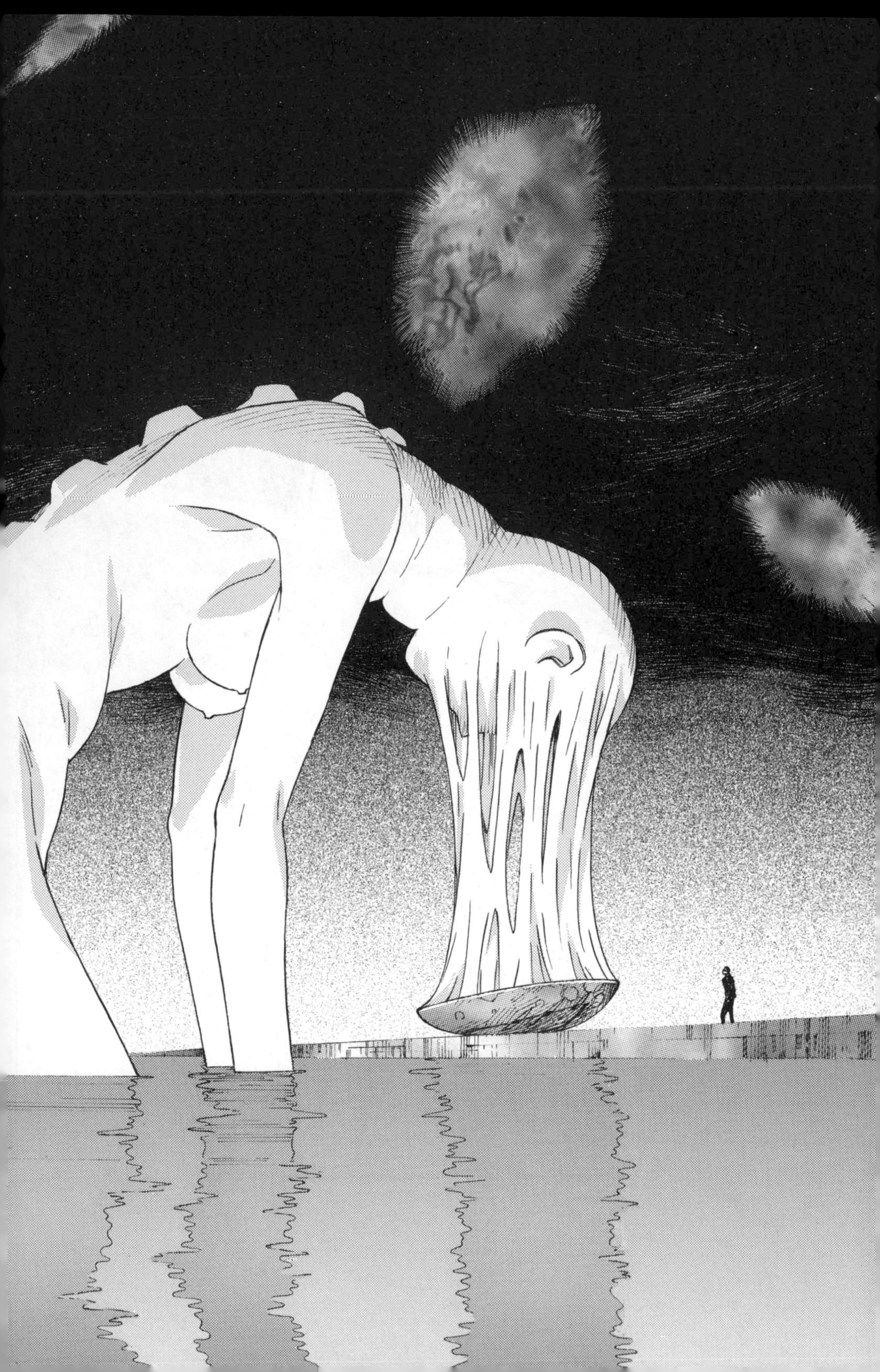

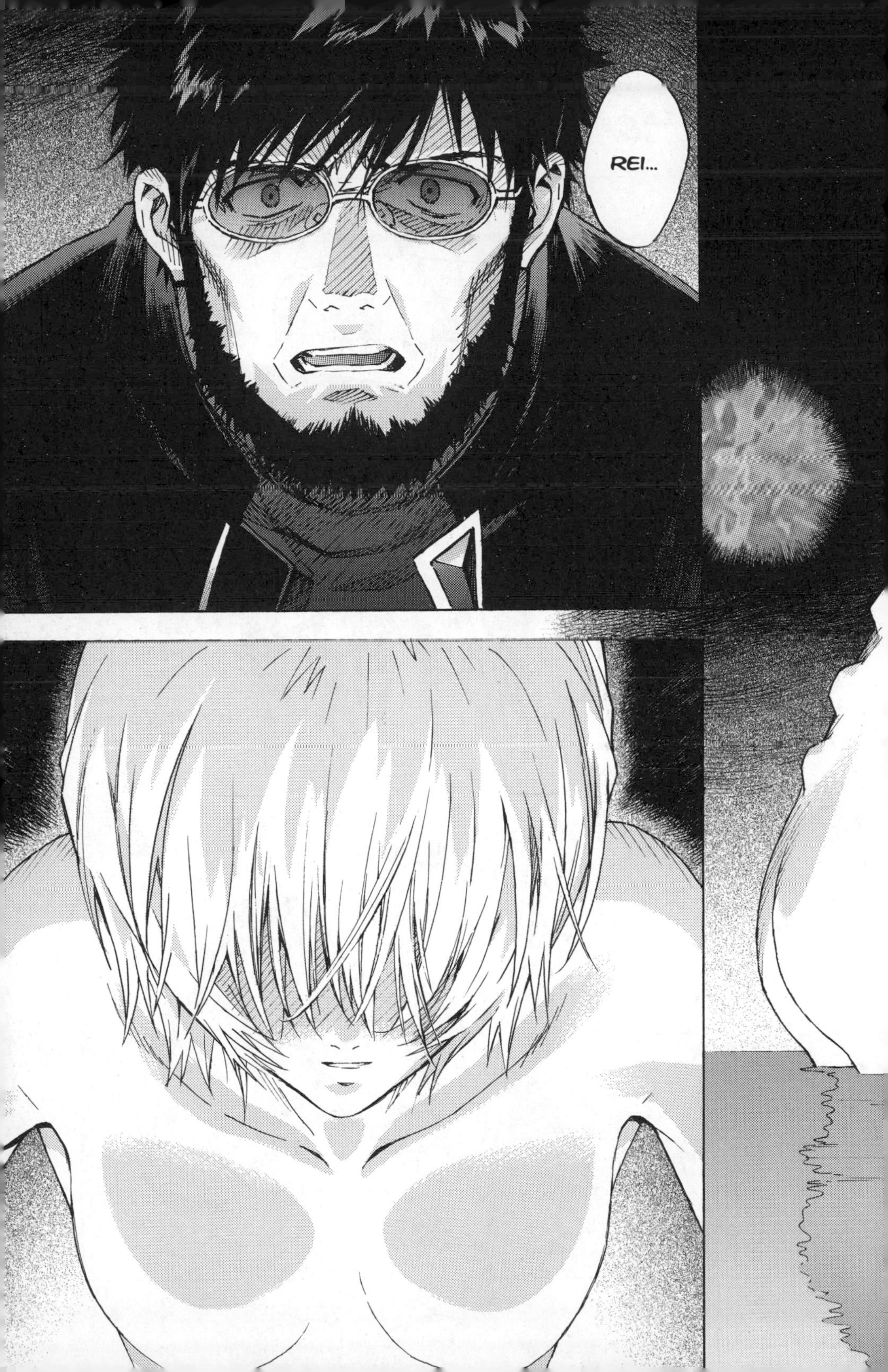
REI...

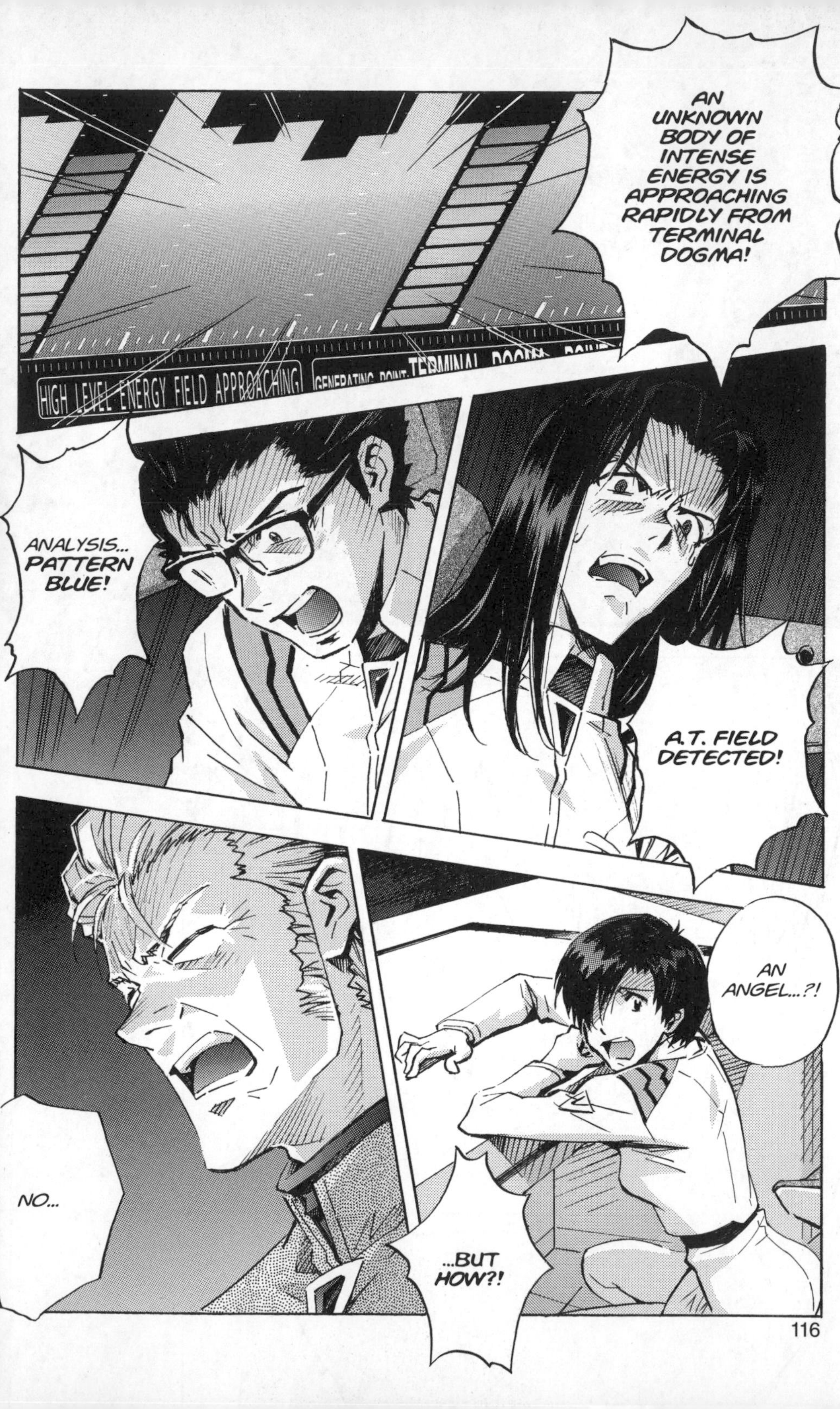
HIGH LEVEL ENERGY FIELD APPROACHING
AN UNKNOWN BODY OF INTENSE ENERGY IS APPROACHING RAPIDLY FROM TERMINAL DOGMA!
A.T. FIELD DETECTED!
ANALYSIS... PATTERN BLUE!
AN ANGEL...?!
NO...
...BUT HOW?!

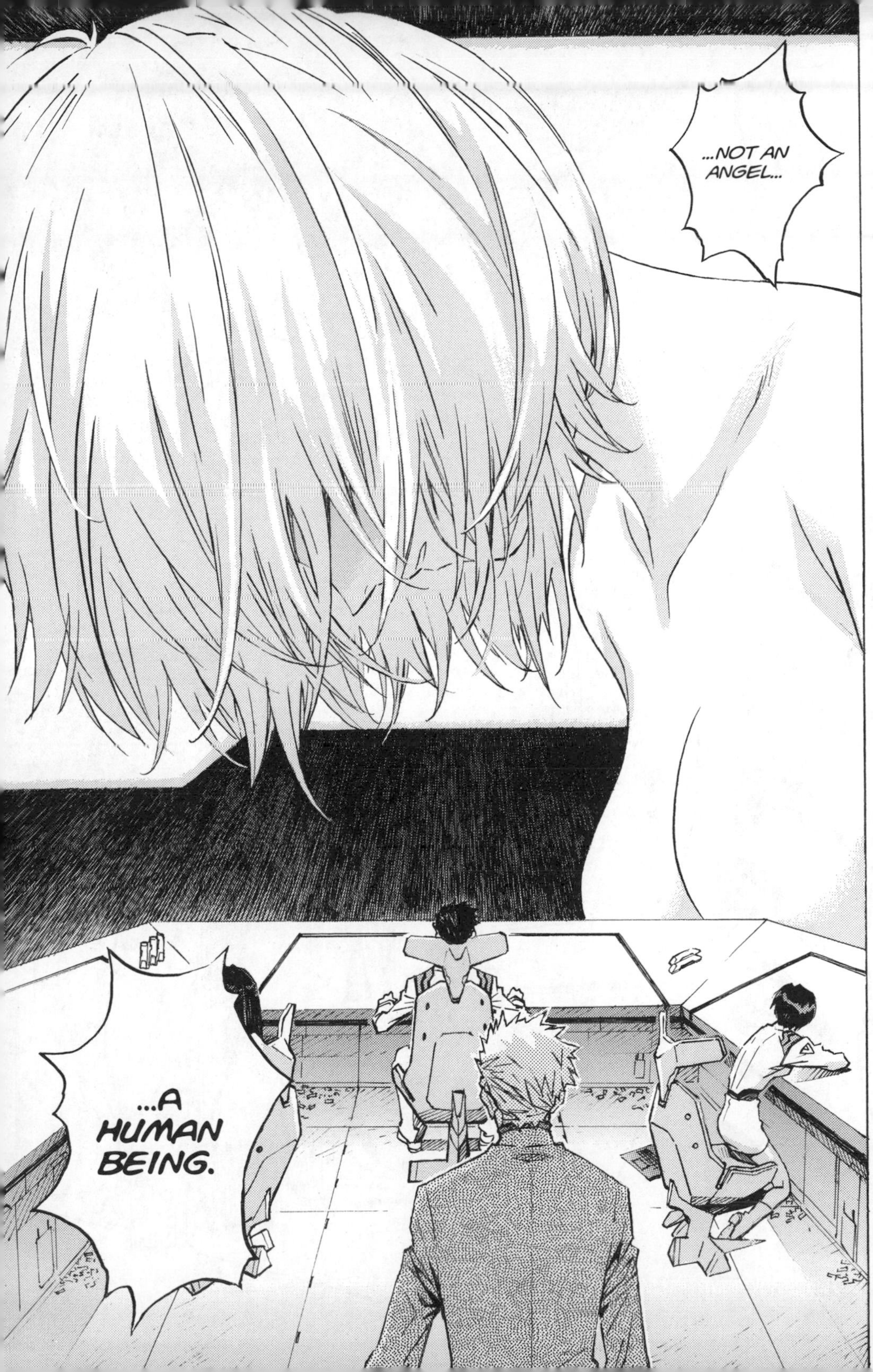
...NOT AN ANGEL...
...A HUMAN BEING.

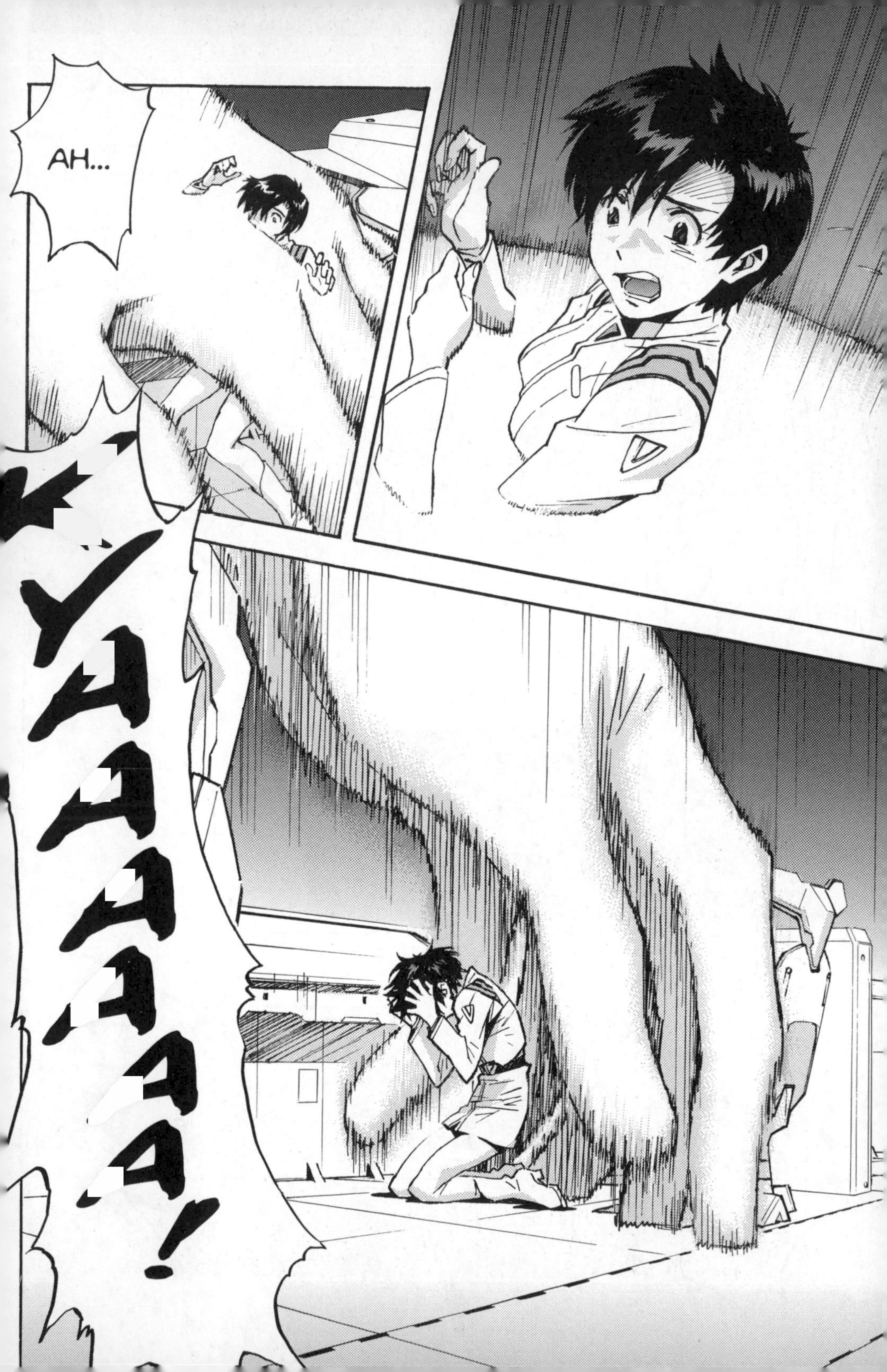
AH...

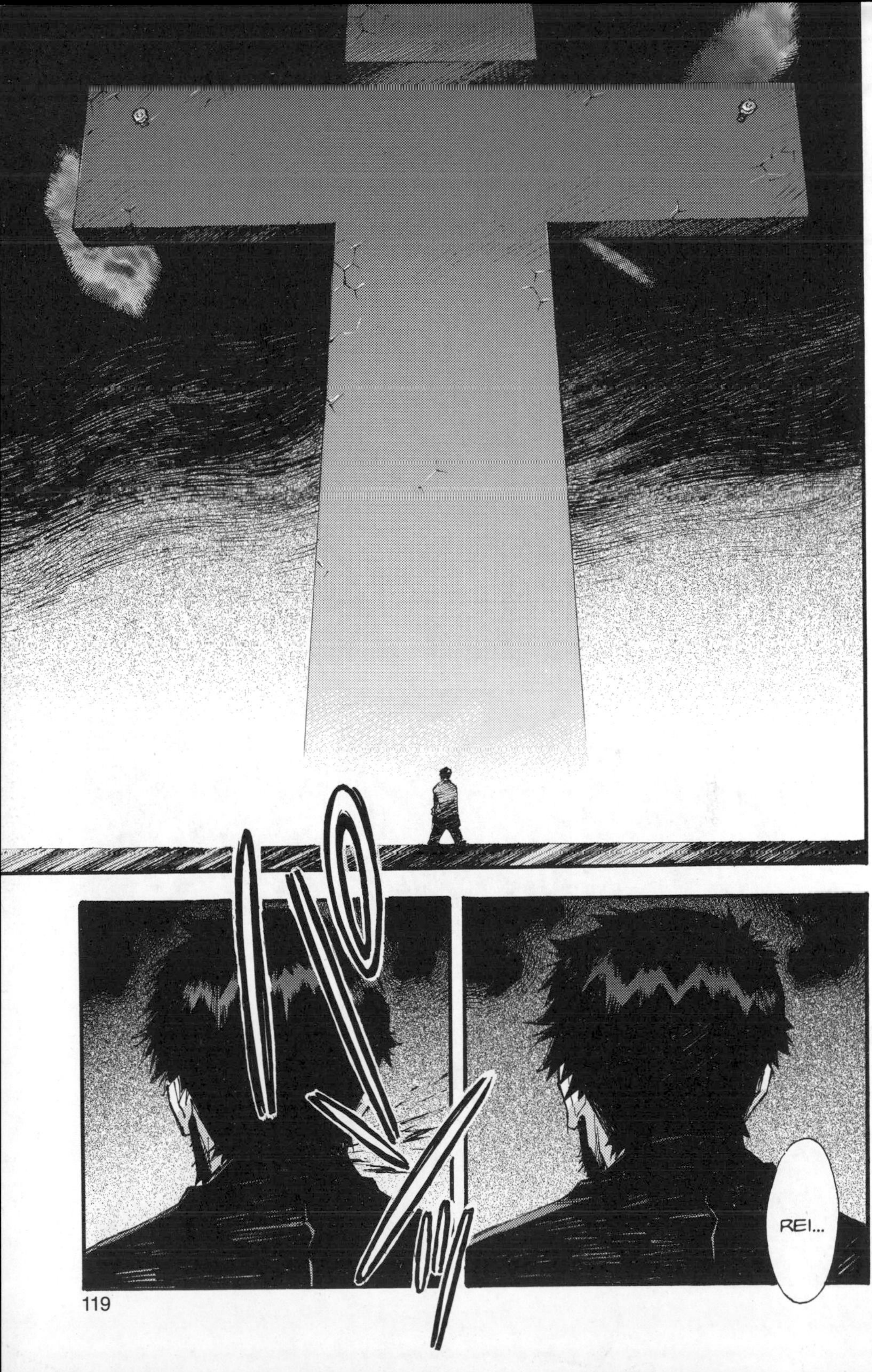
REI...

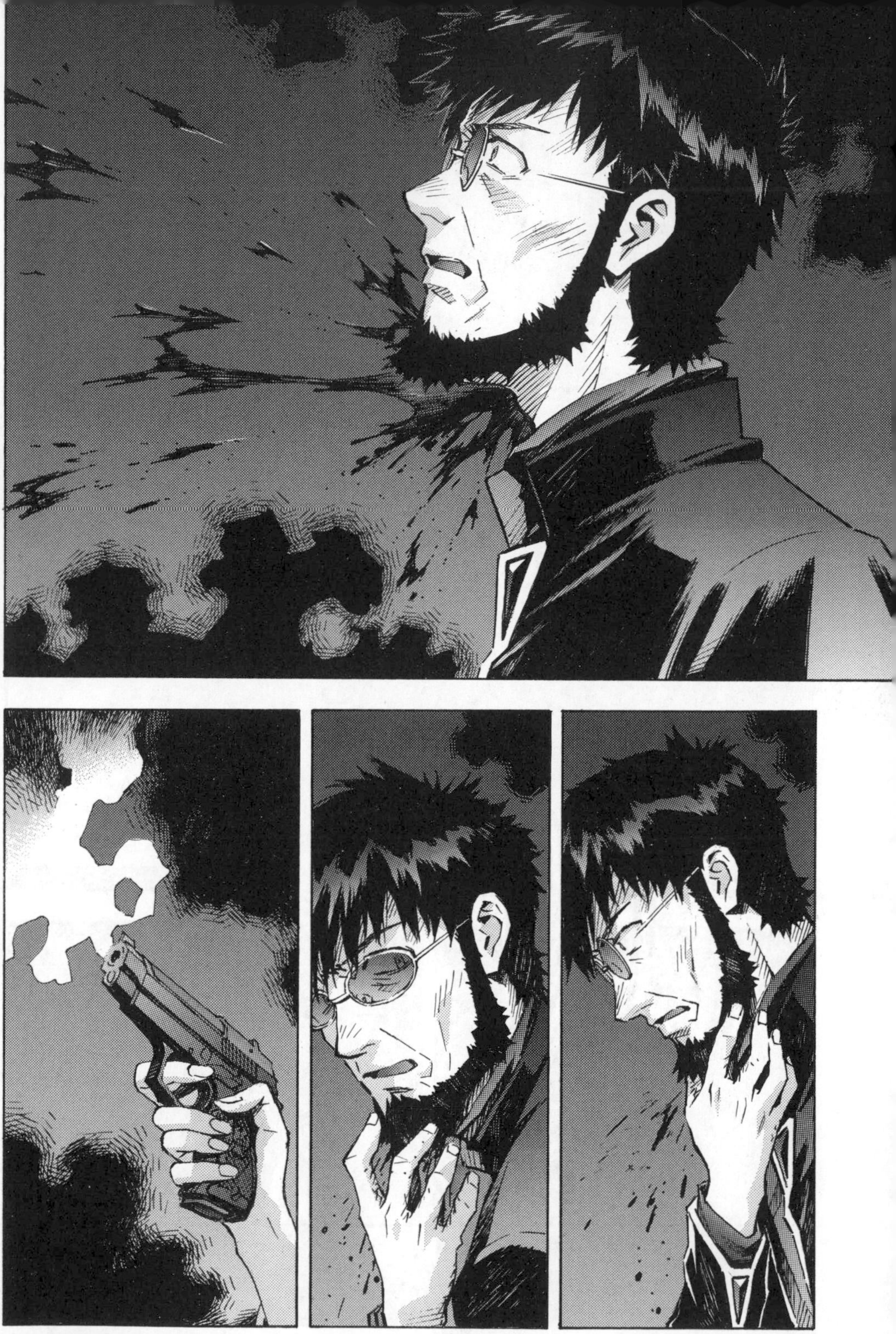

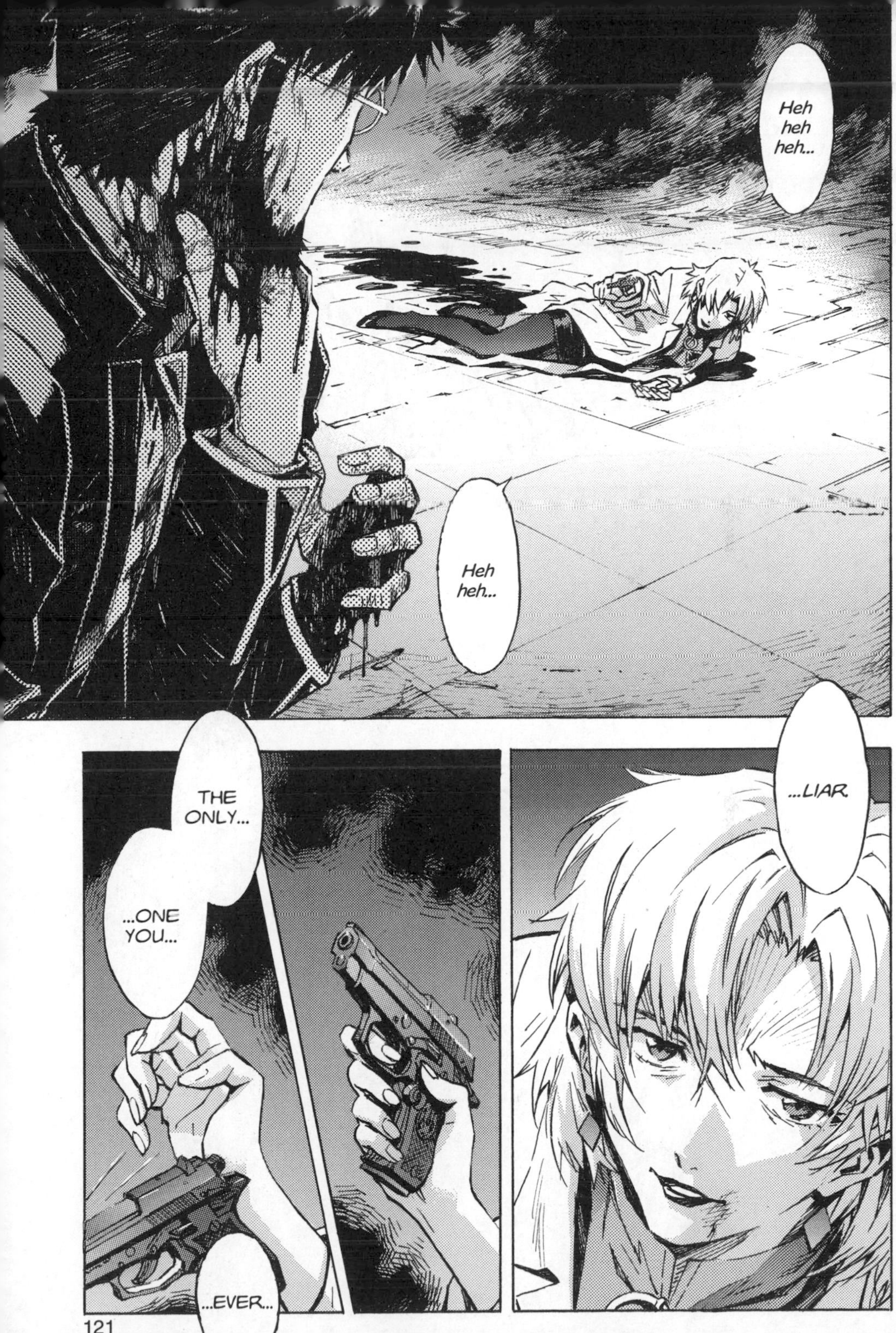
Heh heh heh...
Heh heh...
...LIAR.
THE ONLY...
...ONE YOU...
...EVER...

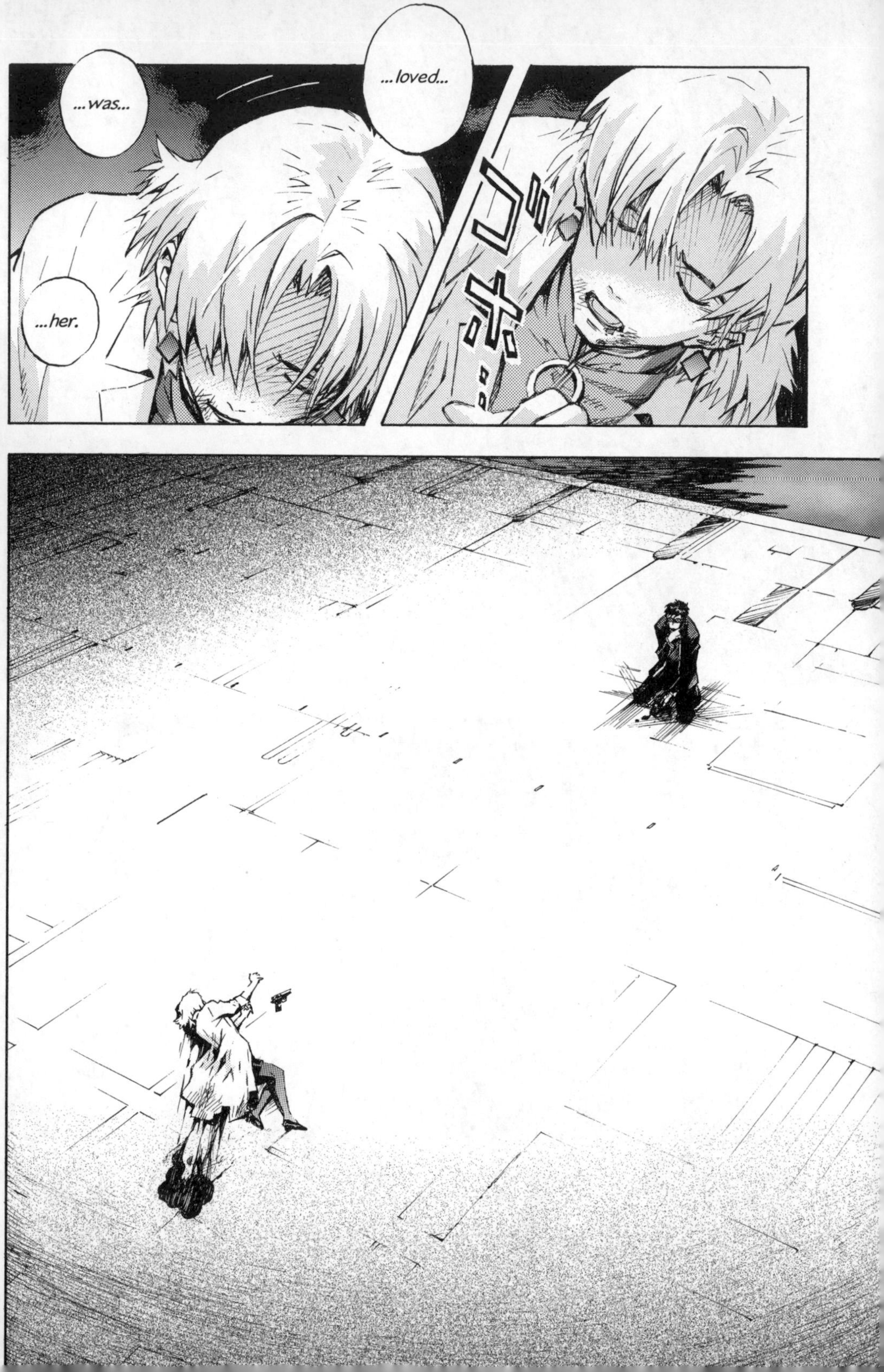
...was...
...loved...
...her.

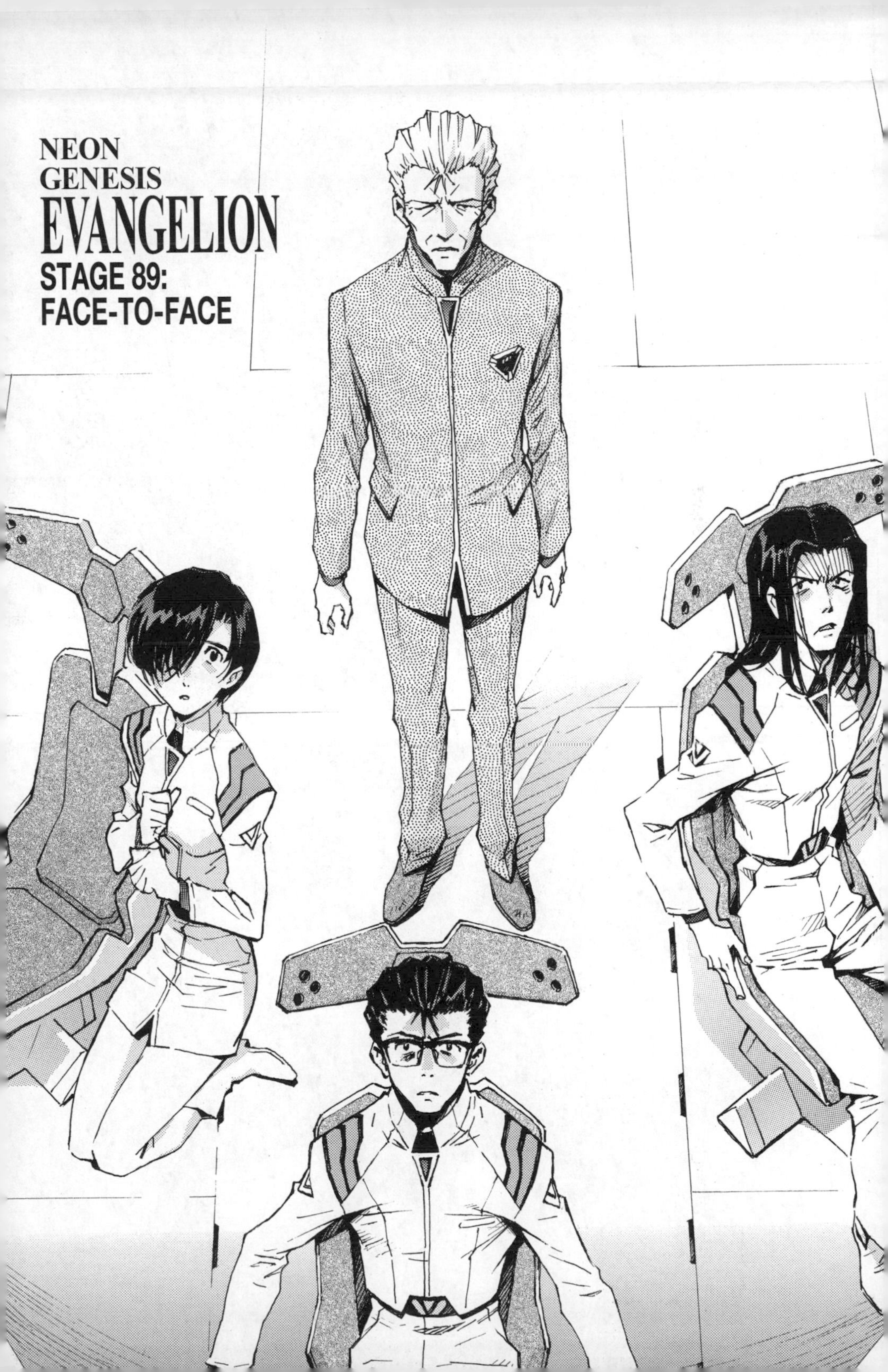
NEON
GENESIS
EVANGELION
STAGE 89:
FACE-TO-FACE

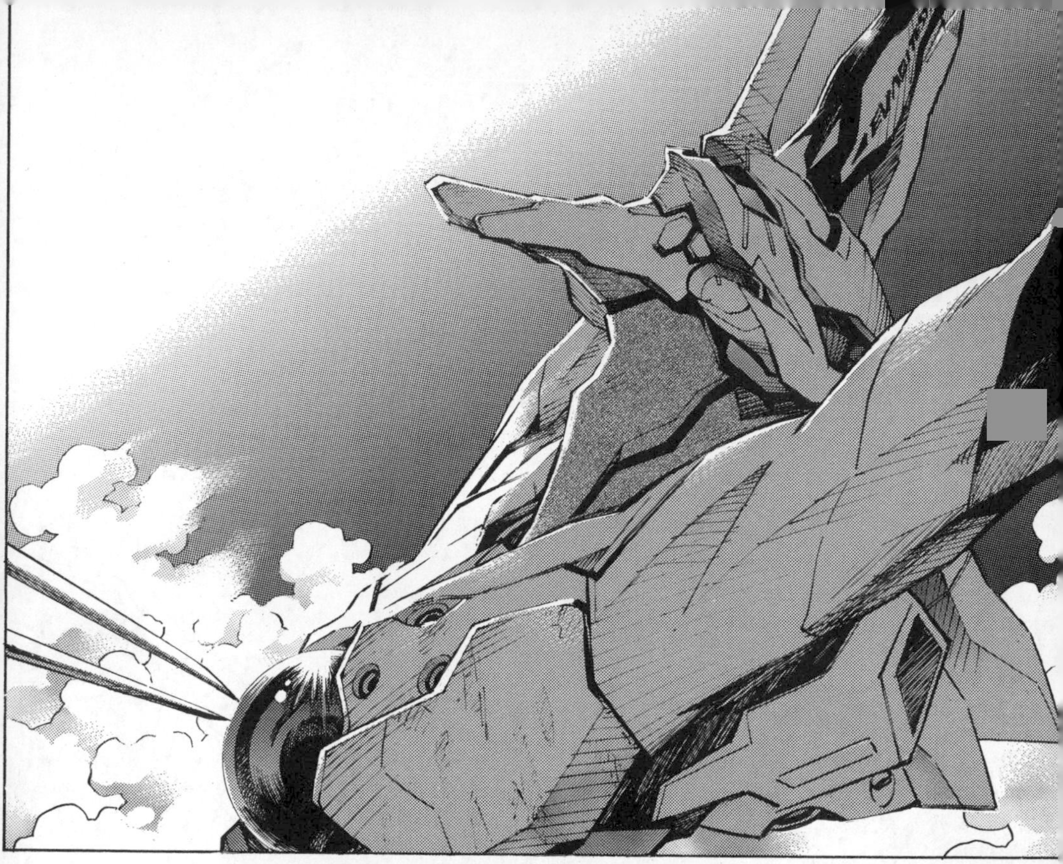
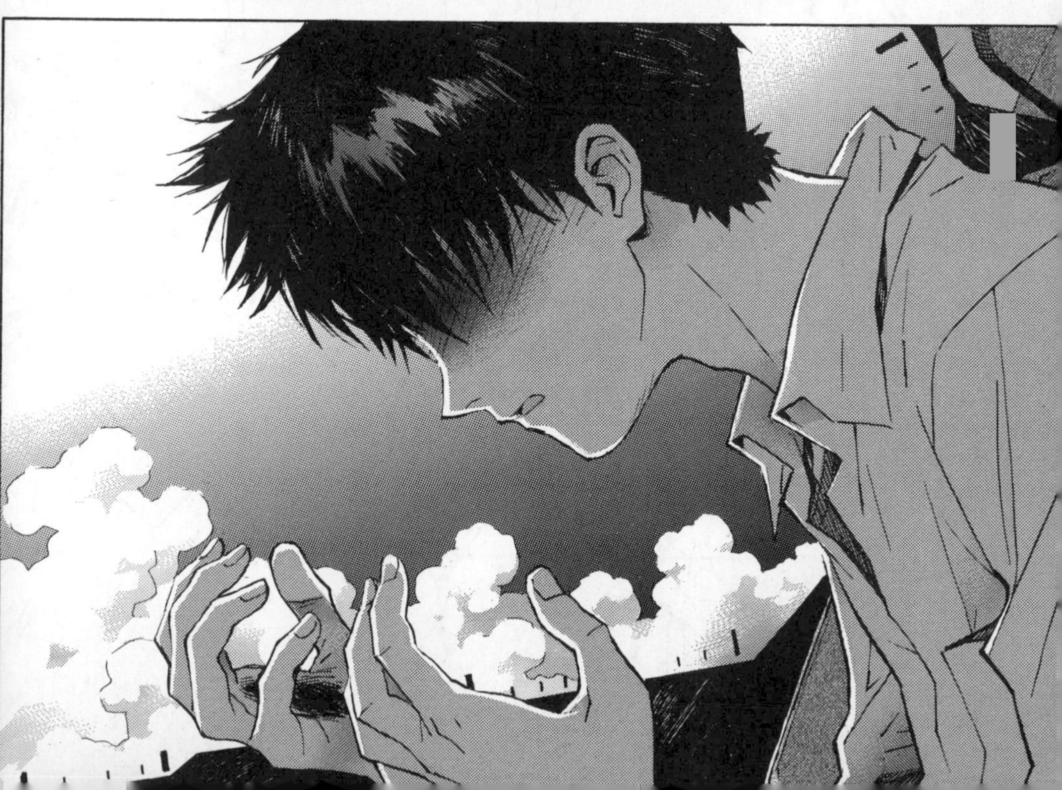

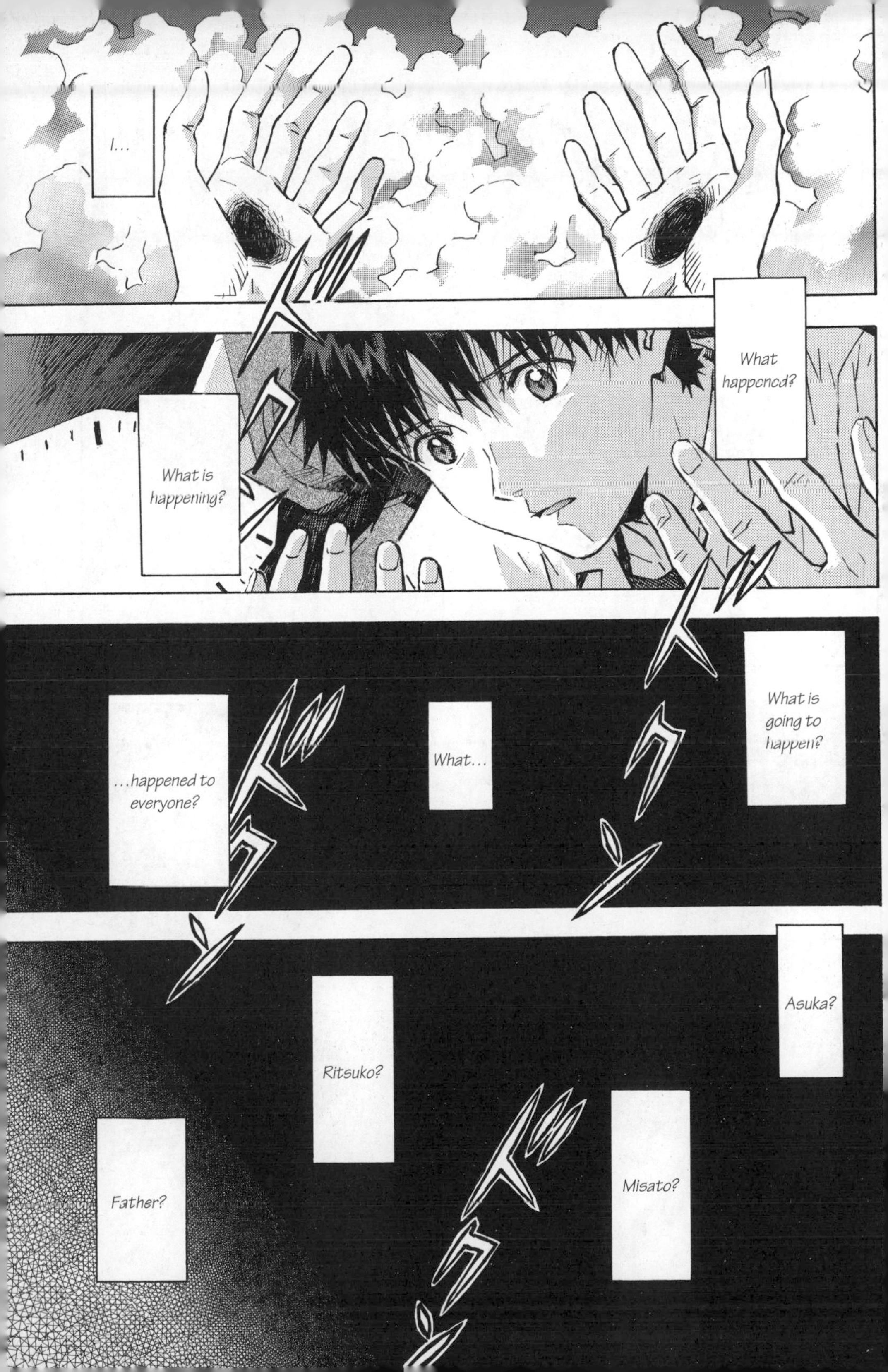
I...
What happened?
What is happening?
What is going to happen?
What...
...happened to everyone?
Asuka?
Misato?
Ritsuko?
Father?

Ayanami
...?

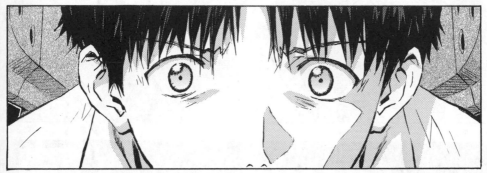

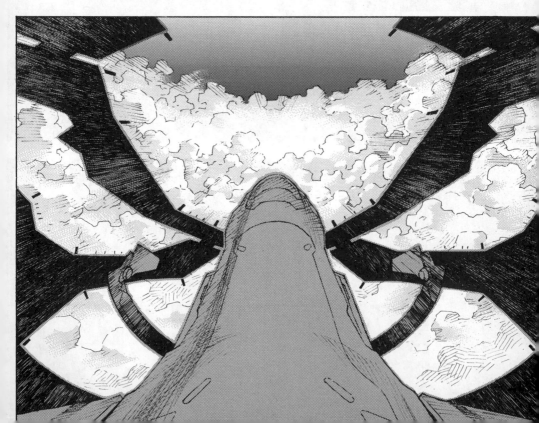

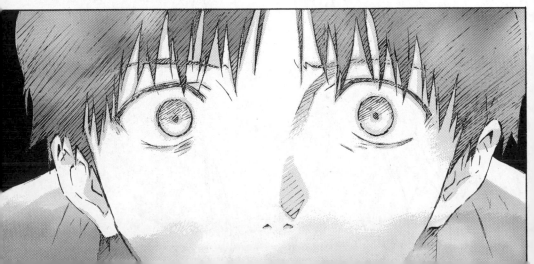

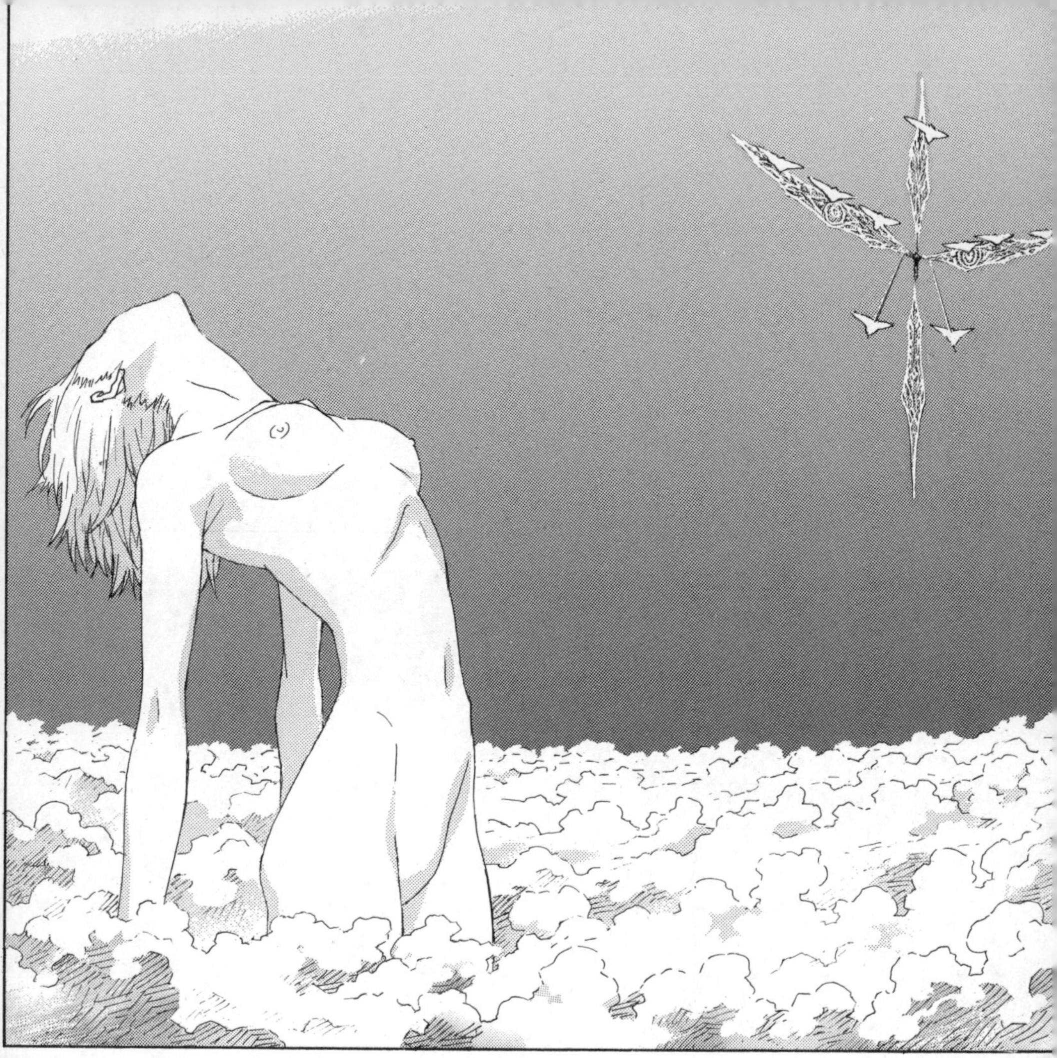
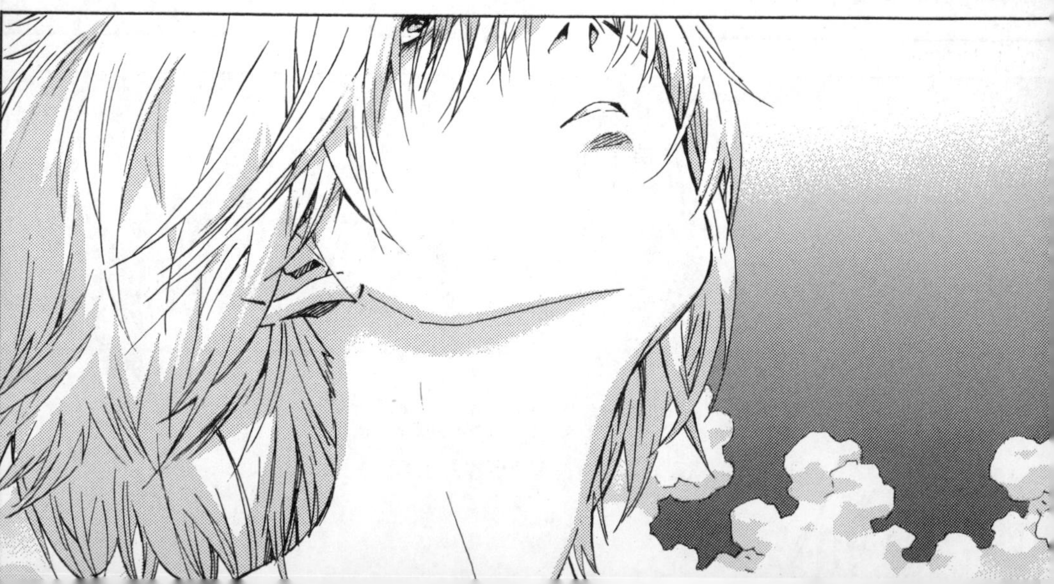

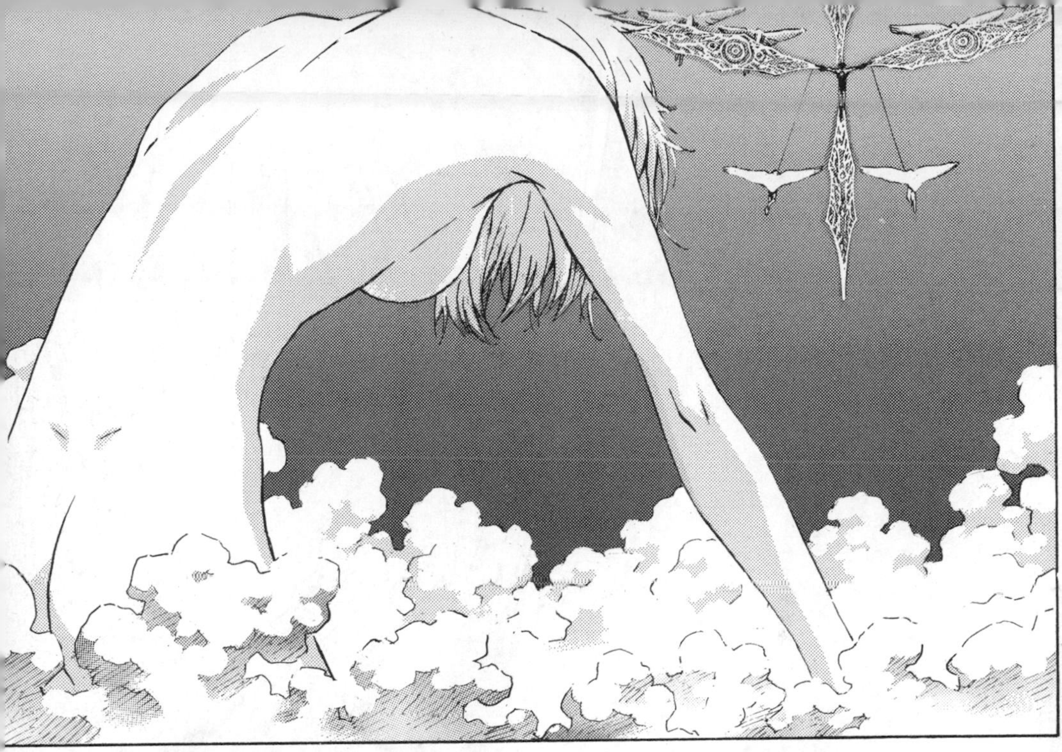

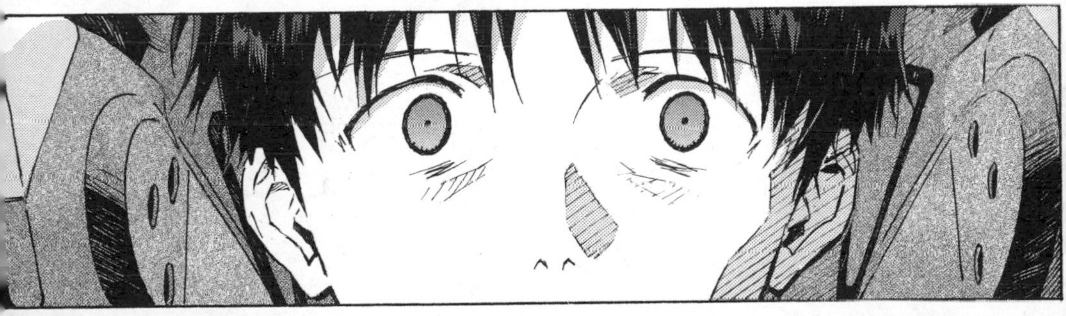

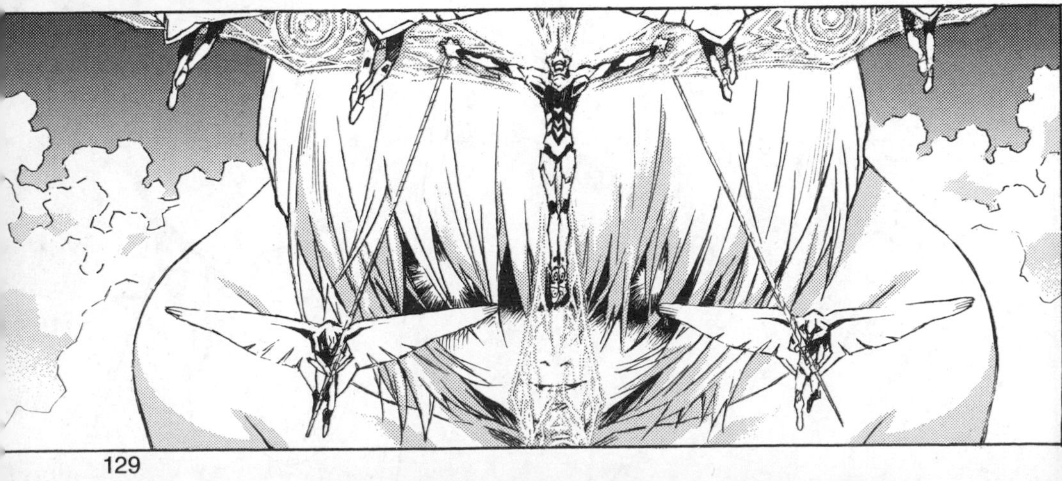

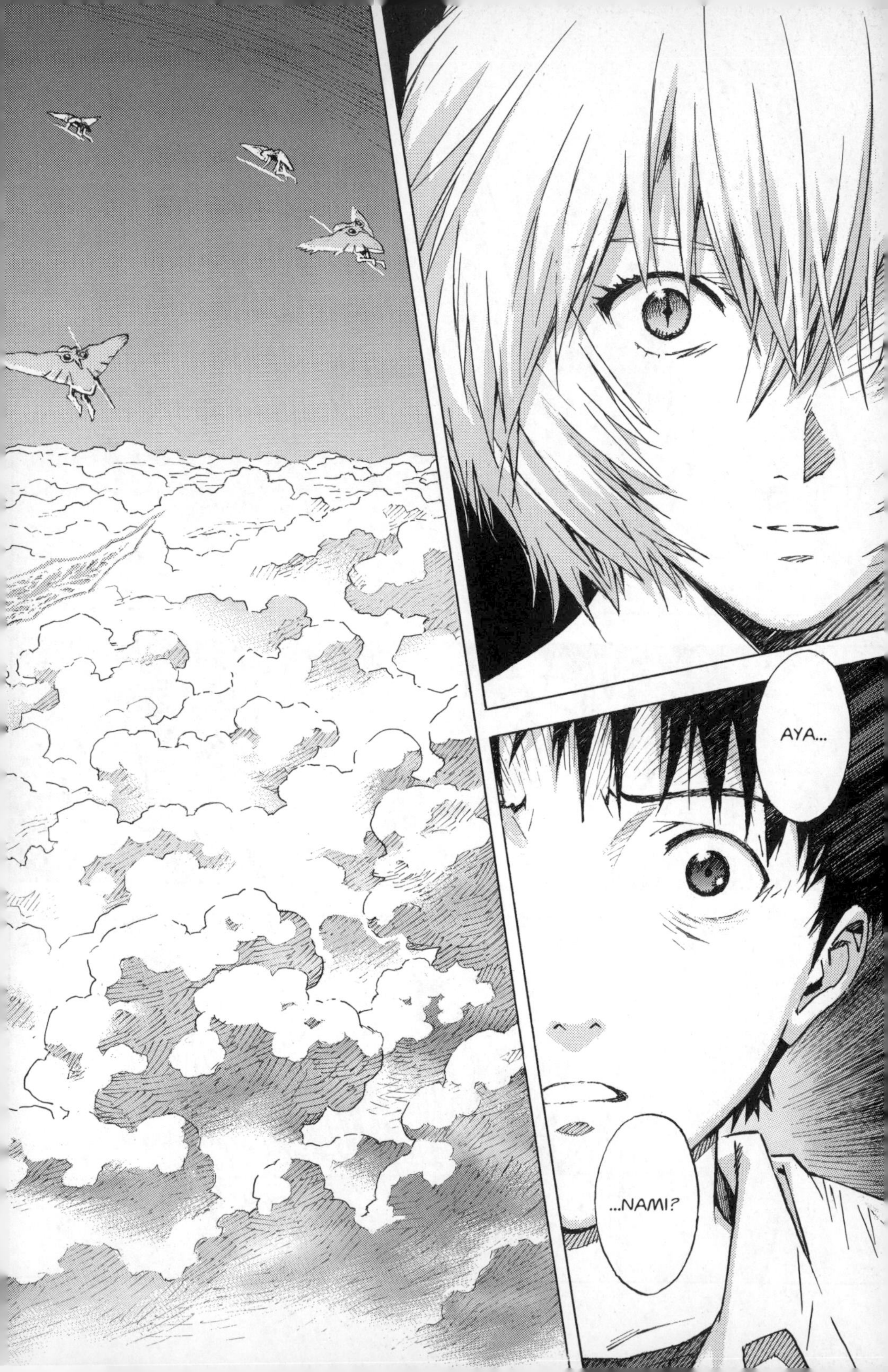
AYA...
...NAMI?

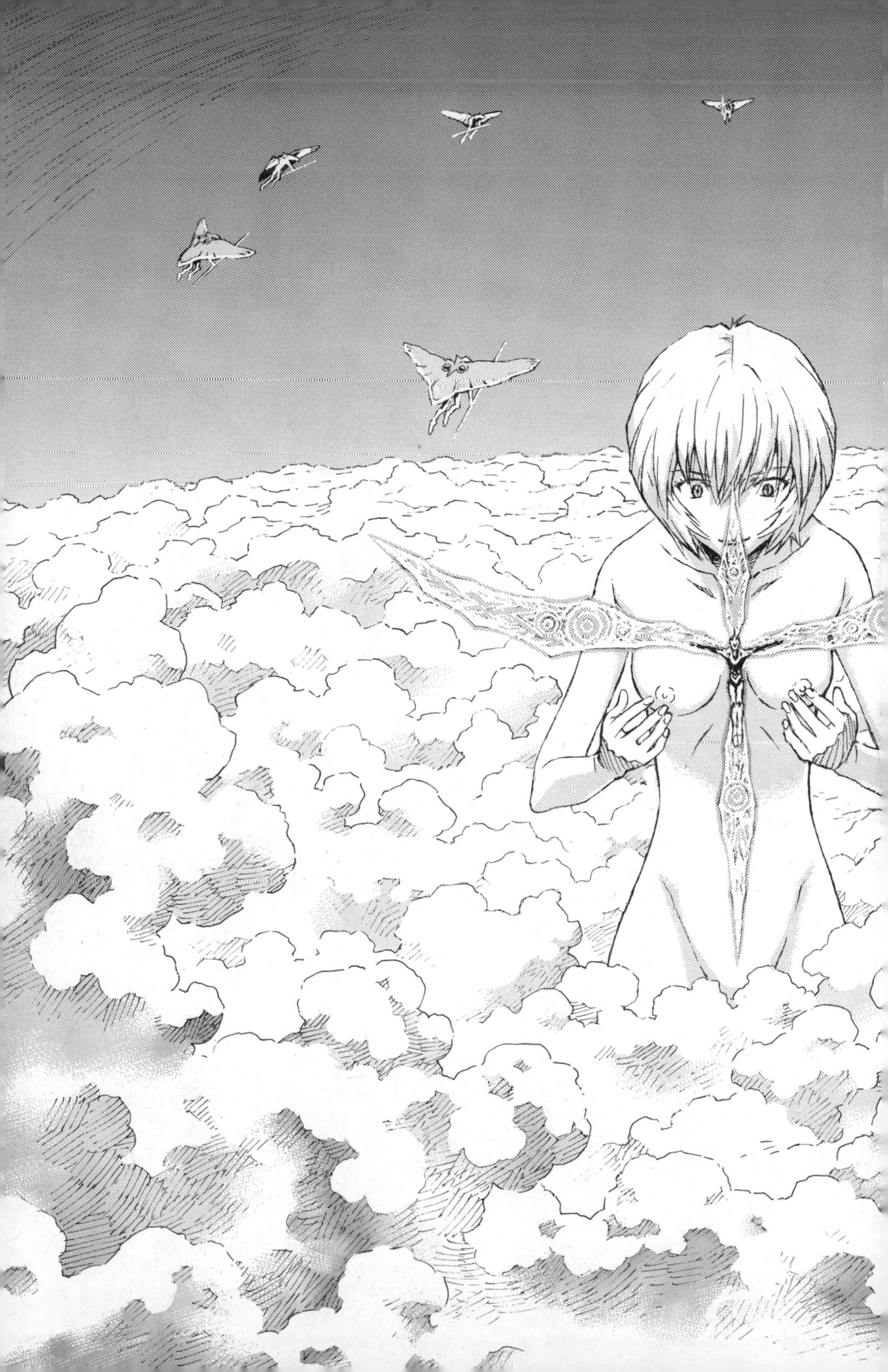

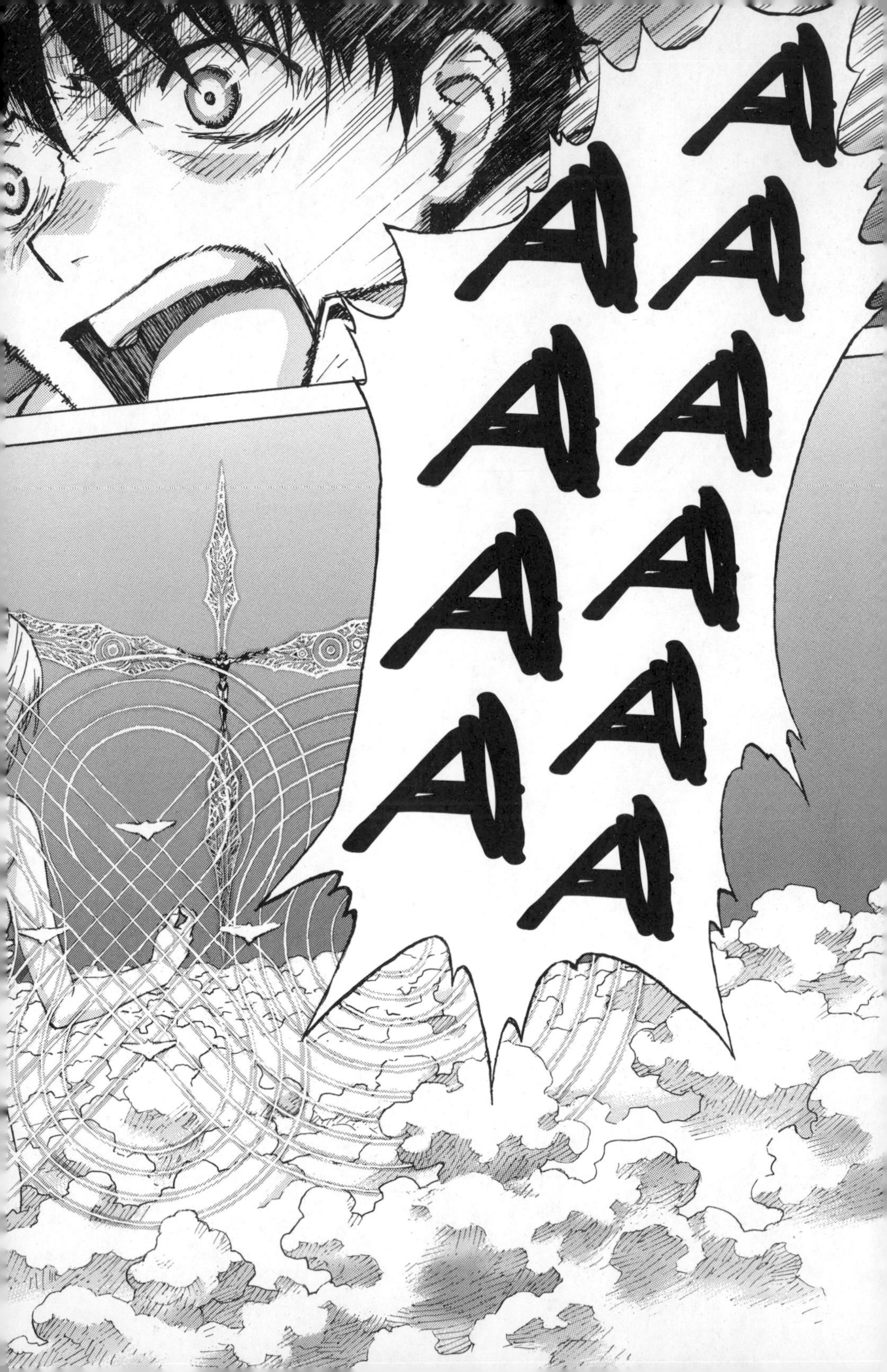
AAAAAAAAAA

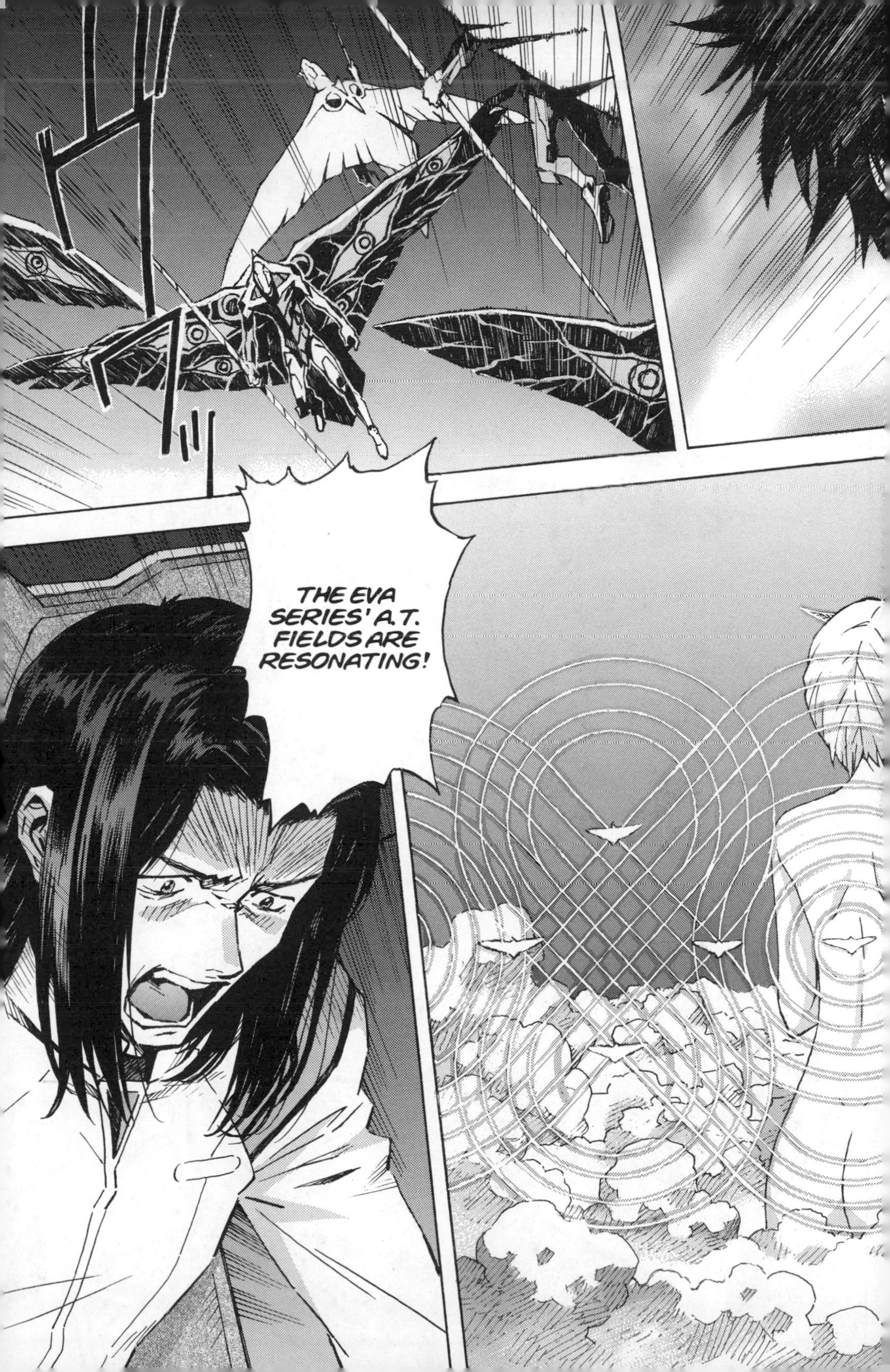
THE EVA SERIES' A.T. FIELDS ARE RESONATING!

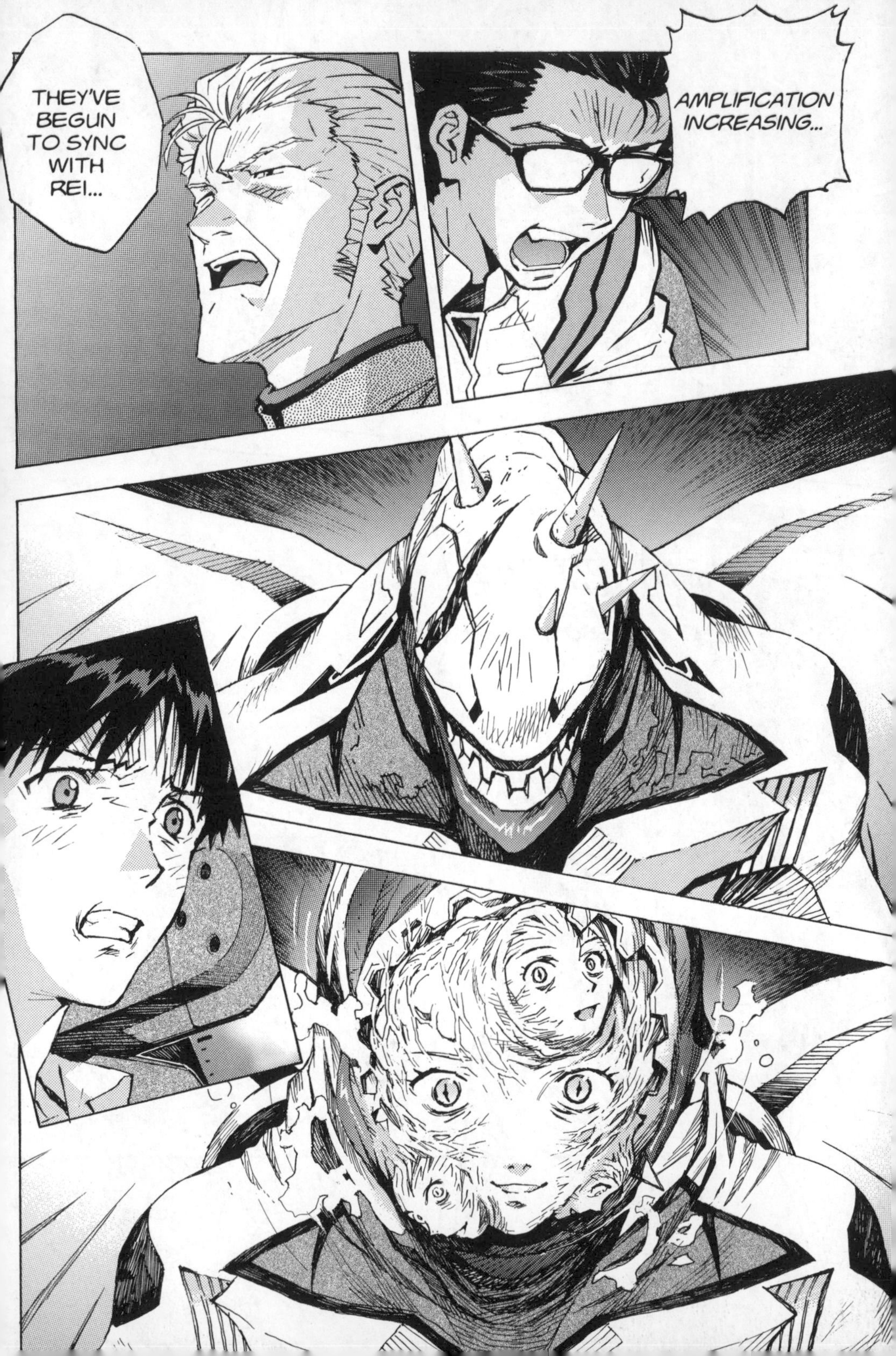
AMPLIFICATION INCREASING...
THEY'VE BEGUN TO SYNC WITH REI...

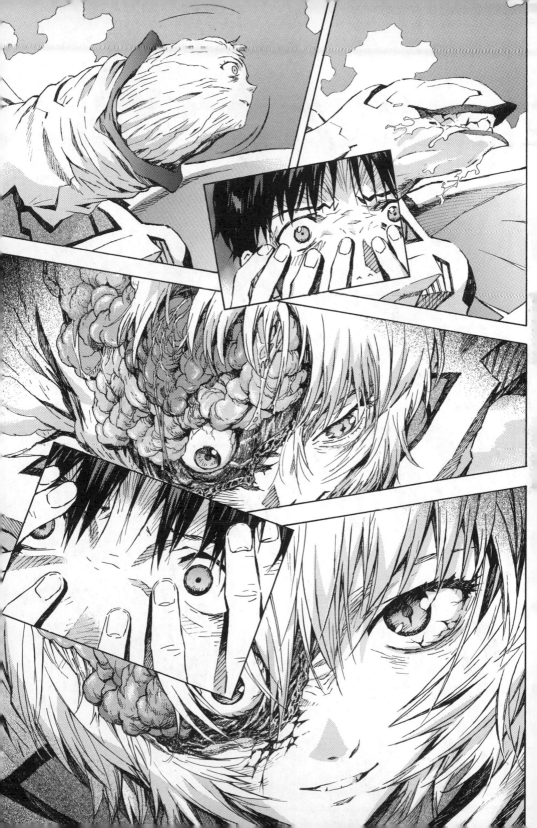

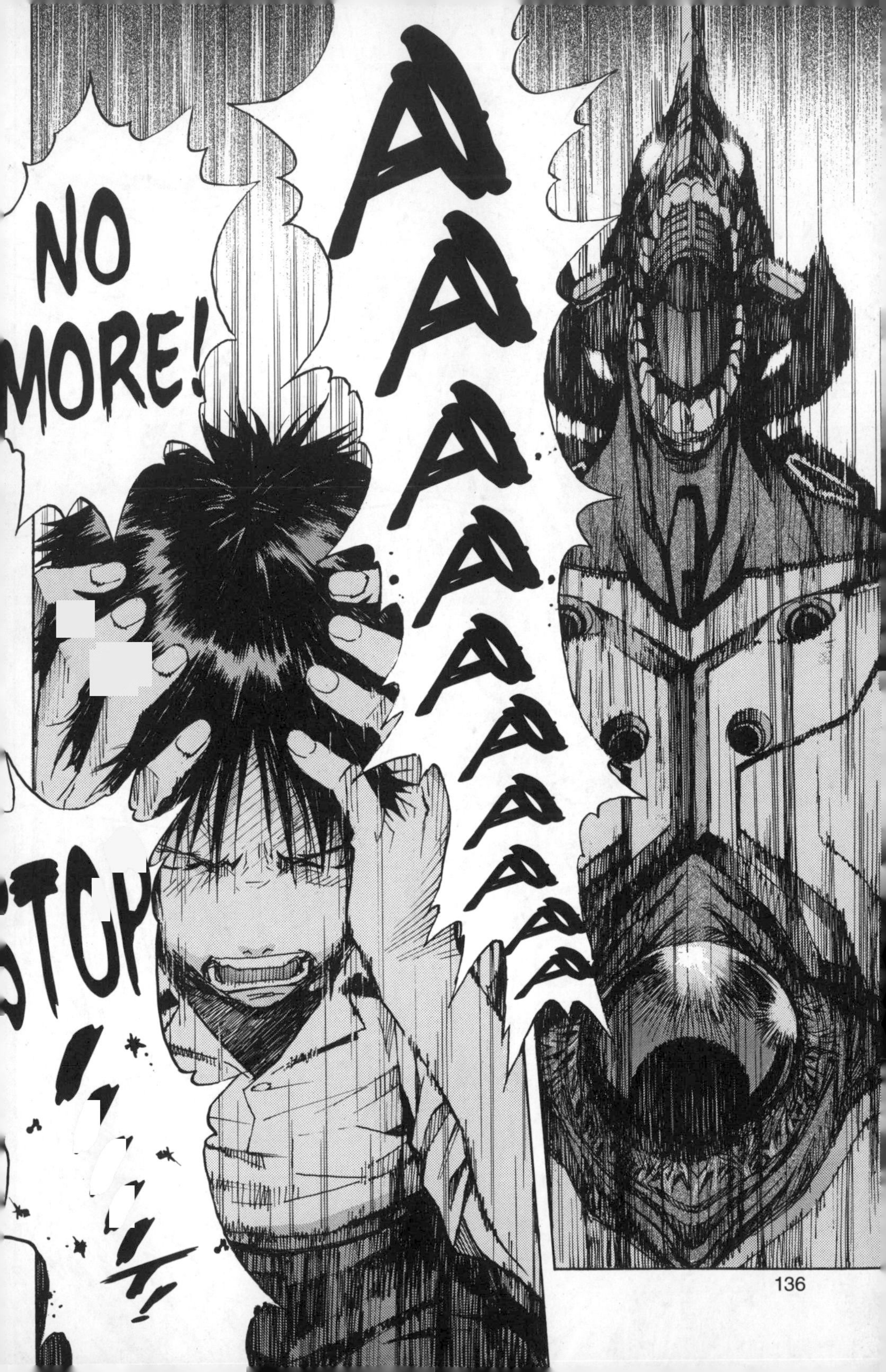
AAAAAAAAAAAA
NO MORE!

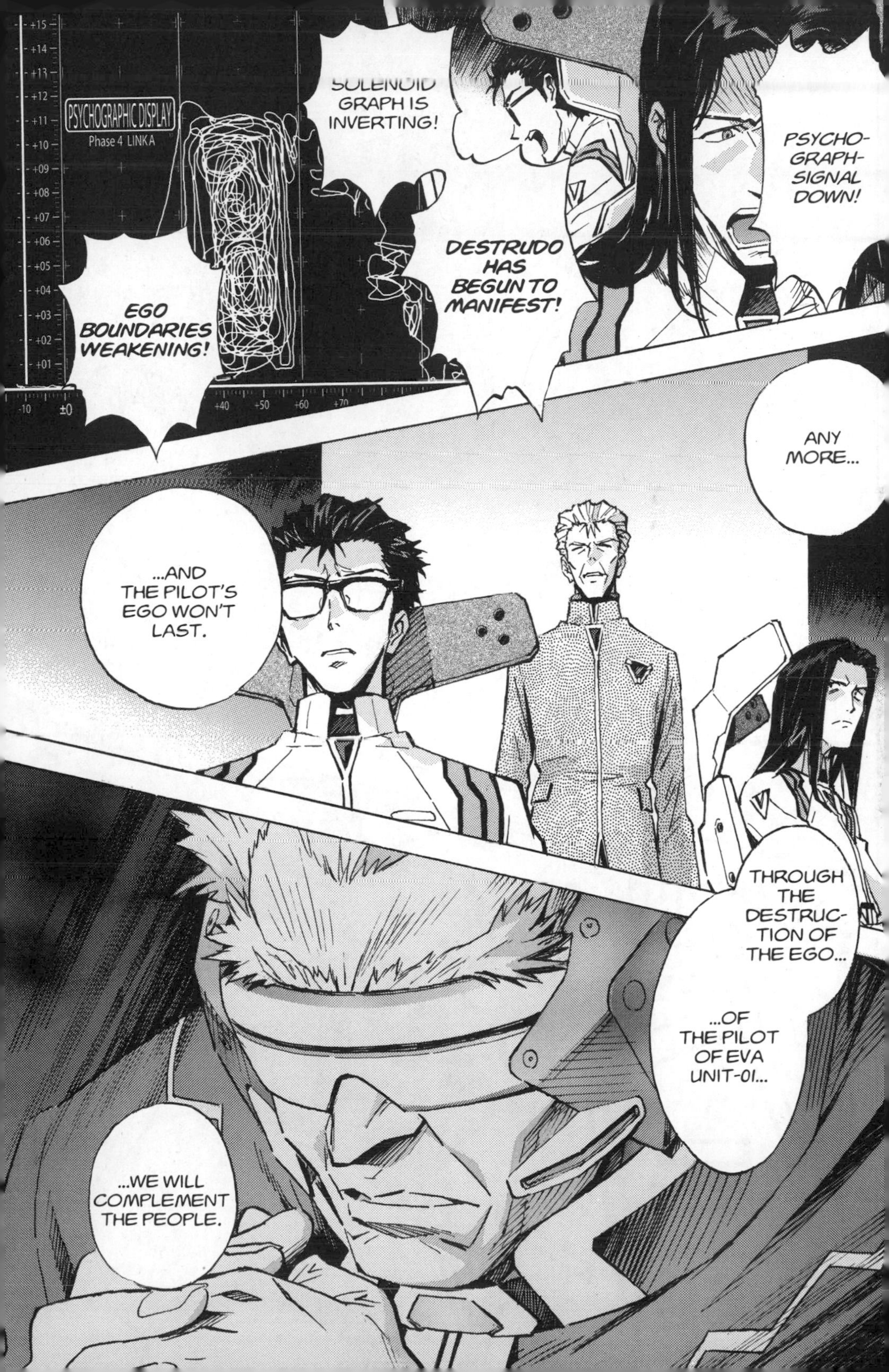
PSYCHO-GRAPH-SIGNAL DOWN!
SOLENOID GRAPH IS INVERTING!
DESTRUDO HAS BEGUN TO MANIFEST!
PSYCHOGRAPHIC DISPLAY
Phase 4 LINKA
EGO BOUNDARIES WEAKENING!
ANY MORE...
...AND THE PILOT'S EGO WON'T LAST.
THROUGH THE DESTRUCTION OF THE EGO...
...OF THE PILOT OF EVA UNIT-01...
...WE WILL COMPLEMENT THE PEOPLE.

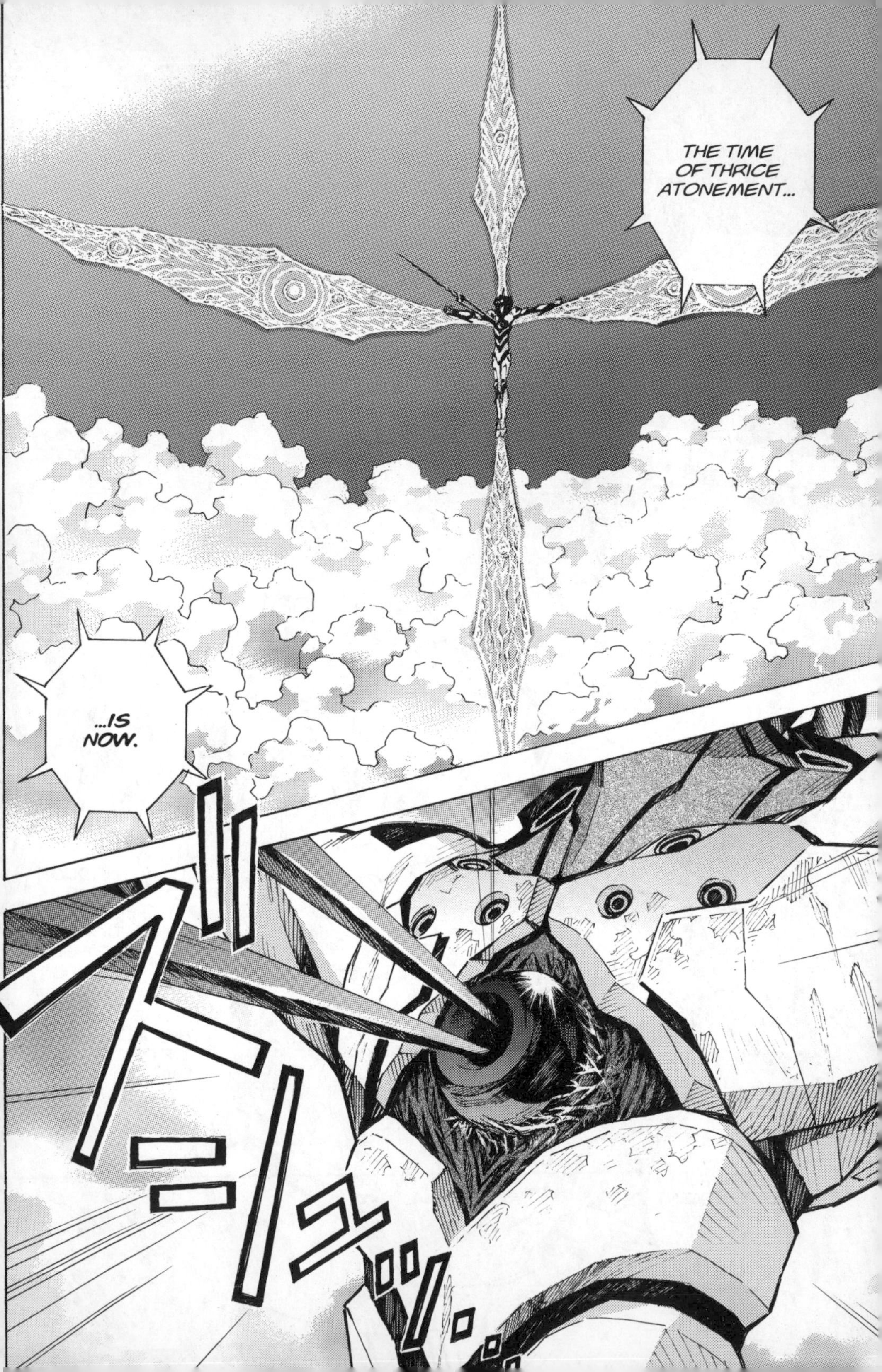
THE TIME OF THRICE ATONEMENT...
...IS NOW.

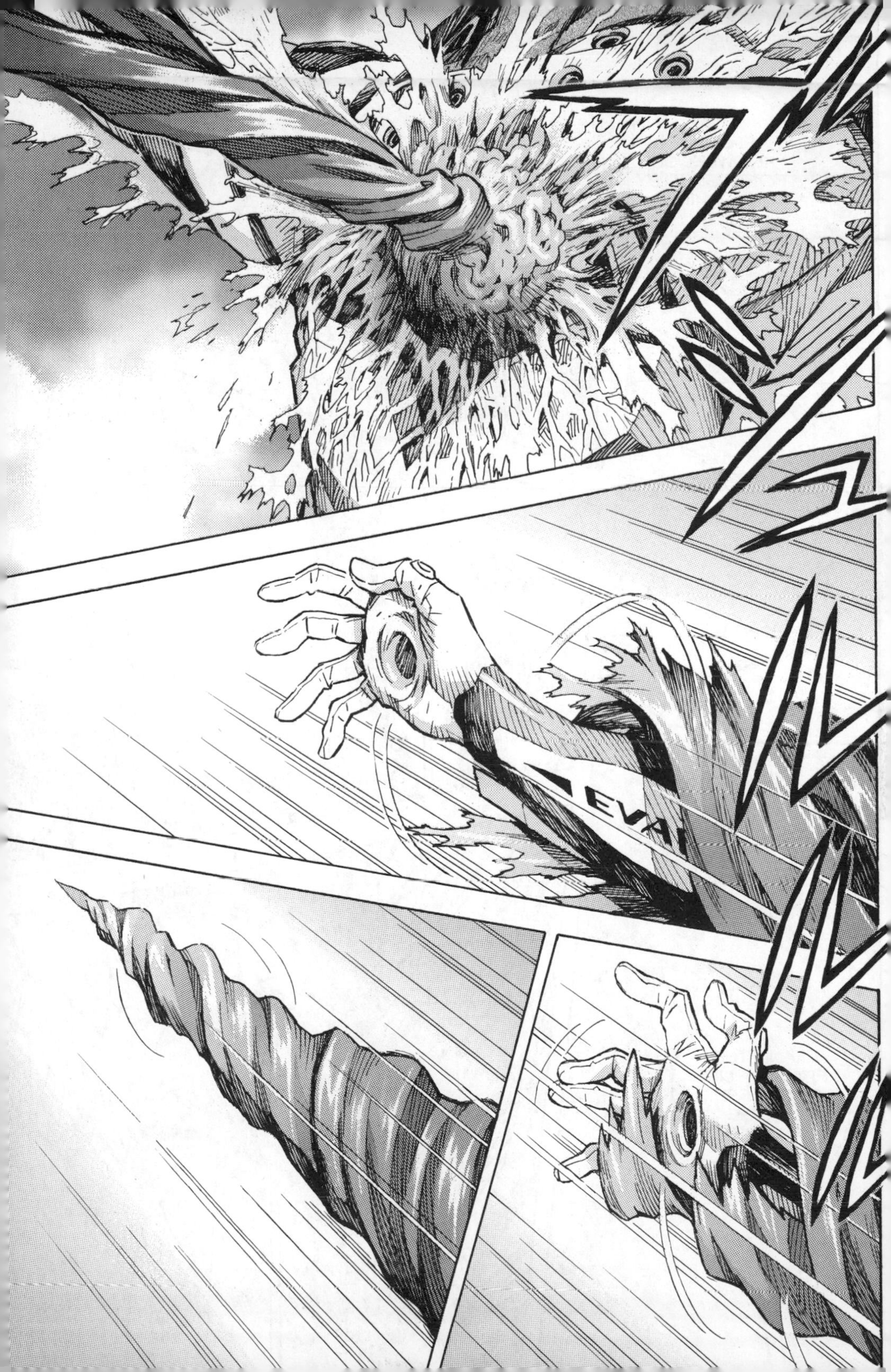
EVA

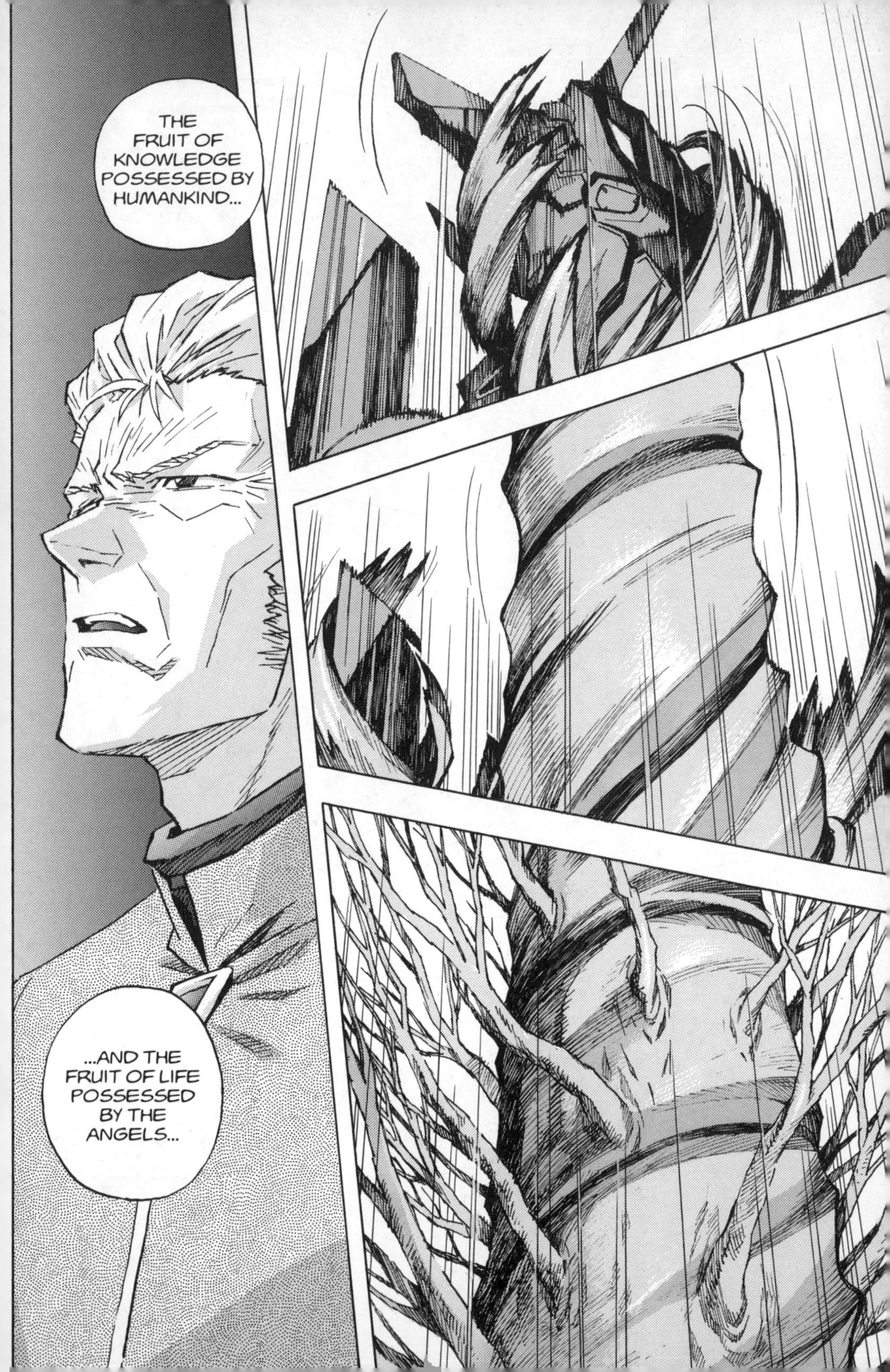
THE FRUIT OF KNOWLEDGE POSSESSED BY HUMANKIND...
...AND THE FRUIT OF LIFE POSSESSED BY THE ANGELS...

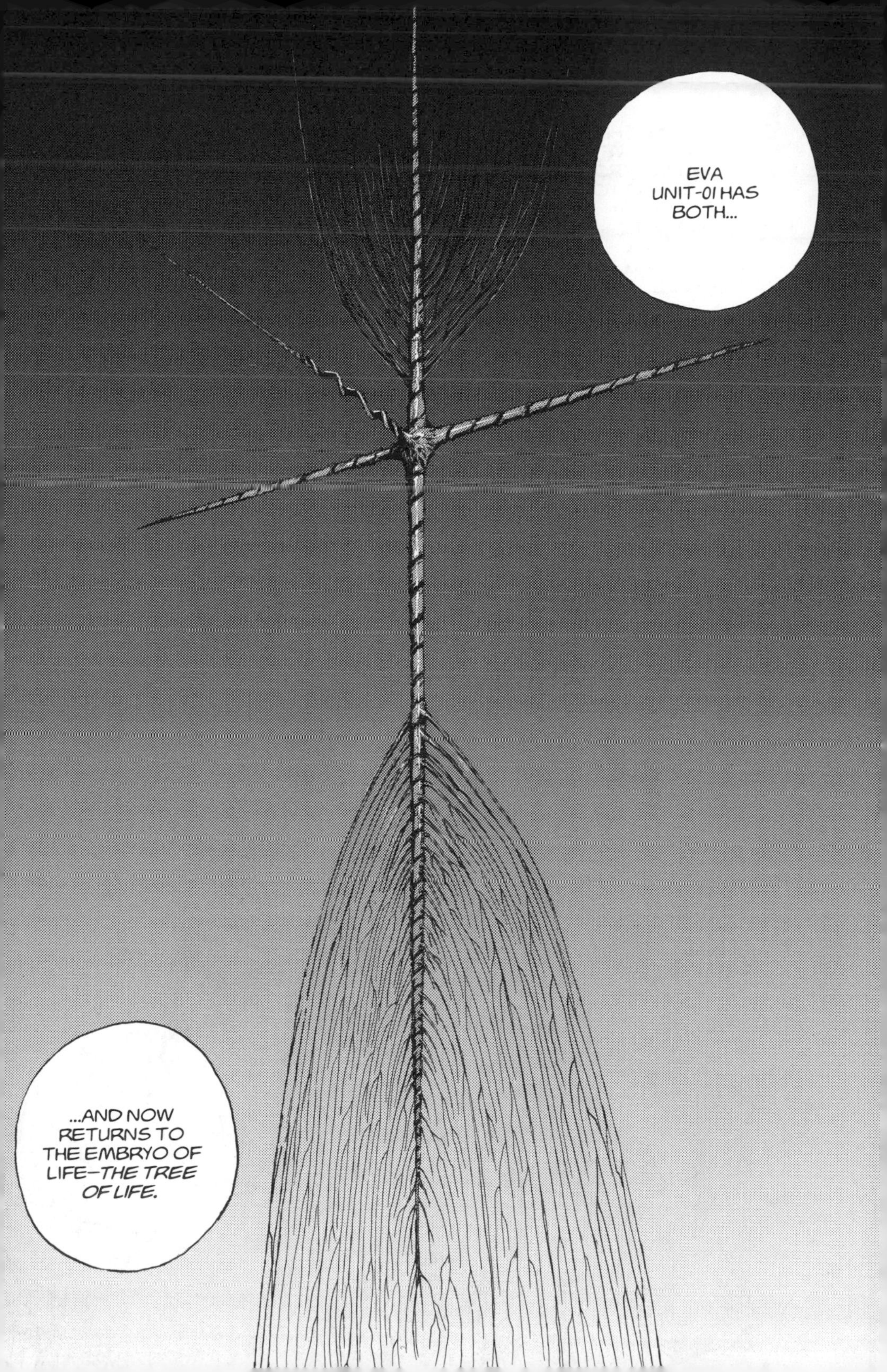
EVA UNIT-01 HAS BOTH...
...AND NOW RETURNS TO THE EMBRYO OF LIFE—THE TREE OF LIFE.

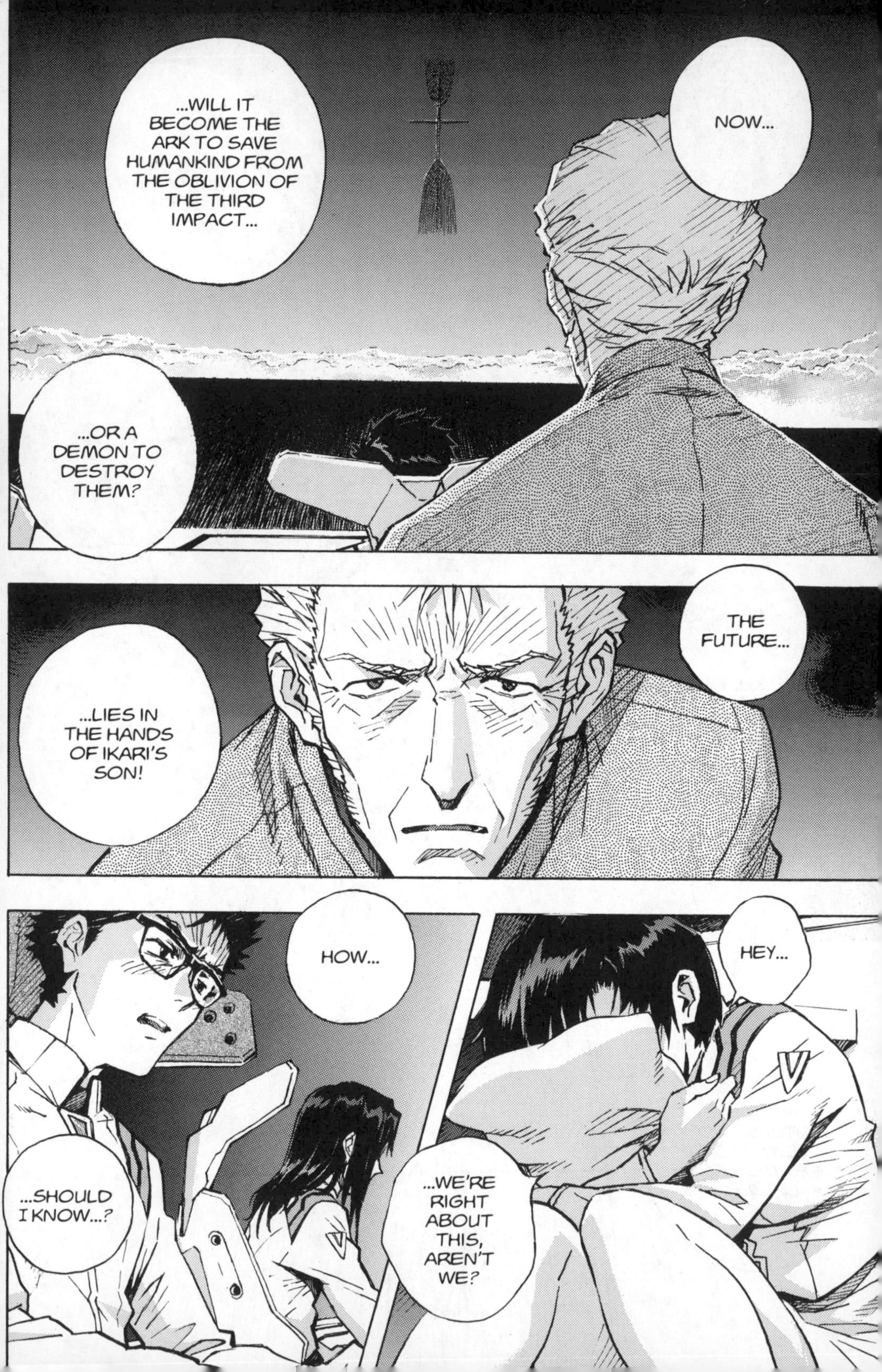
NOW...
...WILL IT BECOME THE ARK TO SAVE HUMANKIND FROM THE OBLIVION OF THE THIRD IMPACT...
...OR A DEMON TO DESTROY THEM?
THE FUTURE...
...LIES IN THE HANDS OF IKARI'S SON!
HEY...
...WE'RE RIGHT ABOUT THIS, AREN'T WE?
HOW...
...SHOULD I KNOW...?

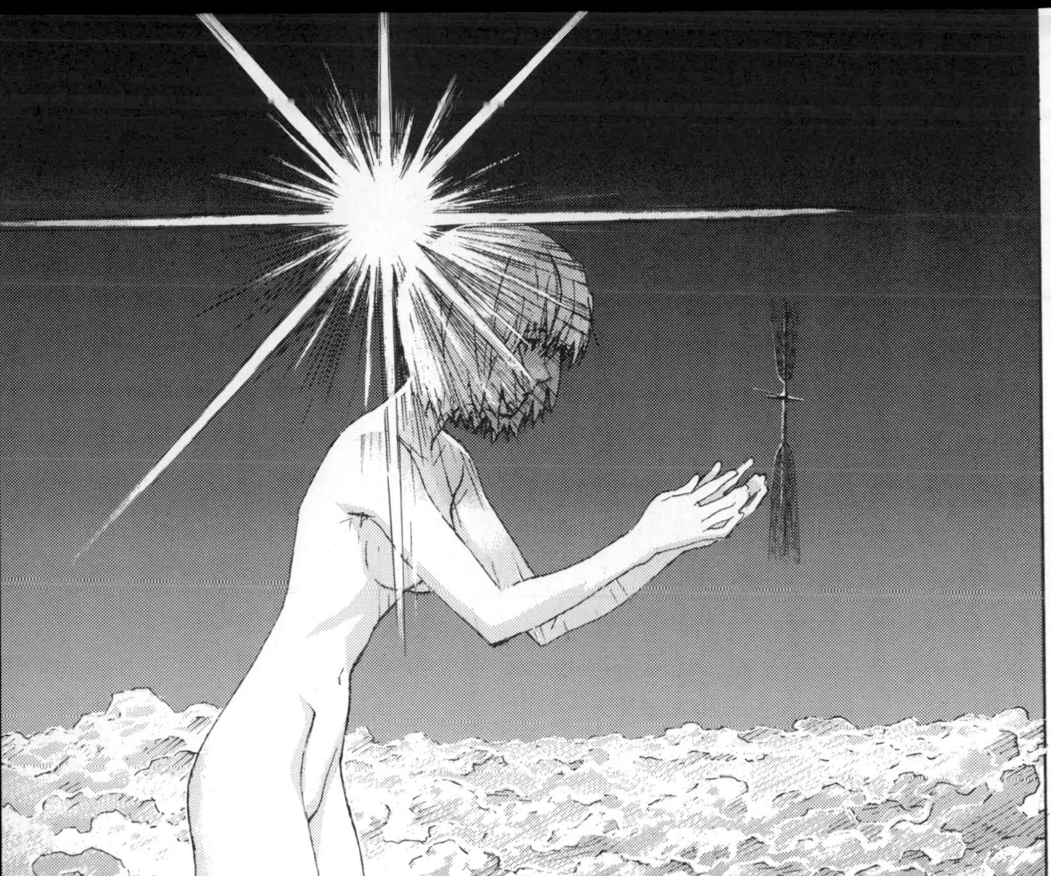
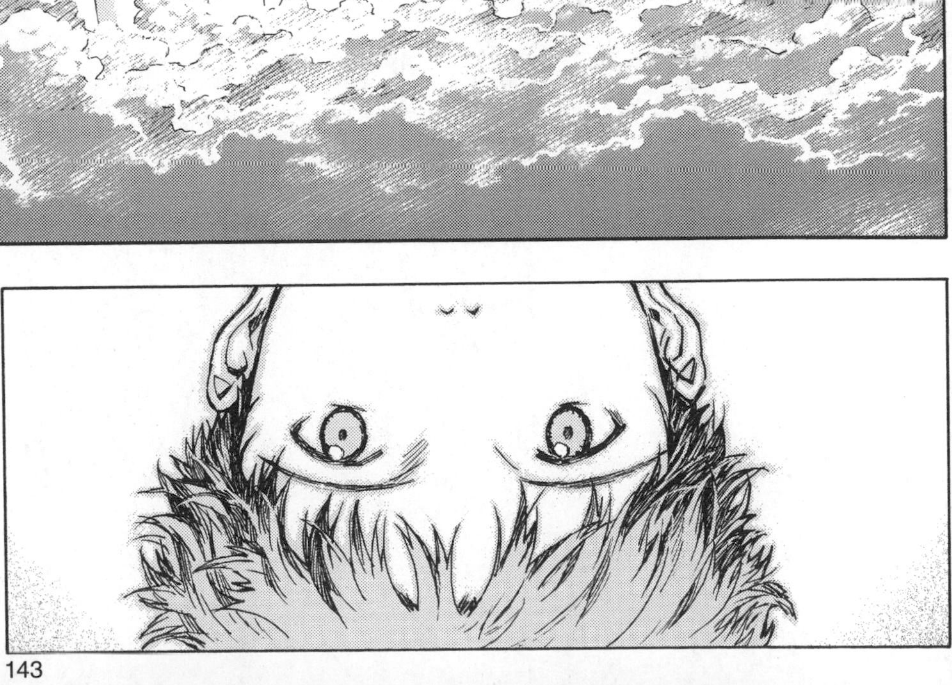

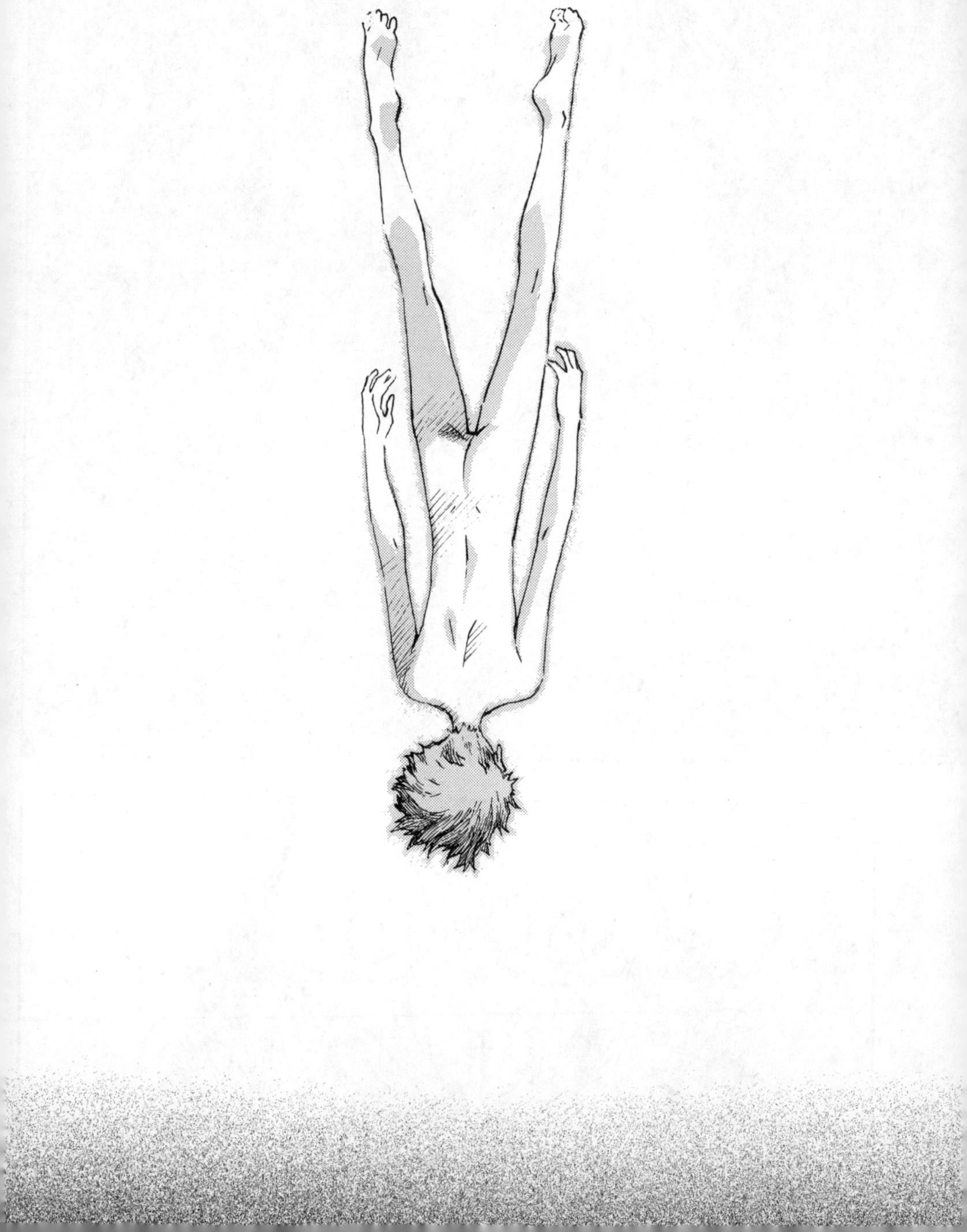

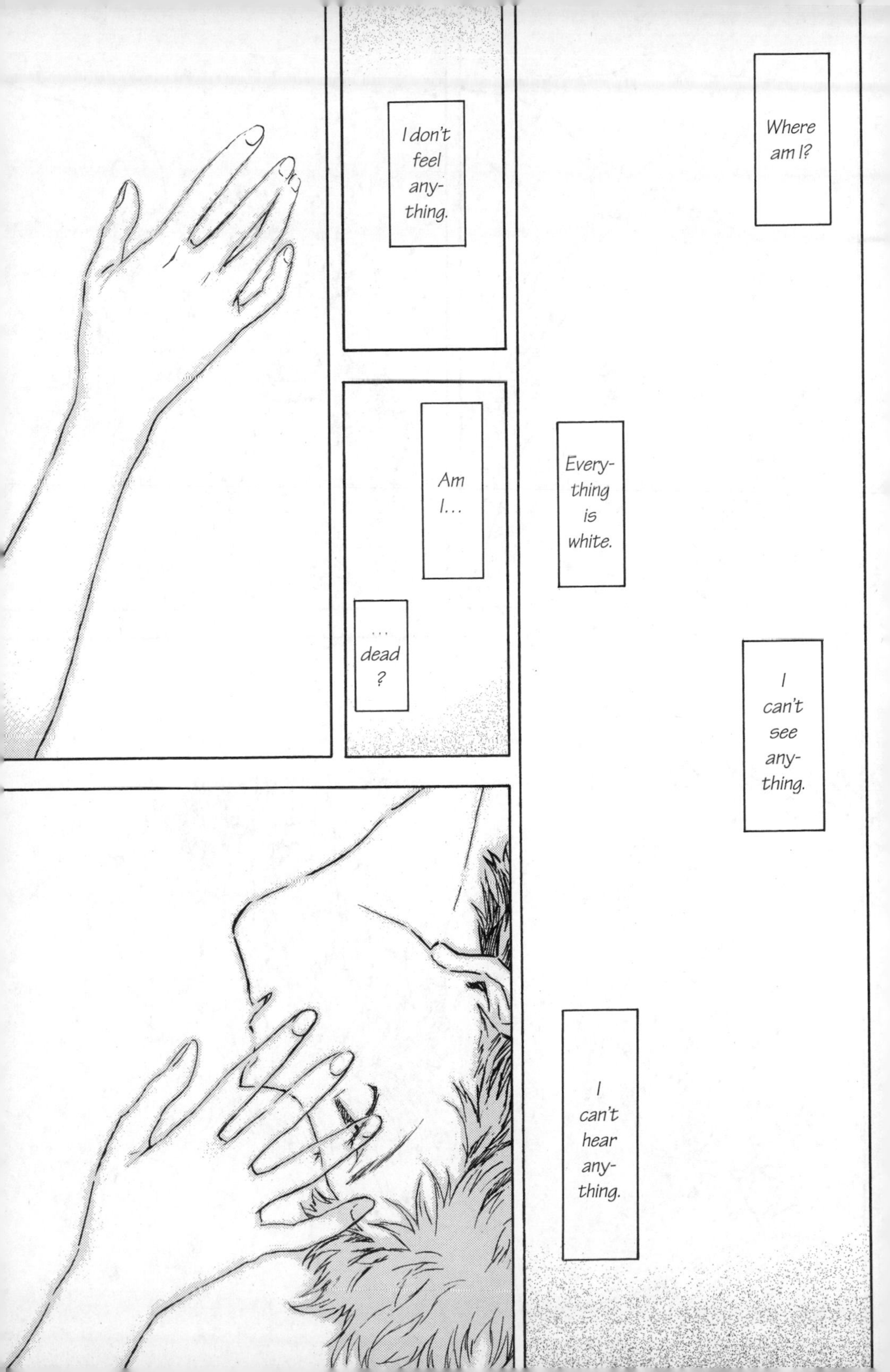
Where am I?
Every-thing is white.
I can't see any-thing.
I can't hear any-thing.
I don't feel any-thing.
Am I…
…dead?

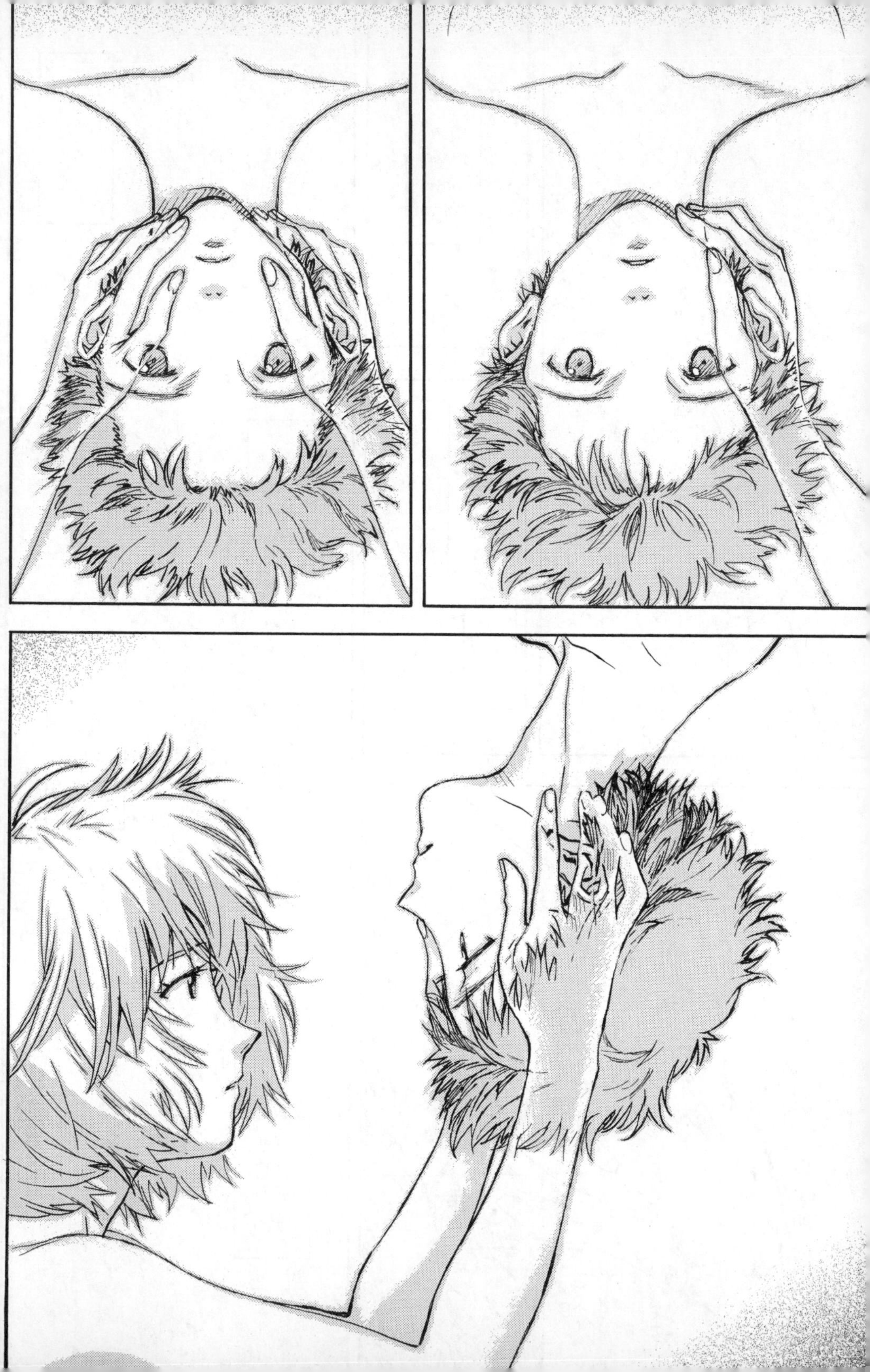

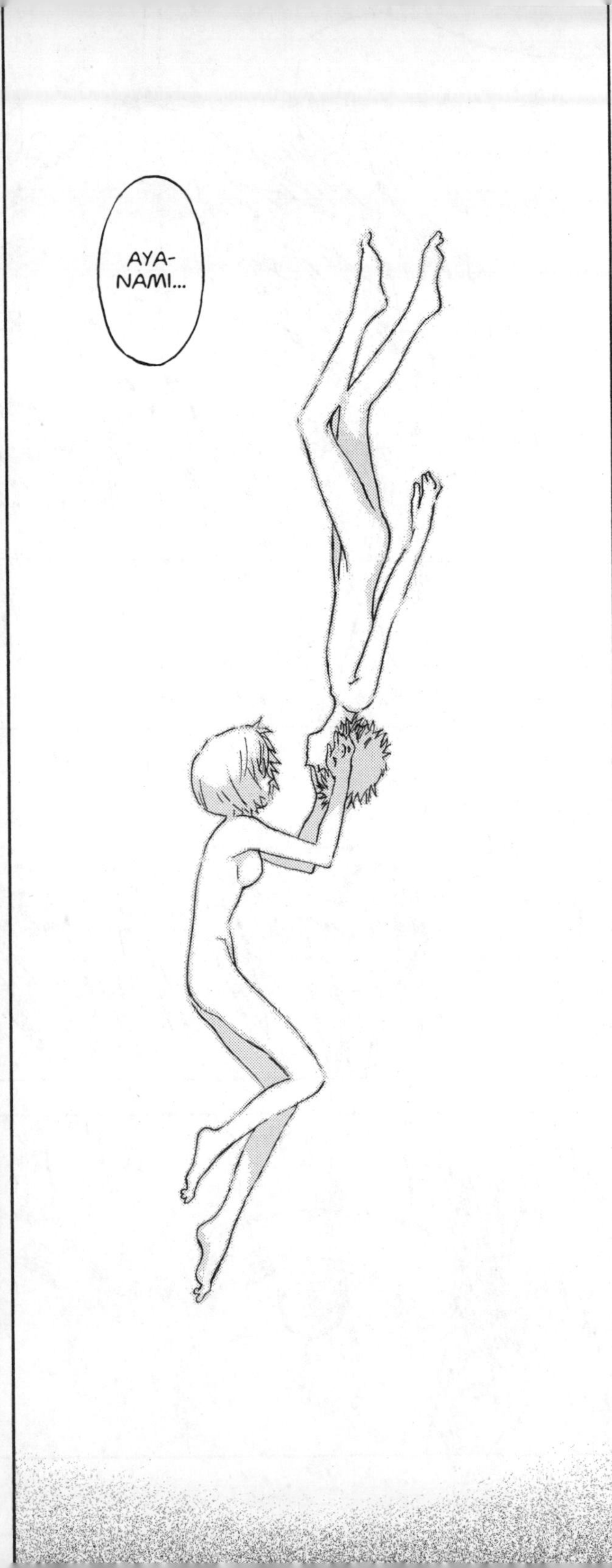
AYA-
NAMI...
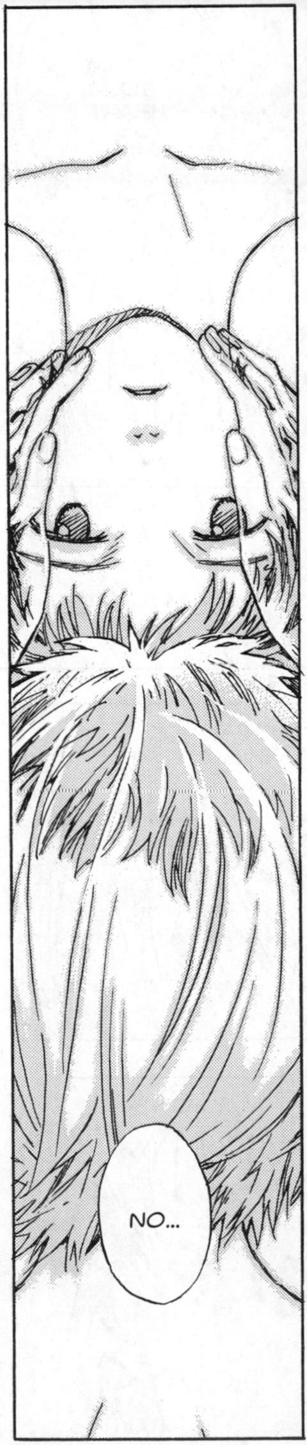
NO...

...I AM YOUR HEART...

...AND YOUR WISHES.

WHAT DO YOU...

...WISH FOR?

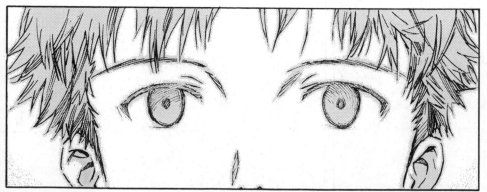

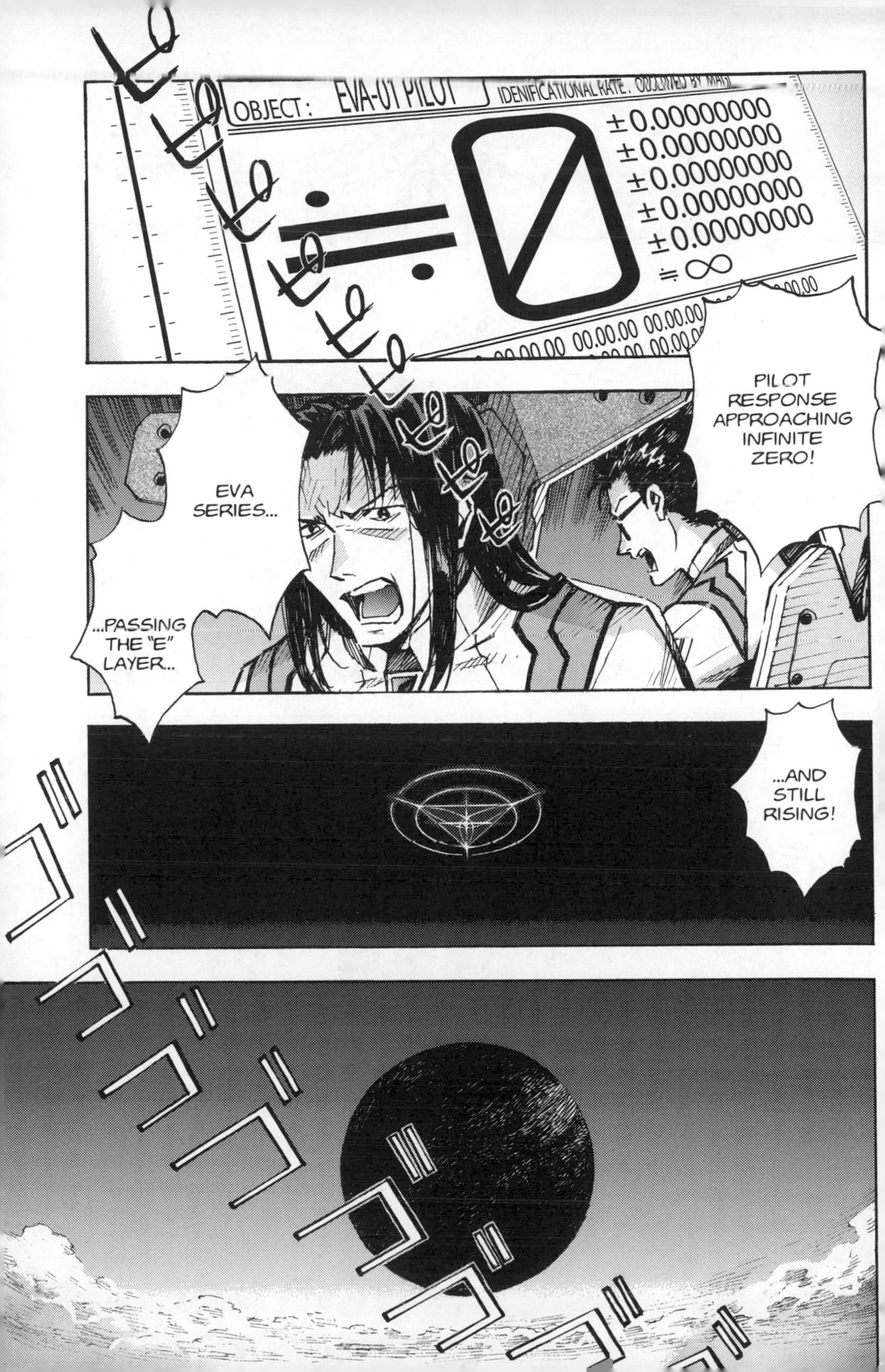
OBJECT : EVA-01 PILOT
IDENIFICATIONAL RATE :
±0.00000000
±0.00000000
±0.00000000
±0.00000000
±0.00000000
≒∞
PILOT RESPONSE APPROACHING INFINITE ZERO!
EVA SERIES...
...PASSING THE "E" LAYER...
...AND STILL RISING!

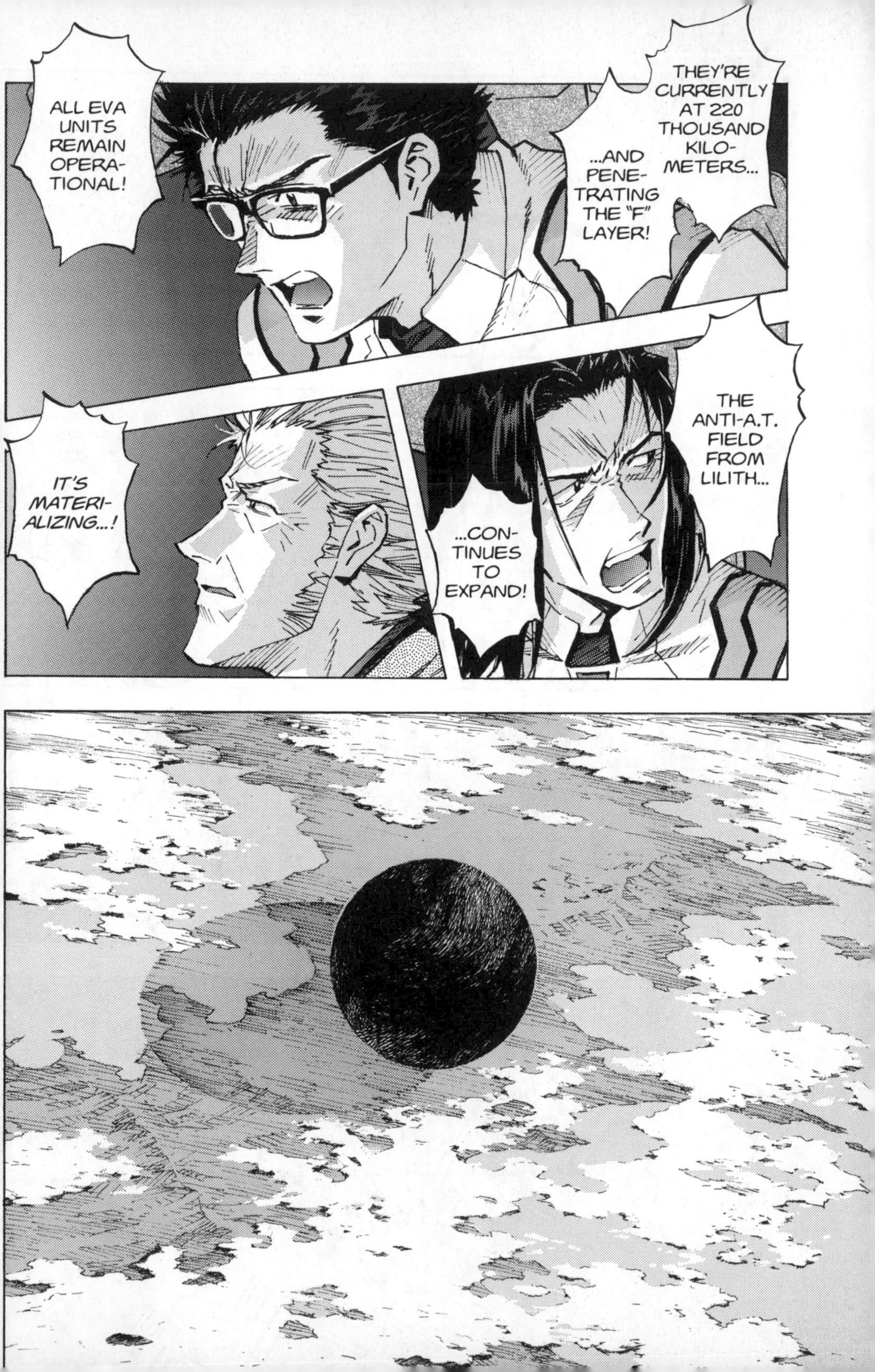
THEY'RE CURRENTLY AT 220 THOUSAND KILO-METERS...
...AND PENE-TRATING THE "F" LAYER!
ALL EVA UNITS REMAIN OPERA-TIONAL!
THE ANTI-A.T. FIELD FROM LILITH...
...CON-TINUES TO EXPAND!
IT'S MATERI-ALIZING...!

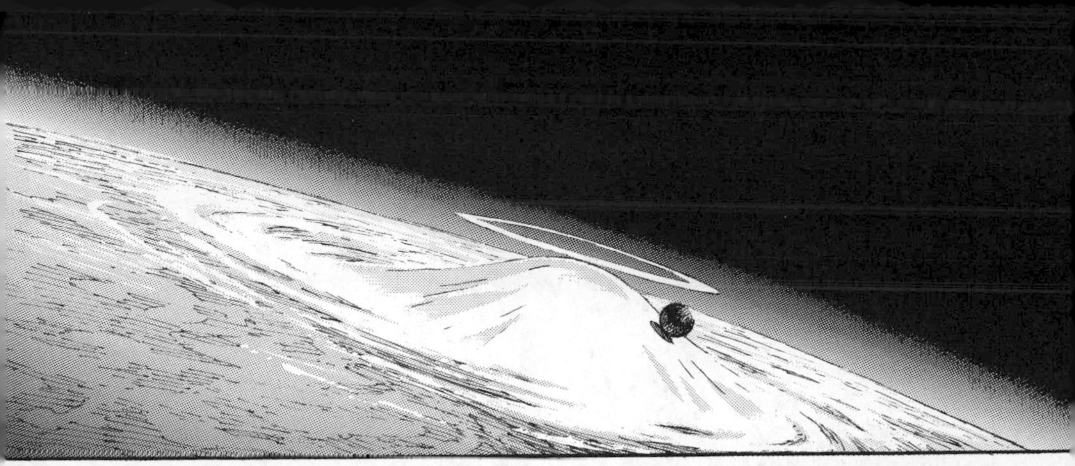
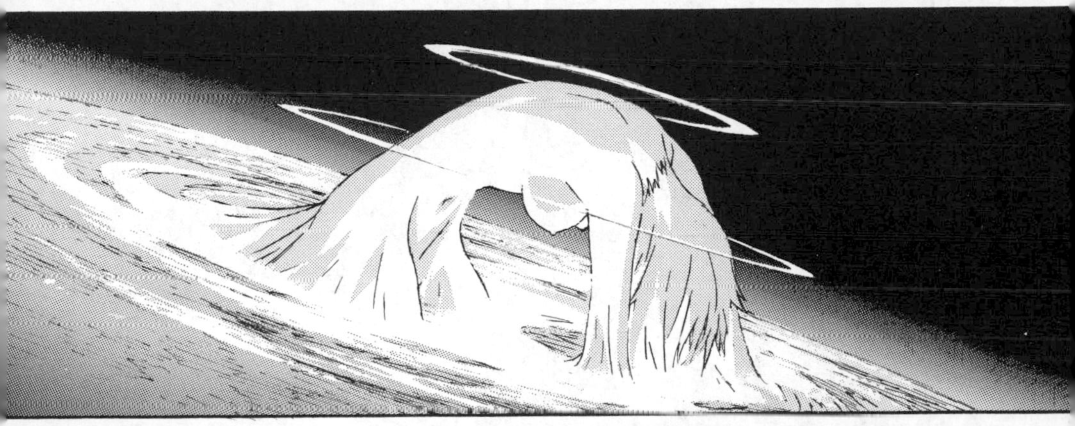
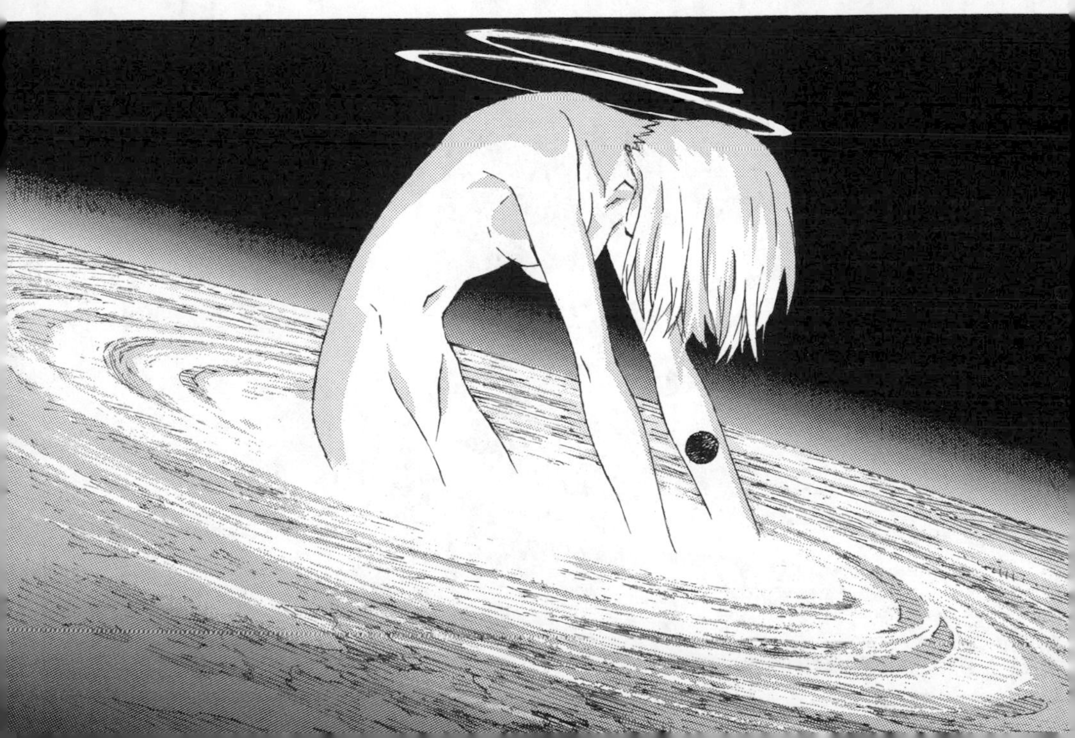

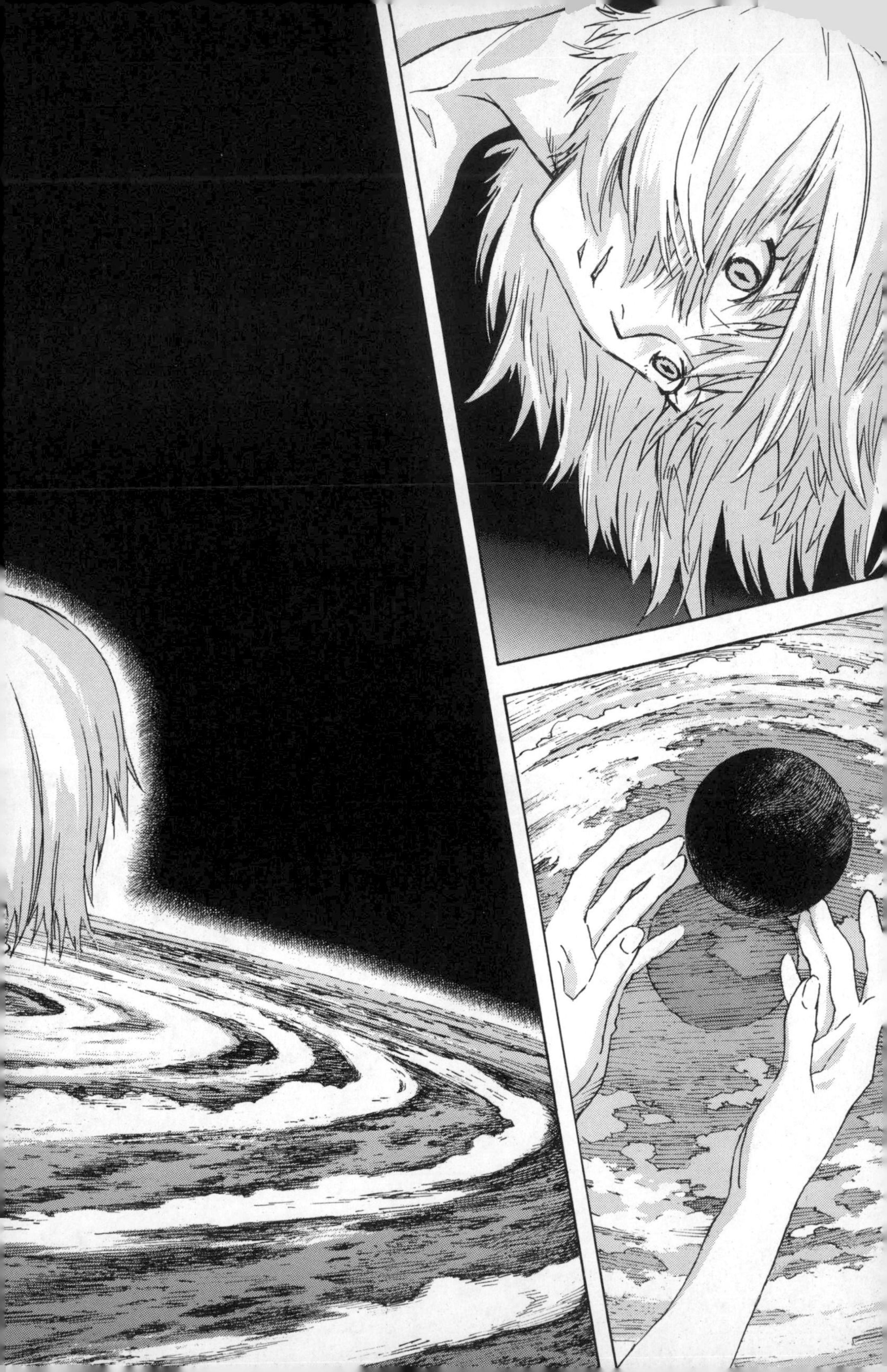

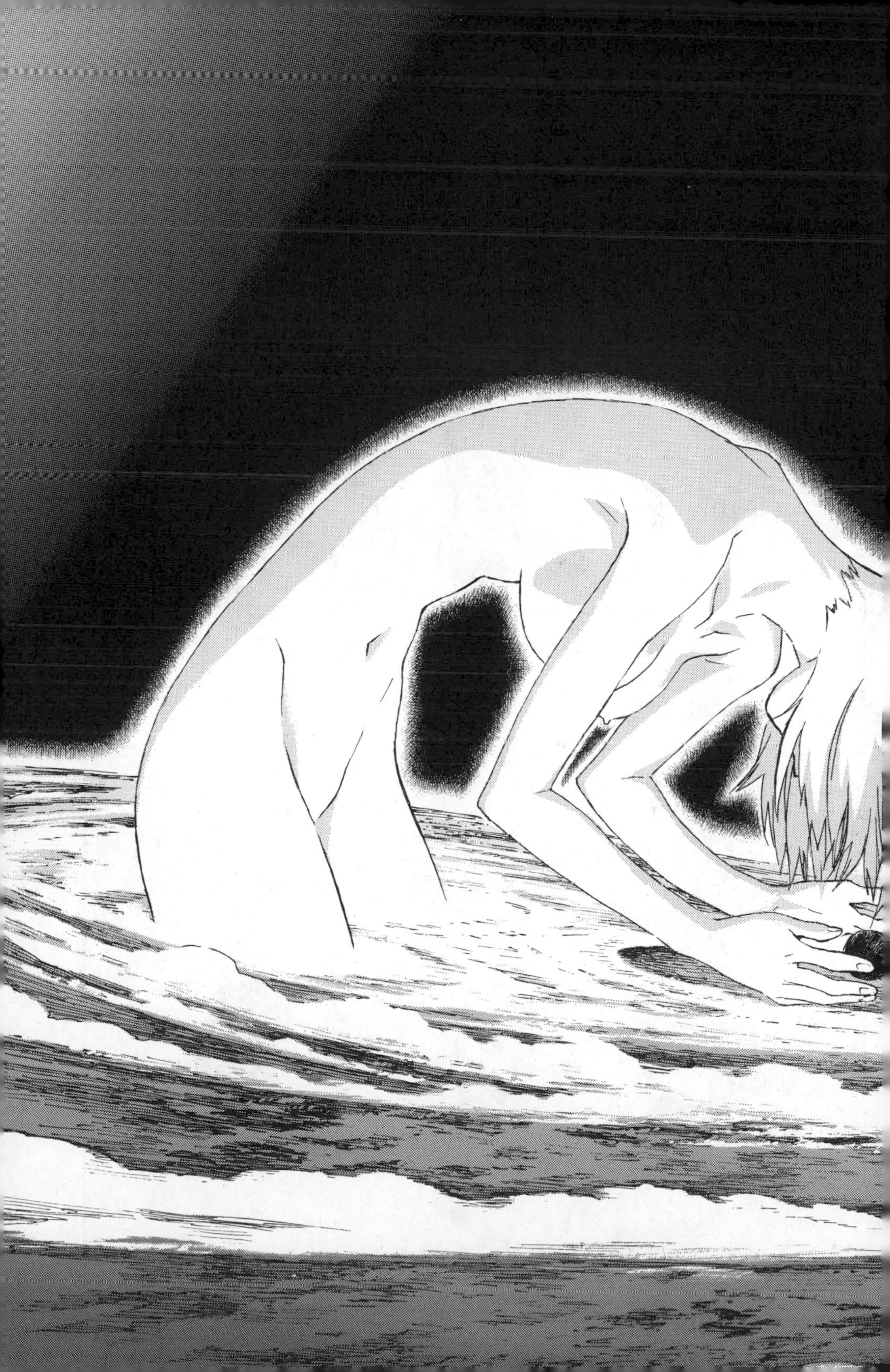

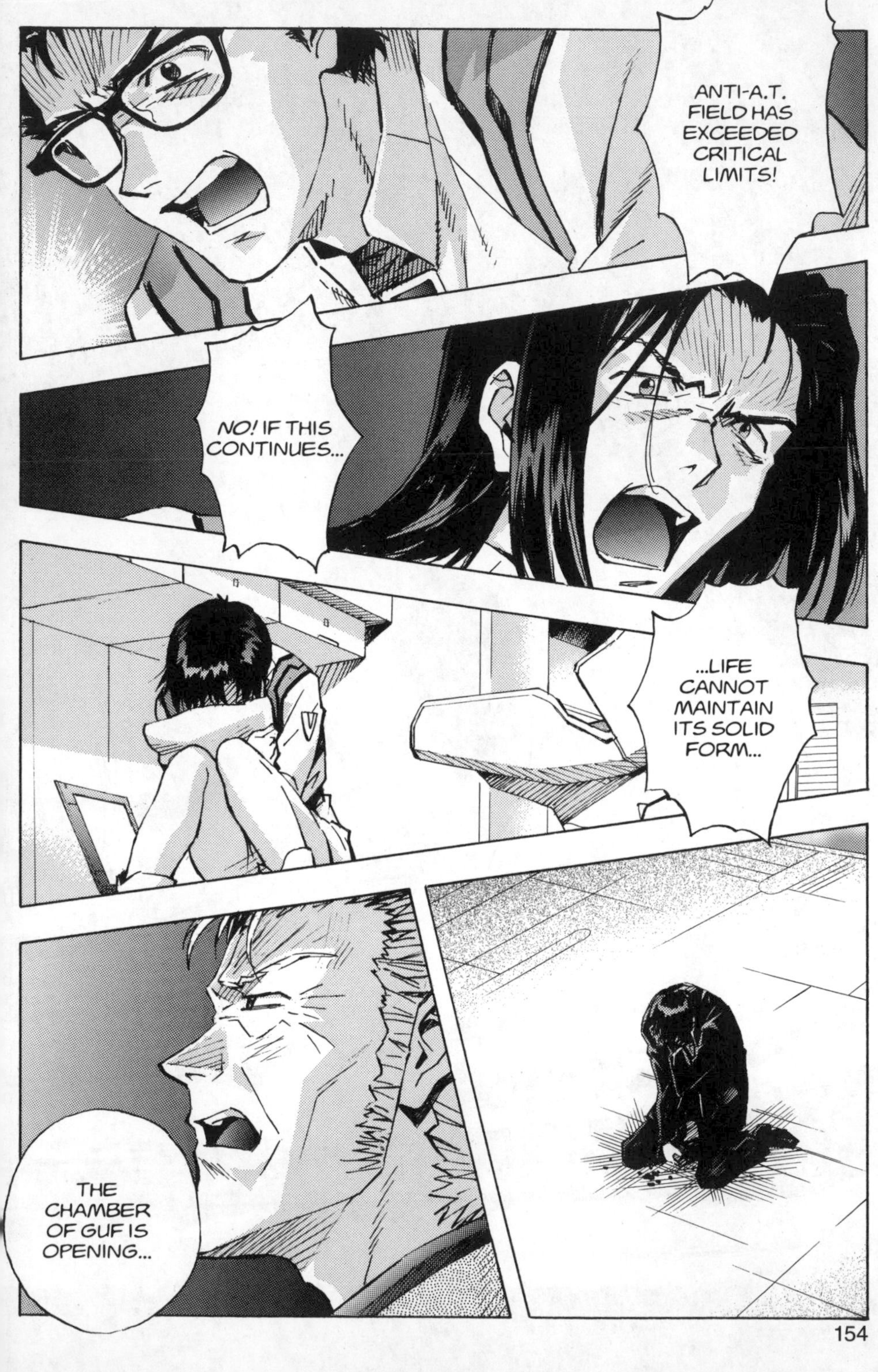
ANTI-A.T. FIELD HAS EXCEEDED CRITICAL LIMITS!
NO! IF THIS CONTINUES...
...LIFE CANNOT MAINTAIN ITS SOLID FORM...
THE CHAMBER OF GUF IS OPENING...

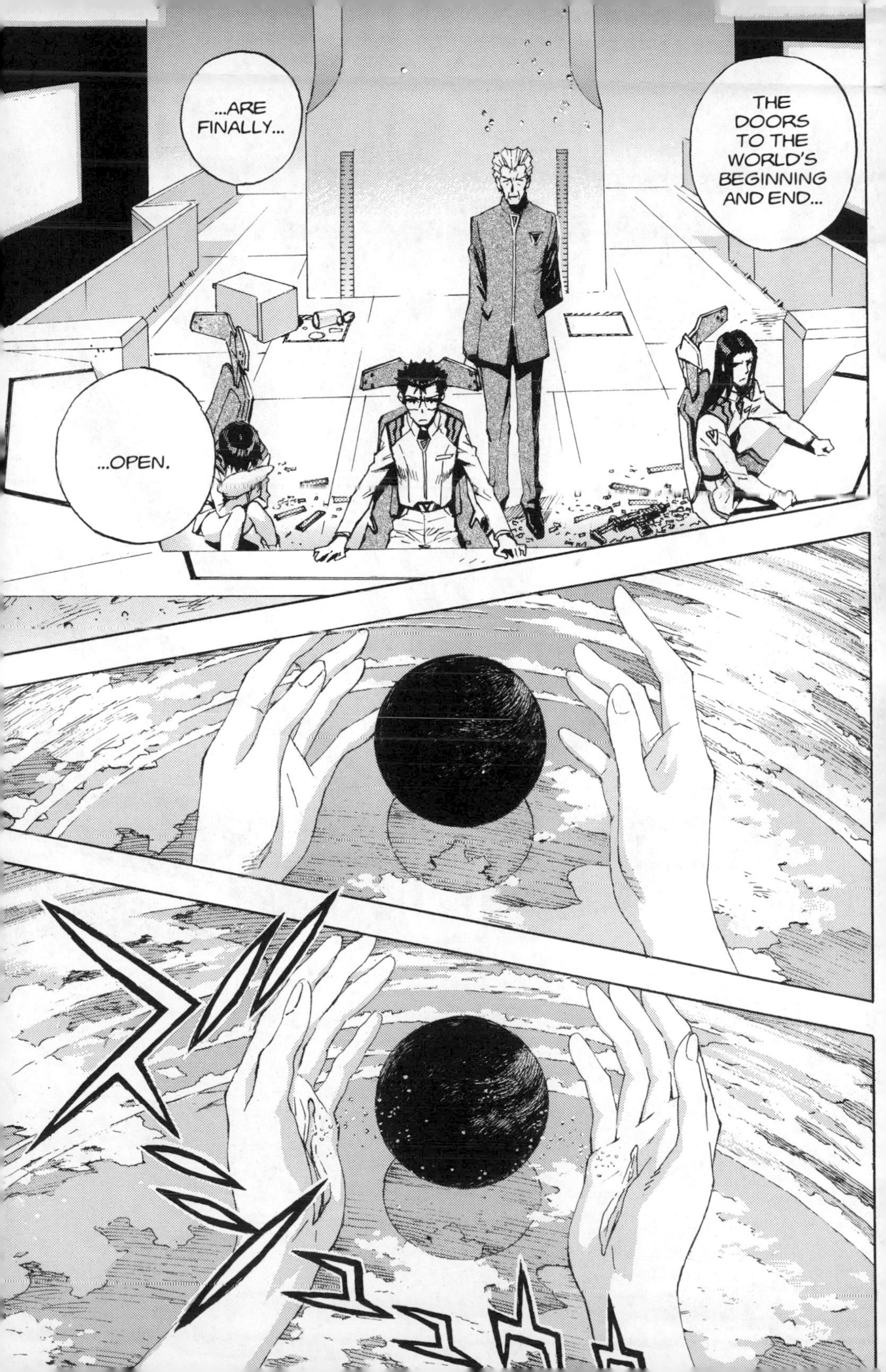
THE DOORS TO THE WORLD'S BEGINNING AND END...
...ARE FINALLY...
...OPEN.

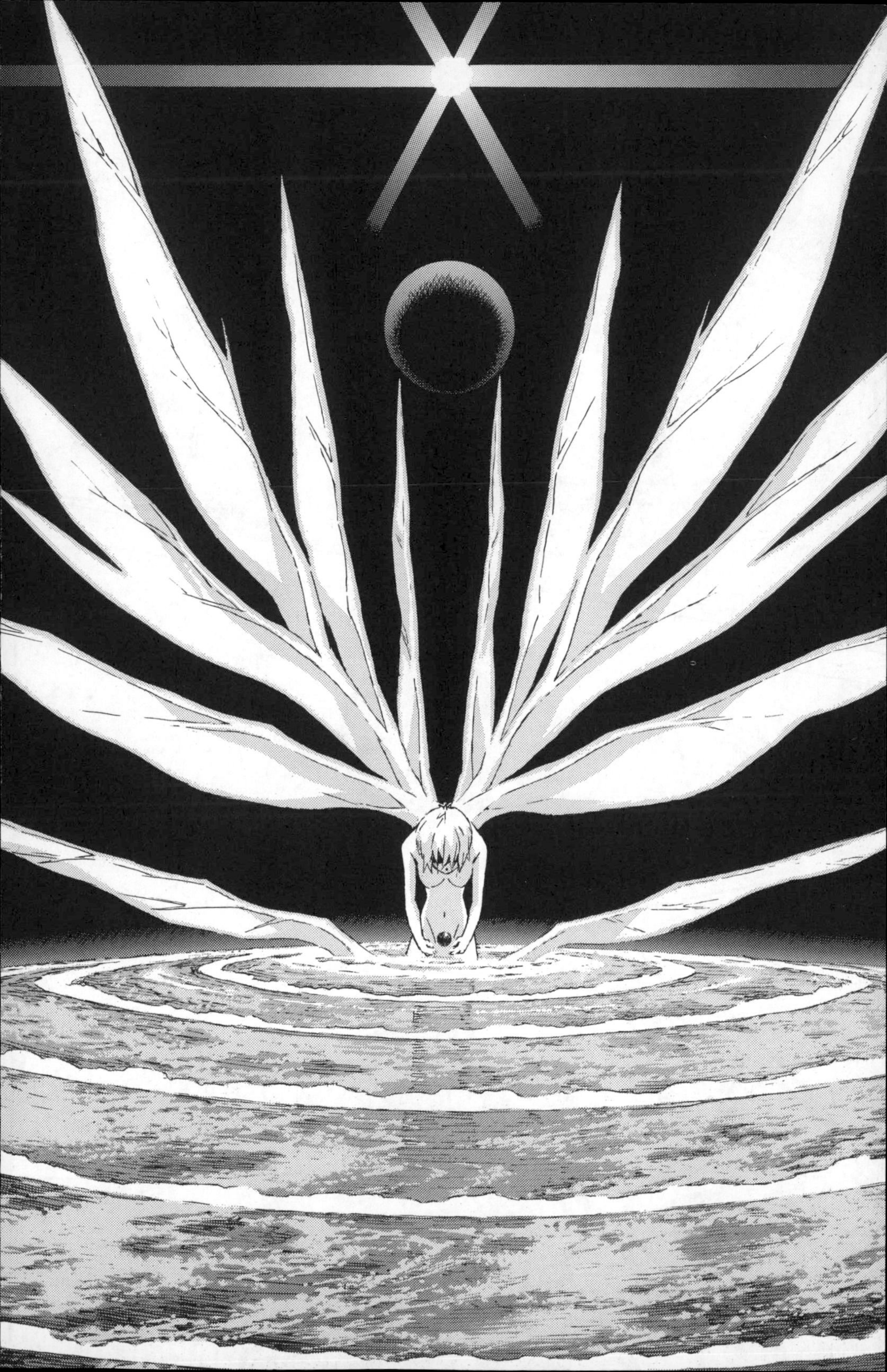

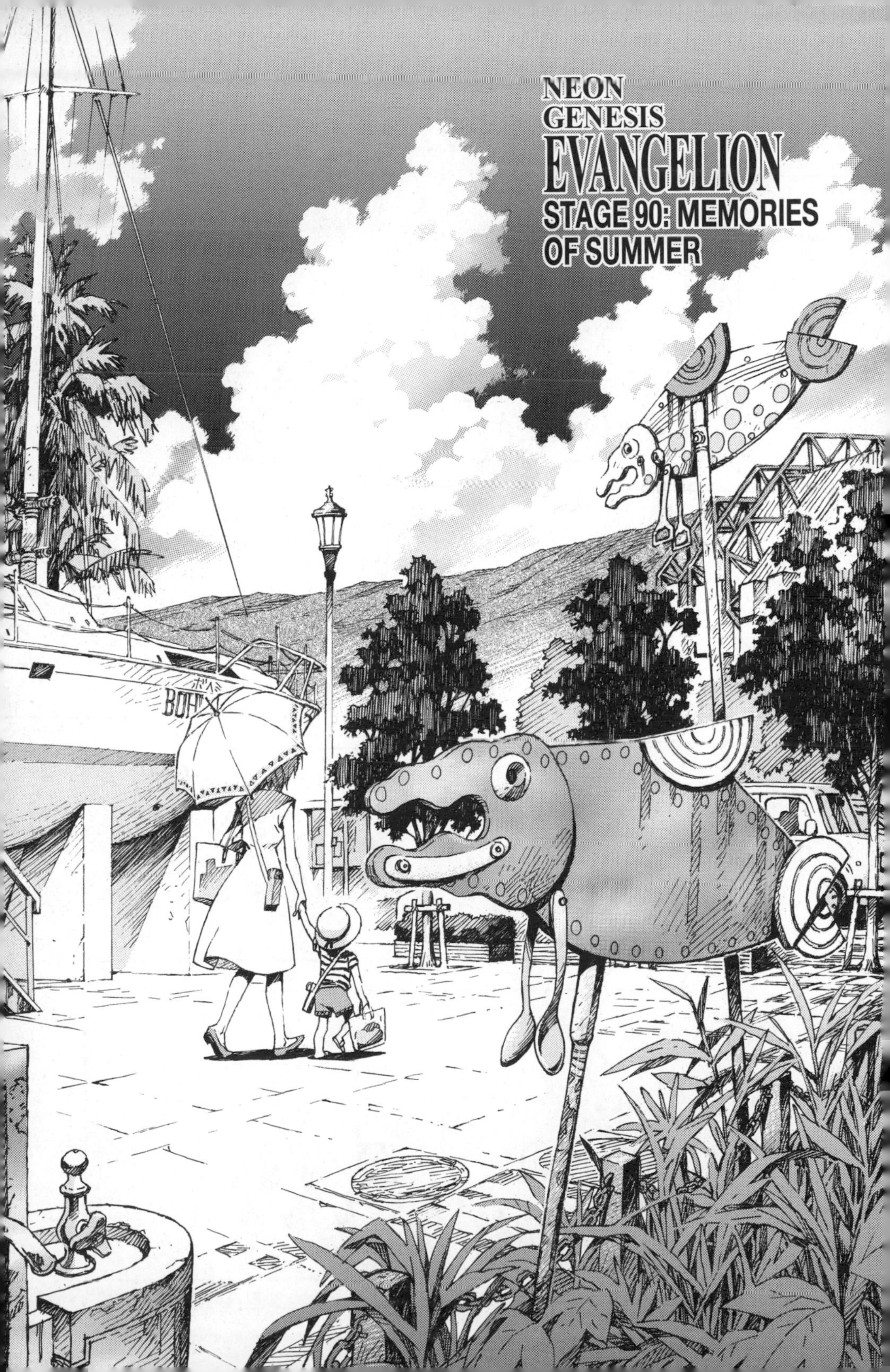
NEON GENESIS EVANGELION
STAGE 90: MEMORIES OF SUMMER

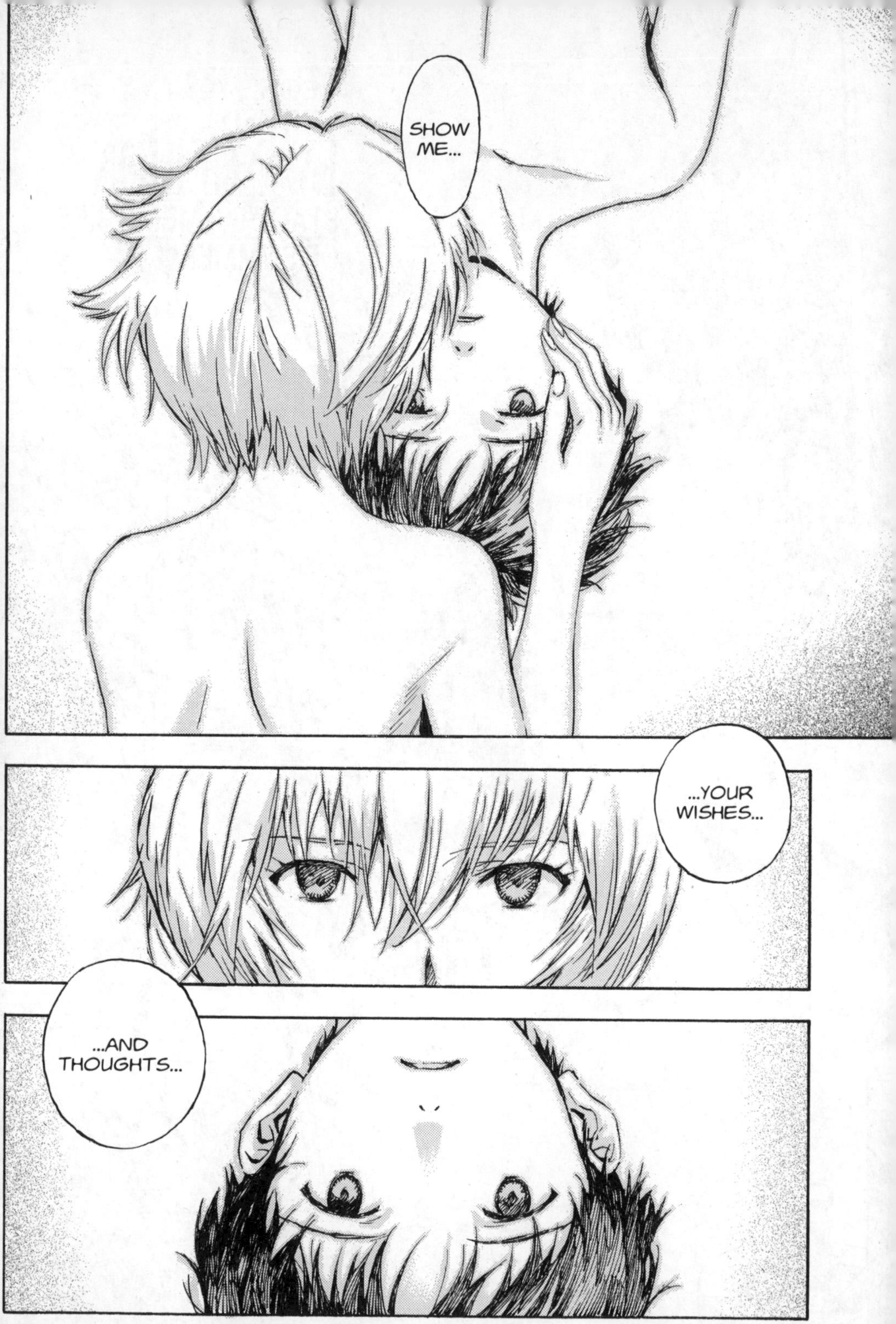
SHOW ME...
...YOUR WISHES...
...AND THOUGHTS...

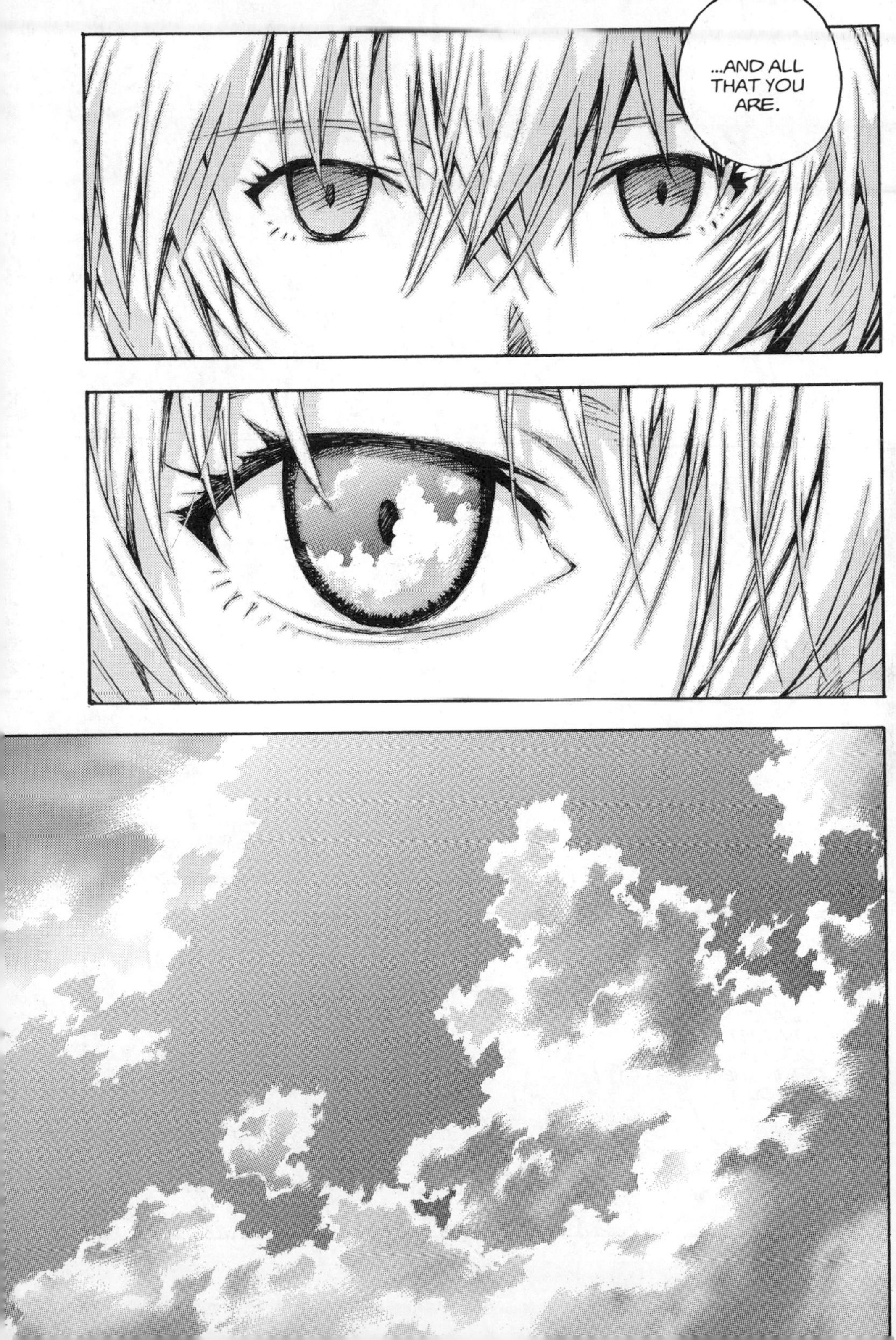
...AND ALL THAT YOU ARE.

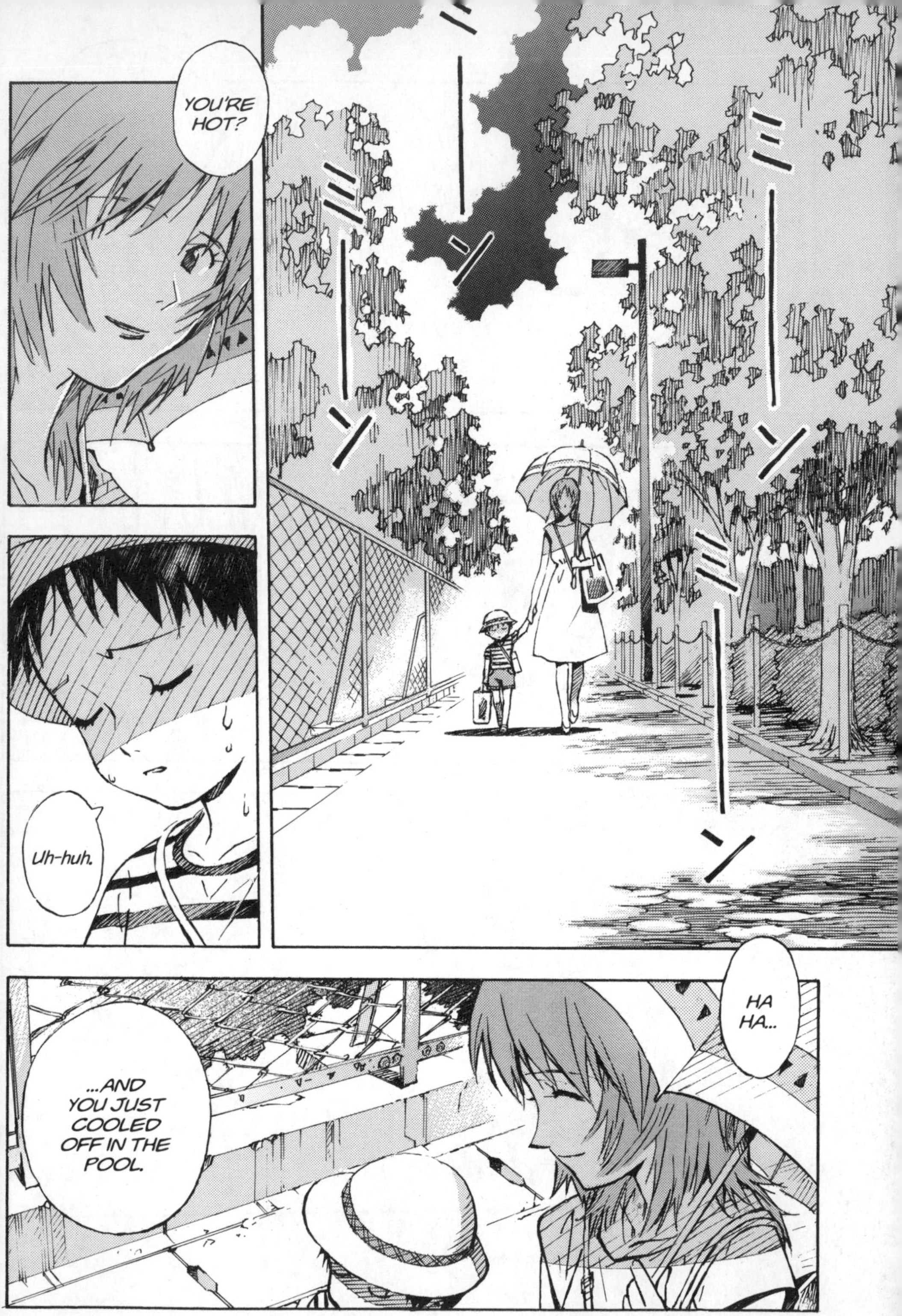
ーン
ミーン
ミーン
ミーン
YOU'RE HOT?
Uh-huh.
HA HA...
...AND YOU JUST COOLED OFF IN THE POOL.

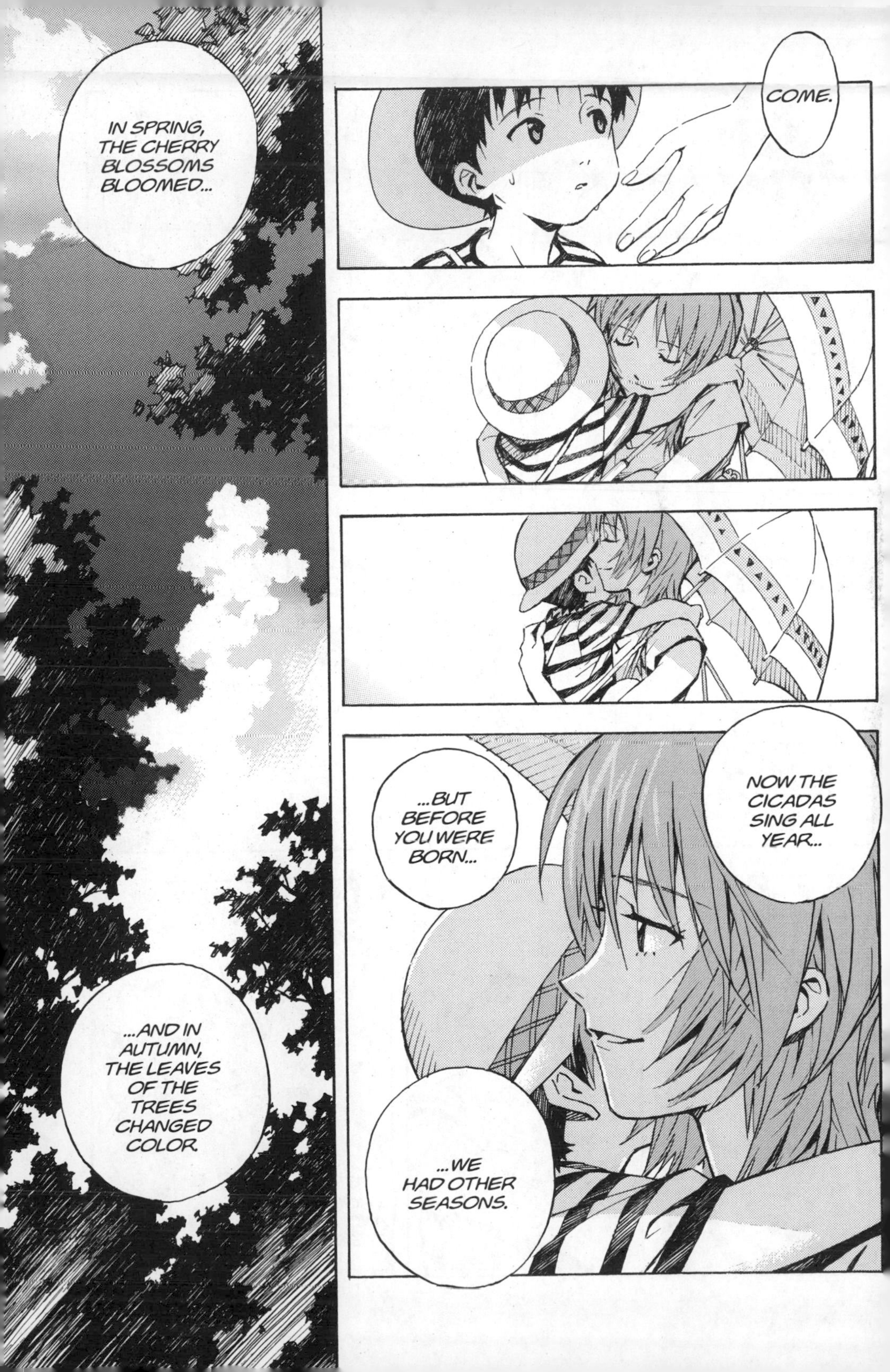
COME.
NOW THE CICADAS SING ALL YEAR...
...BUT BEFORE YOU WERE BORN...
...WE HAD OTHER SEASONS.
IN SPRING, THE CHERRY BLOSSOMS BLOOMED...
...AND IN AUTUMN, THE LEAVES OF THE TREES CHANGED COLOR.

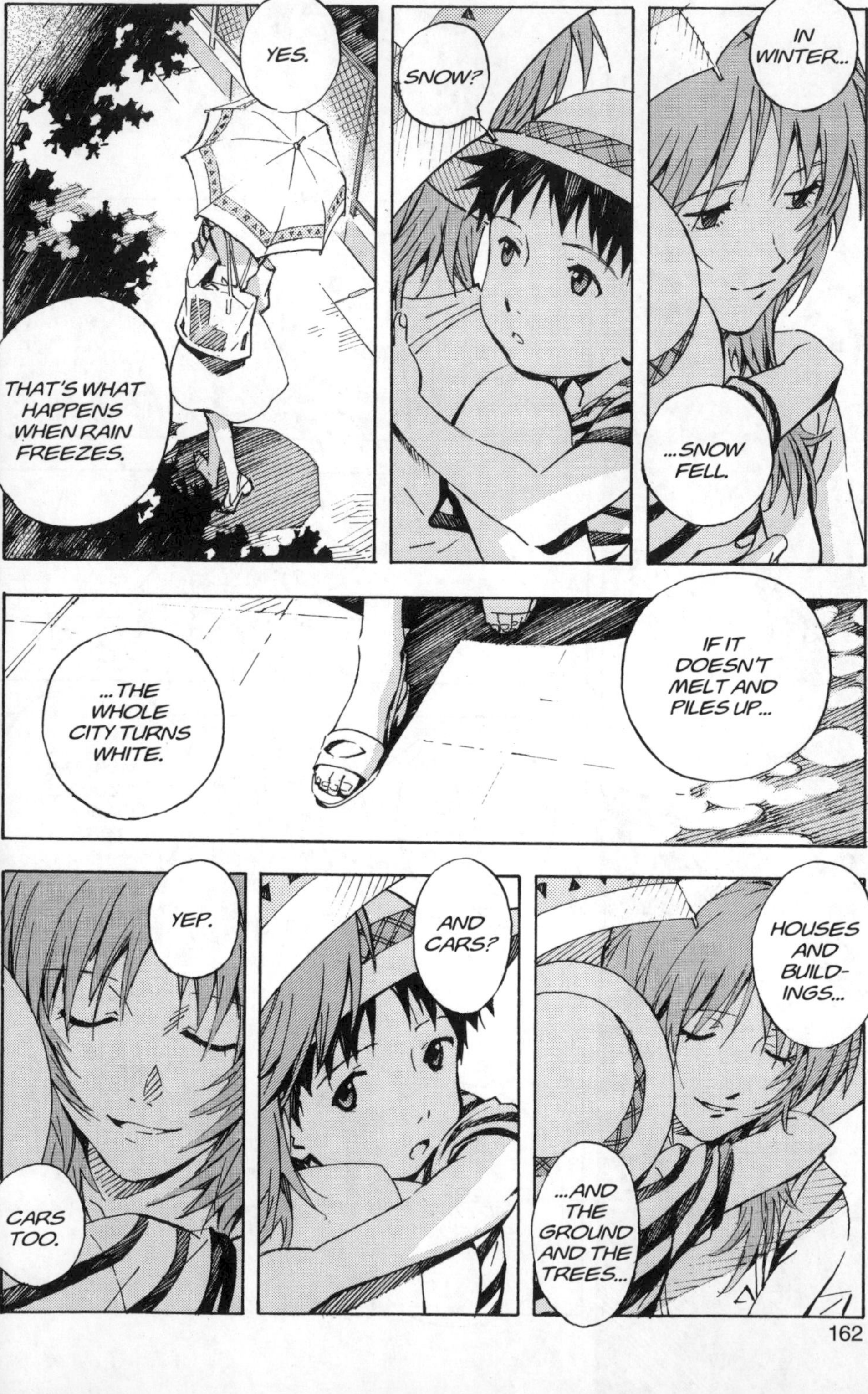
IN WINTER...
...SNOW FELL.
SNOW?
YES.
THAT'S WHAT HAPPENS WHEN RAIN FREEZES.
IF IT DOESN'T MELT AND PILES UP...
...THE WHOLE CITY TURNS WHITE.
HOUSES AND BUILD-INGS...
...AND THE GROUND AND THE TREES...
AND CARS?
YEP.
CARS TOO.

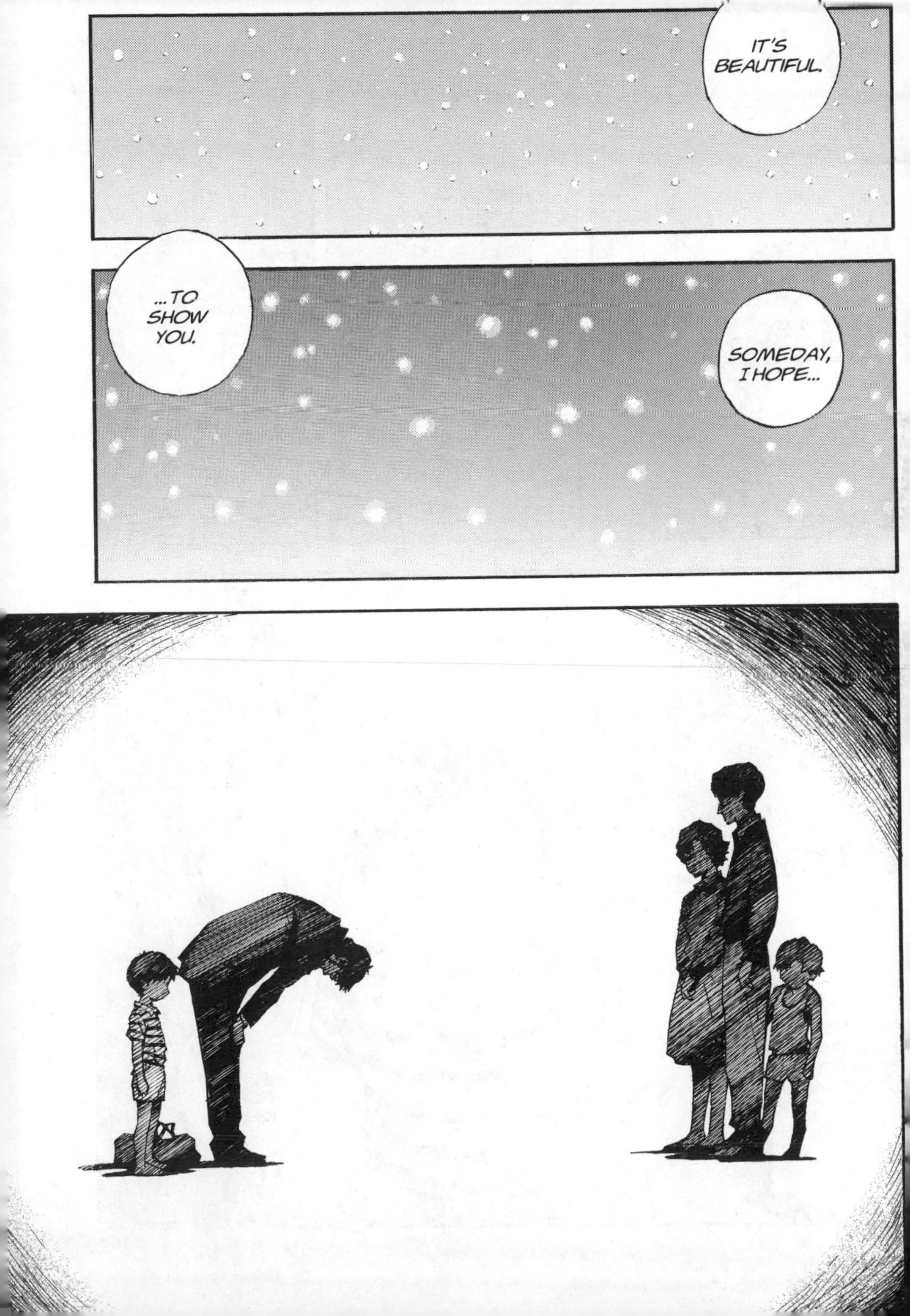
IT'S BEAUTIFUL.
SOMEDAY, I HOPE...
...TO SHOW YOU.

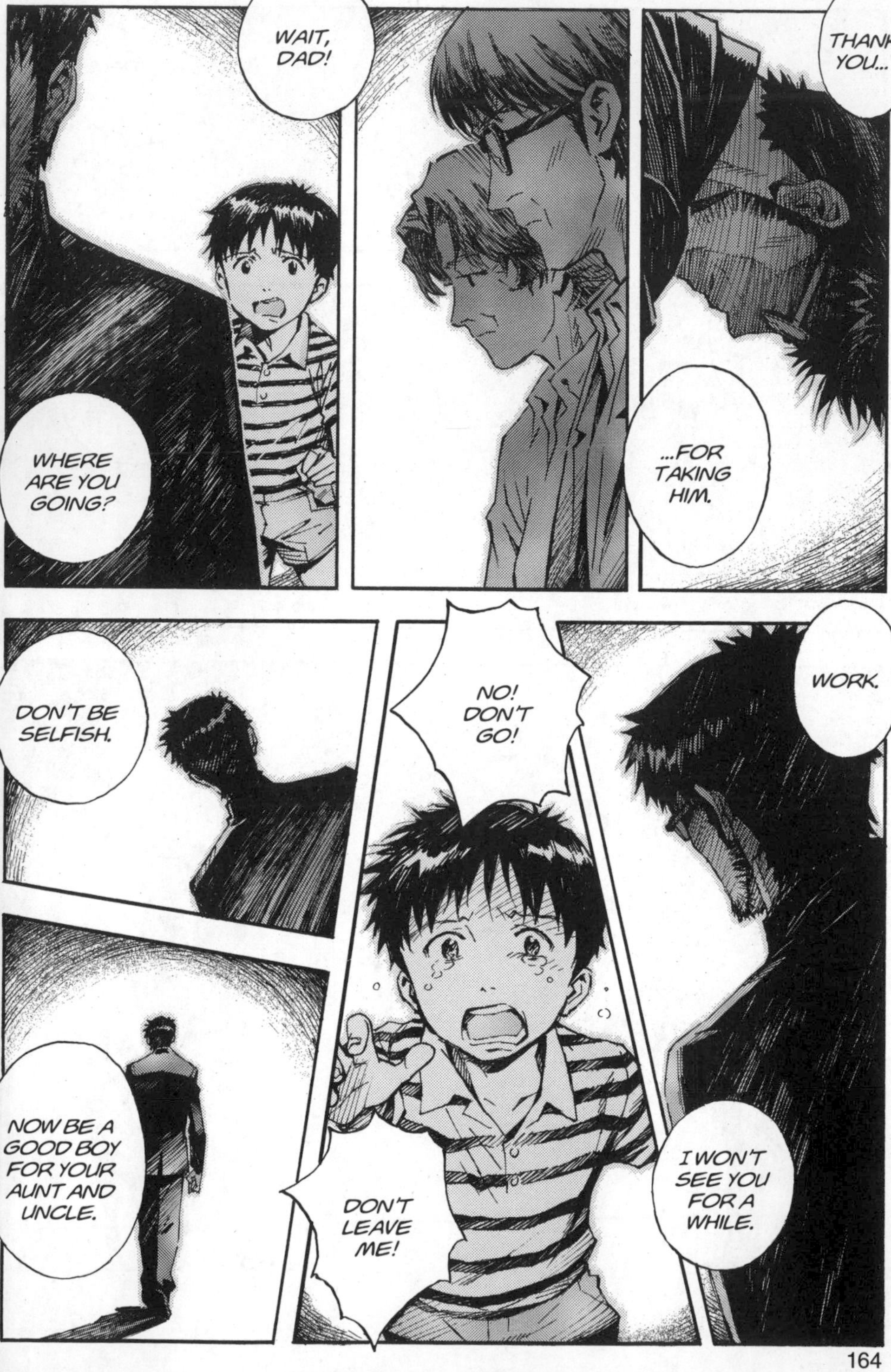
THANK YOU...
...FOR TAKING HIM.
WAIT, DAD!
WHERE ARE YOU GOING?
WORK.
I WON'T SEE YOU FOR A WHILE.
NO! DON'T GO!
DON'T LEAVE ME!
DON'T BE SELFISH.
NOW BE A GOOD BOY FOR YOUR AUNT AND UNCLE.

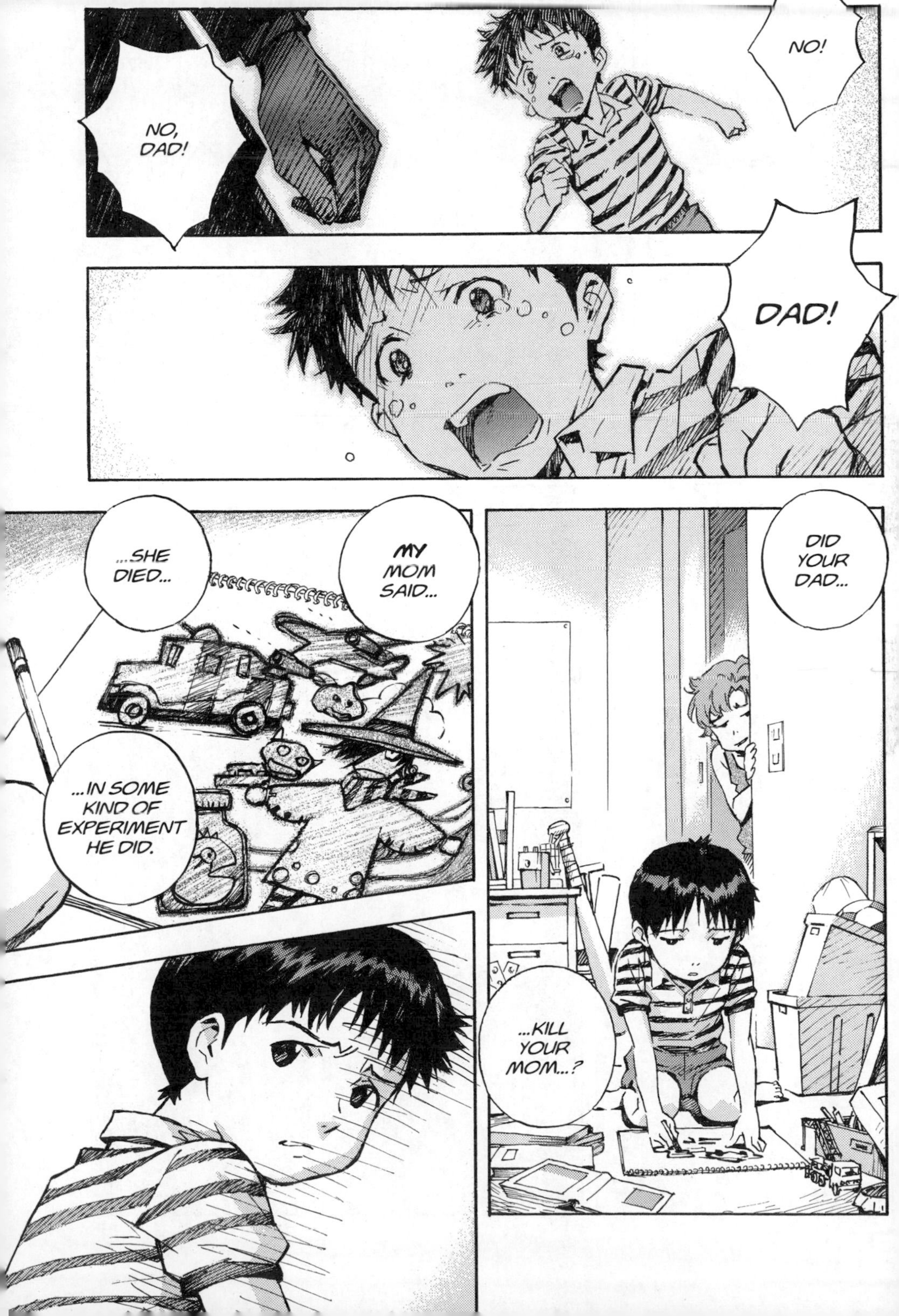
NO!
NO, DAD!
DAD!
DID YOUR DAD...
...KILL YOUR MOM...?
MY MOM SAID...
...SHE DIED...
...IN SOME KIND OF EXPERIMENT HE DID.

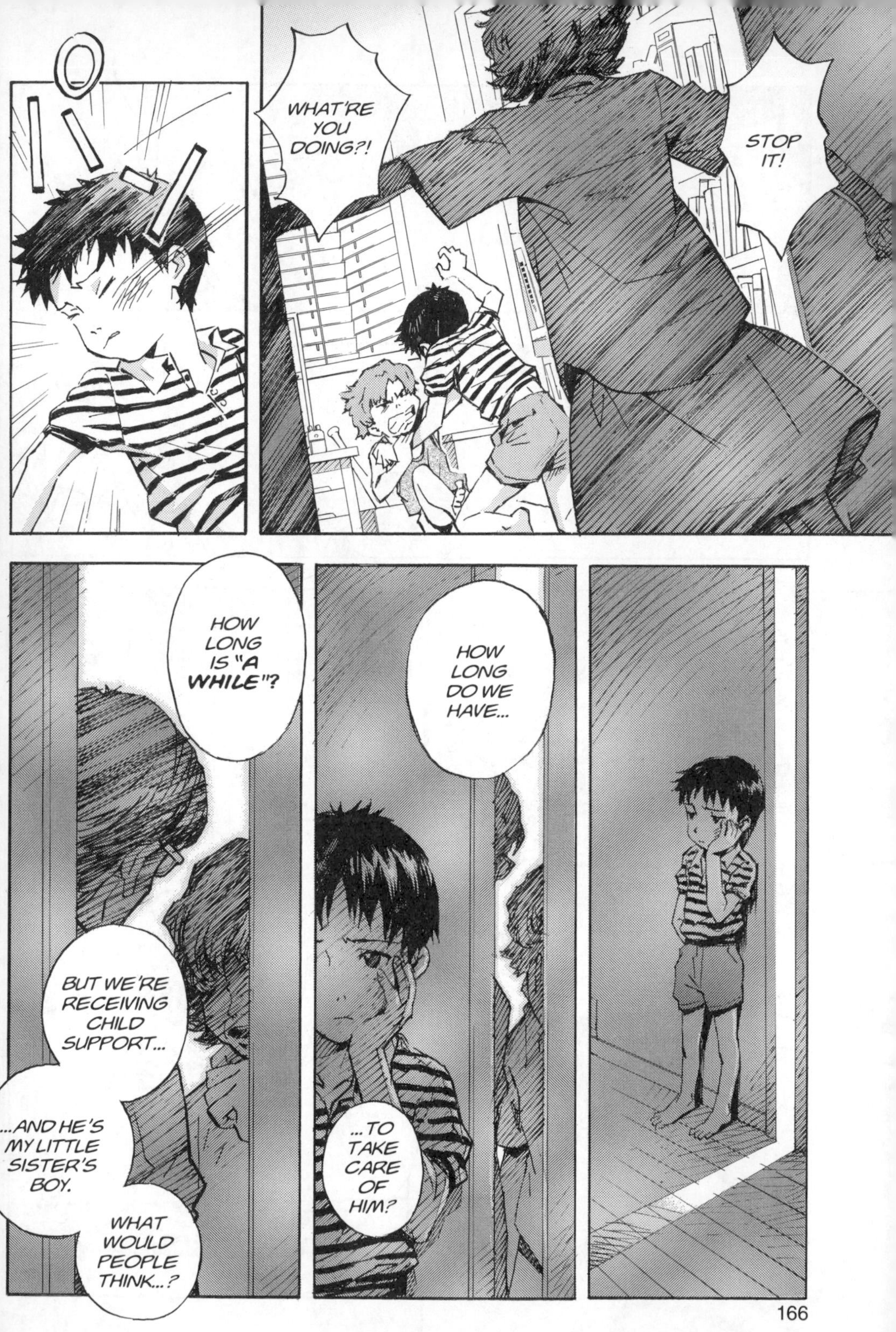
WHAT'RE YOU DOING?!
STOP IT!
HOW LONG DO WE HAVE...
...TO TAKE CARE OF HIM?
HOW LONG IS "A WHILE"?
BUT WE'RE RECEIVING CHILD SUPPORT...
...AND HE'S MY LITTLE SISTER'S BOY.
WHAT WOULD PEOPLE THINK...?

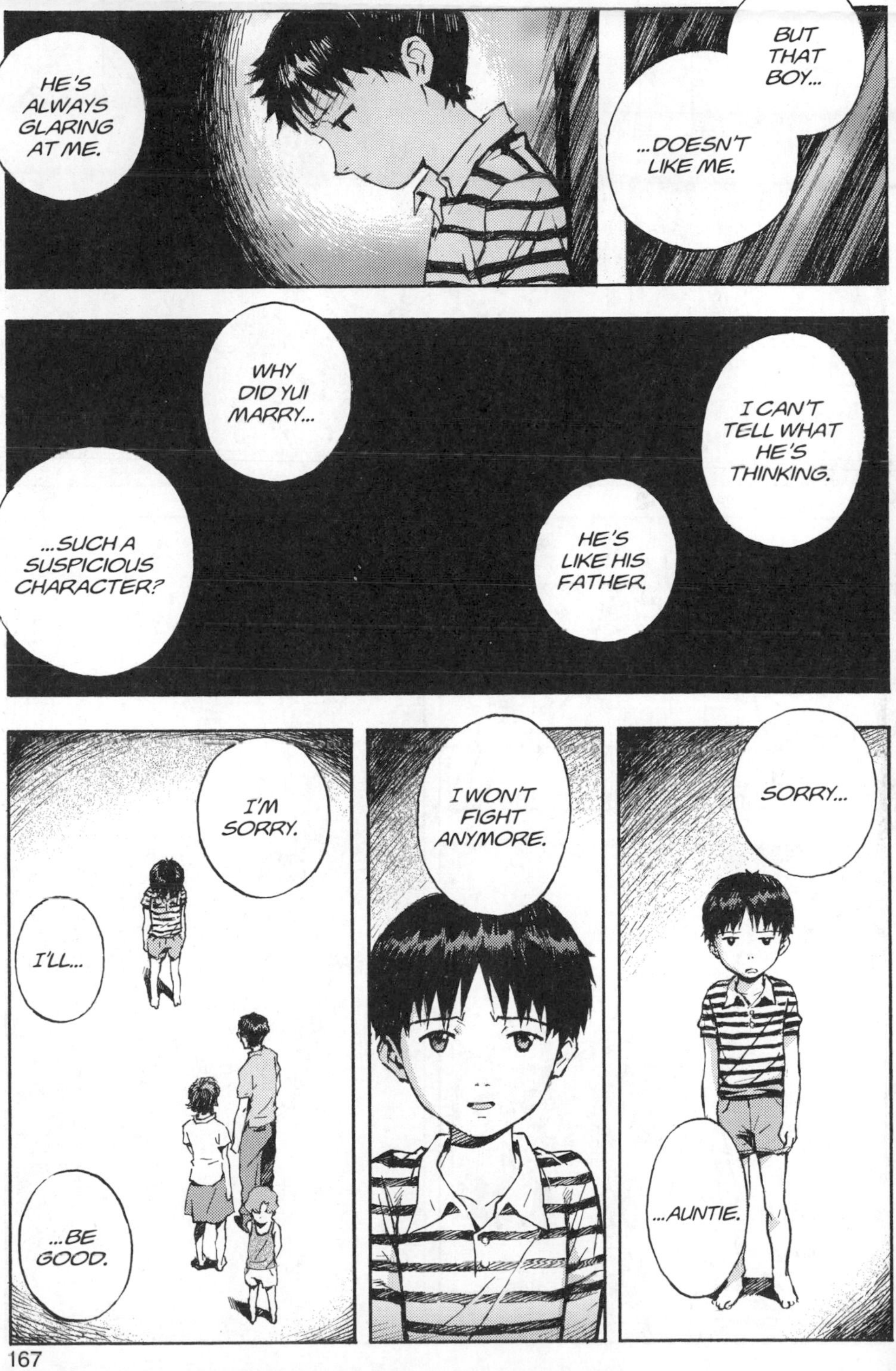
BUT THAT BOY...
...DOESN'T LIKE ME.
HE'S ALWAYS GLARING AT ME.
I CAN'T TELL WHAT HE'S THINKING.
HE'S LIKE HIS FATHER.
WHY DID YUI MARRY...
...SUCH A SUSPICIOUS CHARACTER?
SORRY...
...AUNTIE.
I WON'T FIGHT ANYMORE.
I'M SORRY.
I'LL...
...BE GOOD.

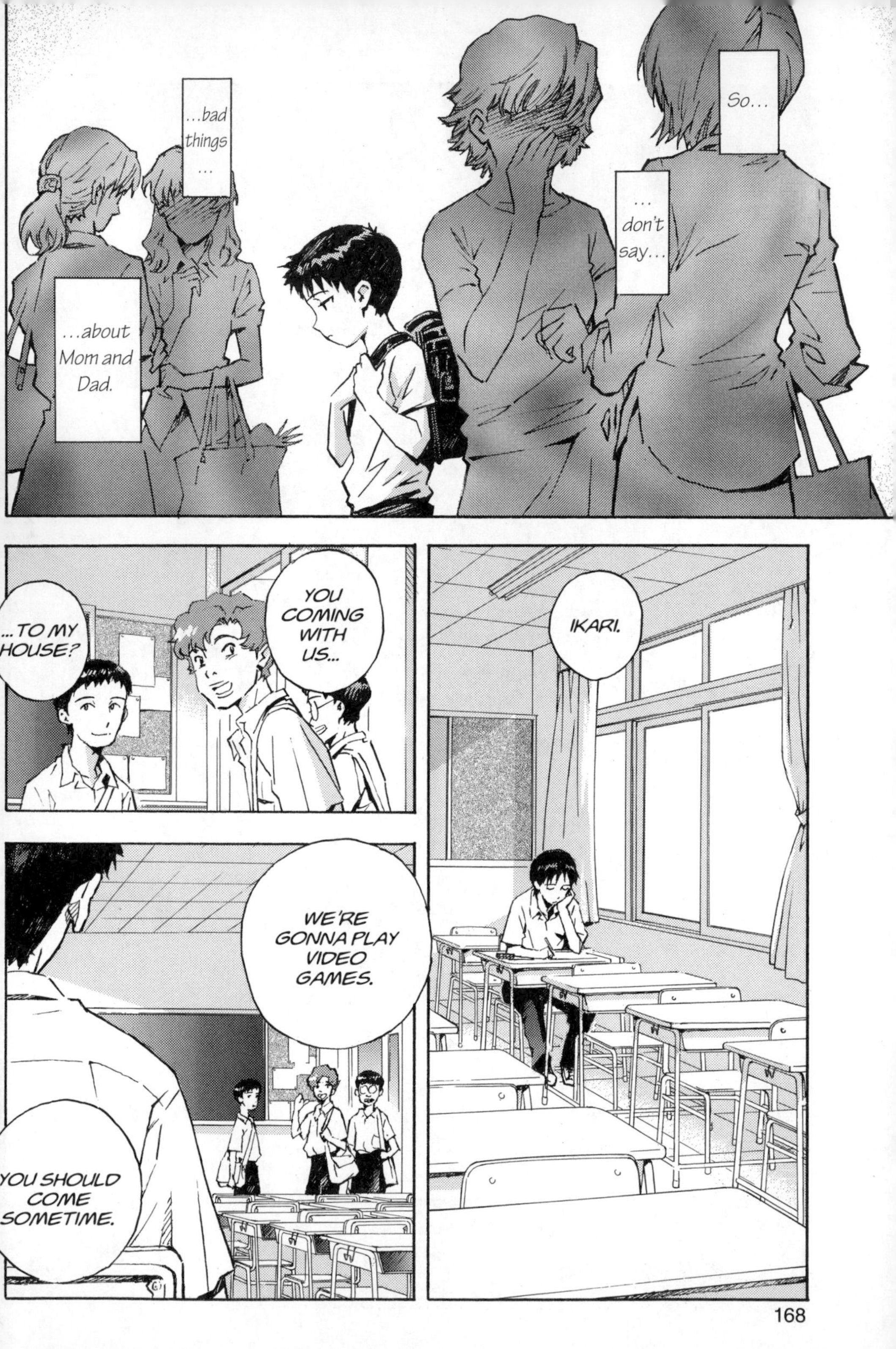
So…
…don't say…
…bad things…
…about Mom and Dad.
IKARI.
YOU COMING WITH US…
…TO MY HOUSE?
WE'RE GONNA PLAY VIDEO GAMES.
YOU SHOULD COME SOMETIME.

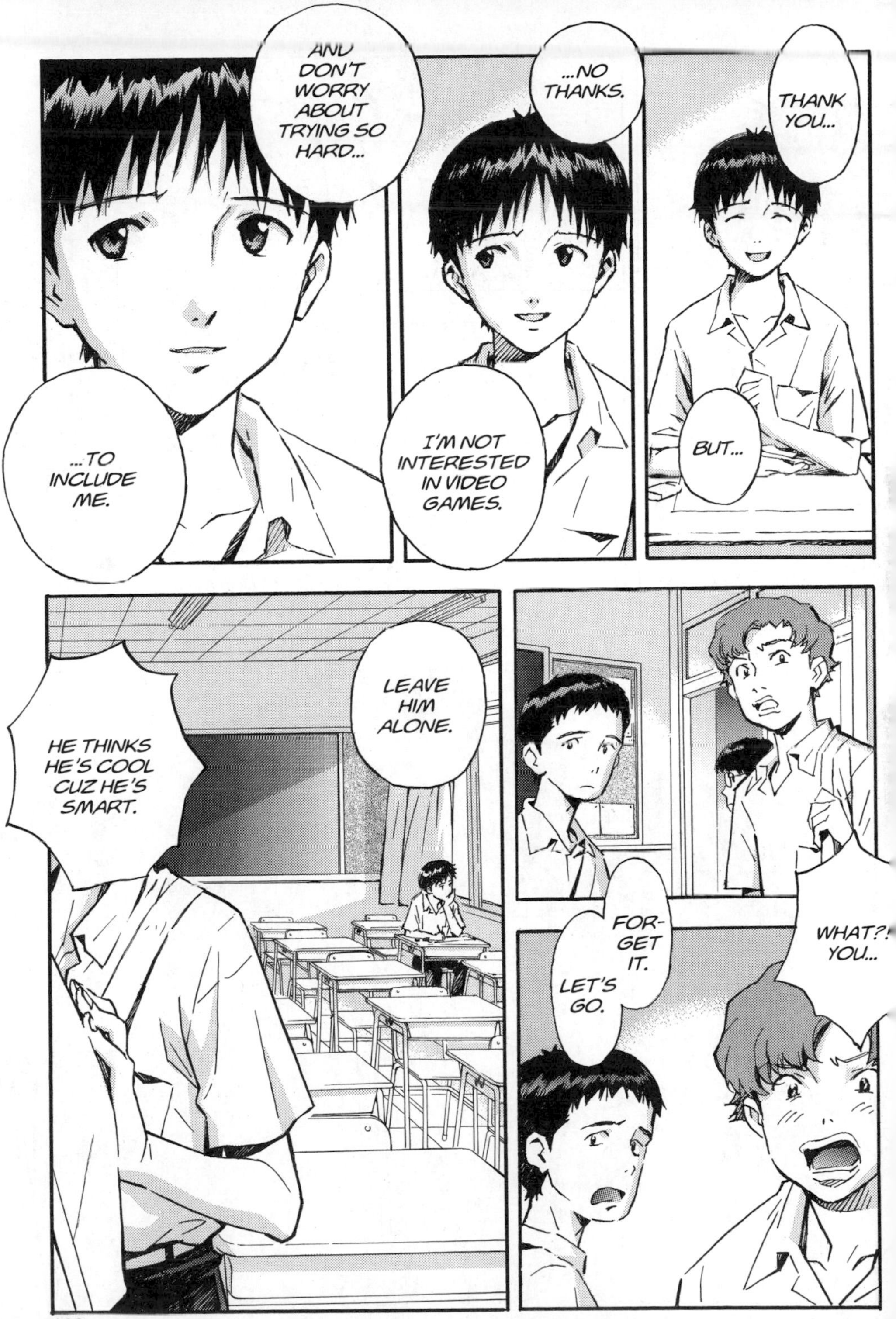
THANK YOU...
BUT...
...NO THANKS.
I'M NOT INTERESTED IN VIDEO GAMES.
AND DON'T WORRY ABOUT TRYING SO HARD...
...TO INCLUDE ME.
WHAT?! YOU...
FOR-GET IT.
LET'S GO.
LEAVE HIM ALONE.
HE THINKS HE'S COOL CUZ HE'S SMART.

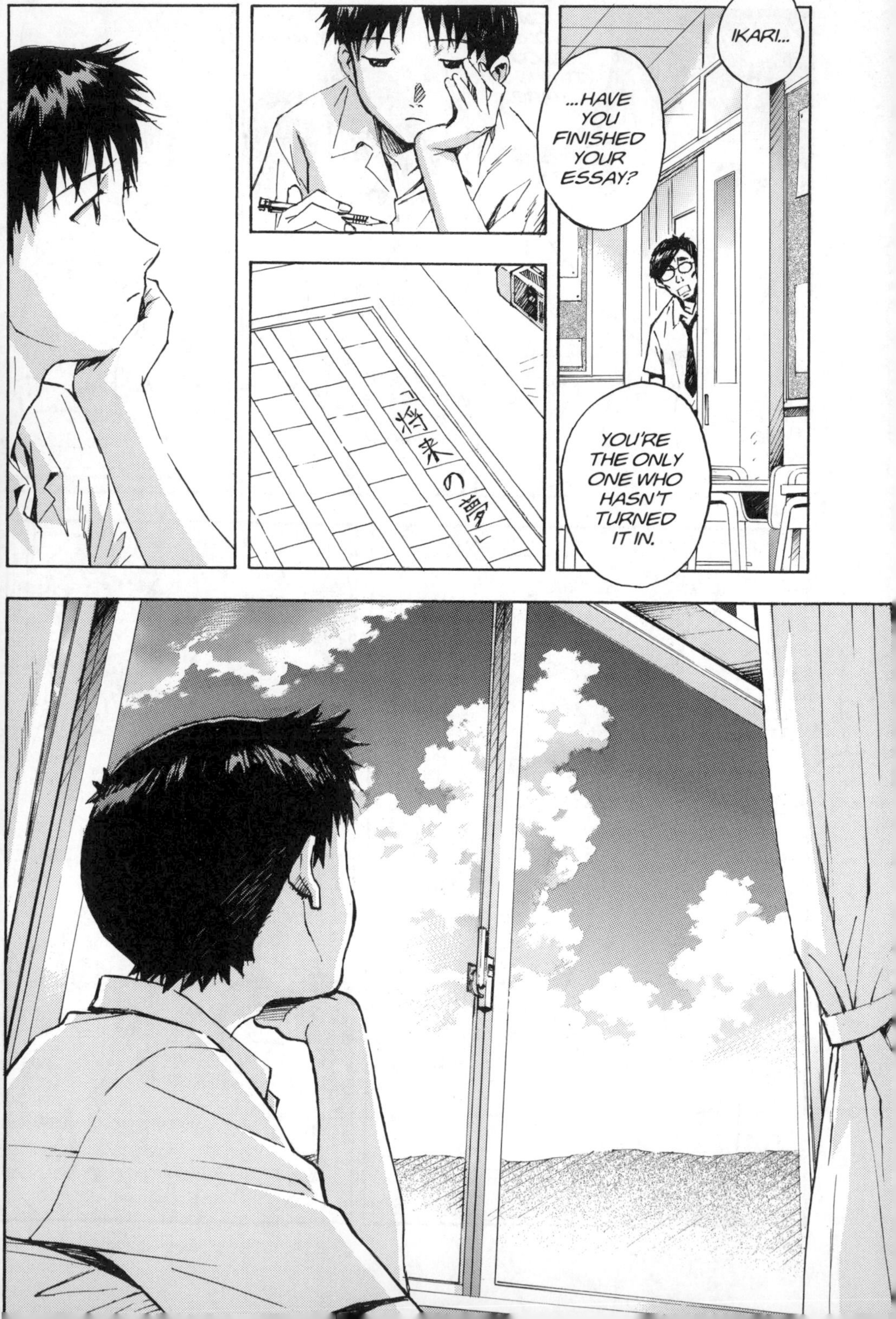
IKARI...
...HAVE YOU FINISHED YOUR ESSAY?
YOU'RE THE ONLY ONE WHO HASN'T TURNED IT IN.
「将来の夢」

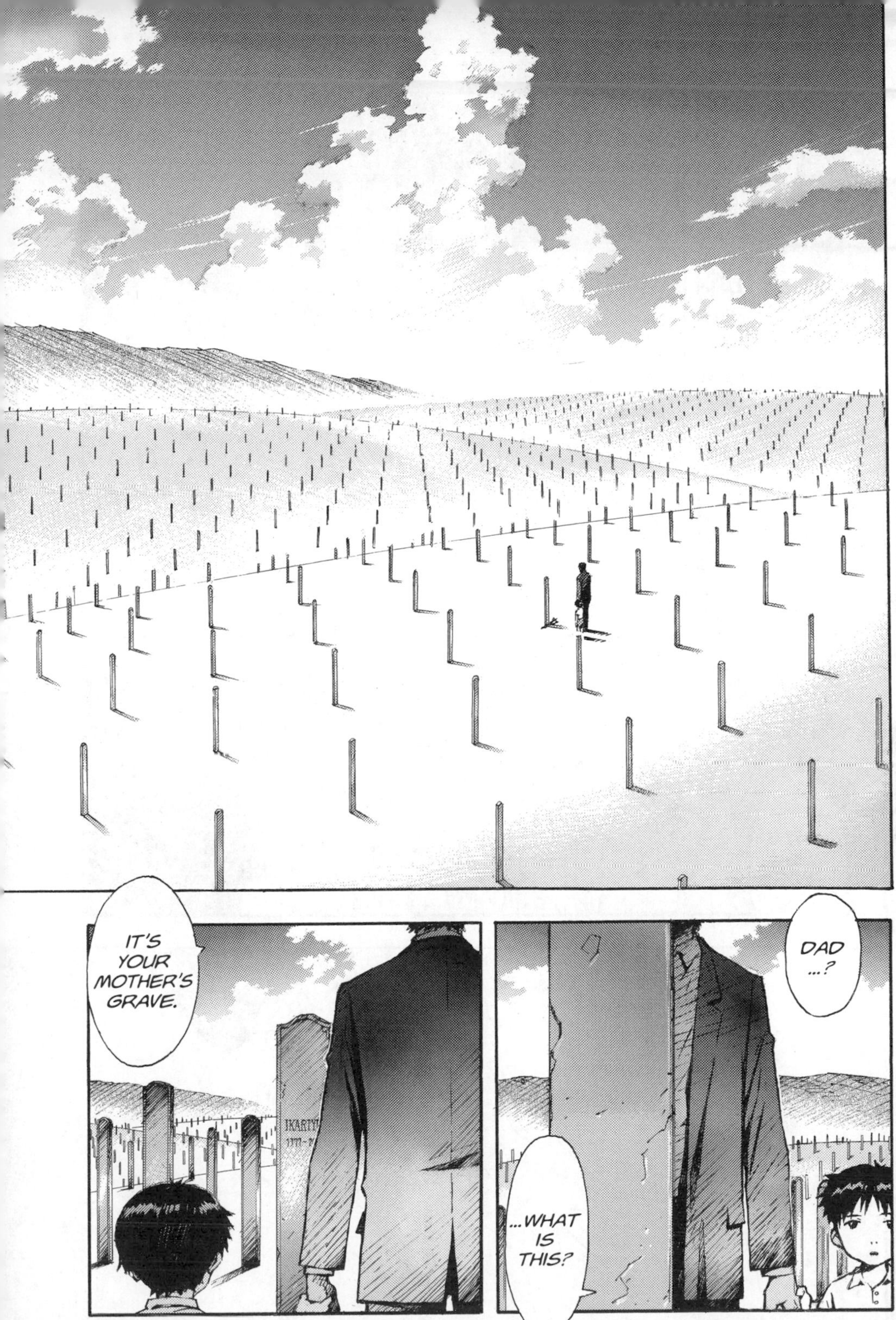
DAD ...?
...WHAT IS THIS?
IT'S YOUR MOTHER'S GRAVE.

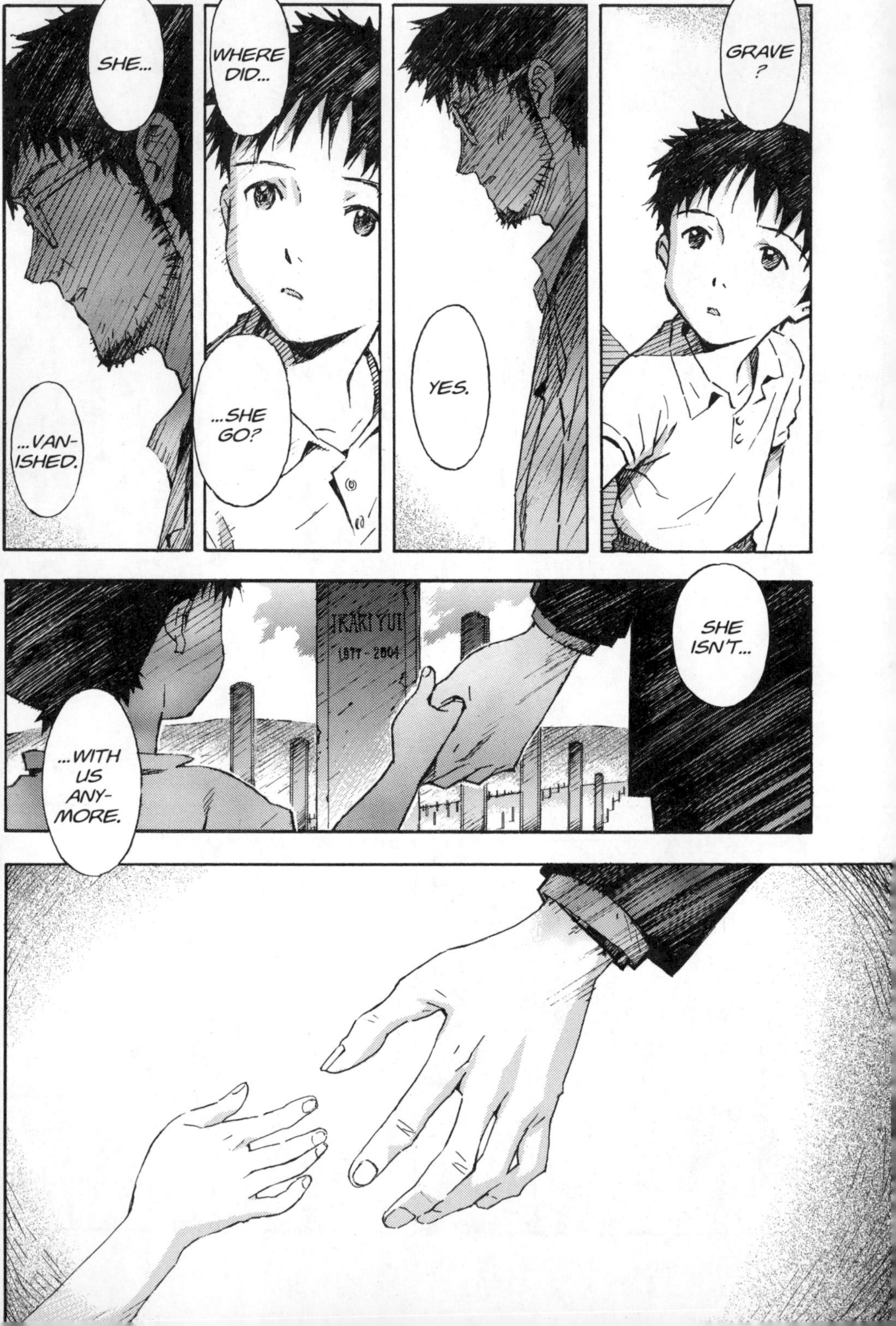
GRAVE ?
YES.
WHERE DID...
...SHE GO?
SHE...
...VAN-ISHED.
SHE ISN'T...
IKARI YUI
1977 - 2004
...WITH US ANYMORE.

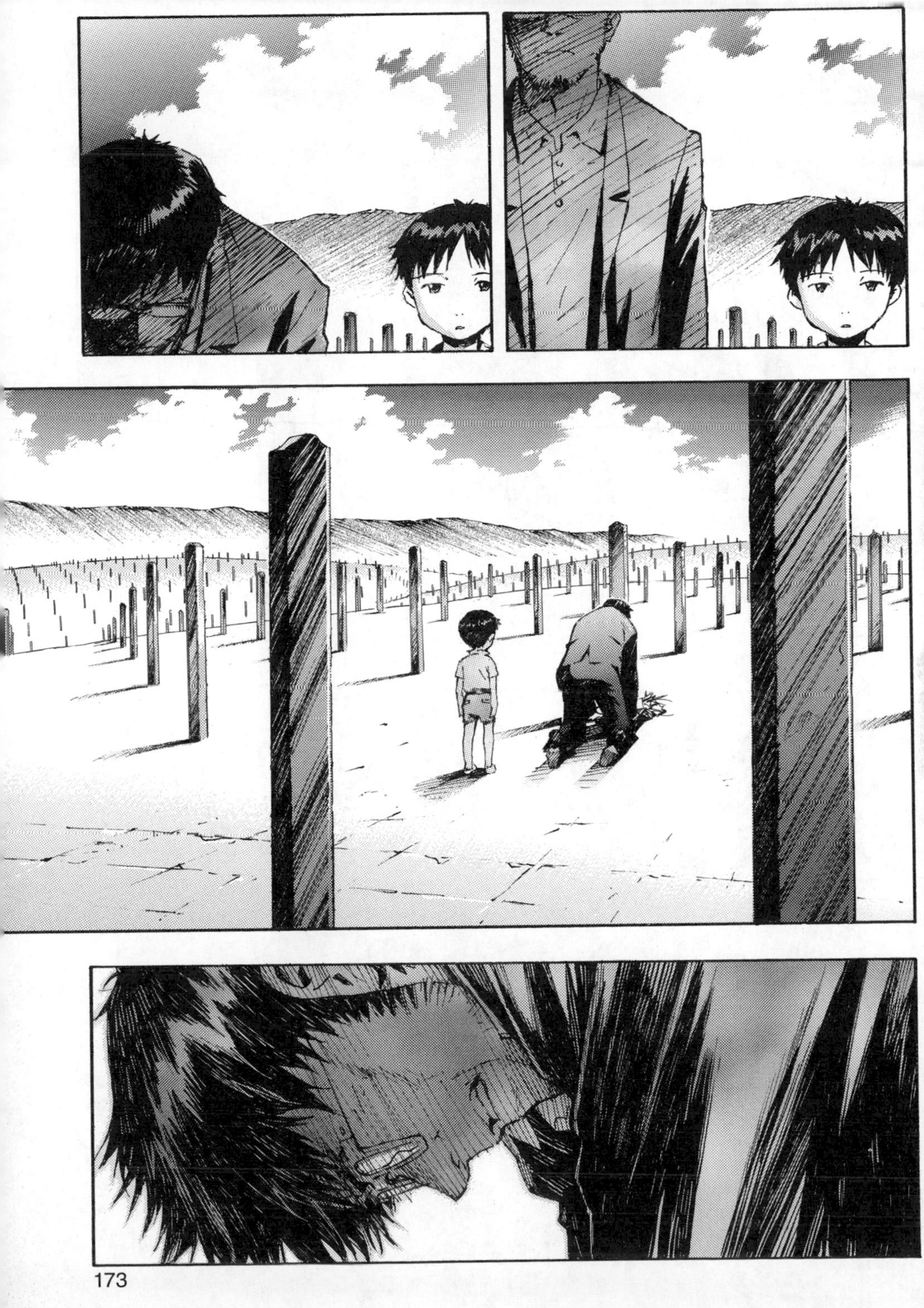

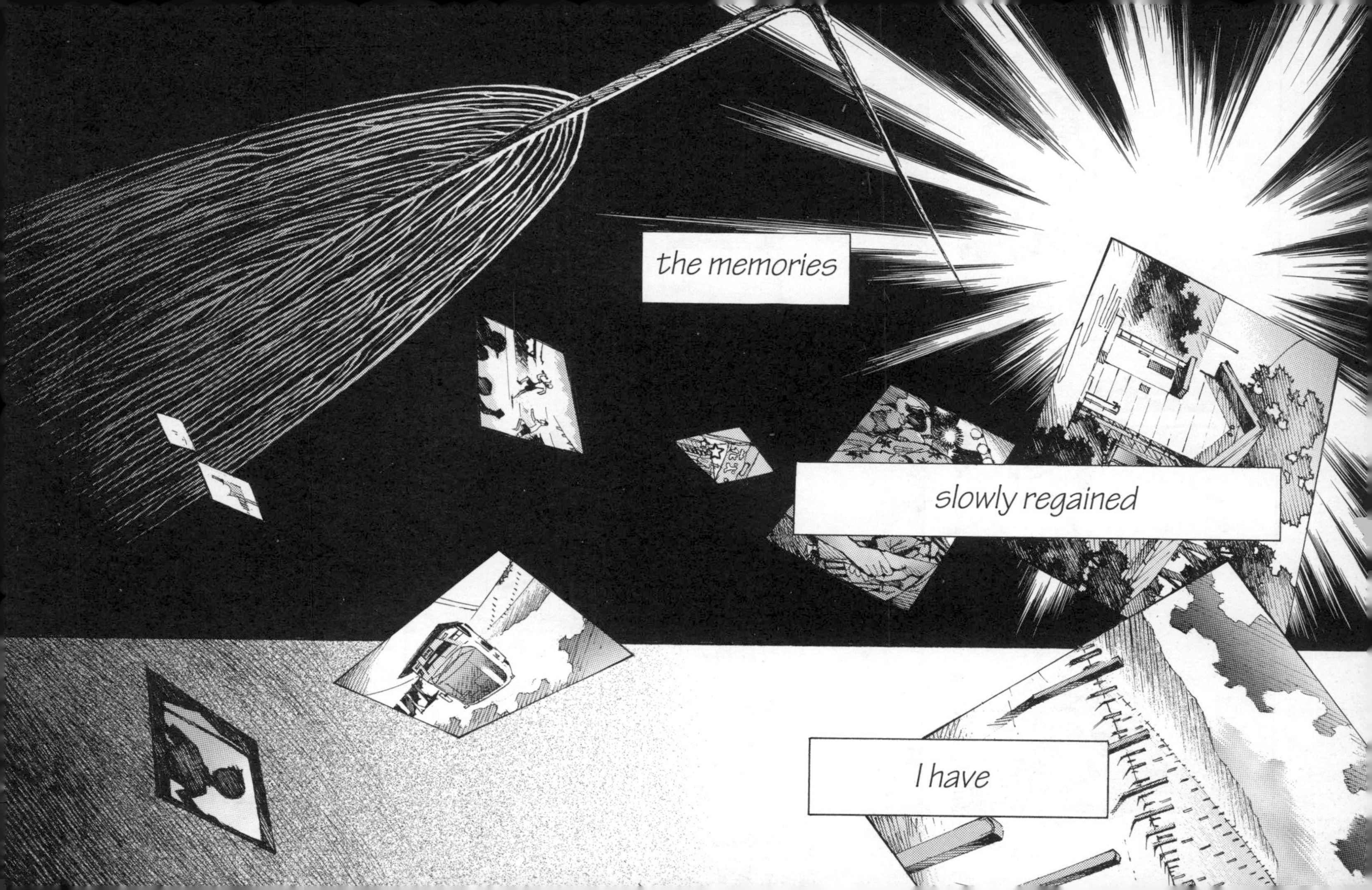
I have
slowly regained
the memories

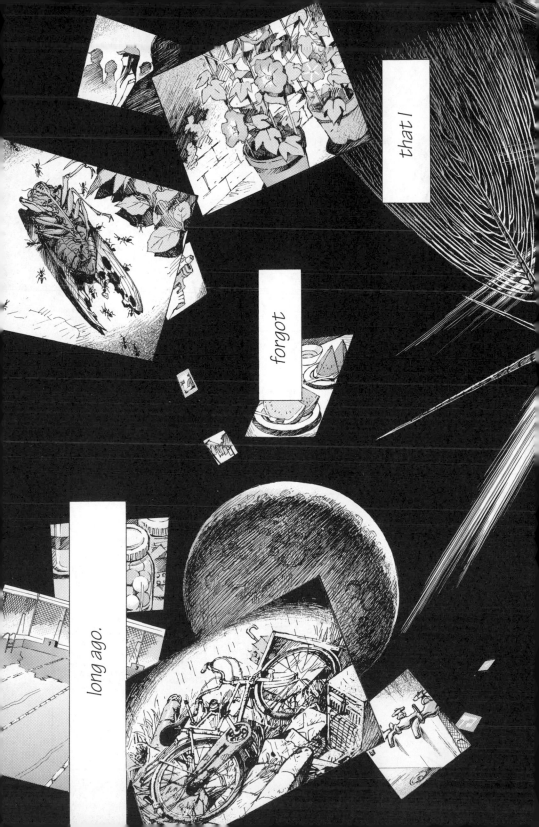

that I

forgot

long ago.

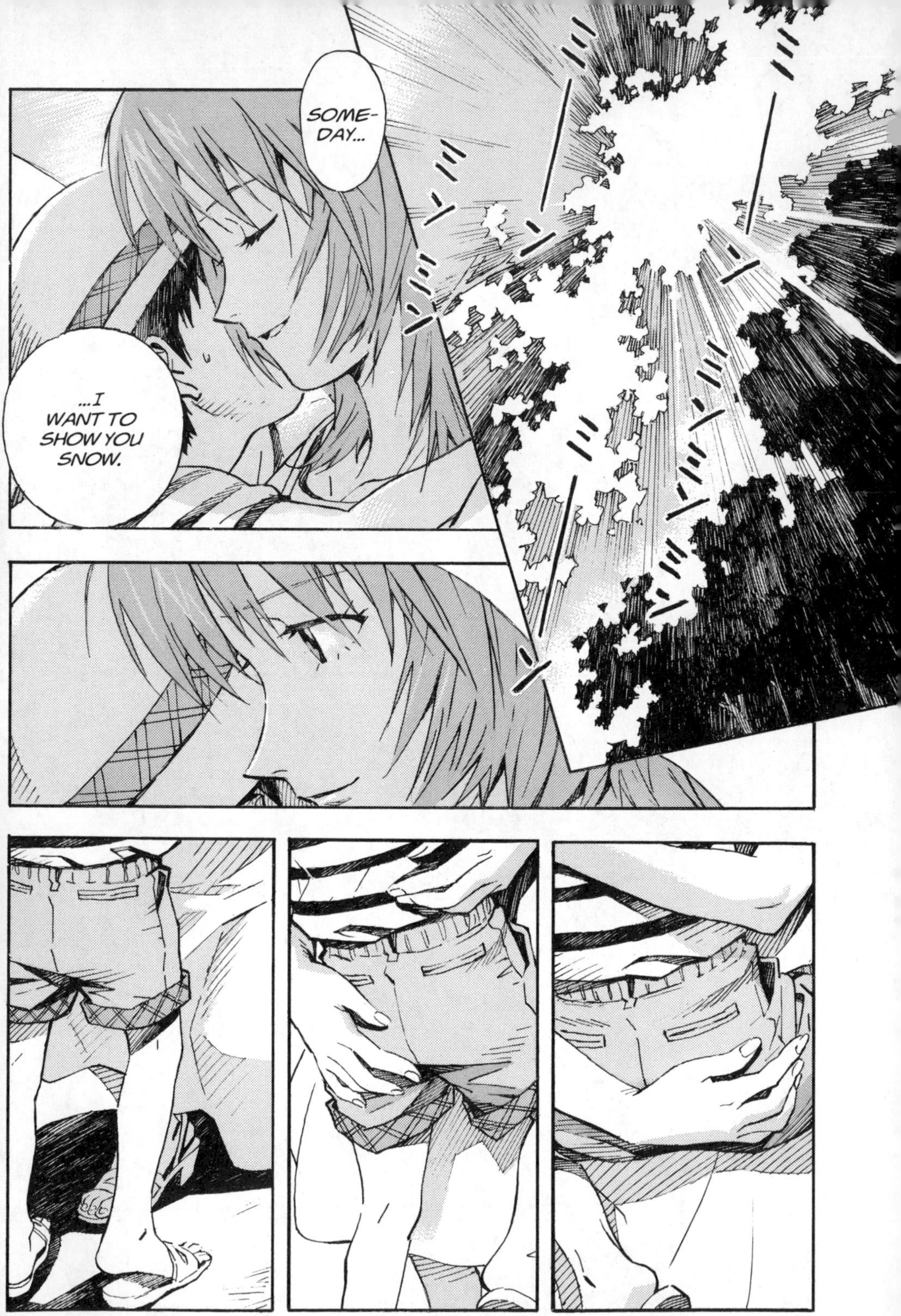
ミーンミンミンミー
ミーンミンミンミー
SOME-DAY...
...I WANT TO SHOW YOU SNOW.

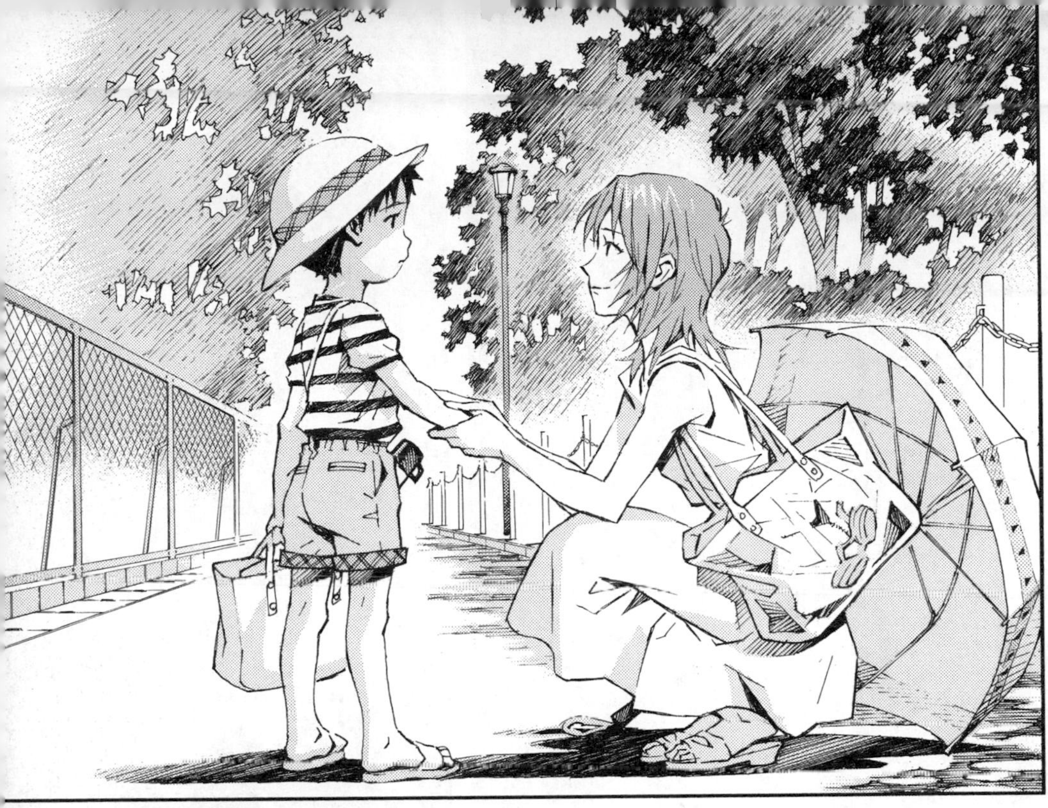
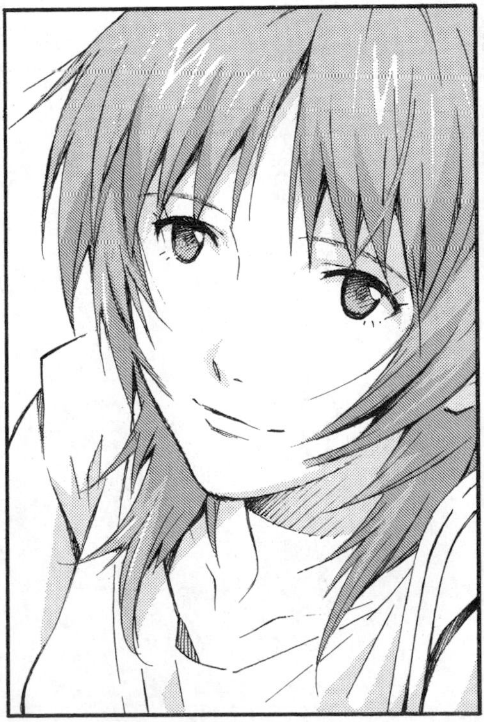
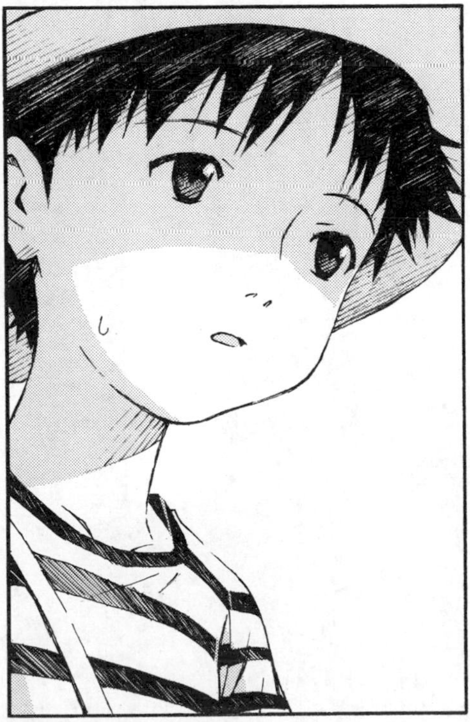

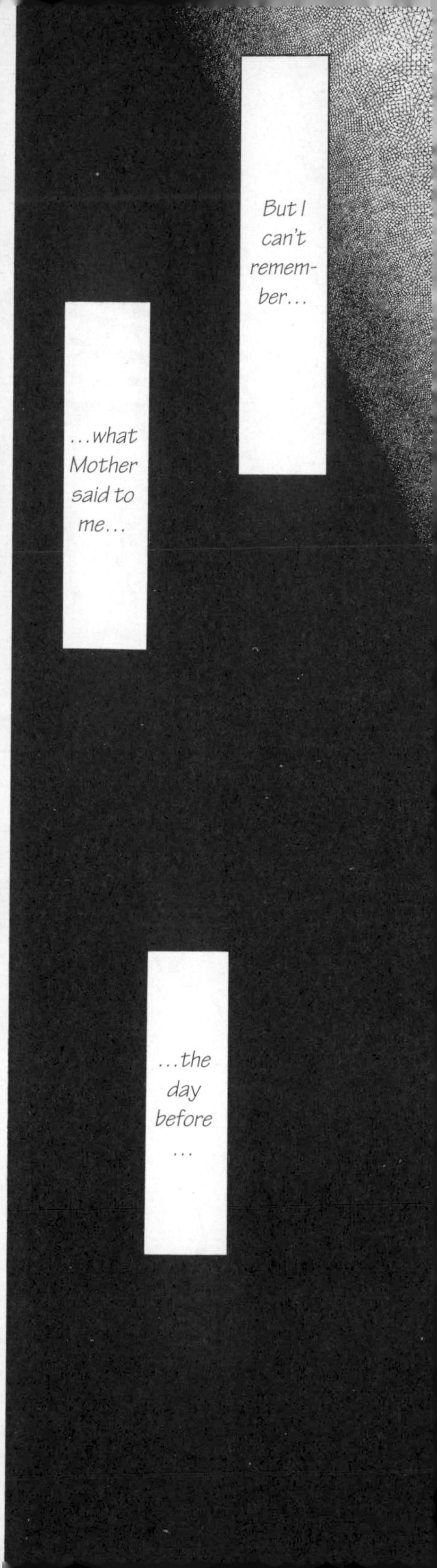
But I can't remem-ber...
...what Mother said to me...
...the day before...
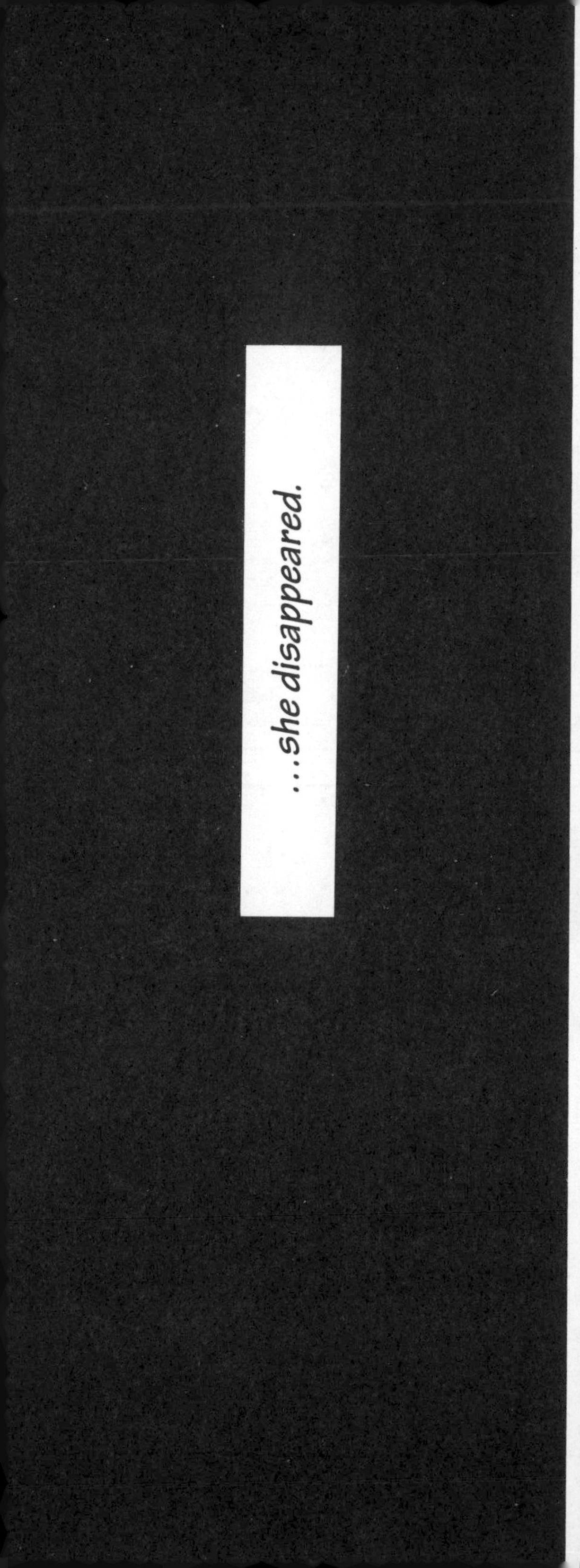
...she disappeared.

YOSHIYUKI SADAMOTO

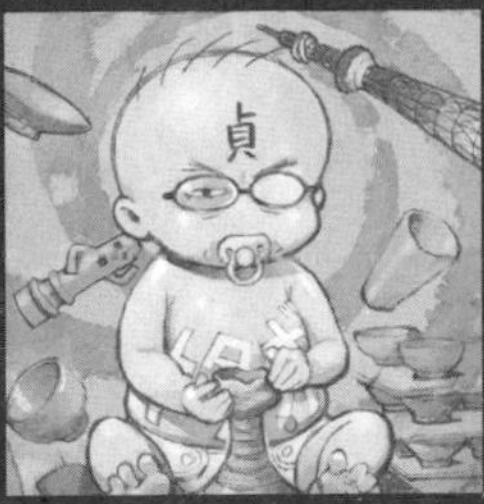
貞
LAX

WRITER AND ARTIST

I'm finally 50. My joints feel numb, my eyesight is going and I need to pee a lot. But to my surprise I also realize that in spirit, I haven't aged a bit. Waaah! So, I'm going to proceed with a fresh outlook on life, just like a baby. Life, like manga, just keeps on going. Onward to volume 14!

NERV

GOD'S IN HIS HEAVEN. ALL'S RIGHT WITH THE WORLD.

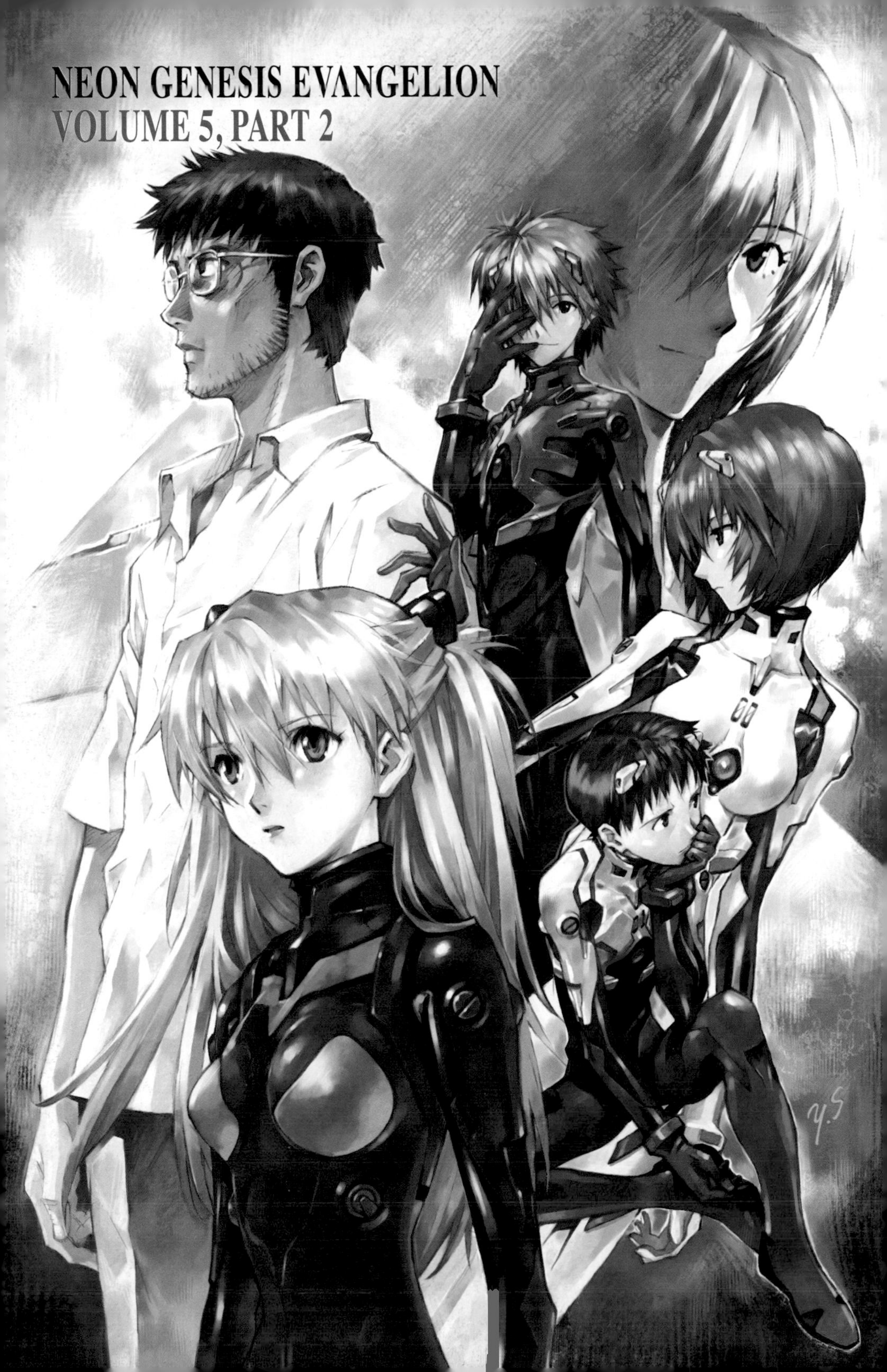
NEON GENESIS EVANGELION
VOLUME 5, PART 2

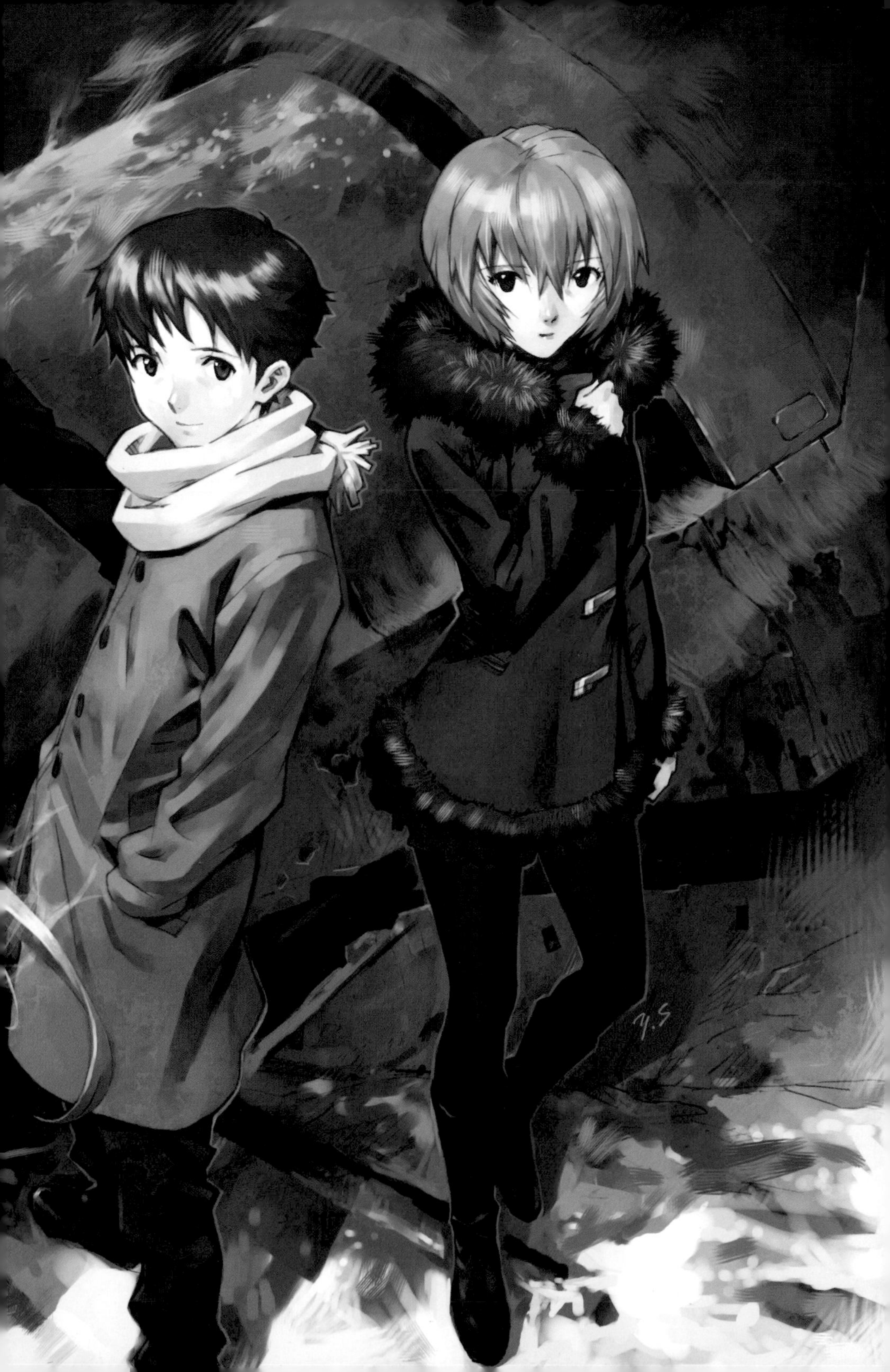

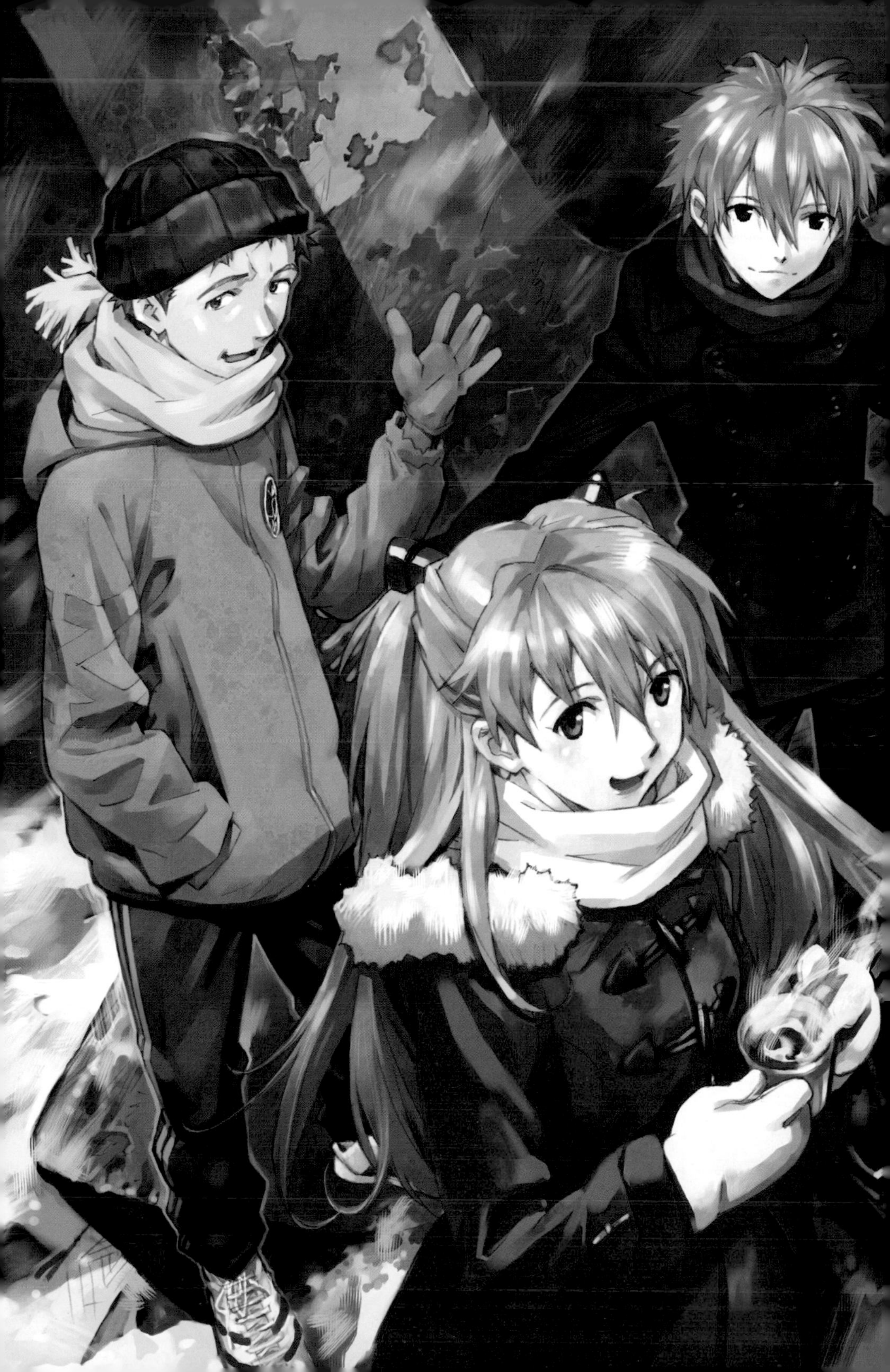

CONTENTS

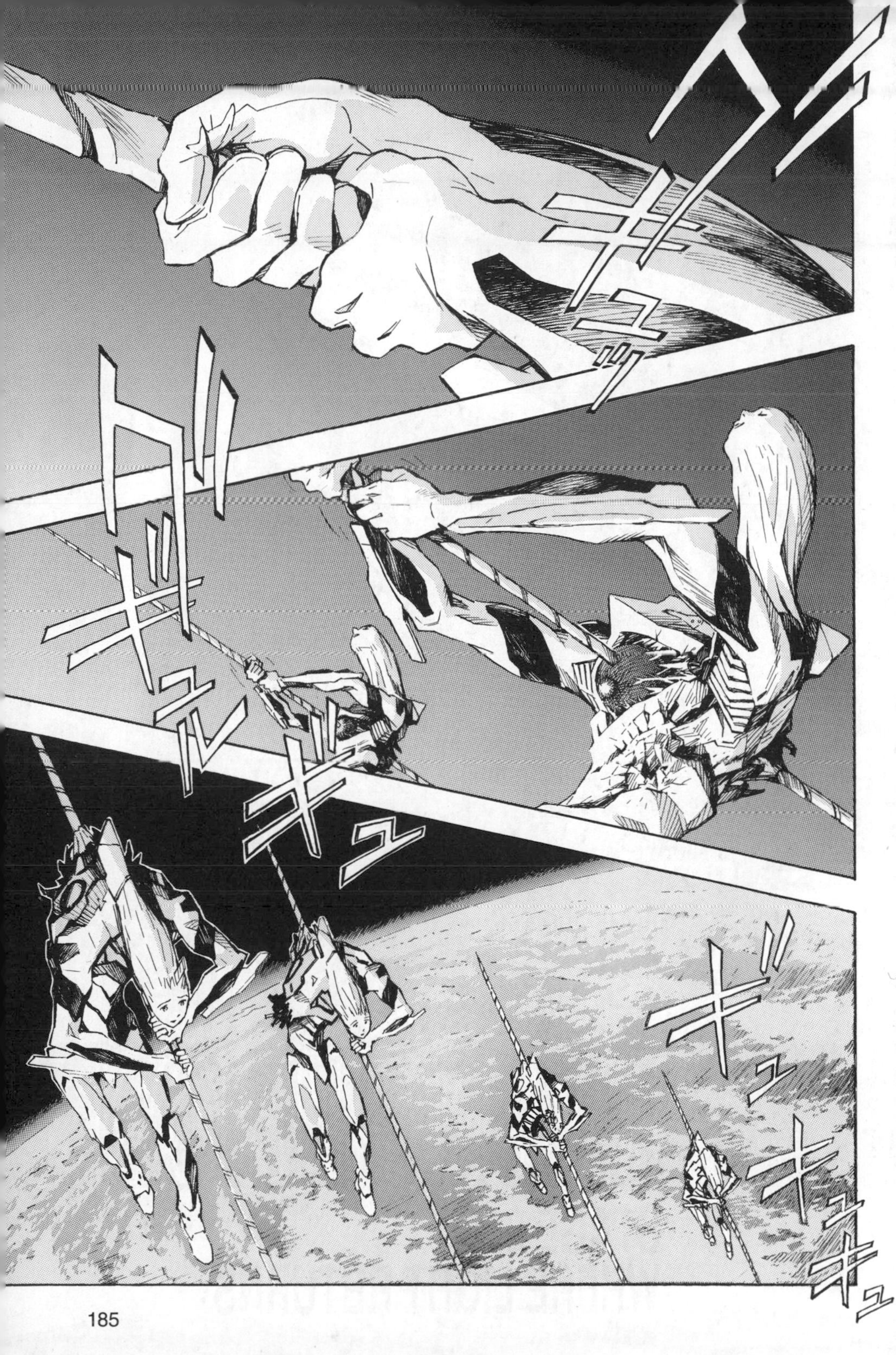
グギュッ
グギュル
ギュ
ギュキュキュ

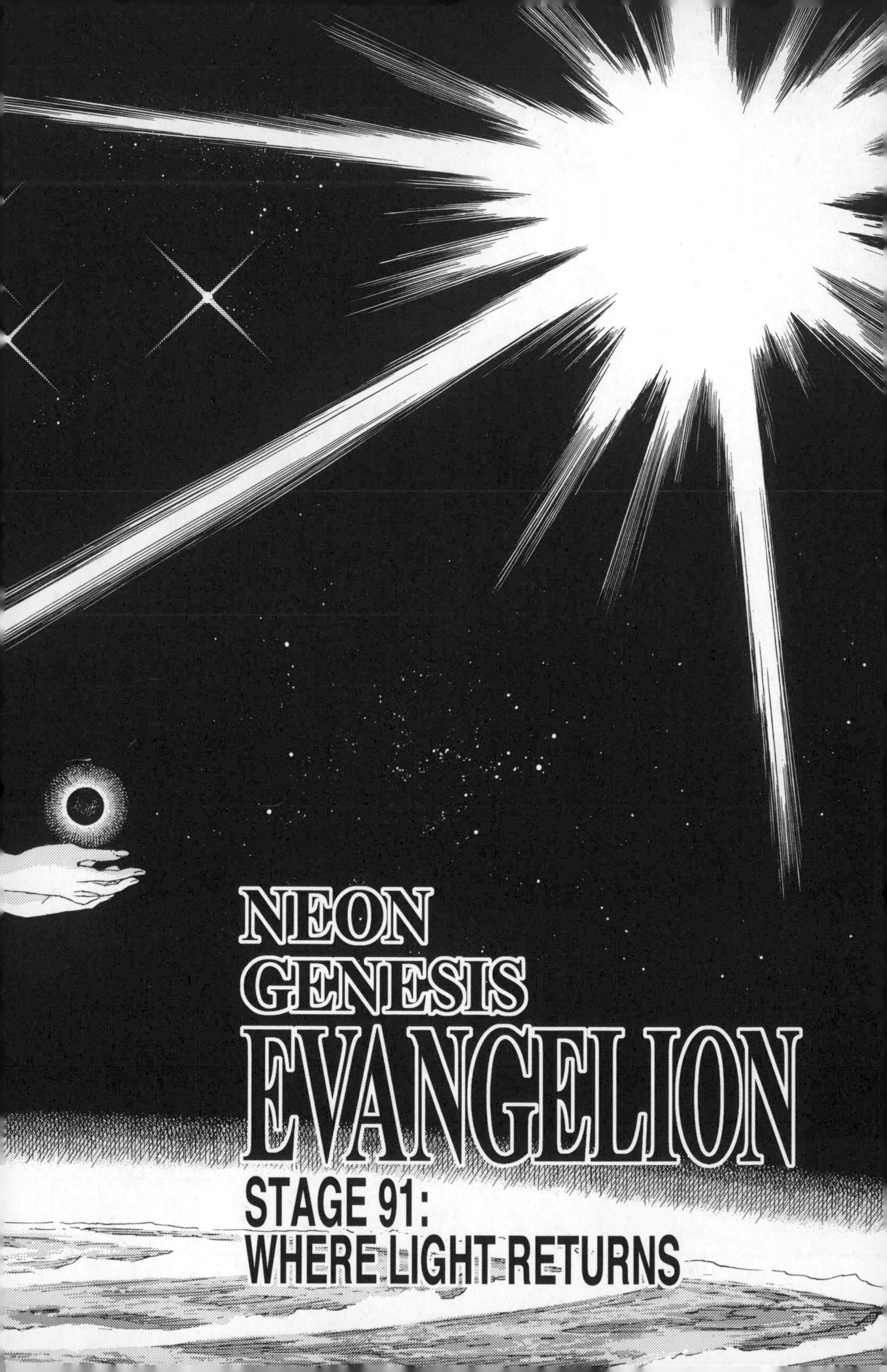
NEON GENESIS EVANGELION
STAGE 91:
WHERE LIGHT RETURNS

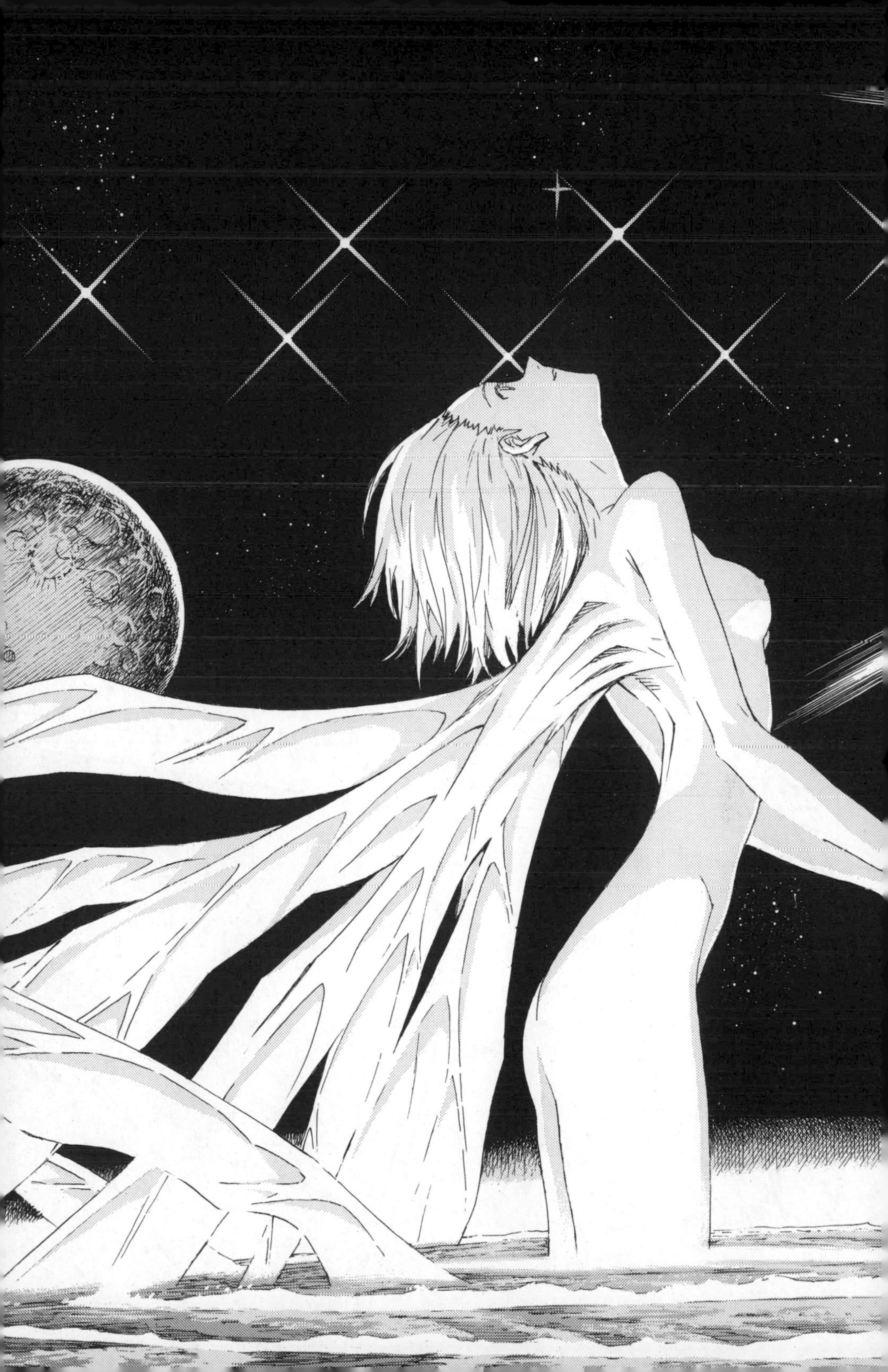

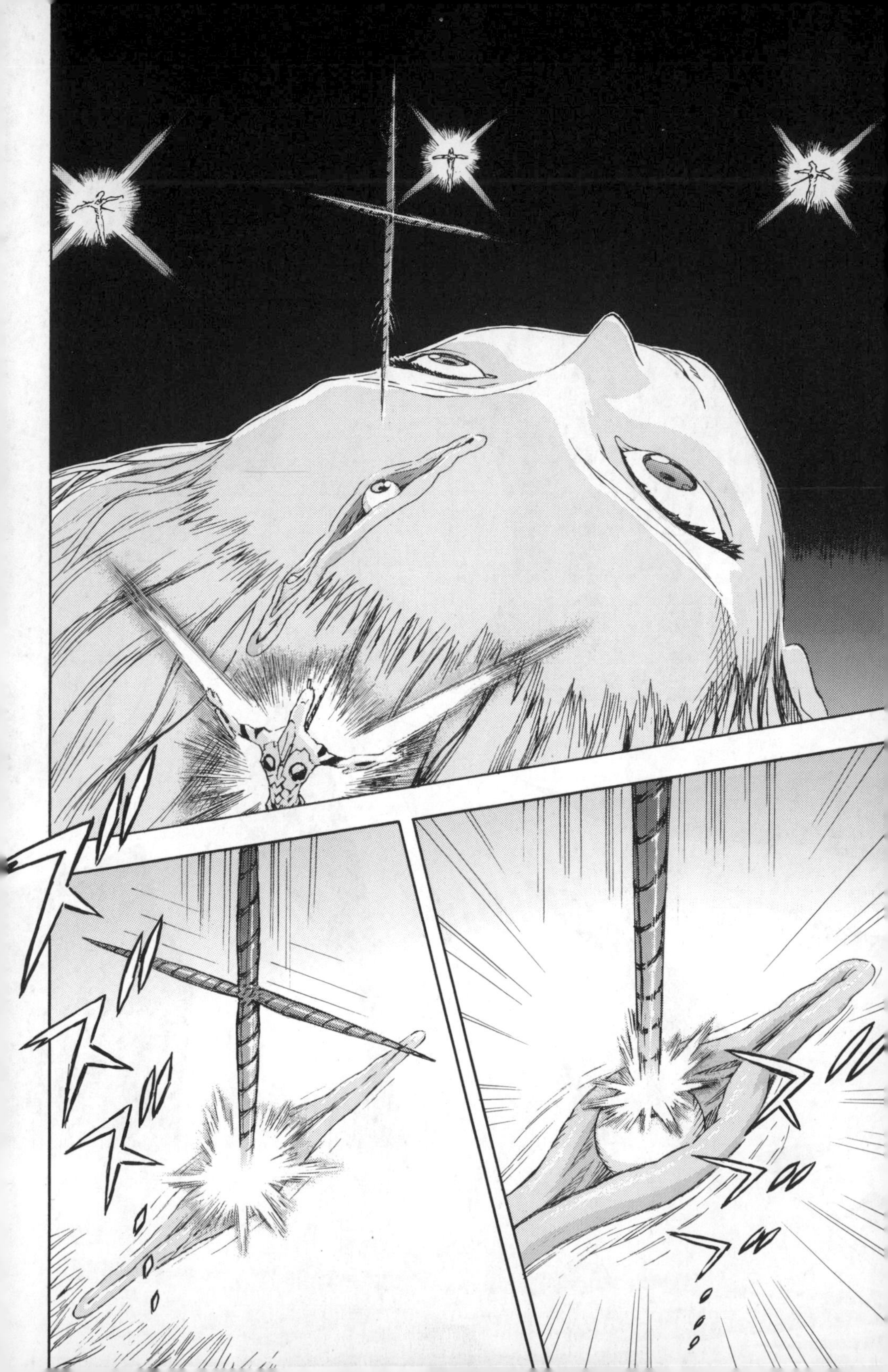
ズズズ…
ズズズズ…

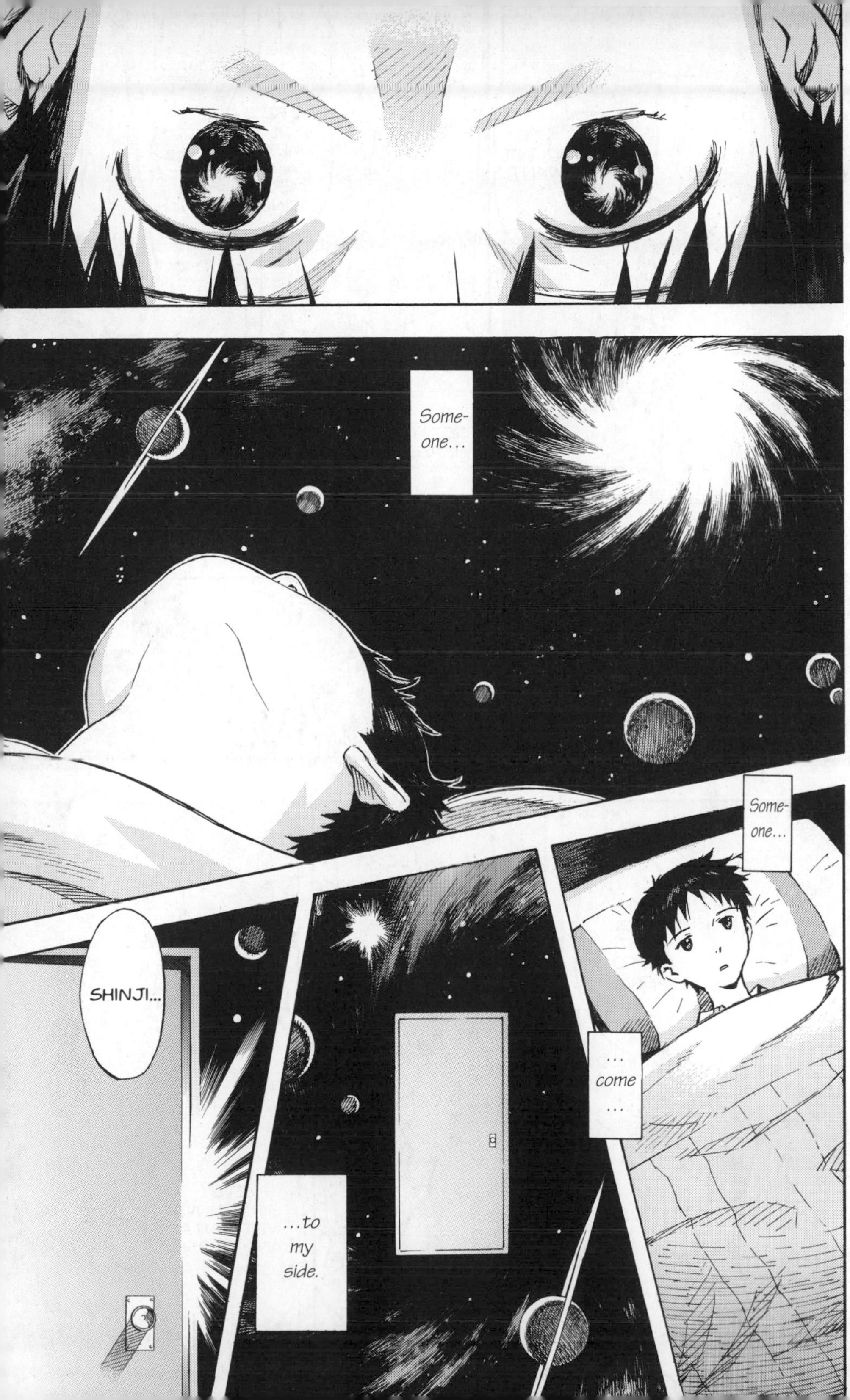
Some-one…
Some-one…
…come…
…to my side.
SHINJI…

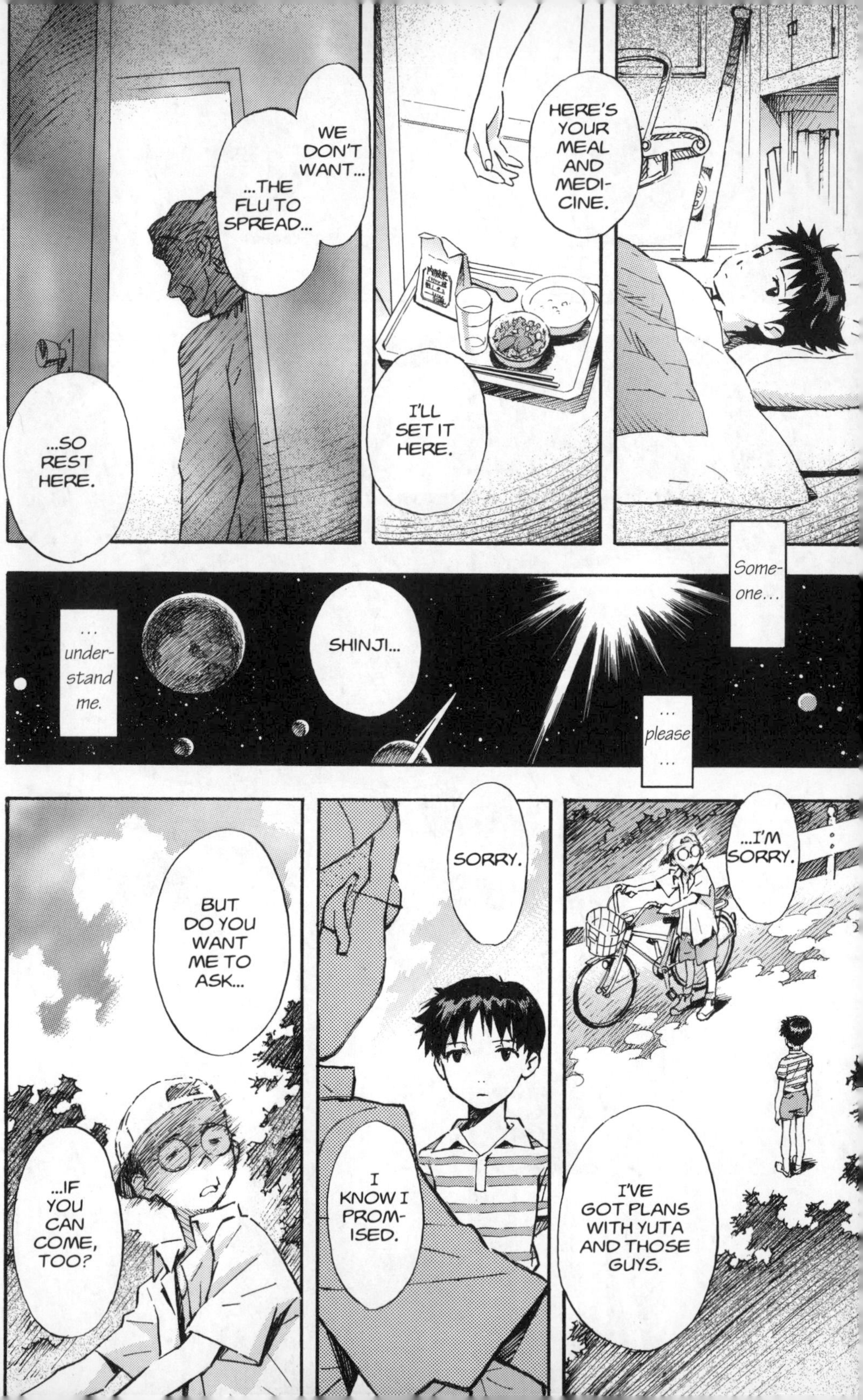
HERE'S YOUR MEAL AND MEDICINE.
I'LL SET IT HERE.
WE DON'T WANT...
...THE FLU TO SPREAD...
...SO REST HERE.
Some-one…
… please …
SHINJI...
… understand me.
...I'M SORRY.
I'VE GOT PLANS WITH YUTA AND THOSE GUYS.
SORRY.
I KNOW I PROMISED.
BUT DO YOU WANT ME TO ASK...
...IF YOU CAN COME, TOO?

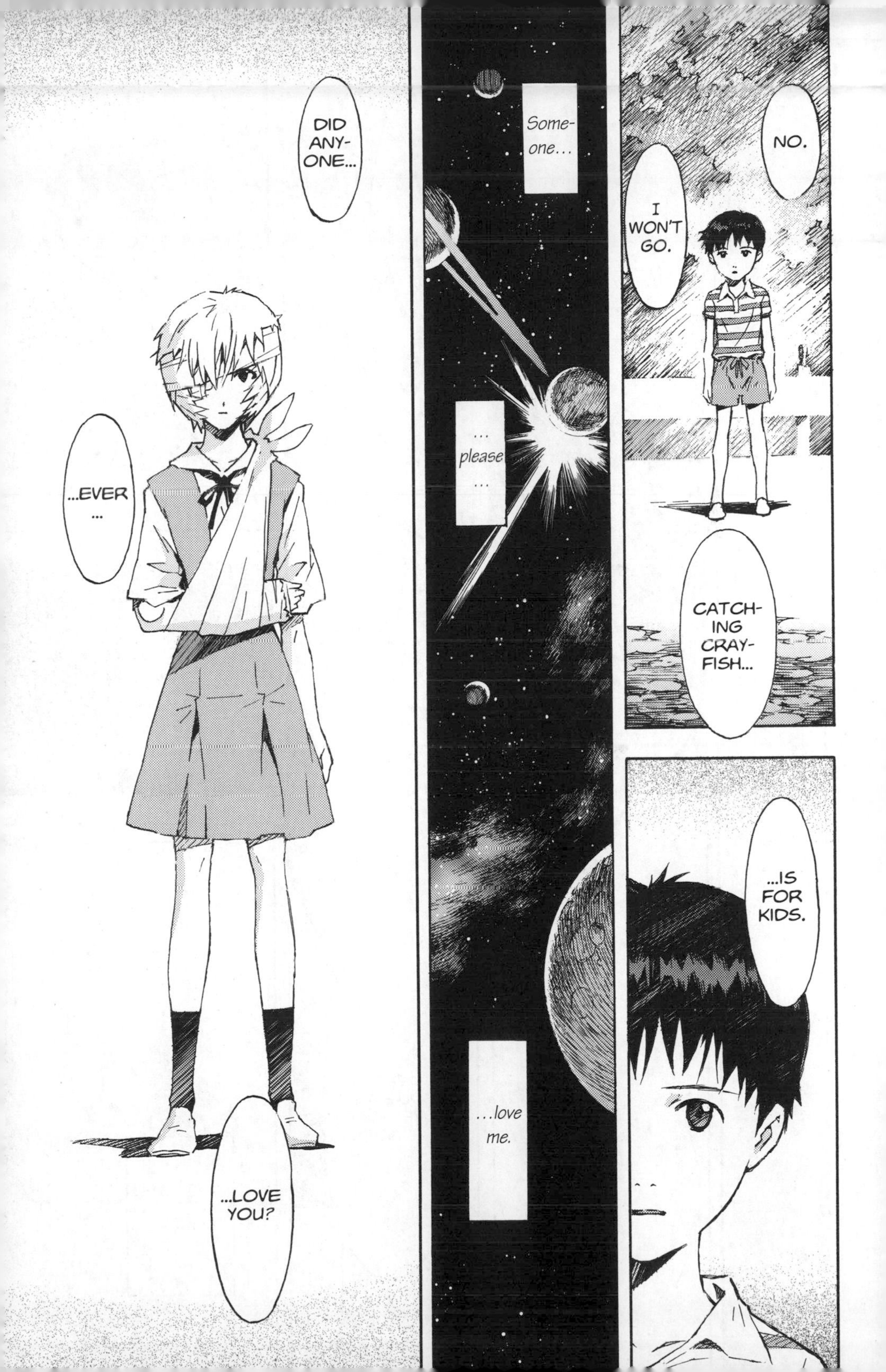
NO.
I WON'T GO.
CATCHING CRAYFISH...
...IS FOR KIDS.
Someone...
...please...
...love me.
DID ANYONE...
...EVER...
...LOVE YOU?

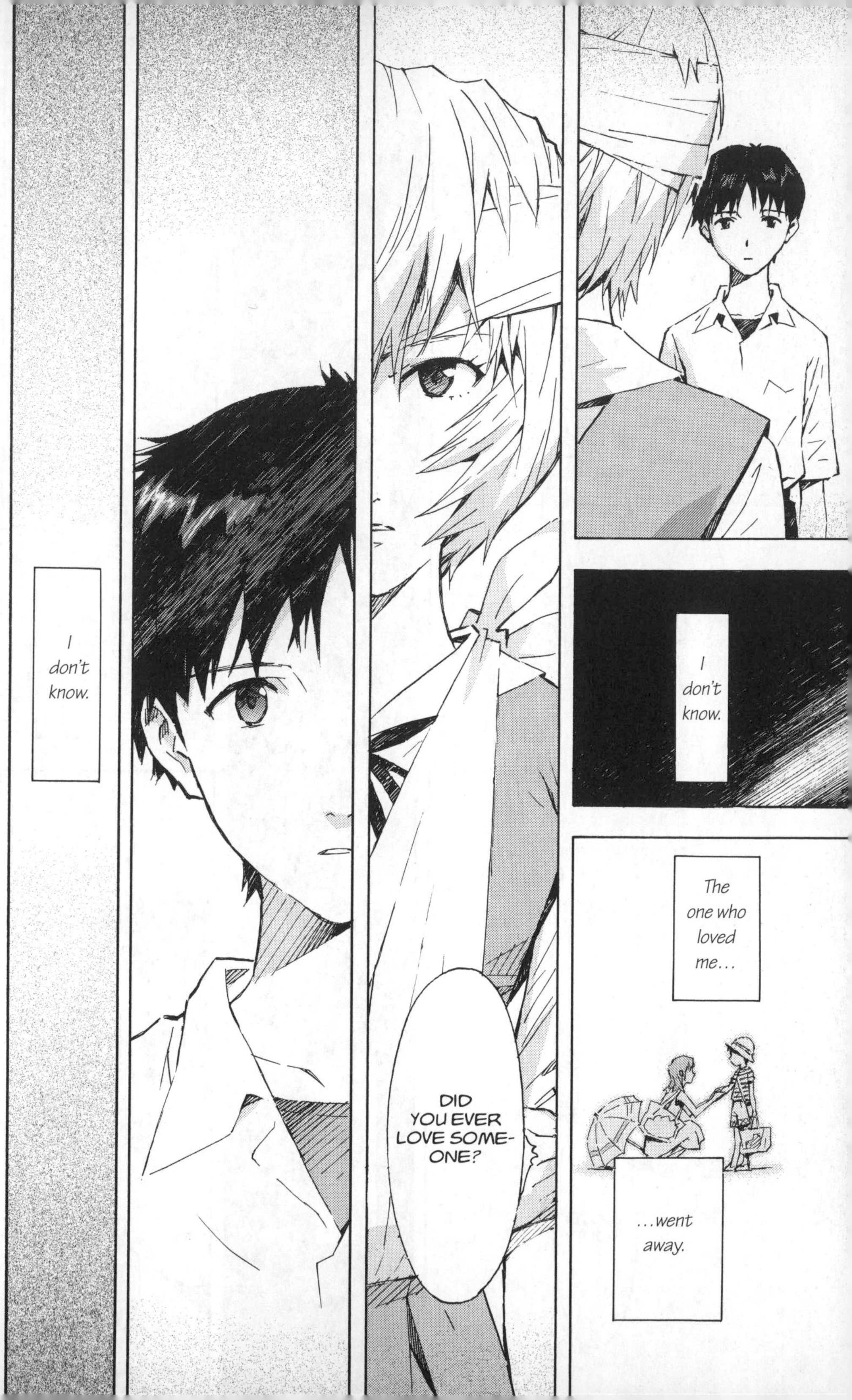
I don't know.
The one who loved me...
...went away.
DID YOU EVER LOVE SOME-ONE?
I don't know.

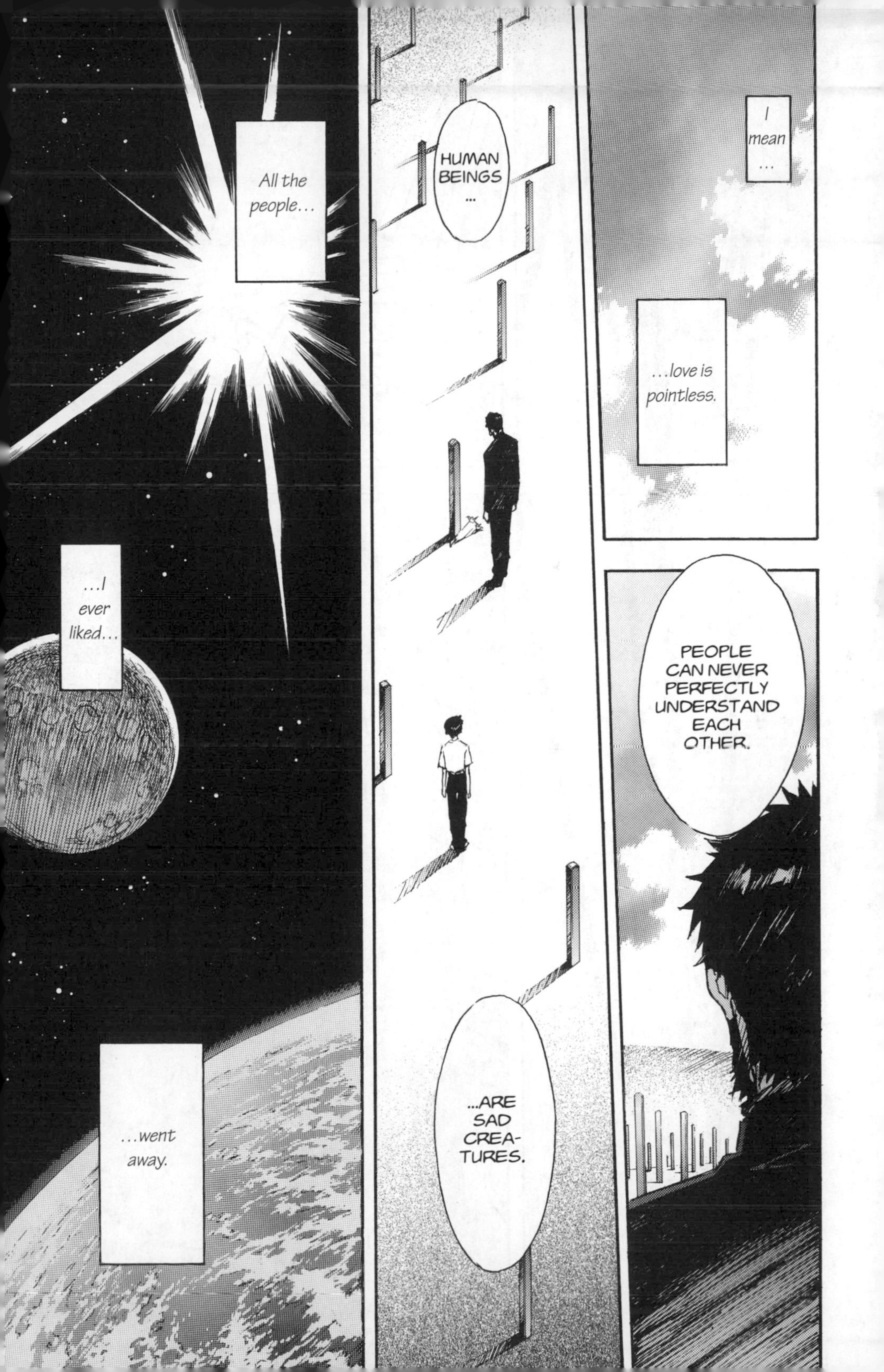
All the people…
…I ever liked…
…went away.
HUMAN BEINGS …
...ARE SAD CREATURES.
I mean …
…love is pointless.
PEOPLE CAN NEVER PERFECTLY UNDERSTAND EACH OTHER.

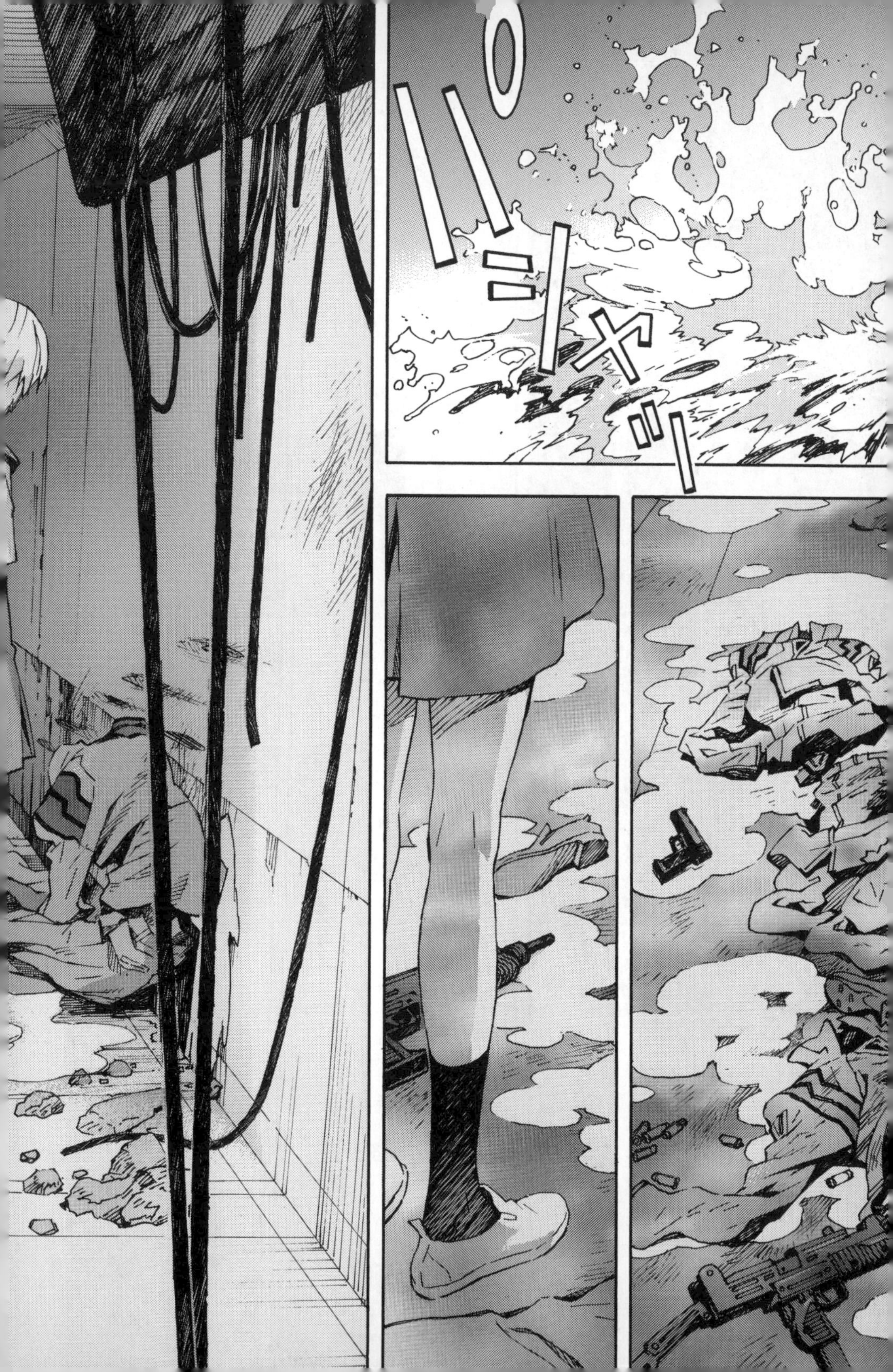

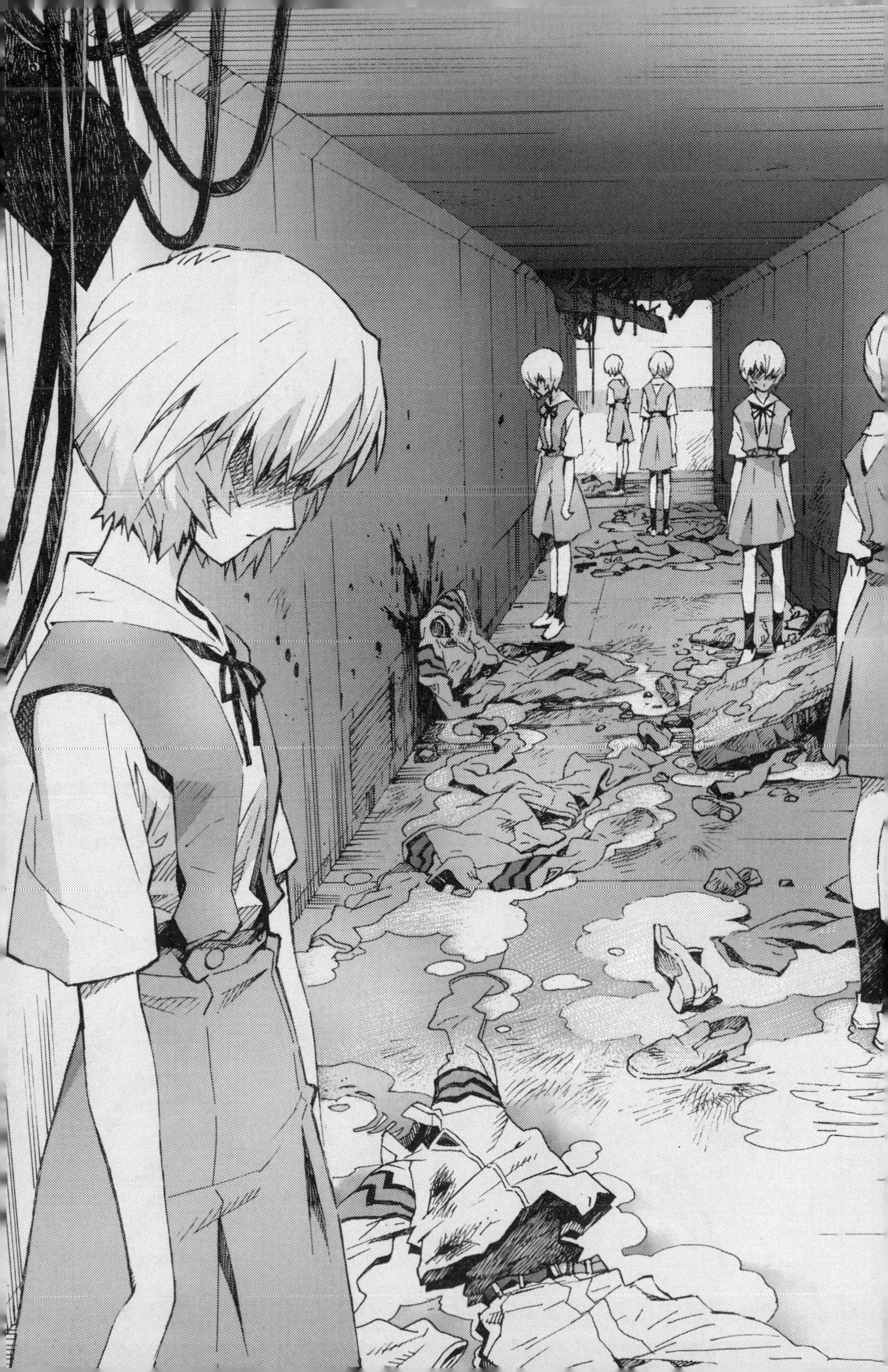

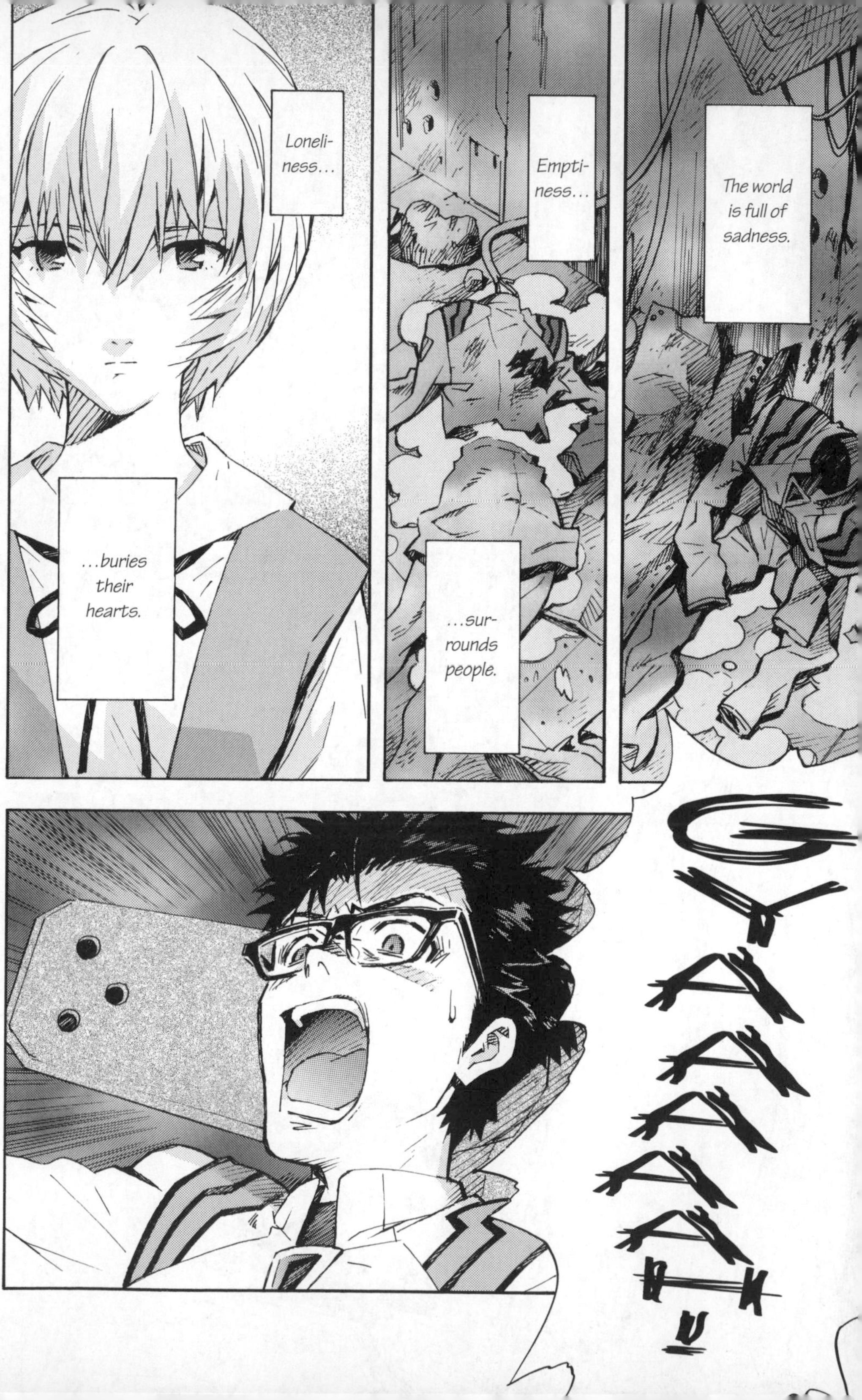
The world is full of sadness.
Emptiness…
…surrounds people.
Loneliness…
…buries their hearts.
GYAAAAAH!

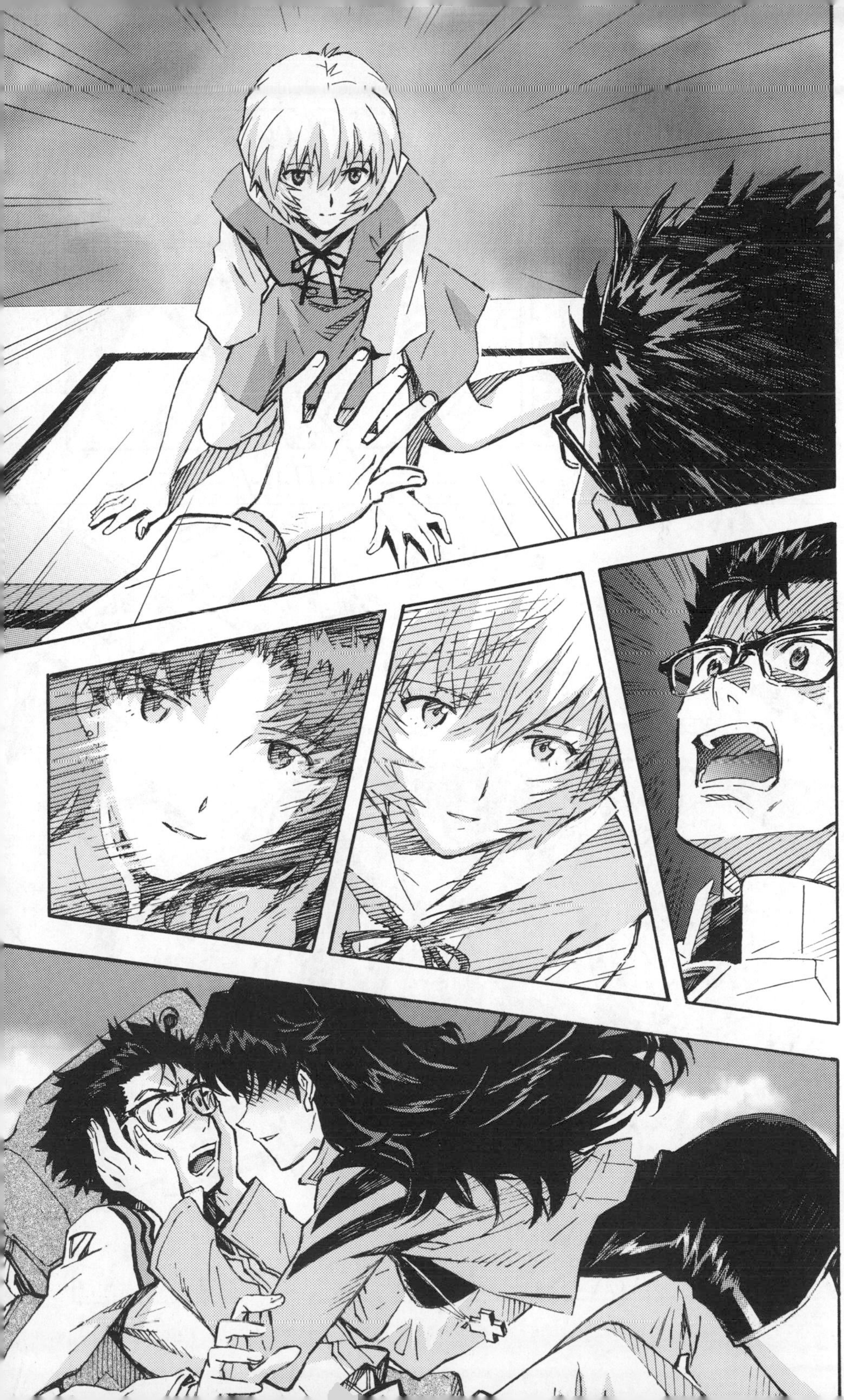

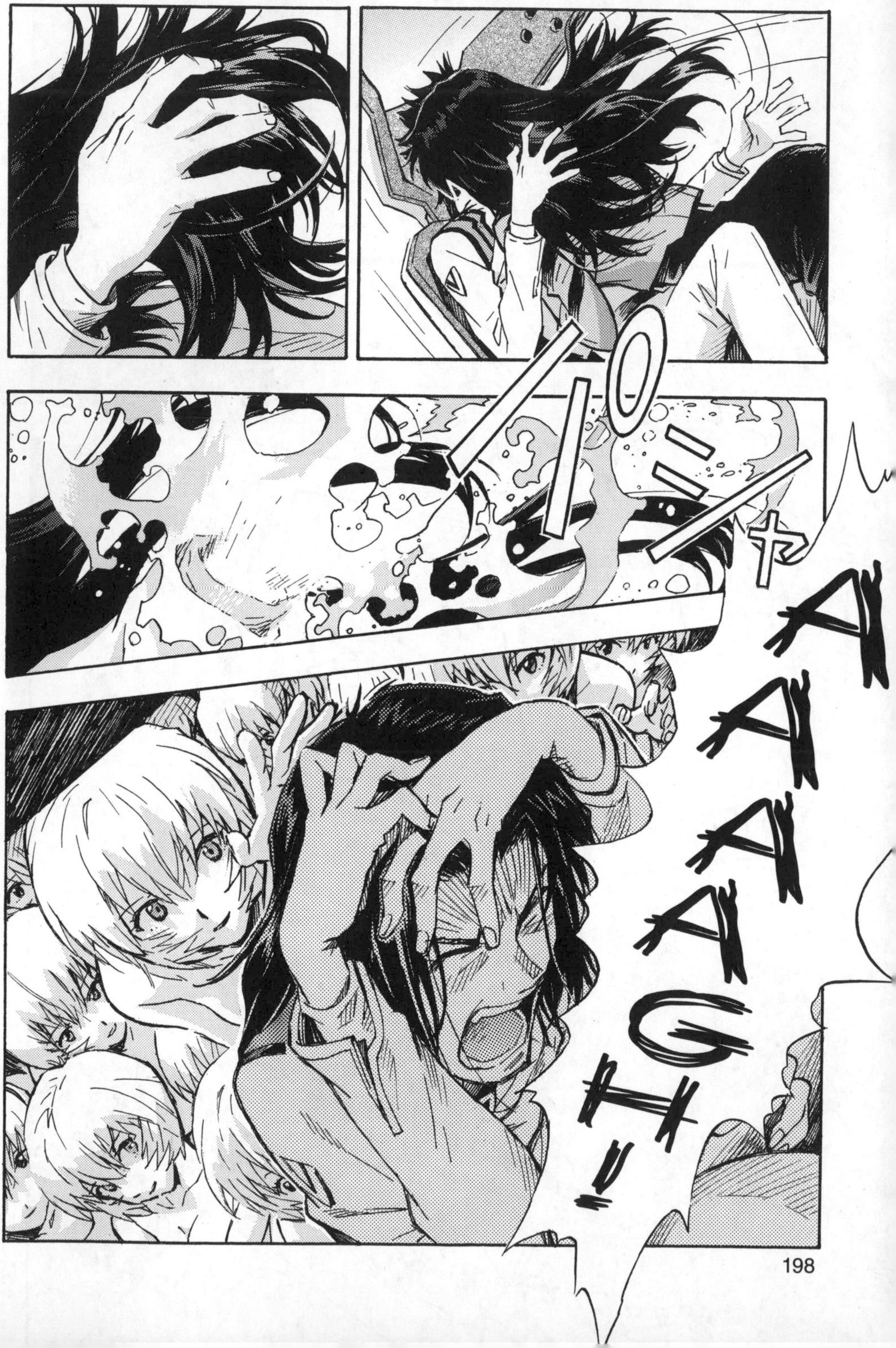
AAAAGH!!

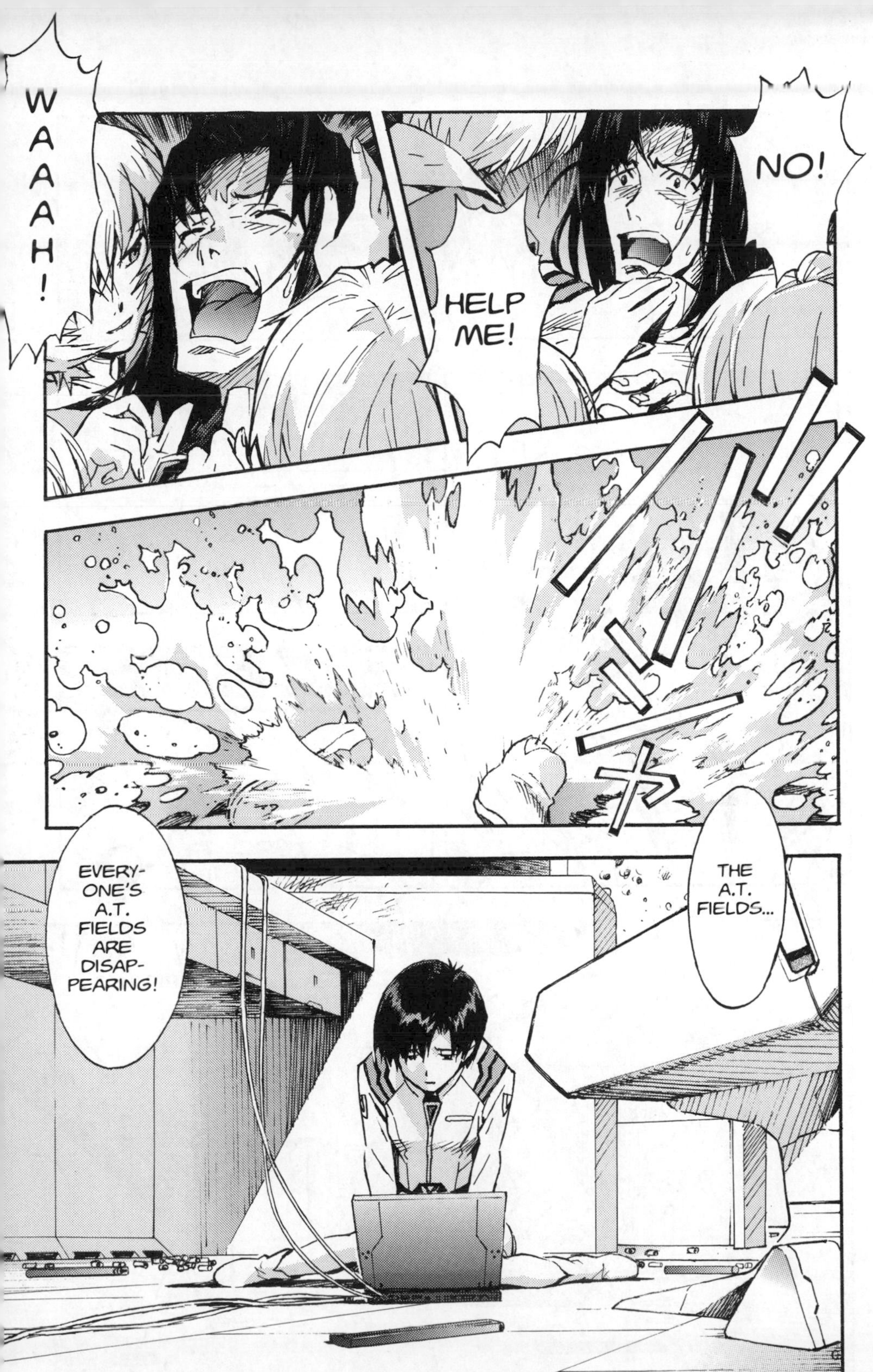
NO!
HELP ME!
WAAAAH!
THE A.T. FIELDS...
EVERYONE'S A.T. FIELDS ARE DISAPPEARING!

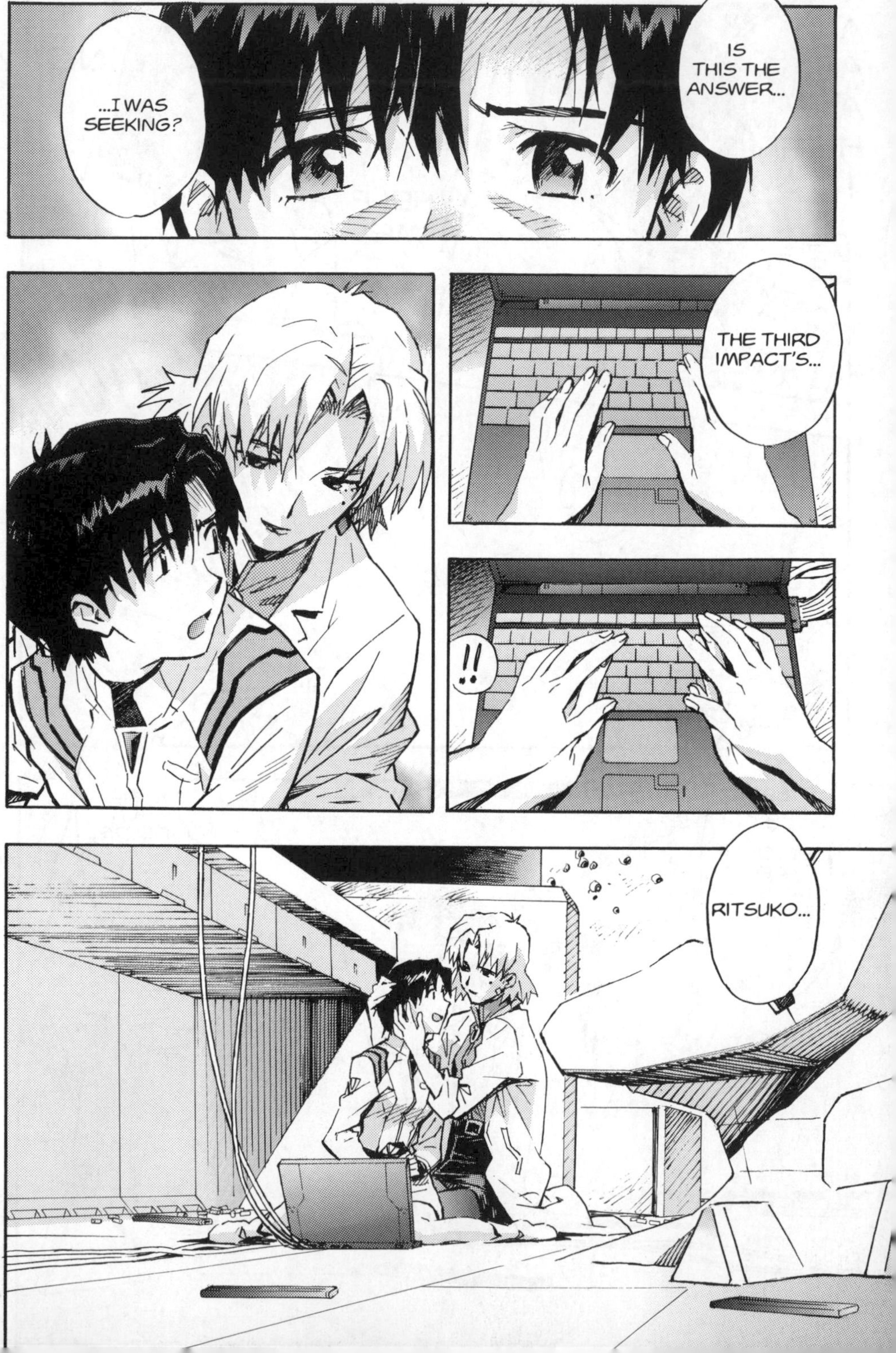
IS THIS THE ANSWER...
...I WAS SEEKING?
THE THIRD IMPACT'S...
!!
RITSUKO...

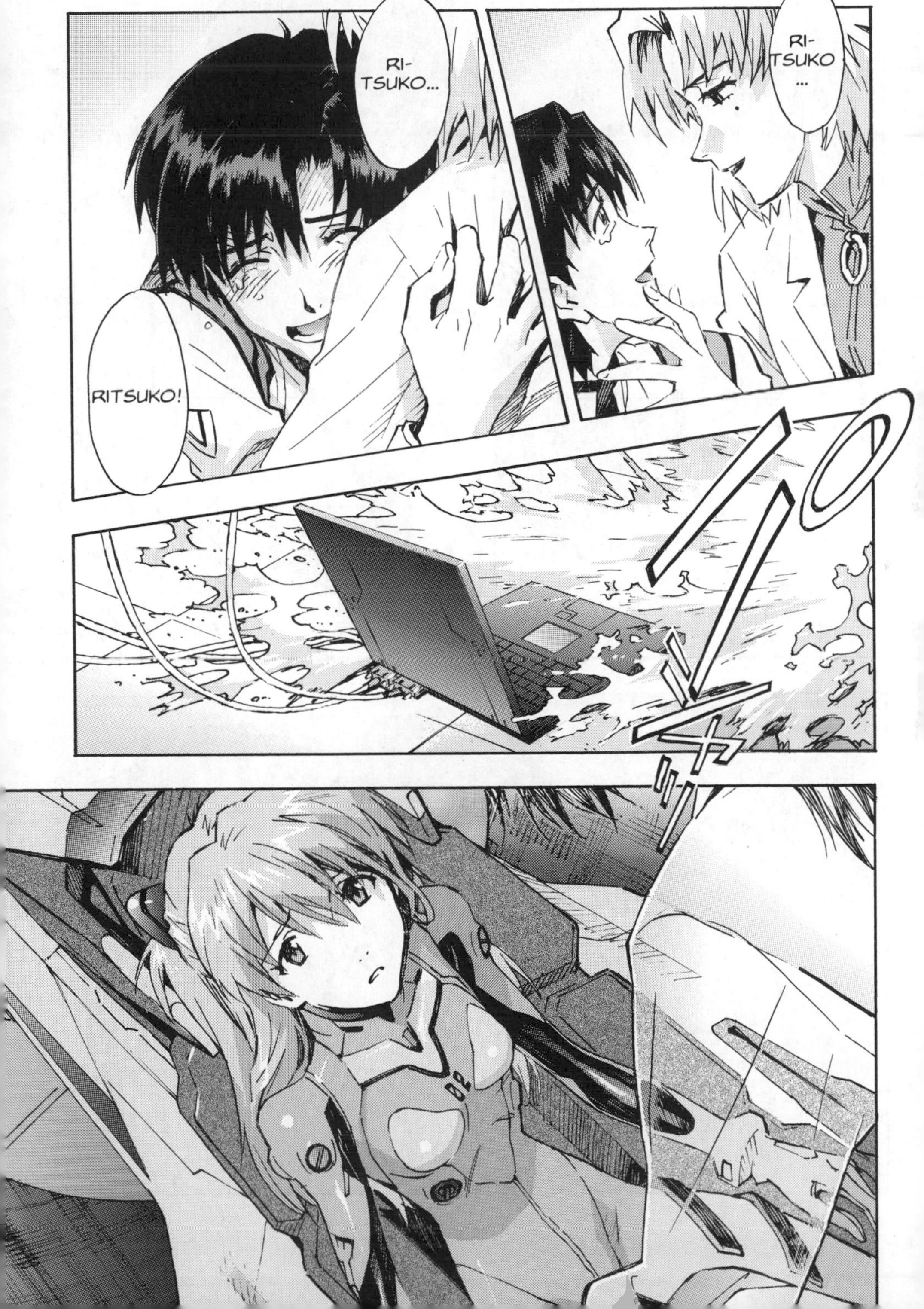
RI-
TSUKO
...
RI-
TSUKO...
RITSUKO!

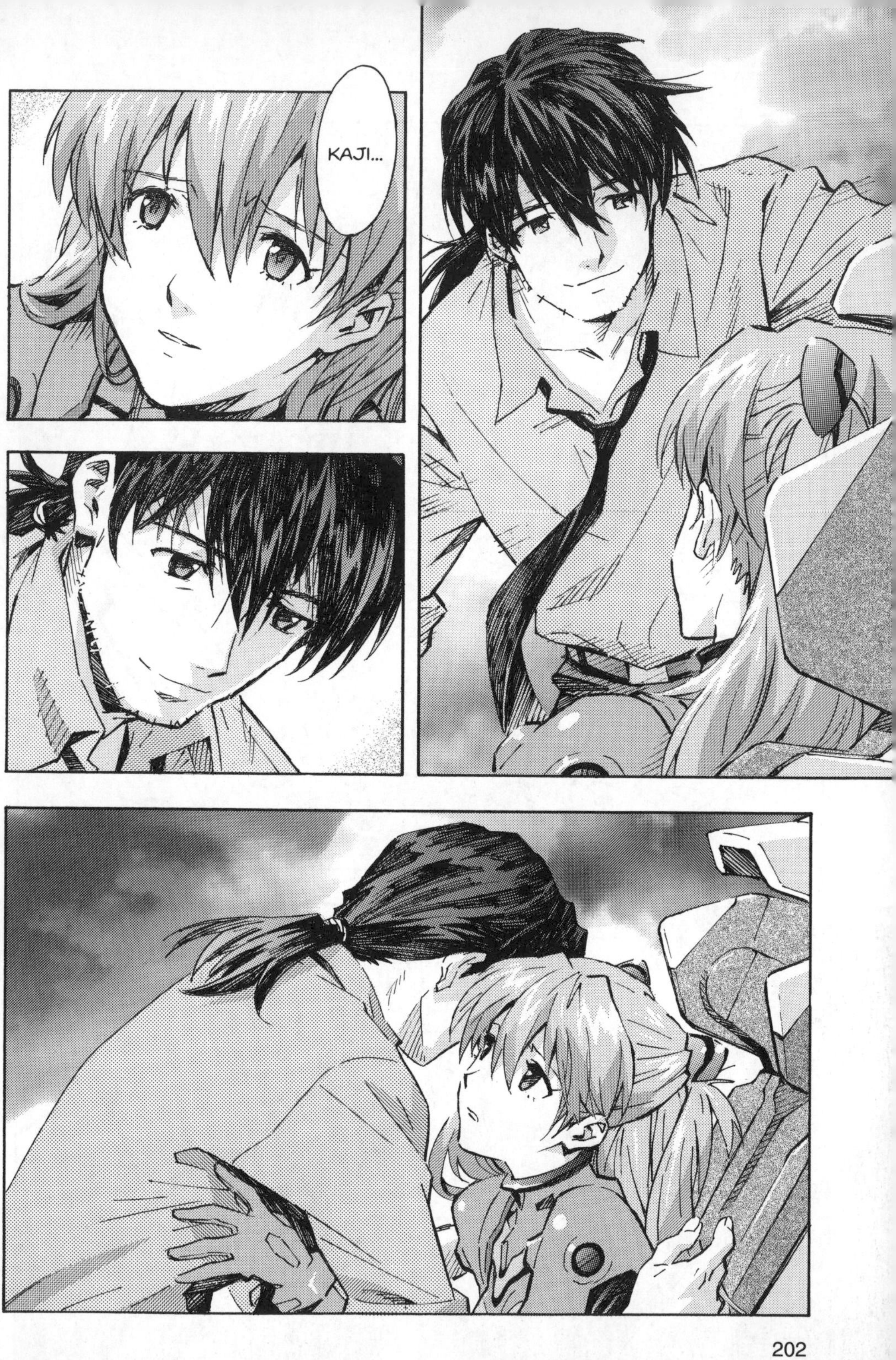
KAJI...

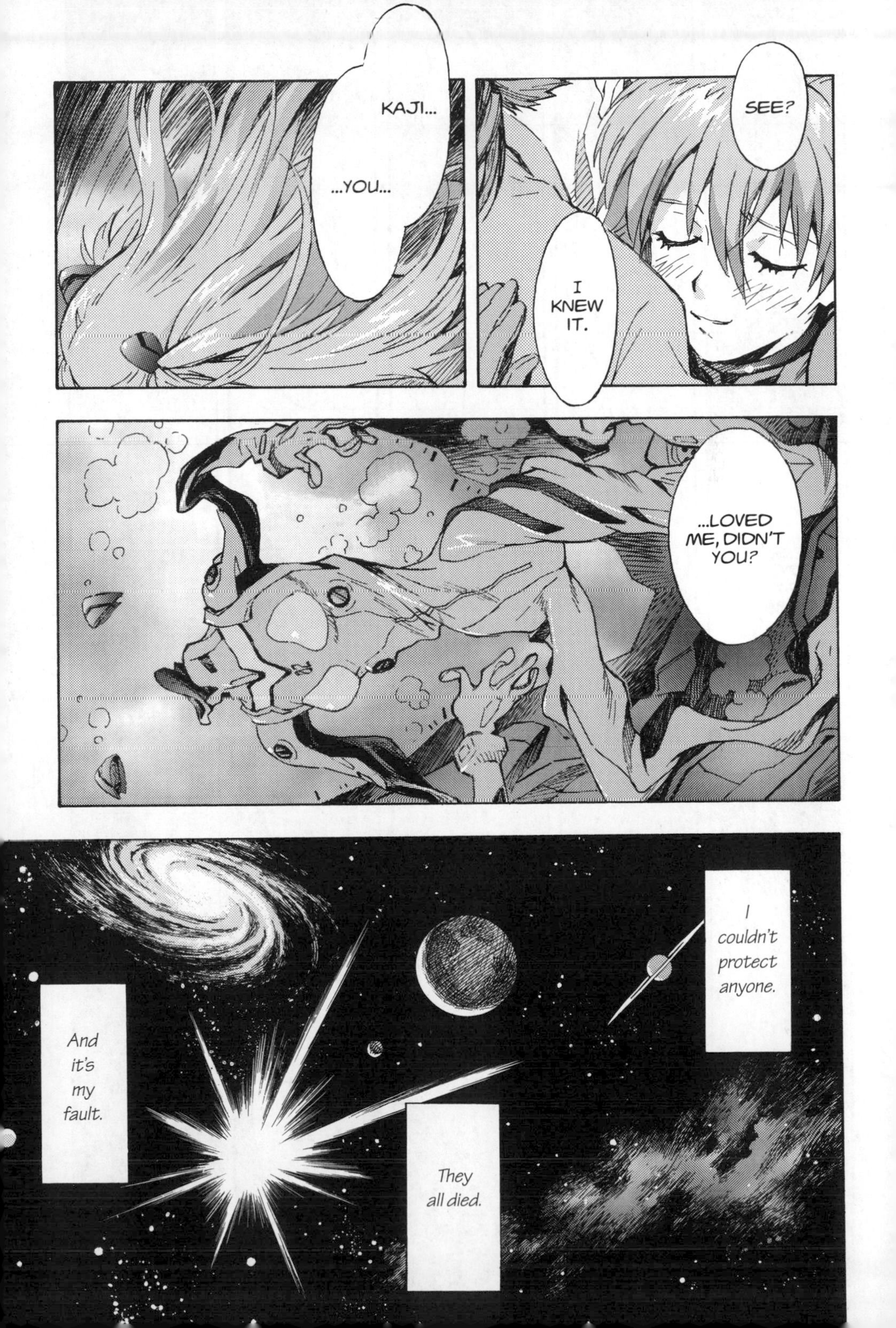
SEE?
I KNEW IT.
KAJI...
...YOU...
...LOVED ME, DIDN'T YOU?
I couldn't protect anyone.
They all died.
And it's my fault.

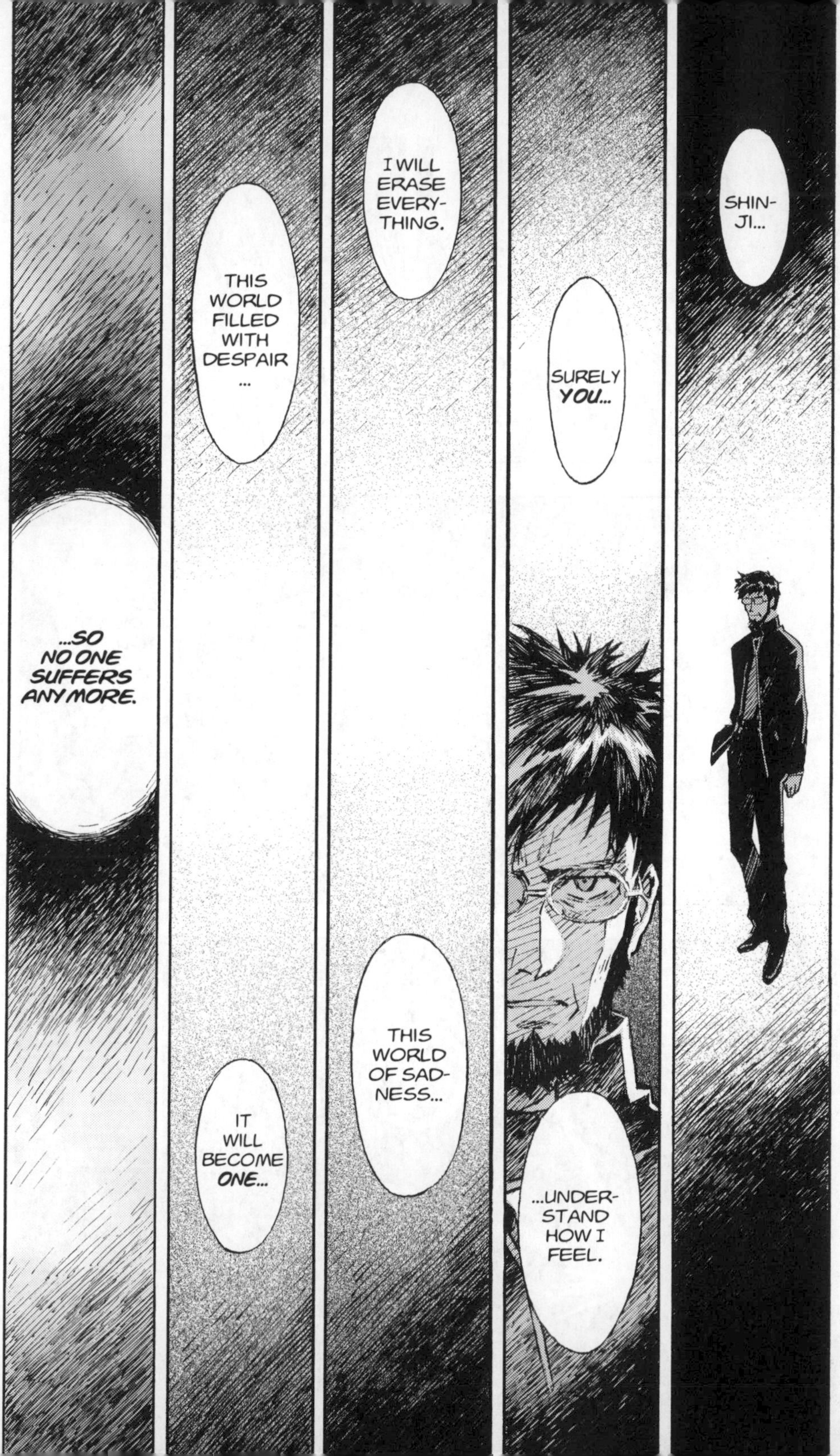
SHIN-JI...
SURELY YOU...
...UNDER-STAND HOW I FEEL.
I WILL ERASE EVERY-THING.
THIS WORLD OF SAD-NESS...
THIS WORLD FILLED WITH DESPAIR ...
IT WILL BECOME ONE...
...SO NO ONE SUFFERS ANYMORE.

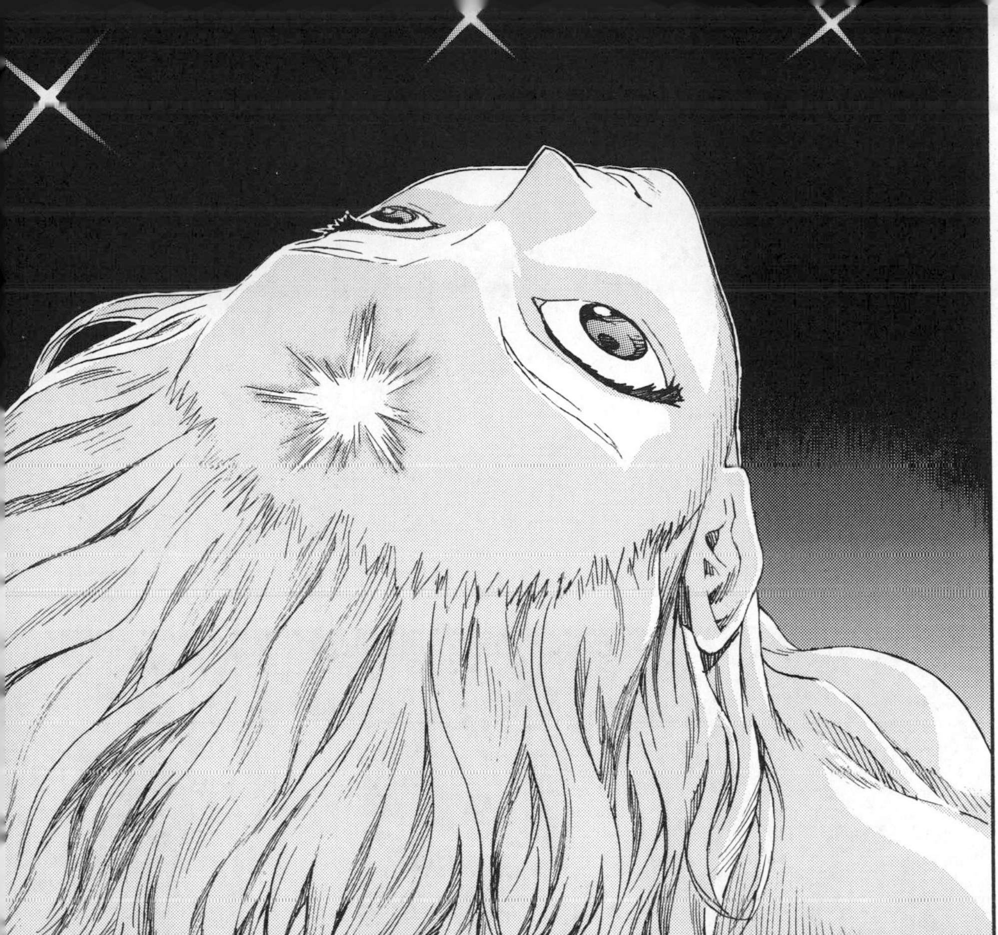
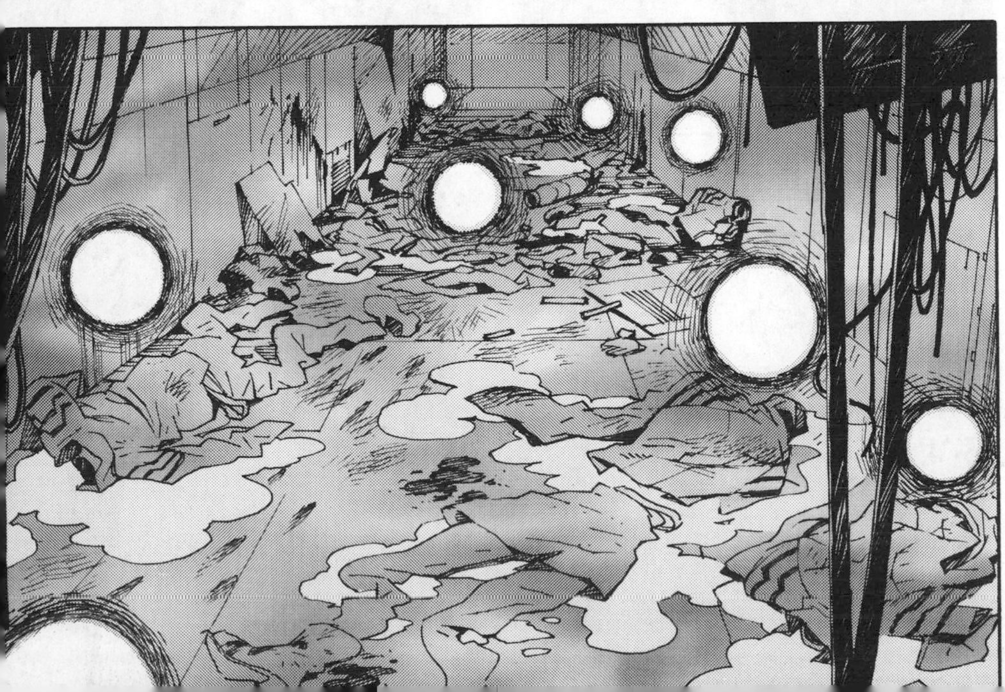

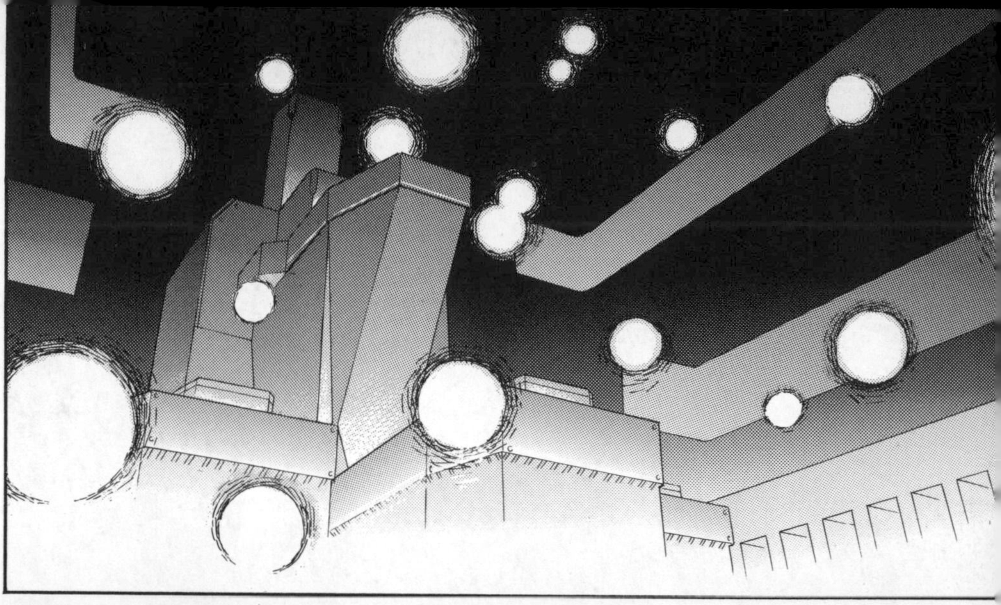
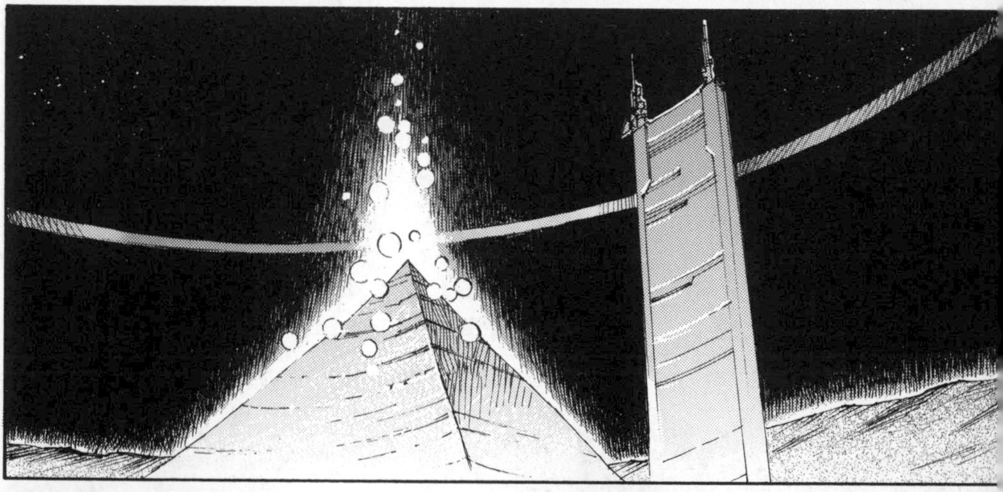
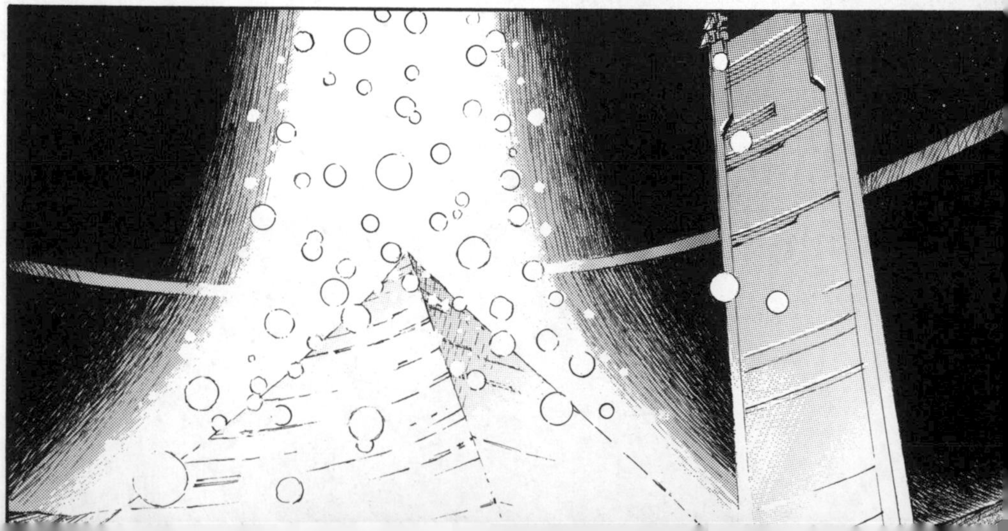

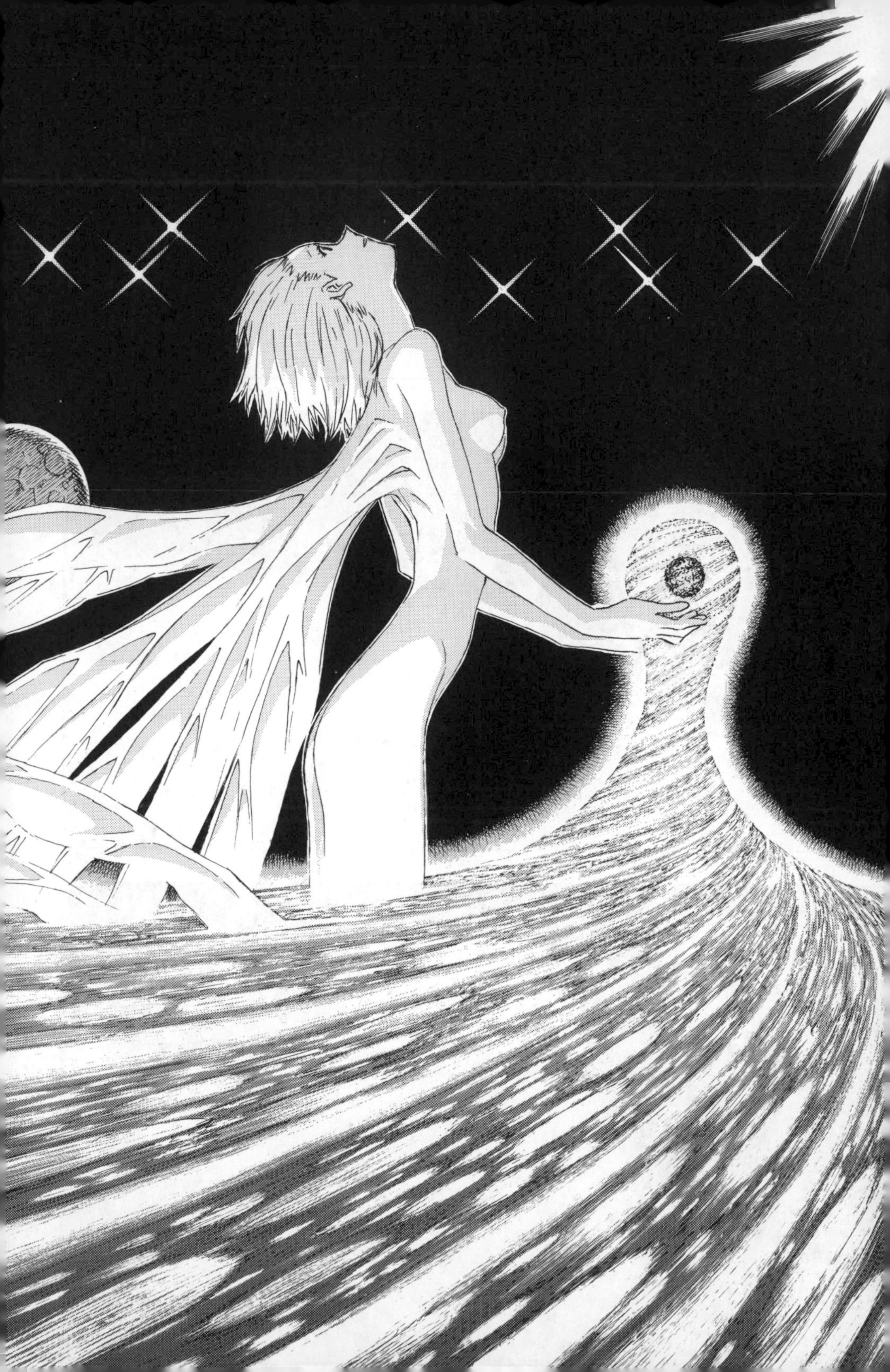

NEON GENESIS EVANGELION

STAGE 92: BIRTHDAY

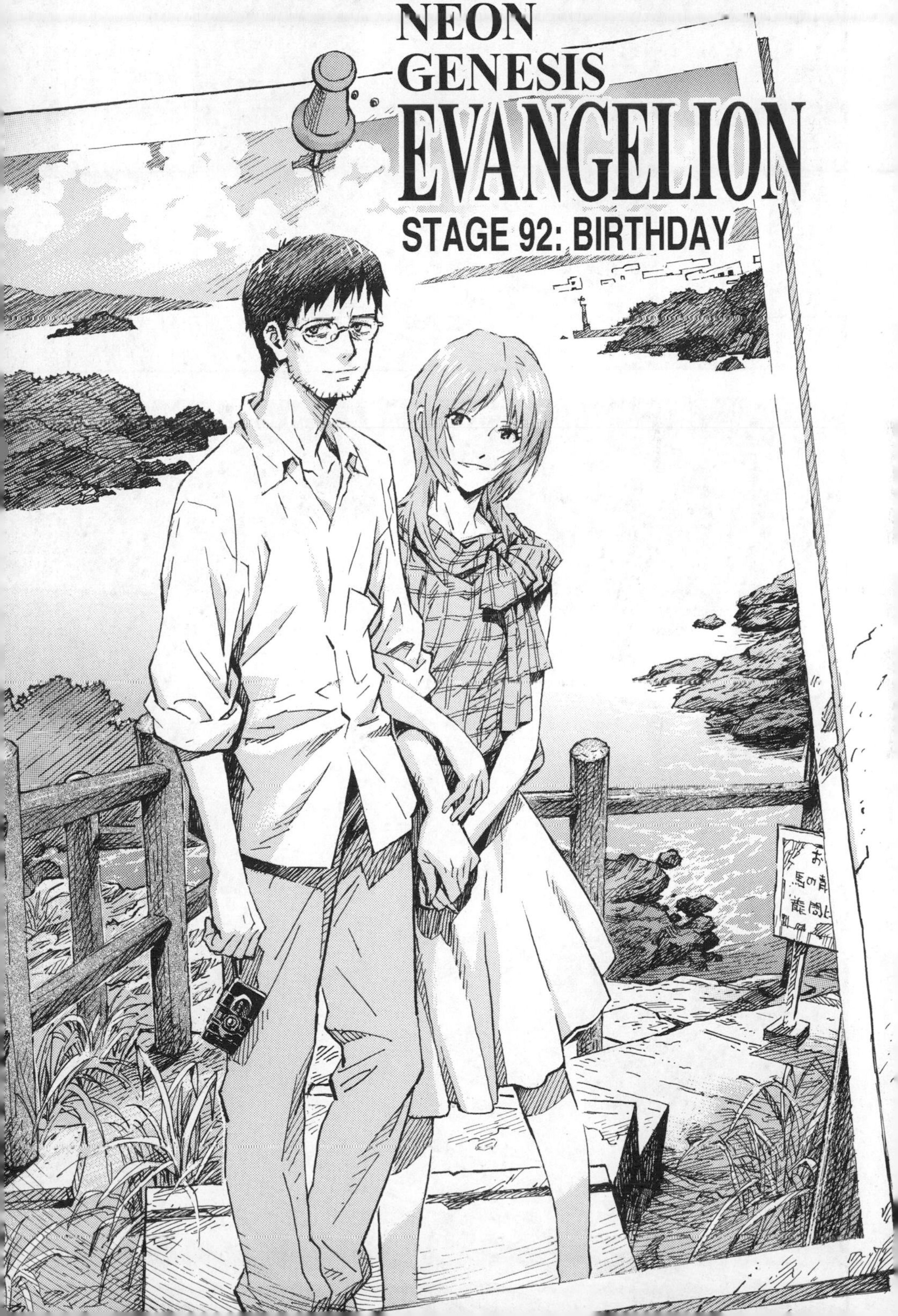

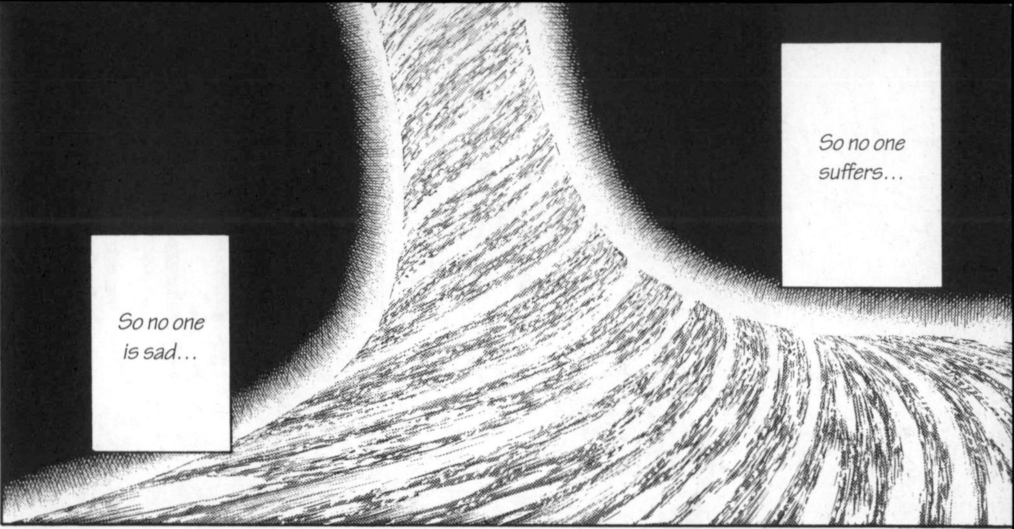
So no one suffers…
So no one is sad…

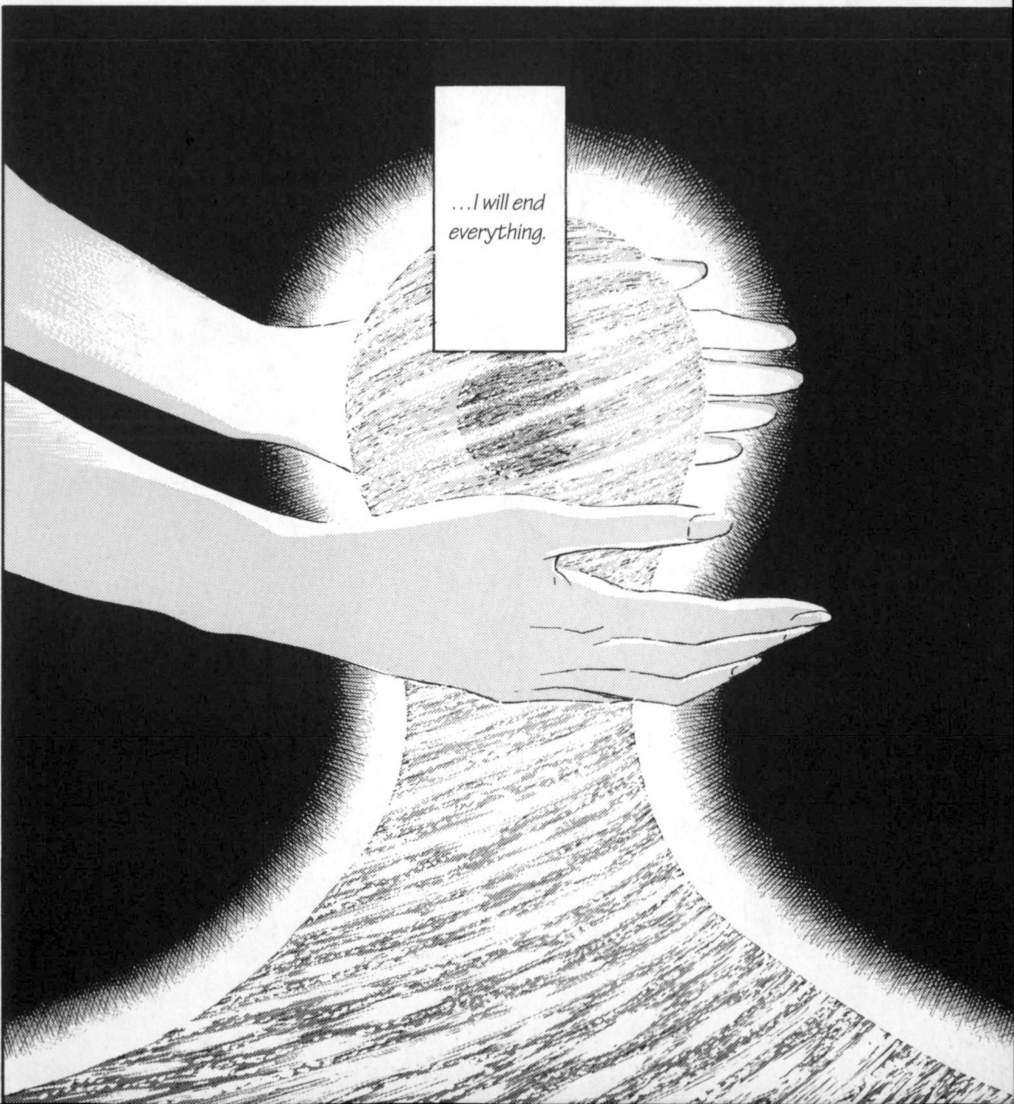
…I will end everything.

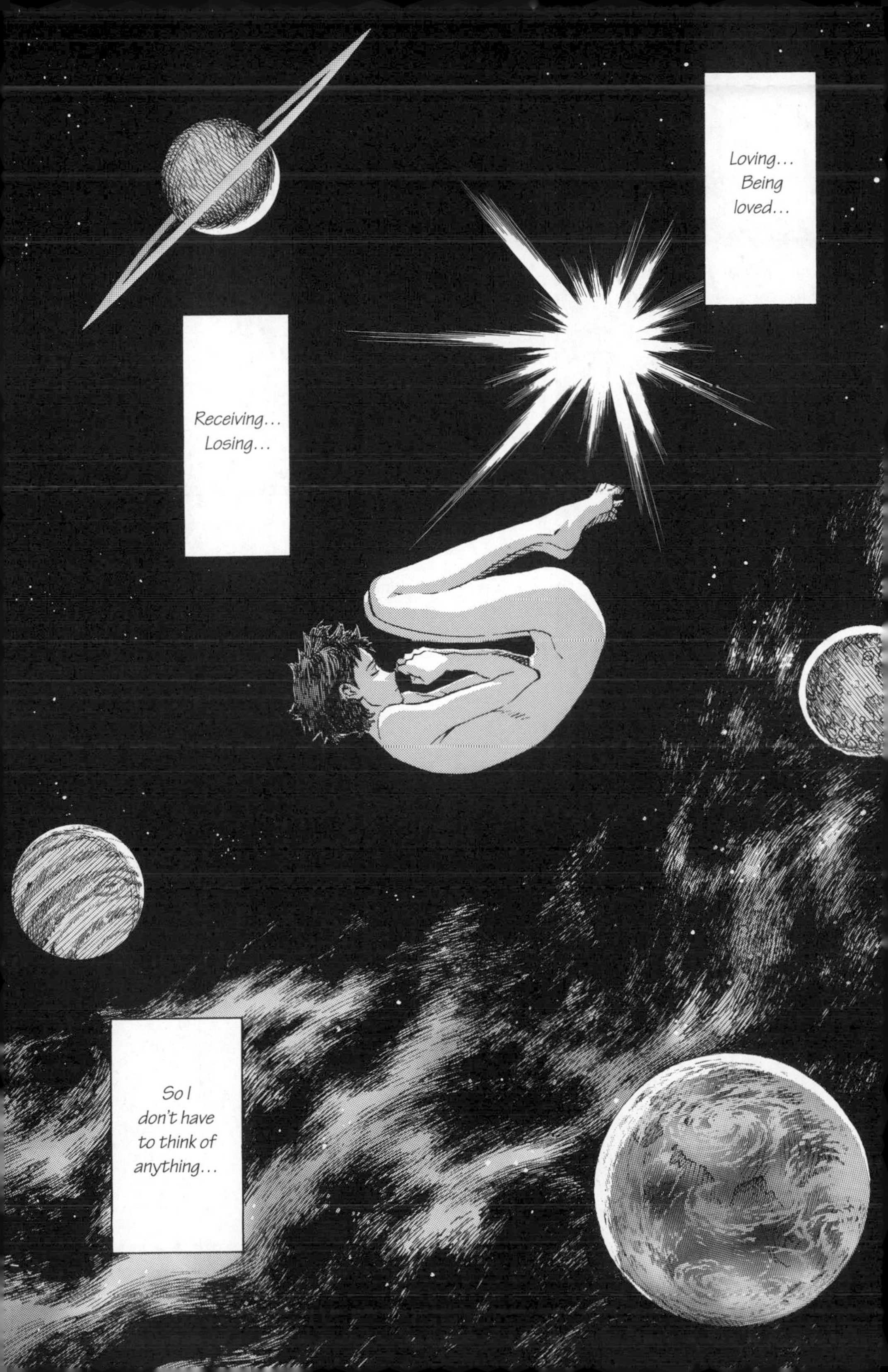
Loving... Being loved...
Receiving... Losing...
So I don't have to think of anything...

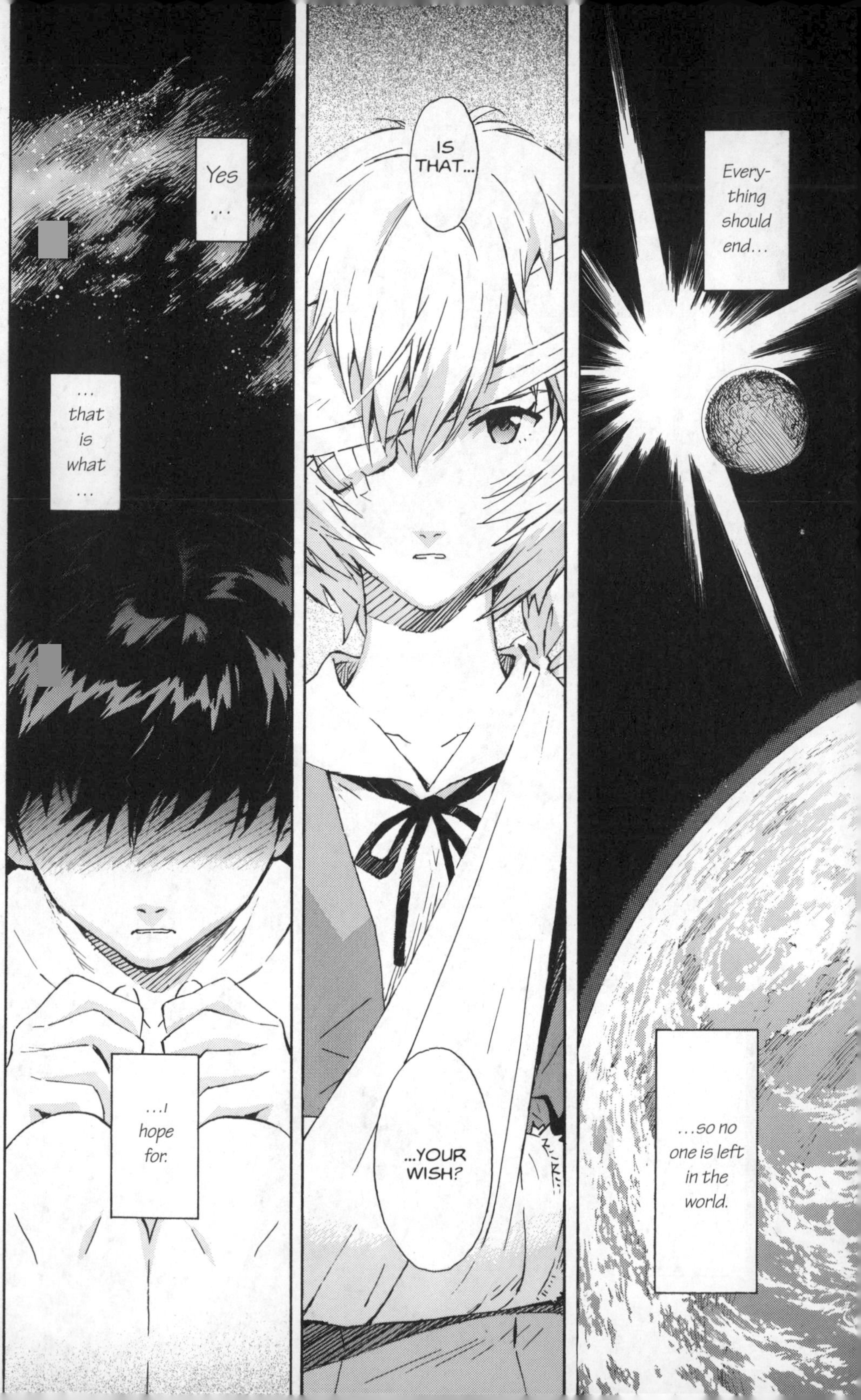
Every-thing should end…
…so no one is left in the world.
IS THAT…
…YOUR WISH?
Yes …
… that is what …
…I hope for.

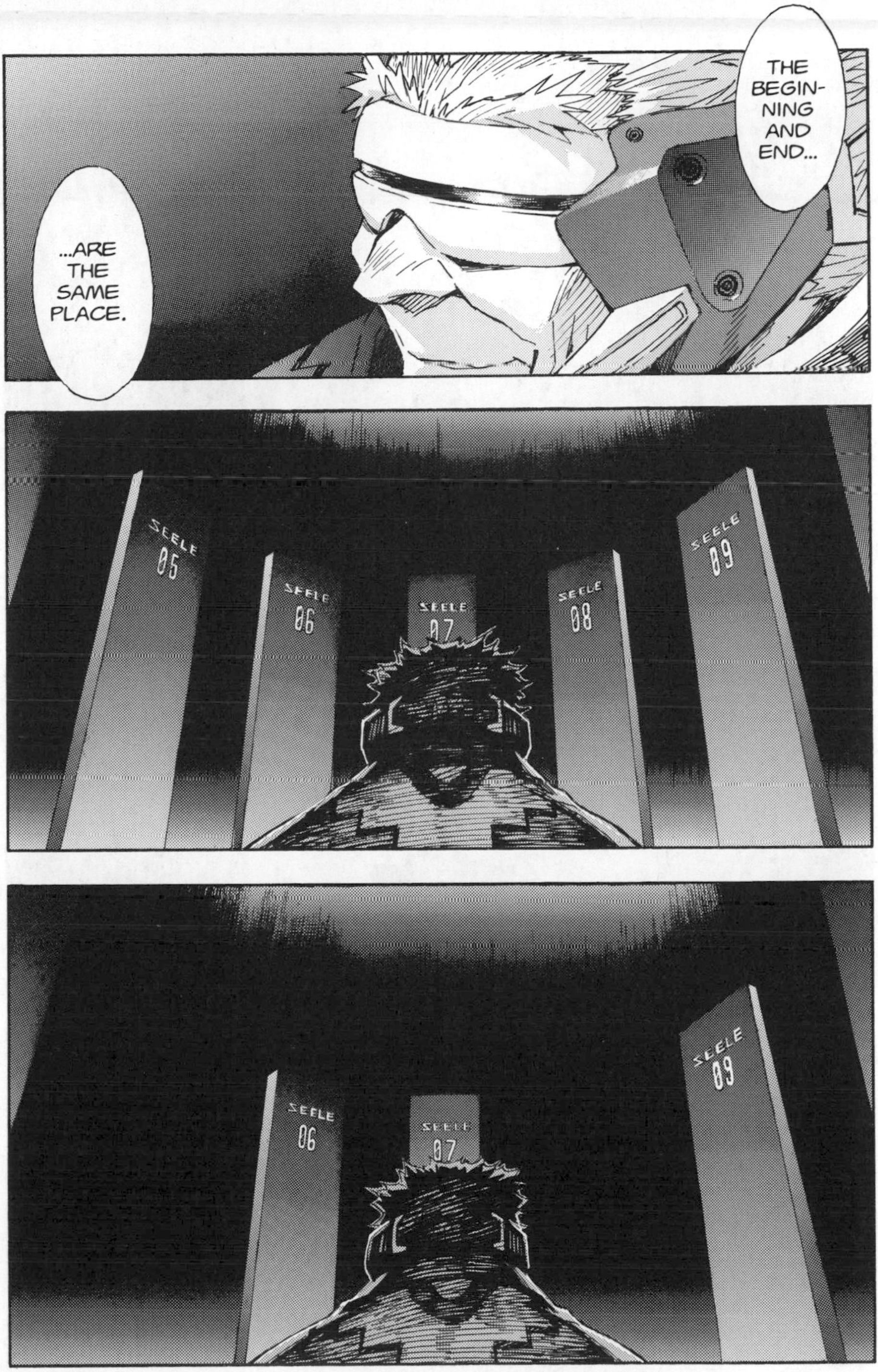
THE BEGIN-NING AND END...
...ARE THE SAME PLACE.
SEELE 09
SEELE 08
SEELE 07
SEELE 06
SEELE 05
SEELE 09
SEELE 07
SEELE 06

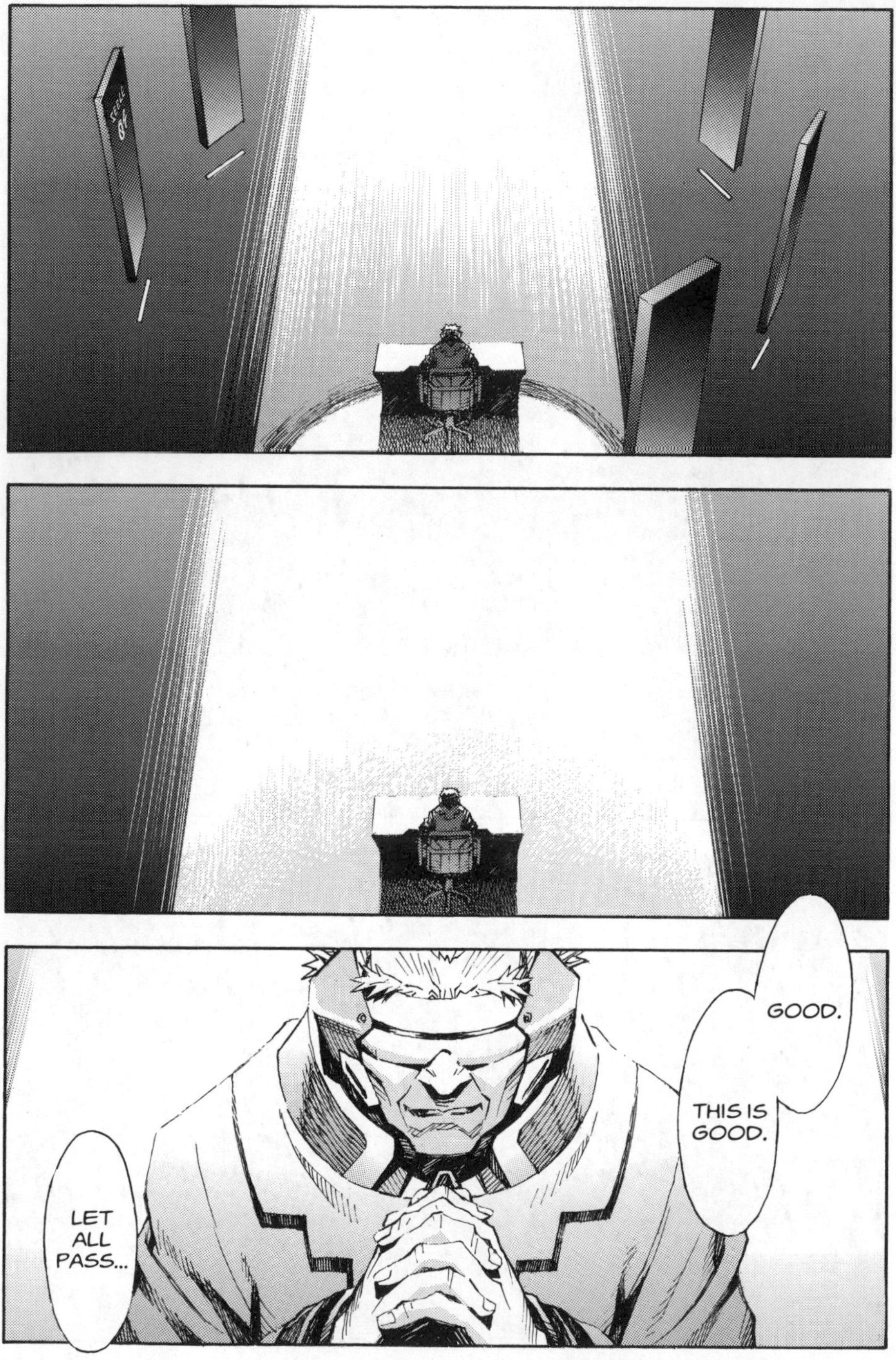
GOOD.
THIS IS GOOD.
LET ALL PASS...

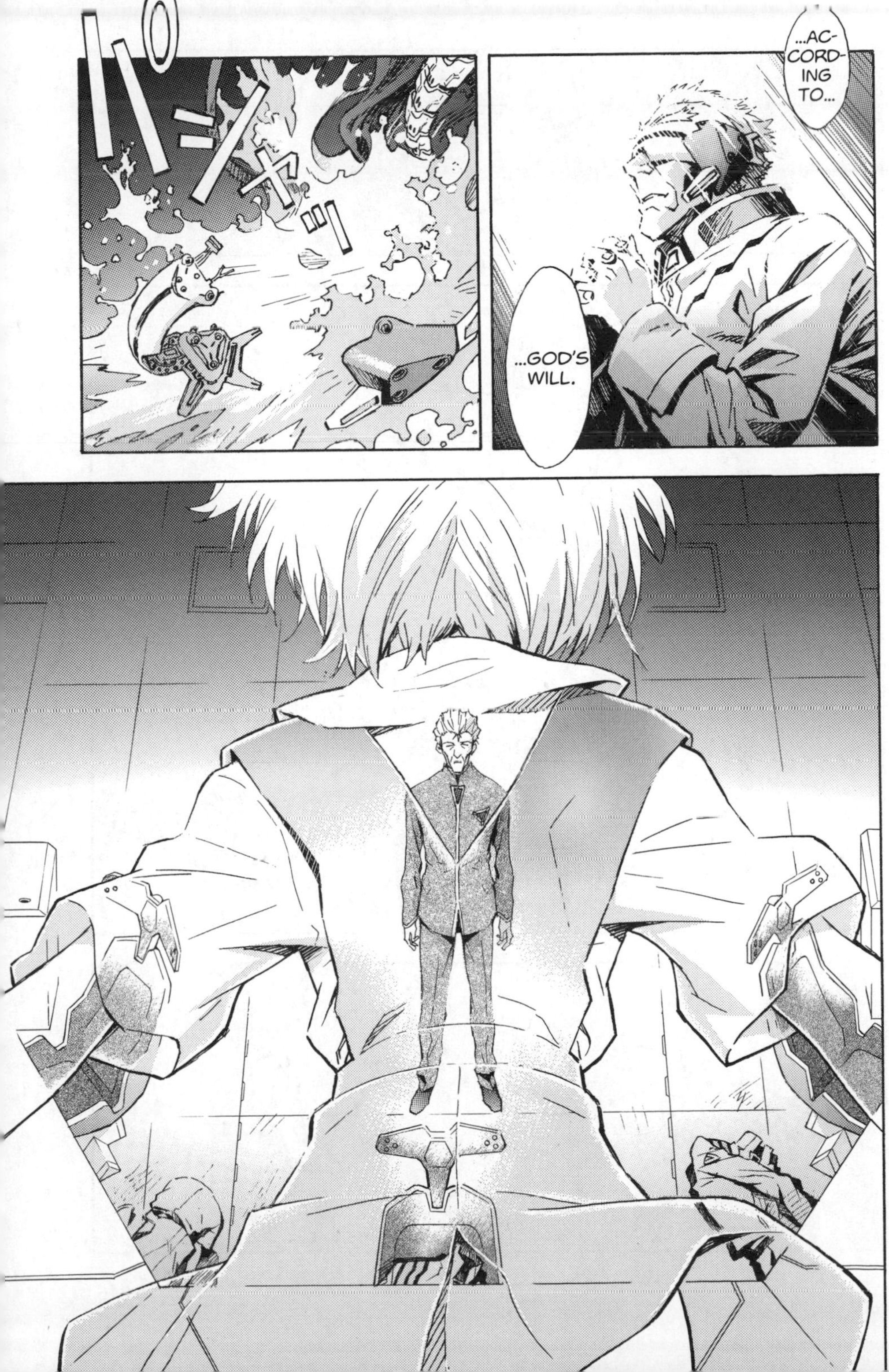
...ACCORDING TO...
...GOD'S WILL.

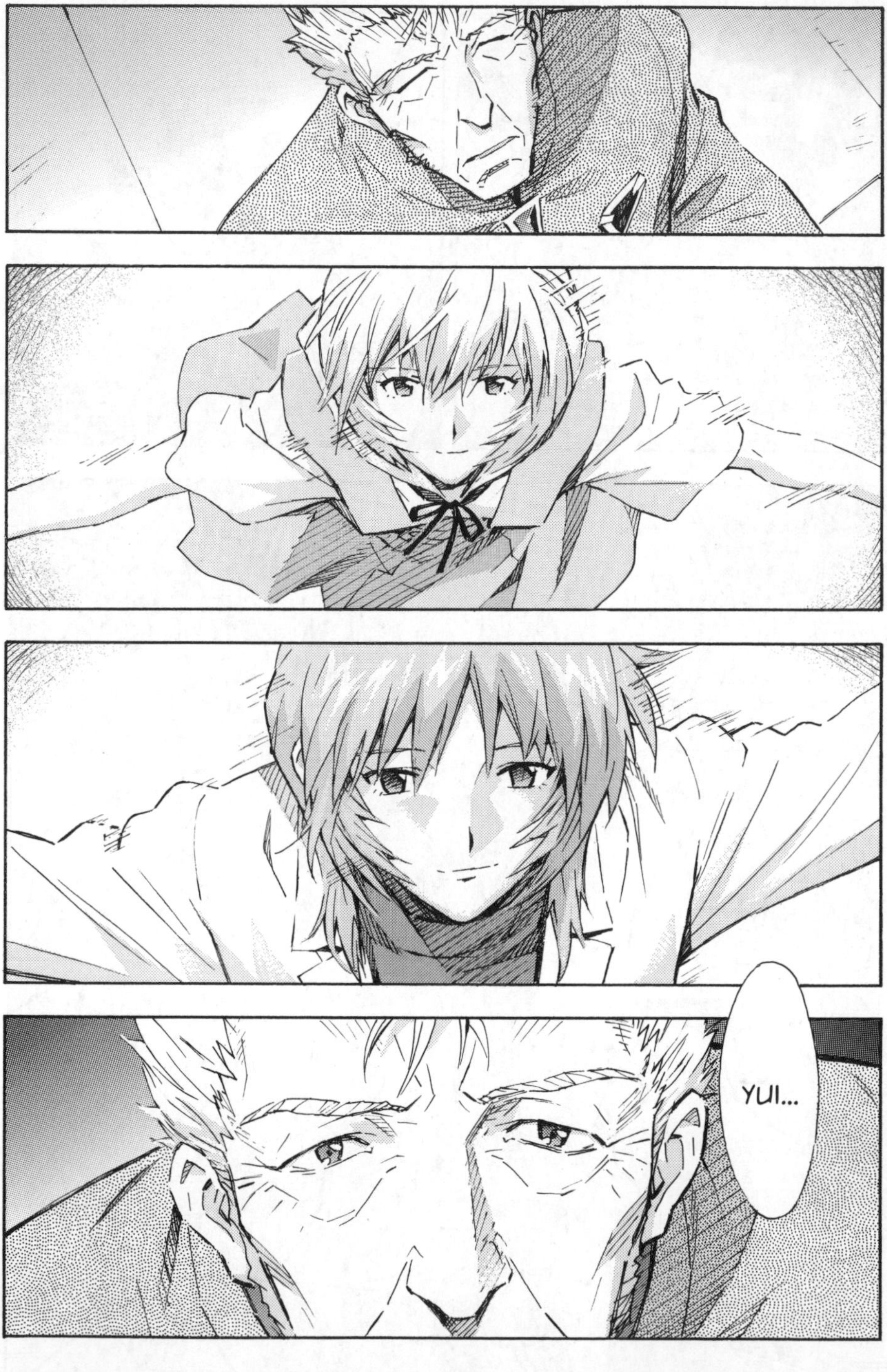
YUI...

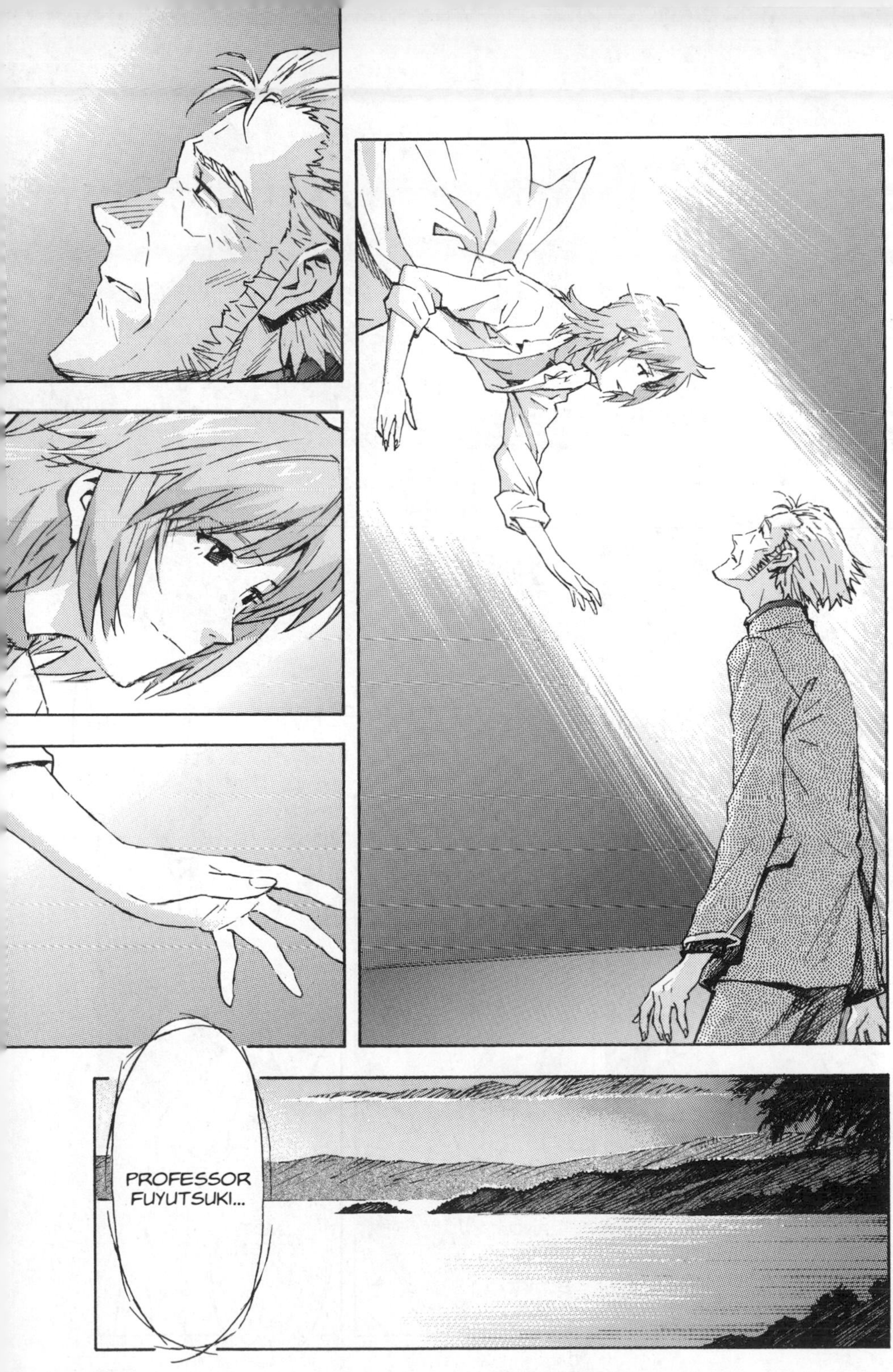
PROFESSOR FUYUTSUKI...

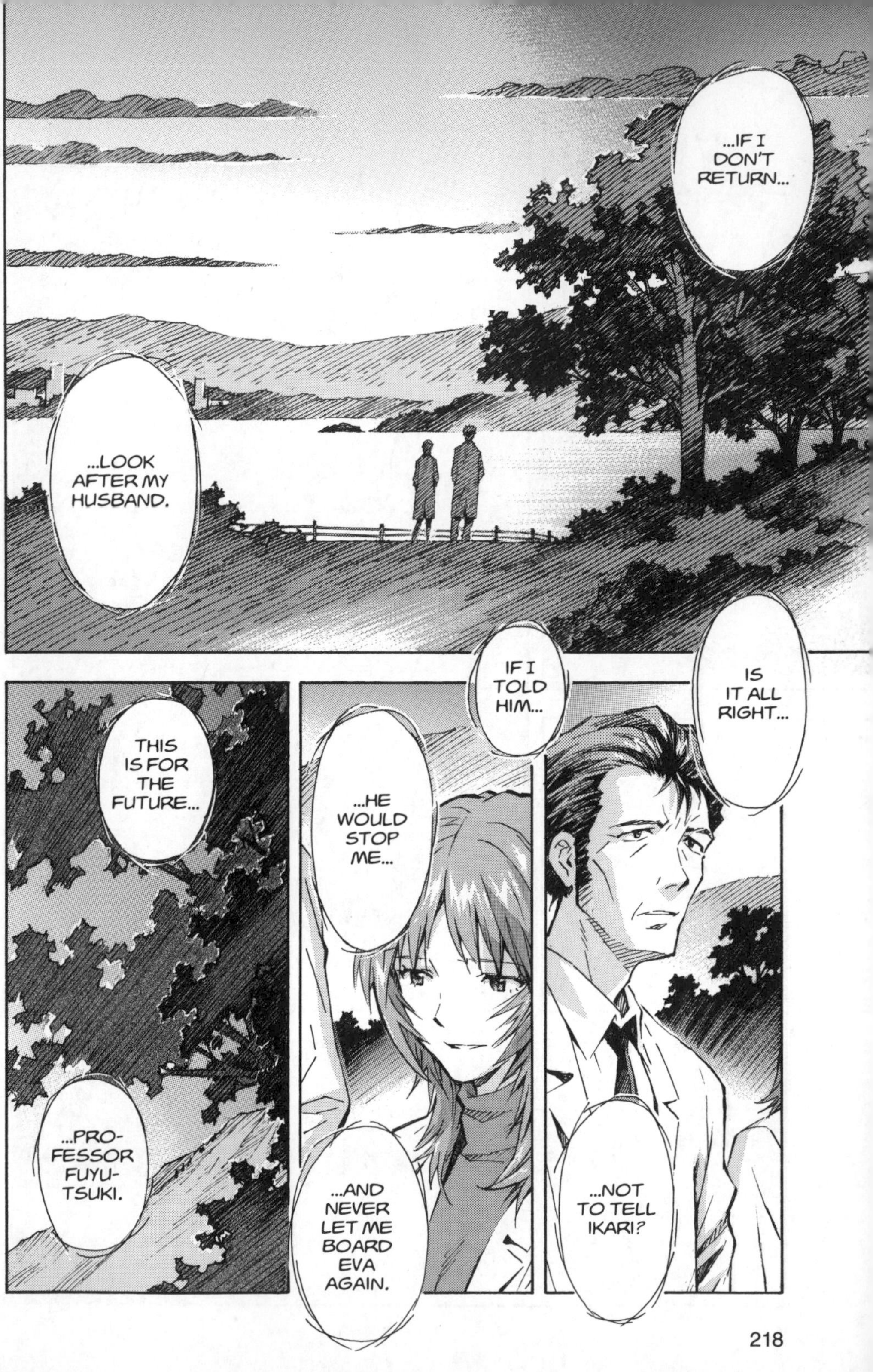
...IF I DON'T RETURN...
...LOOK AFTER MY HUSBAND.
IS IT ALL RIGHT...
...NOT TO TELL IKARI?
IF I TOLD HIM...
...HE WOULD STOP ME...
...AND NEVER LET ME BOARD EVA AGAIN.
THIS IS FOR THE FUTURE...
...PRO-FESSOR FUYU-TSUKI.

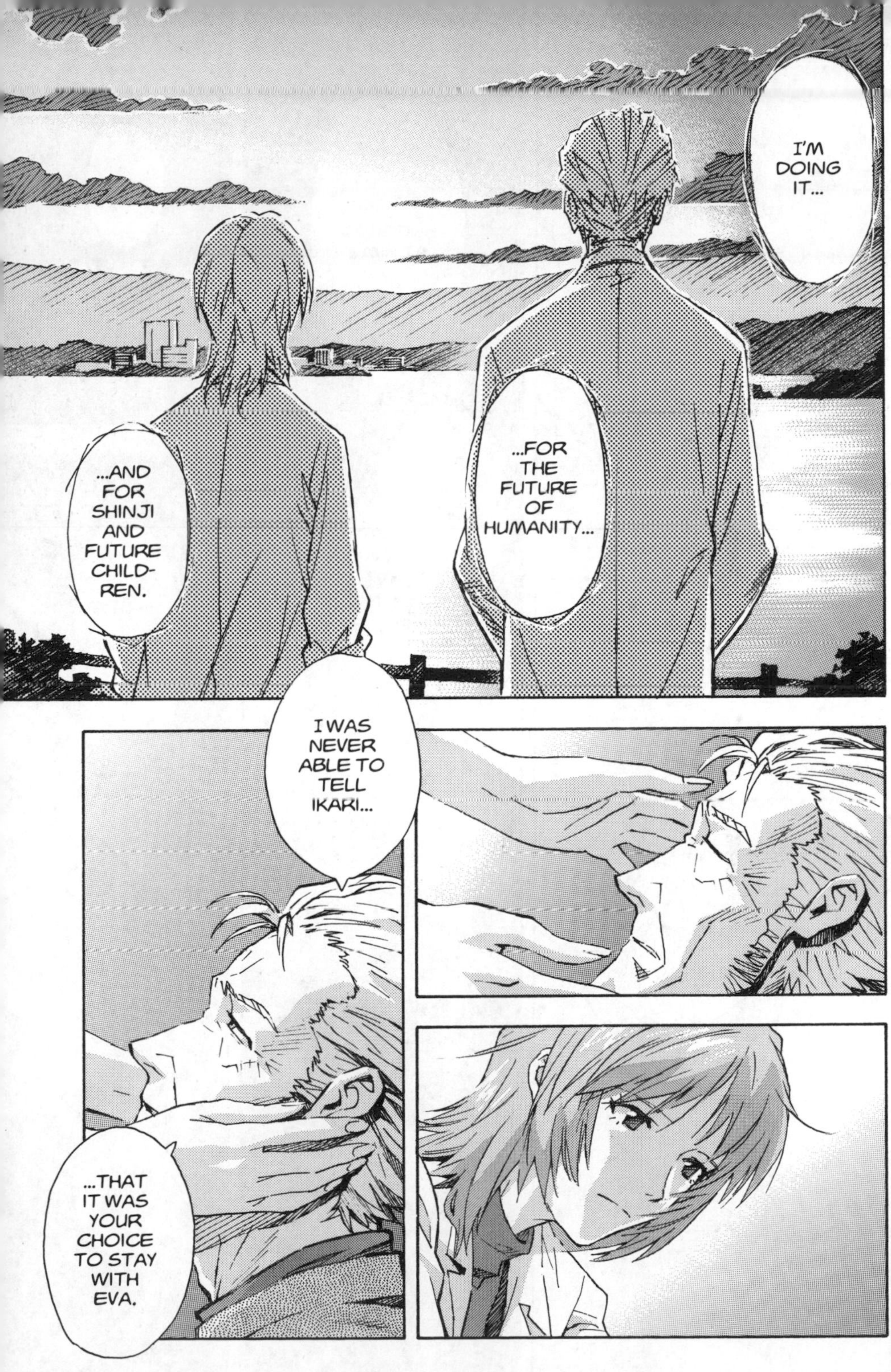
I'M DOING IT...
...FOR THE FUTURE OF HUMANITY...
...AND FOR SHINJI AND FUTURE CHILD-REN.
I WAS NEVER ABLE TO TELL IKARI...
...THAT IT WAS YOUR CHOICE TO STAY WITH EVA.

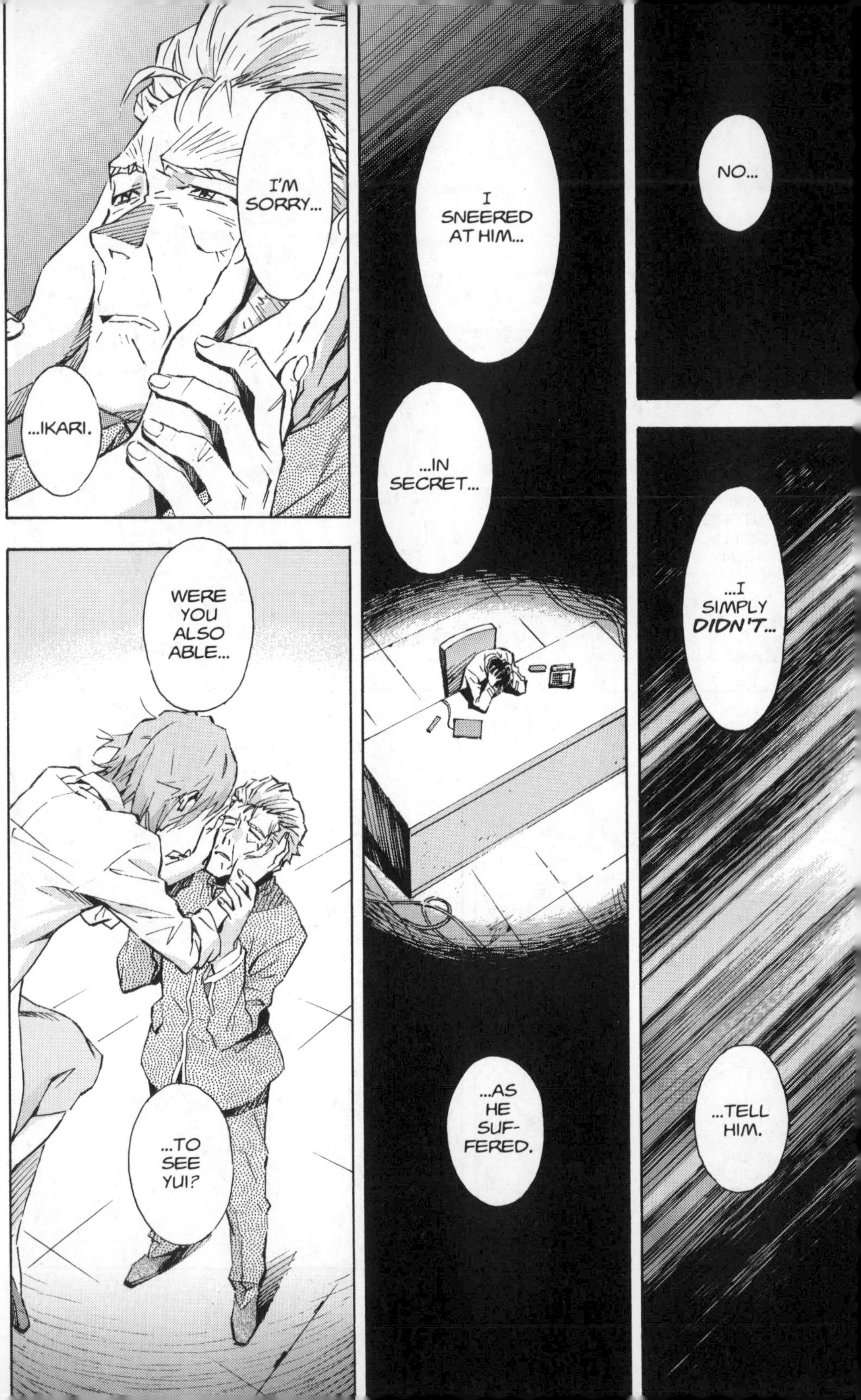
I'M SORRY...
...IKARI.
WERE YOU ALSO ABLE...
...TO SEE YUI?
I SNEERED AT HIM...
...IN SECRET...
...AS HE SUF-FERED.
NO...
...I SIMPLY DIDN'T...
...TELL HIM.

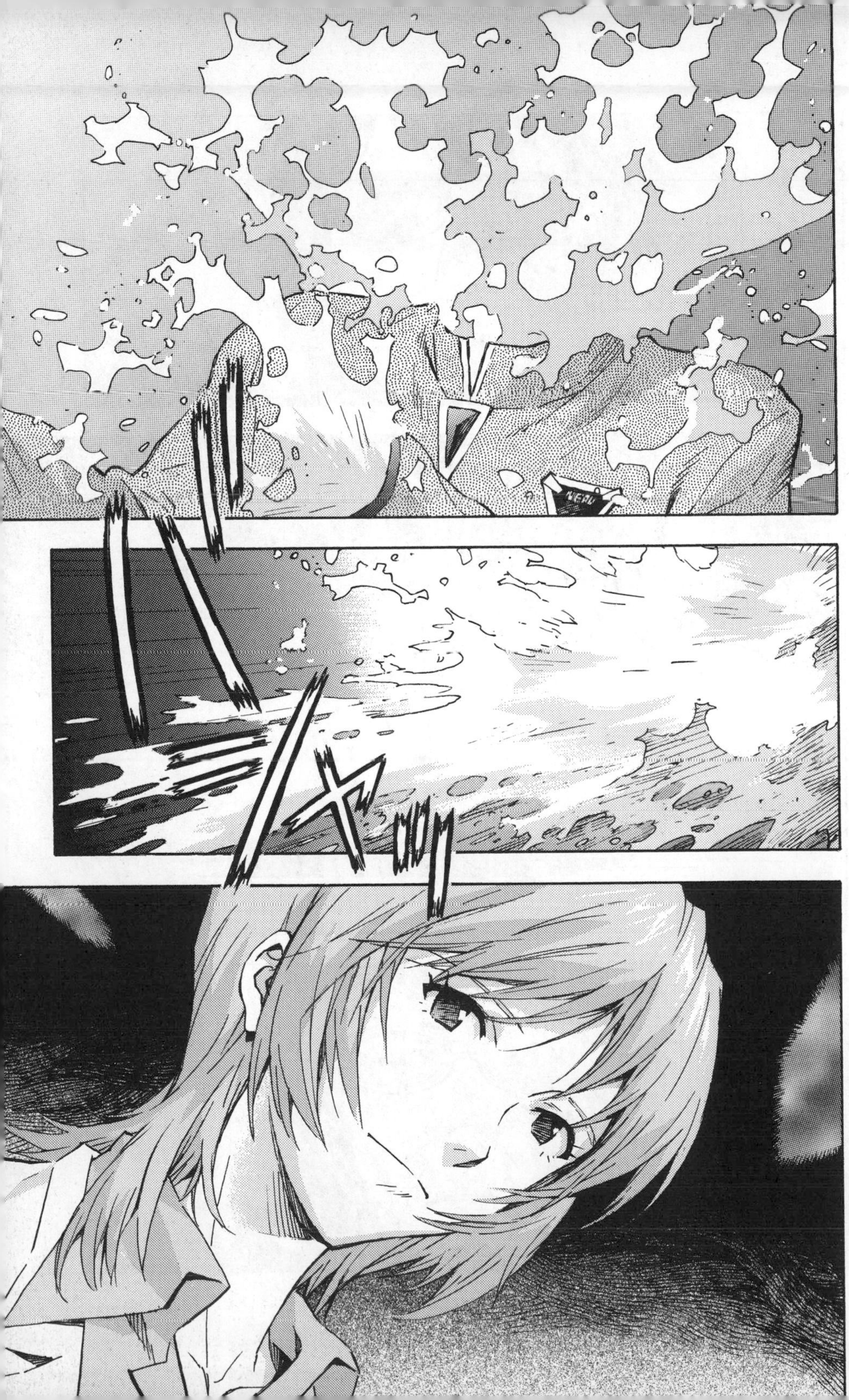

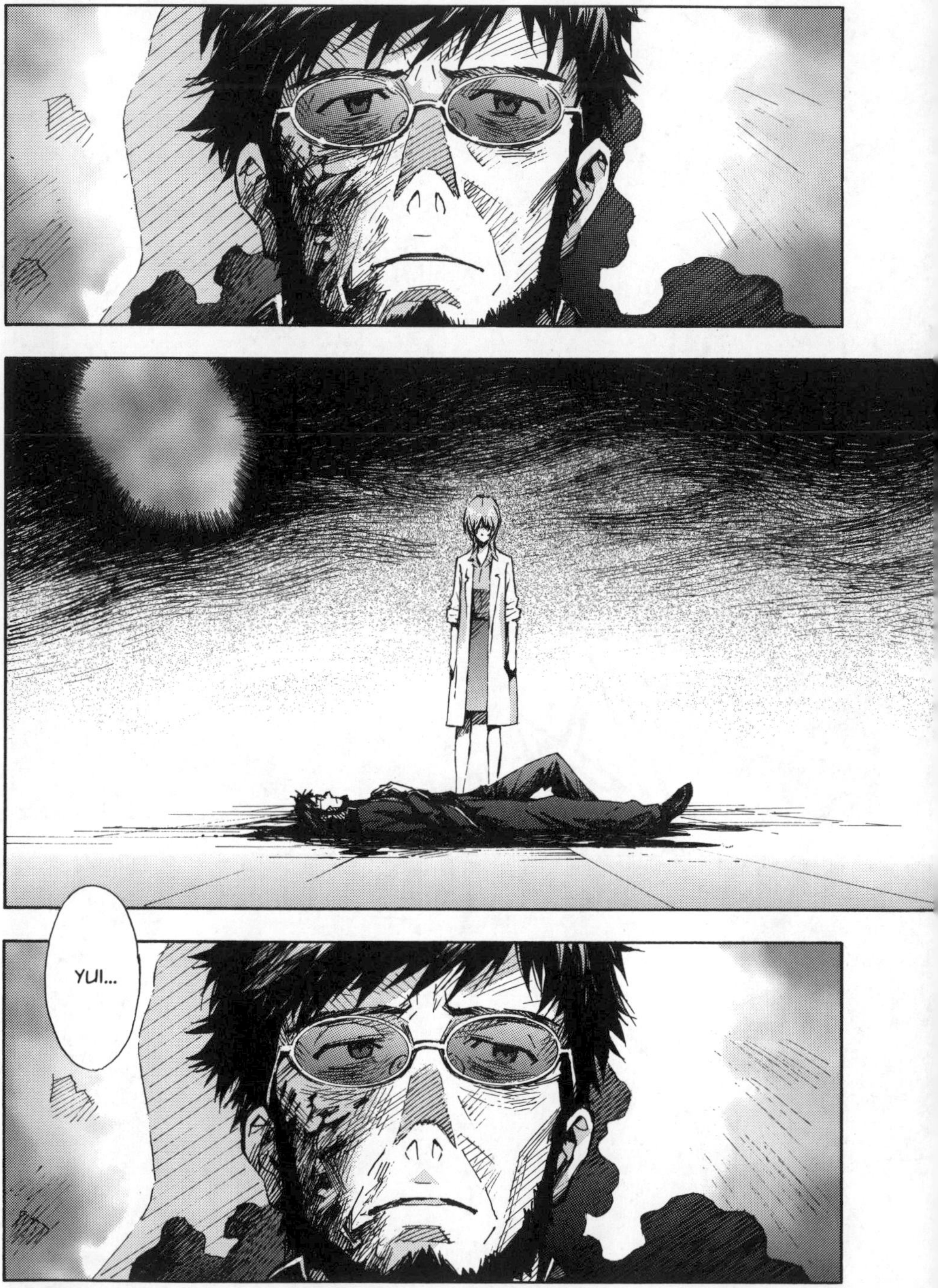
YUI...

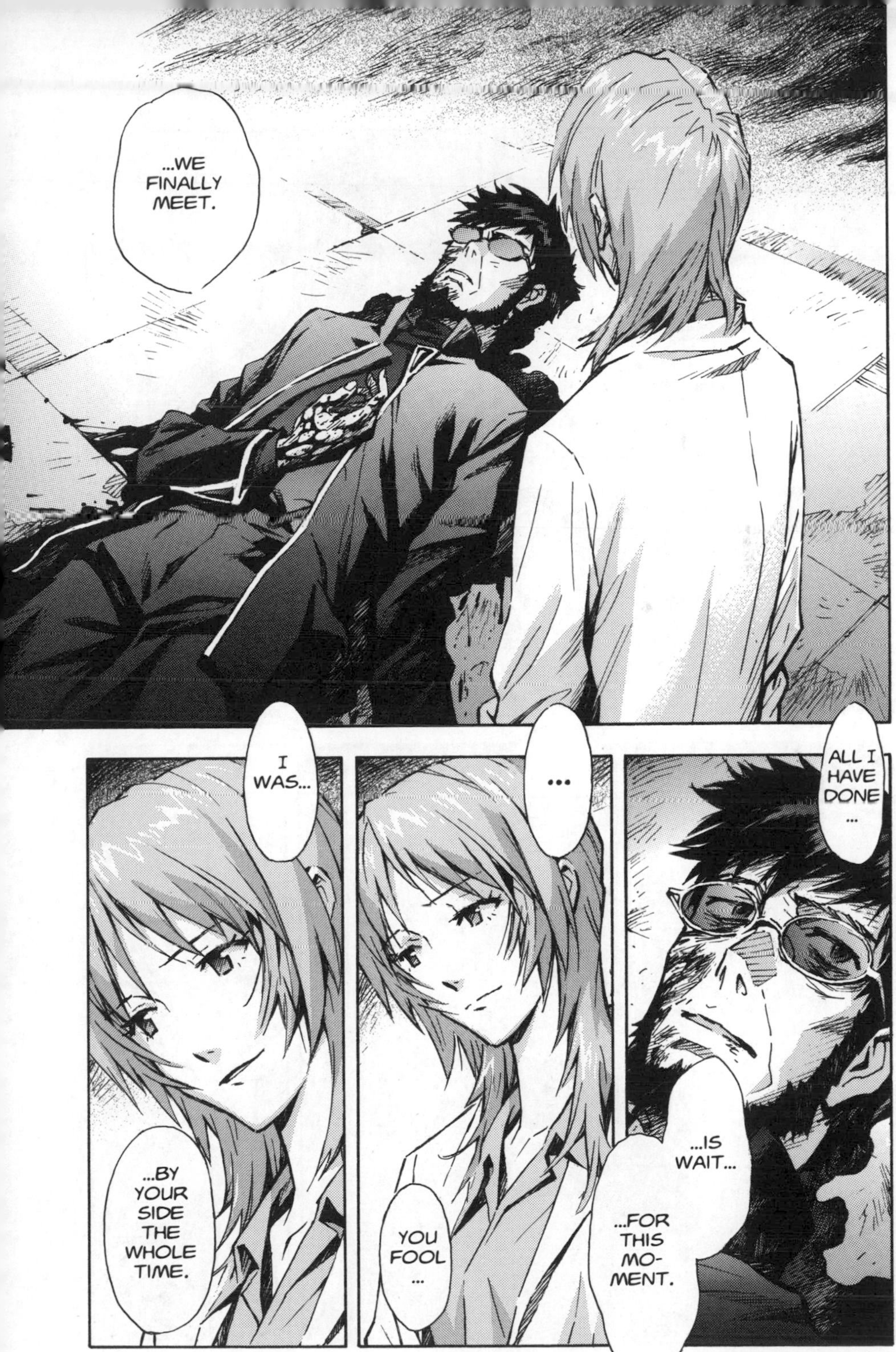
...WE FINALLY MEET.
ALL I HAVE DONE ...
...IS WAIT...
...FOR THIS MO-MENT.
...
YOU FOOL ...
I WAS...
...BY YOUR SIDE THE WHOLE TIME.

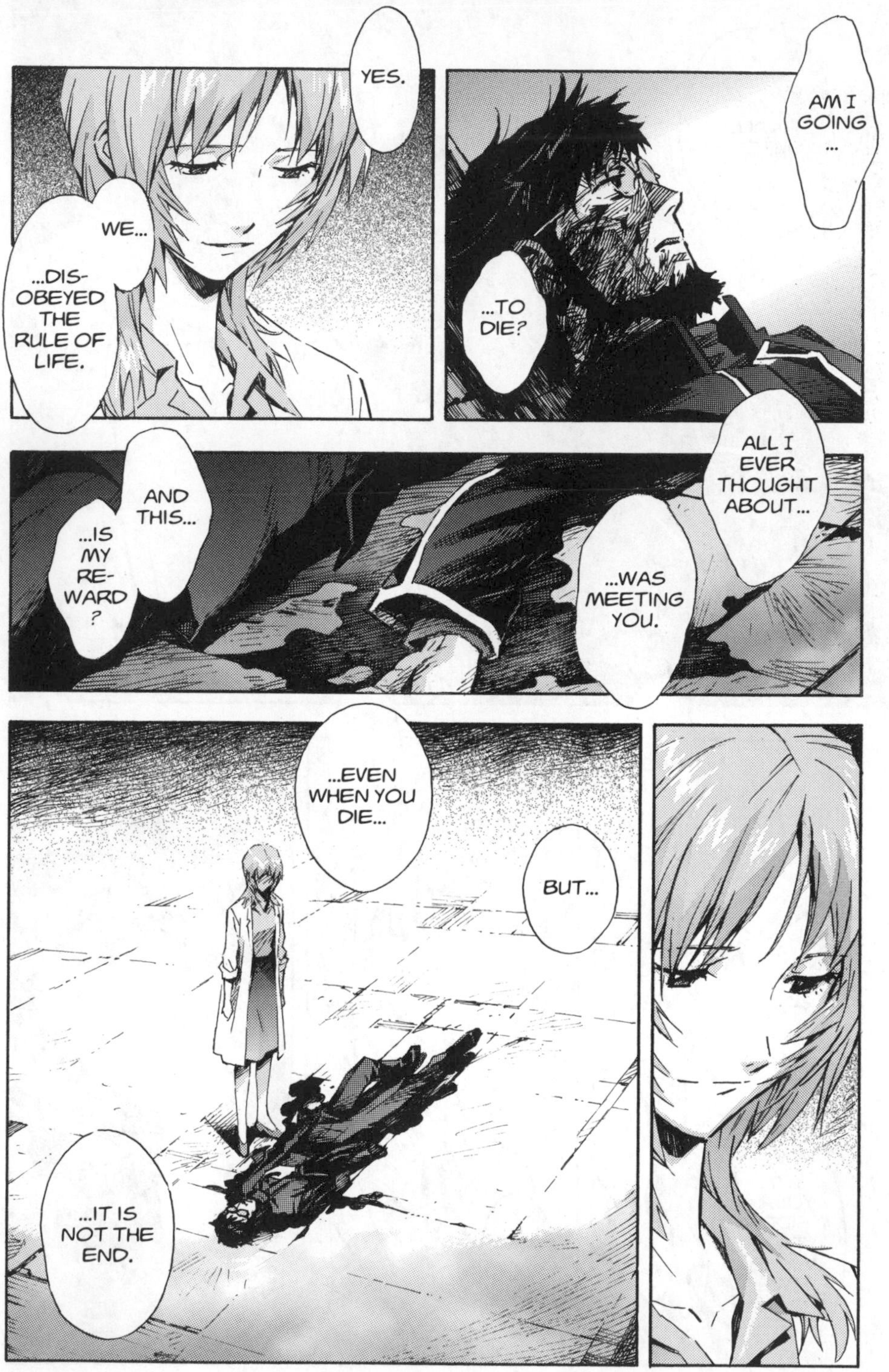
AM I GOING ...
...TO DIE?
YES.
WE...
...DIS-OBEYED THE RULE OF LIFE.
ALL I EVER THOUGHT ABOUT...
...WAS MEETING YOU.
AND THIS...
...IS MY RE-WARD?
BUT...
...EVEN WHEN YOU DIE...
...IT IS NOT THE END.

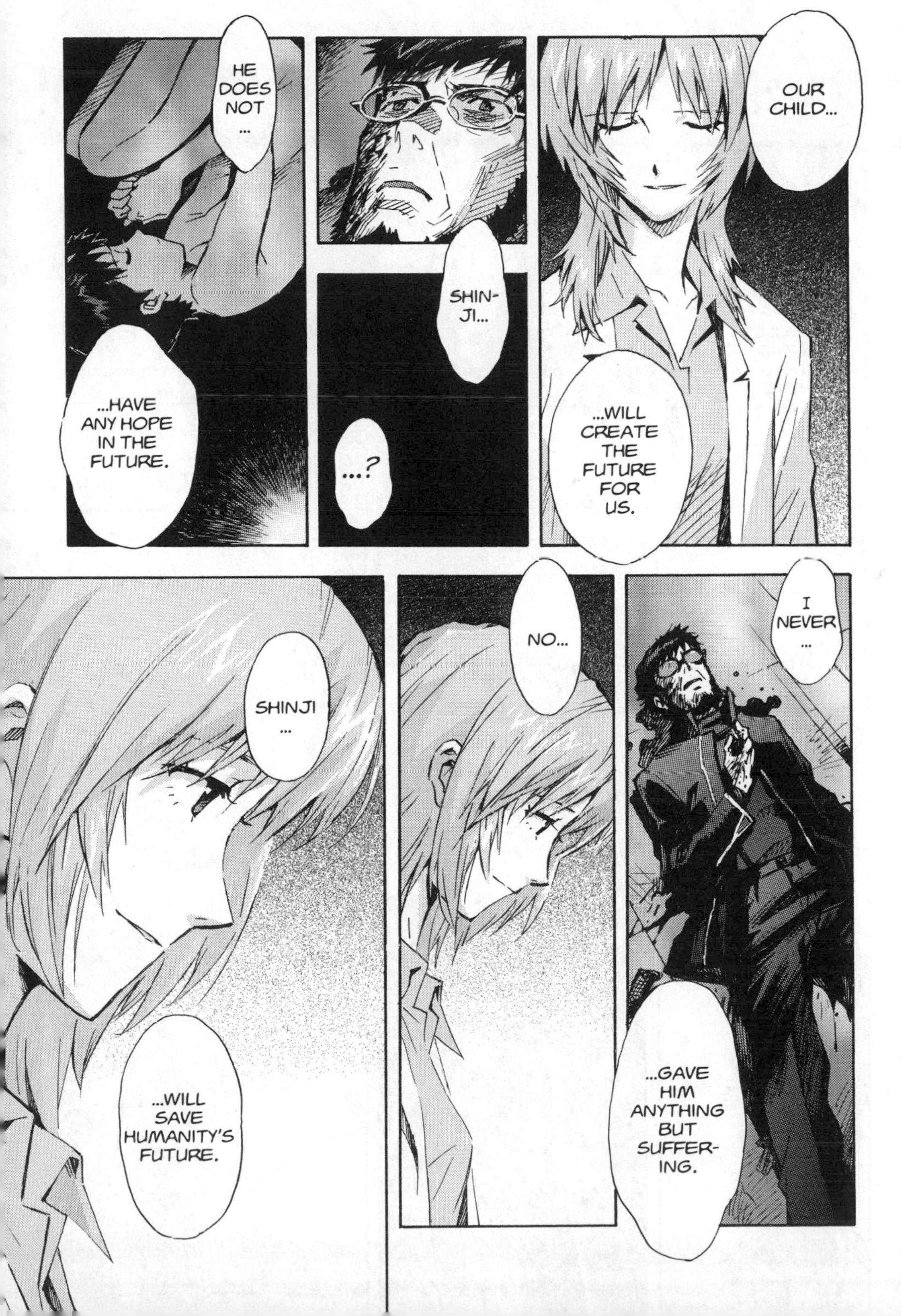
OUR CHILD...
...WILL CREATE THE FUTURE FOR US.
SHIN-JI...
...?
HE DOES NOT ...
...HAVE ANY HOPE IN THE FUTURE.
I NEVER ...
...GAVE HIM ANYTHING BUT SUFFER-ING.
NO...
SHINJI ...
...WILL SAVE HUMANITY'S FUTURE.

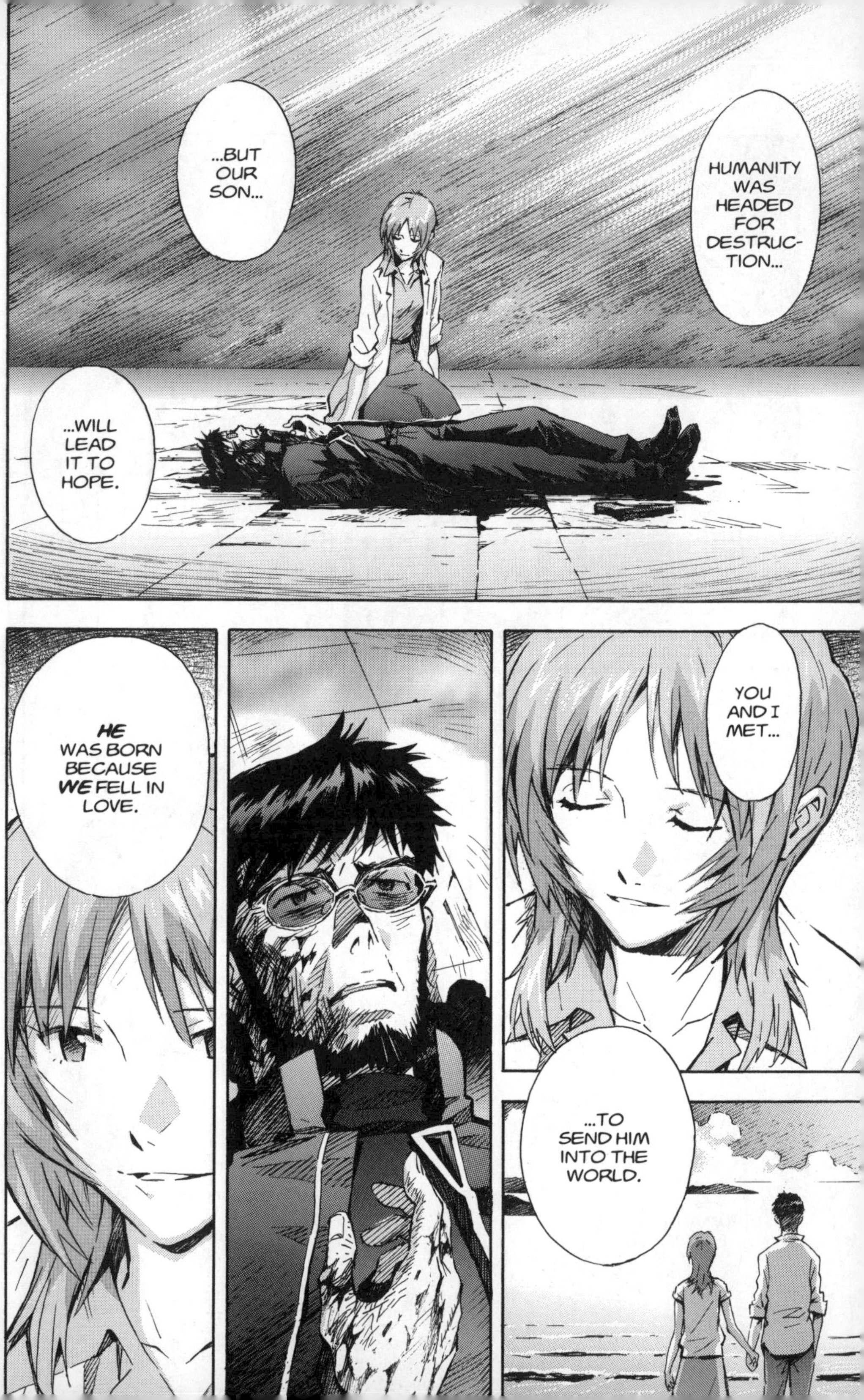
HUMANITY WAS HEADED FOR DESTRUCTION...
...BUT OUR SON...
...WILL LEAD IT TO HOPE.
YOU AND I MET...
...TO SEND HIM INTO THE WORLD.
HE WAS BORN BECAUSE WE FELL IN LOVE.

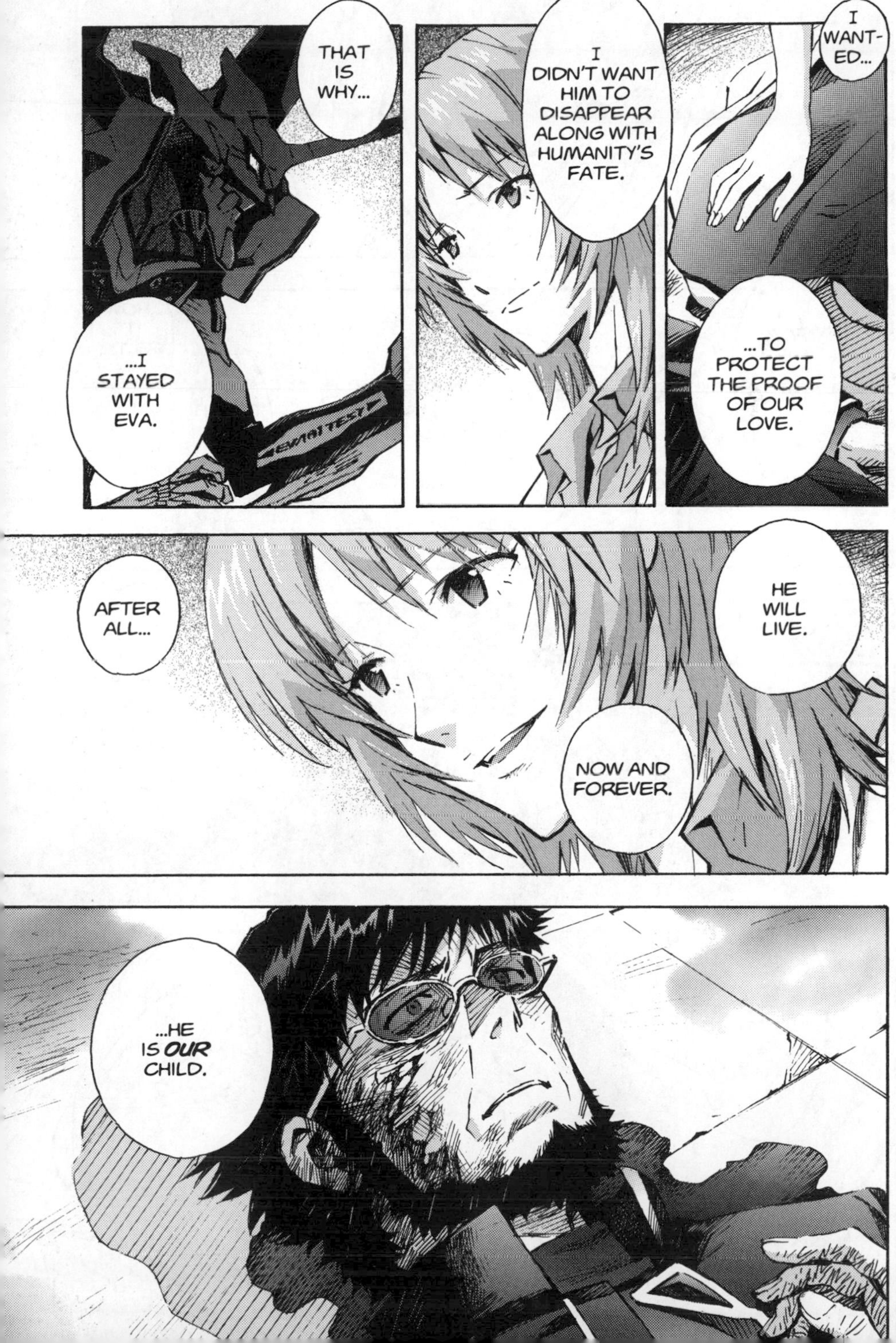
I WANT-ED...
...TO PROTECT THE PROOF OF OUR LOVE.
I DIDN'T WANT HIM TO DISAPPEAR ALONG WITH HUMANITY'S FATE.
THAT IS WHY...
...I STAYED WITH EVA.
HE WILL LIVE.
NOW AND FOREVER.
AFTER ALL...
...HE IS ***OUR*** CHILD.

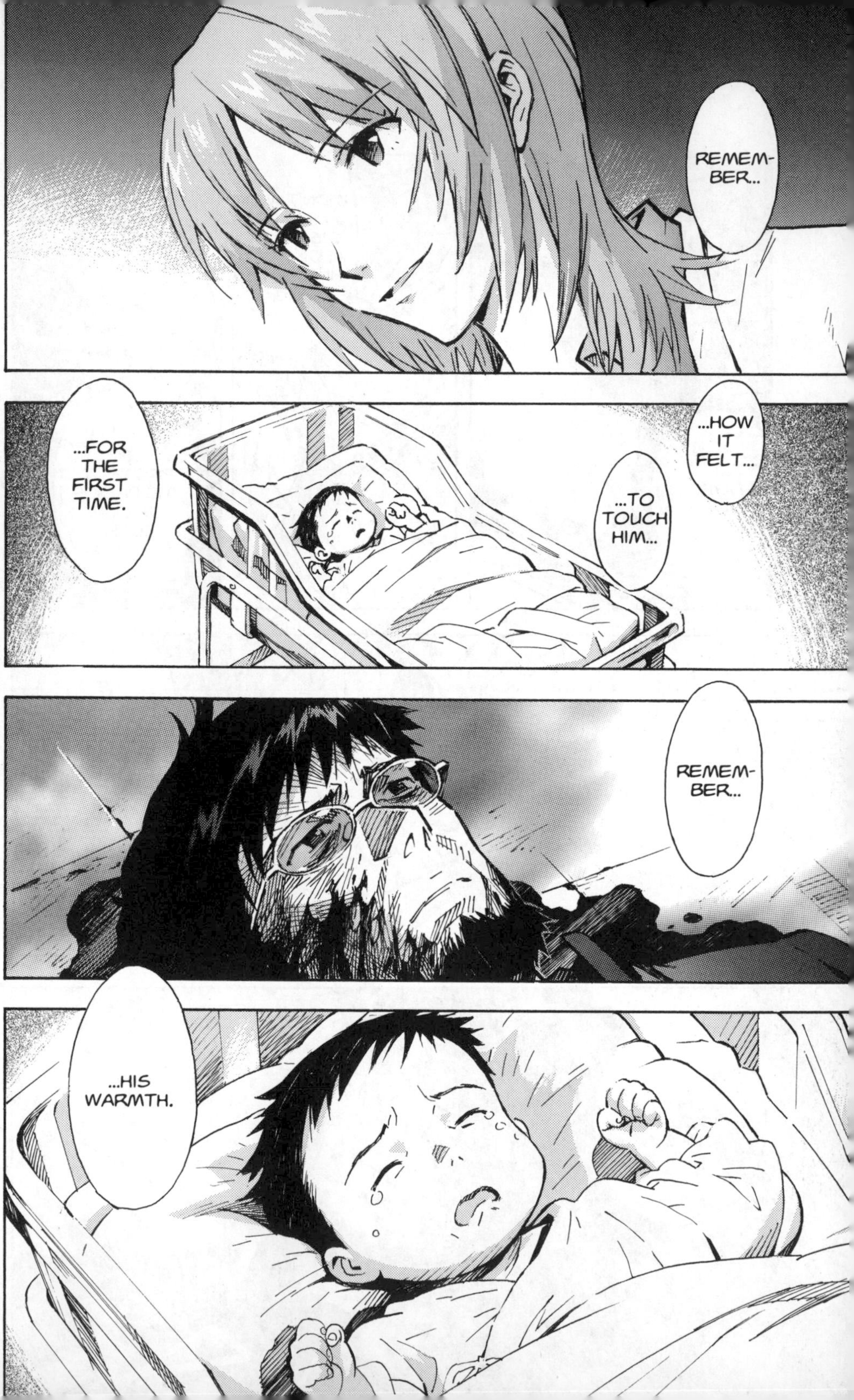
REMEM-
BER...
...HOW IT FELT...
...TO TOUCH HIM...
...FOR THE FIRST TIME.
REMEM-
BER...
...HIS WARMTH.

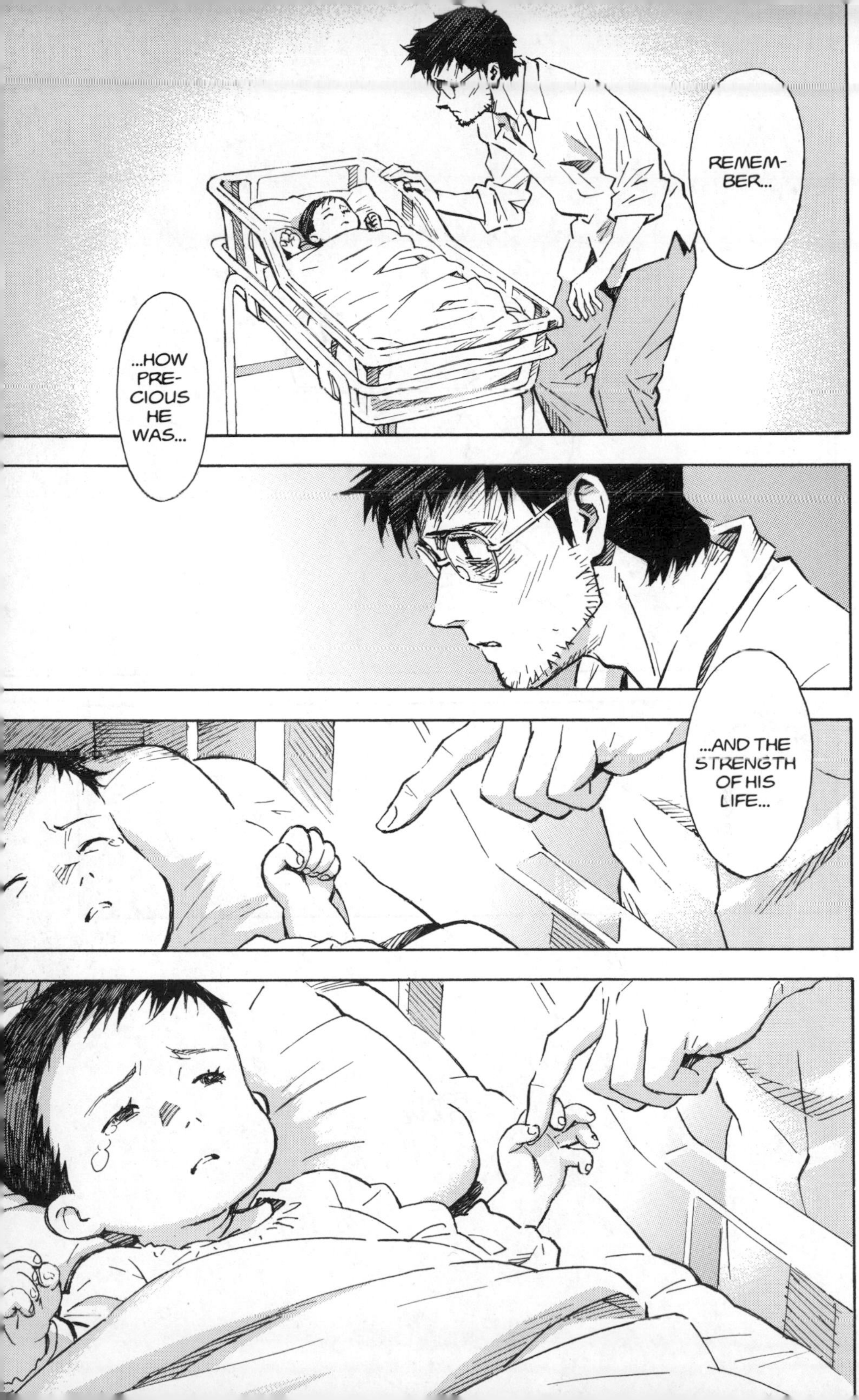
REMEMBER...
...HOW PRECIOUS HE WAS...
...AND THE STRENGTH OF HIS LIFE...

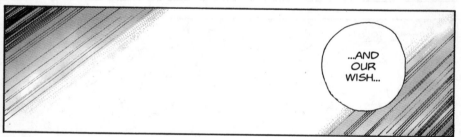

...AND OUR WISH...

...FOR HIM TO *LIVE*.

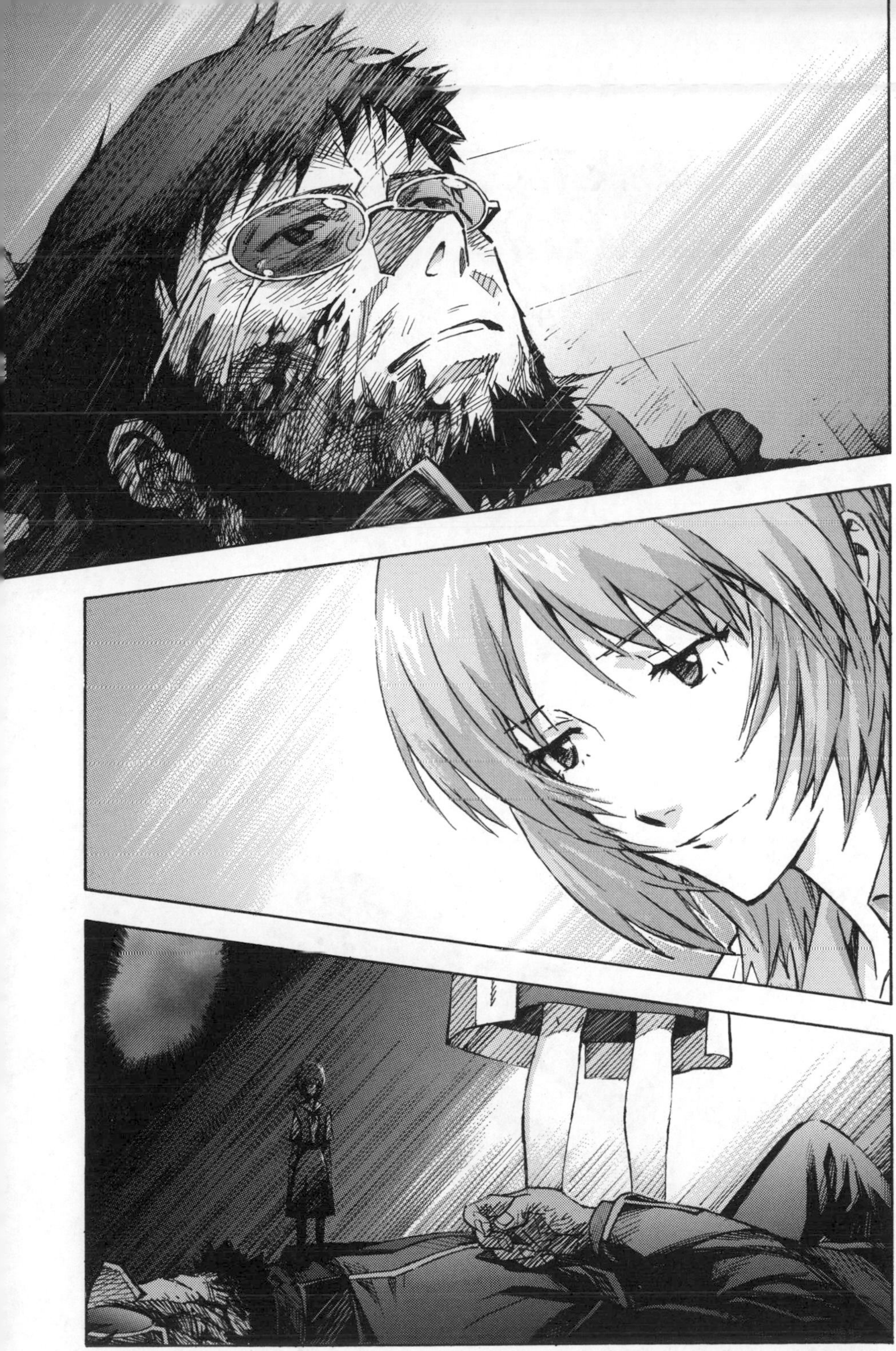

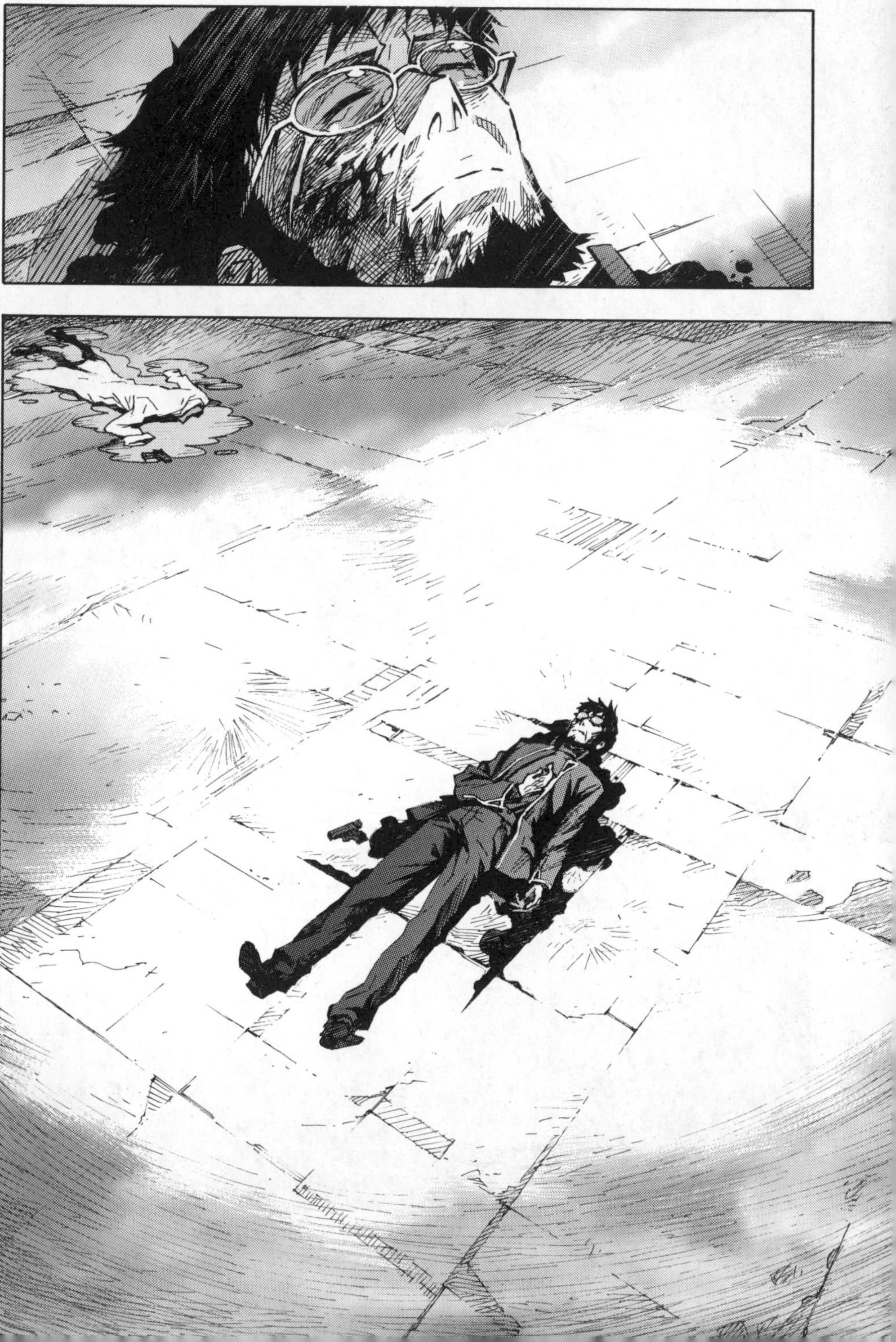

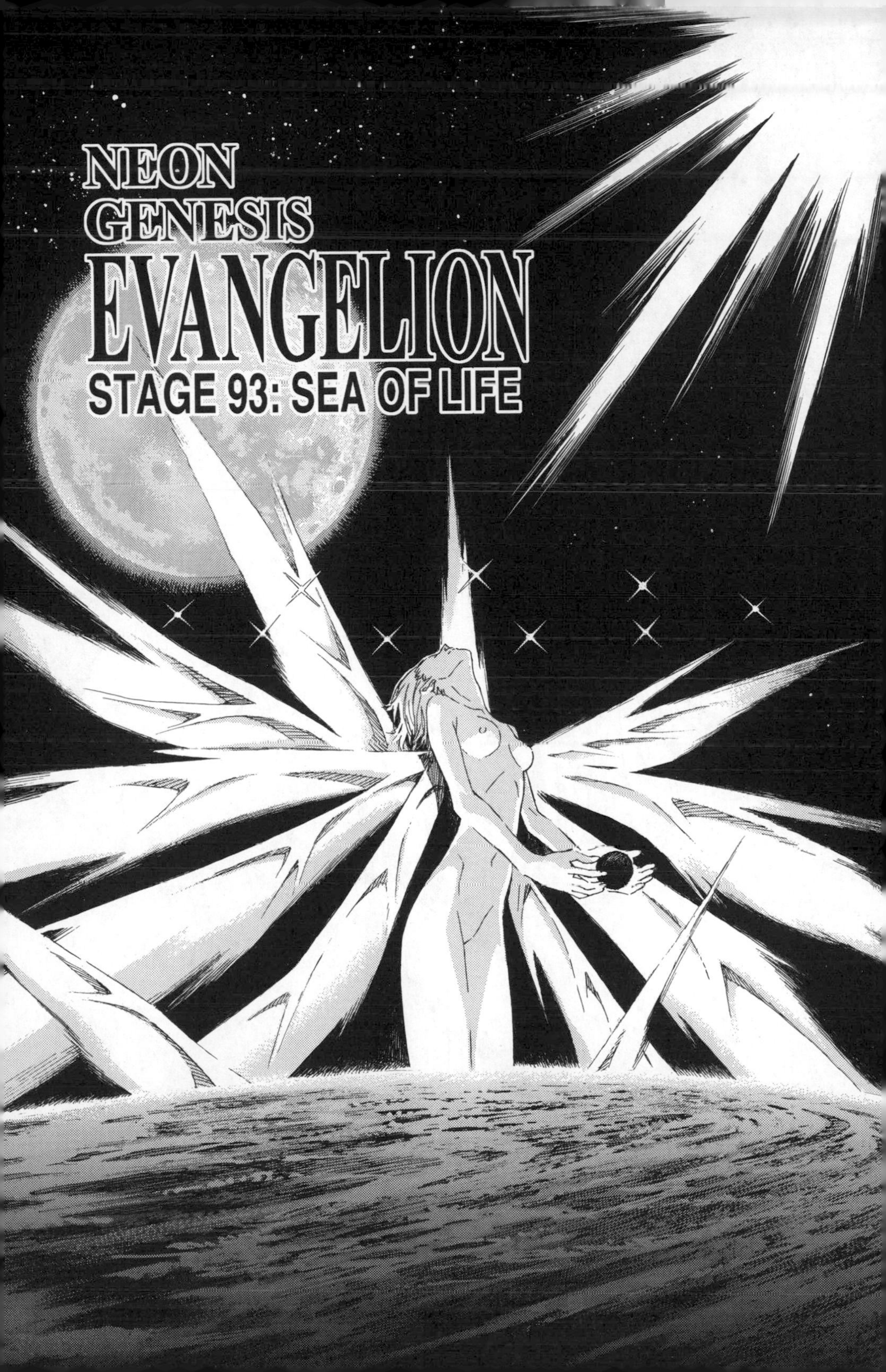
NEON GENESIS EVANGELION
STAGE 93: SEA OF LIFE

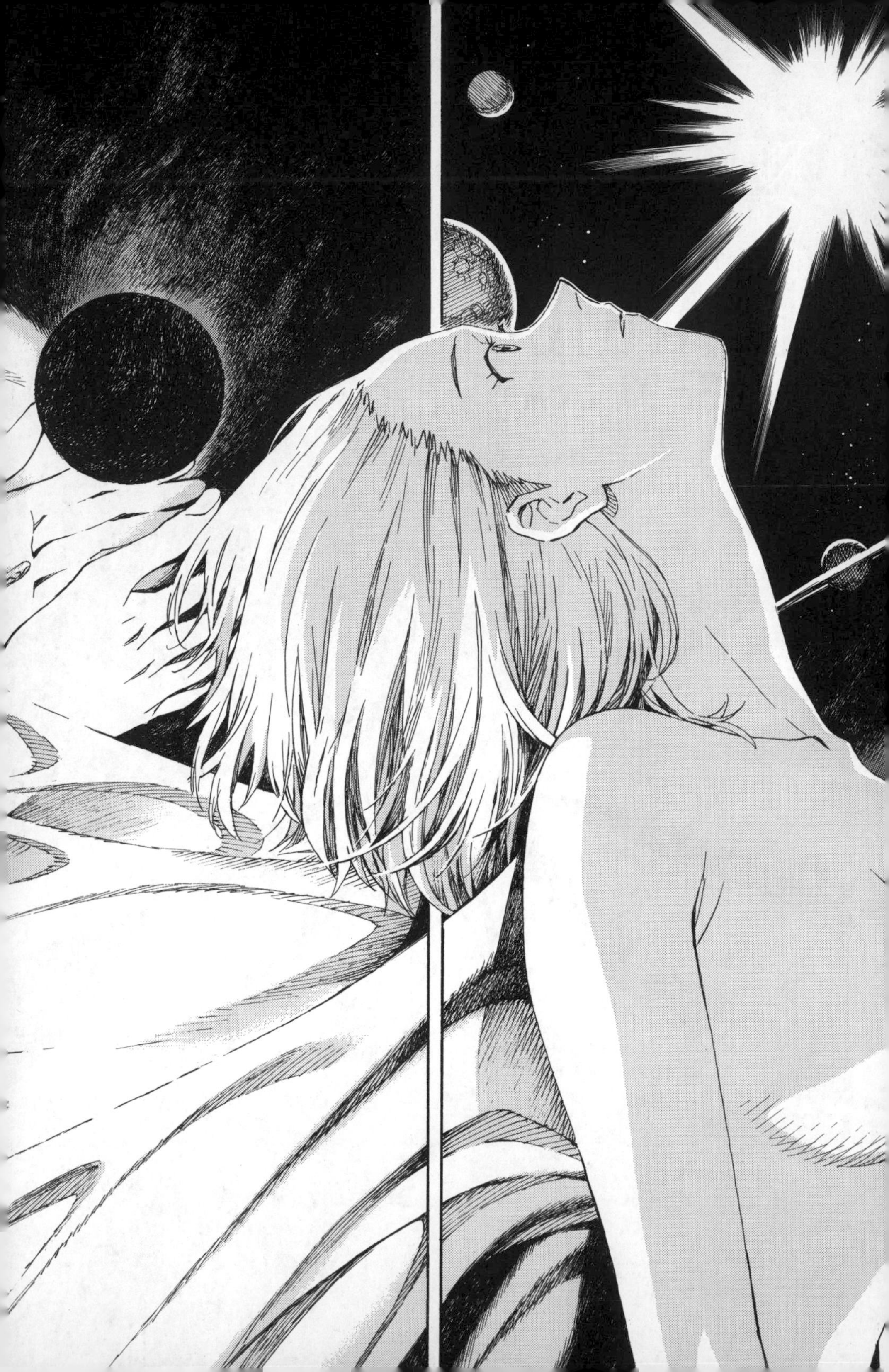

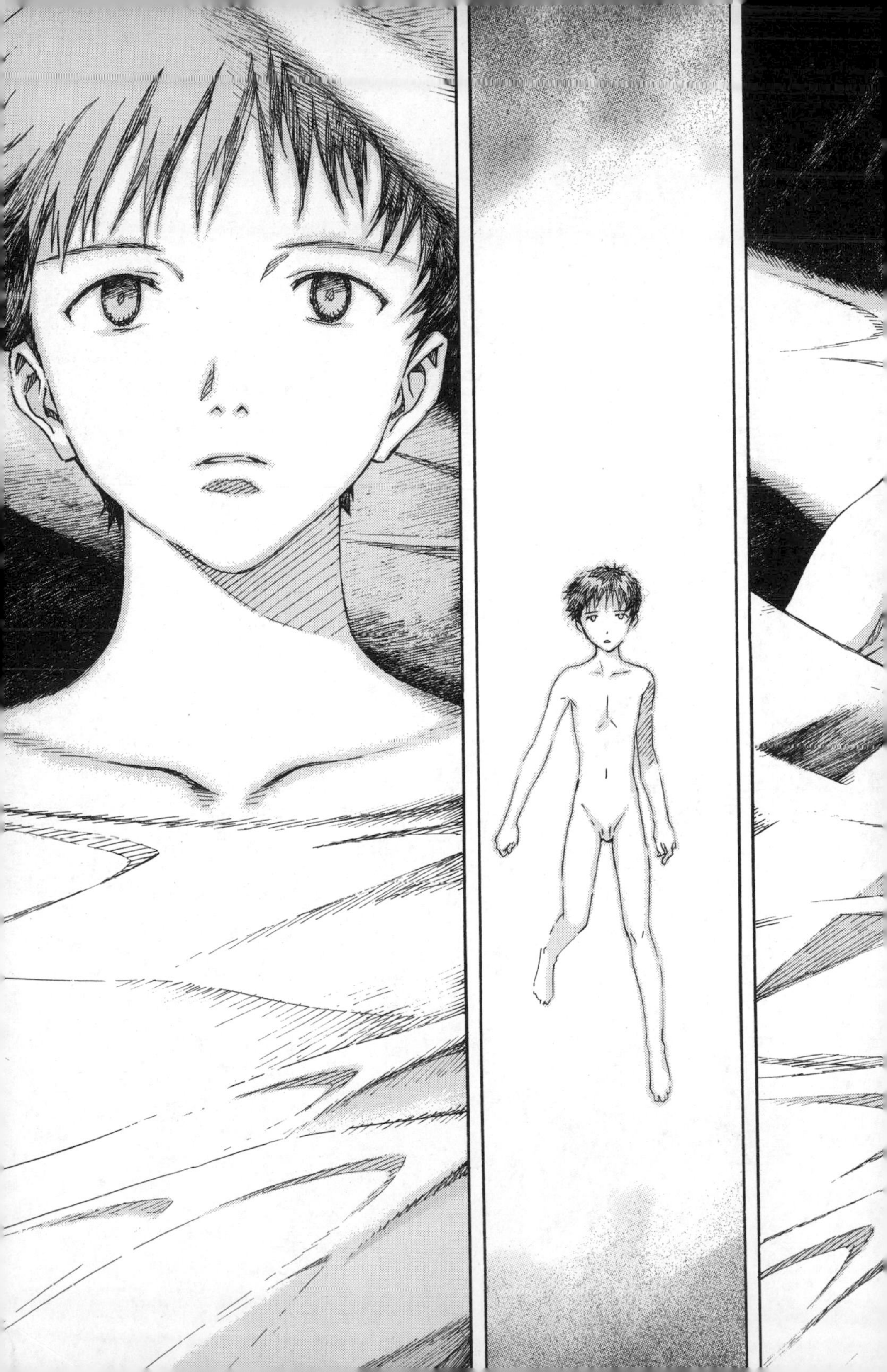

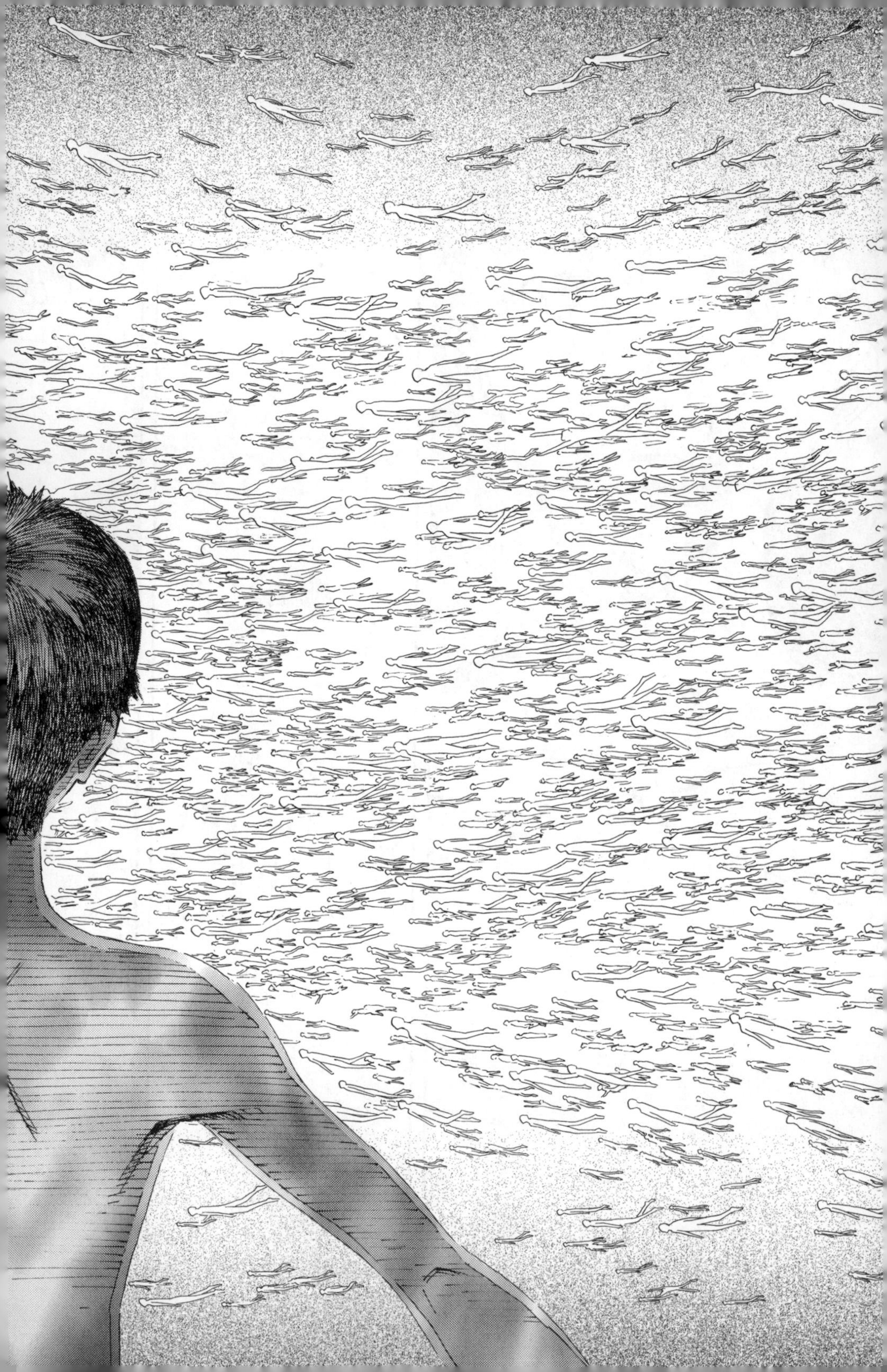

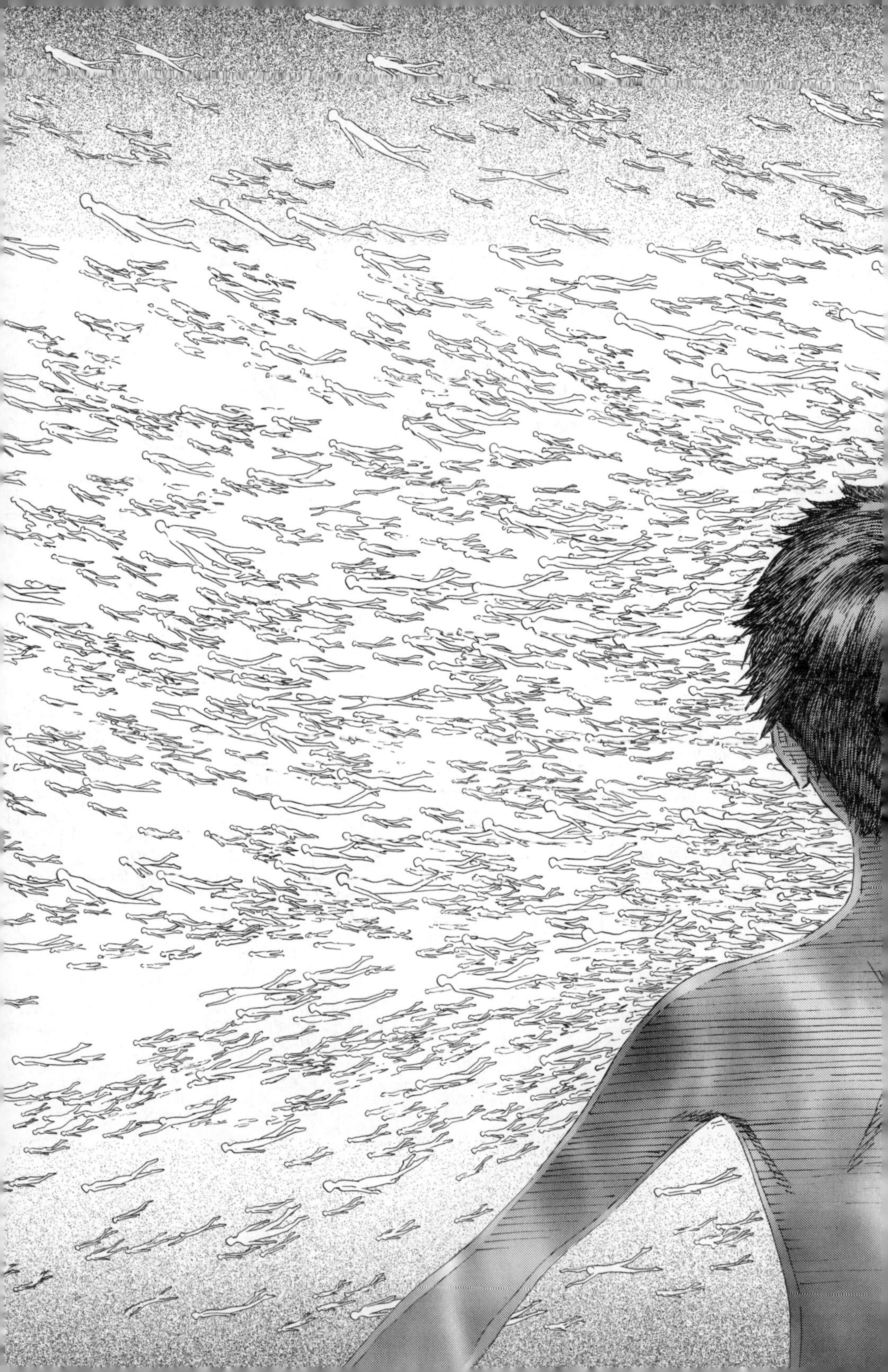

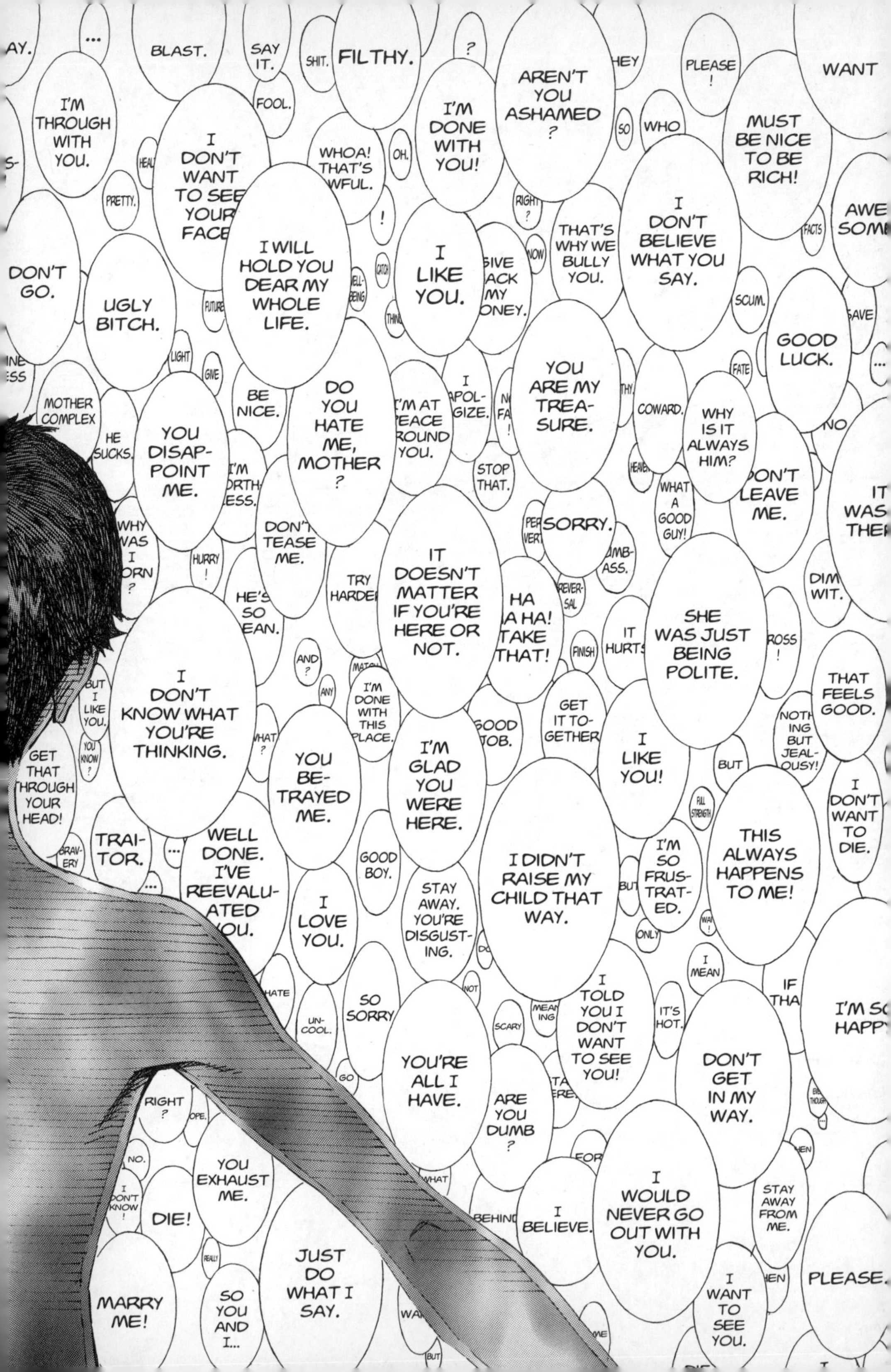
WANT
PLEASE !
AREN'T YOU ASHAMED ?
?
FILTHY.
SHIT.
SAY IT.
BLAST.
...
MUST BE NICE TO BE RICH!
WHO
SO
I'M DONE WITH YOU!
OH.
FOOL.
I DON'T WANT TO SEE YOUR FACE
I'M THROUGH WITH YOU.
PRETTY.
FACTS
I DON'T BELIEVE WHAT YOU SAY.
THAT'S WHY WE BULLY YOU.
RIGHT ?
NOW
I LIKE YOU.
!
CATCH
I WILL HOLD YOU DEAR MY WHOLE LIFE.
FUTURE
UGLY BITCH.
DON'T GO.
GOOD LUCK.
SCUM.
...
FATE
YOU ARE MY TREASURE.
I APOLOGIZE.
DO YOU HATE ME, MOTHER ?
BE NICE.
GIVE
LIGHT
MOTHER COMPLEX
NO
WHY IS IT ALWAYS HIM?
COWARD.
STOP THAT.
YOU DISAPPOINT ME.
HE SUCKS.
WHAT A GOOD GUY!
SORRY.
IT DOESN'T MATTER IF YOU'RE HERE OR NOT.
HURRY !
DIMWIT.
SHE WAS JUST BEING POLITE.
FINISH
AND ?
ANY
THAT FEELS GOOD.
NOTHING BUT JEALOUSY!
BUT
I LIKE YOU!
GET IT TOGETHER
I'M DONE WITH THIS PLACE.
I DON'T KNOW WHAT YOU'RE THINKING.
BUT I LIKE YOU.
YOU KNOW ?
GET THAT THROUGH YOUR HEAD!
I DON'T WANT TO DIE.
THIS ALWAYS HAPPENS TO ME!
FULL STRENGTH
I'M SO FRUSTRATED.
I DIDN'T RAISE MY CHILD THAT WAY.
I'M GLAD YOU WERE HERE.
YOU BETRAYED ME.
GOOD BOY.
TRAITOR.
...
BRAVERY
ONLY
STAY AWAY. YOU'RE DISGUSTING.
I LOVE YOU.
I MEAN
I TOLD YOU I DON'T WANT TO SEE YOU!
IT'S HOT.
SCARY
NOT
SO SORRY
UNCOOL.
HATE
DON'T GET IN MY WAY.
YOU'RE ALL I HAVE.
ARE YOU DUMB ?
GO
RIGHT ?
NO.
YOU EXHAUST ME.
I DON'T KNOW !
DIE!
PLEASE.
STAY AWAY FROM ME.
I WOULD NEVER GO OUT WITH YOU.
I BELIEVE.
WHAT
I WANT TO SEE YOU.
JUST DO WHAT I SAY.
REALLY
SO YOU AND I...
MARRY ME!
BUT

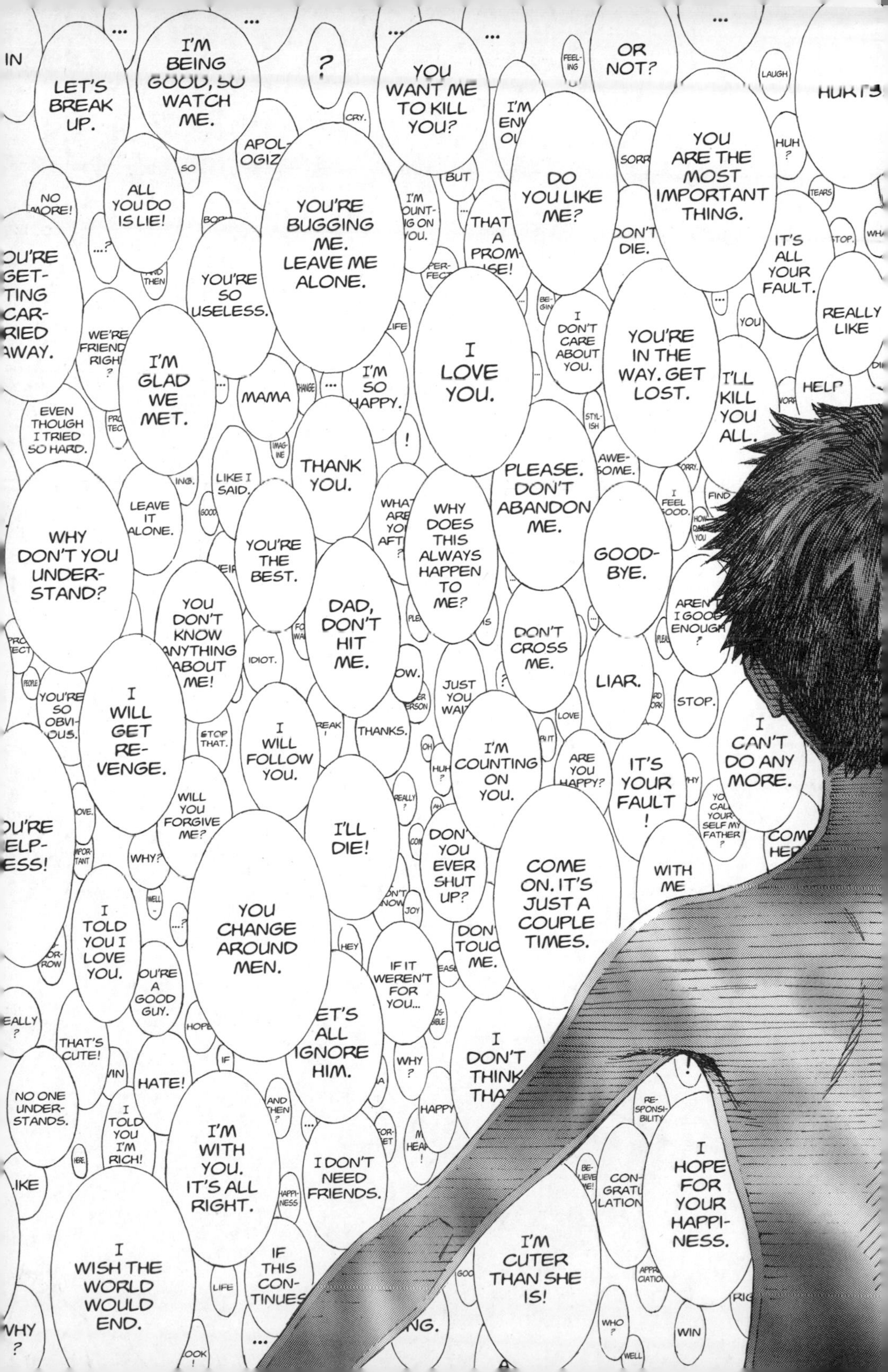
LAUGH
OR NOT?
FEEL-ING
...
YOU WANT ME TO KILL YOU?
...
?
...
I'M BEING GOOD, SO WATCH ME.
...
LET'S BREAK UP.
HUH ?
YOU ARE THE MOST IMPORTANT THING.
DO YOU LIKE ME?
BUT
CRY.
SO
ALL YOU DO IS LIE!
NO MORE!
TEARS
STOP.
IT'S ALL YOUR FAULT.
YOU'RE BUGGING ME. LEAVE ME ALONE.
...?
AND THEN
YOU'RE SO USELESS.
REALLY LIKE
YOU
...
YOU'RE IN THE WAY. GET LOST.
I DON'T CARE ABOUT YOU.
I LOVE YOU.
LIFE
I'M SO HAPPY.
...
MAMA
I'M GLAD WE MET.
EVEN THOUGH I TRIED SO HARD.
HELP
I'LL KILL YOU ALL.
STYL-ISH
AWE-SOME.
PLEASE. DON'T ABANDON ME.
!
THANK YOU.
IMAG-INE
LIKE I SAID.
LEAVE IT ALONE.
WHY DON'T YOU UNDER-STAND?
GOOD-BYE.
WHY DOES THIS ALWAYS HAPPEN TO ME?
YOU'RE THE BEST.
IDIOT.
YOU DON'T KNOW ANYTHING ABOUT ME!
DAD, DON'T HIT ME.
AREN'T I GOOD ENOUGH ?
DON'T CROSS ME.
LIAR.
STOP.
I CAN'T DO ANY MORE.
IT'S YOUR FAULT !
ARE YOU HAPPY?
LOVE
I'M COUNTING ON YOU.
THANKS.
I WILL FOLLOW YOU.
STOP THAT.
I WILL GET RE-VENGE.
PEOPLE
WITH ME
COME ON. IT'S JUST A COUPLE TIMES.
I'LL DIE!
YOU CHANGE AROUND MEN.
WILL YOU FORGIVE ME?
WHY?
I TOLD YOU I LOVE YOU.
JOY
HEY
IF IT WEREN'T FOR YOU...
RE-SPONSI-BILITY
I HOPE FOR YOUR HAPPI-NESS.
HAPPY
WHY ?
I DON'T NEED FRIENDS.
I'M WITH YOU. IT'S ALL RIGHT.
HATE!
IF
I TOLD YOU I'M RICH!
THAT'S CUTE!
NO ONE UNDER-STANDS.
HERE.
I'M CUTER THAN SHE IS!
WIN
WHO ?
WELL
LIFE
IF THIS CON-TINUES
HAPPI-NESS
I WISH THE WORLD WOULD END.
...

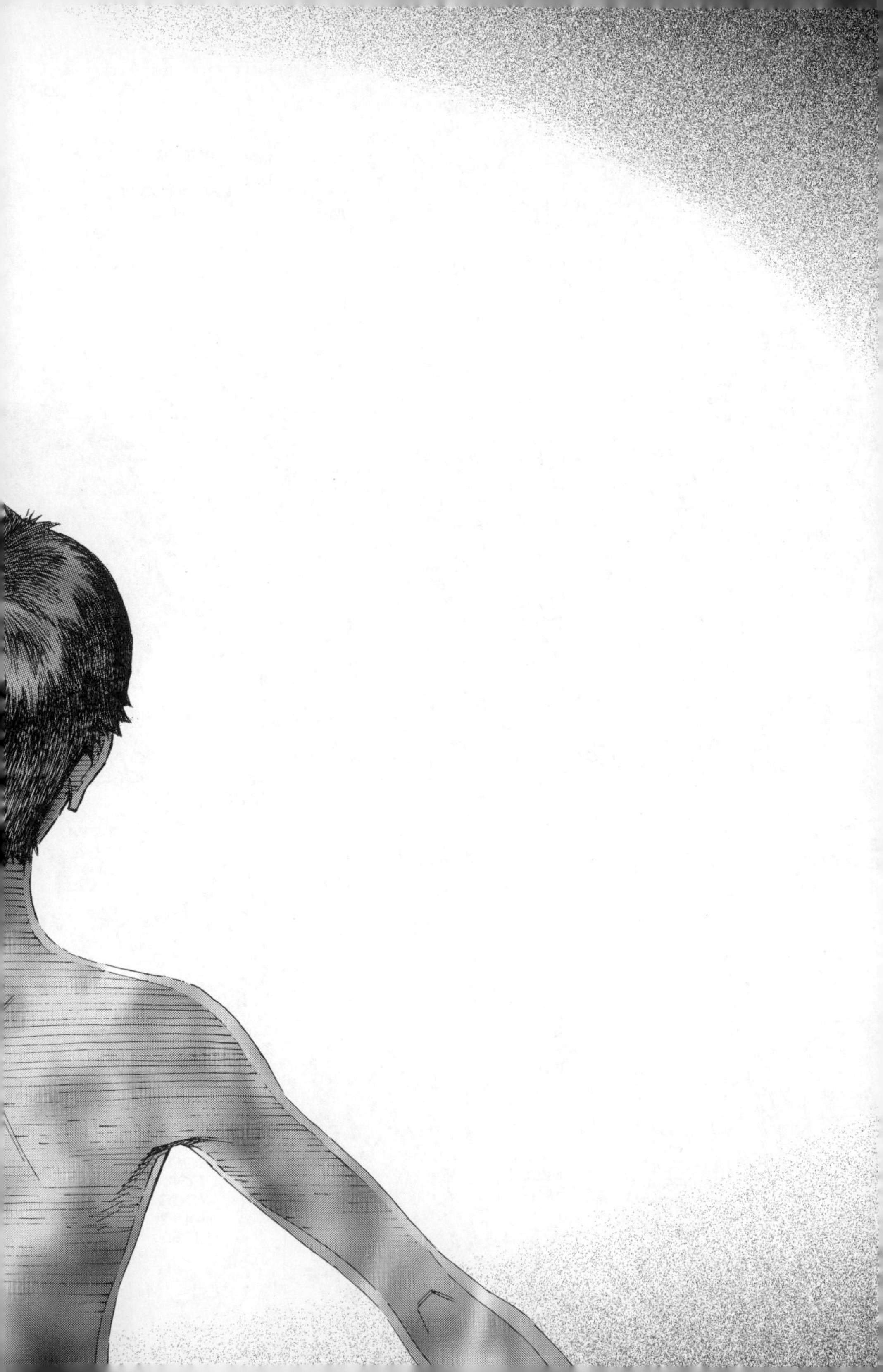

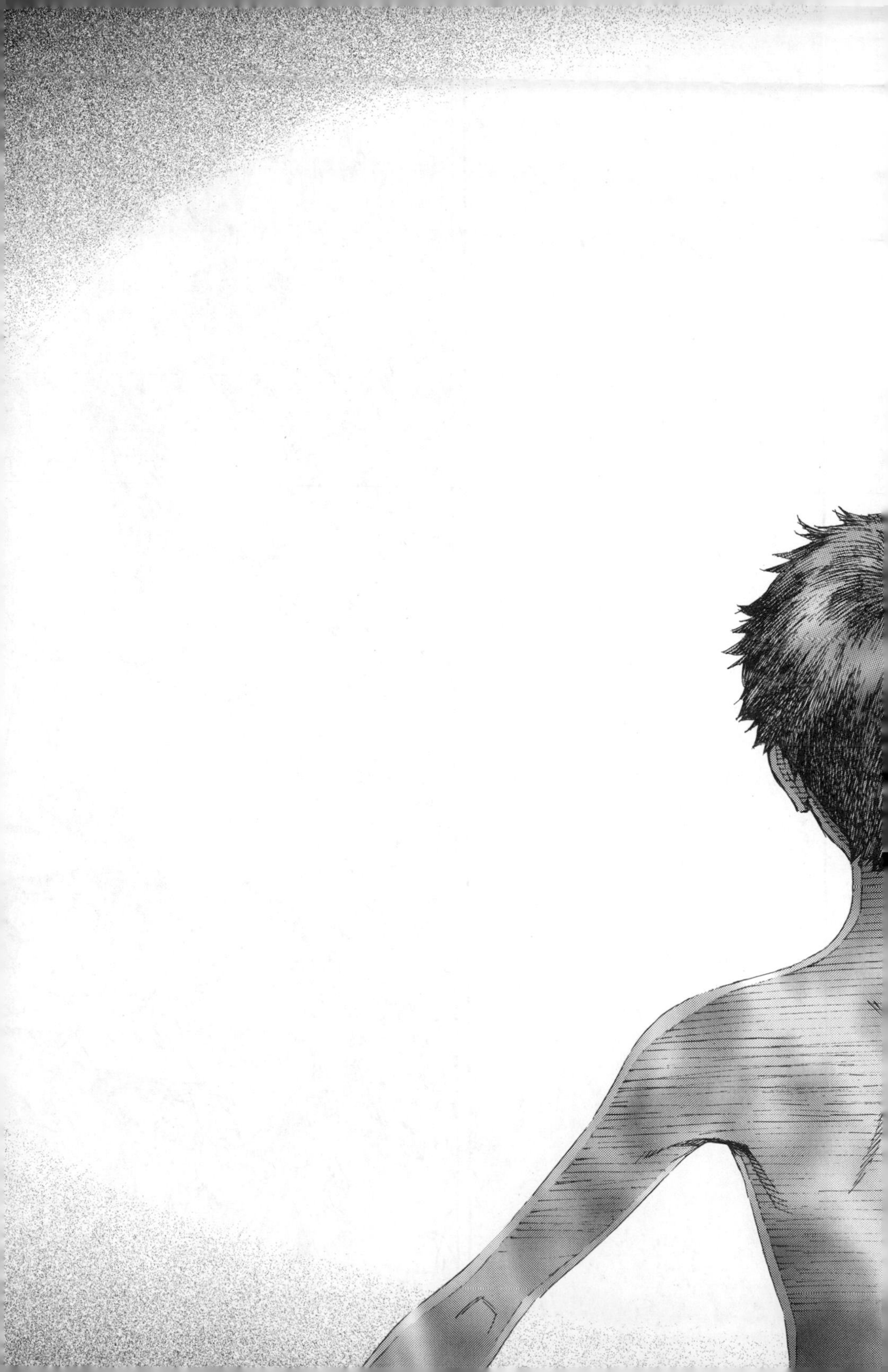

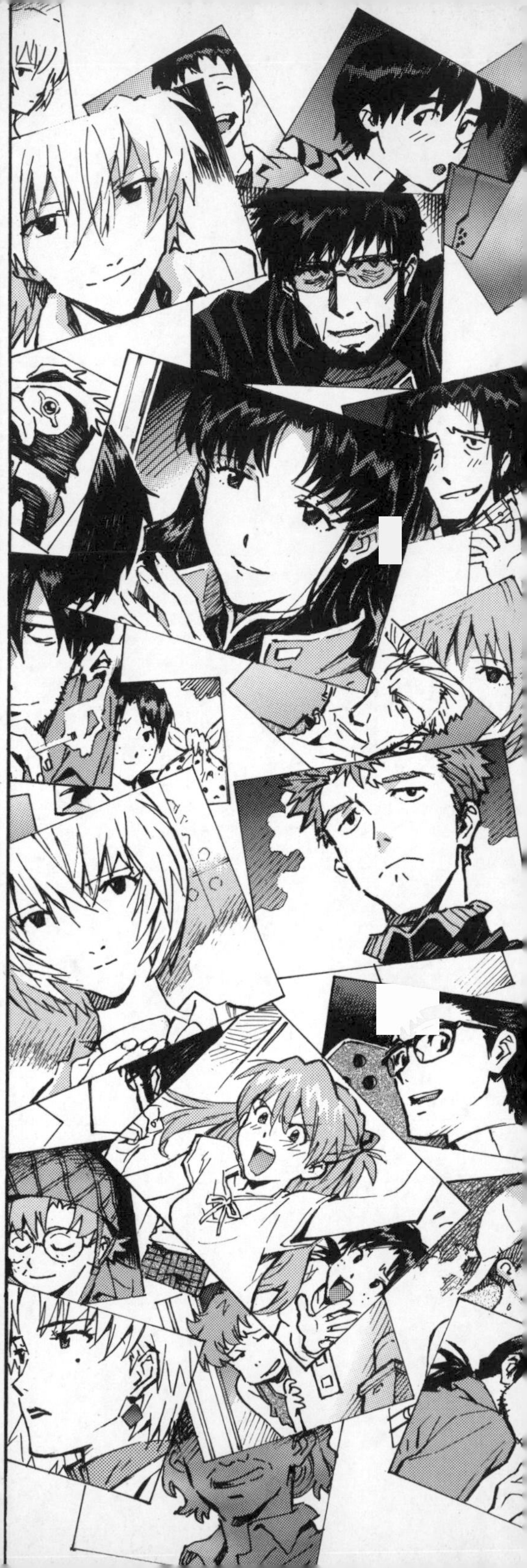
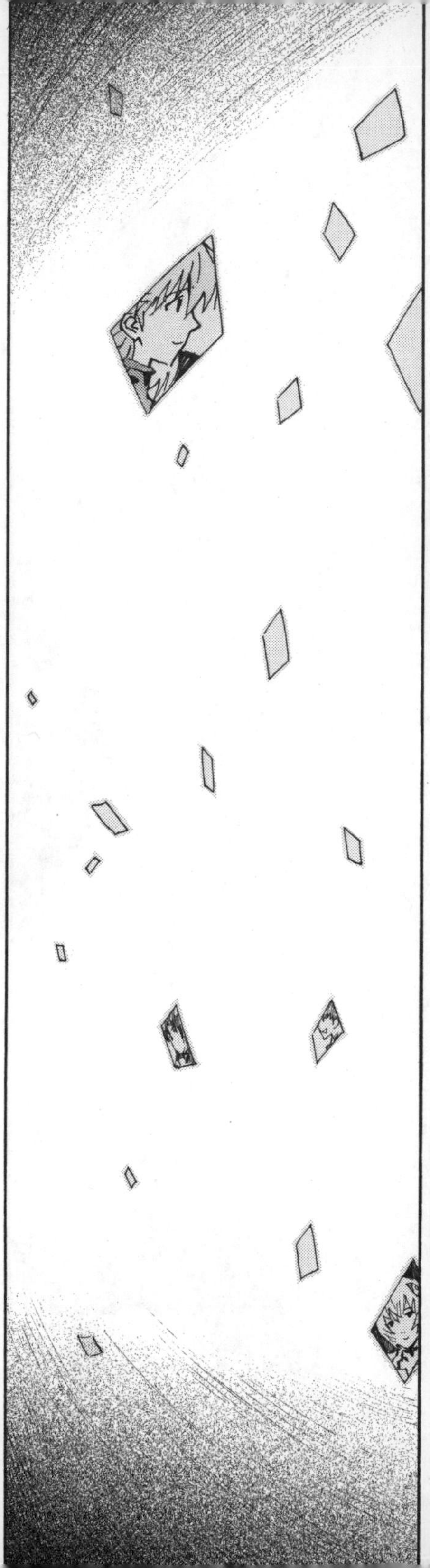

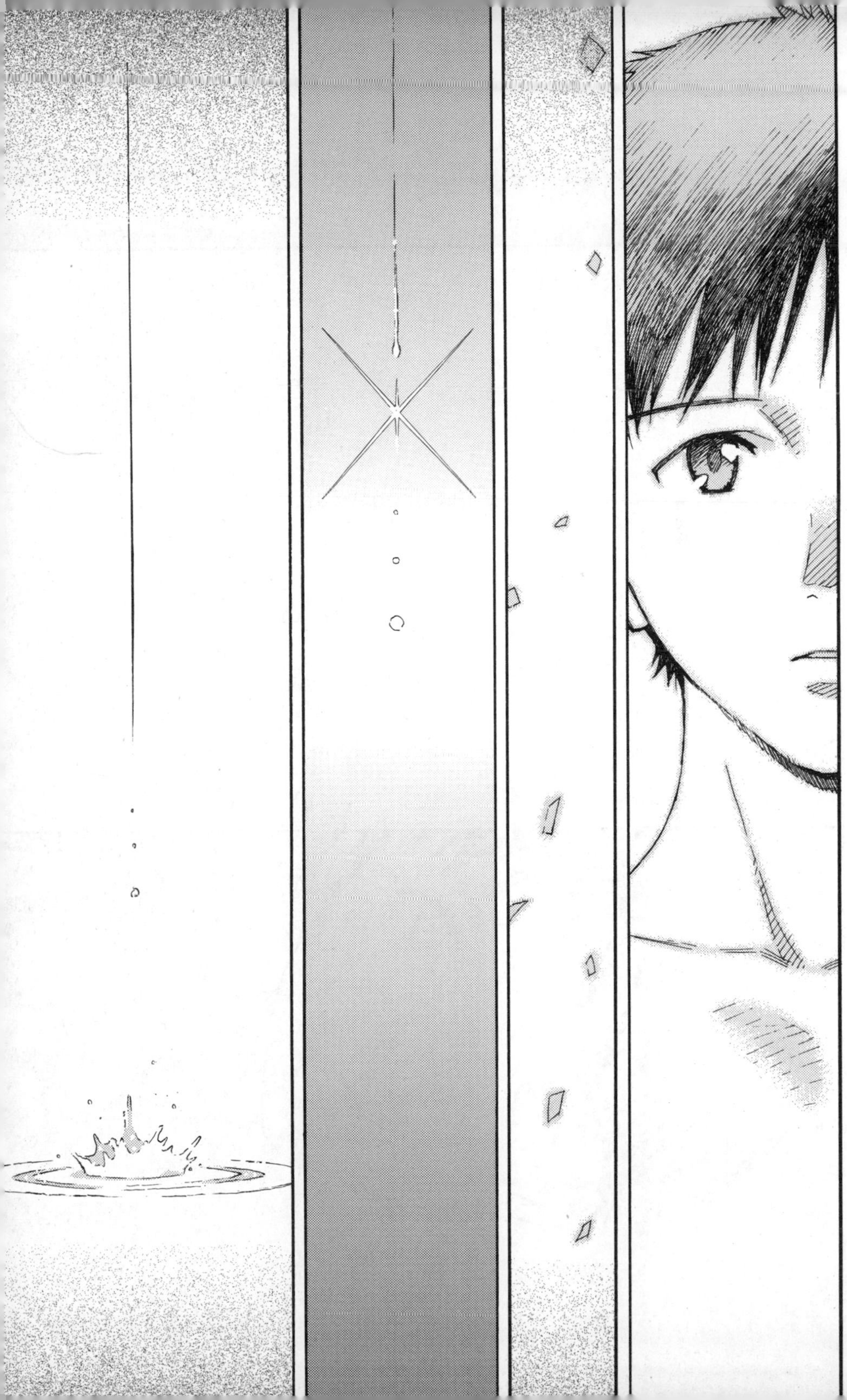

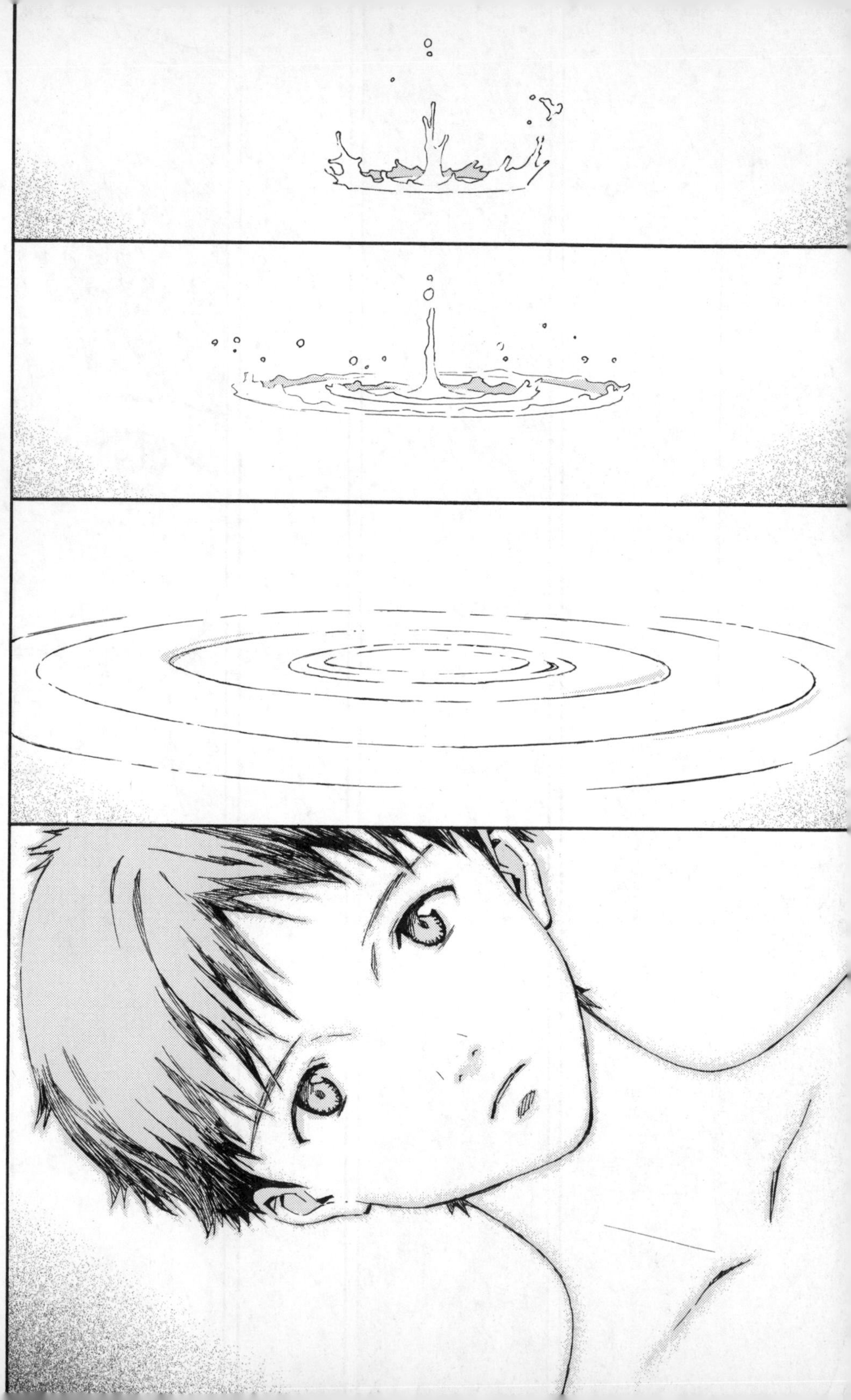

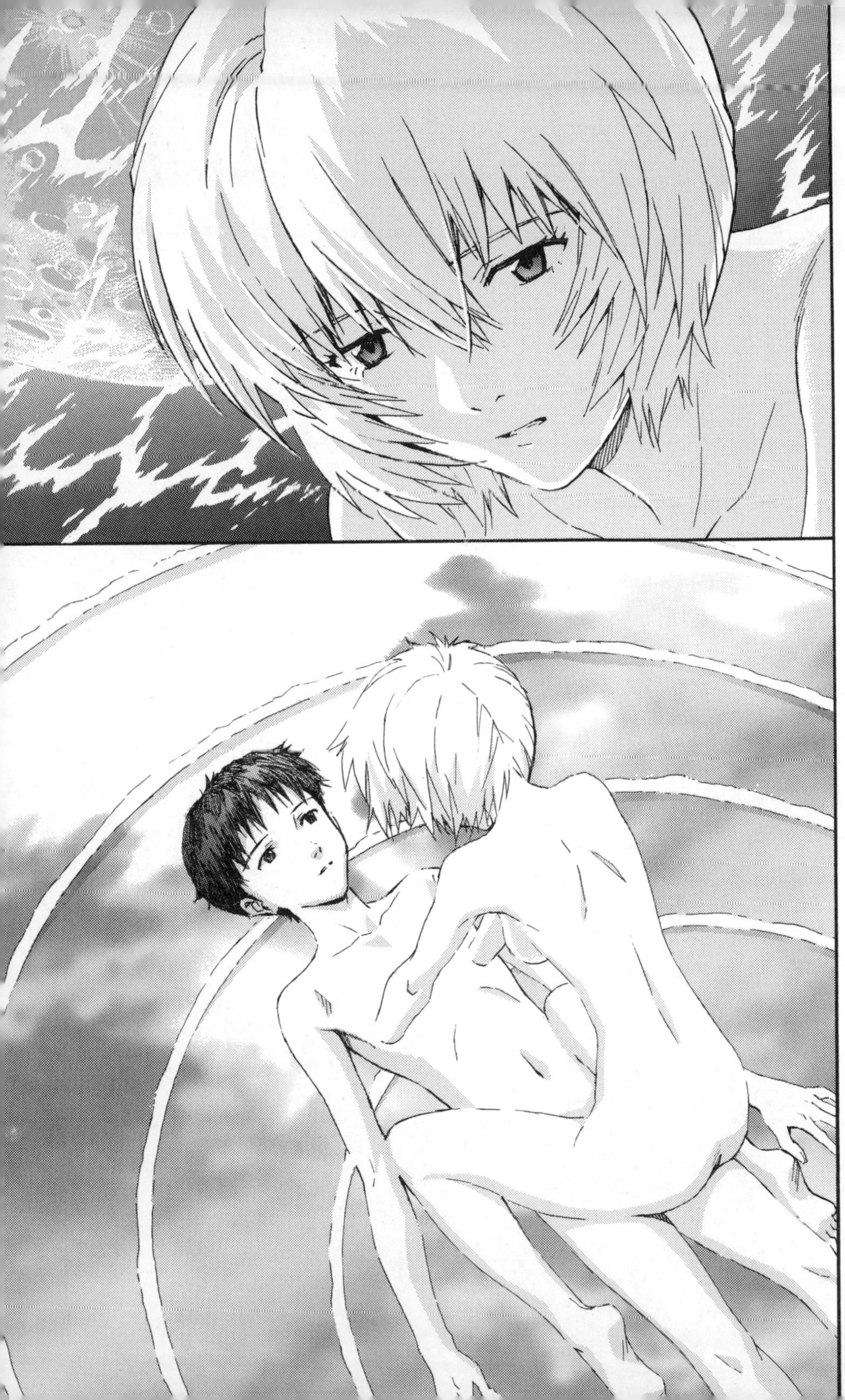

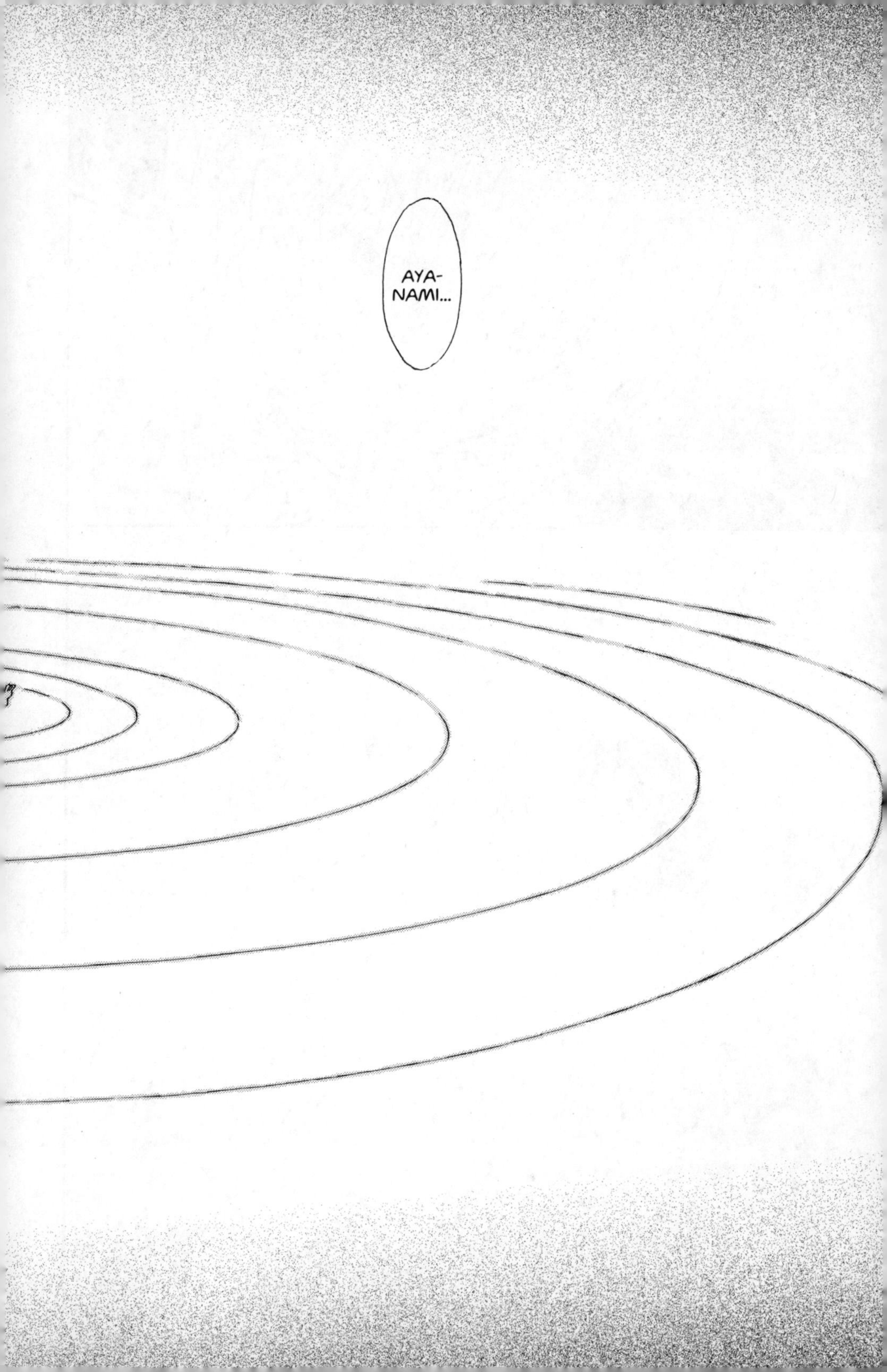
AYA-NAMI...

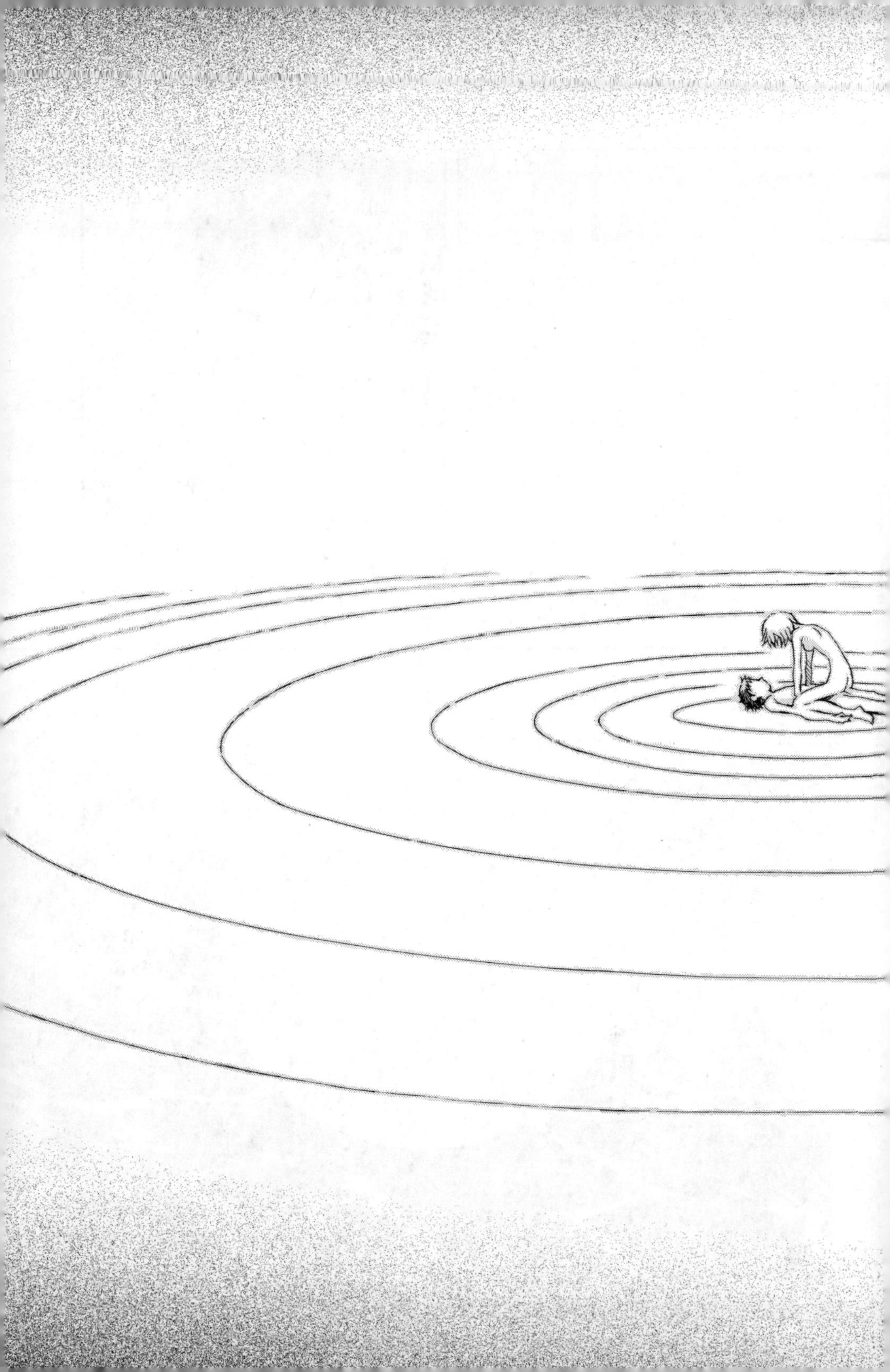

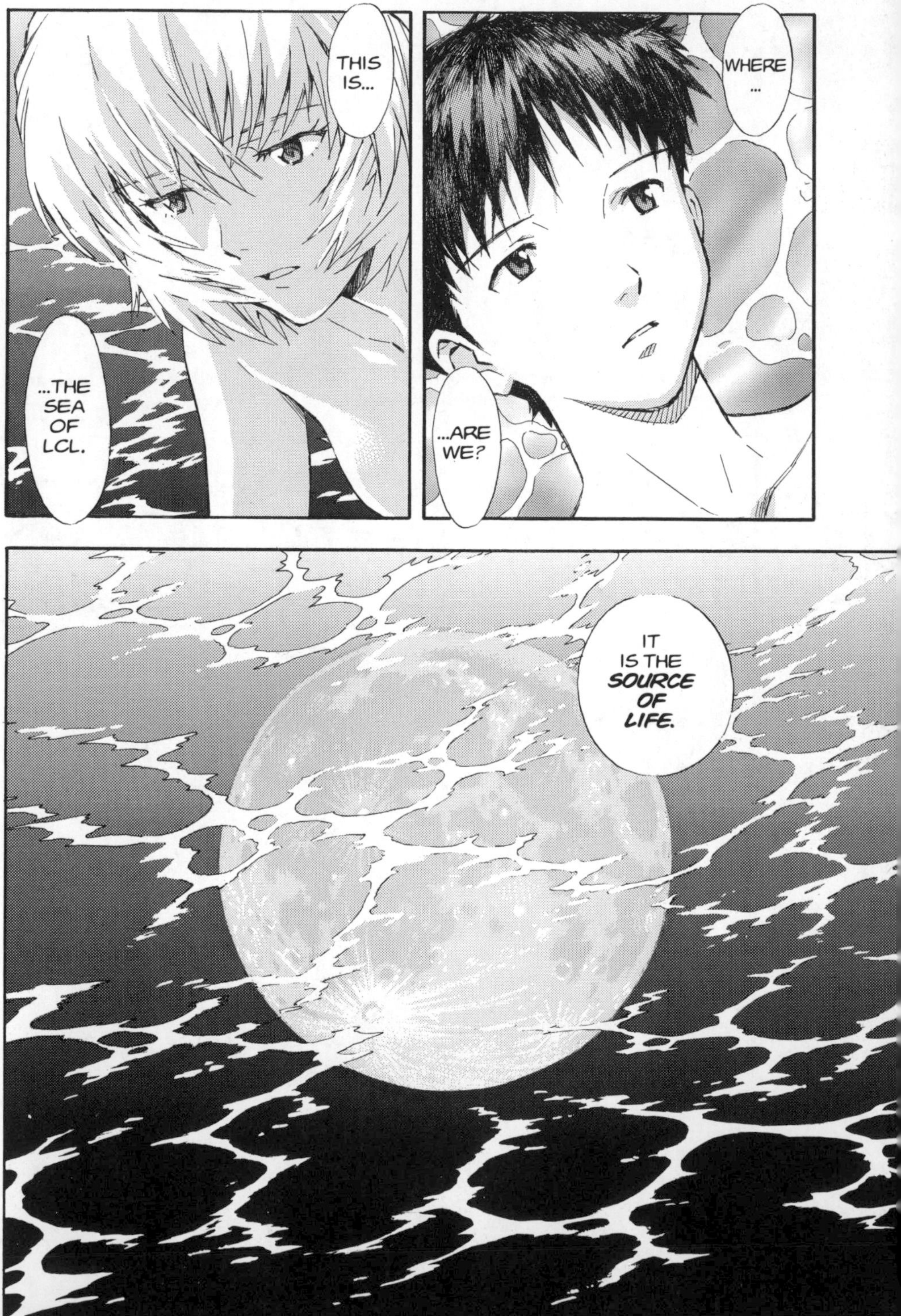
WHERE ...
...ARE WE?
THIS IS...
...THE SEA OF LCL.
IT IS THE ***SOURCE OF LIFE.***

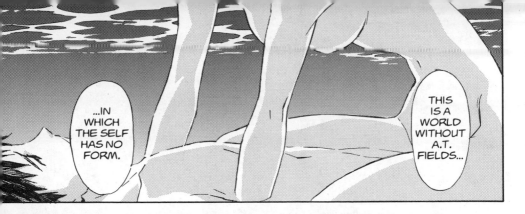

THIS IS A WORLD WITHOUT A.T. FIELDS...
...IN WHICH THE SELF HAS NO FORM.
WHERE ONE PERSON ENDS...
...AND ANOTHER BEGINS IS UNCLEAR.
IT IS A **VAGUE** WORLD...
YOU EXTEND EVERYWHERE...
...AND ARE NOWHERE AT ONCE.
THIS IS A **FRAGILE** WORLD.

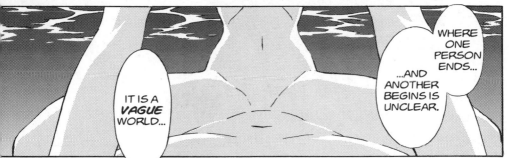

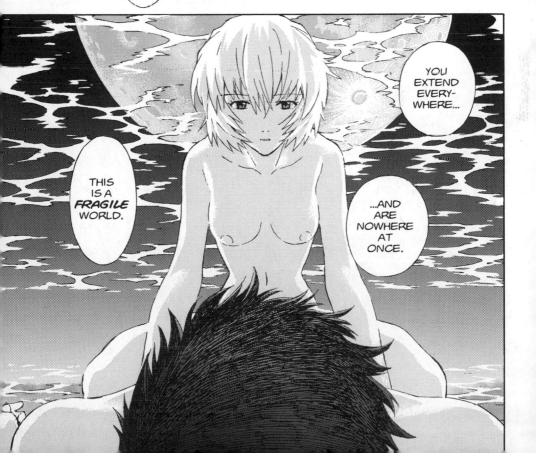

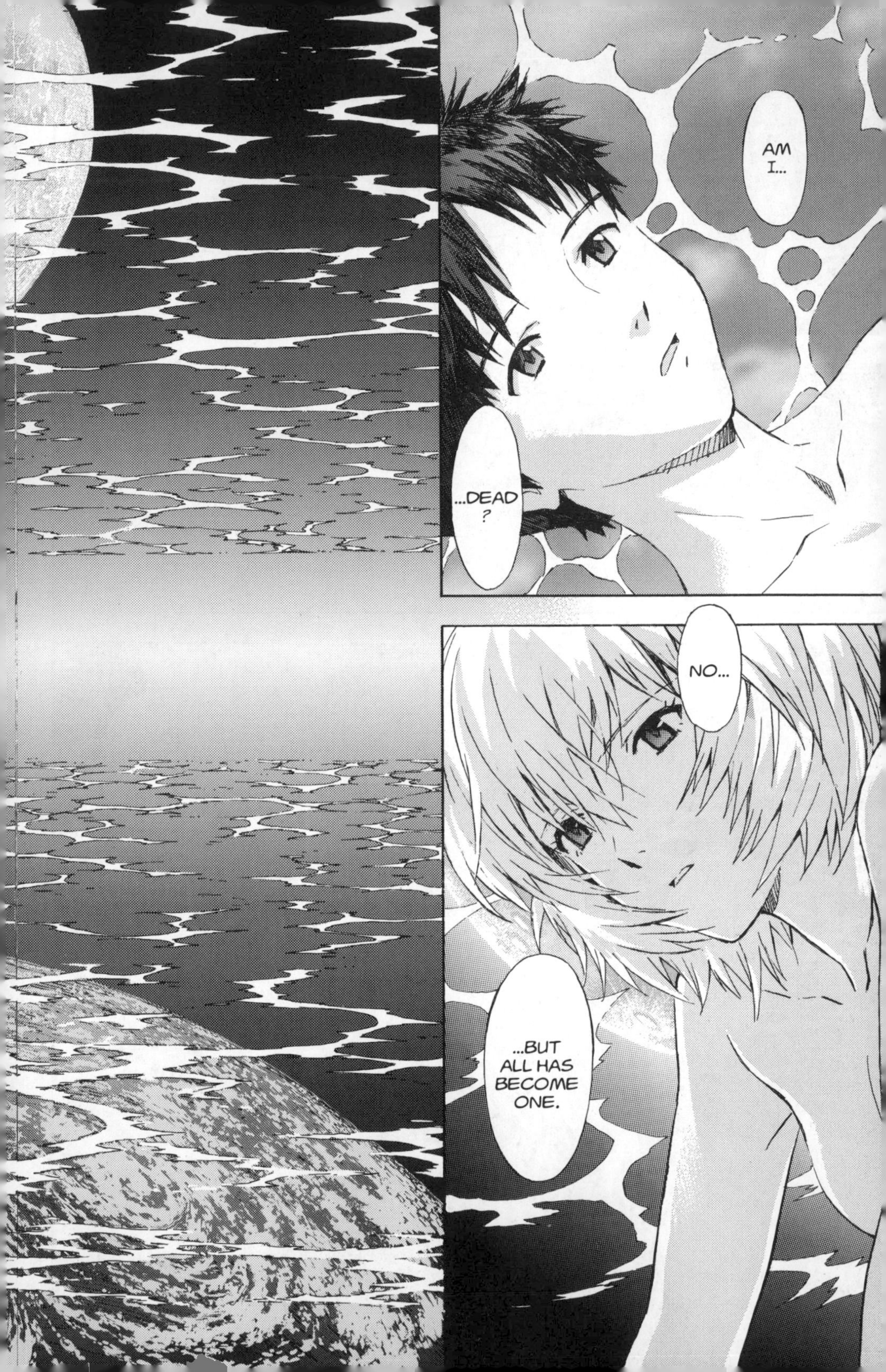
AM I...
...DEAD?
NO...
...BUT ALL HAS BECOME ONE.

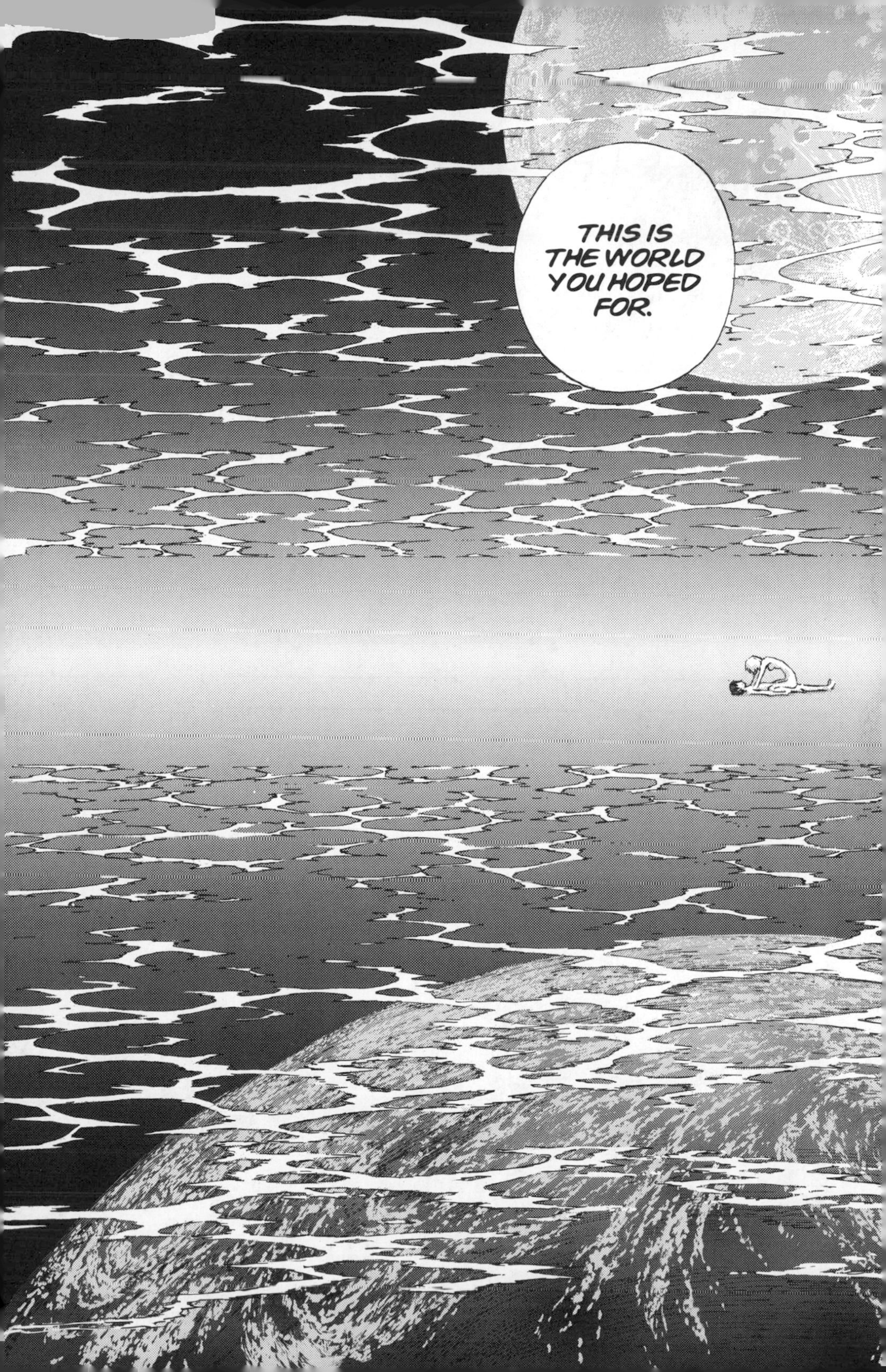
THIS IS THE WORLD YOU HOPED FOR.

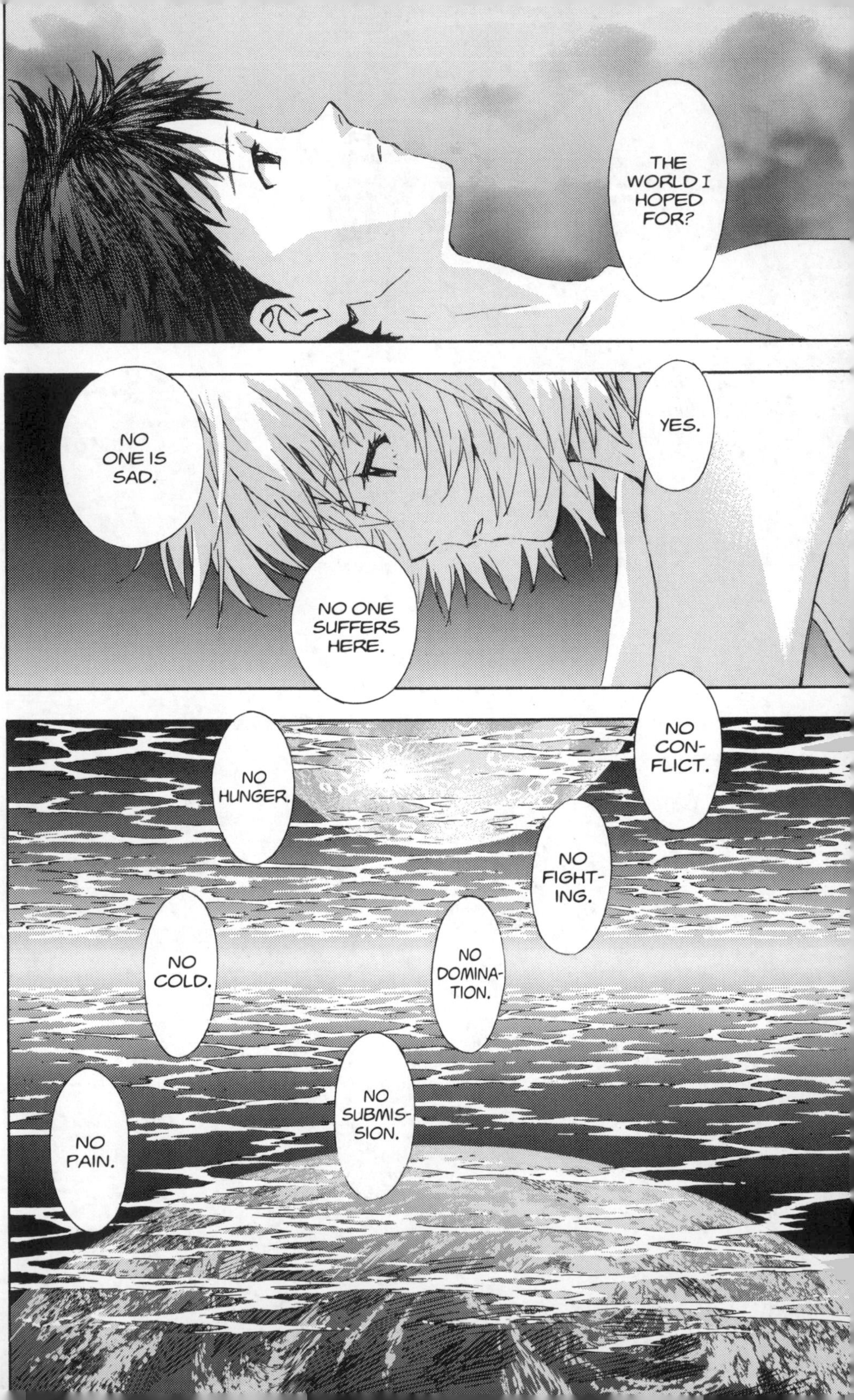
THE WORLD I HOPED FOR?
YES.
NO ONE IS SAD.
NO ONE SUFFERS HERE.
NO CONFLICT.
NO HUNGER.
NO FIGHTING.
NO DOMINATION.
NO COLD.
NO SUBMISSION.
NO PAIN.

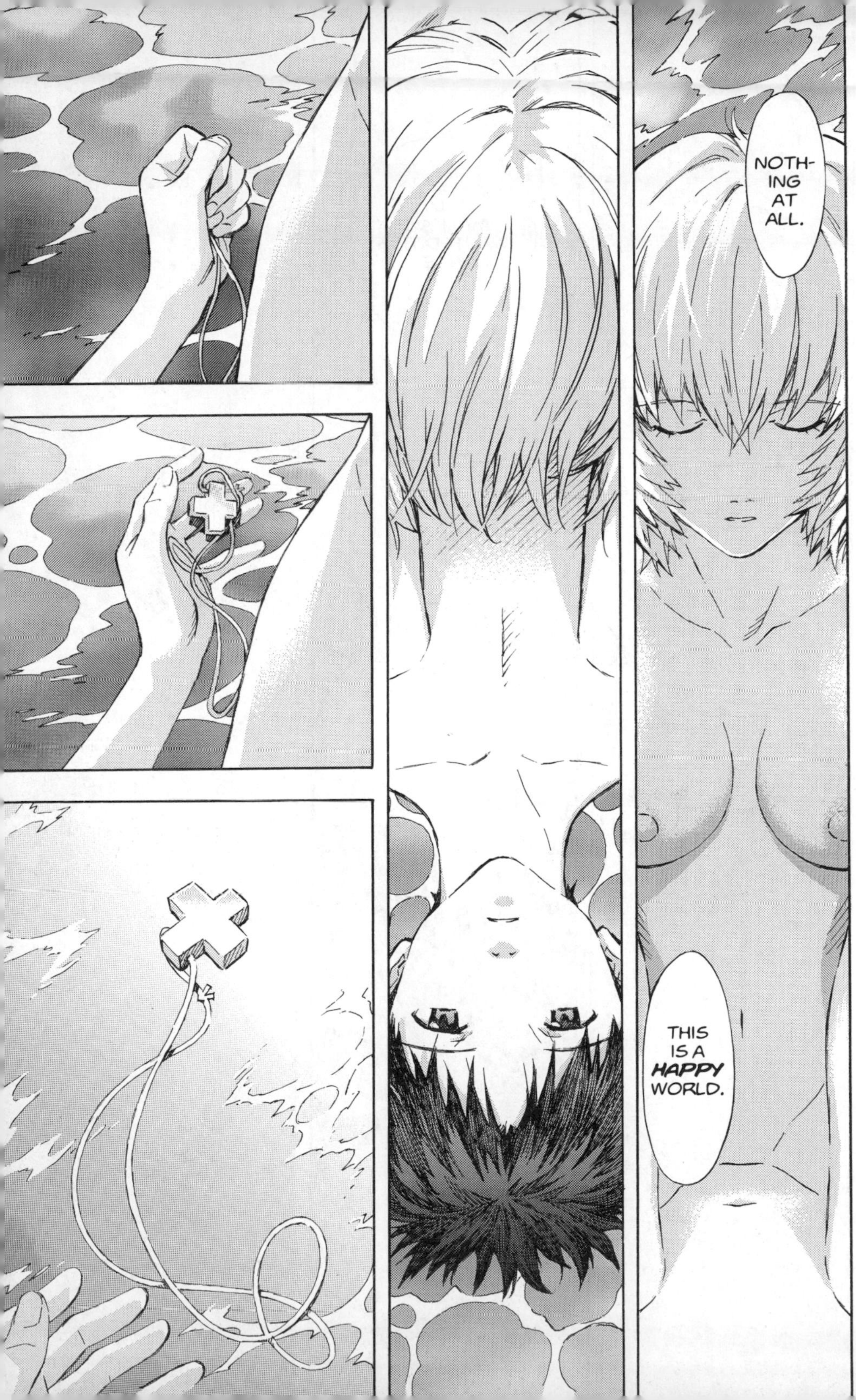
NOTH-ING AT ALL.
THIS IS A *HAPPY* WORLD.

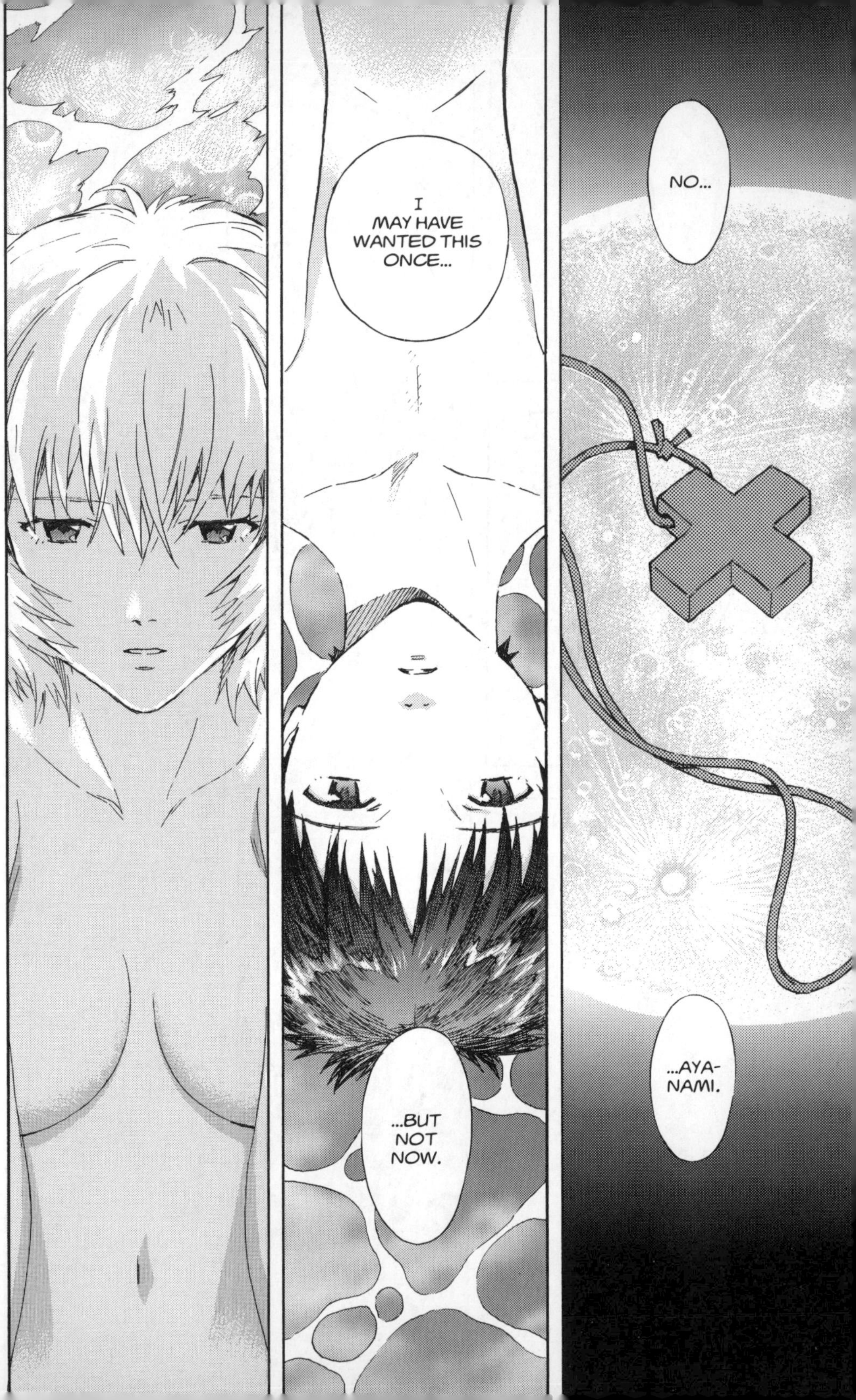
NO...
...AYA-NAMI.
I MAY HAVE WANTED THIS ONCE...
...BUT NOT NOW.

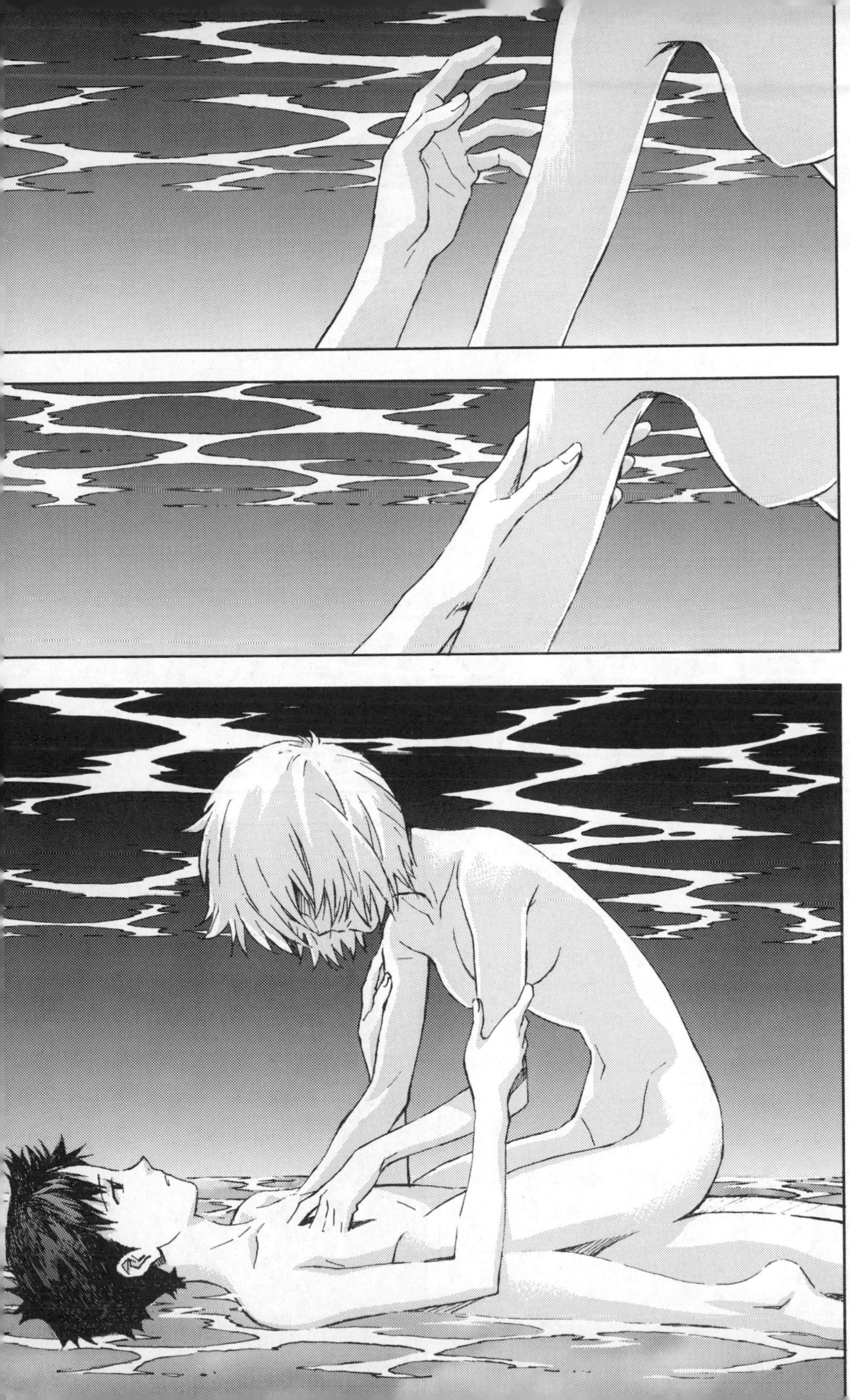

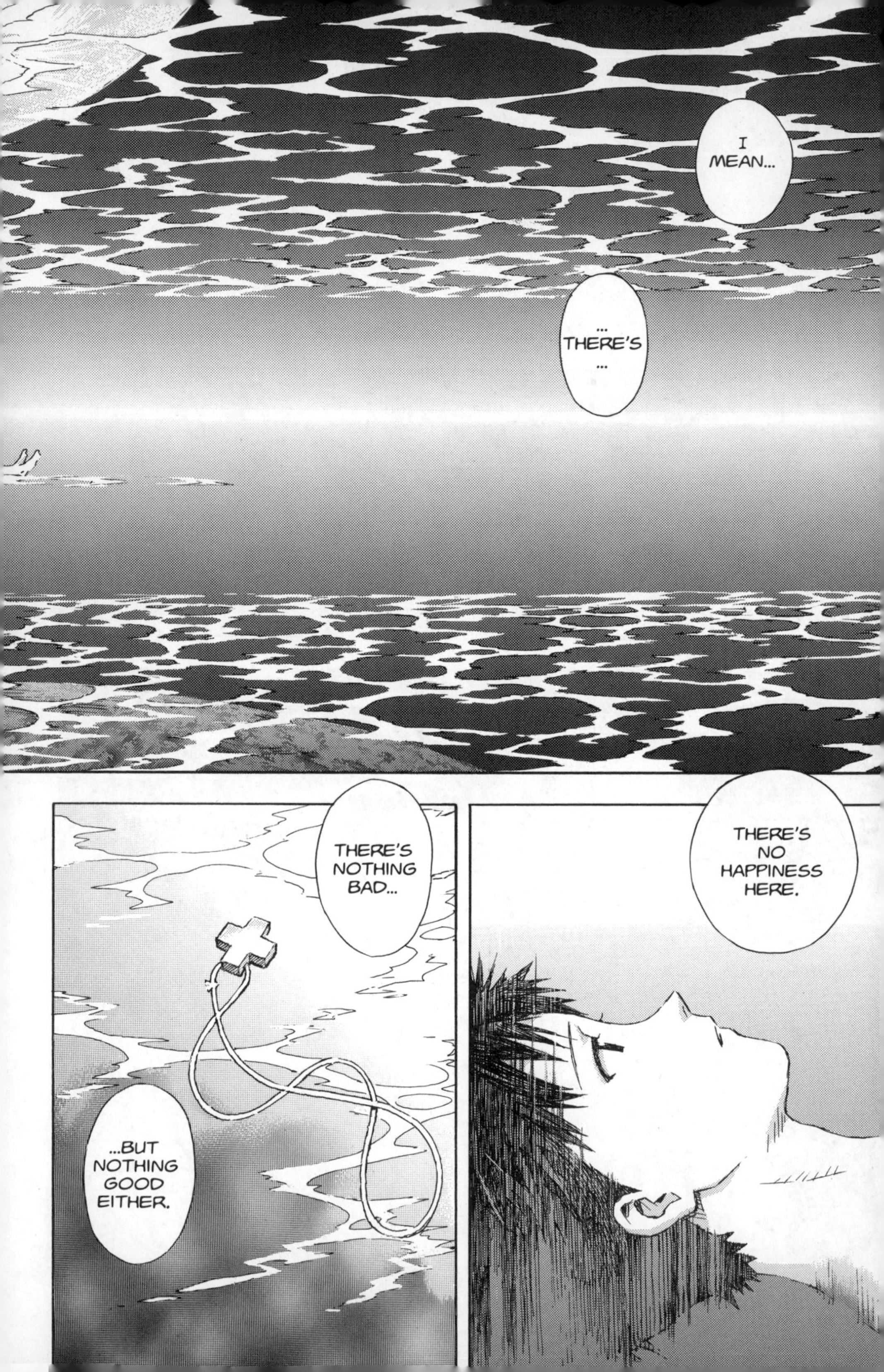
I MEAN...
... THERE'S ...
THERE'S NO HAPPINESS HERE.
THERE'S NOTHING BAD...
...BUT NOTHING GOOD EITHER.

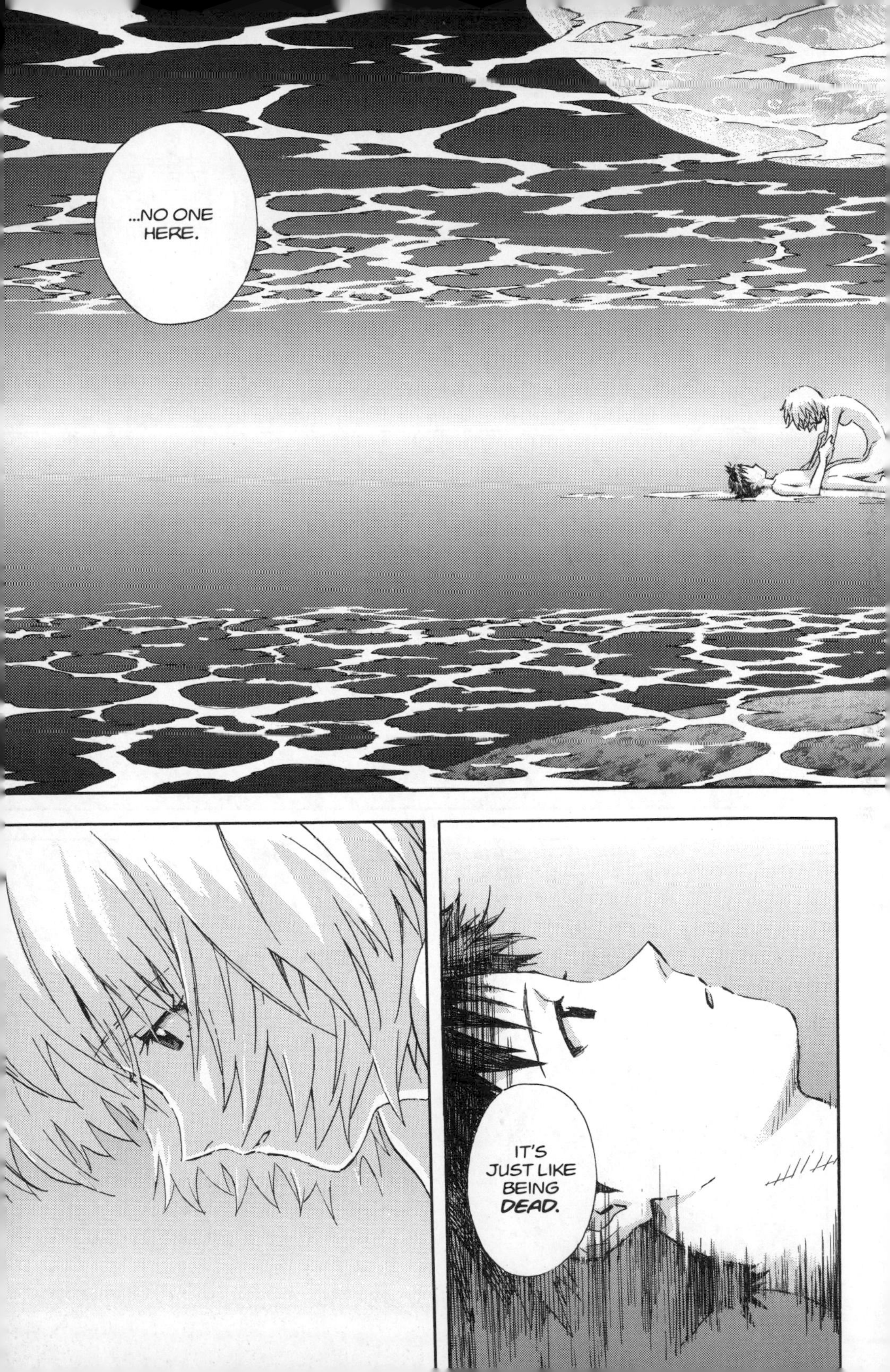
...NO ONE HERE.
IT'S JUST LIKE BEING DEAD.

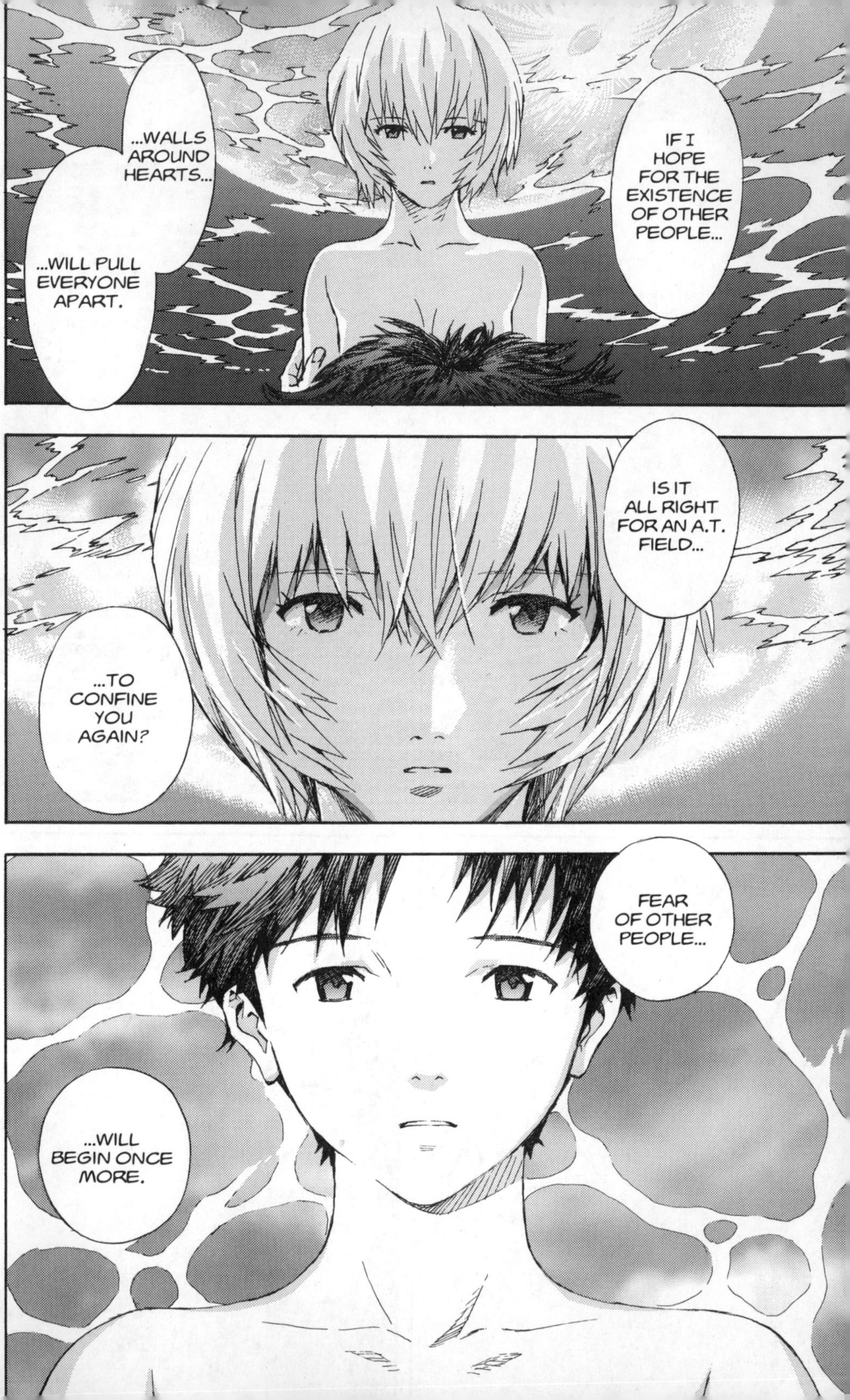
IF I HOPE FOR THE EXISTENCE OF OTHER PEOPLE...
...WALLS AROUND HEARTS...
...WILL PULL EVERYONE APART.
IS IT ALL RIGHT FOR AN A.T. FIELD...
...TO CONFINE YOU AGAIN?
FEAR OF OTHER PEOPLE...
...WILL BEGIN ONCE MORE.

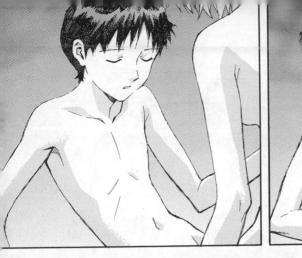
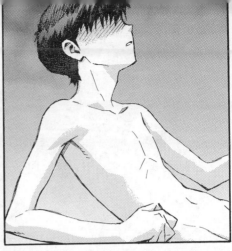

IT'S ALL RIGHT.

...IT'S IMPOSSIBLE FOR PEOPLE TO FULLY UNDERSTAND EACH OTHER.

MY FA-THER...

...TOLD ME...

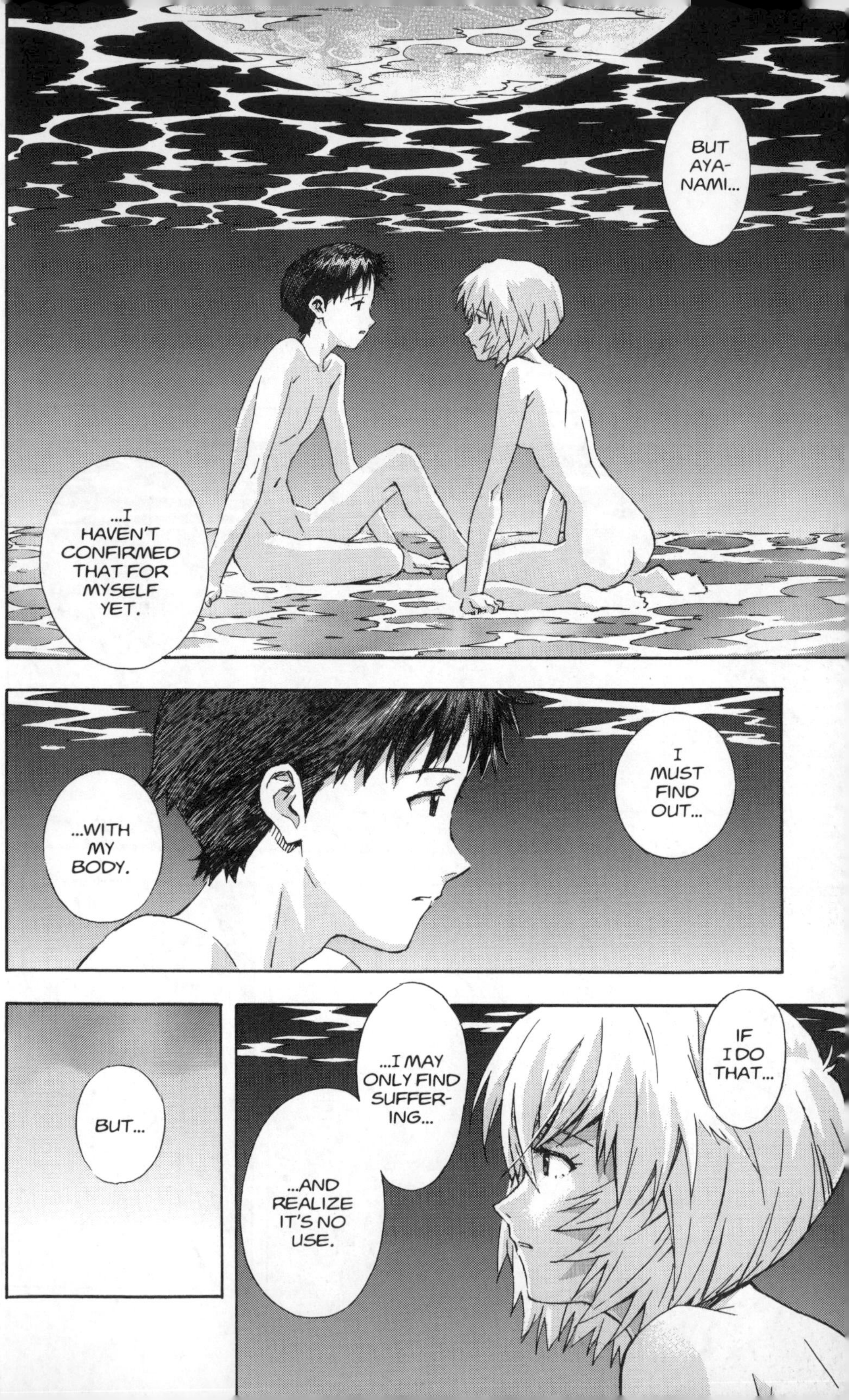
BUT AYA- NAMI...
...I HAVEN'T CONFIRMED THAT FOR MYSELF YET.
I MUST FIND OUT...
...WITH MY BODY.
IF I DO THAT...
...I MAY ONLY FIND SUFFER- ING...
...AND REALIZE IT'S NO USE.
BUT...

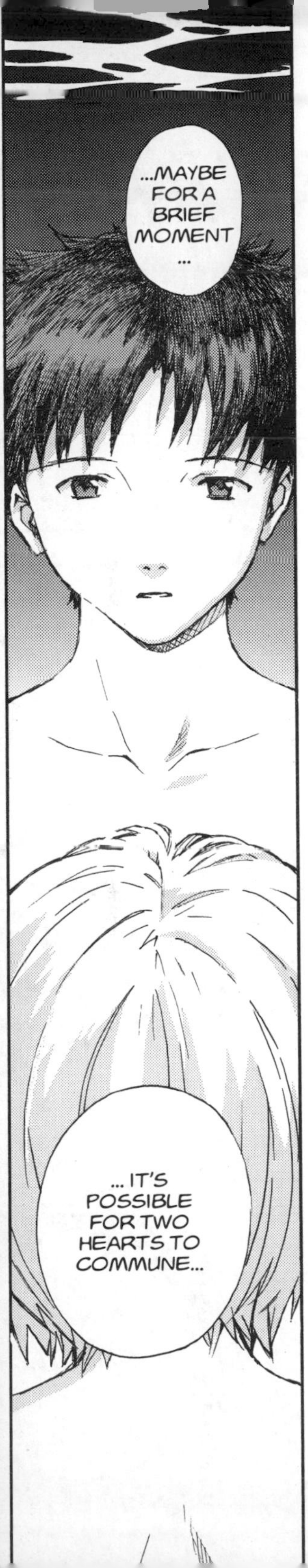
...MAYBE FOR A BRIEF MOMENT ...
... IT'S POSSIBLE FOR TWO HEARTS TO COMMUNE...
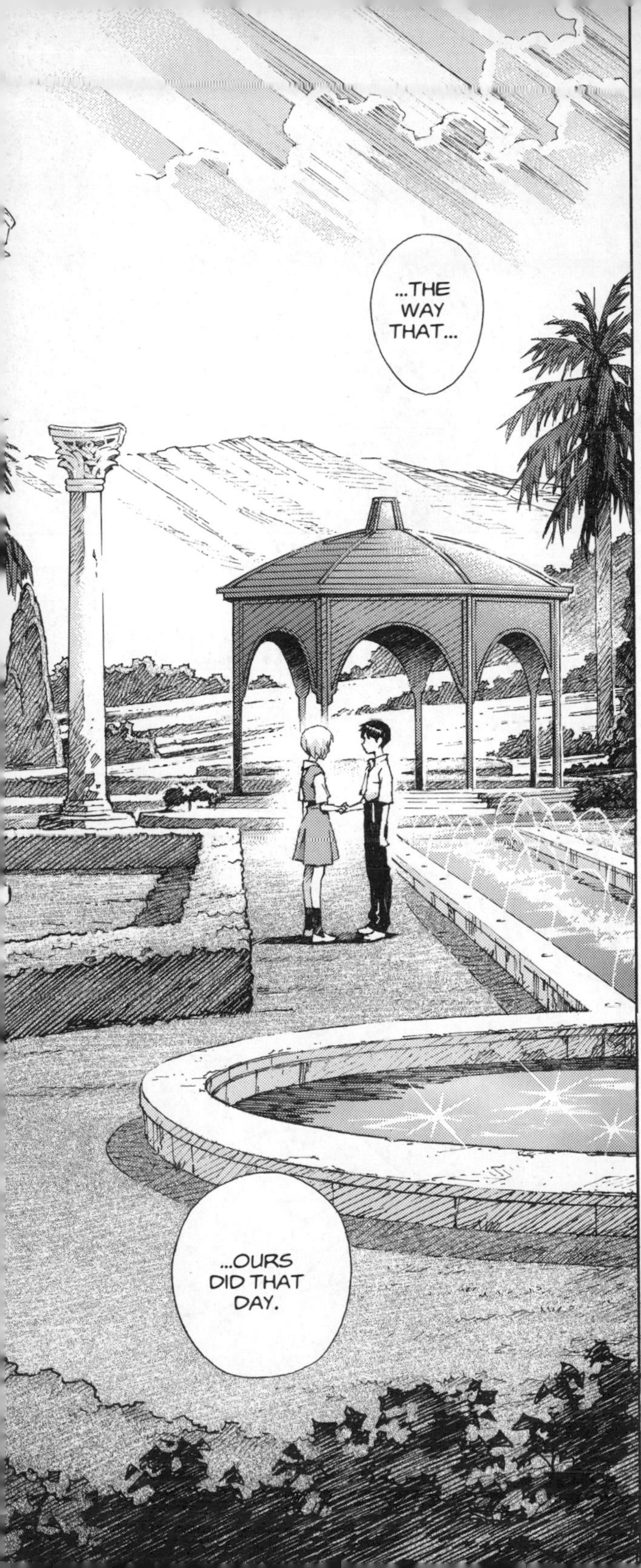
...THE WAY THAT...
...OURS DID THAT DAY.

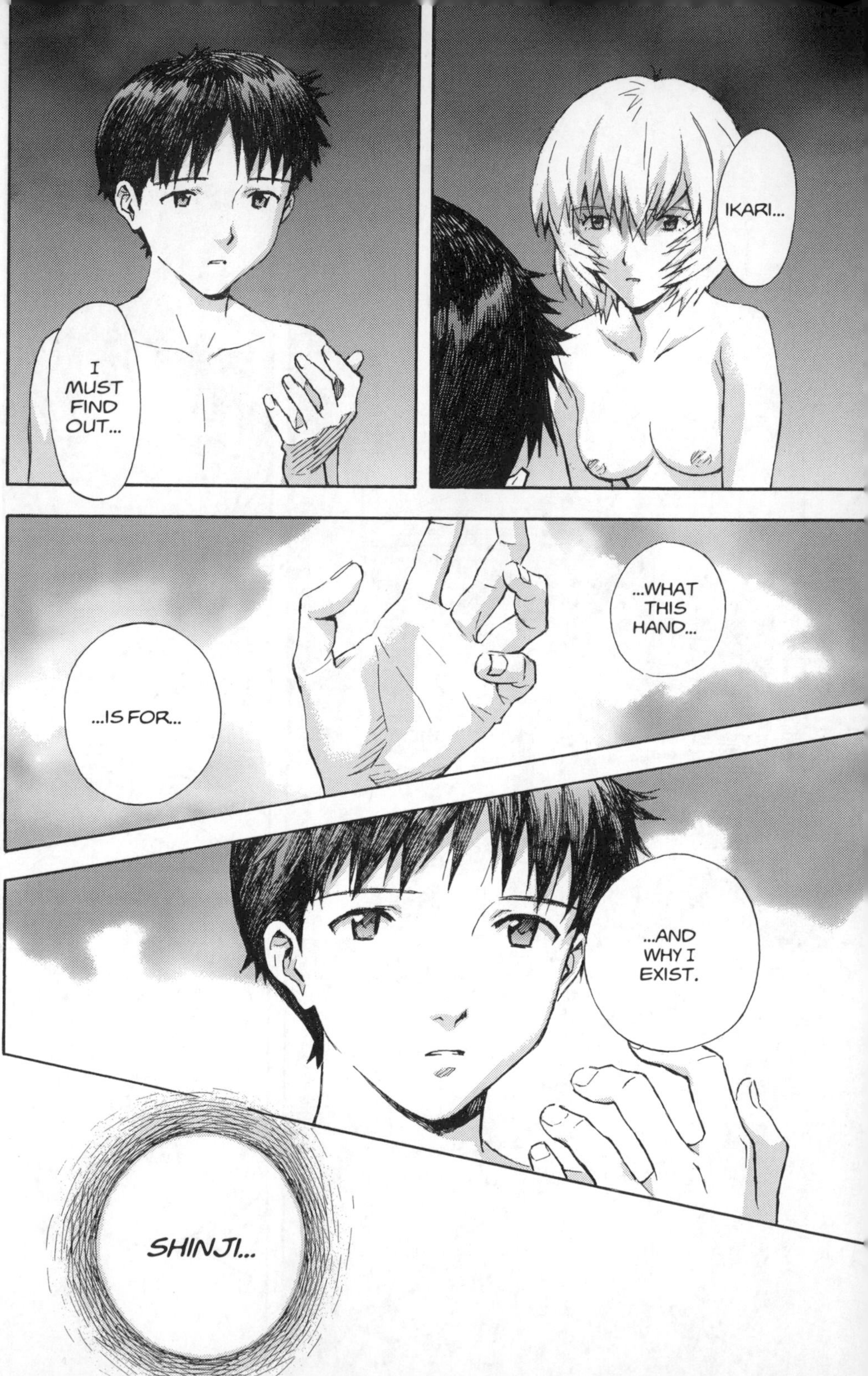
IKARI...
I MUST FIND OUT...
...WHAT THIS HAND...
...IS FOR...
...AND WHY I EXIST.
SHINJI...

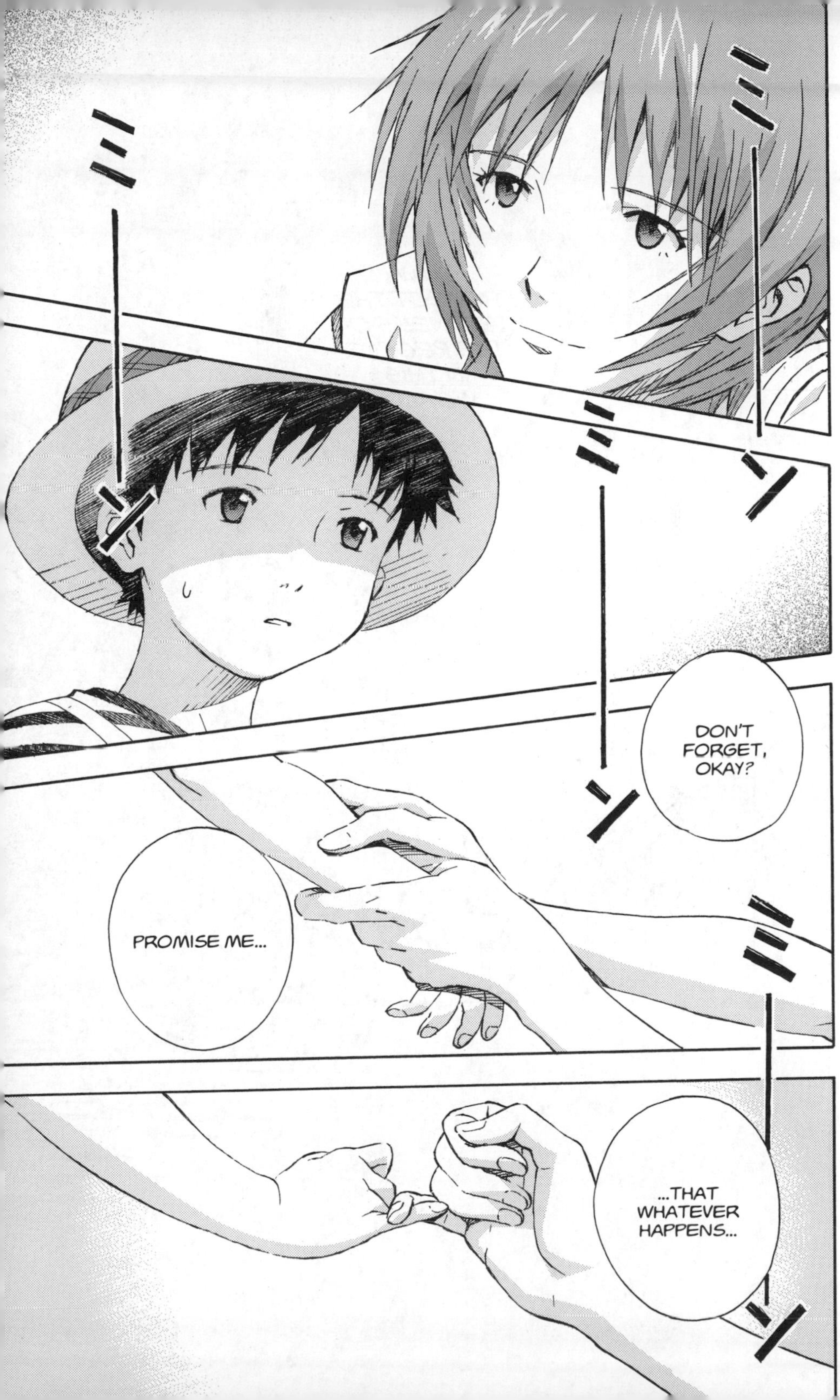
DON'T FORGET, OKAY?
PROMISE ME...
...THAT WHATEVER HAPPENS...

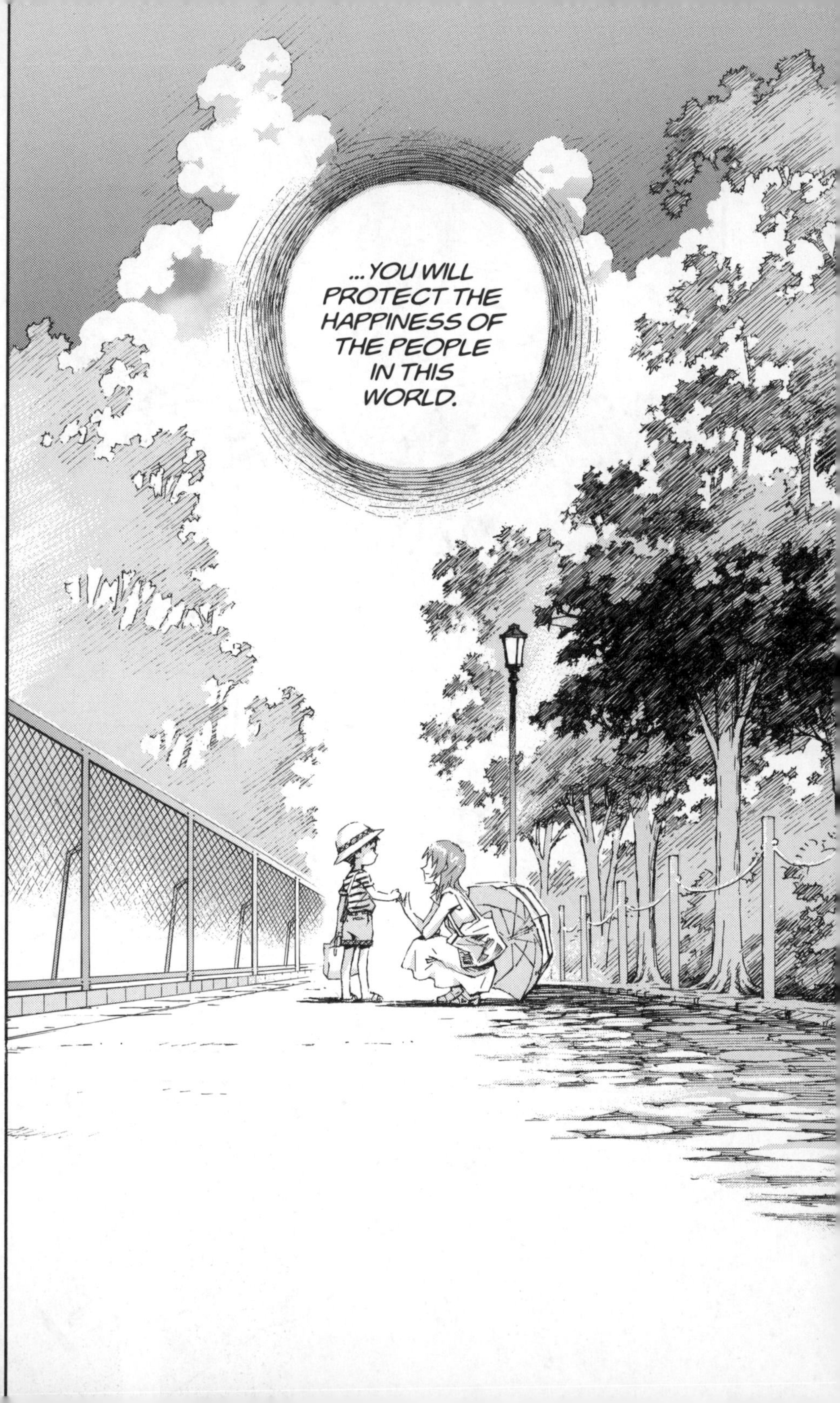
...YOU WILL PROTECT THE HAPPINESS OF THE PEOPLE IN THIS WORLD.

NEON GENESIS EVANGELION

STAGE 94: PALMS

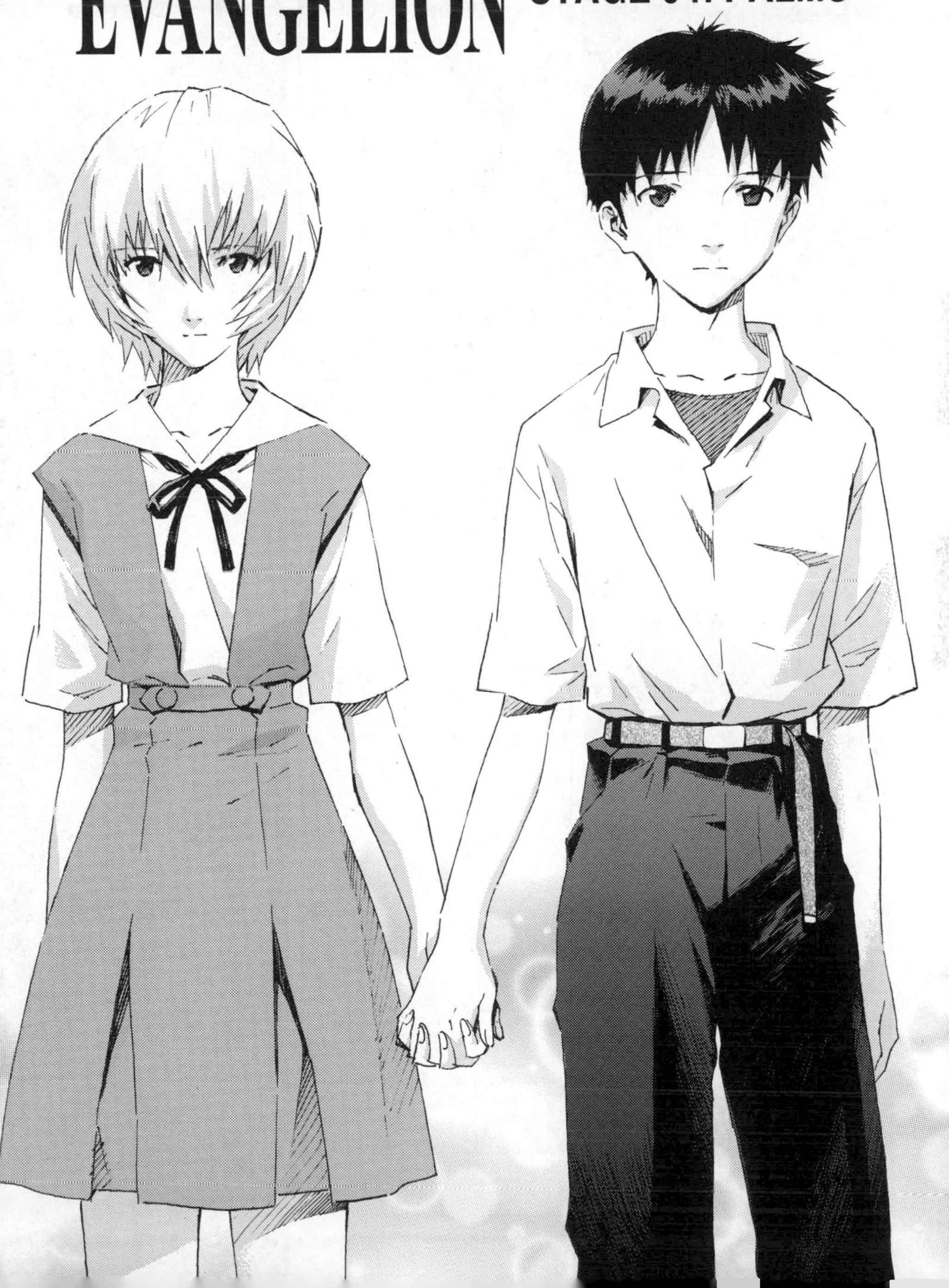

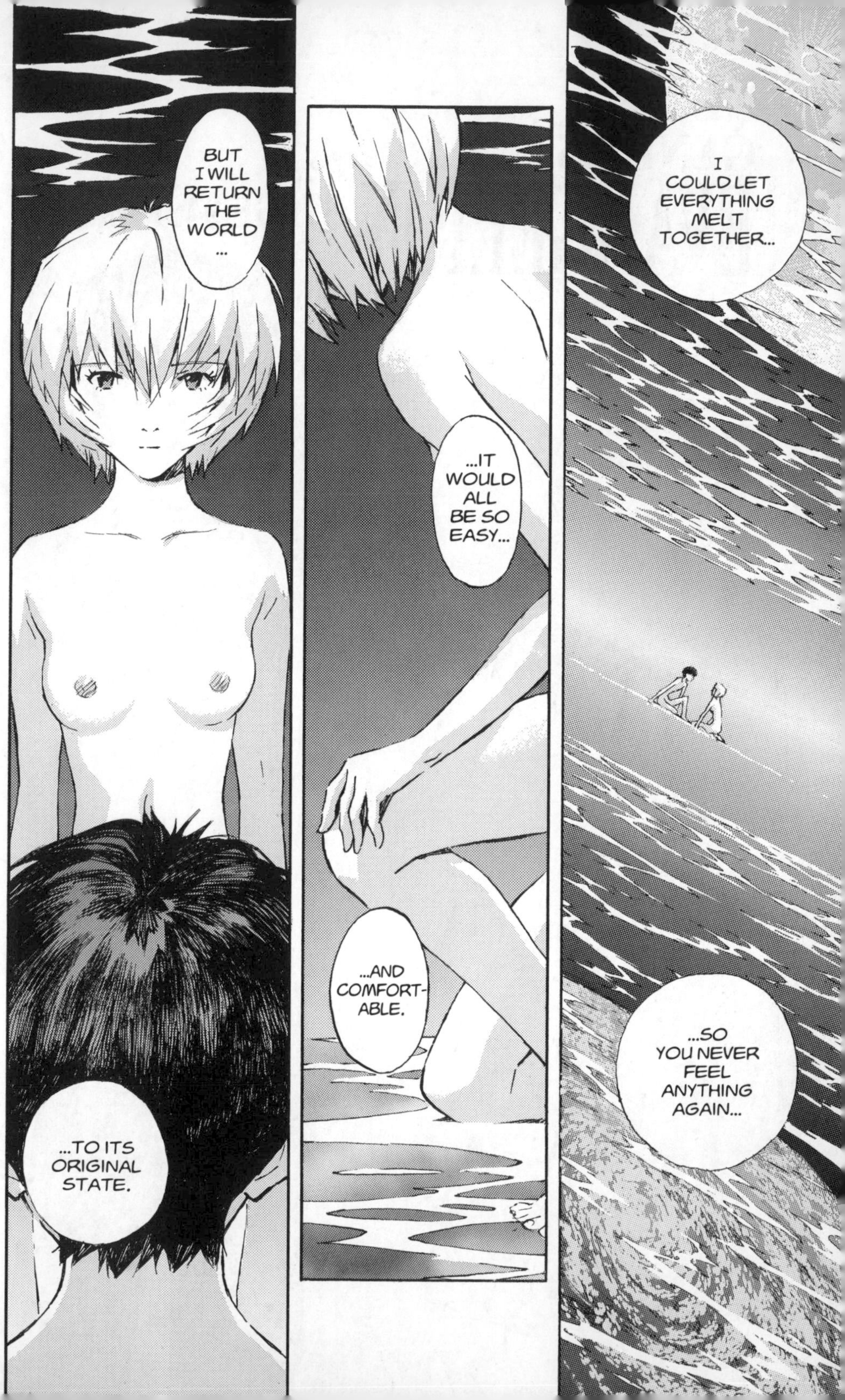
I COULD LET EVERYTHING MELT TOGETHER...
...SO YOU NEVER FEEL ANYTHING AGAIN...
...IT WOULD ALL BE SO EASY...
...AND COMFORTABLE.
BUT I WILL RETURN THE WORLD ...
...TO ITS ORIGINAL STATE.

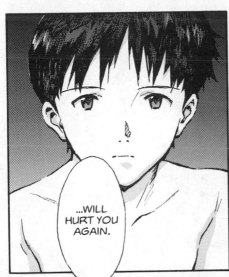

PEOPLE'S HANDS...
...AND VOICES ...
...WILL HURT YOU AGAIN.
THAT'S ALL RIGHT.

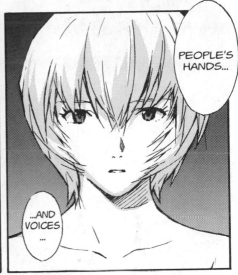

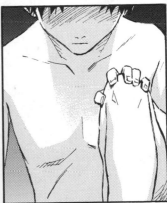

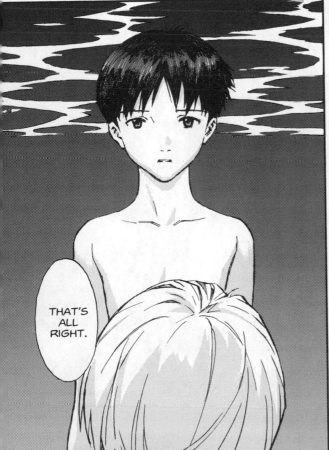

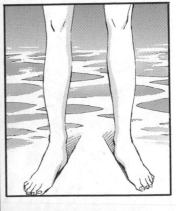

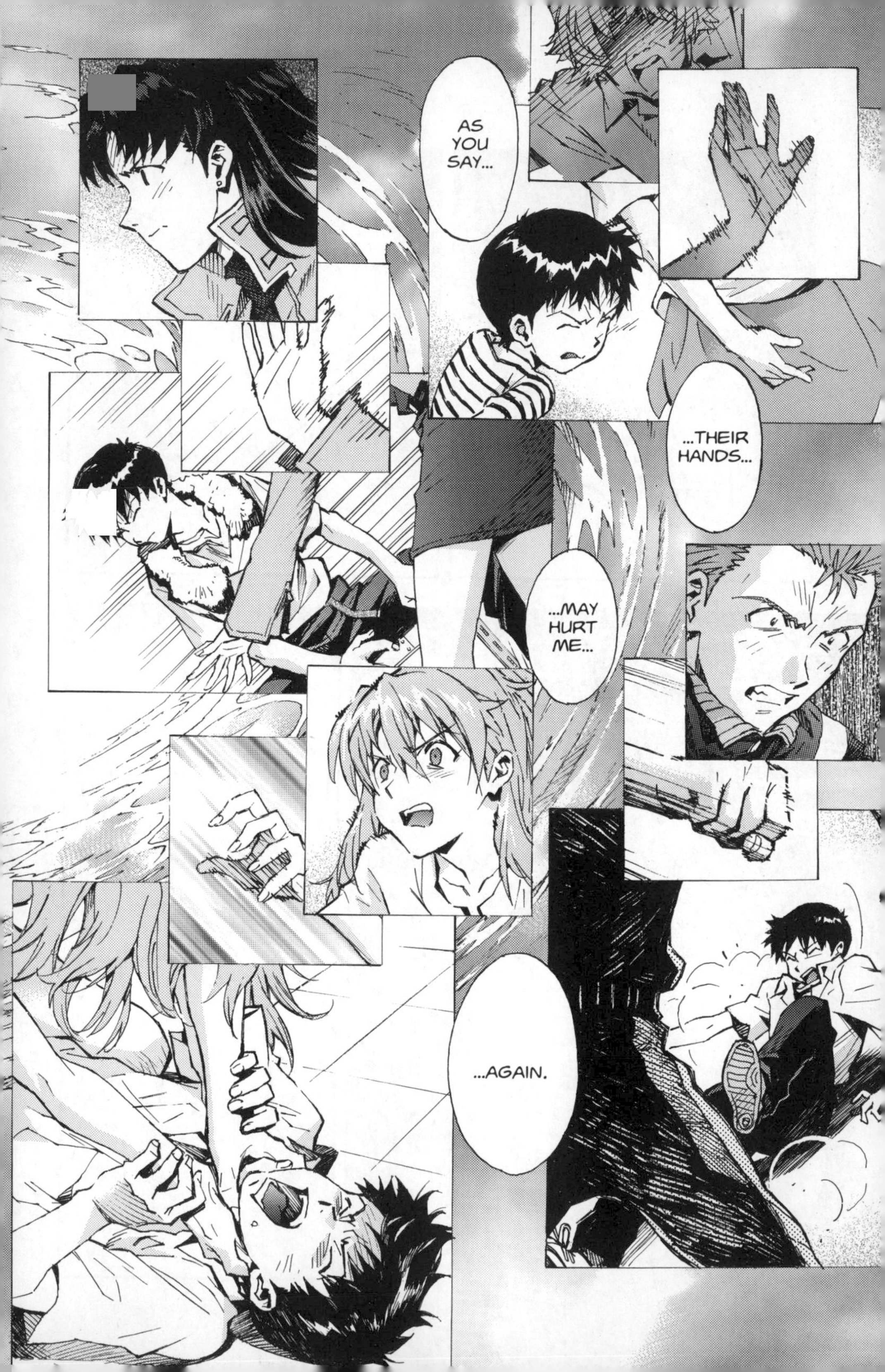
AS YOU SAY...
...THEIR HANDS...
...MAY HURT ME...
...AGAIN.

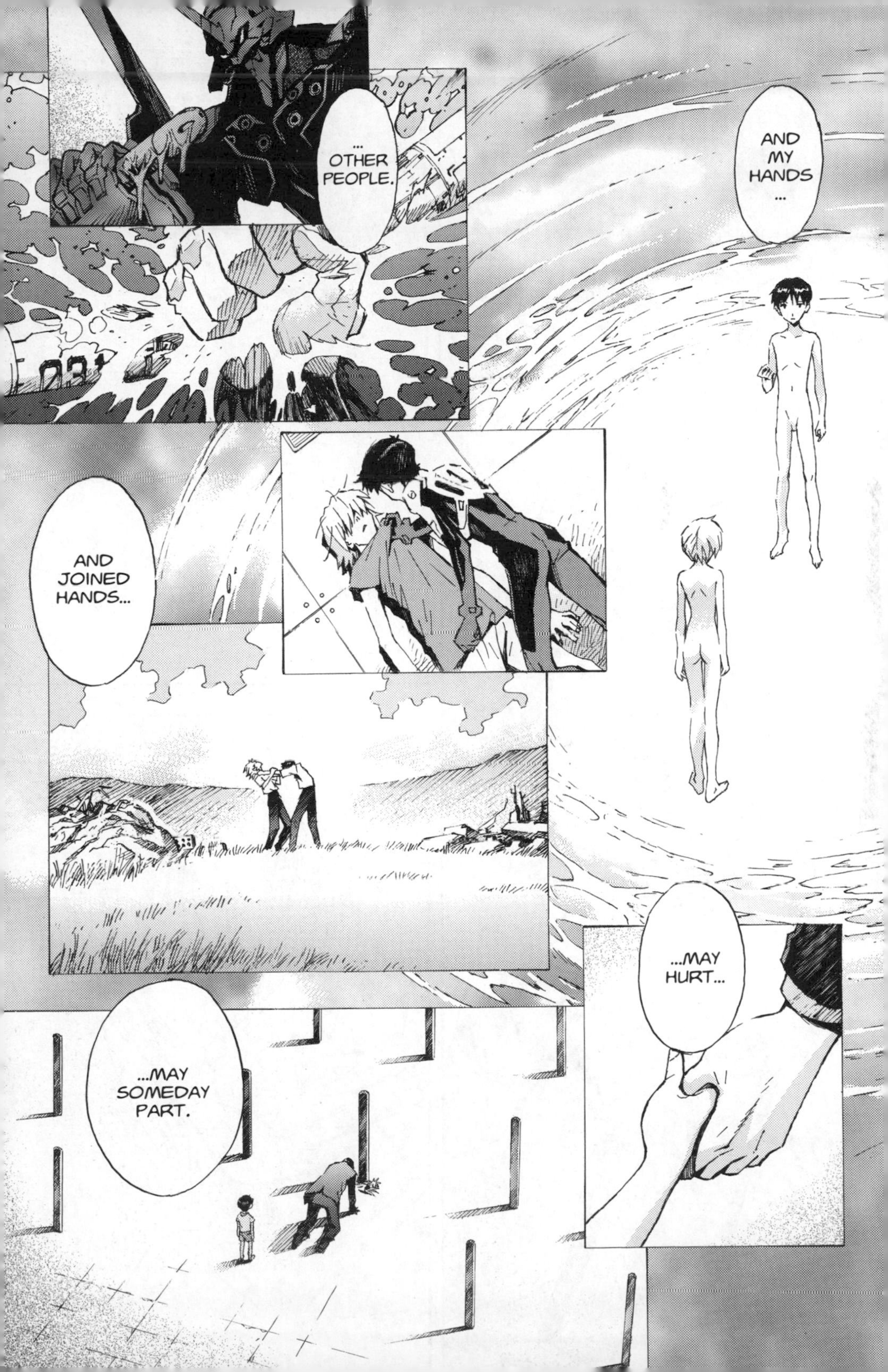
AND MY HANDS ...
... OTHER PEOPLE.
AND JOINED HANDS...
...MAY HURT...
...MAY SOMEDAY PART.

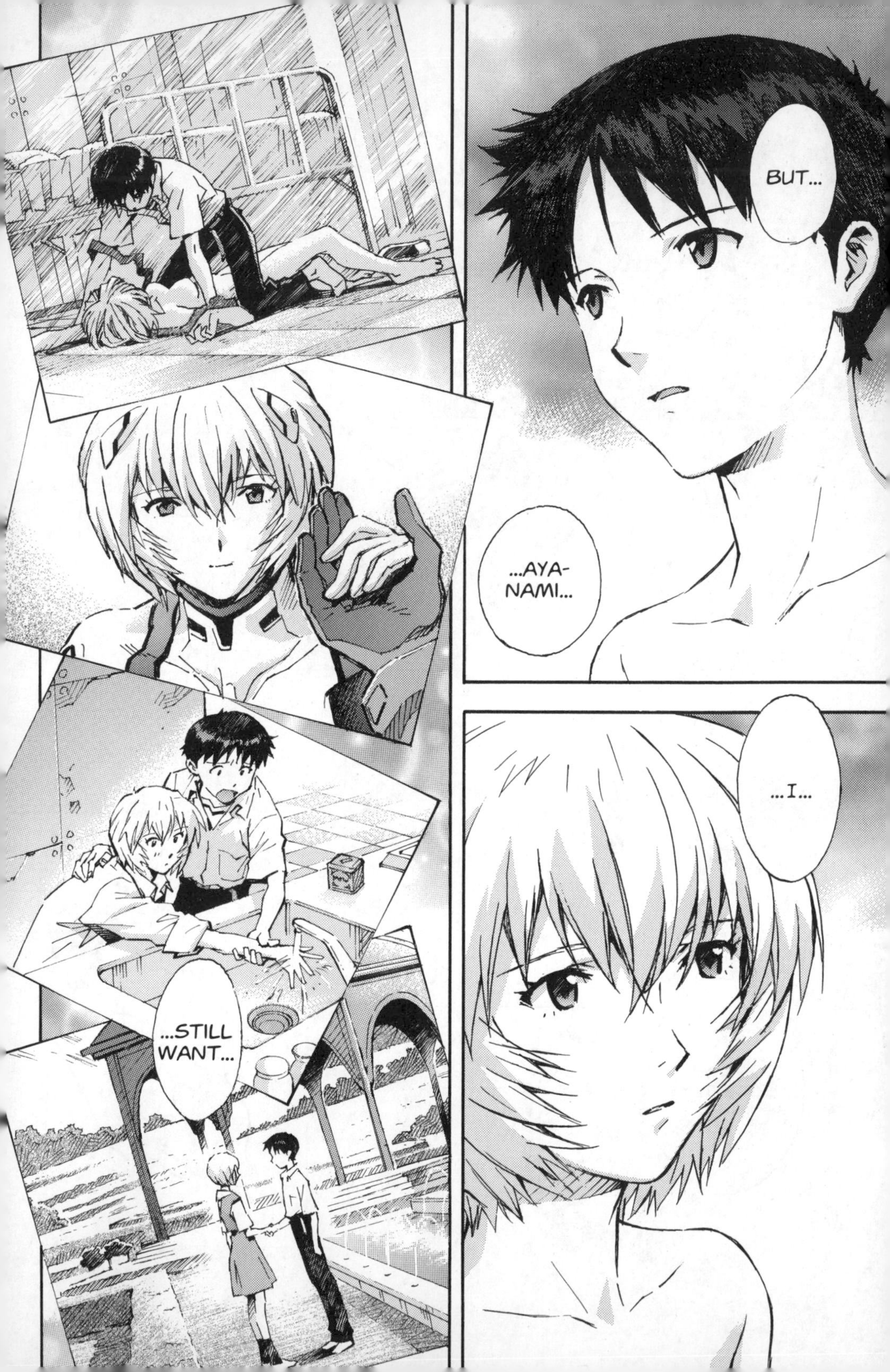
BUT...
...AYA-
NAMI...
...I...
...STILL
WANT...

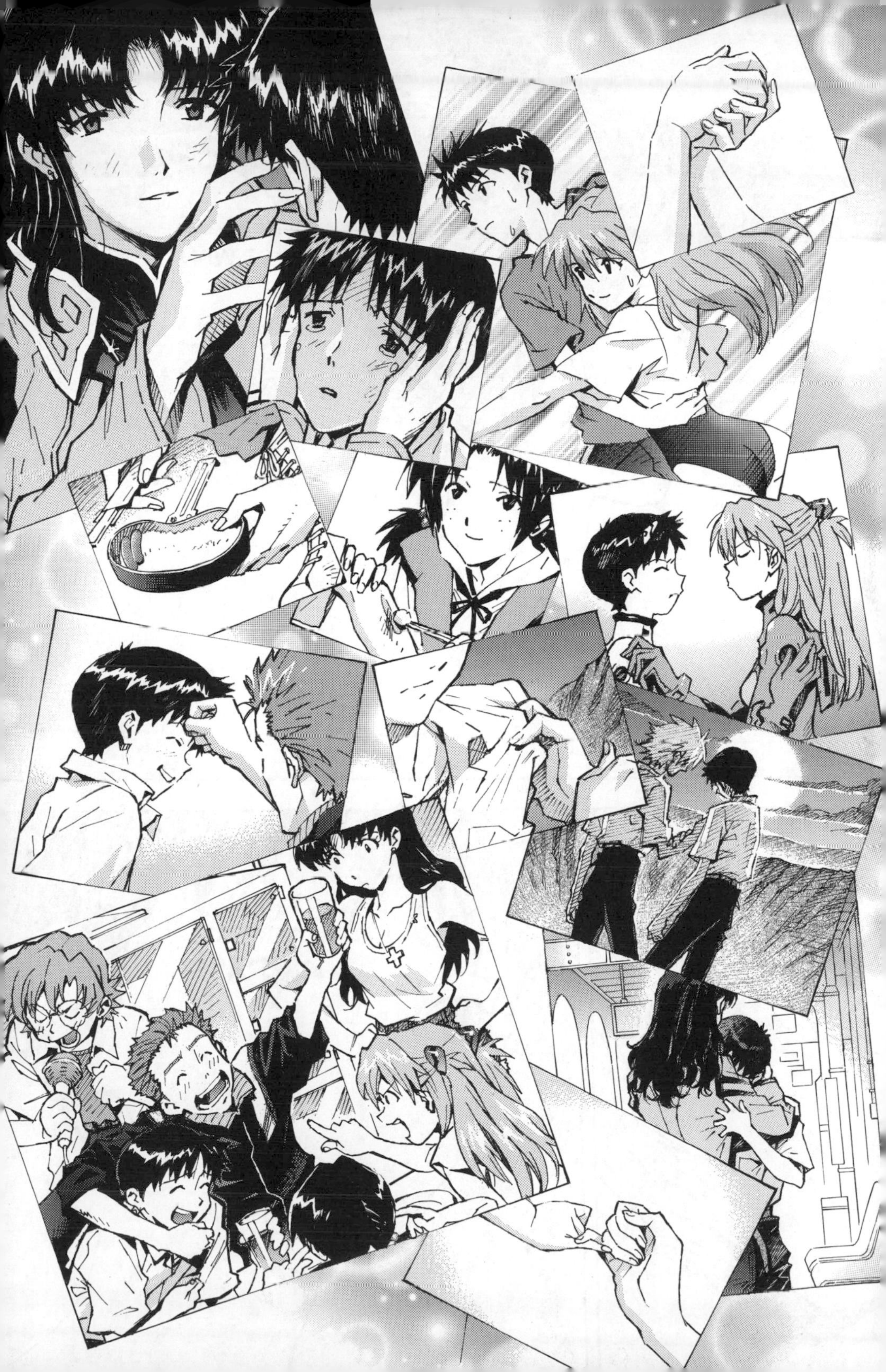

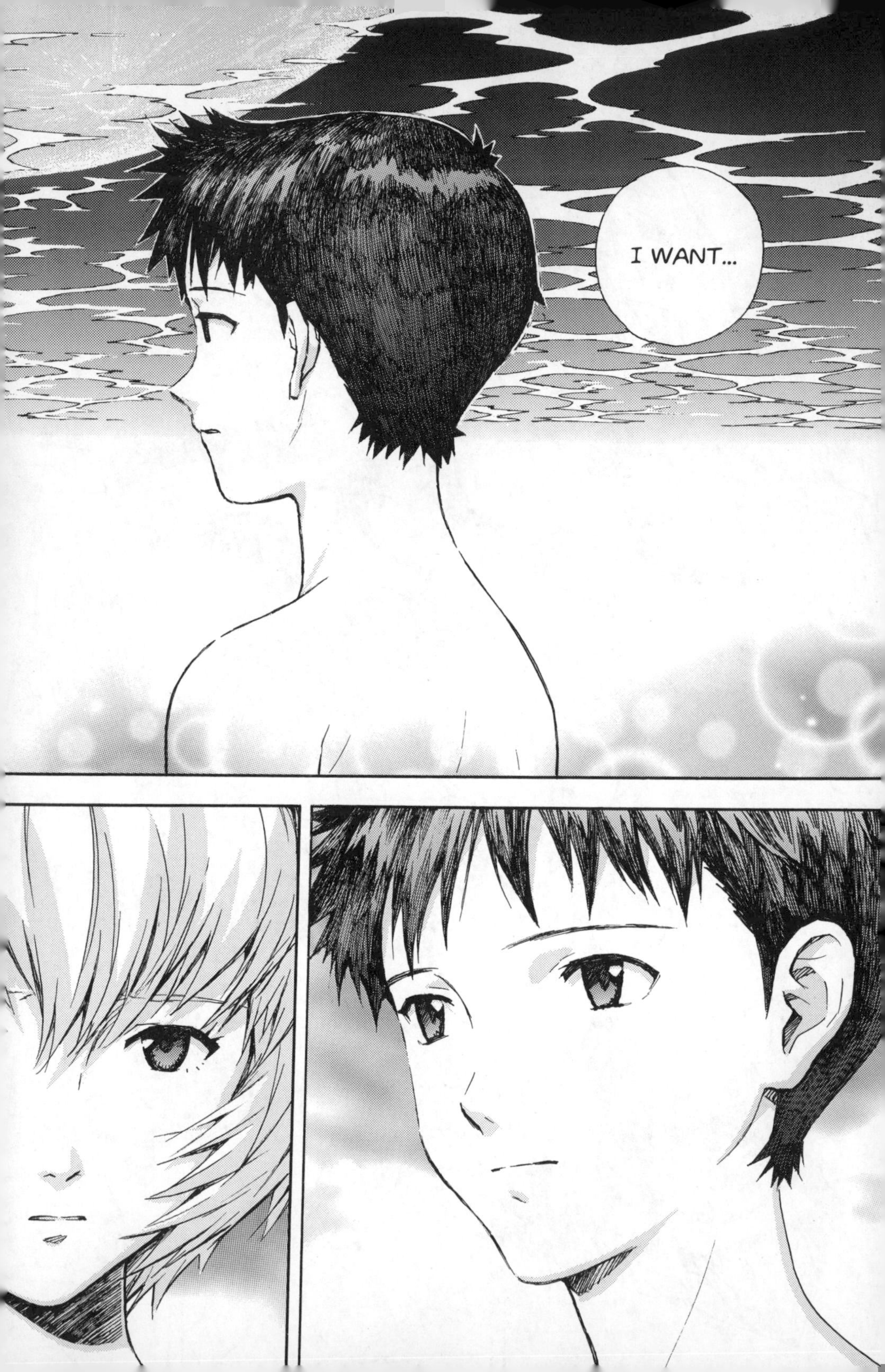
I WANT...

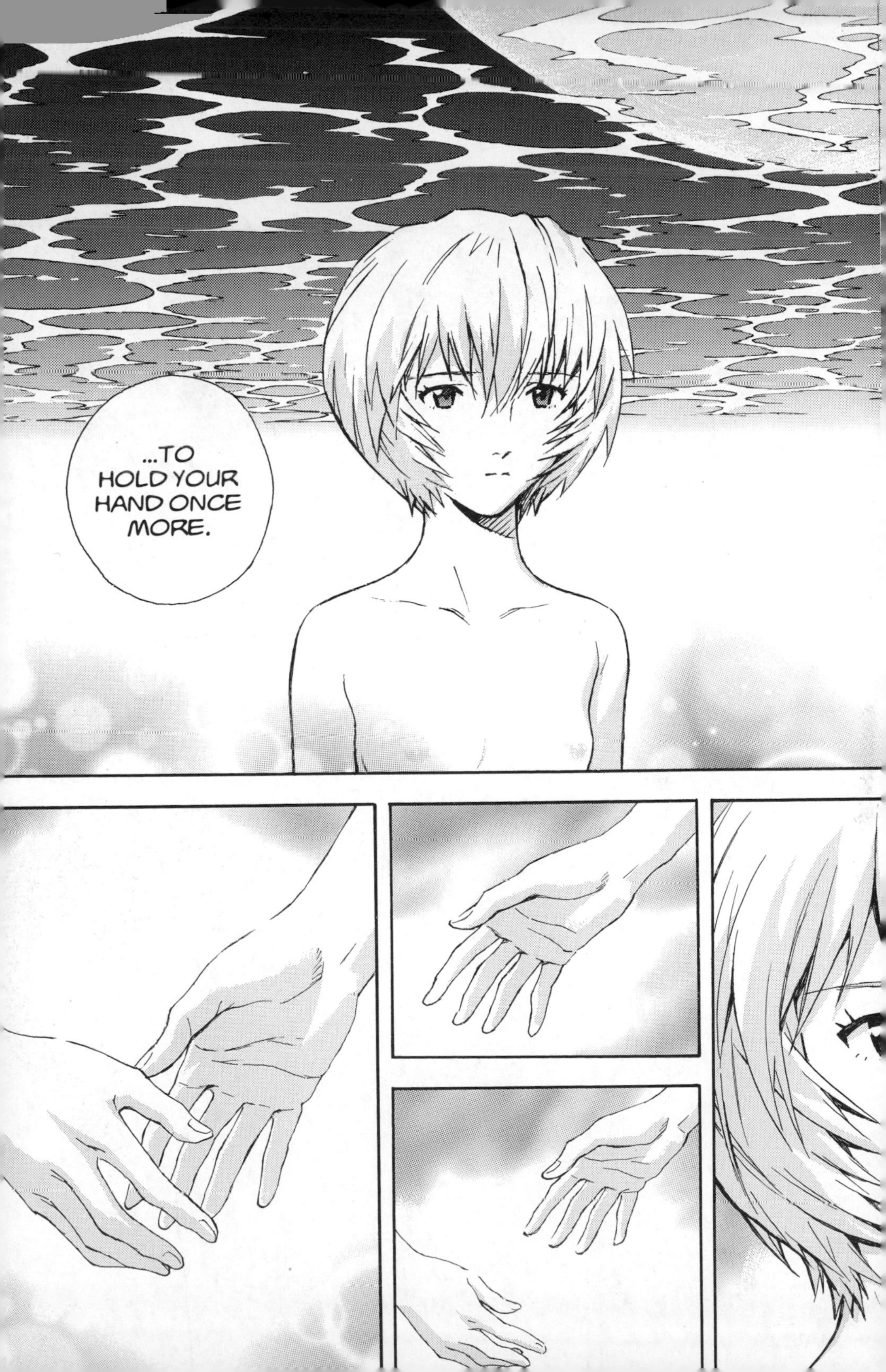
...TO HOLD YOUR HAND ONCE MORE.

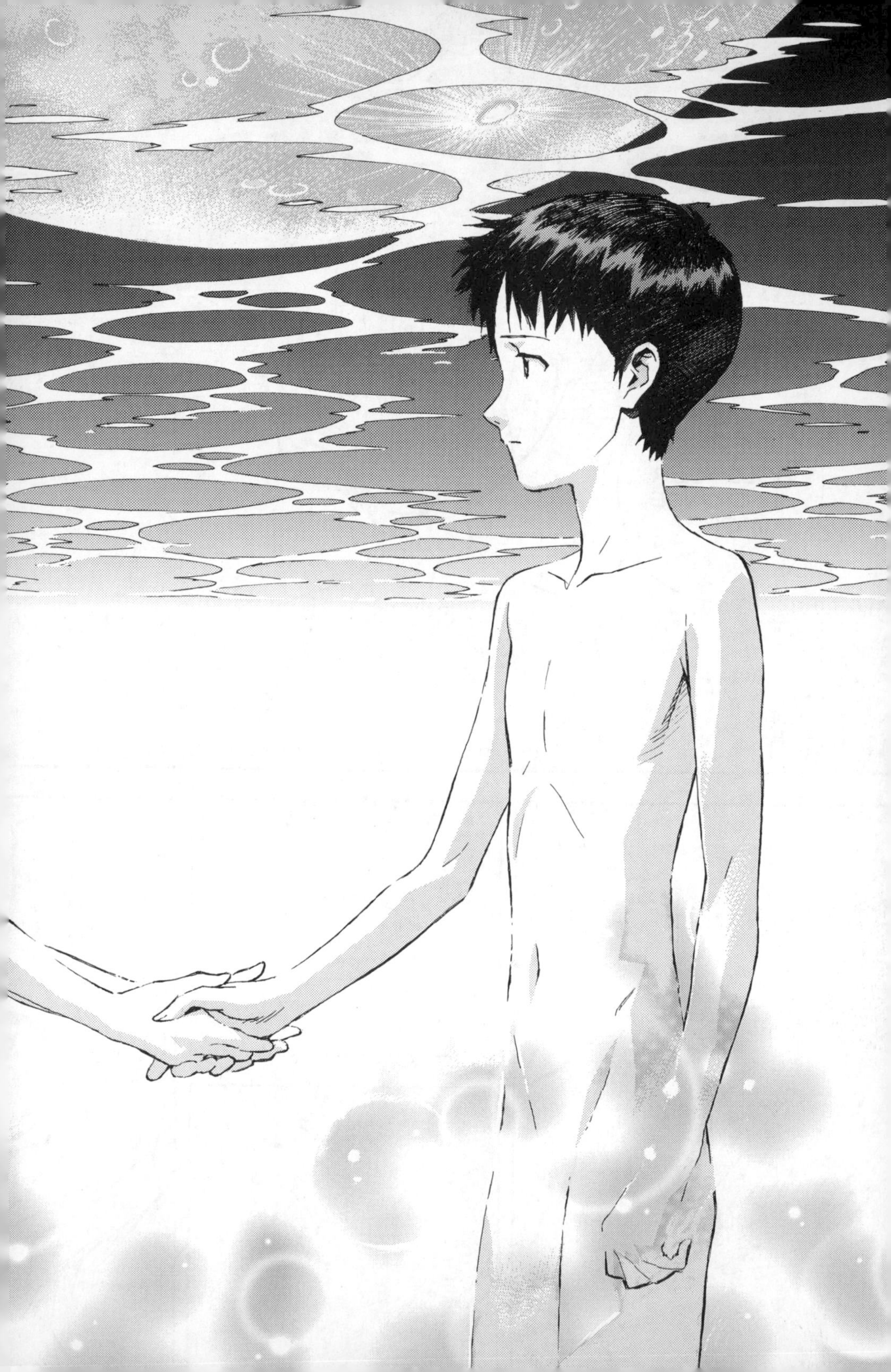

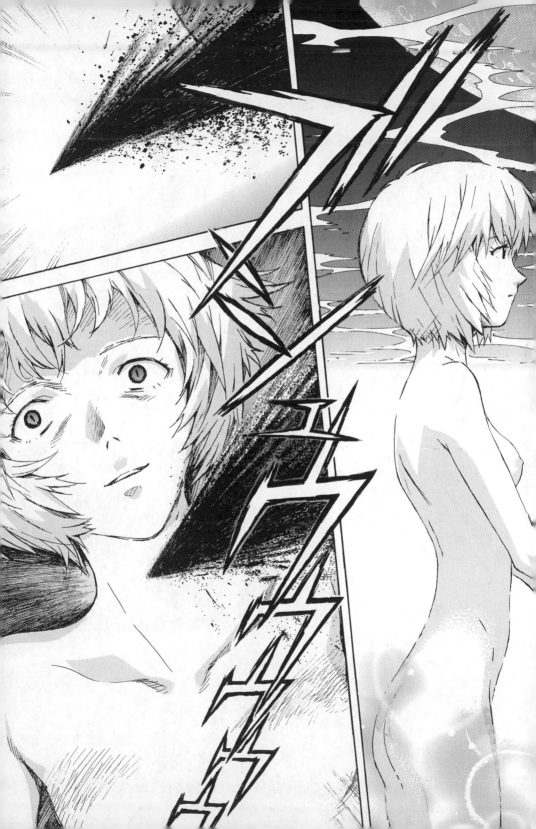

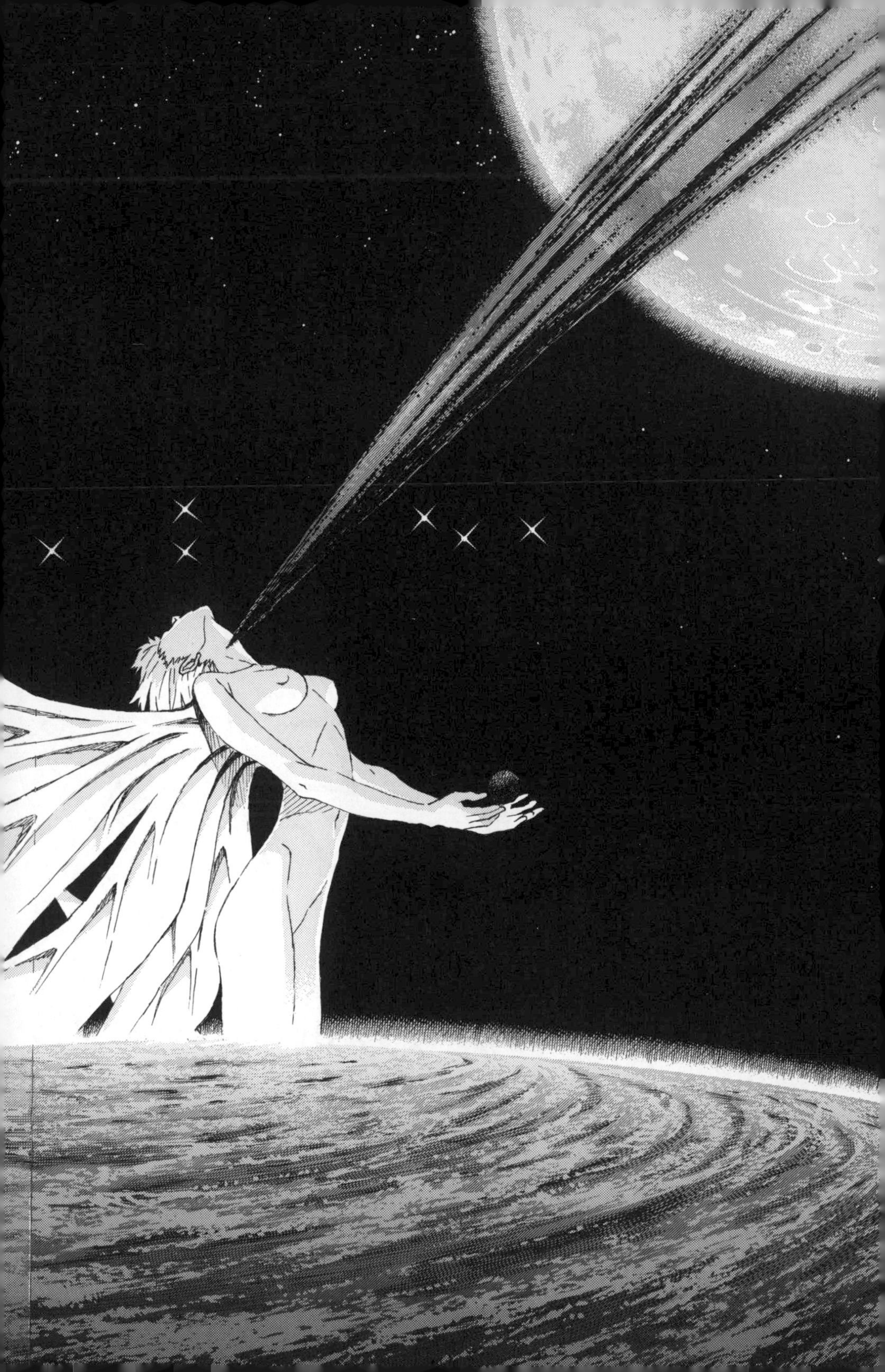

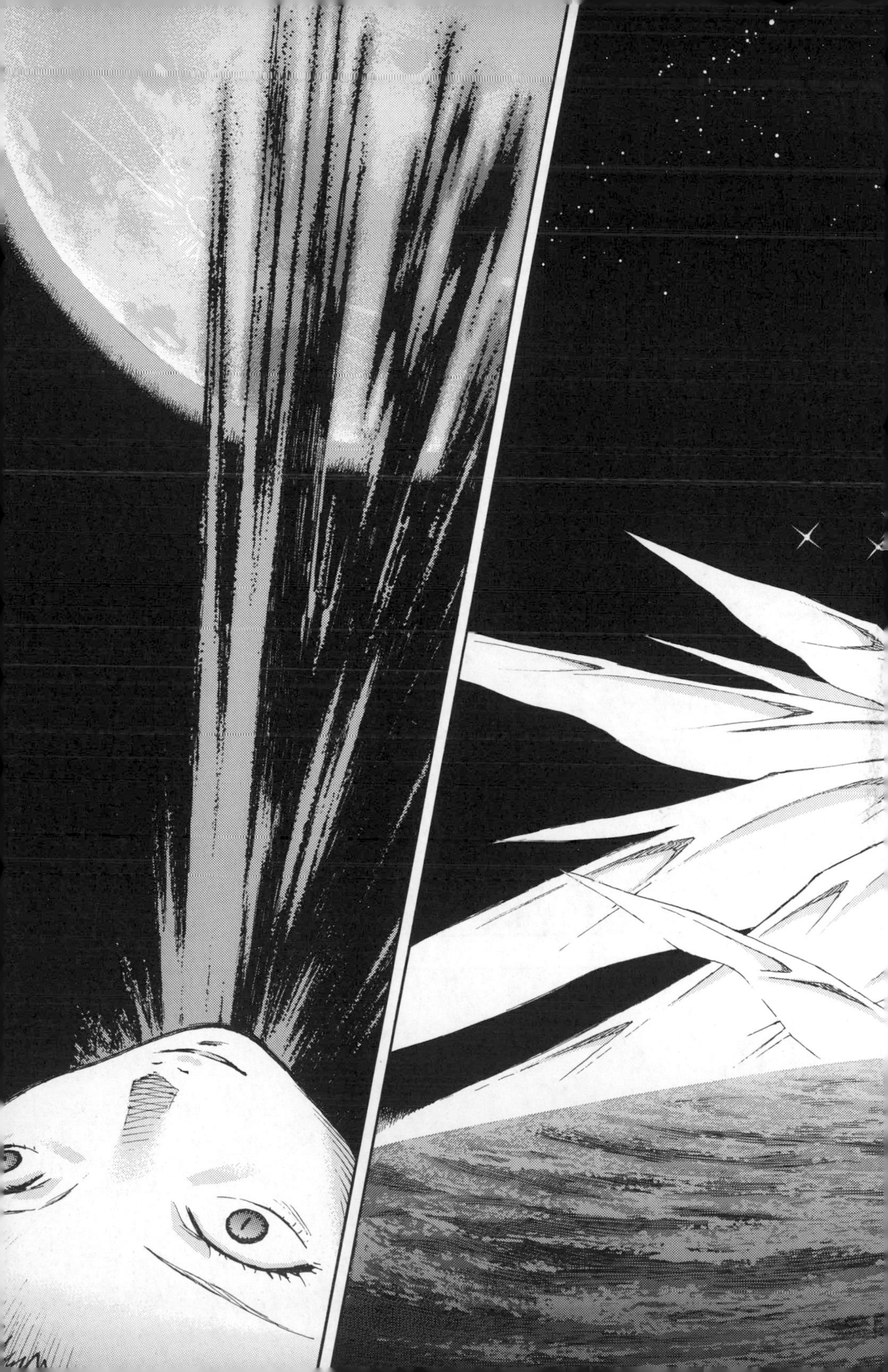

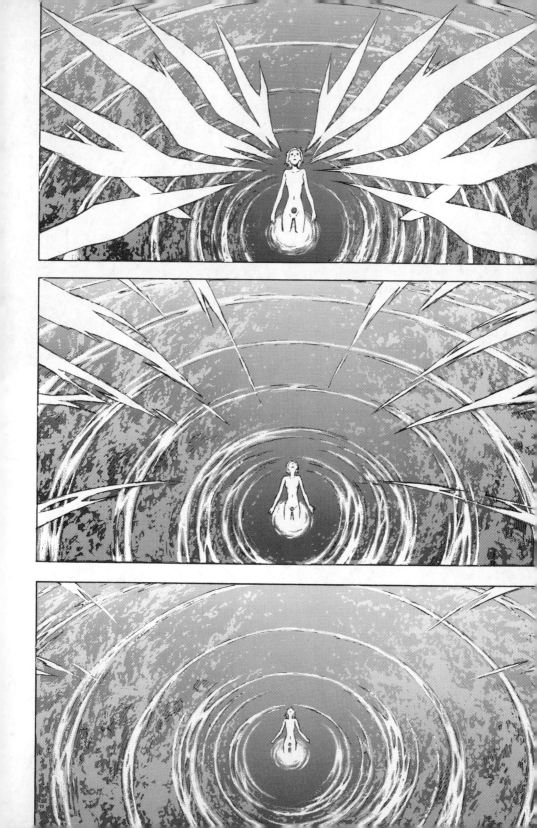

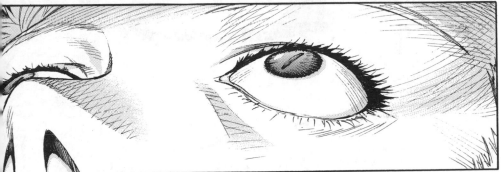

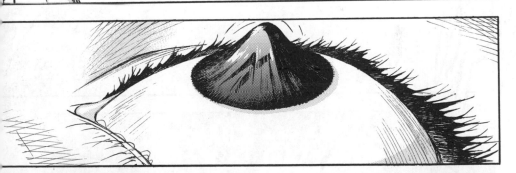

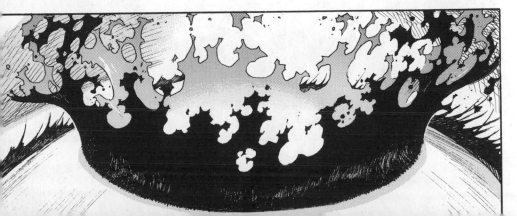

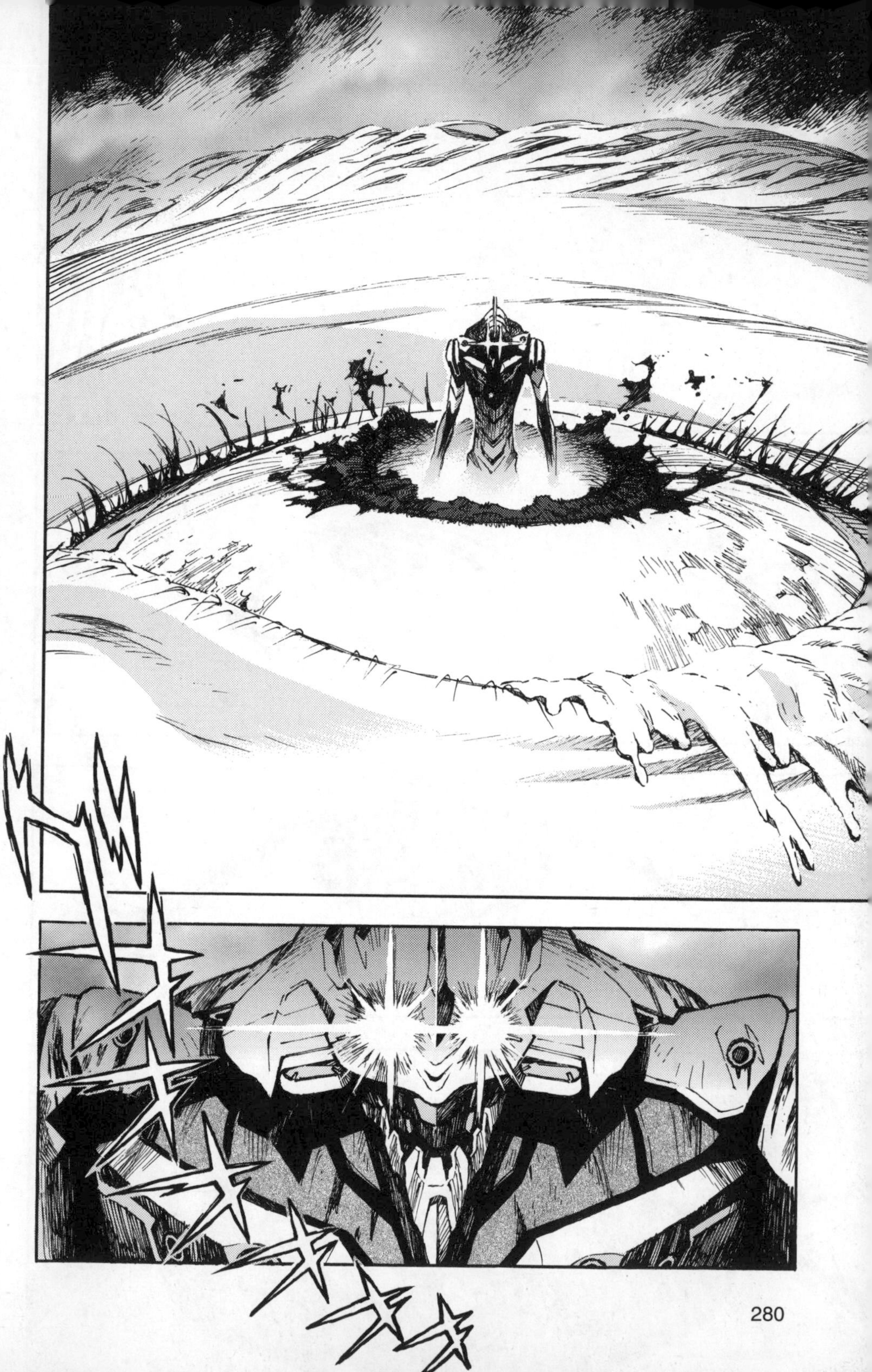

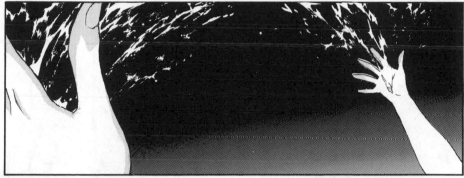

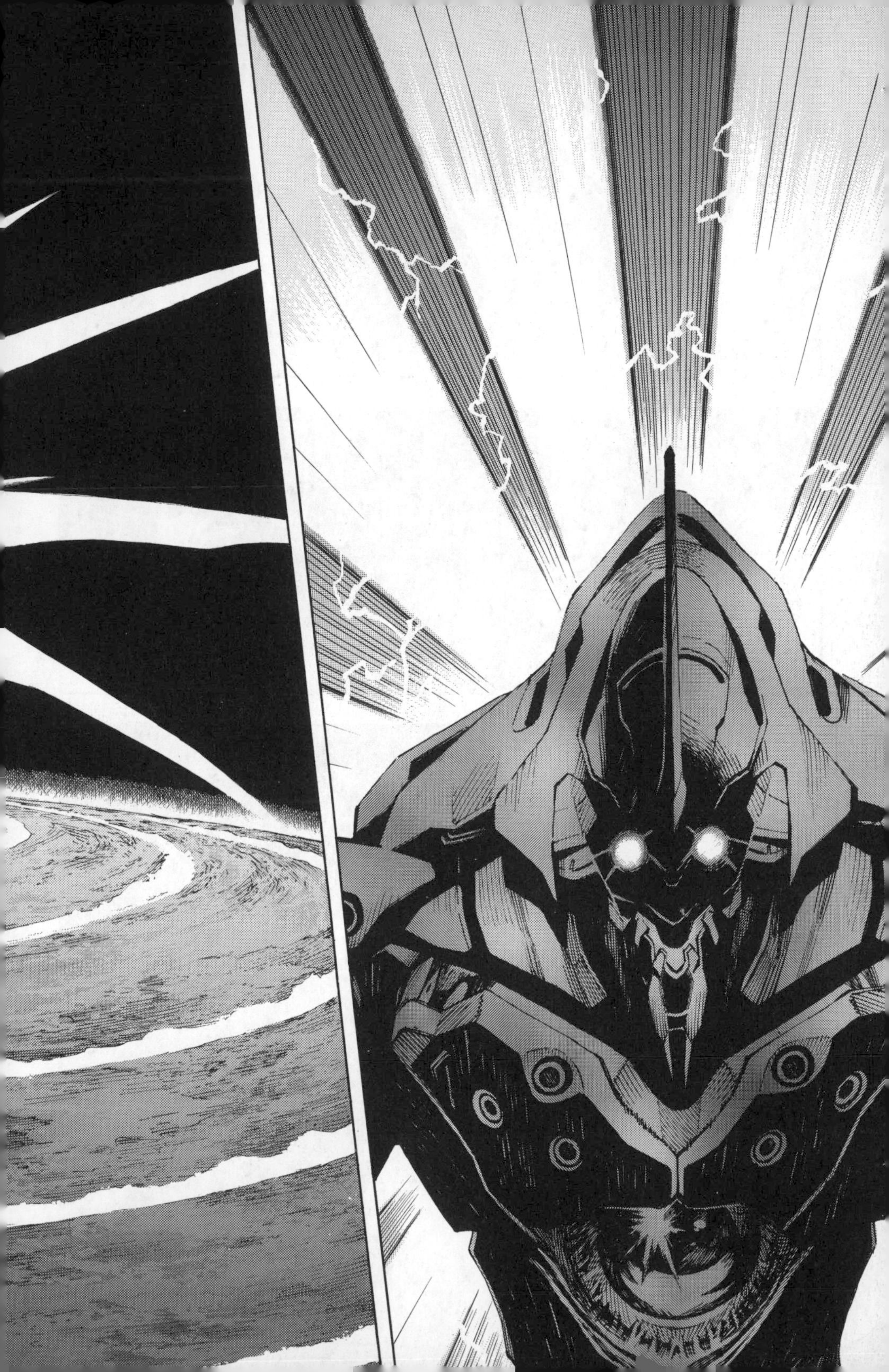

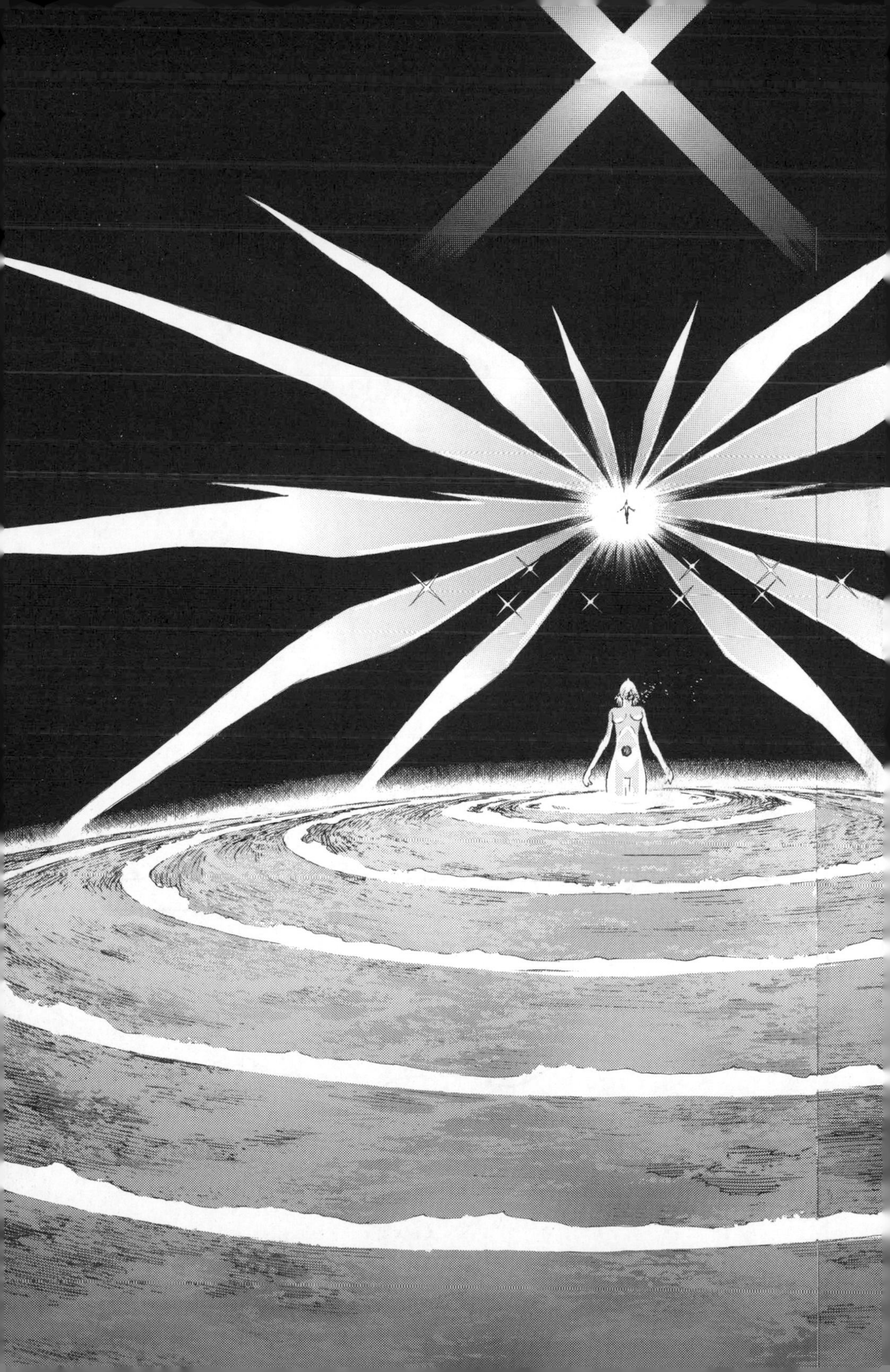

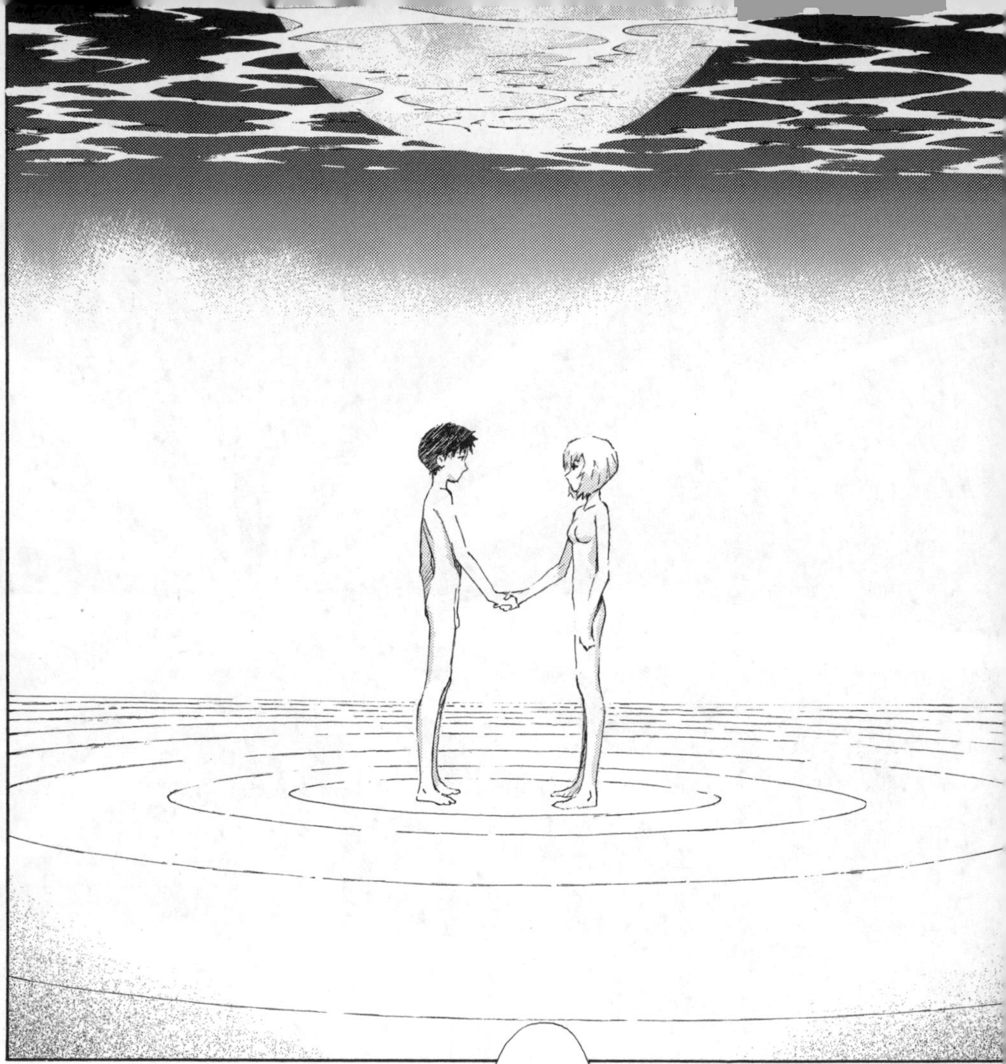

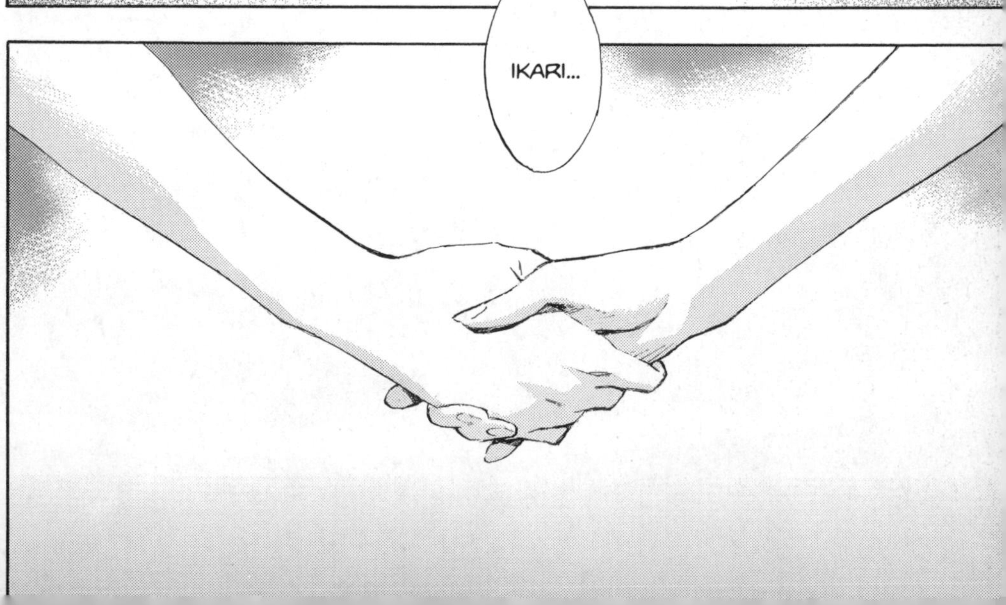
IKARI...

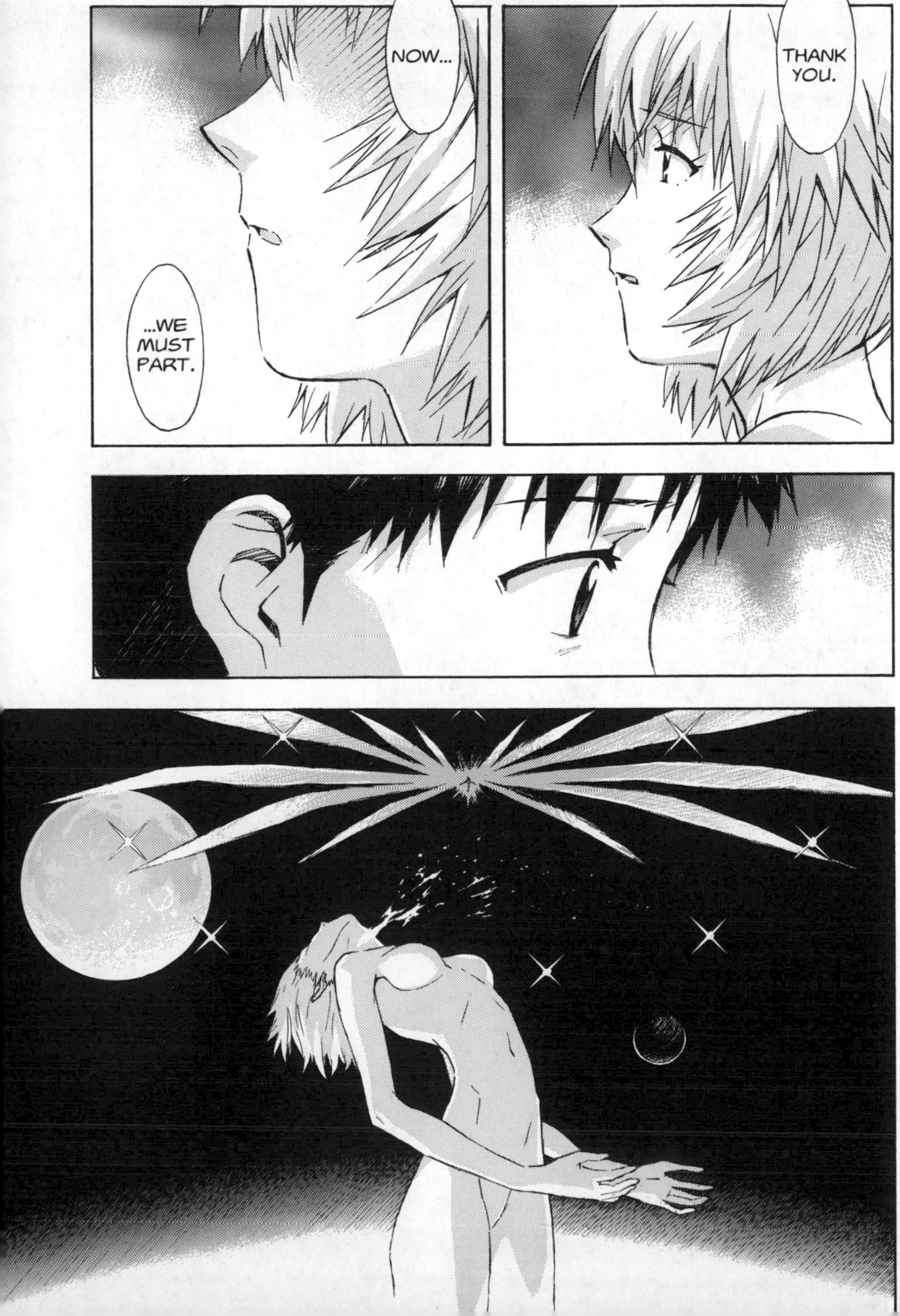
THANK YOU.
NOW...
...WE MUST PART.

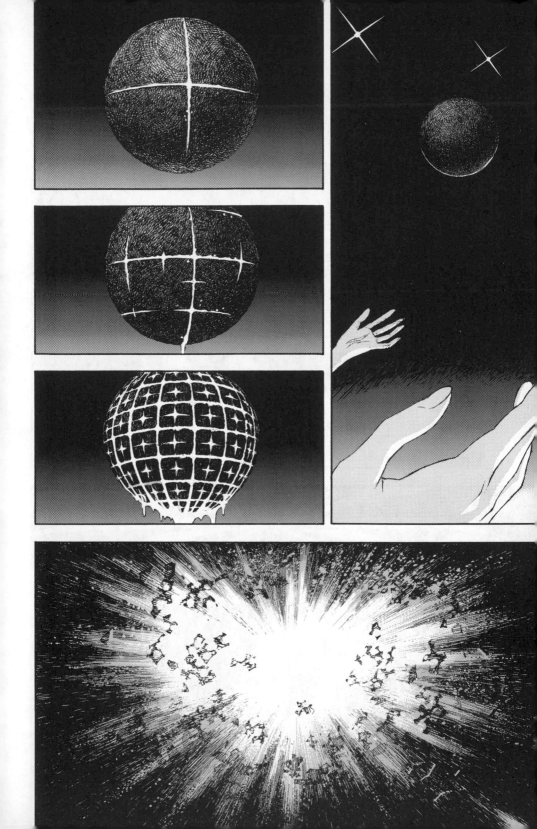

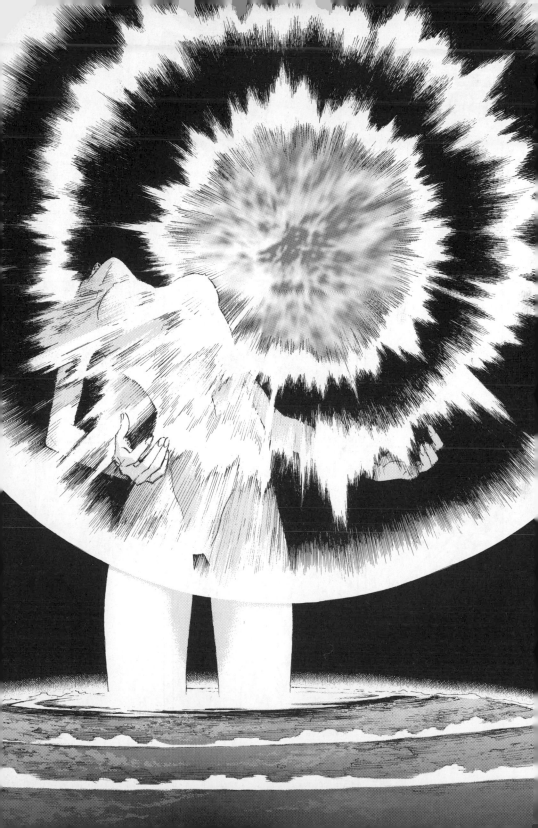

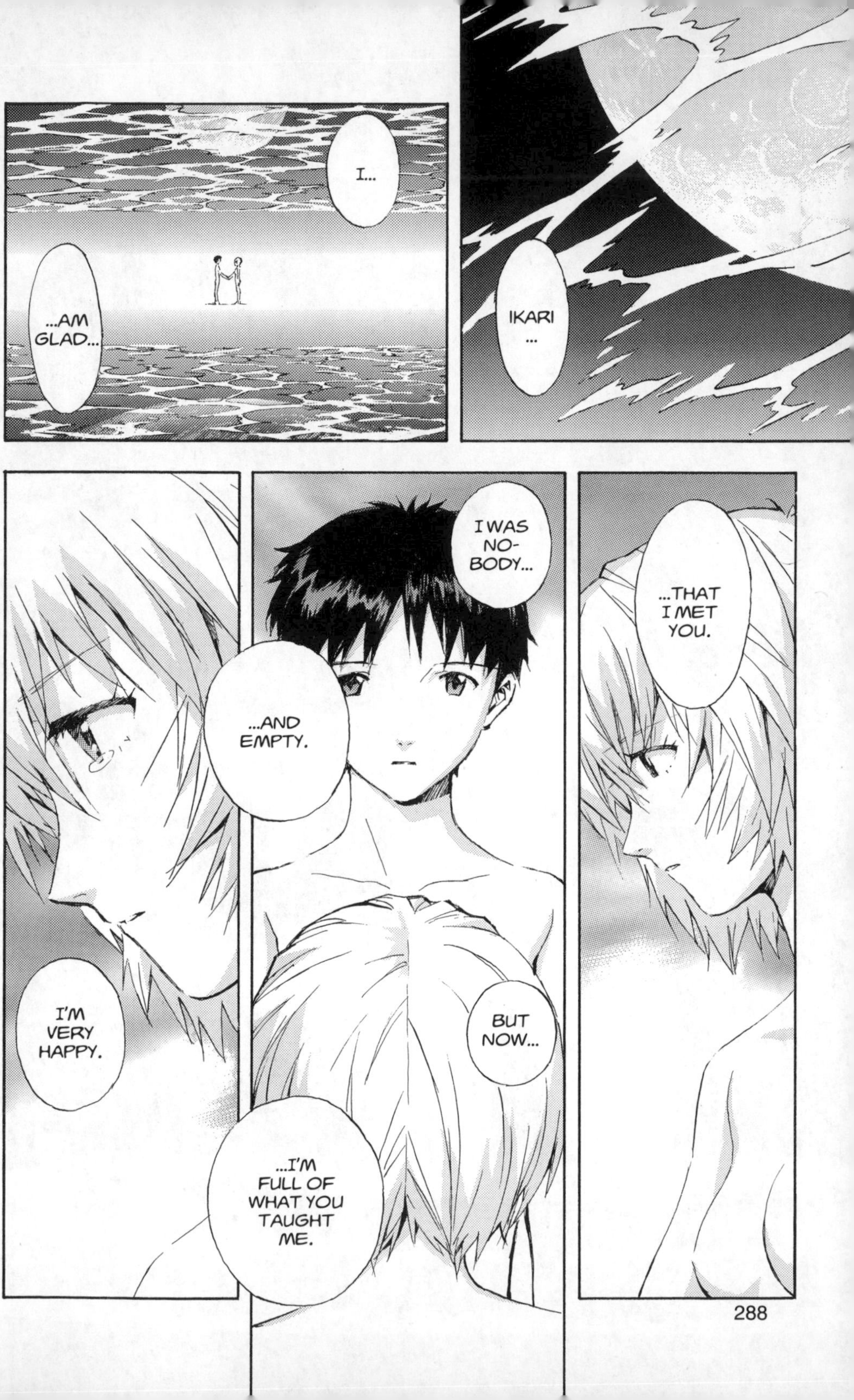
IKARI ...
I...
...AM GLAD...
...THAT I MET YOU.
I WAS NO-BODY...
...AND EMPTY.
BUT NOW...
...I'M FULL OF WHAT YOU TAUGHT ME.
I'M VERY HAPPY.

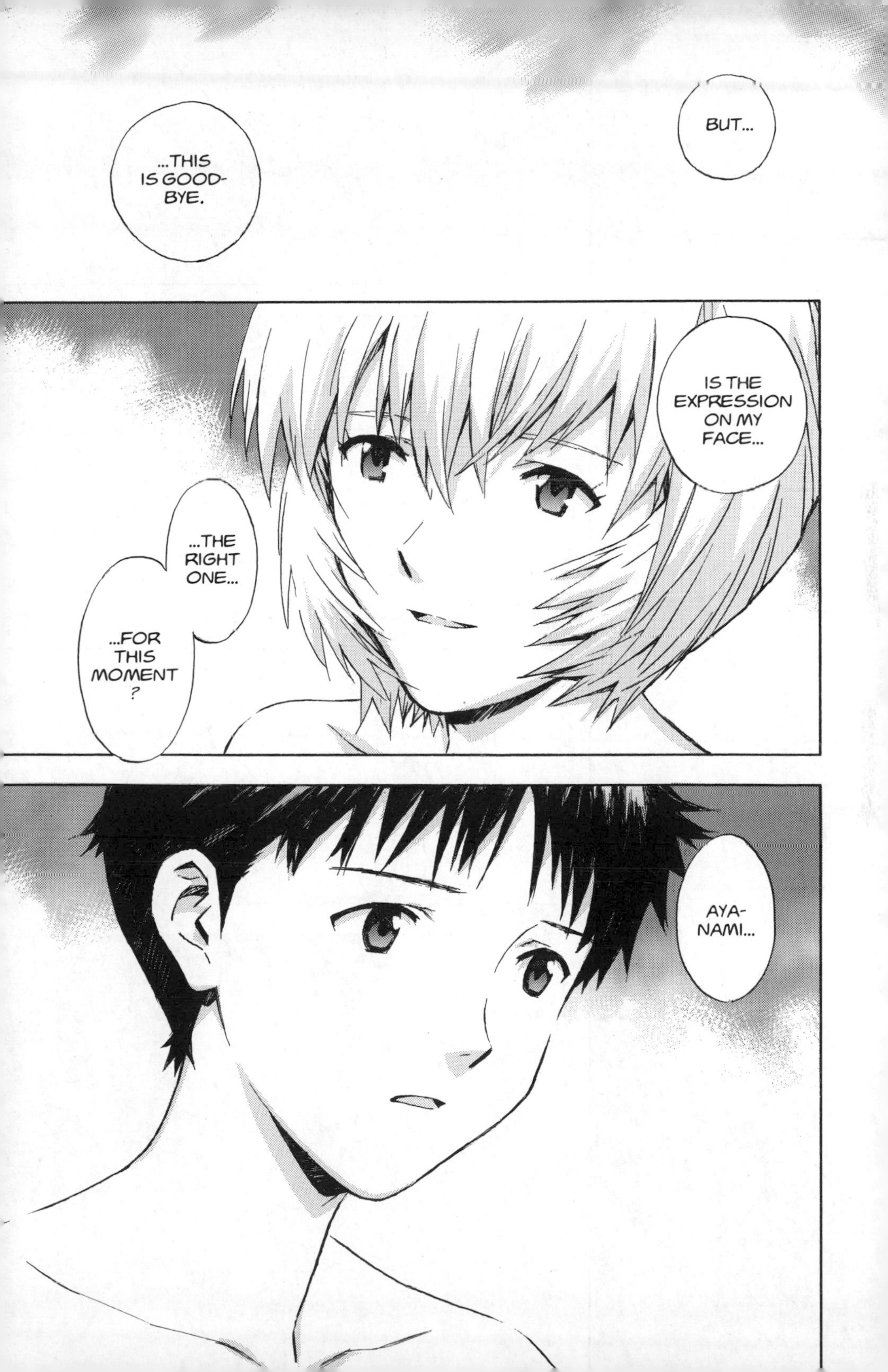
BUT...
...THIS IS GOOD-BYE.
IS THE EXPRESSION ON MY FACE...
...THE RIGHT ONE...
...FOR THIS MOMENT?
AYA-NAMI...

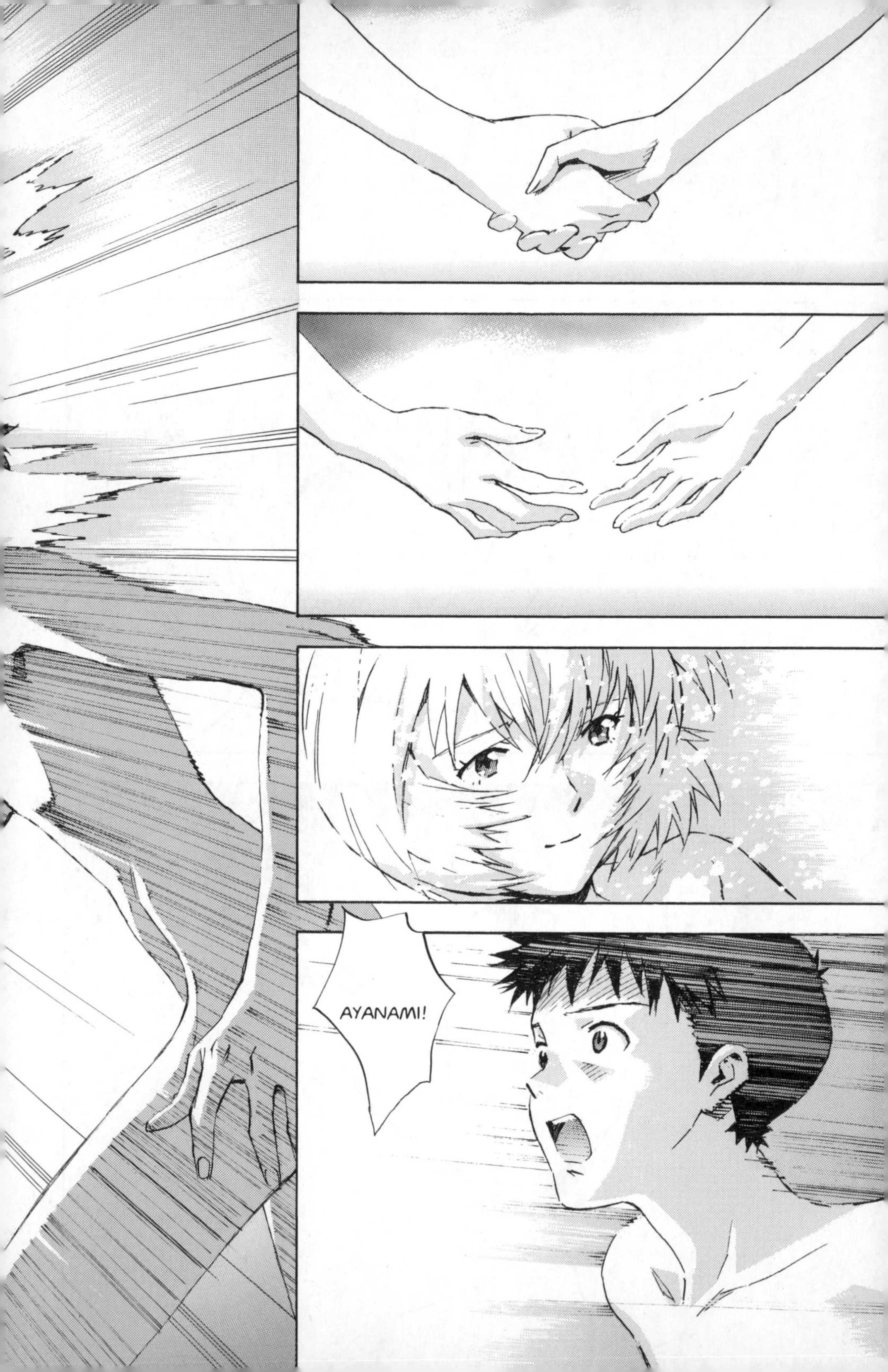
AYANAMI!

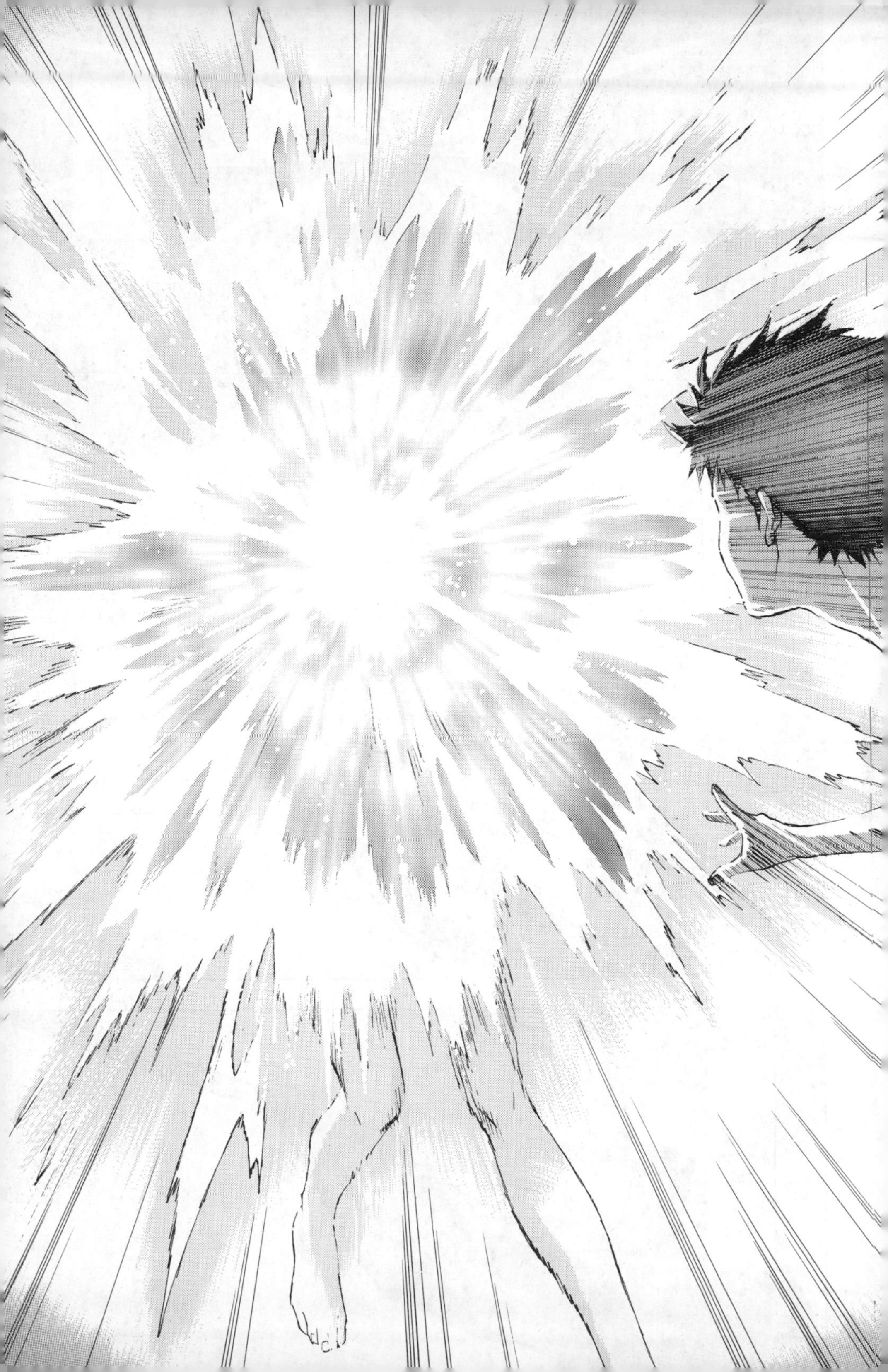

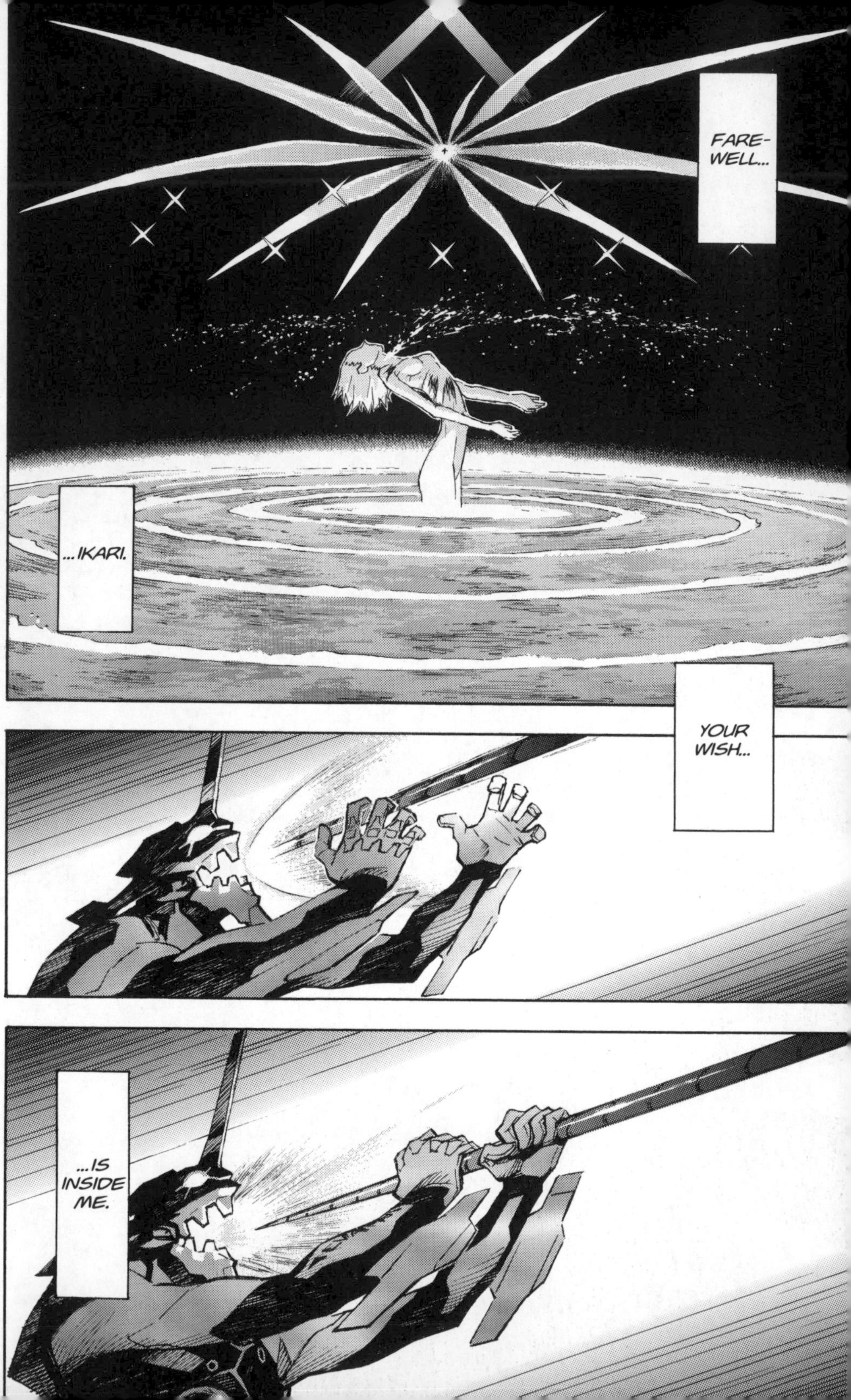
FARE-WELL...
...IKARI.
YOUR WISH...
...IS INSIDE ME.

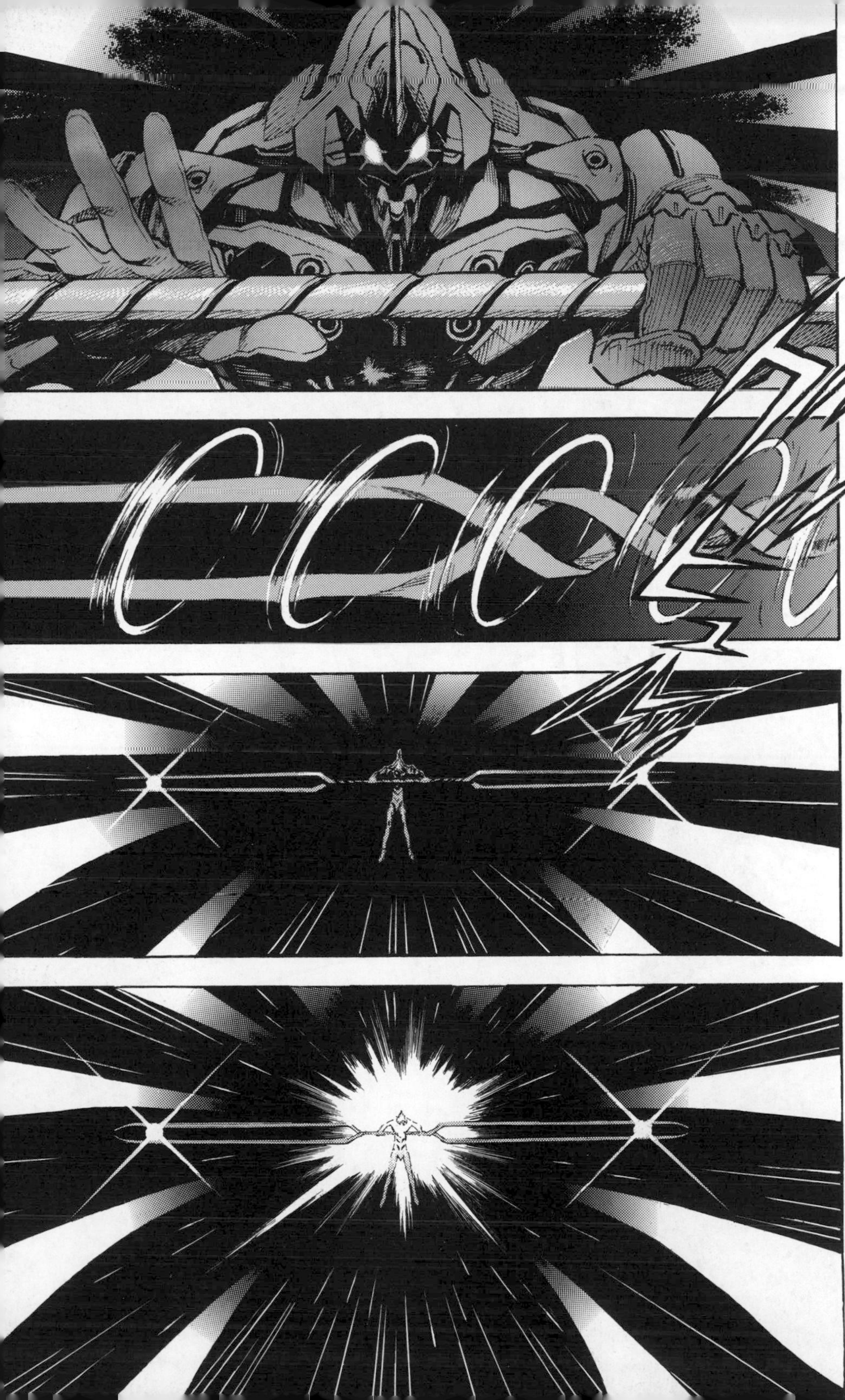

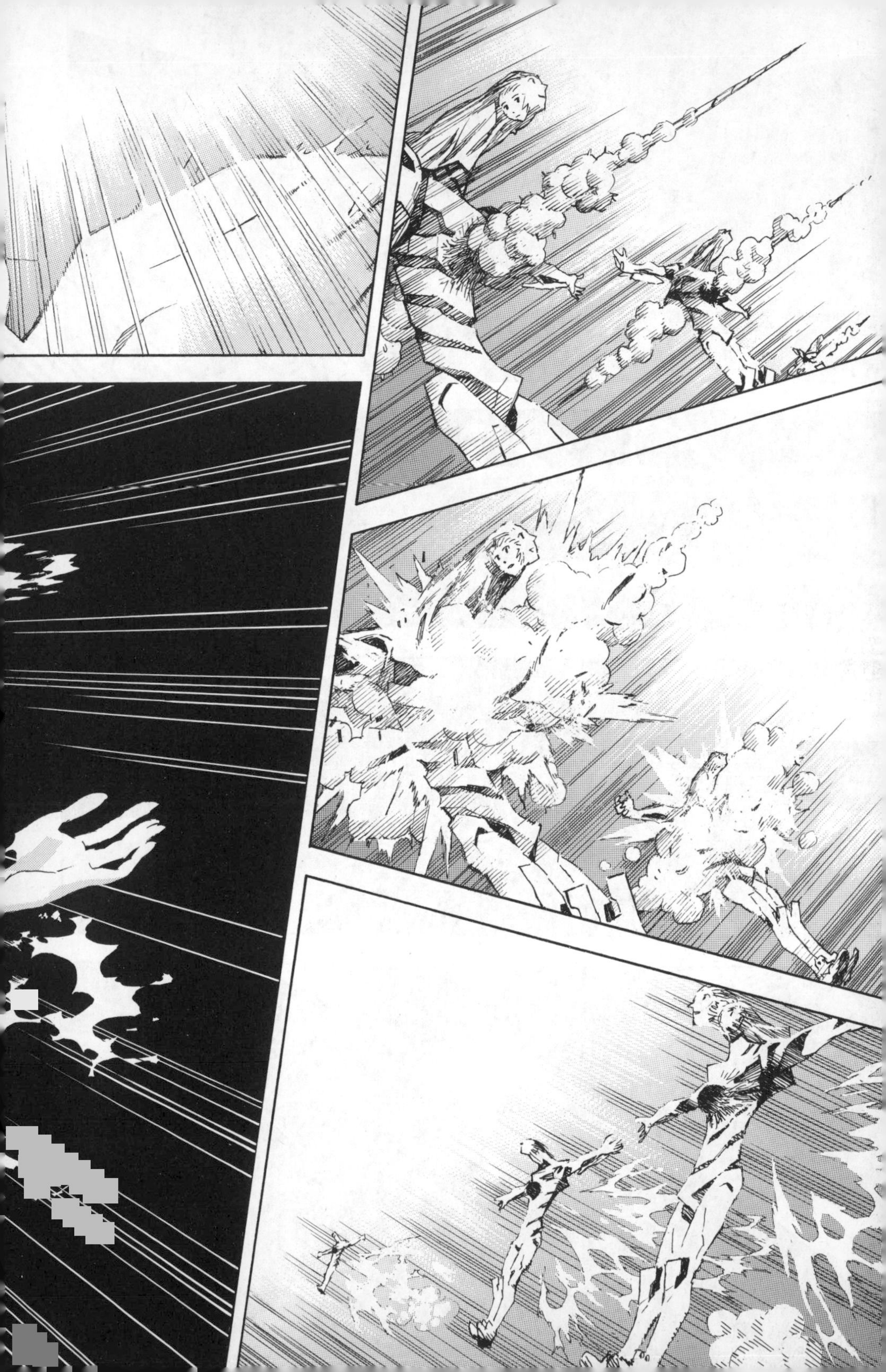

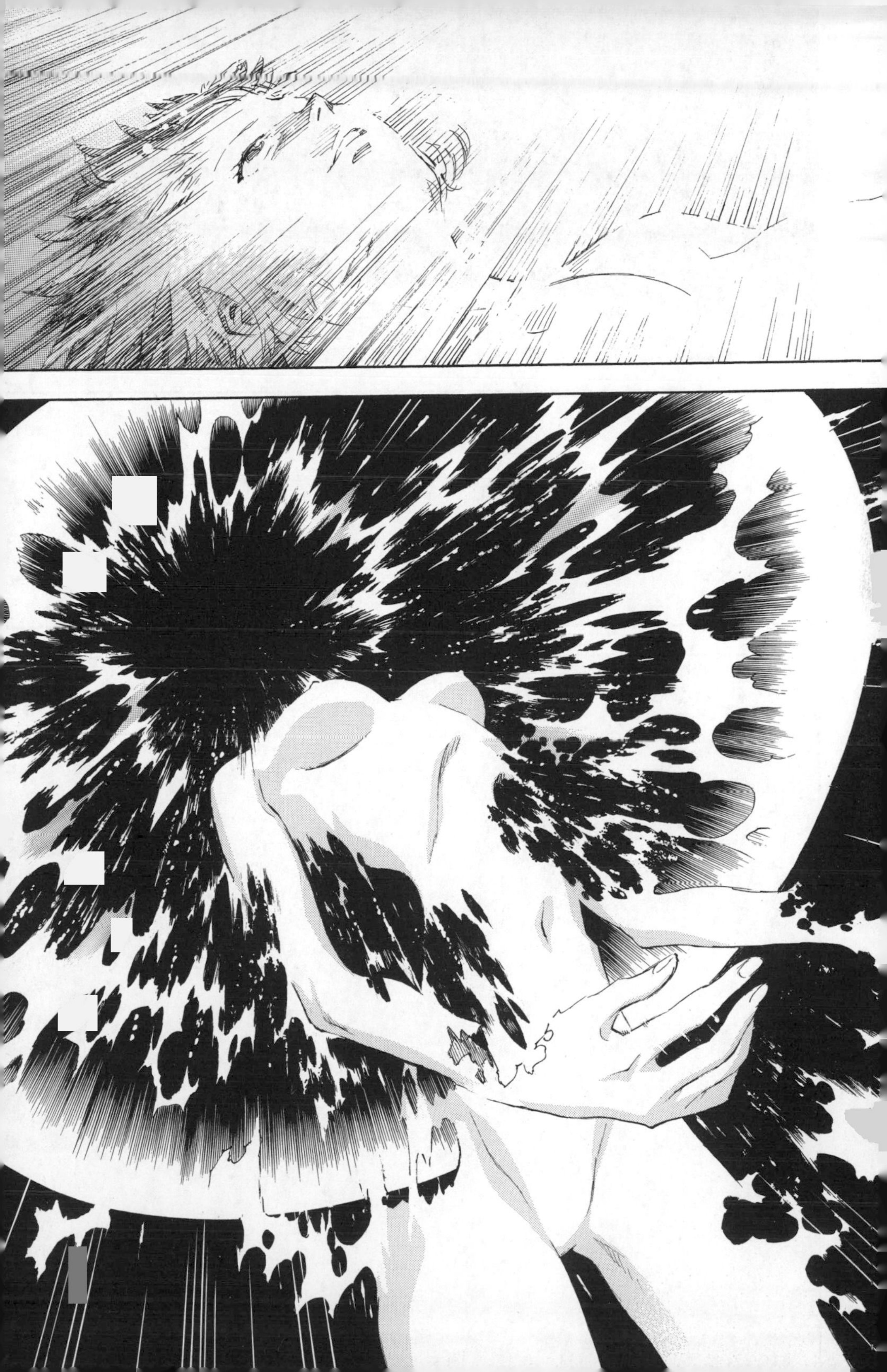

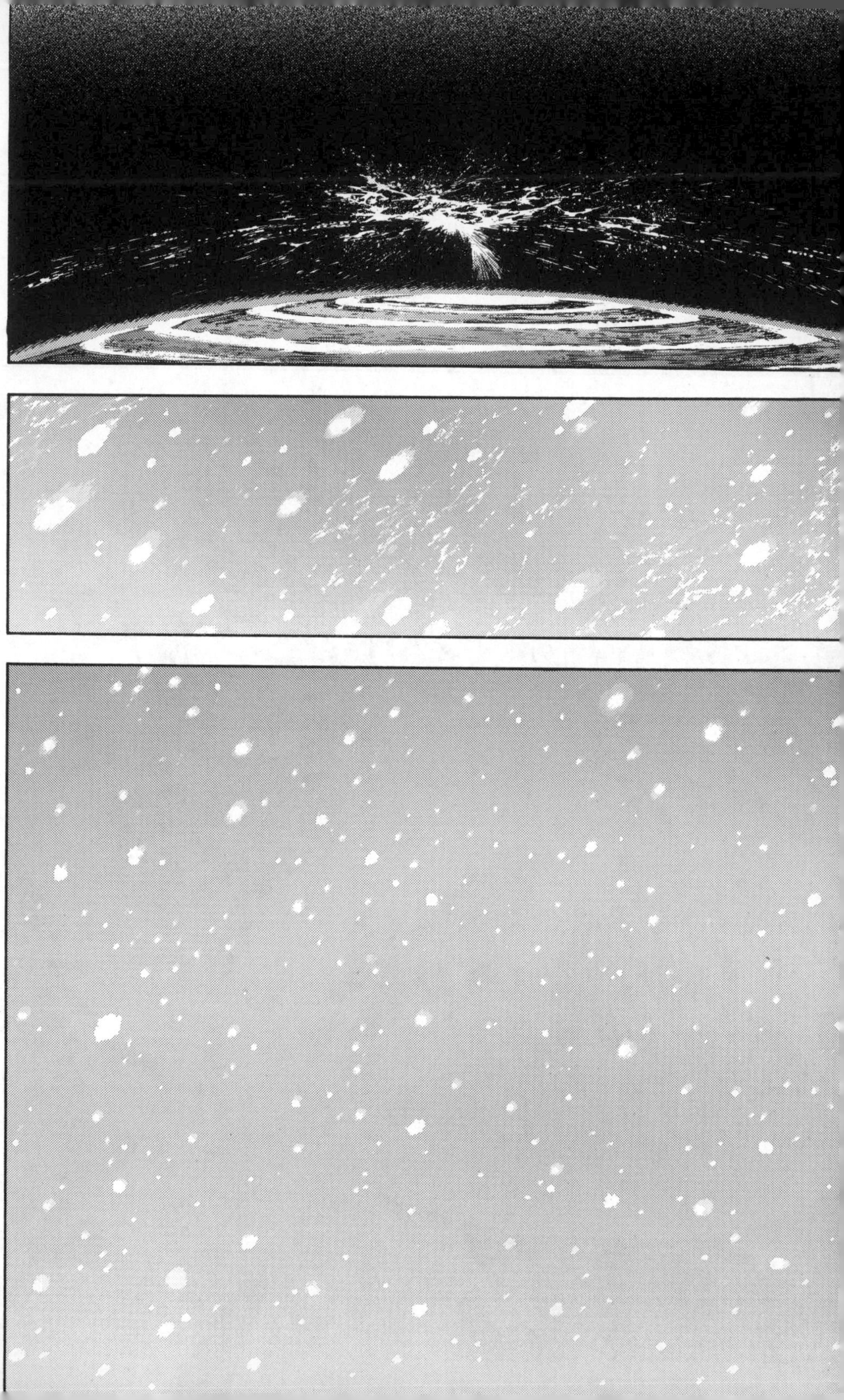

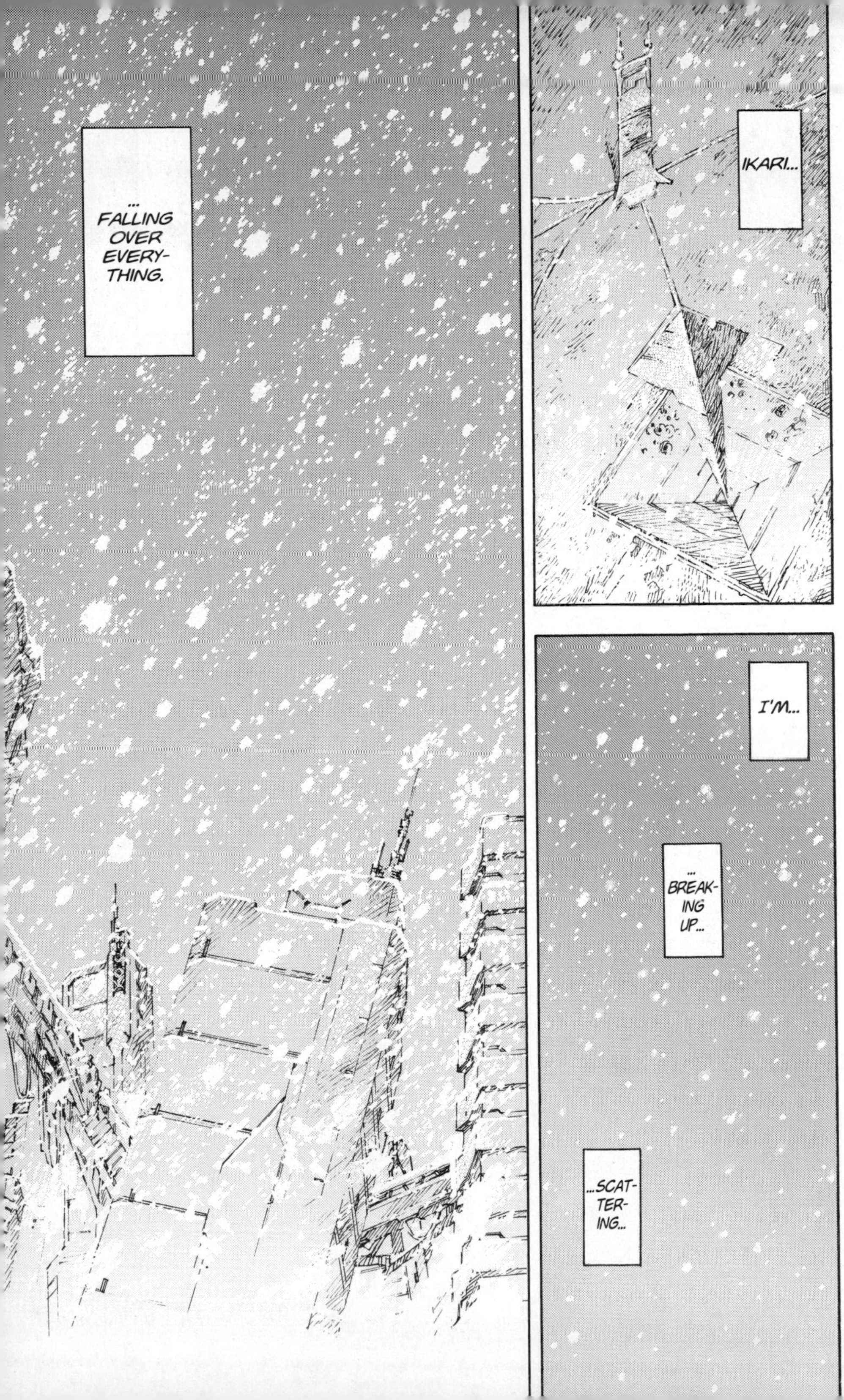
IKARI...
I'M...
... BREAKING UP...
...SCATTERING...
... FALLING OVER EVERYTHING.

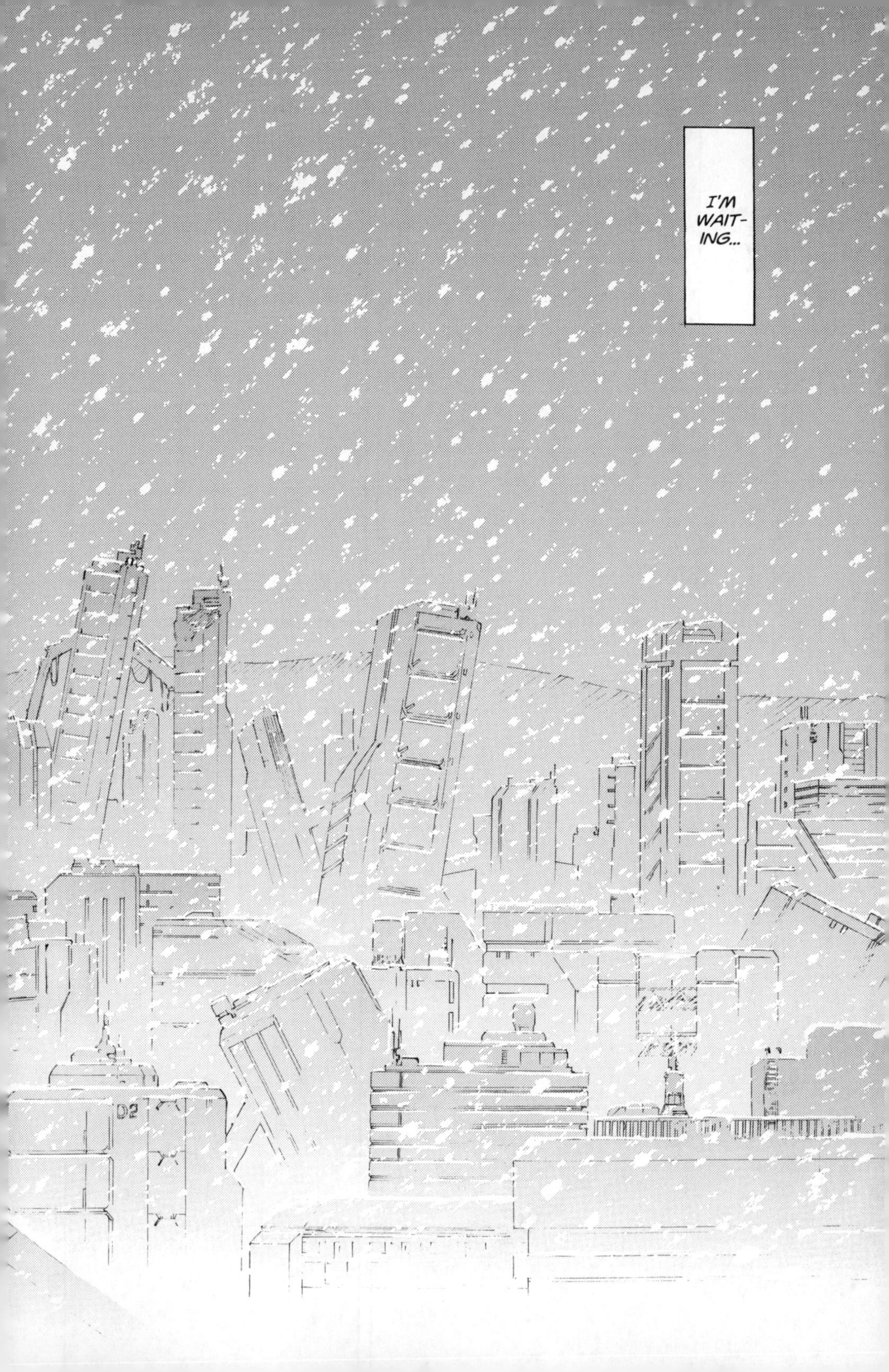
I'M WAIT- ING...

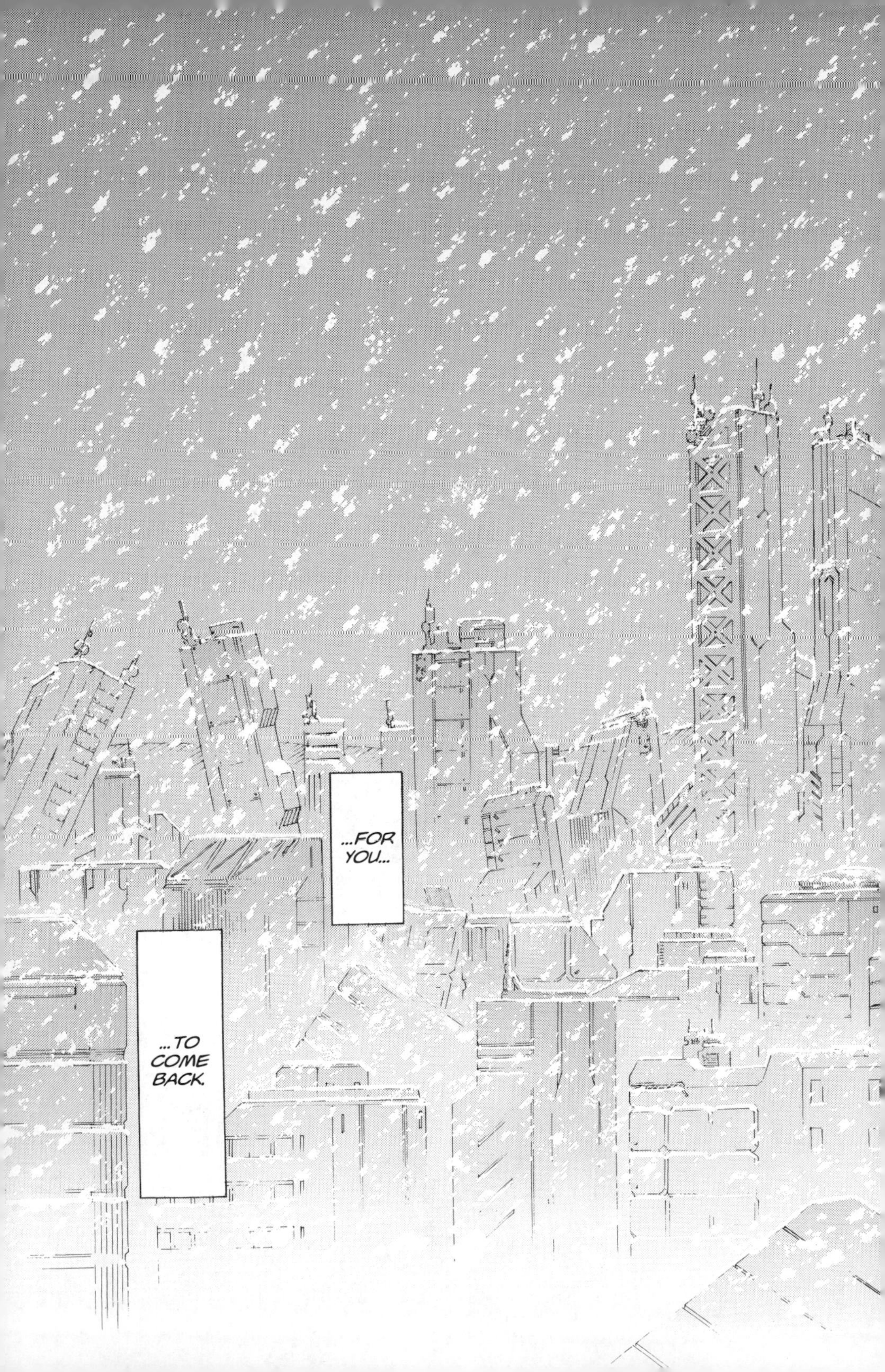
...FOR YOU...
...TO COME BACK.

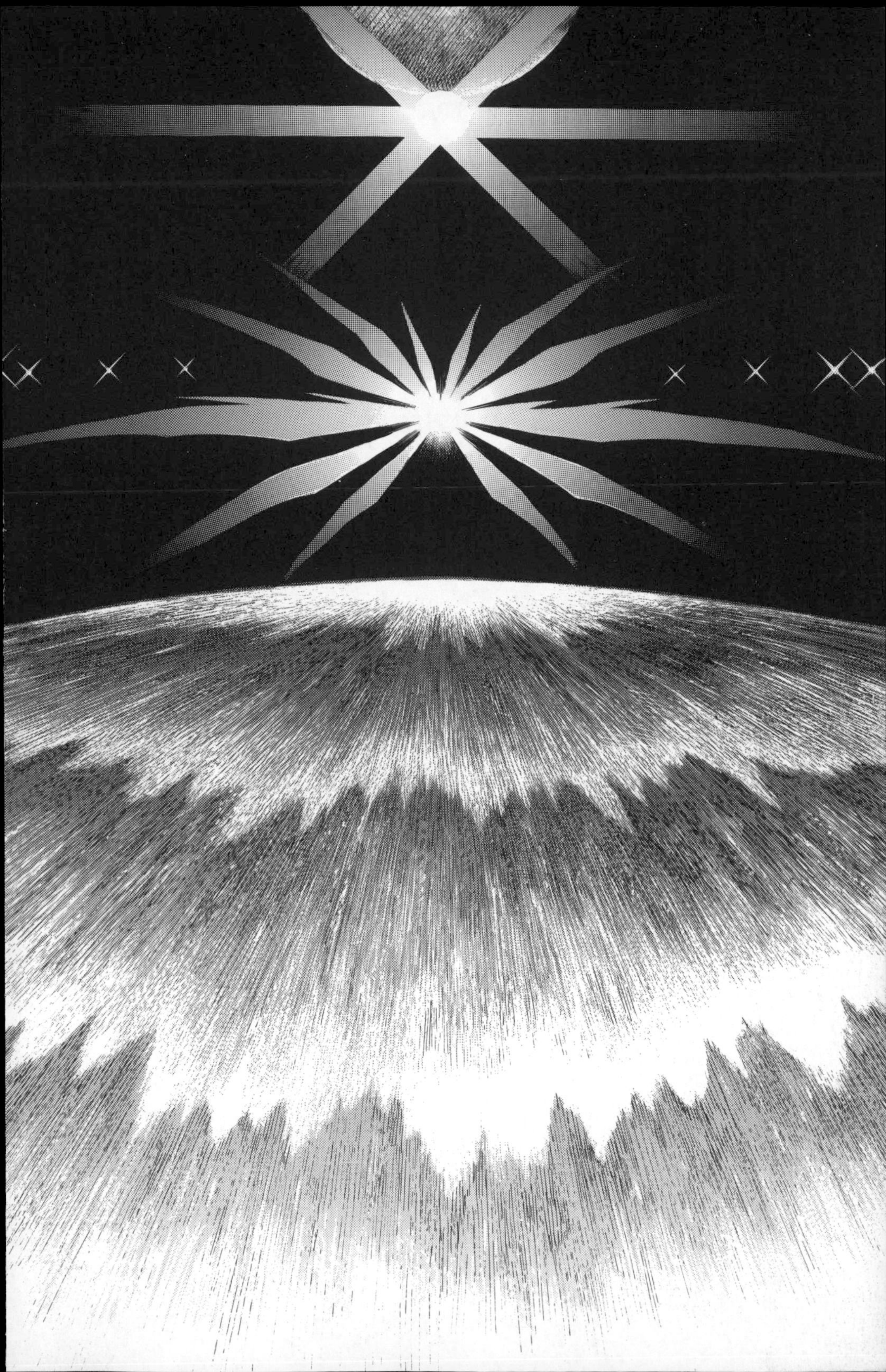

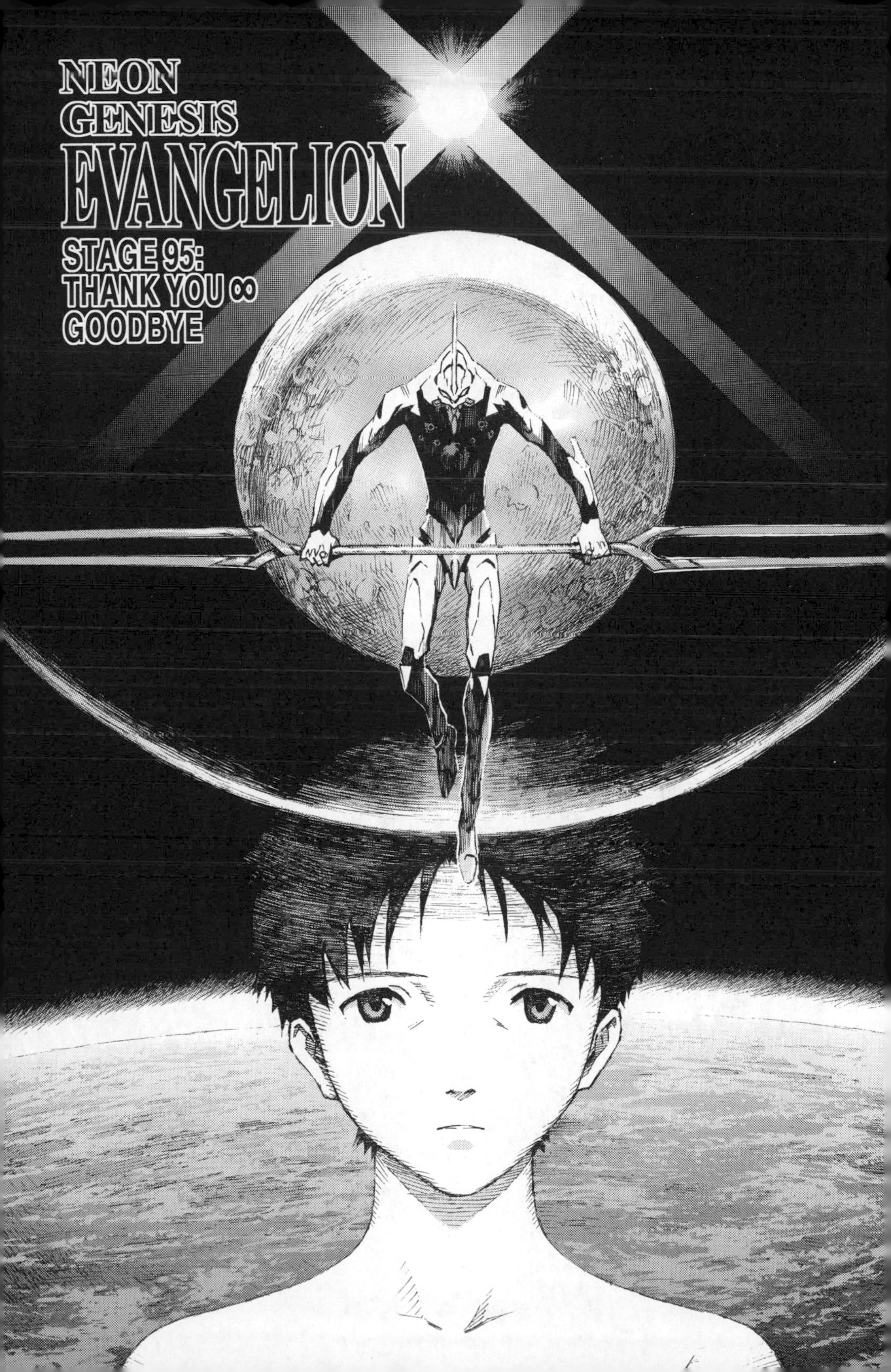
NEON GENESIS EVANGELION
STAGE 95: THANK YOU ∞ GOODBYE

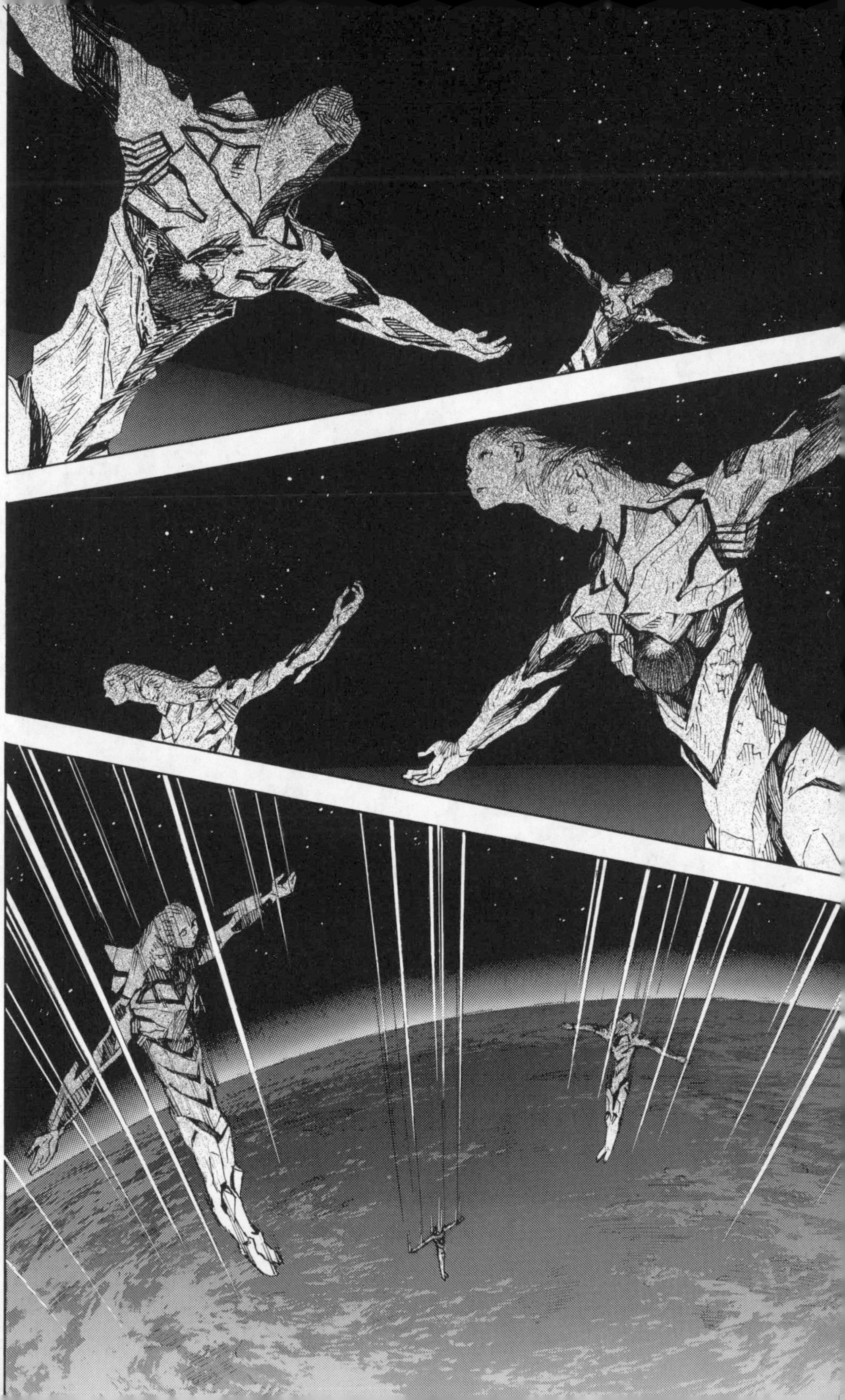

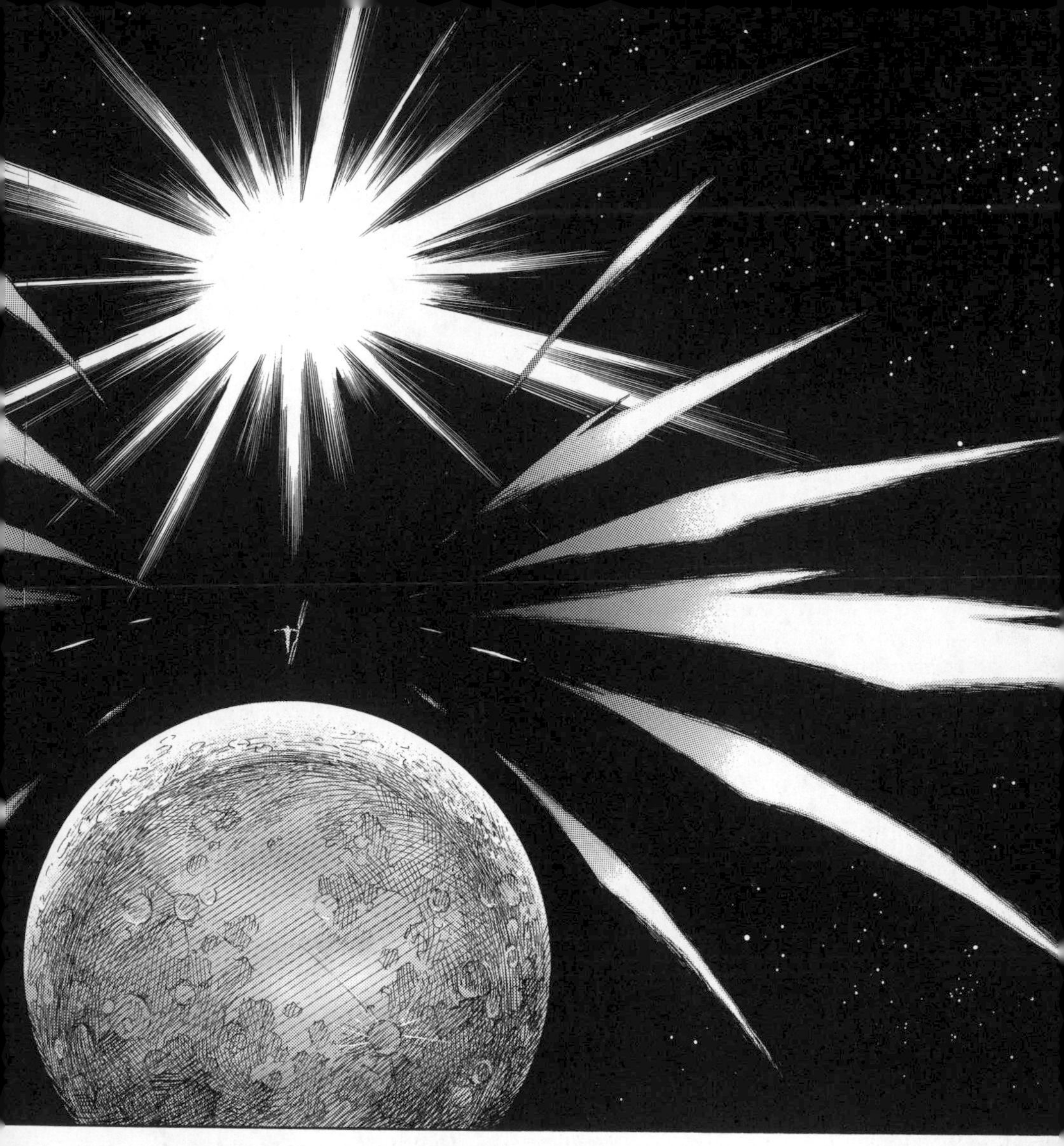
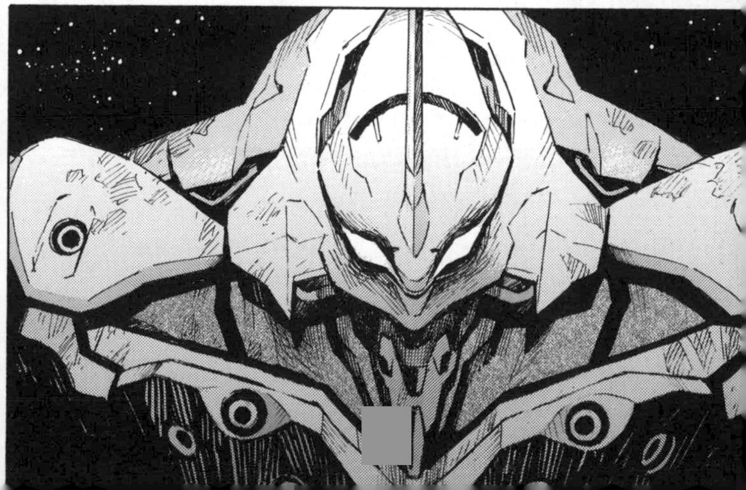
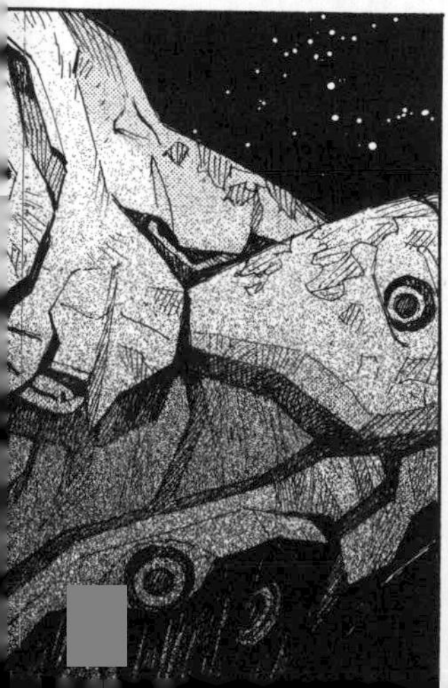

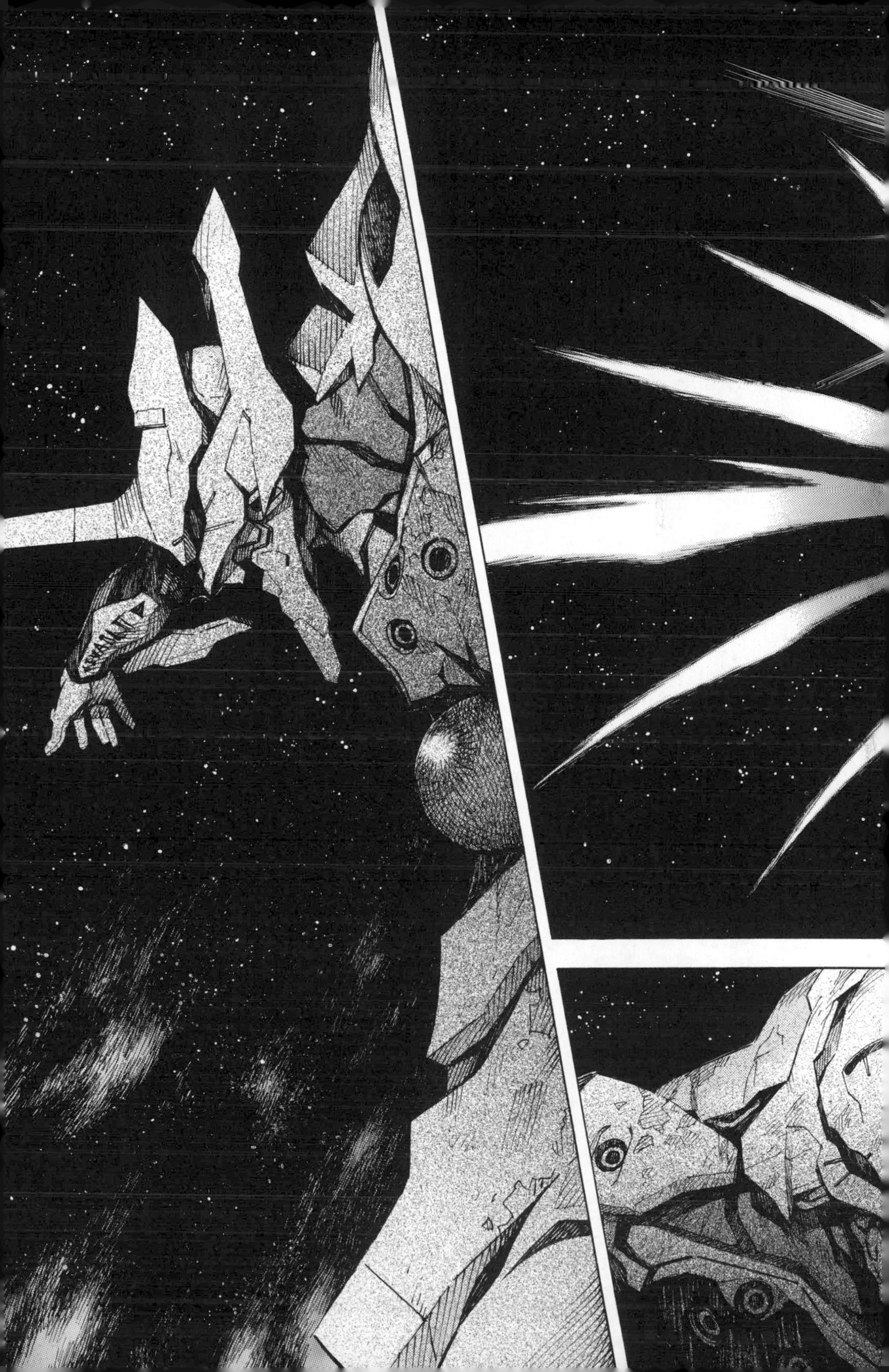

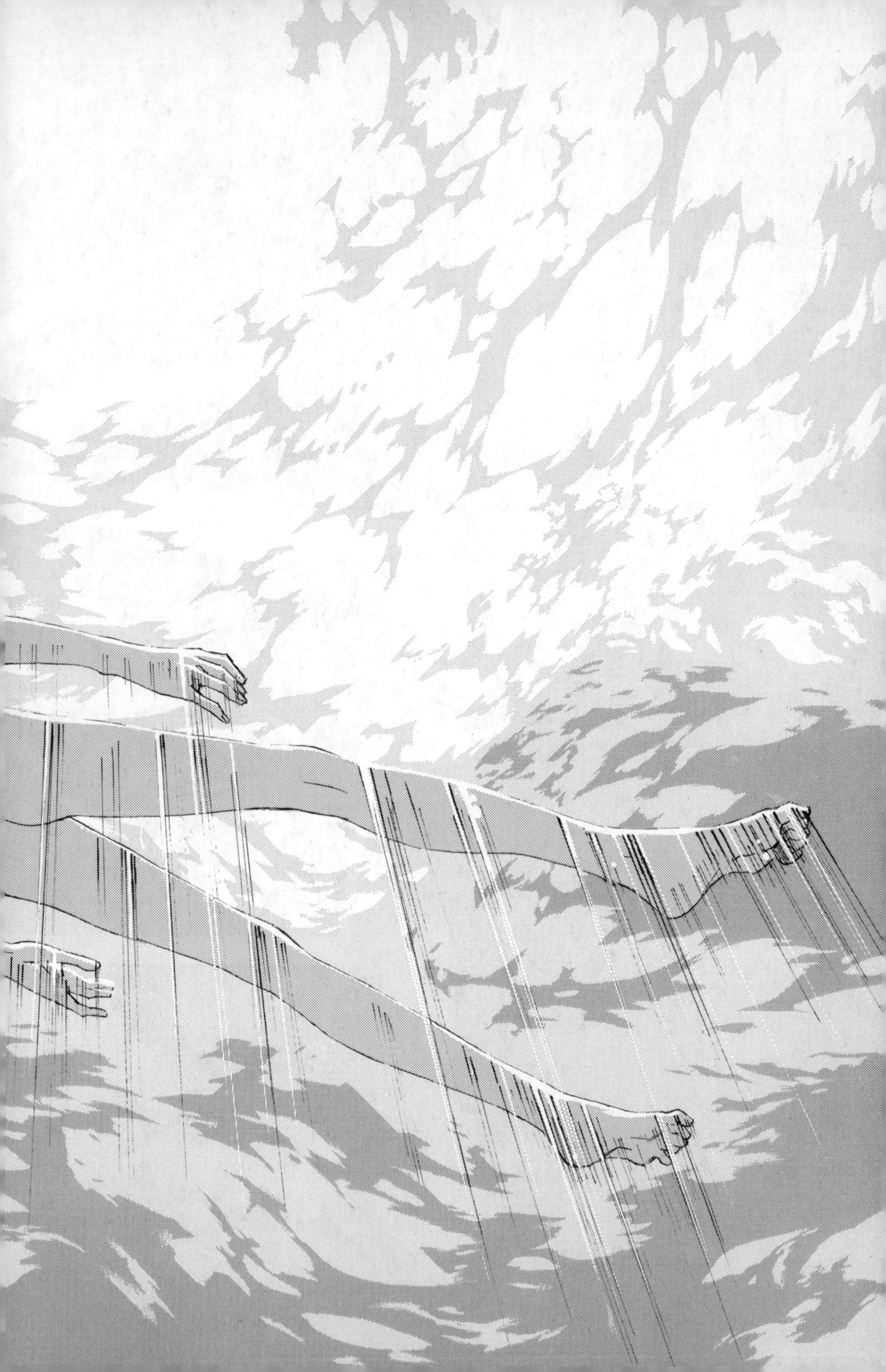

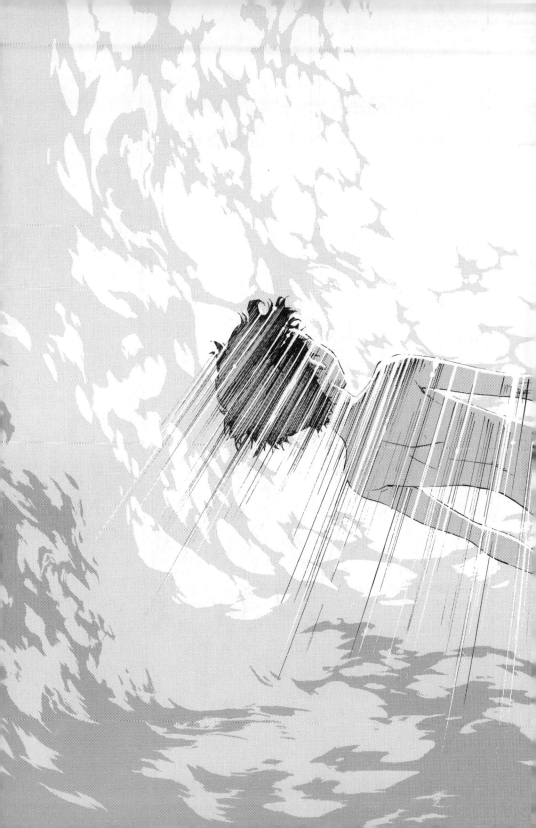

THANK
YOU...

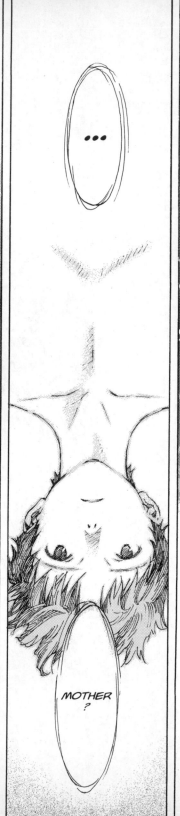

...FOR
REMEMBERING
YOUR PROMISE.

SHINJI...

MOTHER
?

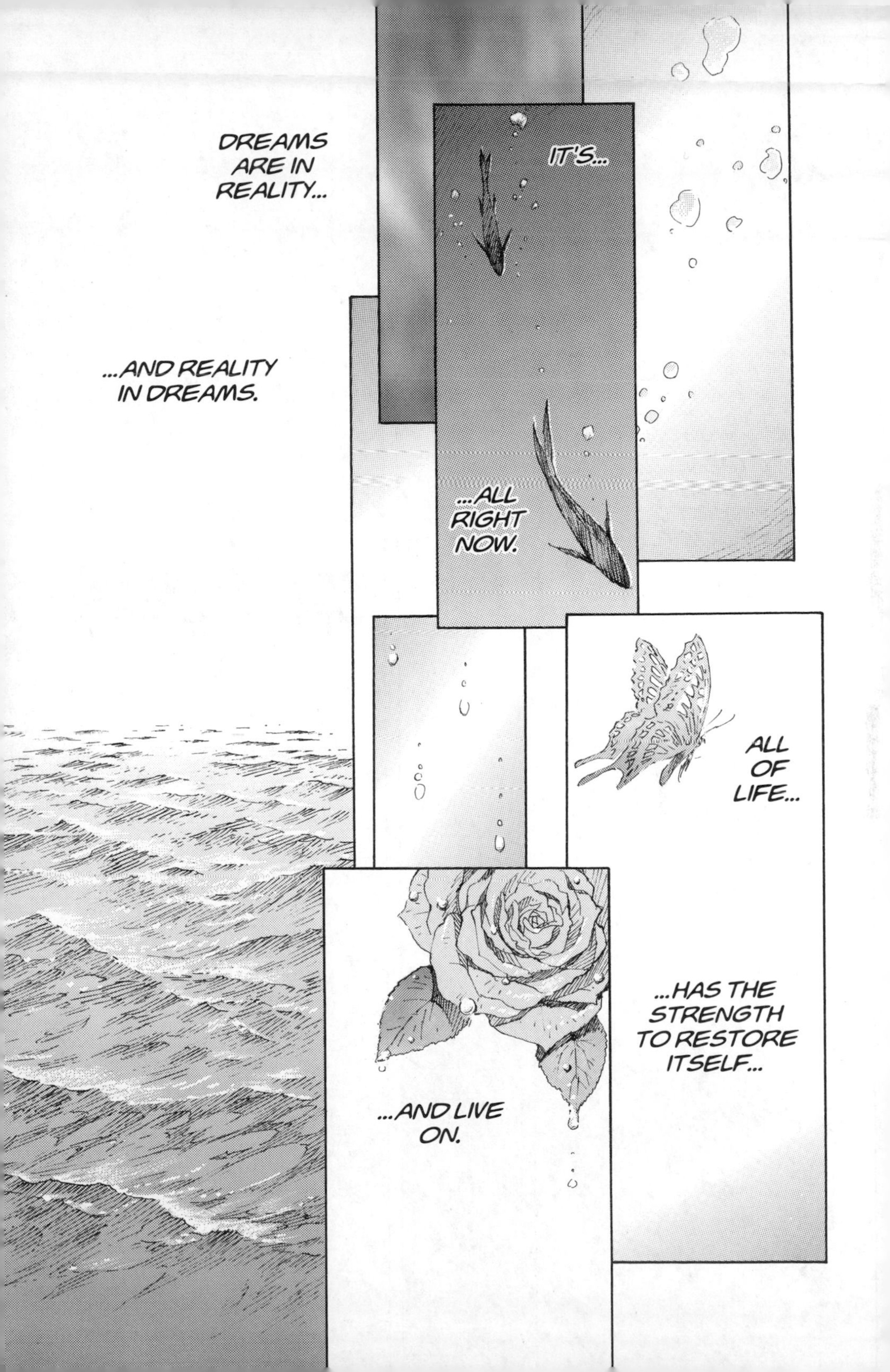
DREAMS ARE IN REALITY...
...AND REALITY IN DREAMS.
IT'S...
...ALL RIGHT NOW.
ALL OF LIFE...
...HAS THE STRENGTH TO RESTORE ITSELF...
...AND LIVE ON.

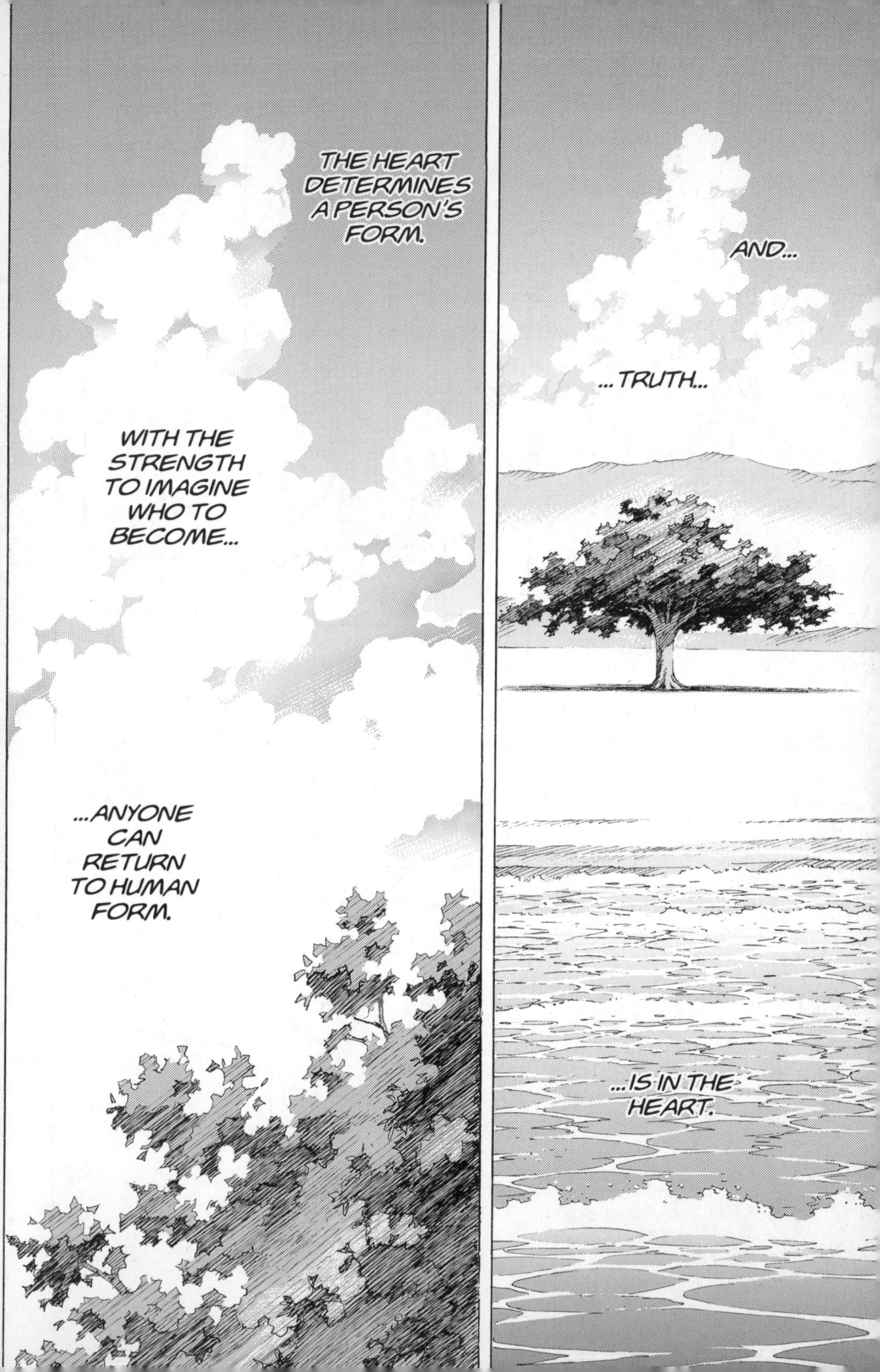
AND...
...TRUTH...
...IS IN THE HEART.
THE HEART DETERMINES A PERSON'S FORM.
WITH THE STRENGTH TO IMAGINE WHO TO BECOME...
...ANYONE CAN RETURN TO HUMAN FORM.

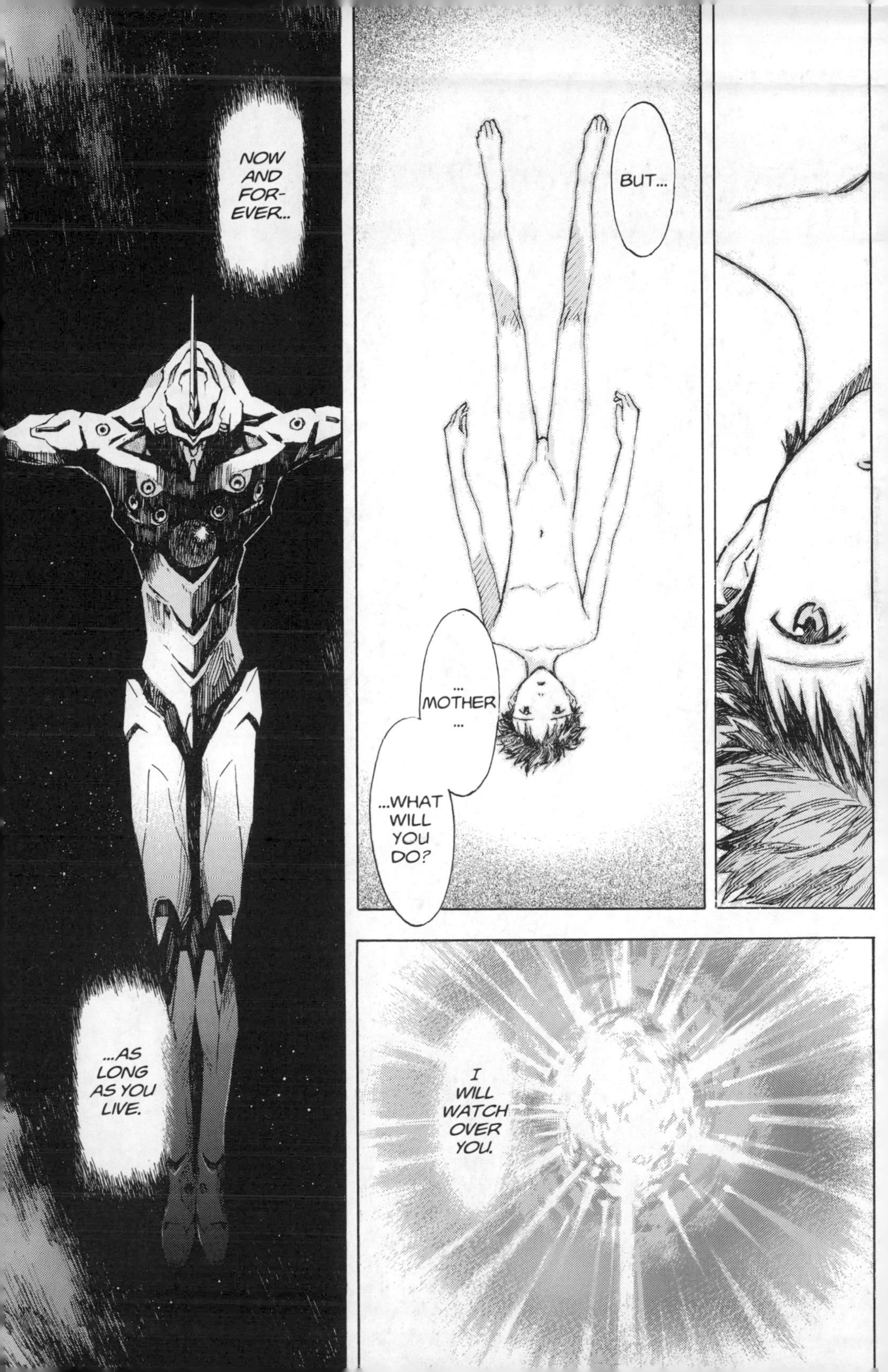
BUT...
... MOTHER ...
...WHAT WILL YOU DO?
I WILL WATCH OVER YOU.
NOW AND FOR-EVER...
...AS LONG AS YOU LIVE.

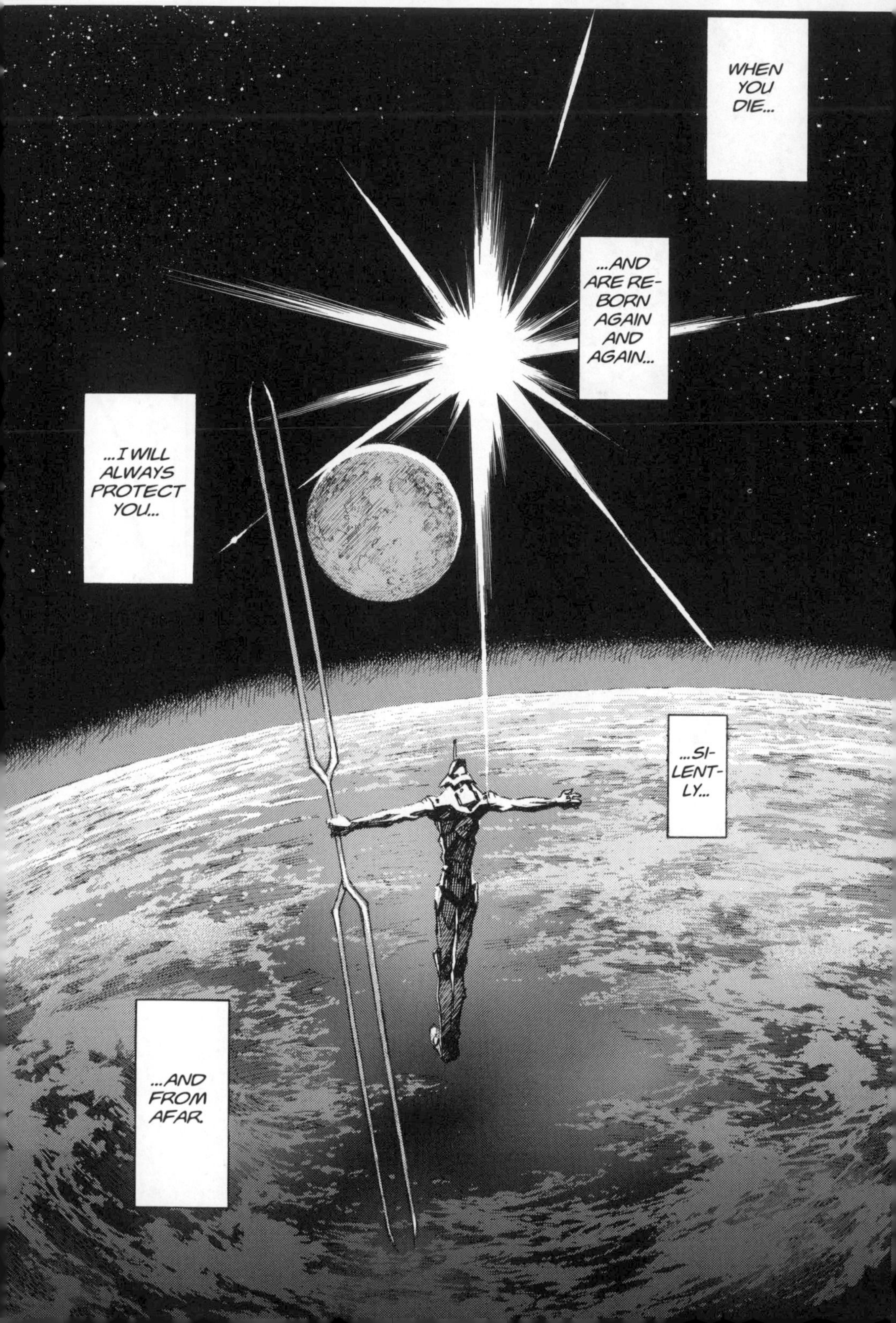
WHEN YOU DIE...
...AND ARE RE-BORN AGAIN AND AGAIN...
...I WILL ALWAYS PROTECT YOU...
...SI-LENT-LY...
...AND FROM AFAR.

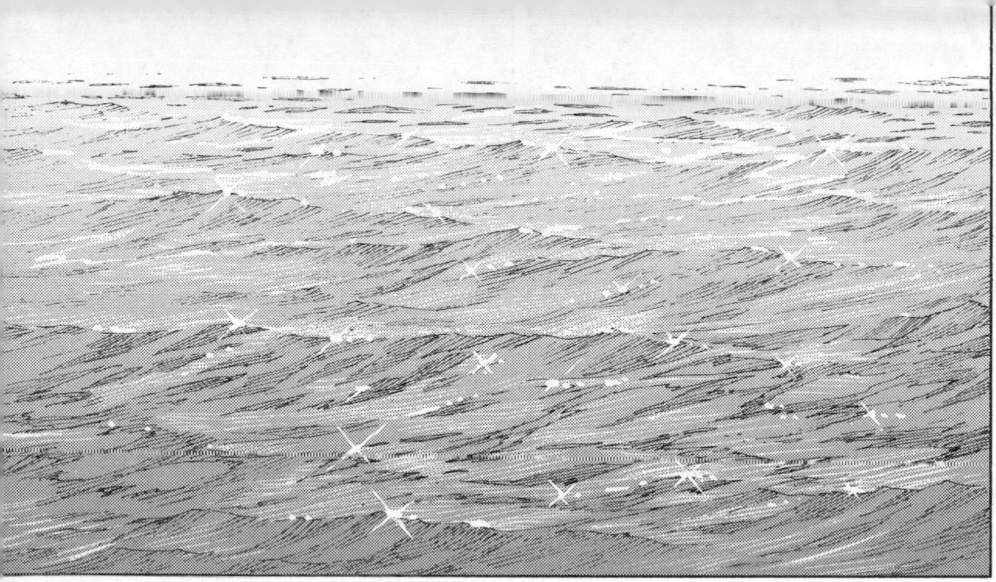
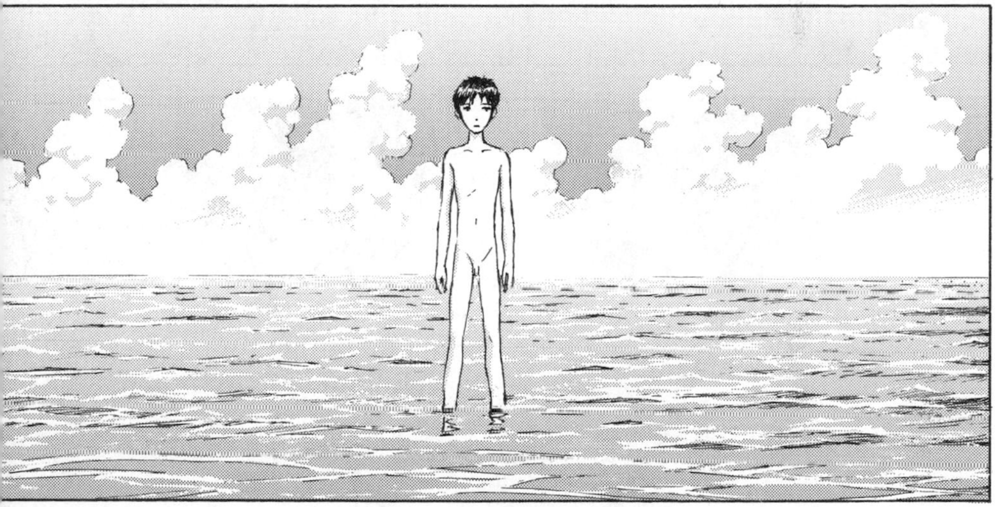
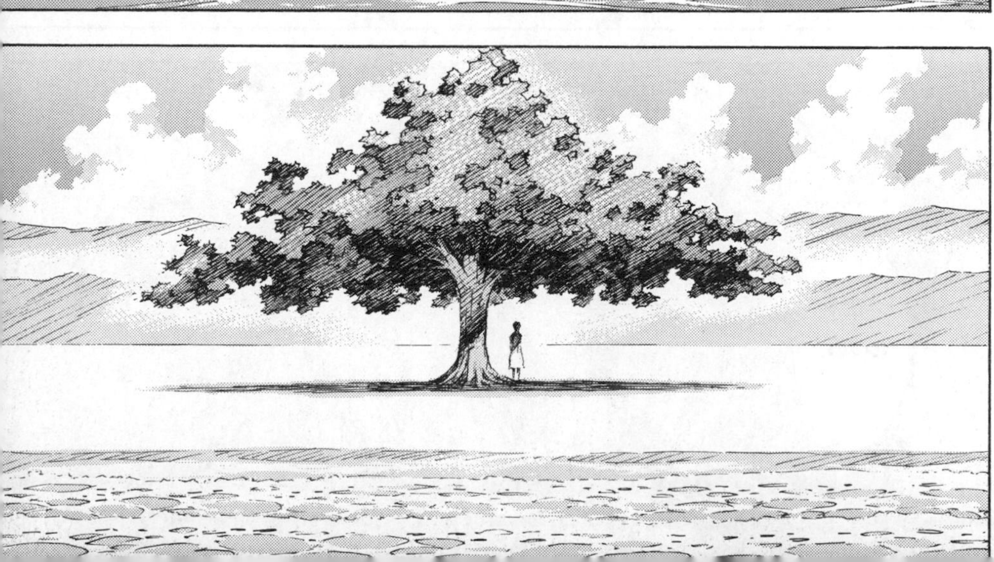

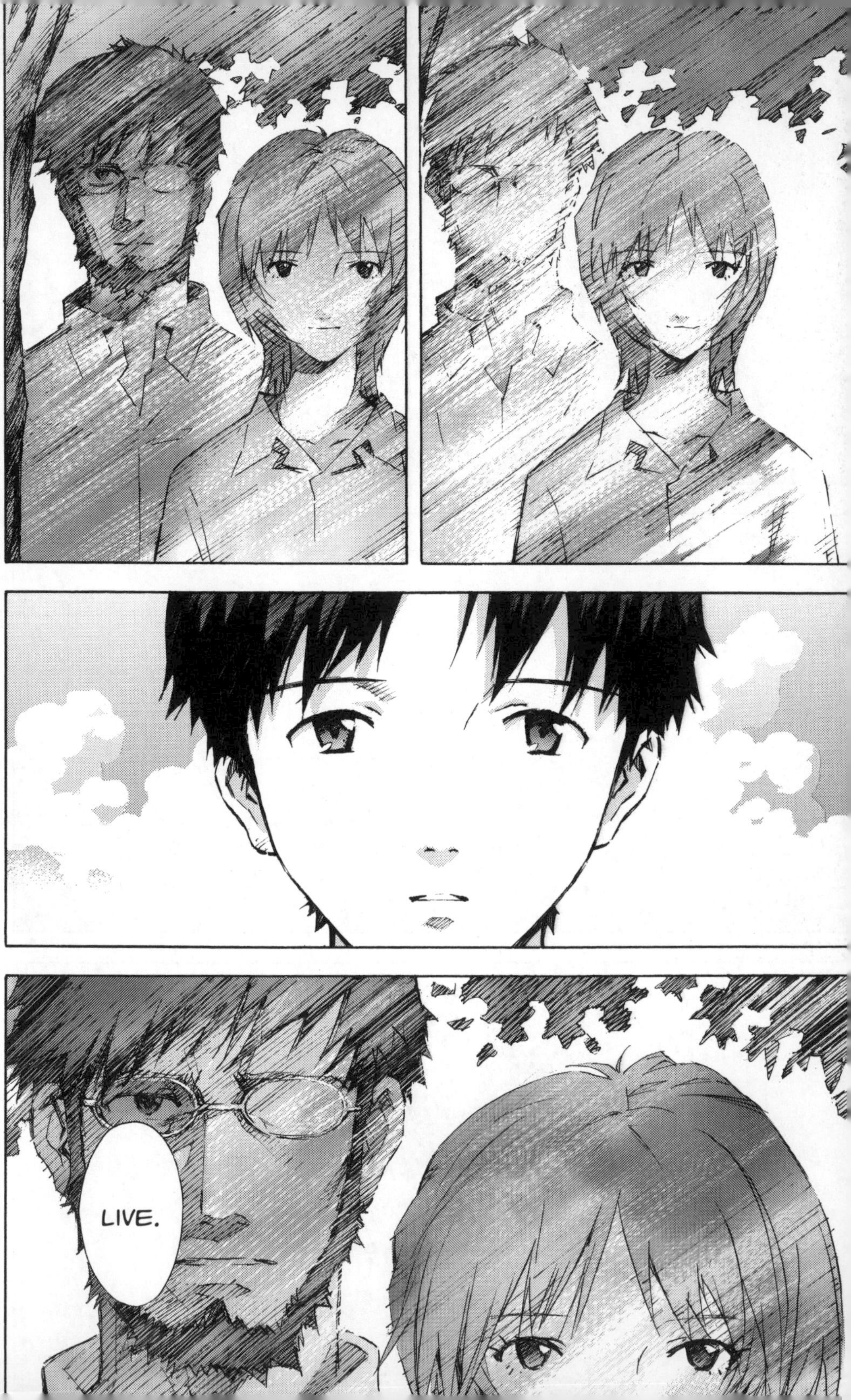
LIVE.

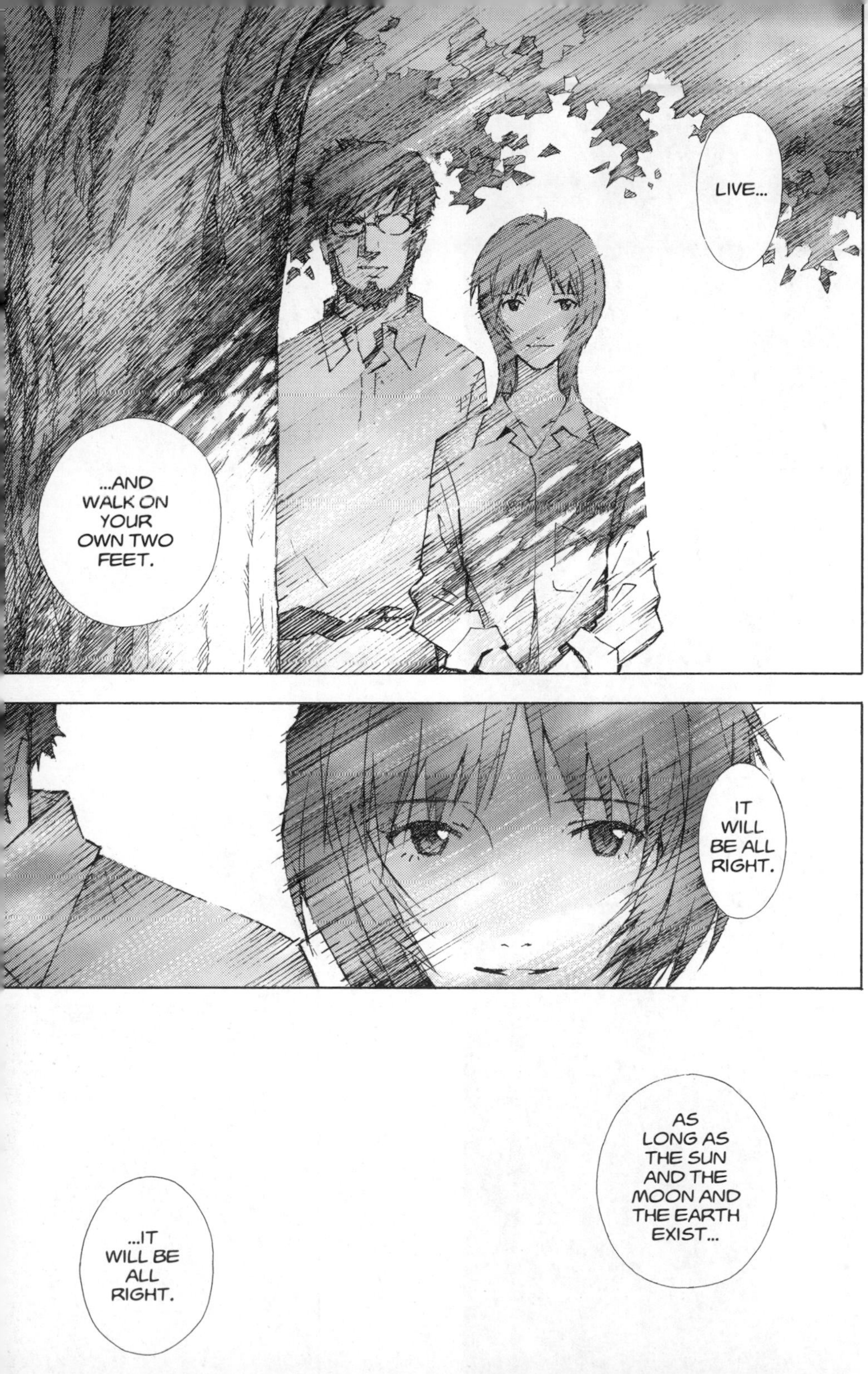
LIVE...
...AND WALK ON YOUR OWN TWO FEET.
IT WILL BE ALL RIGHT.
AS LONG AS THE SUN AND THE MOON AND THE EARTH EXIST...
...IT WILL BE ALL RIGHT.

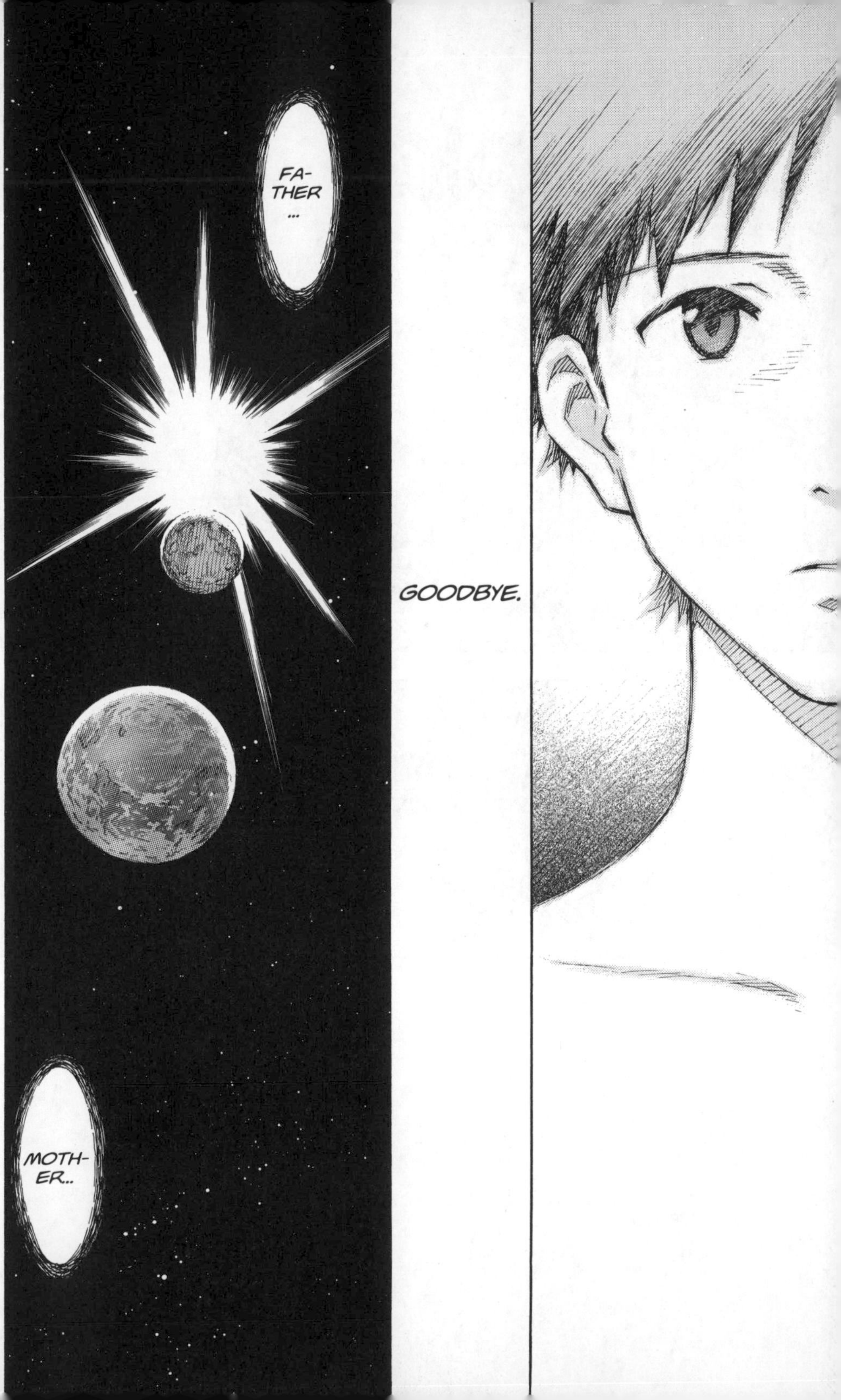
GOODBYE.
FA-
THER
...
MOTH-
ER..

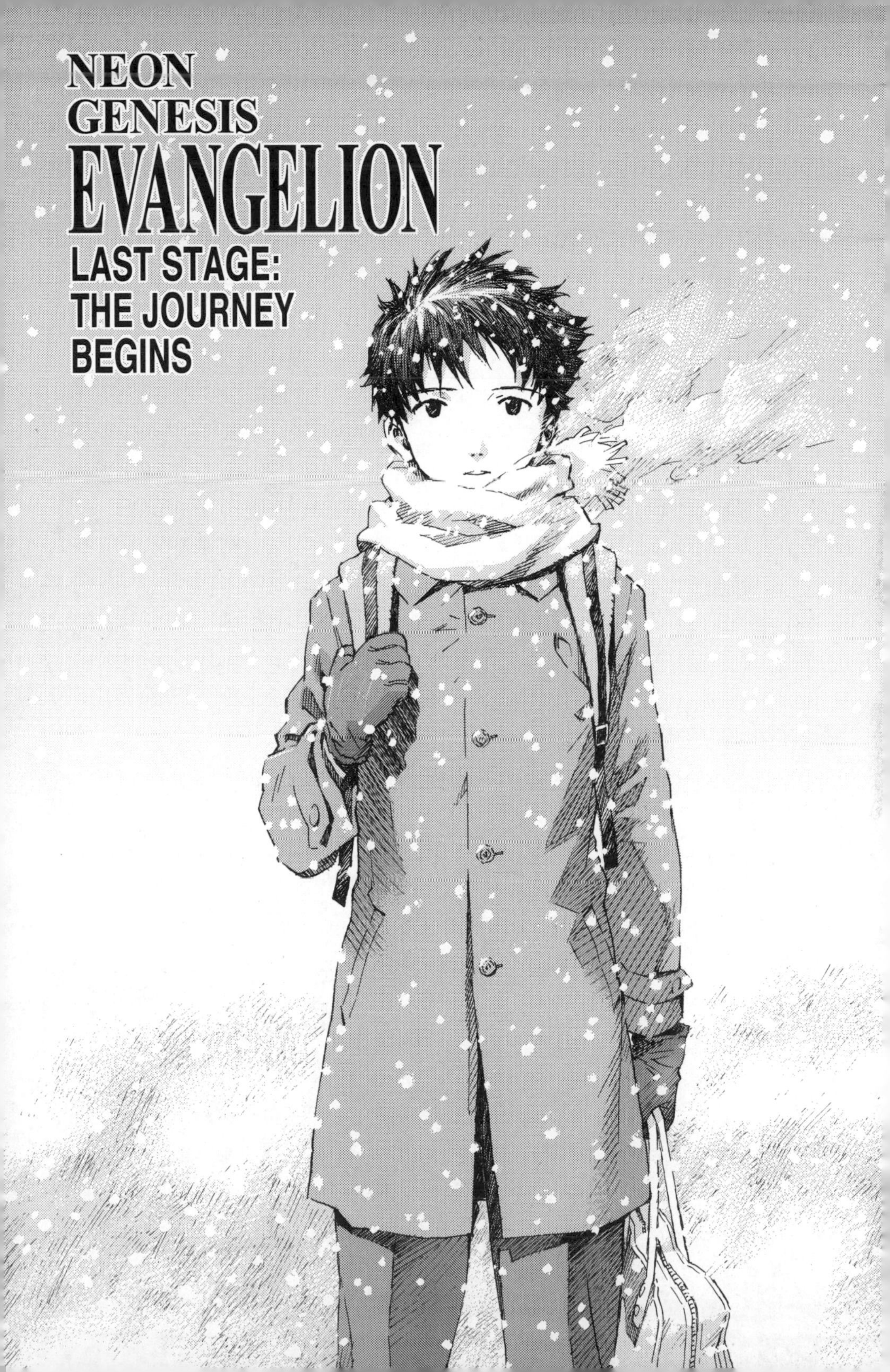
NEON GENESIS EVANGELION
LAST STAGE: THE JOURNEY BEGINS

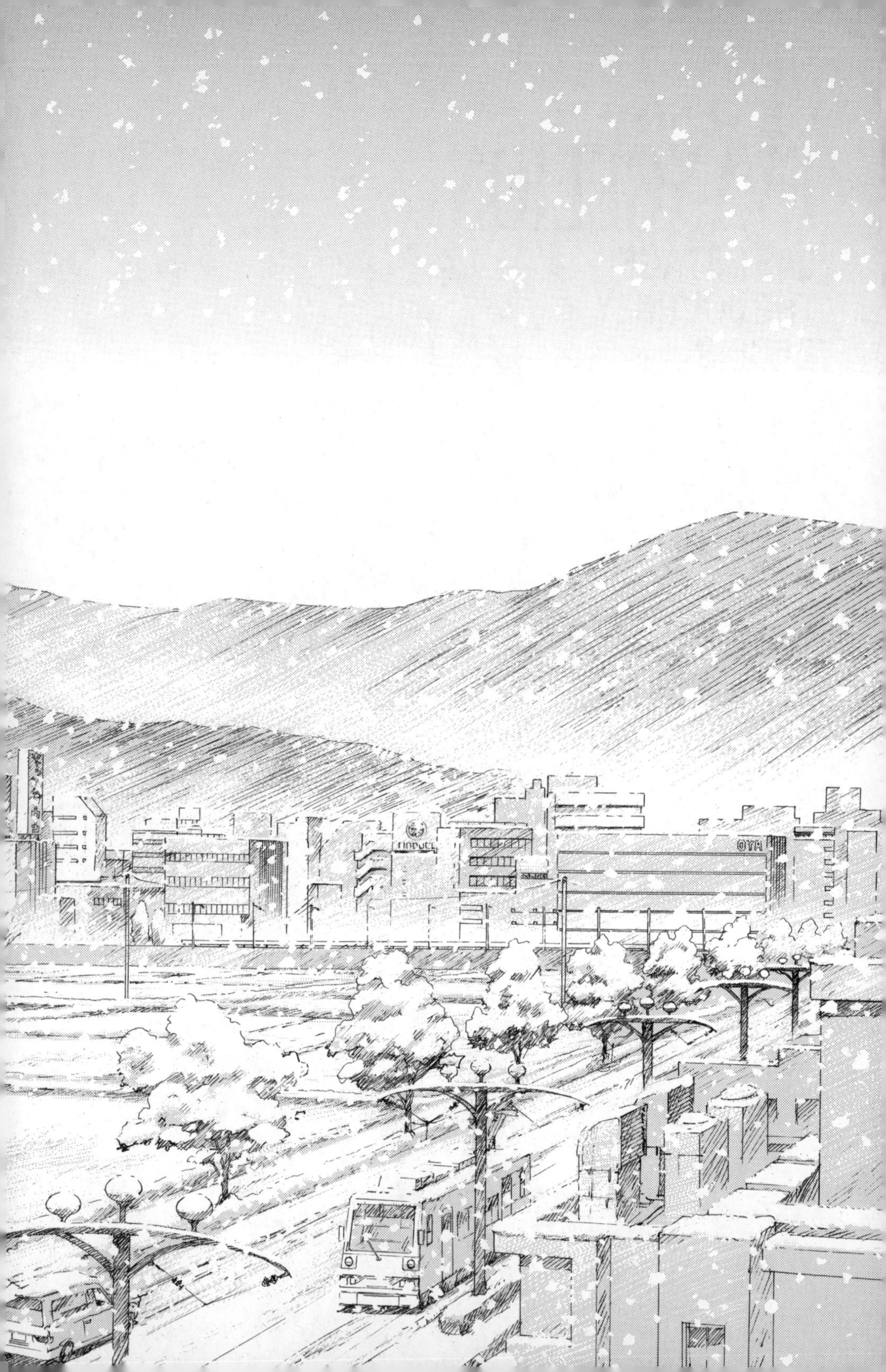
OYA

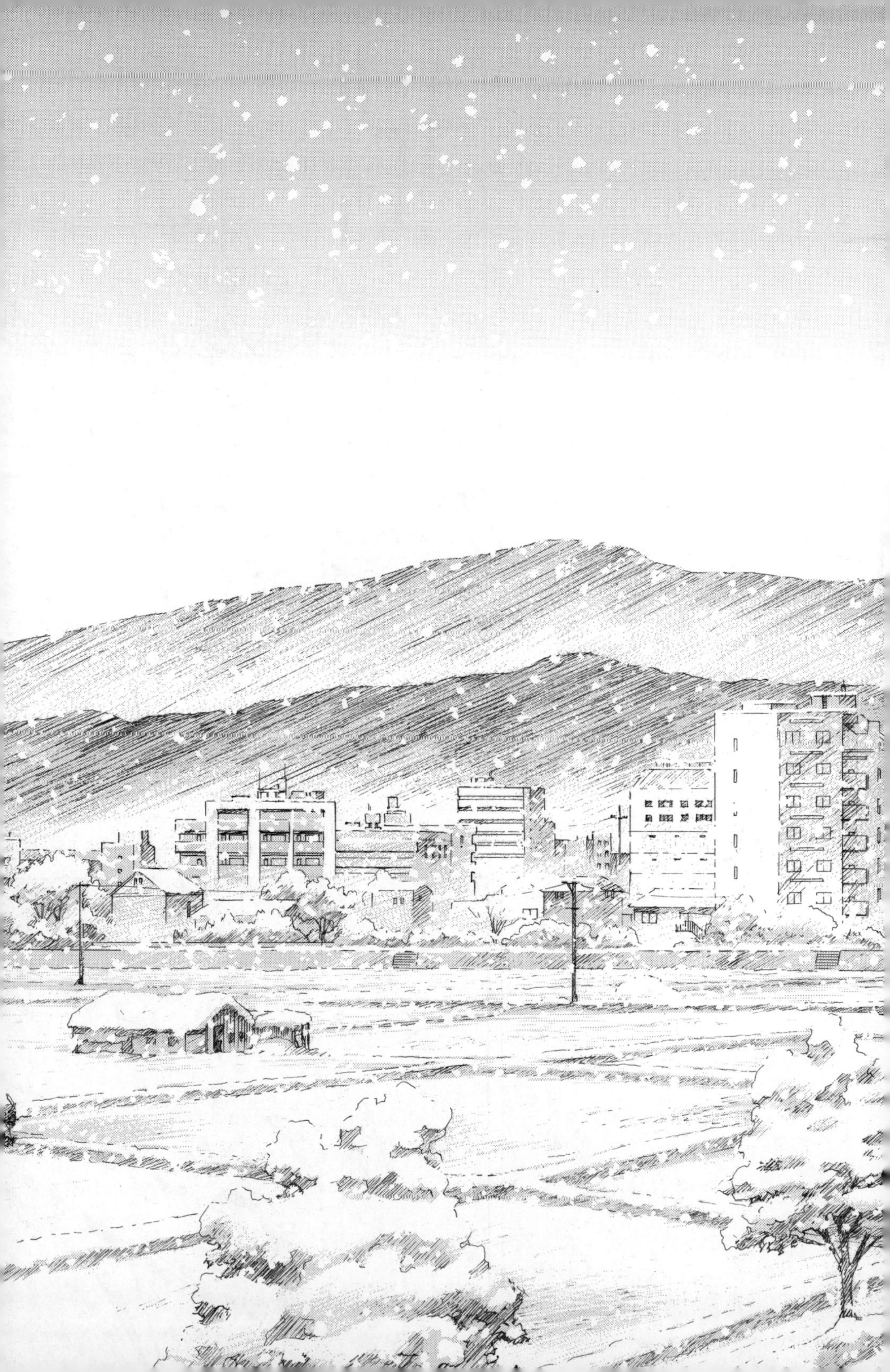

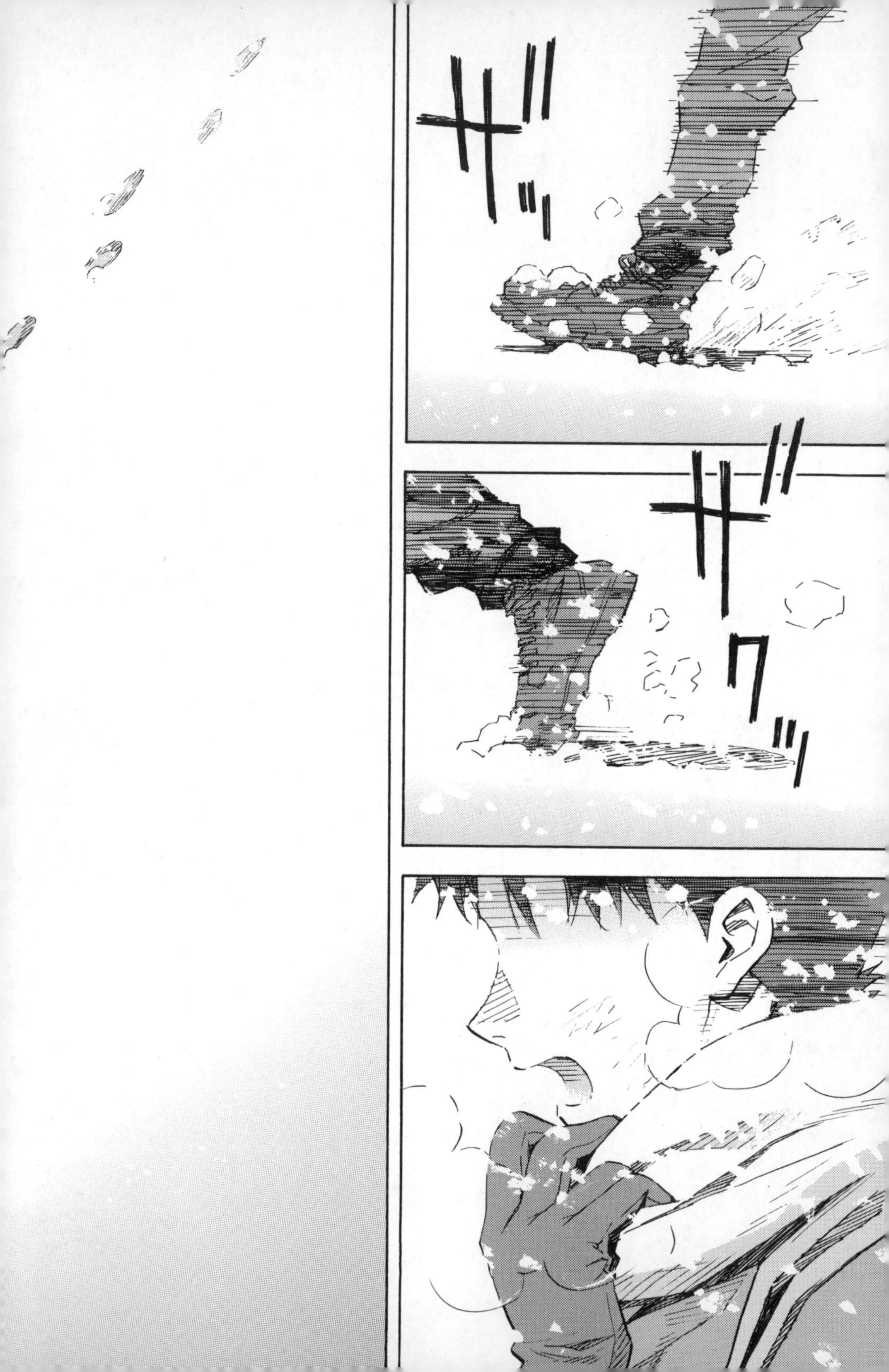
ザッ
ザクッ

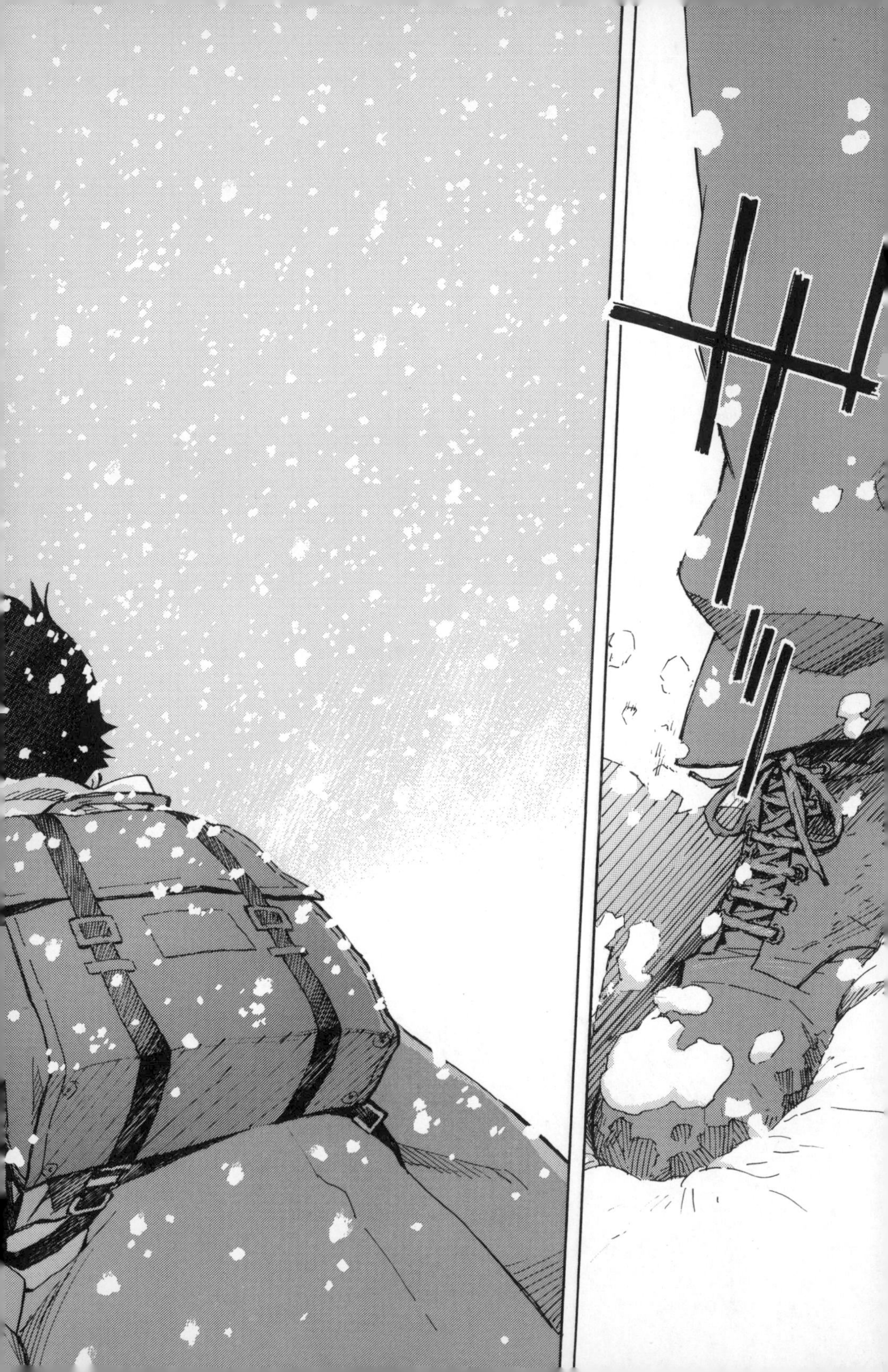

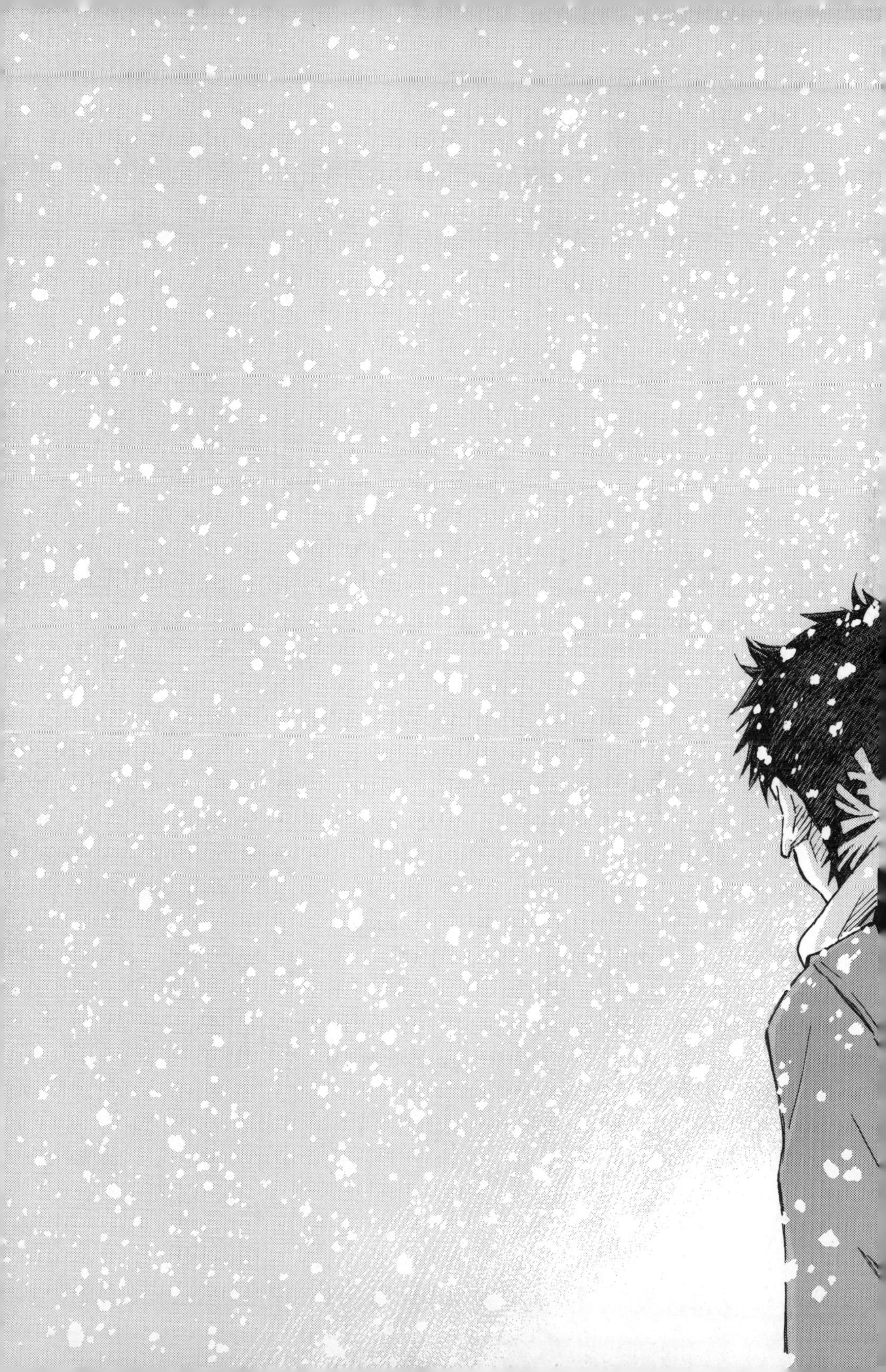

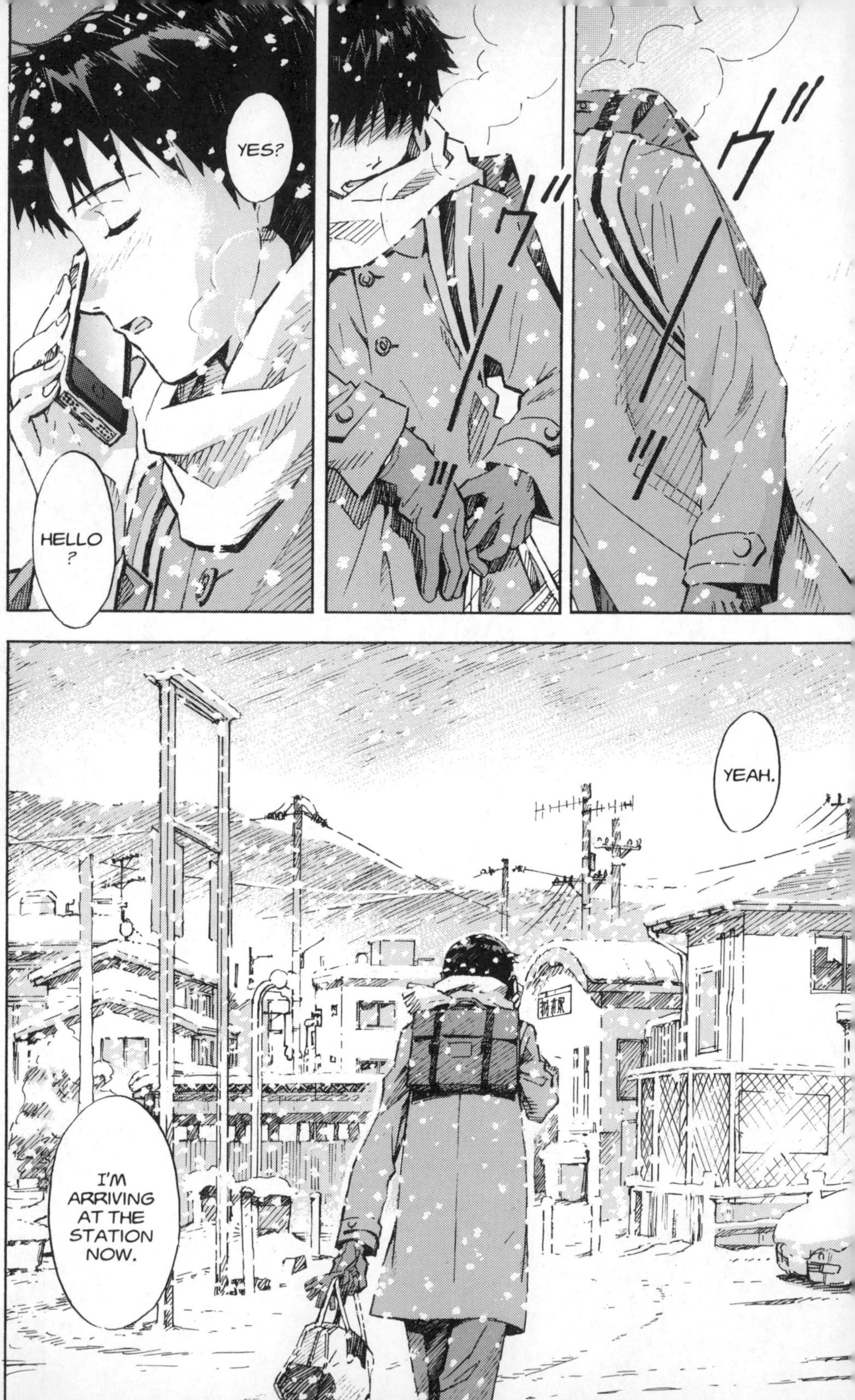
YES?
HELLO ?
YEAH.
I'M ARRIVING AT THE STATION NOW.

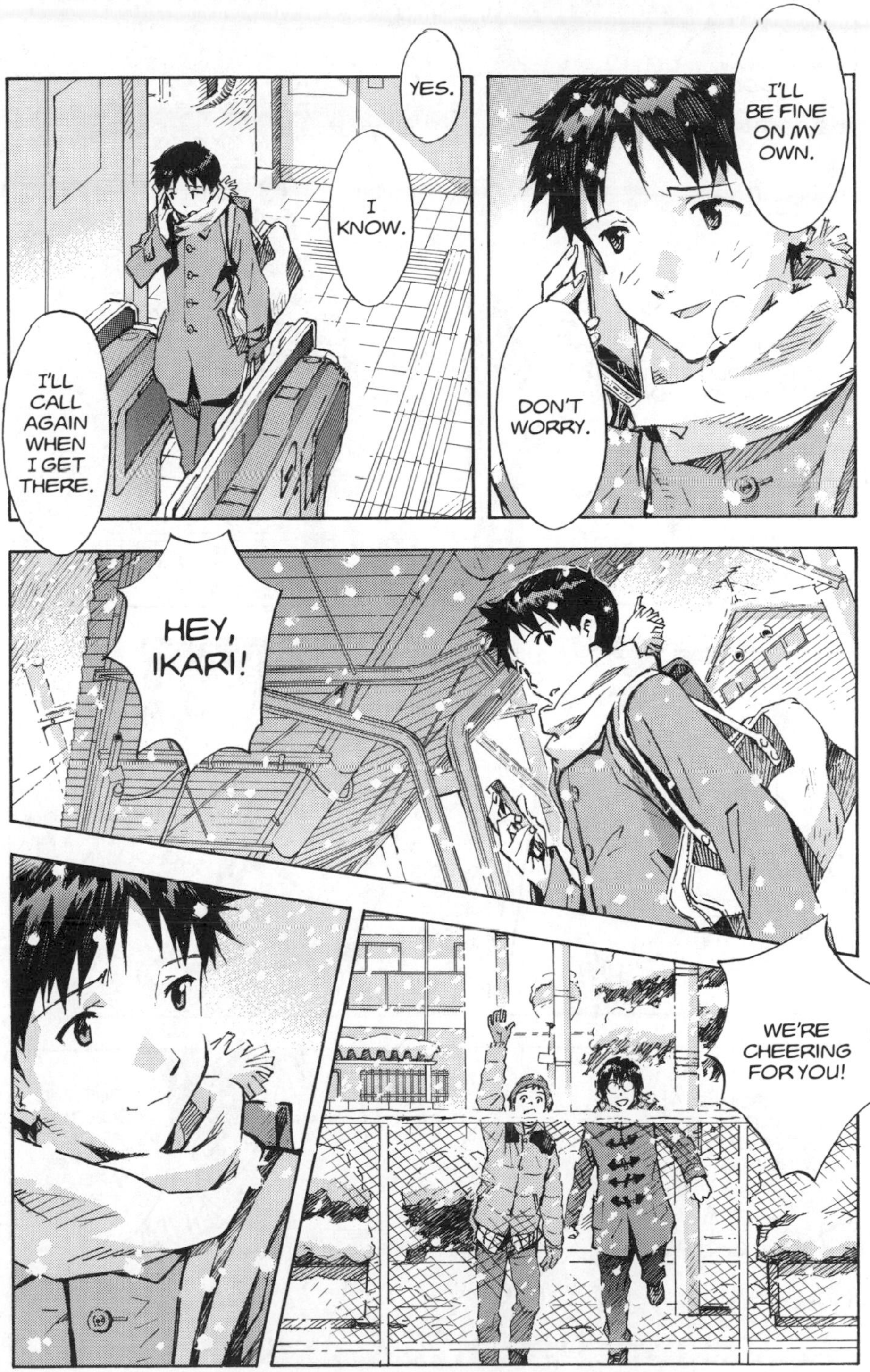
I'LL BE FINE ON MY OWN.
DON'T WORRY.
YES.
I KNOW.
I'LL CALL AGAIN WHEN I GET THERE.
HEY, IKARI!
WE'RE CHEERING FOR YOU!

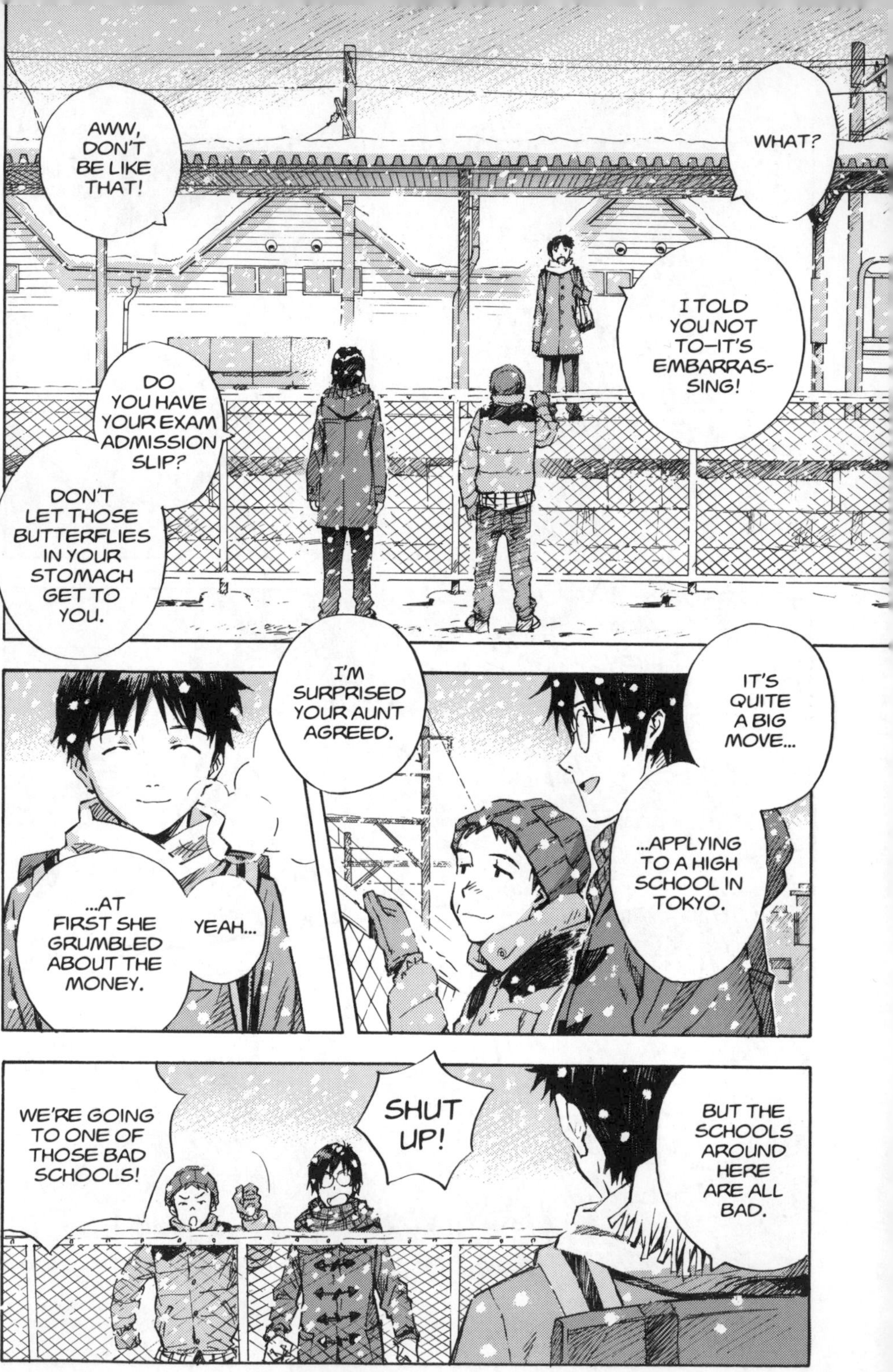
WHAT?
I TOLD YOU NOT TO—IT'S EMBARRAS-SING!
AWW, DON'T BE LIKE THAT!
DO YOU HAVE YOUR EXAM ADMISSION SLIP?
DON'T LET THOSE BUTTERFLIES IN YOUR STOMACH GET TO YOU.
IT'S QUITE A BIG MOVE...
...APPLYING TO A HIGH SCHOOL IN TOKYO.
I'M SURPRISED YOUR AUNT AGREED.
YEAH...
...AT FIRST SHE GRUMBLED ABOUT THE MONEY.
BUT THE SCHOOLS AROUND HERE ARE ALL BAD.
WE'RE GOING TO ONE OF THOSE BAD SCHOOLS!
SHUT UP!

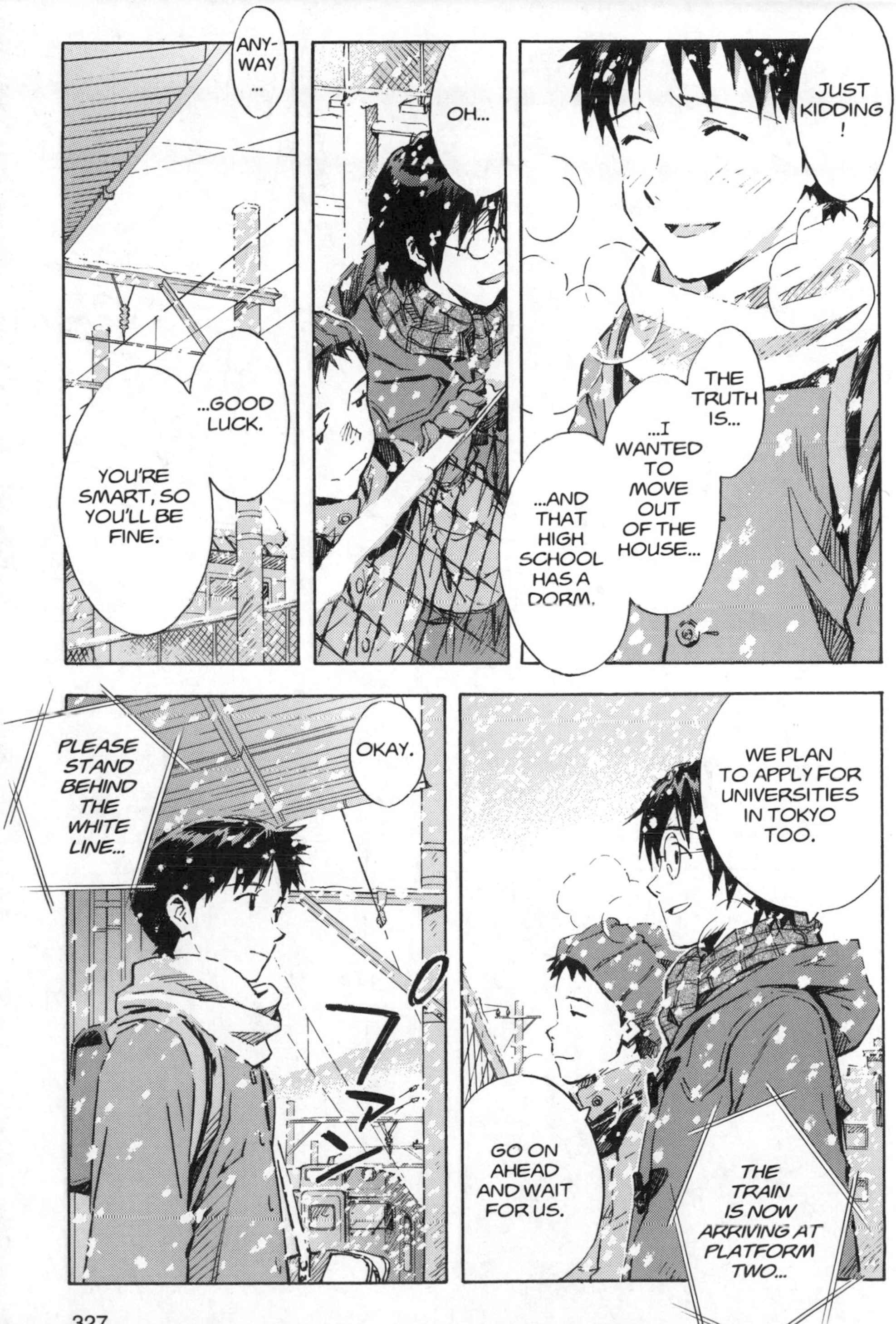
JUST KIDDING!
THE TRUTH IS...
...I WANTED TO MOVE OUT OF THE HOUSE...
...AND THAT HIGH SCHOOL HAS A DORM.
OH...
ANYWAY...
...GOOD LUCK.
YOU'RE SMART, SO YOU'LL BE FINE.
WE PLAN TO APPLY FOR UNIVERSITIES IN TOKYO TOO.
GO ON AHEAD AND WAIT FOR US.
THE TRAIN IS NOW ARRIVING AT PLATFORM TWO...
OKAY.
PLEASE STAND BEHIND THE WHITE LINE...

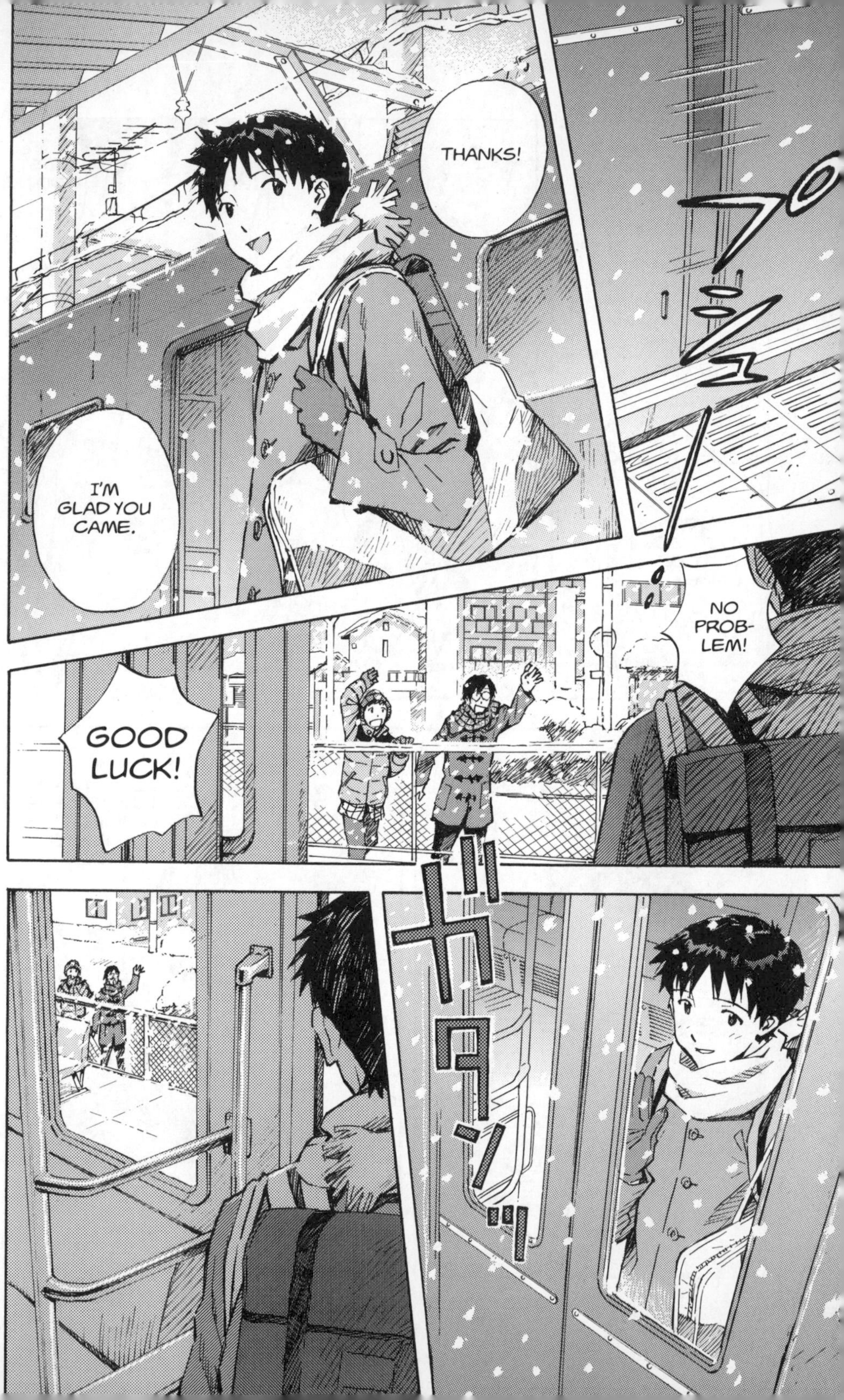
THANKS!
I'M GLAD YOU CAME.
NO PROB-LEM!
GOOD LUCK!

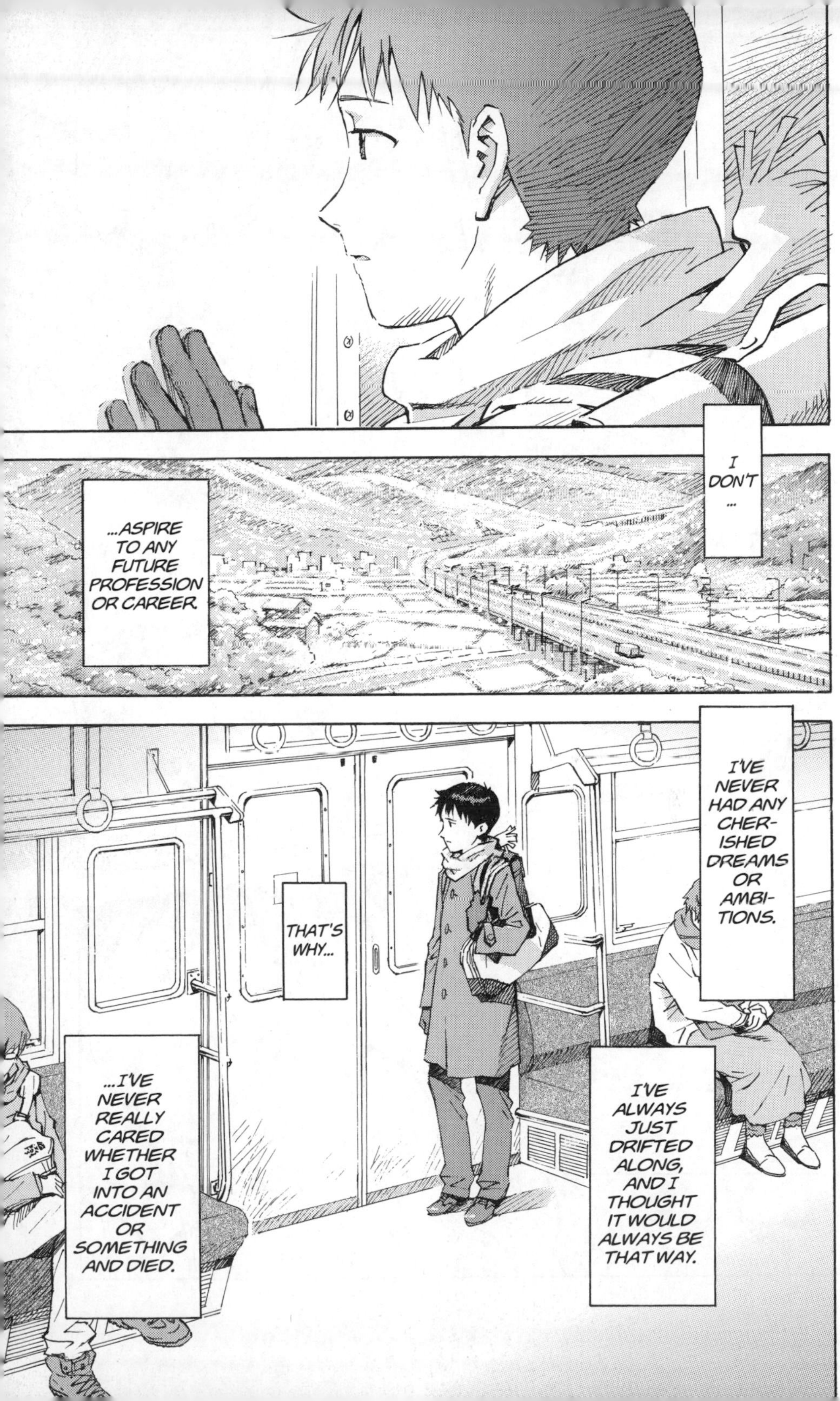
I DON'T ...
...ASPIRE TO ANY FUTURE PROFESSION OR CAREER.
I'VE NEVER HAD ANY CHERISHED DREAMS OR AMBITIONS.
I'VE ALWAYS JUST DRIFTED ALONG, AND I THOUGHT IT WOULD ALWAYS BE THAT WAY.
THAT'S WHY...
...I'VE NEVER REALLY CARED WHETHER I GOT INTO AN ACCIDENT OR SOMETHING AND DIED.

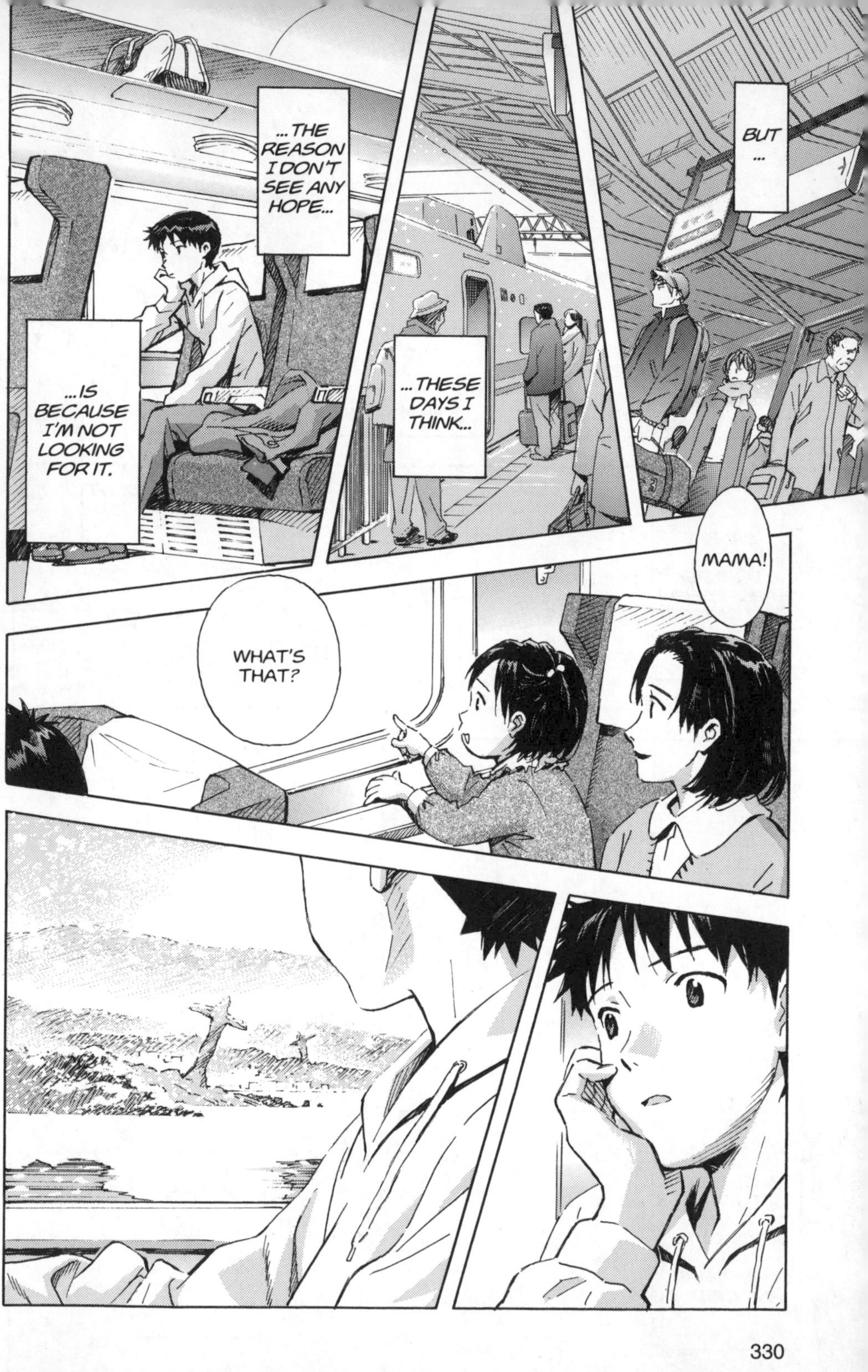
BUT ...
...THESE DAYS I THINK...
...THE REASON I DON'T SEE ANY HOPE...
...IS BECAUSE I'M NOT LOOKING FOR IT.
MAMA!
WHAT'S THAT?

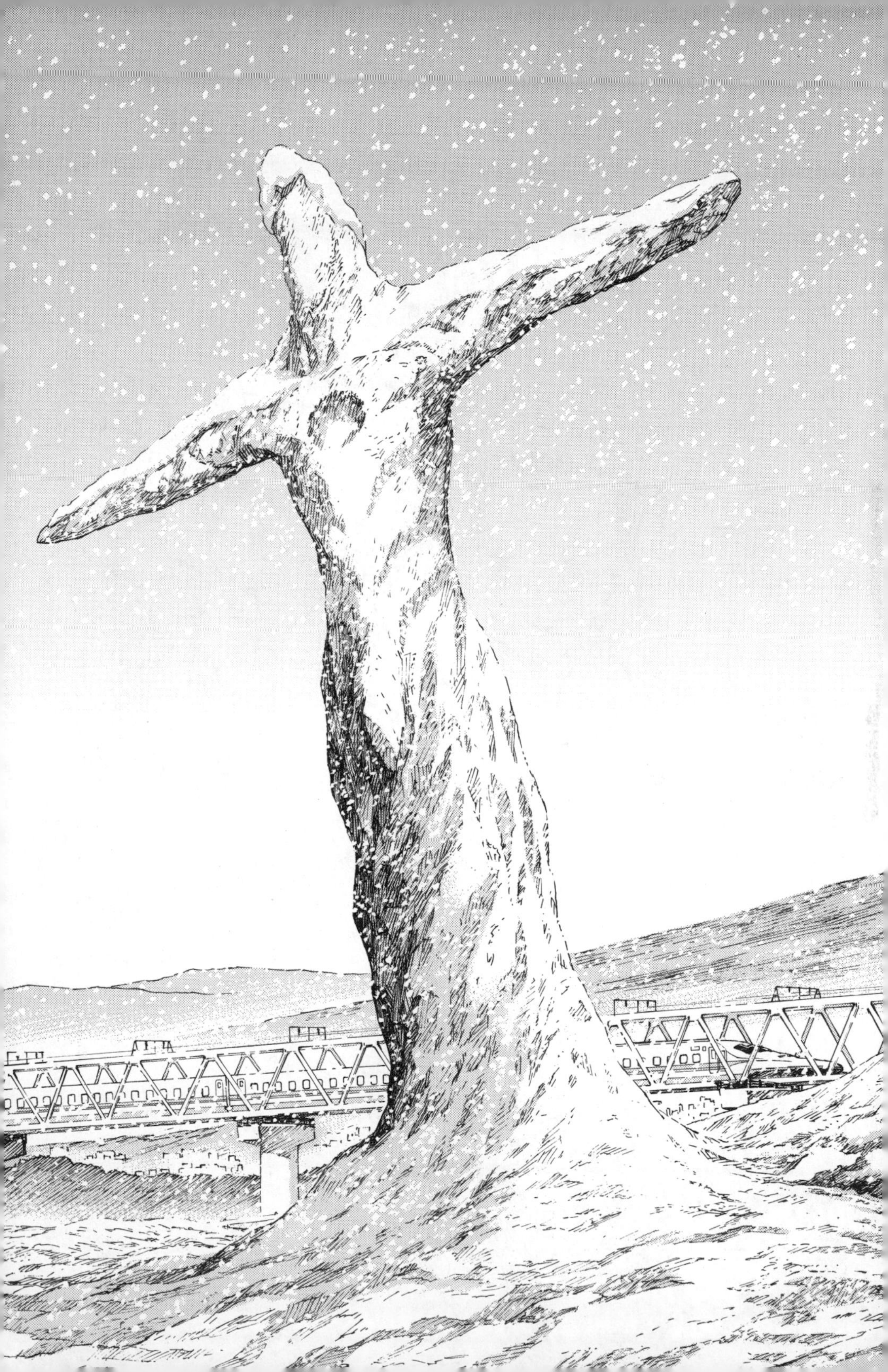

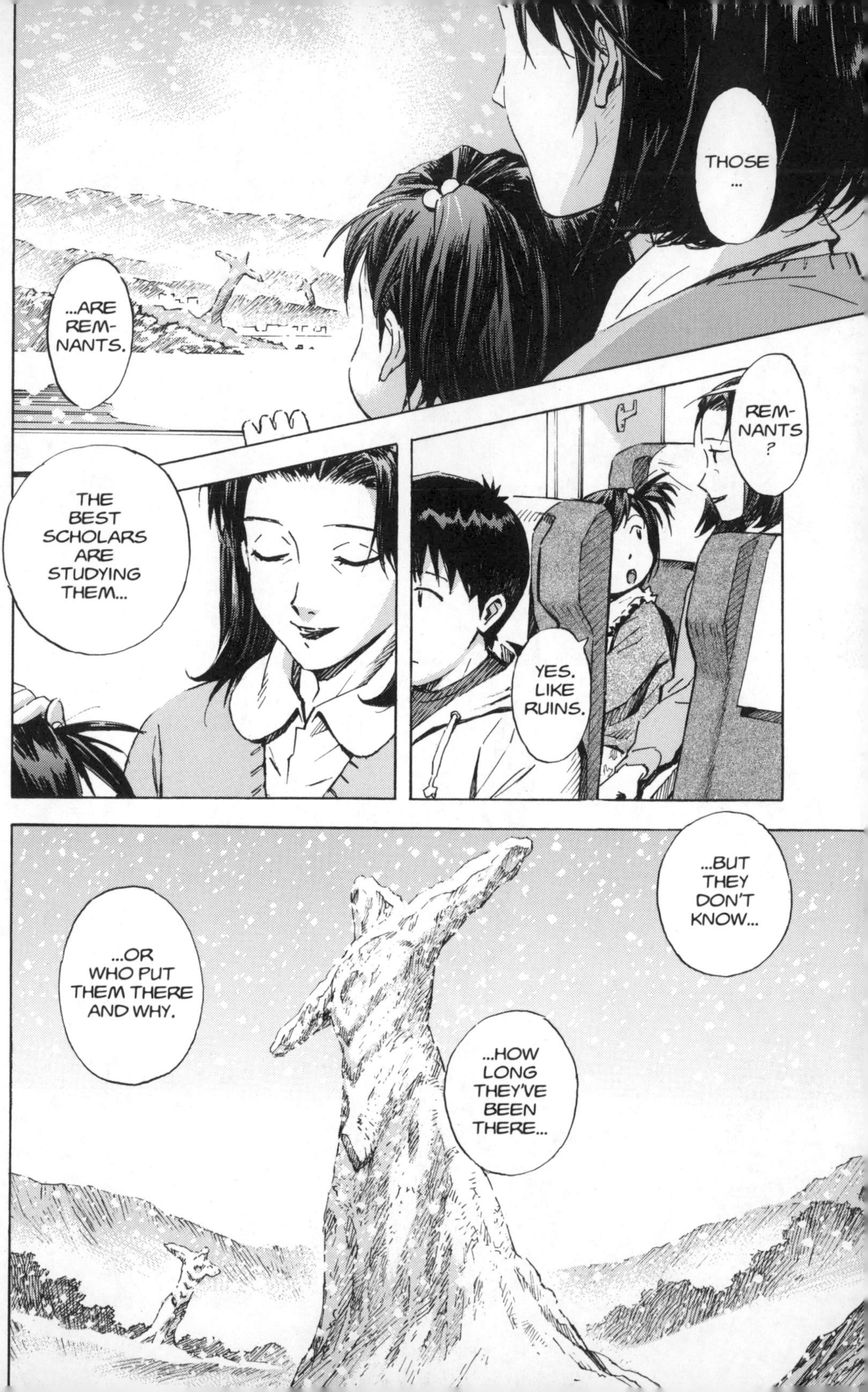
THOSE ...
...ARE REMNANTS.
REMNANTS?
YES. LIKE RUINS.
THE BEST SCHOLARS ARE STUDYING THEM...
...BUT THEY DON'T KNOW...
...HOW LONG THEY'VE BEEN THERE...
...OR WHO PUT THEM THERE AND WHY.

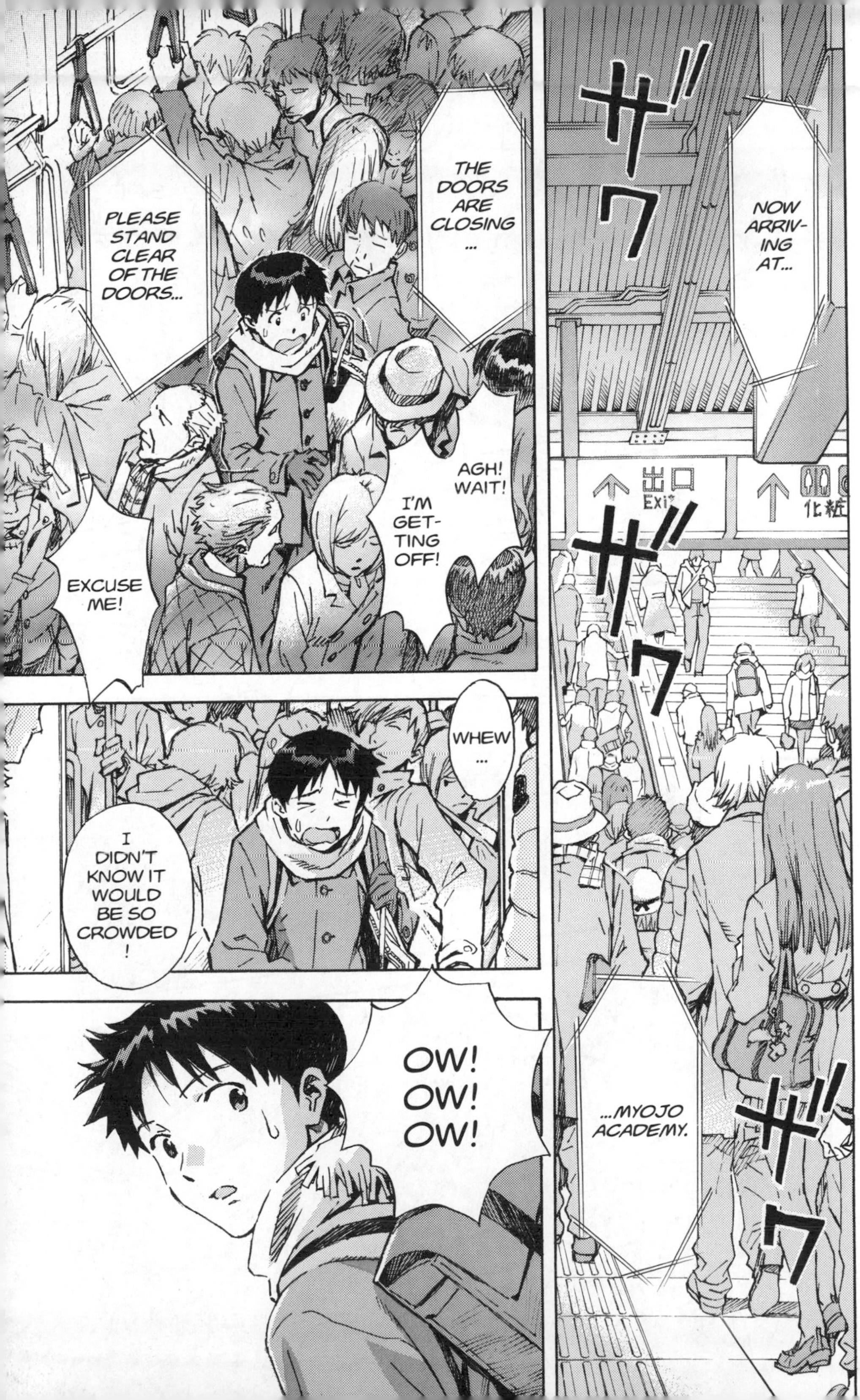

ザワ
NOW ARRIVING AT...
出口
Exit
ザワ
...MYOJO ACADEMY.
ザワ
THE DOORS ARE CLOSING...
PLEASE STAND CLEAR OF THE DOORS...
AGH! WAIT!
I'M GETTING OFF!
EXCUSE ME!
WHEW...
I DIDN'T KNOW IT WOULD BE SO CROWDED!
OW! OW! OW!

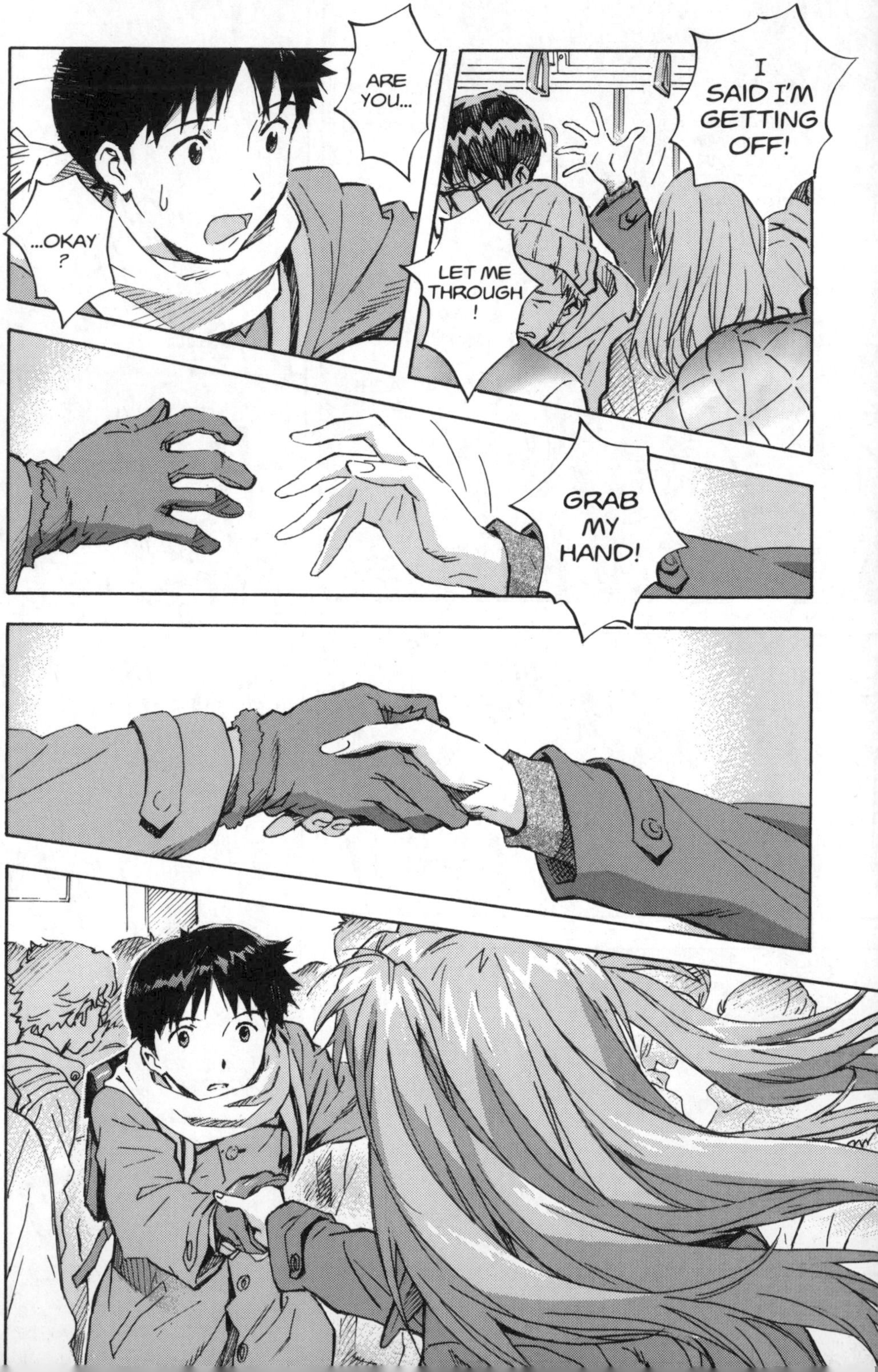
I SAID I'M GETTING OFF!
LET ME THROUGH!
ARE YOU...
...OKAY?
GRAB MY HAND!

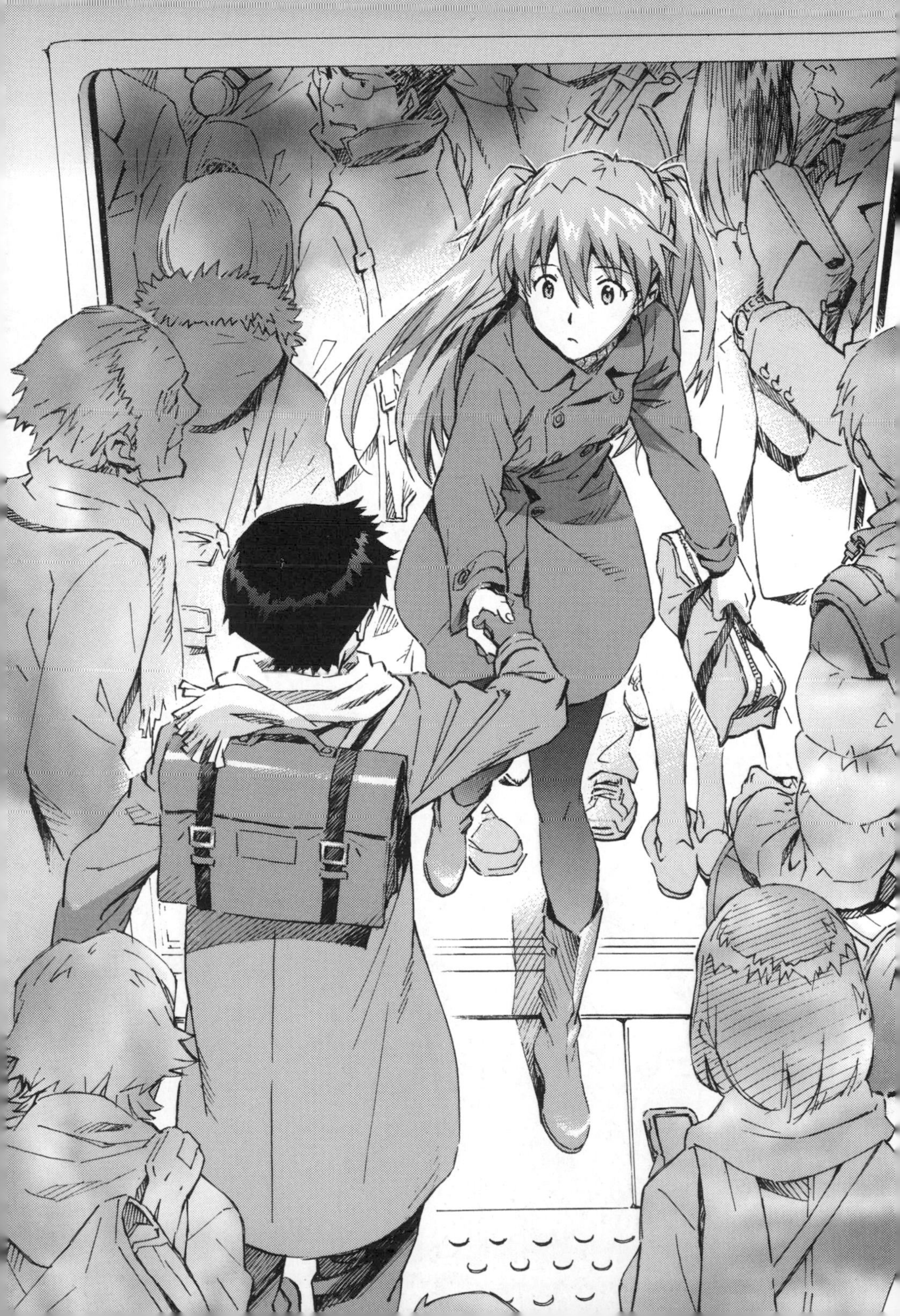

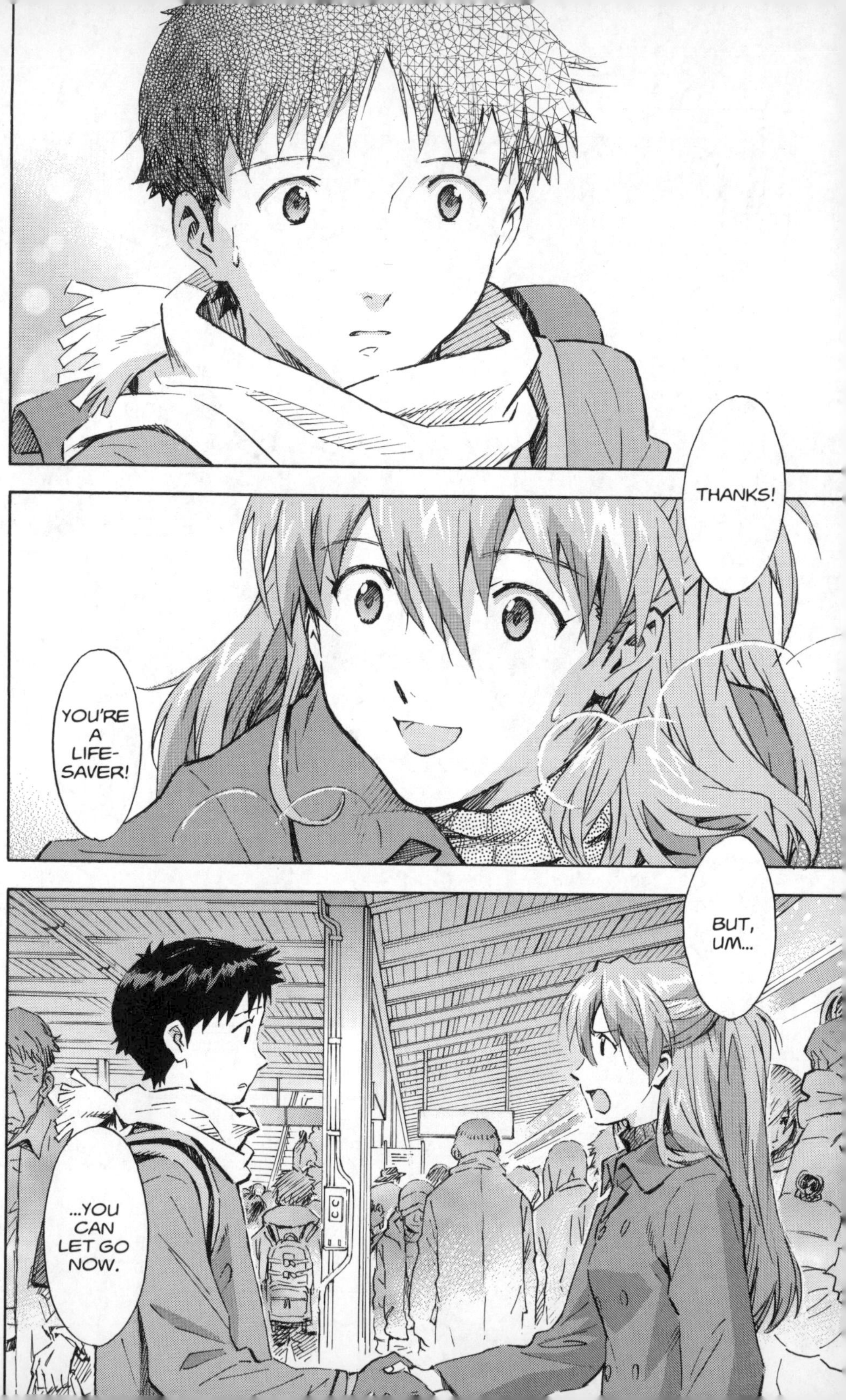
THANKS!
YOU'RE A LIFE-SAVER!
BUT, UM...
...YOU CAN LET GO NOW.

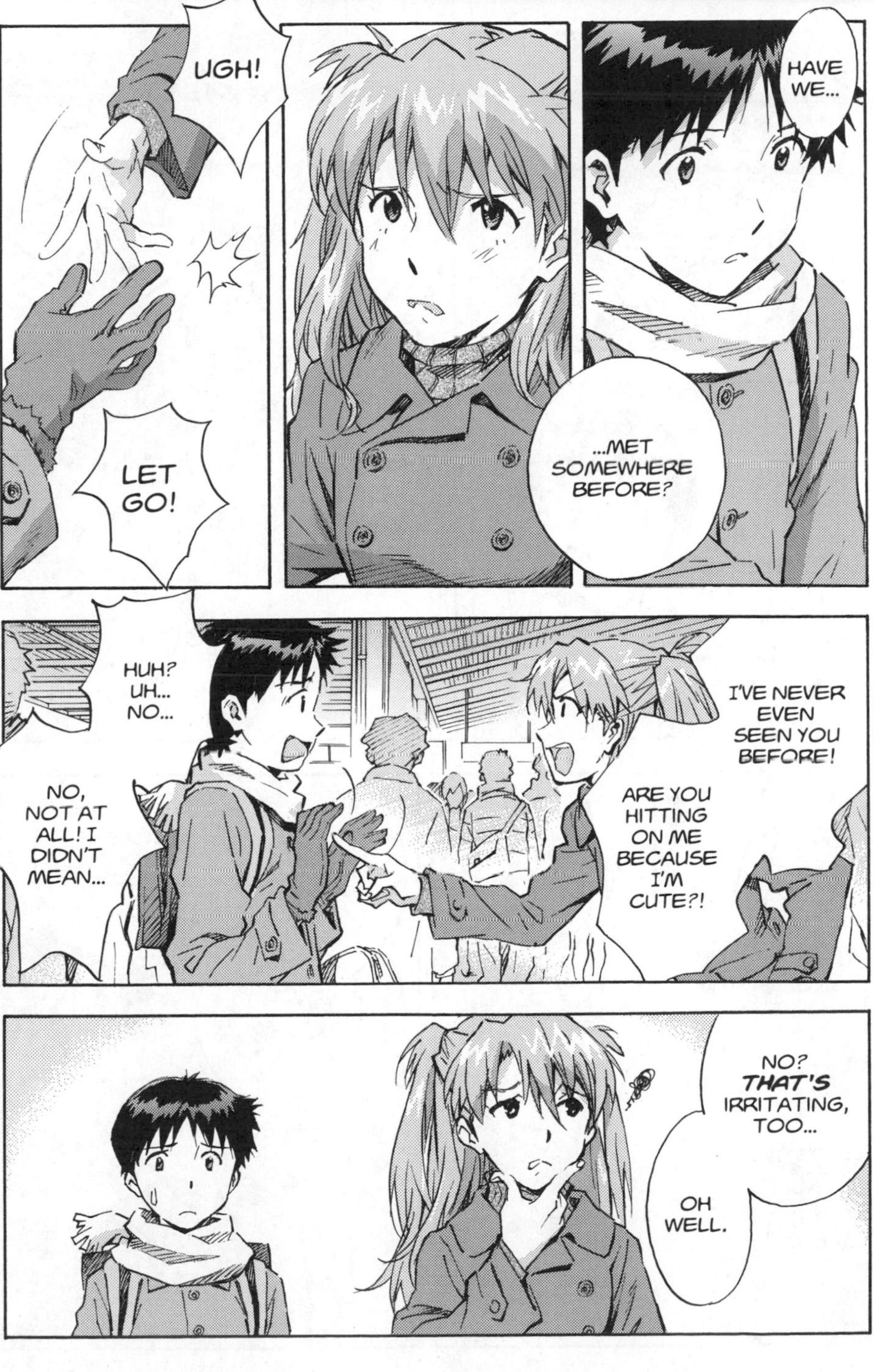
HAVE WE...
...MET SOMEWHERE BEFORE?
UGH!
LET GO!
I'VE NEVER EVEN SEEN YOU BEFORE!
ARE YOU HITTING ON ME BECAUSE I'M CUTE?!
HUH? UH... NO...
NO, NOT AT ALL! I DIDN'T MEAN...
NO? ***THAT'S*** IRRITATING, TOO...
OH WELL.

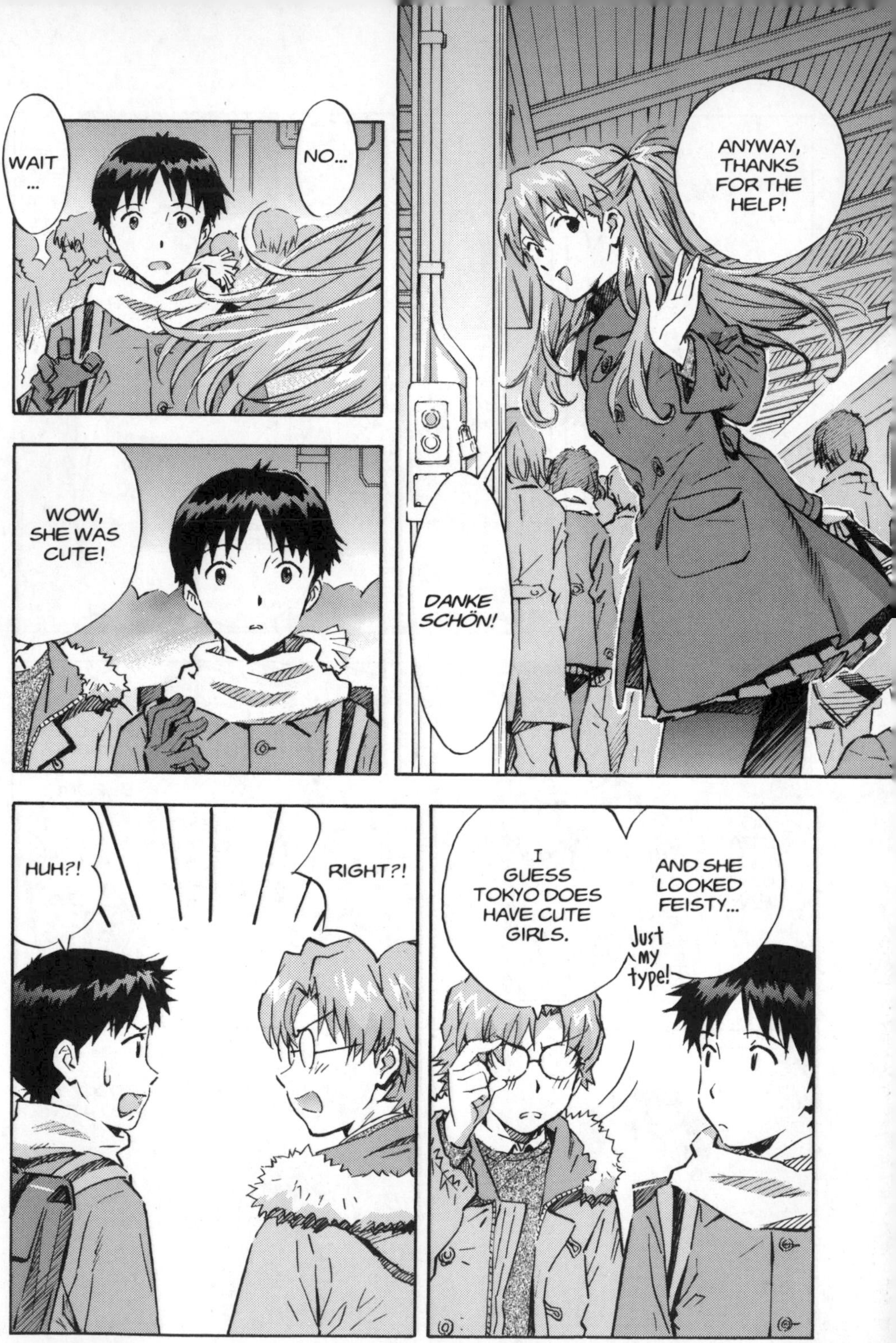
ANYWAY, THANKS FOR THE HELP!
DANKE SCHÖN!
NO...
WAIT ...
WOW, SHE WAS CUTE!
I GUESS TOKYO DOES HAVE CUTE GIRLS.
AND SHE LOOKED FEISTY...
Just my type!
RIGHT?!
HUH?!

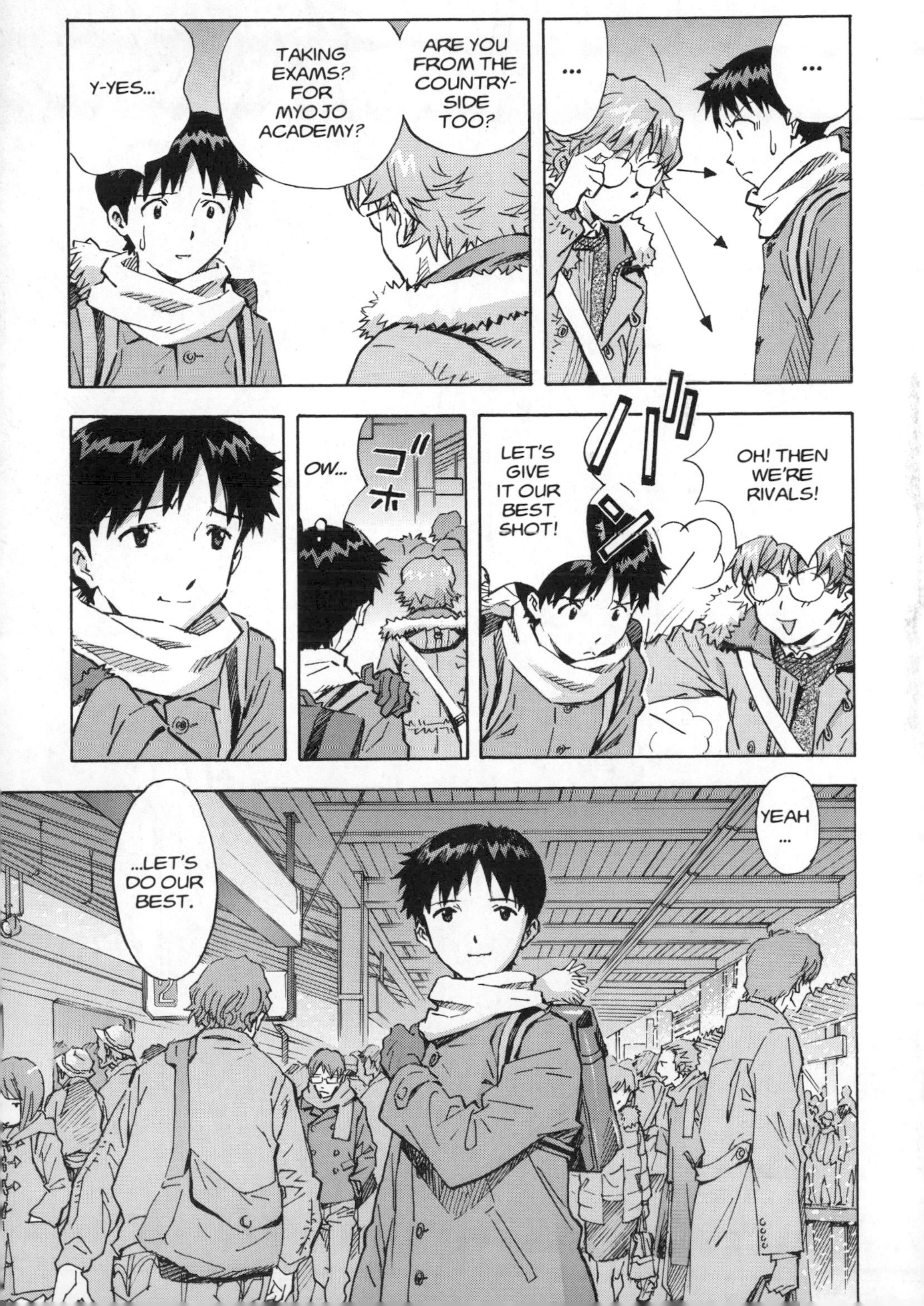
...
...
ARE YOU FROM THE COUNTRY-SIDE TOO?
TAKING EXAMS? FOR MYOJO ACADEMY?
Y-YES...
OH! THEN WE'RE RIVALS!
LET'S GIVE IT OUR BEST SHOT!
ゴホ
OW...
YEAH ...
...LET'S DO OUR BEST.

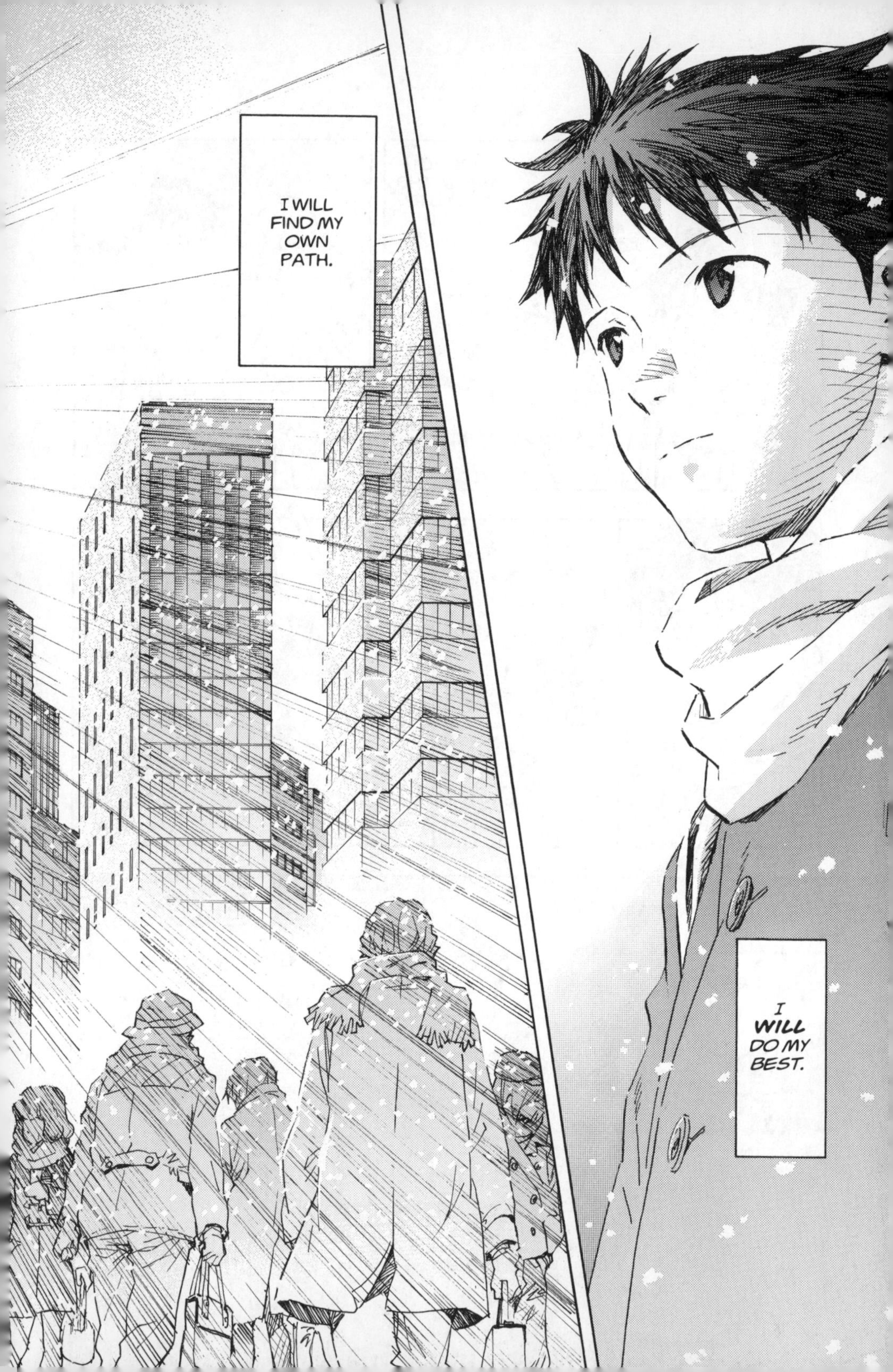
I WILL DO MY BEST.
I WILL FIND MY OWN PATH.

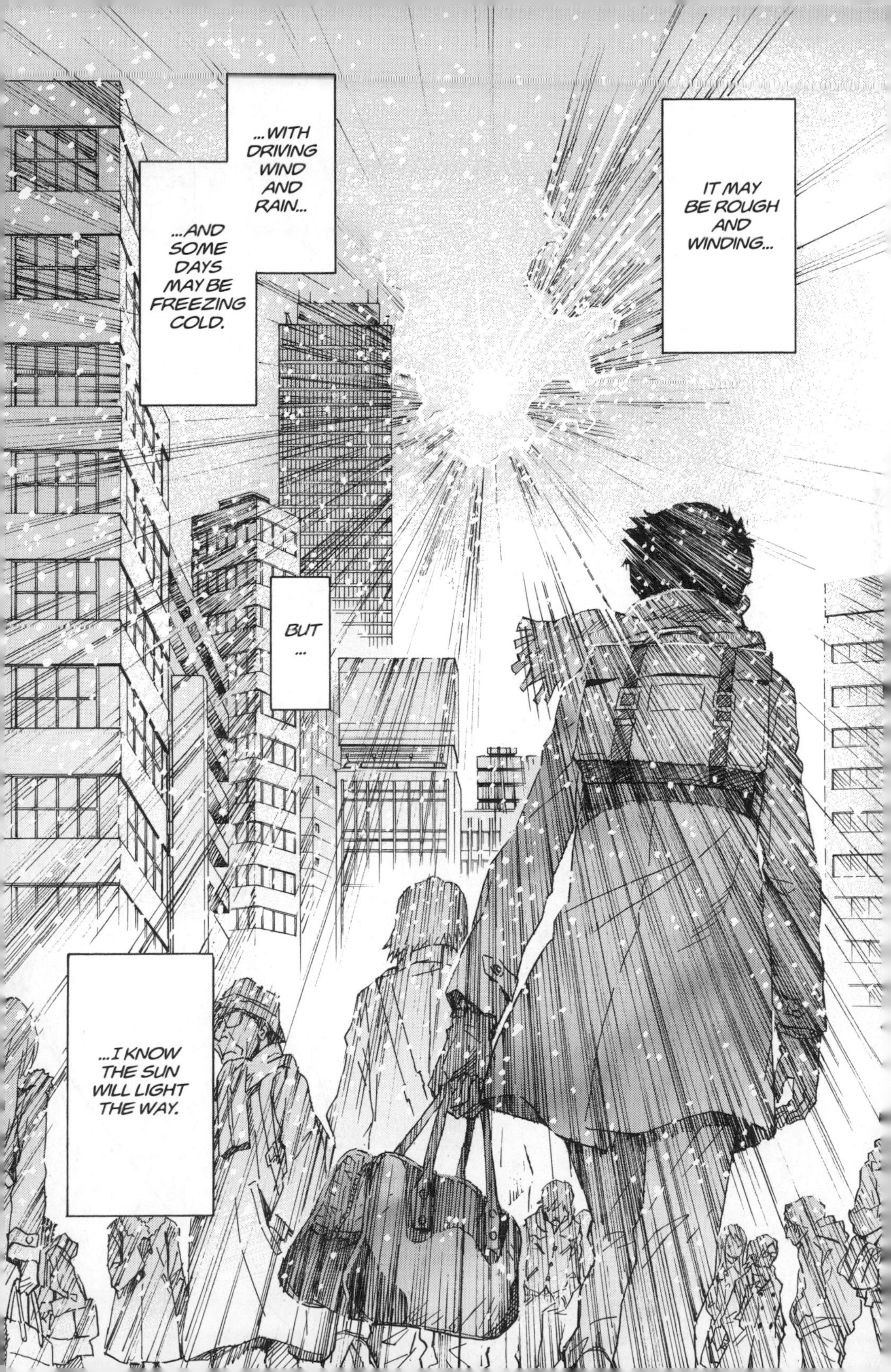
IT MAY BE ROUGH AND WINDING...
...WITH DRIVING WIND AND RAIN...
...AND SOME DAYS MAY BE FREEZING COLD.
BUT ...
...I KNOW THE SUN WILL LIGHT THE WAY.

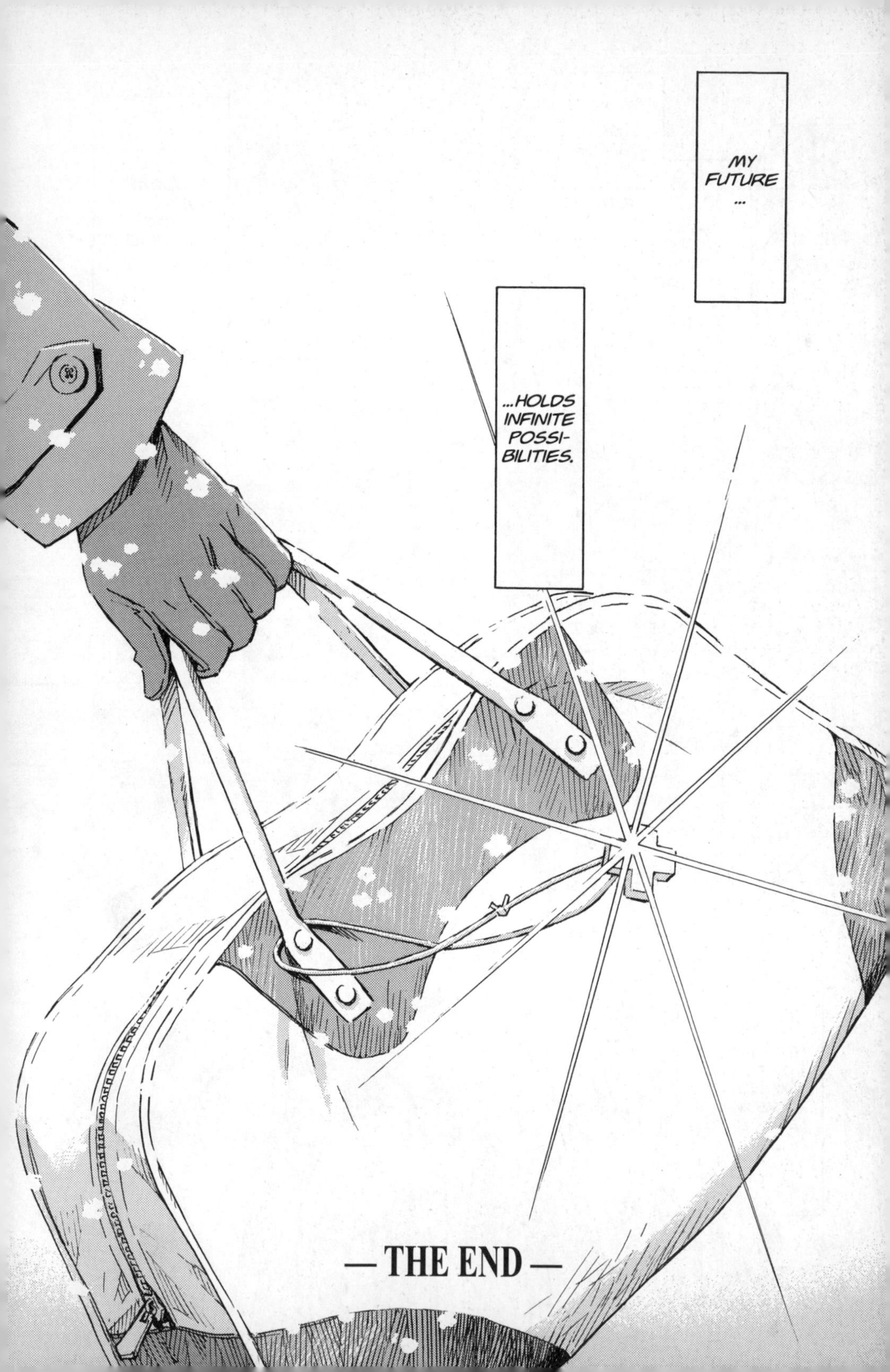
MY FUTURE ...
...HOLDS INFINITE POSSI-BILITIES.
— THE END —

NERV

GOD'S IN HIS HEAVEN. ALL'S RIGHT WITH THE WORLD.

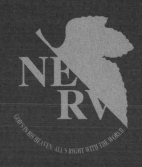

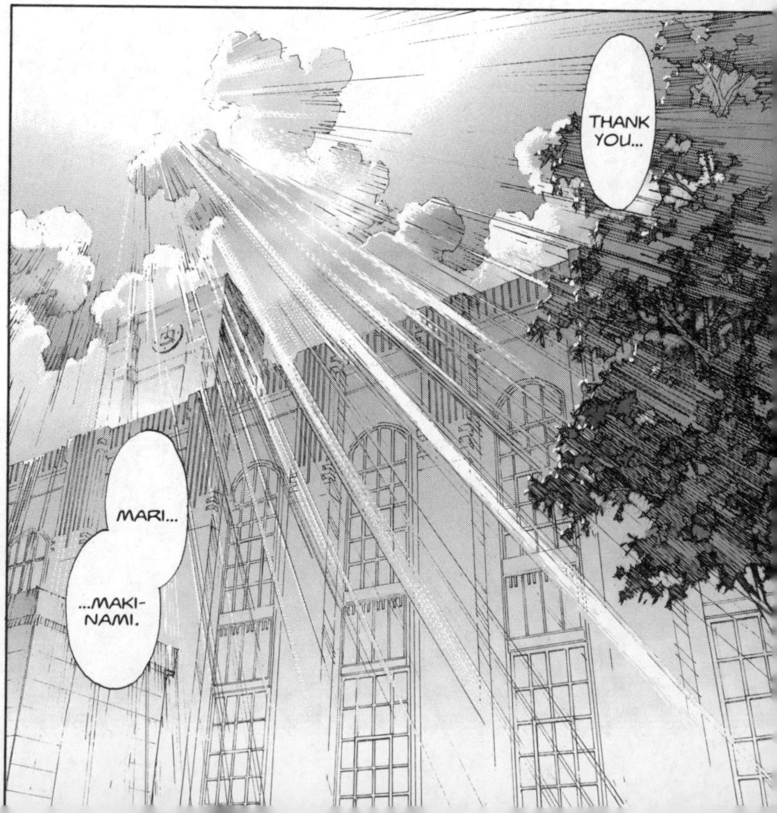
THANK YOU...
MARI...
...MAKI-NAMI.

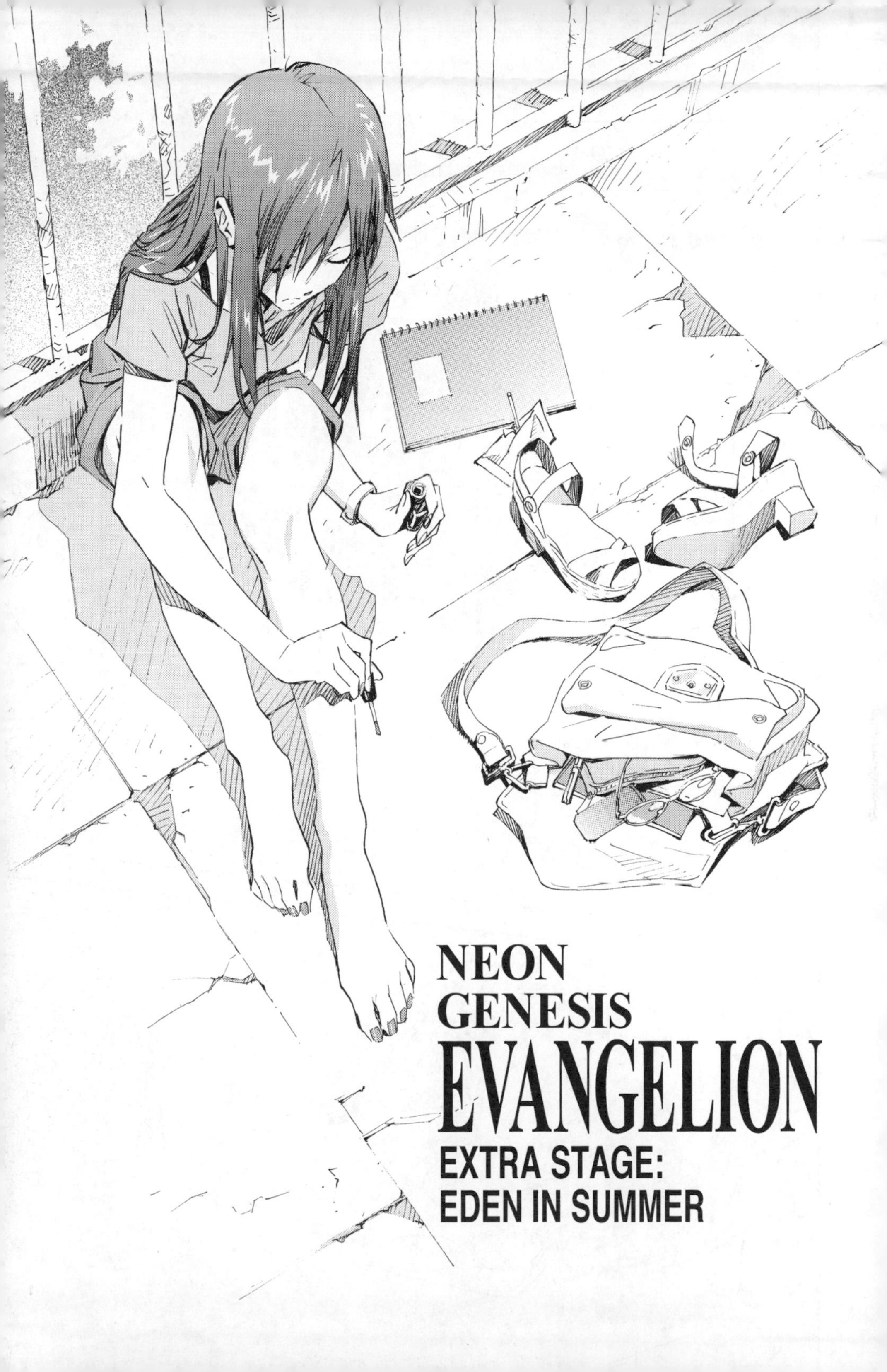

NEON GENESIS EVANGELION

EXTRA STAGE: EDEN IN SUMMER

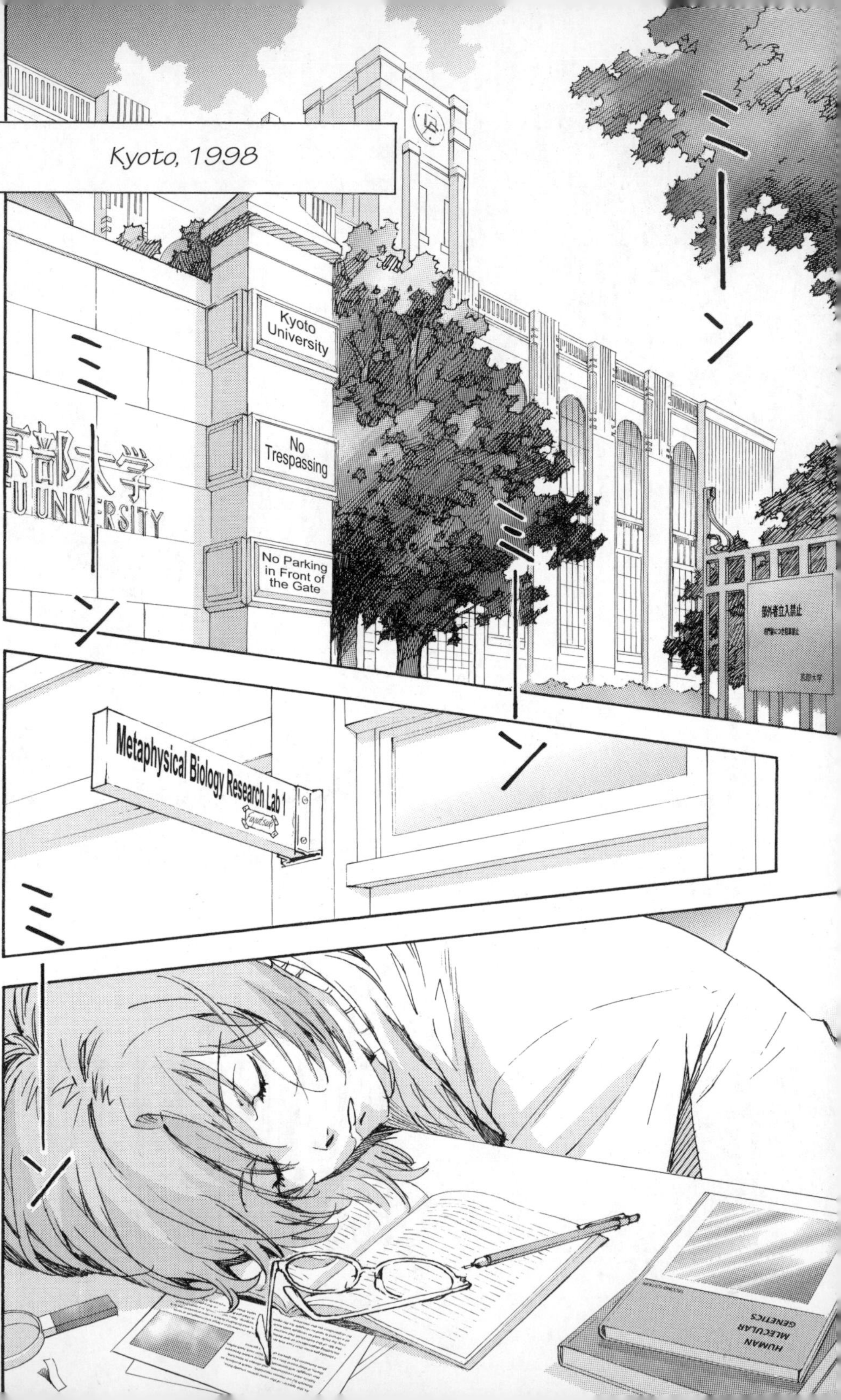
Kyoto, 1998
ミーン
Kyoto University
No Trespassing
No Parking in Front of the Gate
ミーン
ミーン
Metaphysical Biology Research Lab 1
ミーン
HUMAN MLECULAR GENETICS

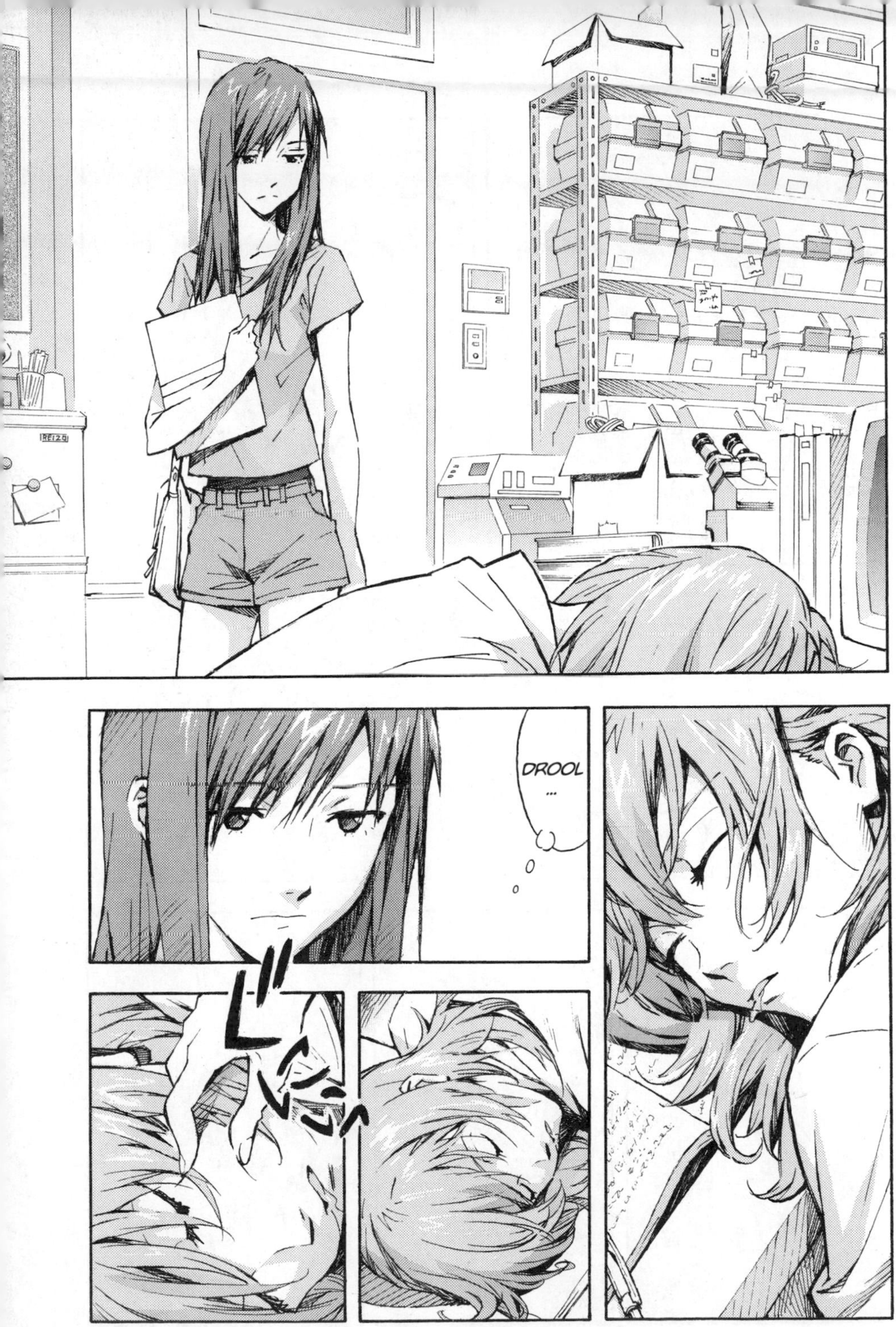
DROOL
...

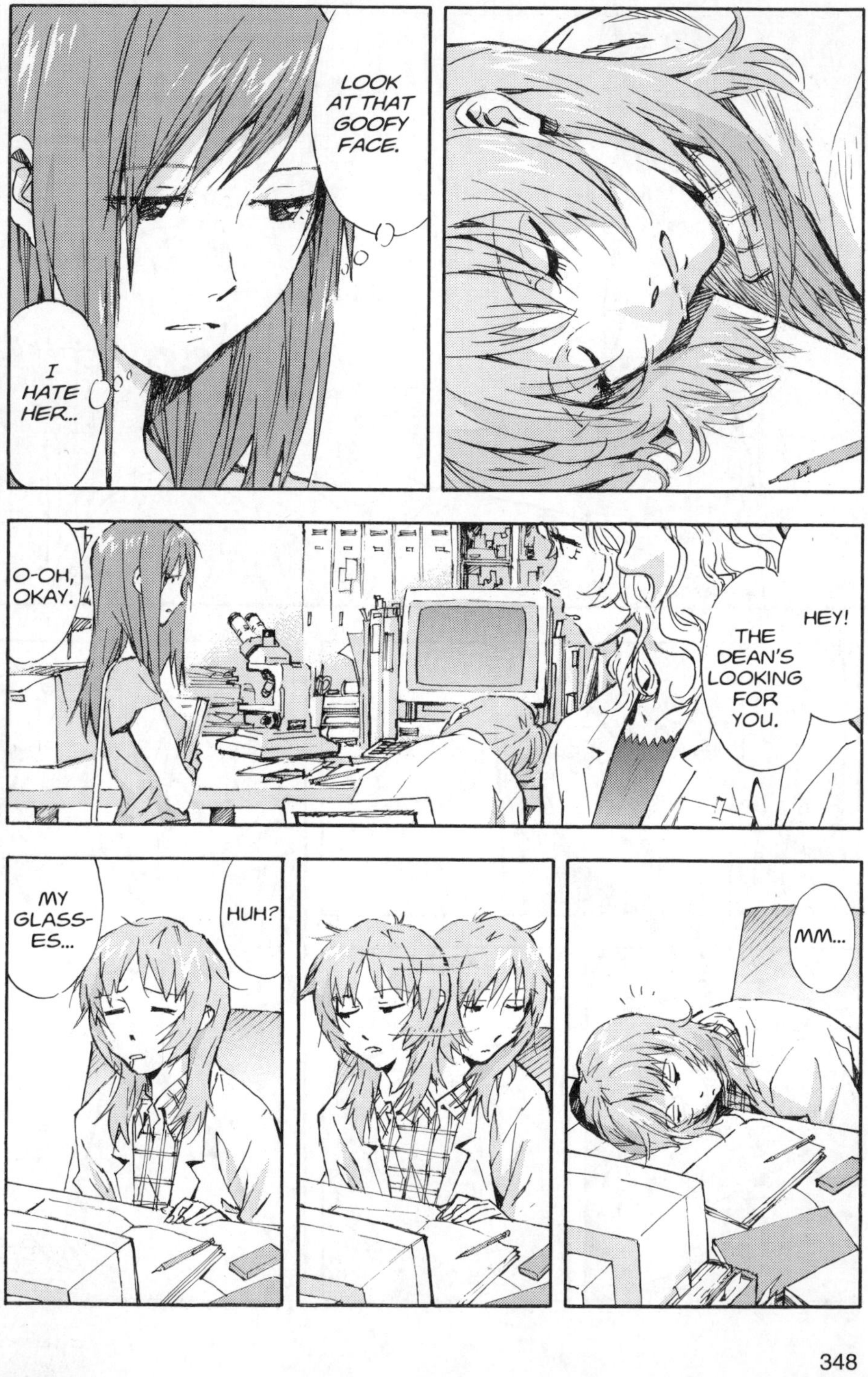
LOOK AT THAT GOOFY FACE.
I HATE HER...
HEY!
THE DEAN'S LOOKING FOR YOU.
O-OH, OKAY.
MM...
HUH?
MY GLASS-ES...

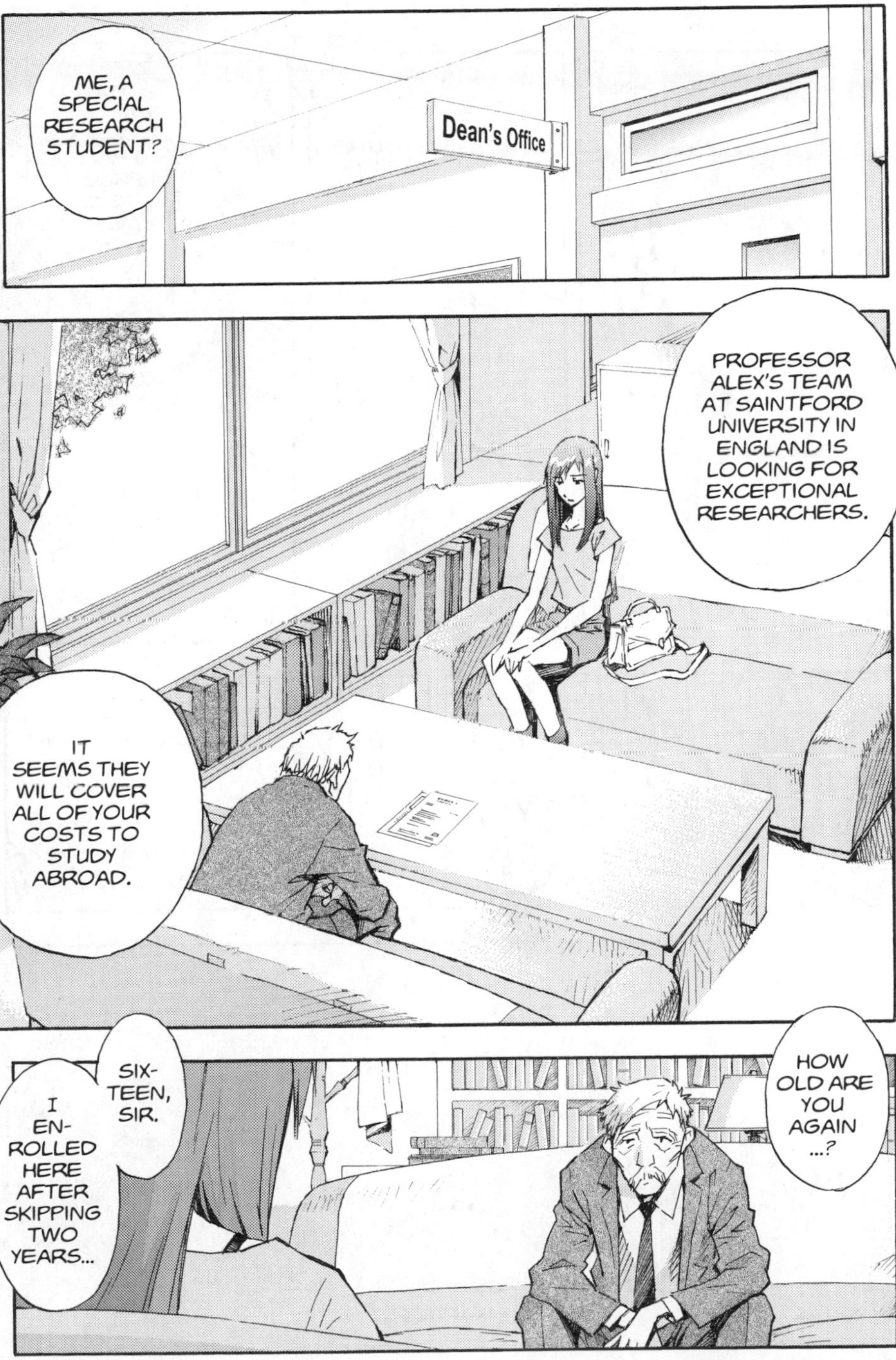
Dean's Office
ME, A SPECIAL RESEARCH STUDENT?
PROFESSOR ALEX'S TEAM AT SAINTFORD UNIVERSITY IN ENGLAND IS LOOKING FOR EXCEPTIONAL RESEARCHERS.
IT SEEMS THEY WILL COVER ALL OF YOUR COSTS TO STUDY ABROAD.
HOW OLD ARE YOU AGAIN ...?
SIX-TEEN, SIR.
I EN-ROLLED HERE AFTER SKIPPING TWO YEARS...

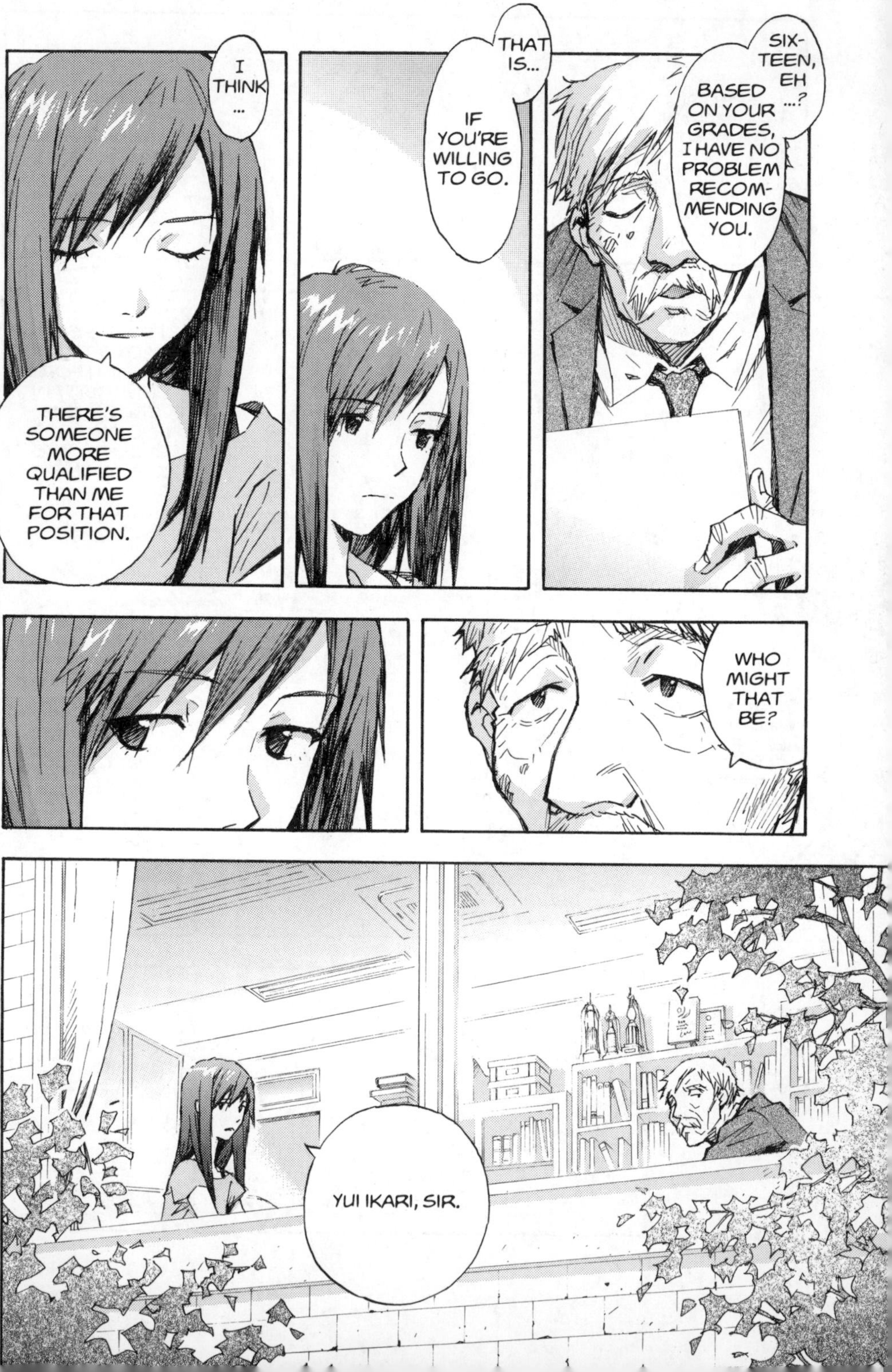
SIXTEEN, EH ...?
BASED ON YOUR GRADES, I HAVE NO PROBLEM RECOMMENDING YOU.
THAT IS...
IF YOU'RE WILLING TO GO.
I THINK ...
THERE'S SOMEONE MORE QUALIFIED THAN ME FOR THAT POSITION.
WHO MIGHT THAT BE?
YUI IKARI, SIR.

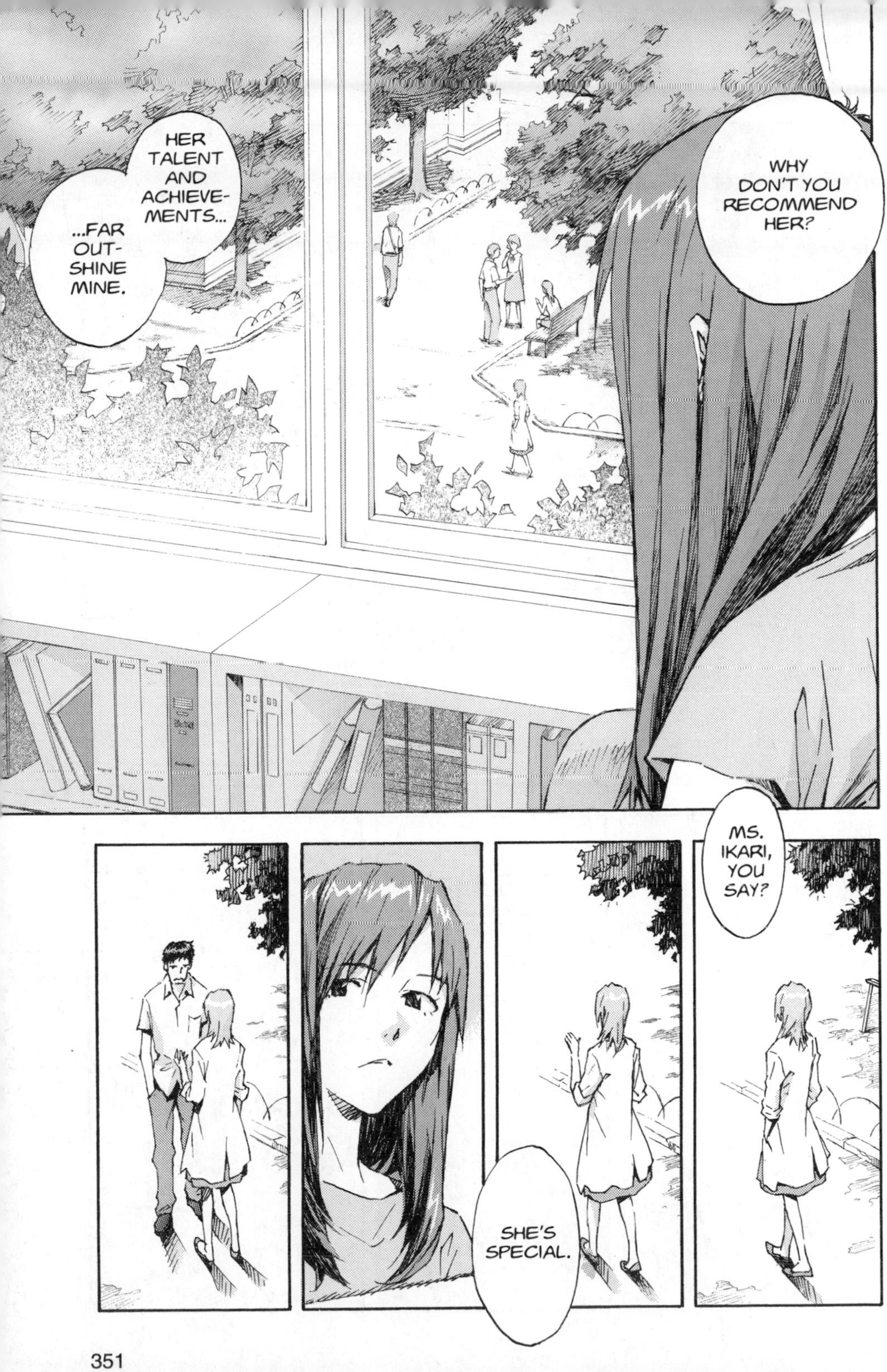
WHY DON'T YOU RECOMMEND HER?
HER TALENT AND ACHIEVE-MENTS...
...FAR OUT-SHINE MINE.
MS. IKARI, YOU SAY?
SHE'S SPECIAL.

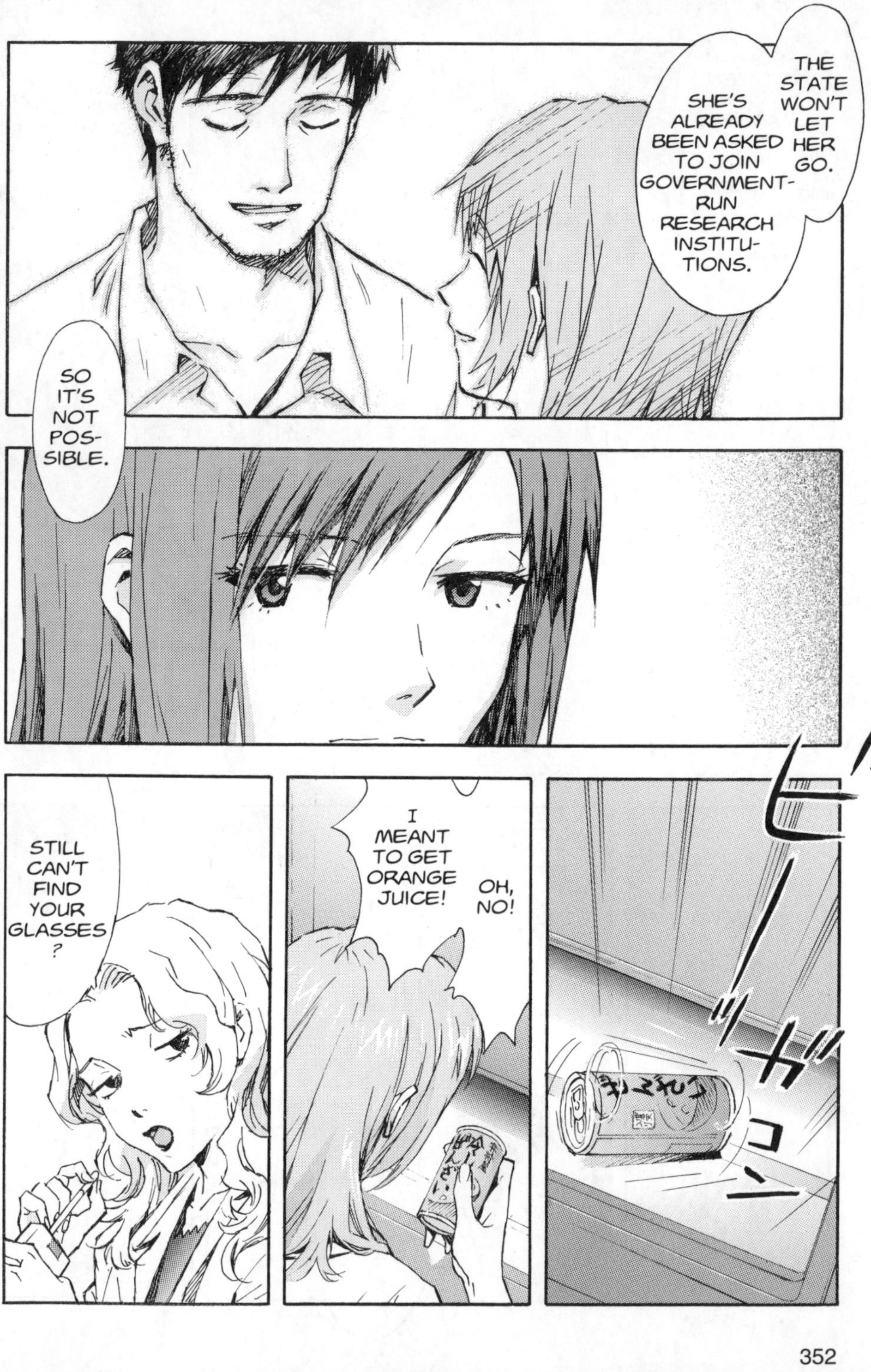
THE STATE WON'T LET HER GO.
SHE'S ALREADY BEEN ASKED TO JOIN GOVERNMENT-RUN RESEARCH INSTITUTIONS.
SO IT'S NOT POSSIBLE.
ビーッ
ガコン
OH, NO!
I MEANT TO GET ORANGE JUICE!
STILL CAN'T FIND YOUR GLASSES?

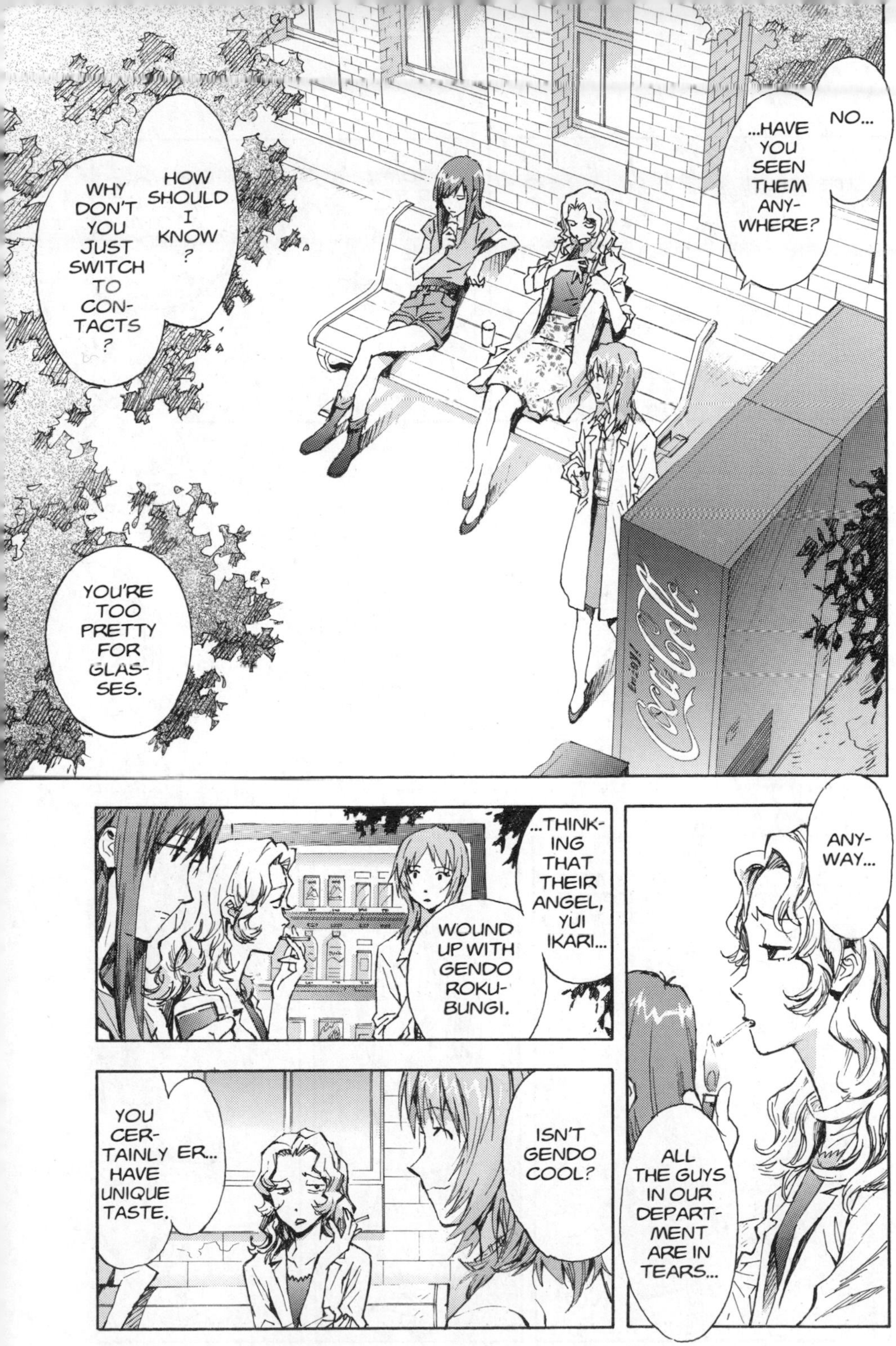
NO...
...HAVE YOU SEEN THEM ANYWHERE?
HOW SHOULD I KNOW?
WHY DON'T YOU JUST SWITCH TO CONTACTS?
YOU'RE TOO PRETTY FOR GLASSES.
ANYWAY...
ALL THE GUYS IN OUR DEPARTMENT ARE IN TEARS...
...THINKING THAT THEIR ANGEL, YUI IKARI...
WOUND UP WITH GENDO ROKUBUNGI.
ISN'T GENDO COOL?
ER...
YOU CERTAINLY HAVE UNIQUE TASTE.

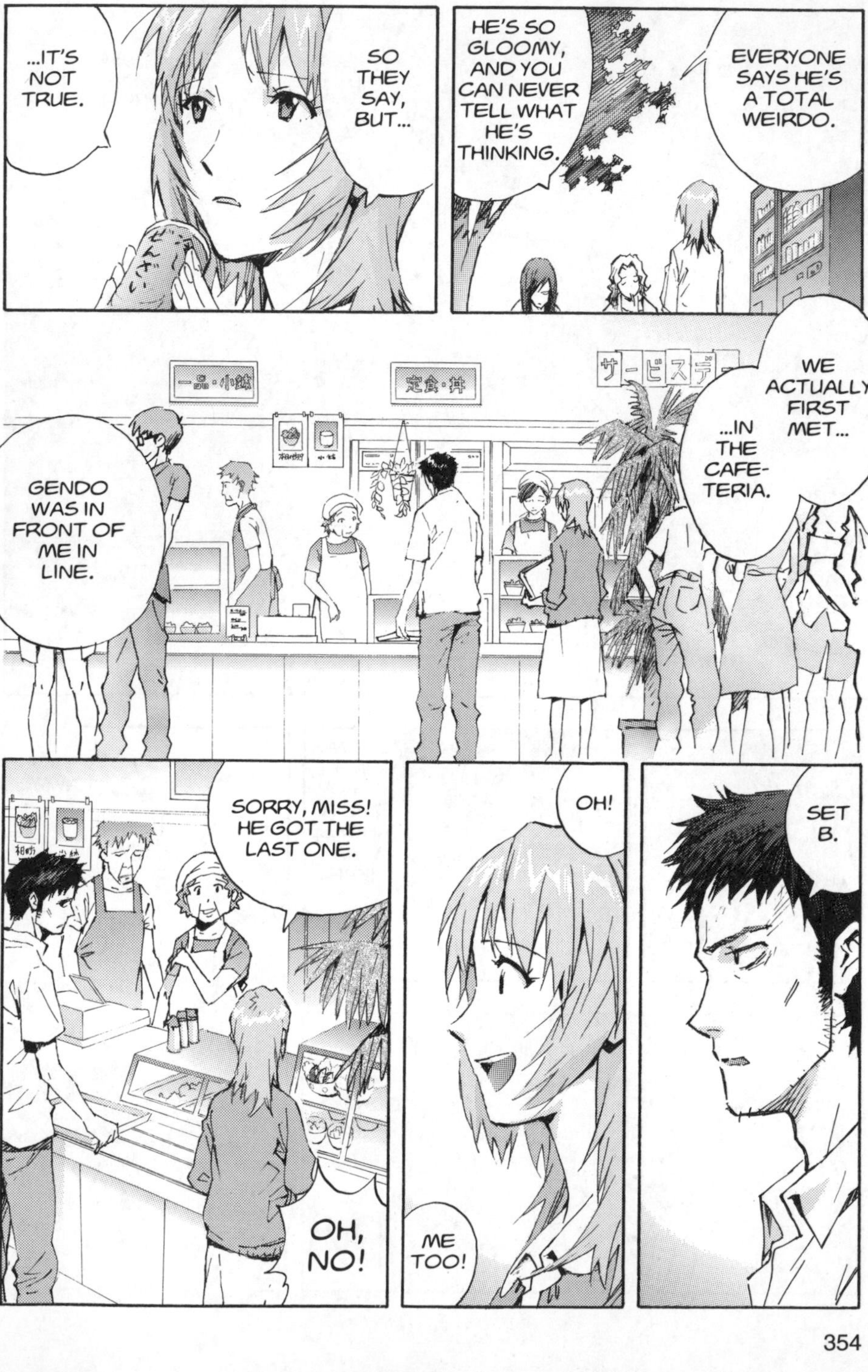
EVERYONE SAYS HE'S A TOTAL WEIRDO.
HE'S SO GLOOMY, AND YOU CAN NEVER TELL WHAT HE'S THINKING.
SO THEY SAY, BUT...
...IT'S NOT TRUE.
WE ACTUALLY FIRST MET...
...IN THE CAFETERIA.
一品・小鉢
定食・丼
GENDO WAS IN FRONT OF ME IN LINE.
SET B.
OH!
ME TOO!
SORRY, MISS! HE GOT THE LAST ONE.
OH, NO!

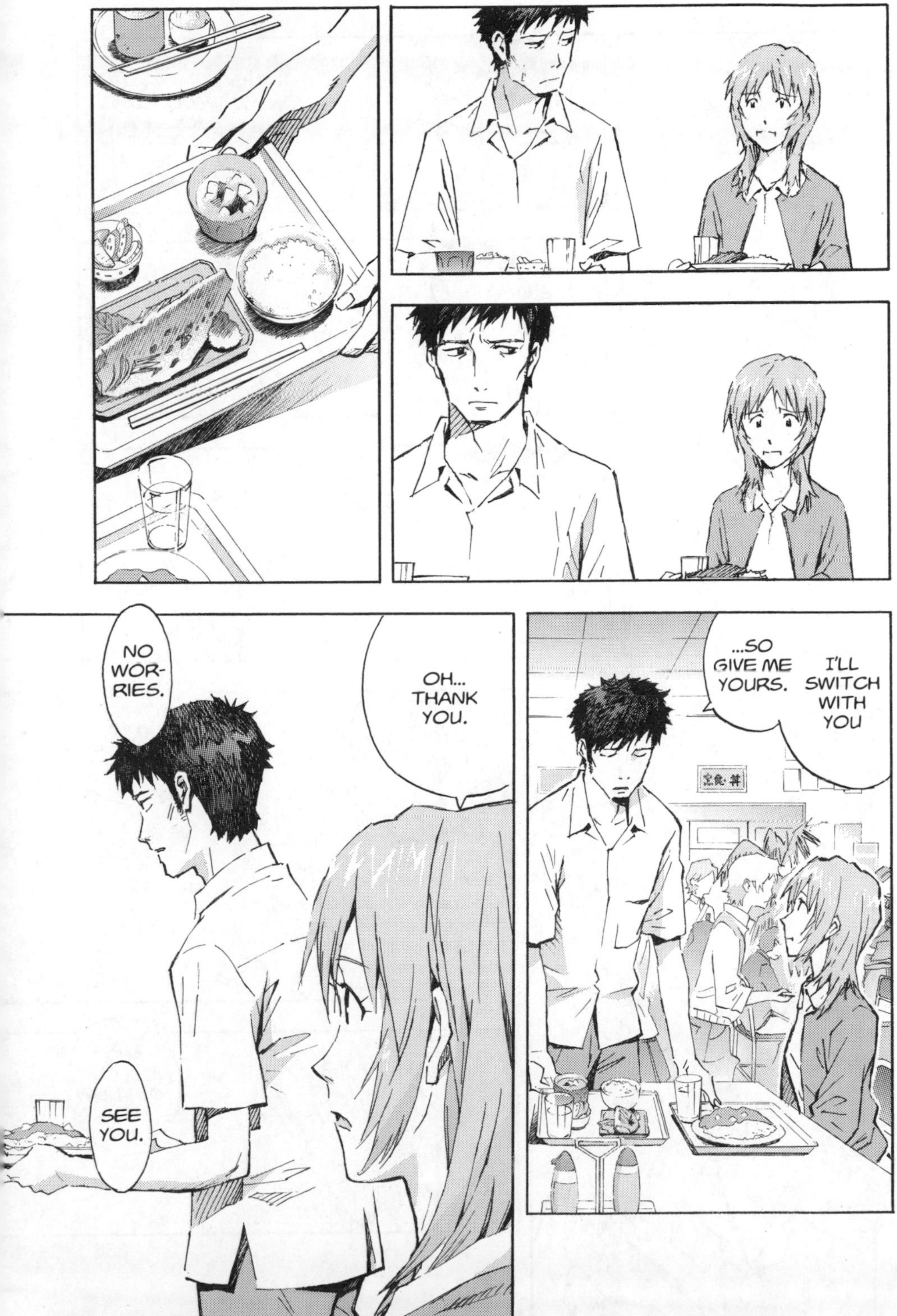
I'LL SWITCH WITH YOU
...SO GIVE ME YOURS.
OH... THANK YOU.
NO WORRIES.
SEE YOU.

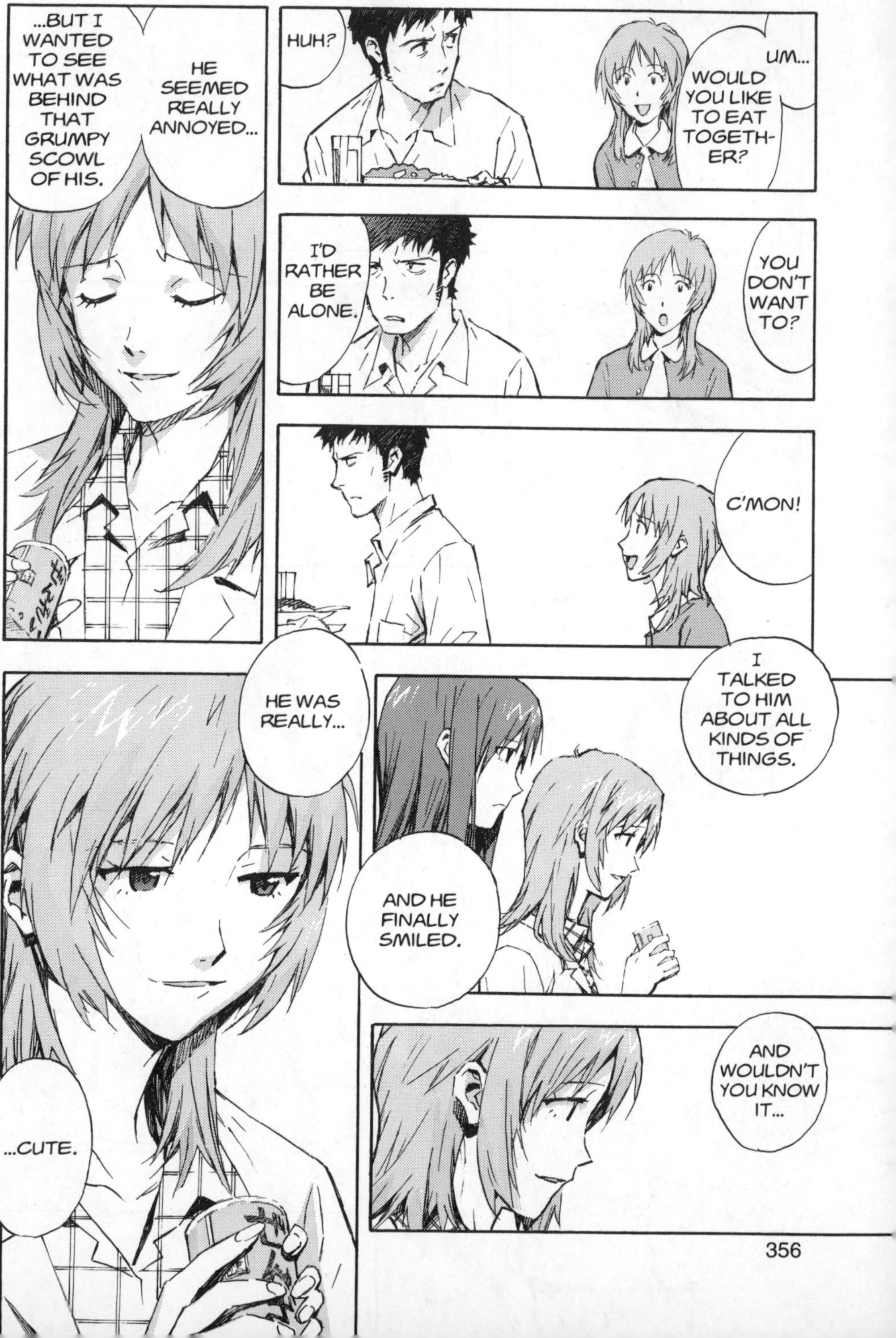
UM... WOULD YOU LIKE TO EAT TOGETH-ER?
HUH?
YOU DON'T WANT TO?
I'D RATHER BE ALONE.
C'MON!
HE SEEMED REALLY ANNOYED...
...BUT I WANTED TO SEE WHAT WAS BEHIND THAT GRUMPY SCOWL OF HIS.
I TALKED TO HIM ABOUT ALL KINDS OF THINGS.
AND HE FINALLY SMILED.
AND WOULDN'T YOU KNOW IT...
HE WAS REALLY...
...CUTE.

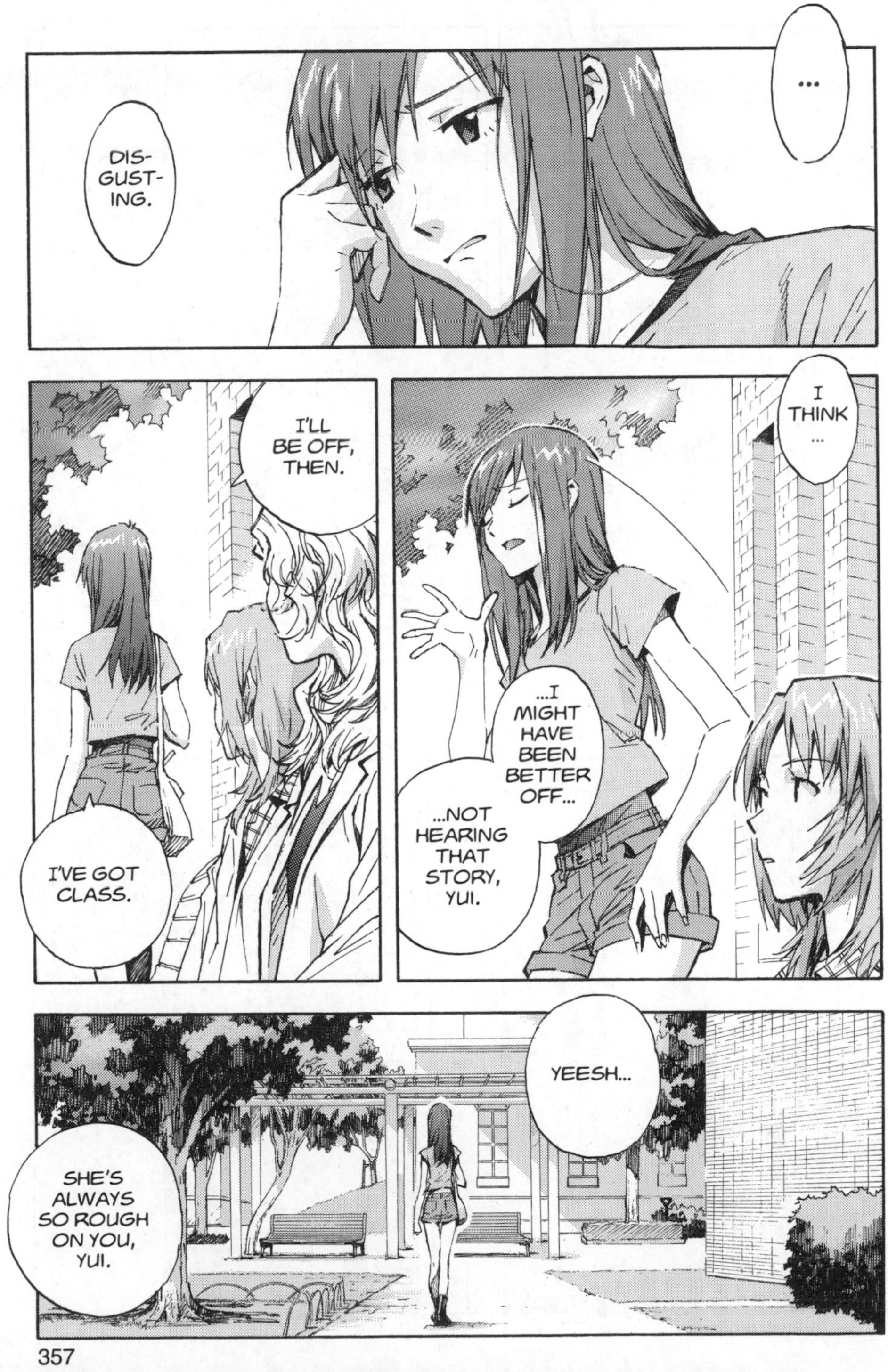
...
DIS-GUSTING.
I THINK ...
...I MIGHT HAVE BEEN BETTER OFF...
...NOT HEARING THAT STORY, YUI.
I'LL BE OFF, THEN.
I'VE GOT CLASS.
YEESH...
SHE'S ALWAYS SO ROUGH ON YOU, YUI.

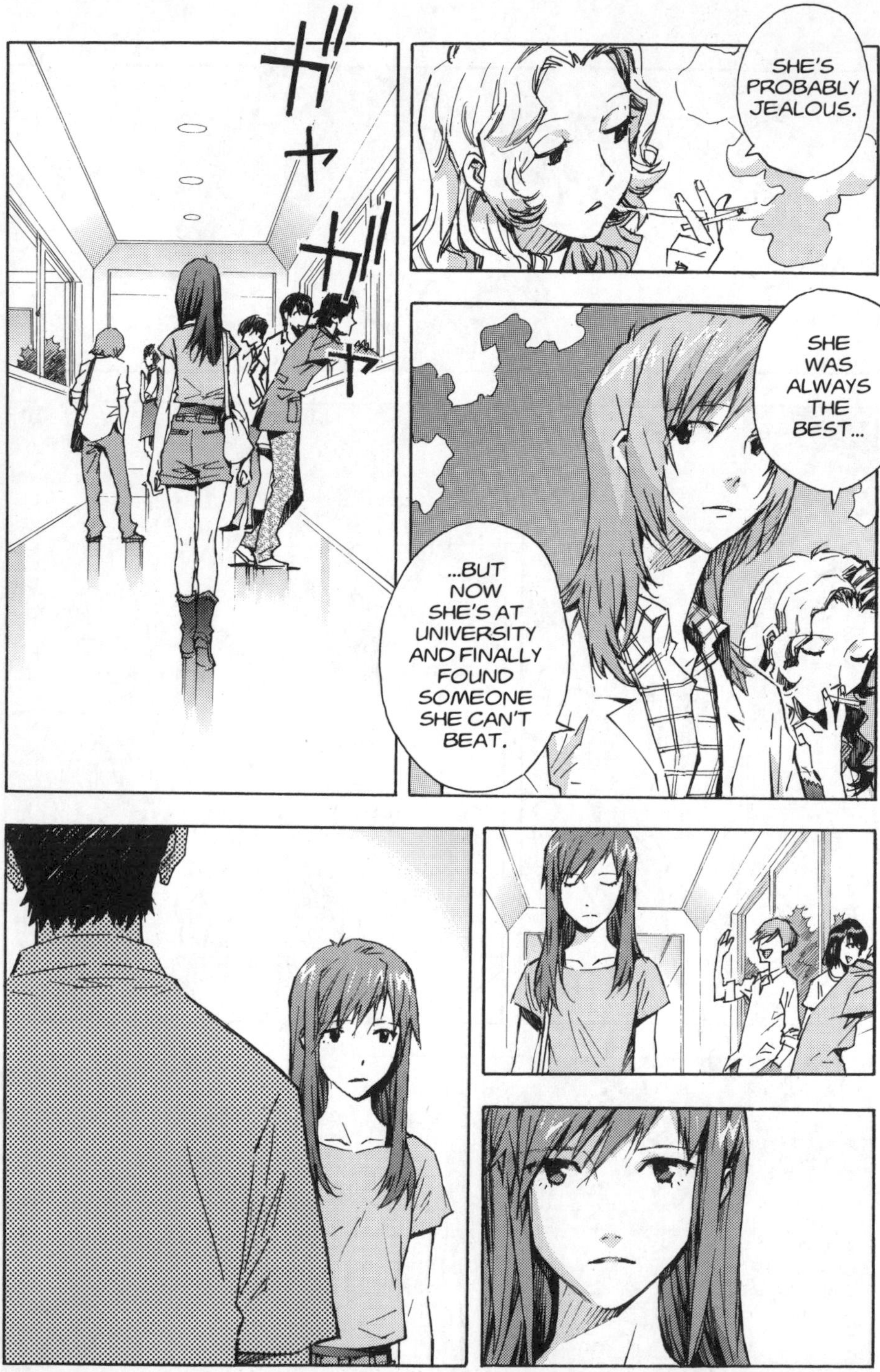
SHE'S PROBABLY JEALOUS.
SHE WAS ALWAYS THE BEST...
...BUT NOW SHE'S AT UNIVERSITY AND FINALLY FOUND SOMEONE SHE CAN'T BEAT.
ガヤガヤ

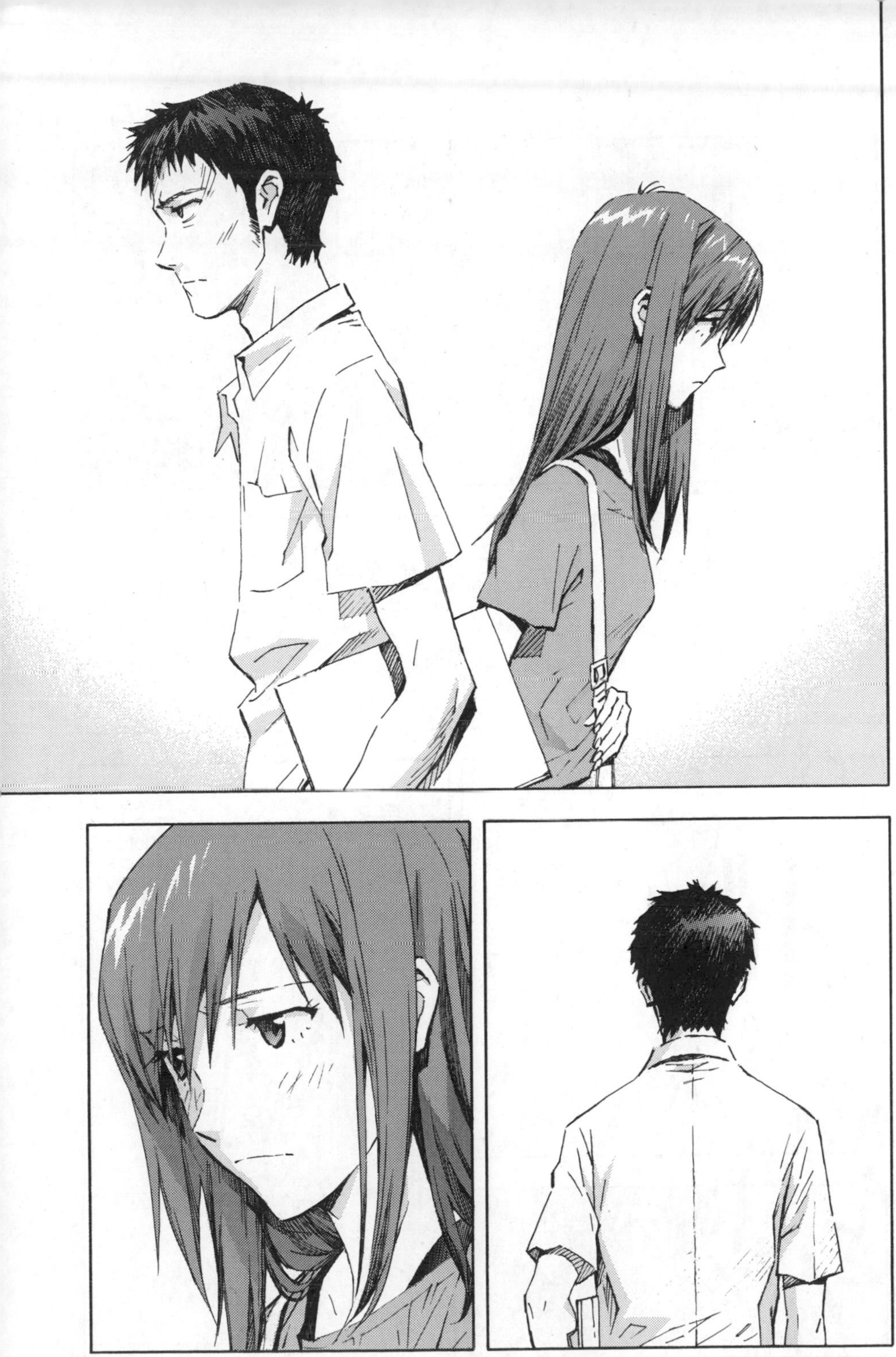

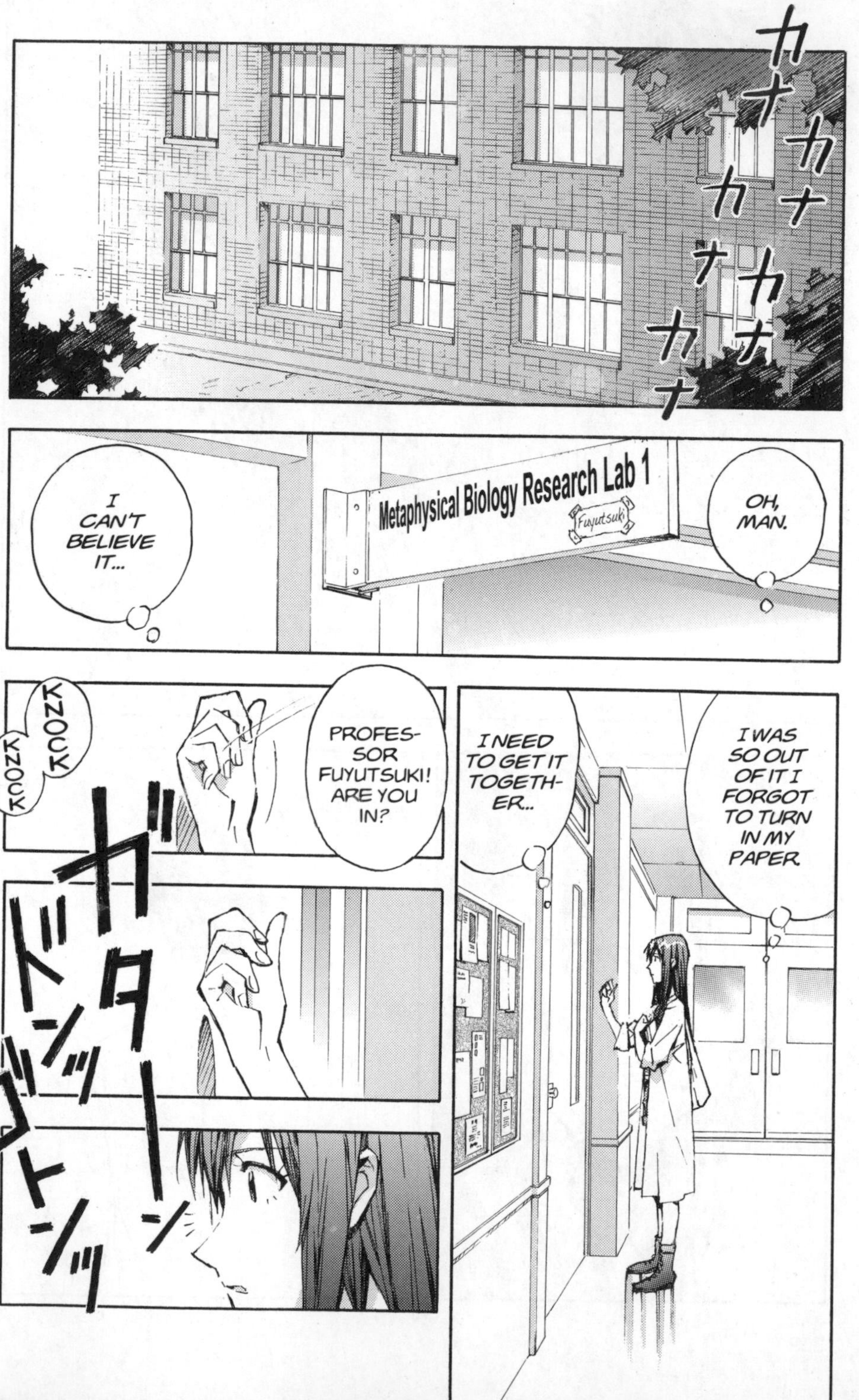
カナカナ
カナカナ
カナカナ
OH, MAN.
Metaphysical Biology Research Lab 1
Fuyutsuki
I CAN'T BELIEVE IT...
I WAS SO OUT OF IT I FORGOT TO TURN IN MY PAPER.
I NEED TO GET IT TOGETHER...
PROFESSOR FUYUTSUKI! ARE YOU IN?
KNOCK KNOCK
ガターン
ドンッ
ゴトンッ

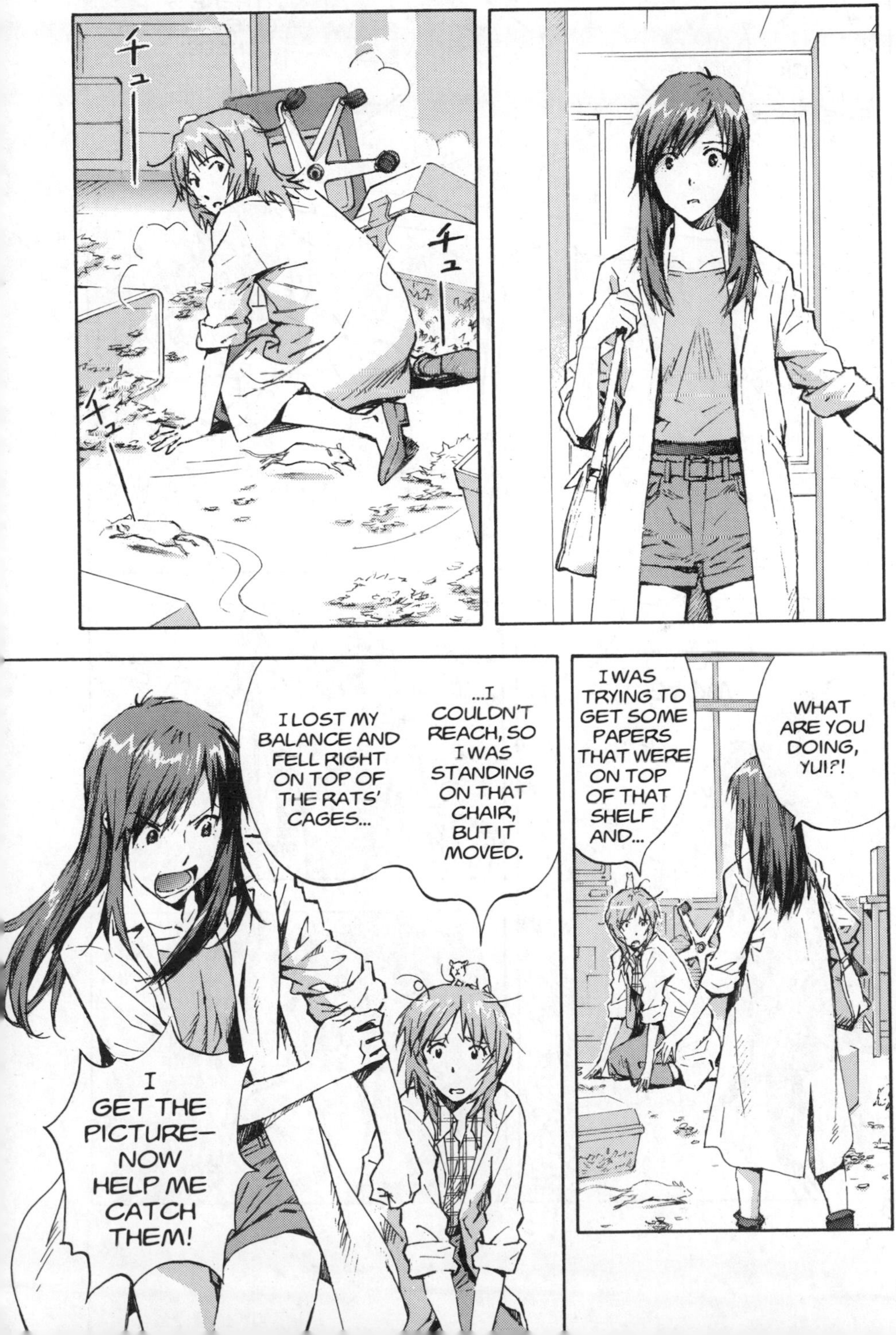
チュー
チュ
チュ
WHAT ARE YOU DOING, YUI?!
I WAS TRYING TO GET SOME PAPERS THAT WERE ON TOP OF THAT SHELF AND...
...I COULDN'T REACH, SO I WAS STANDING ON THAT CHAIR, BUT IT MOVED.
I LOST MY BALANCE AND FELL RIGHT ON TOP OF THE RATS' CAGES...
I GET THE PICTURE— NOW HELP ME CATCH THEM!

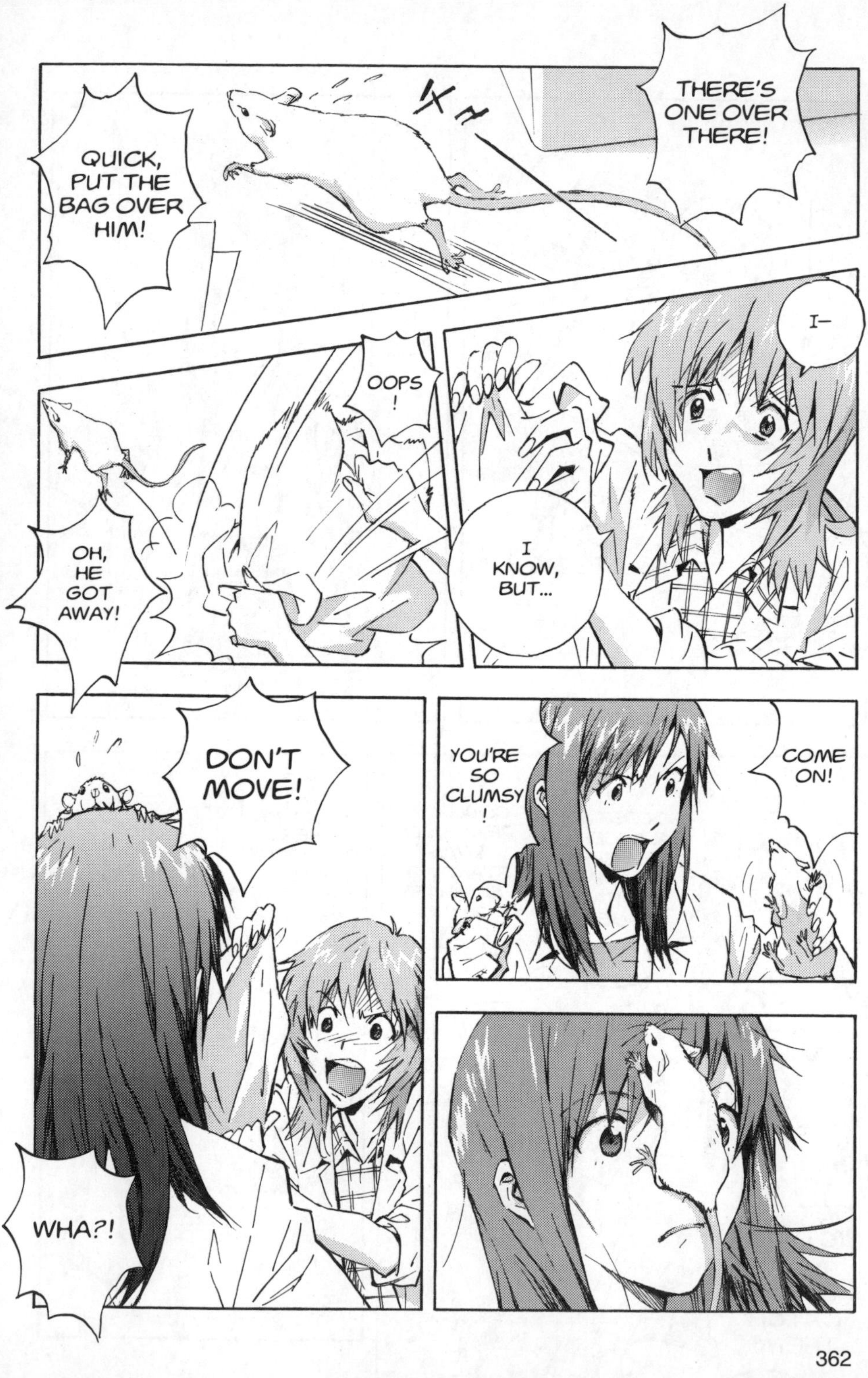
THERE'S ONE OVER THERE!
QUICK, PUT THE BAG OVER HIM!
I—
I KNOW, BUT...
OOPS!
OH, HE GOT AWAY!
COME ON!
YOU'RE SO CLUMSY!
DON'T MOVE!
WHA?!

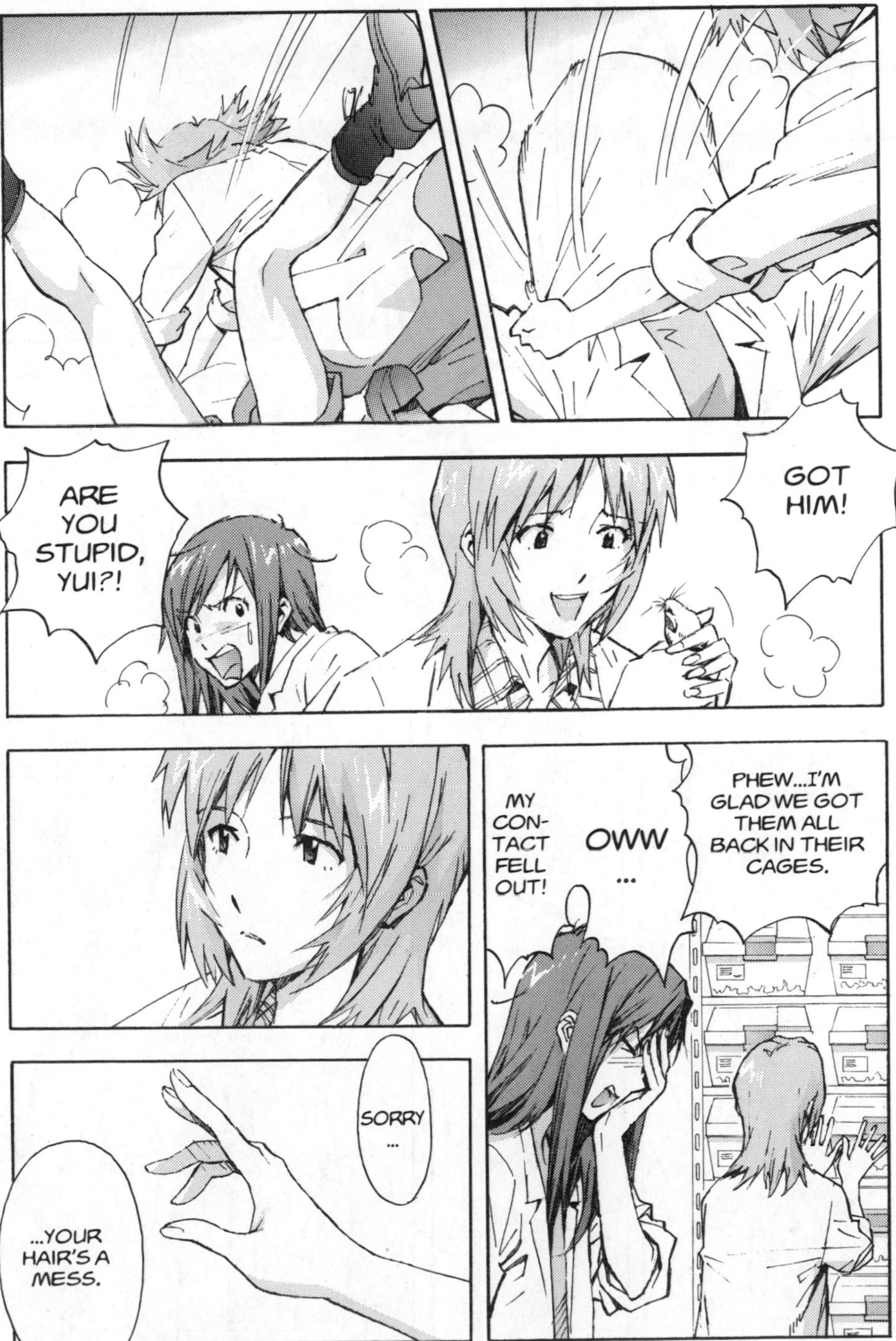
GOT HIM!
ARE YOU STUPID, YUI?!
PHEW...I'M GLAD WE GOT THEM ALL BACK IN THEIR CAGES.
OWW ...
MY CONTACT FELL OUT!
SORRY ...
...YOUR HAIR'S A MESS.

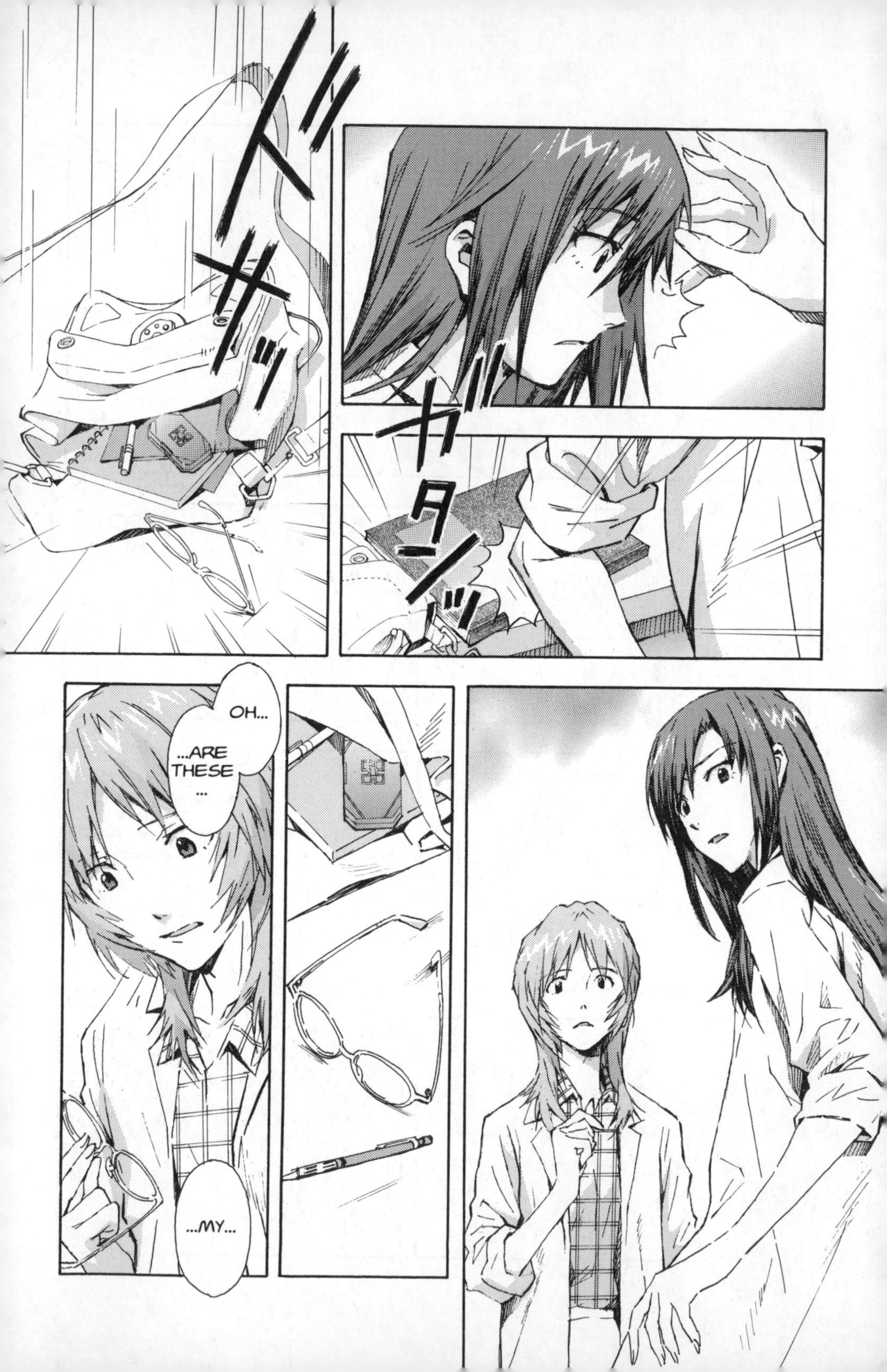
ガタンッ
OH... ...ARE THESE ...
...MY...

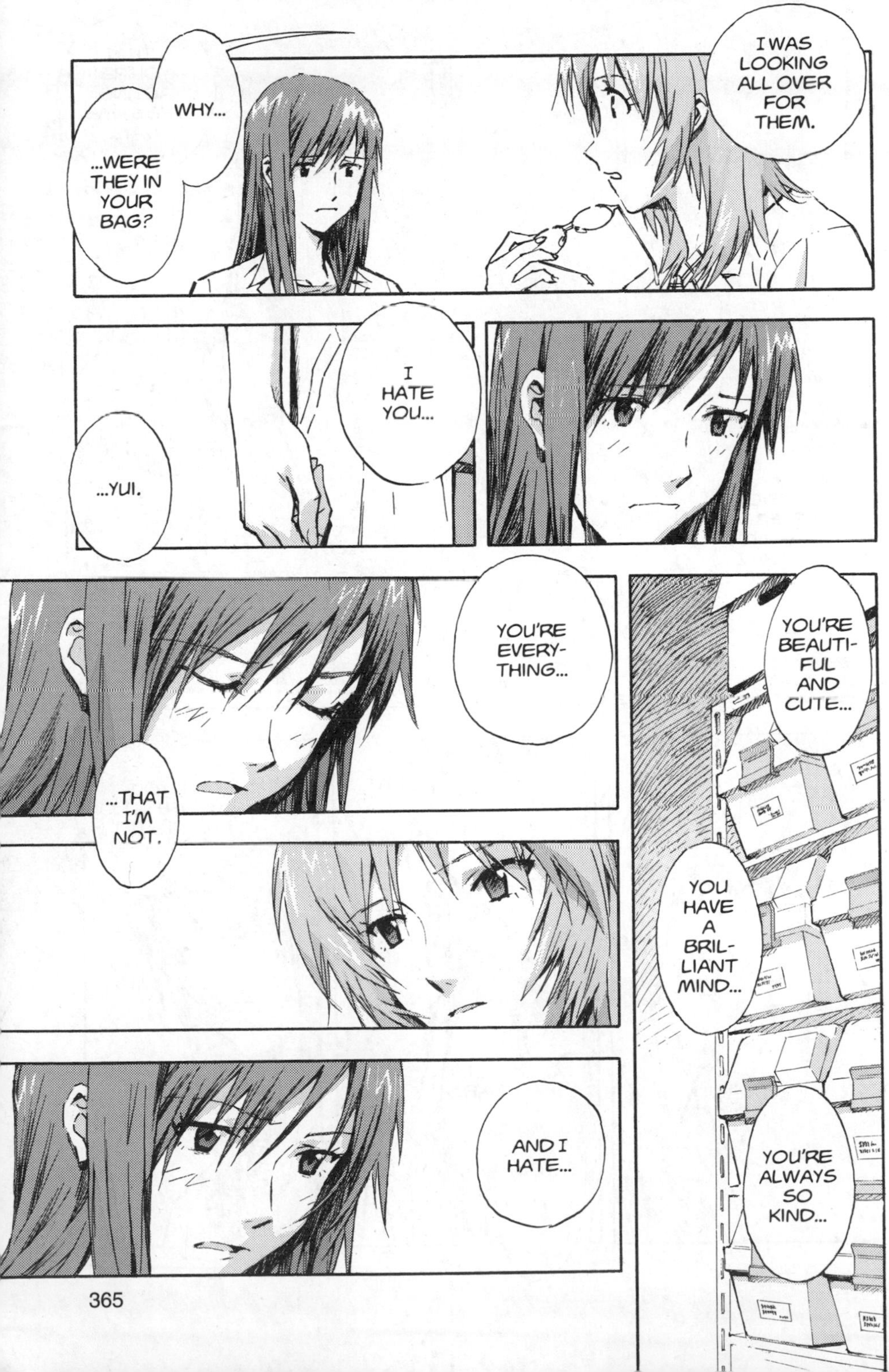
I WAS LOOKING ALL OVER FOR THEM.
WHY...
...WERE THEY IN YOUR BAG?
I HATE YOU...
...YUI.
YOU'RE BEAUTIFUL AND CUTE...
YOU HAVE A BRILLIANT MIND...
YOU'RE ALWAYS SO KIND...
YOU'RE EVERYTHING...
...THAT I'M NOT.
AND I HATE...

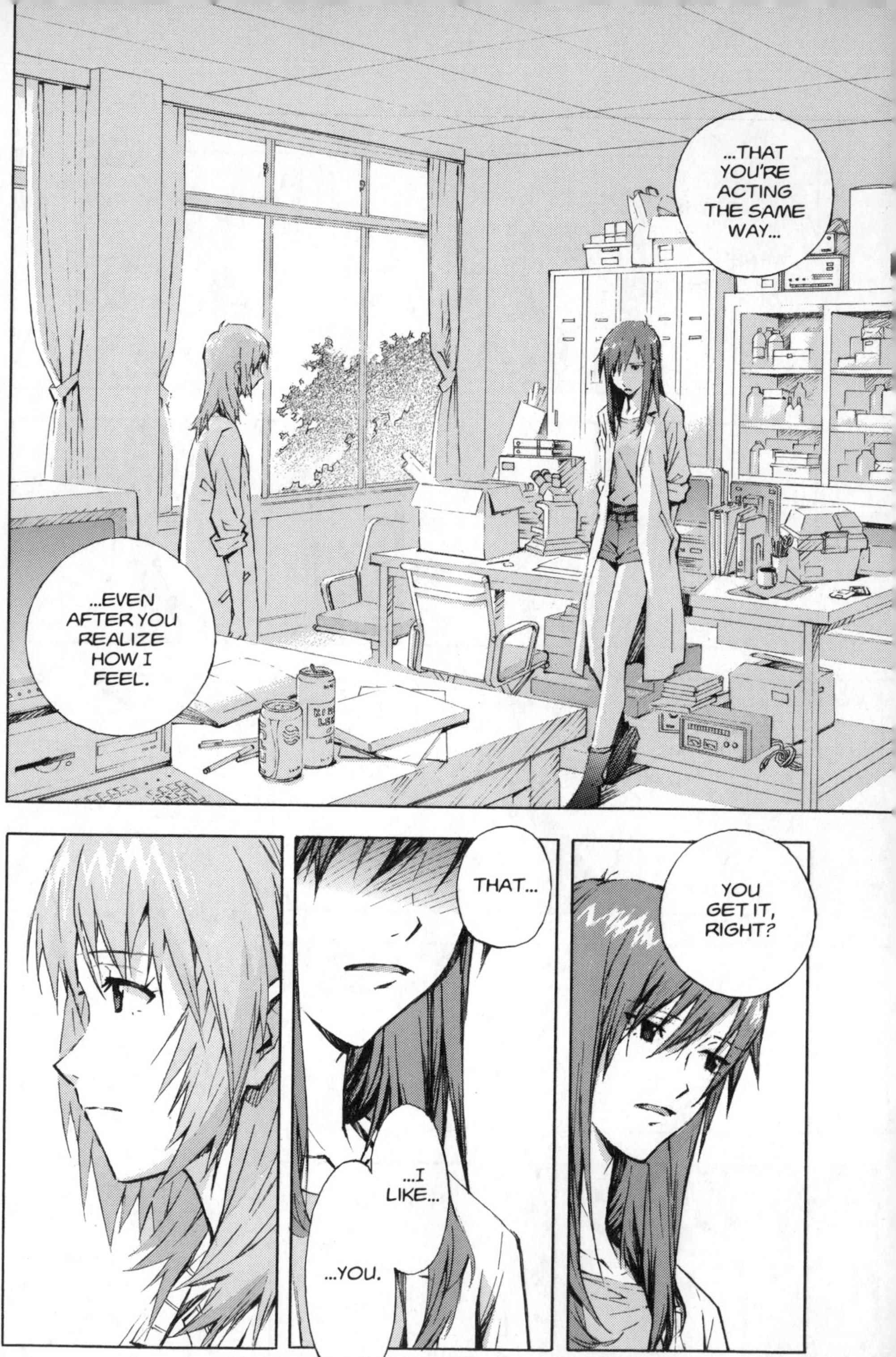
...THAT YOU'RE ACTING THE SAME WAY...
...EVEN AFTER YOU REALIZE HOW I FEEL.
YOU GET IT, RIGHT?
THAT...
...I LIKE...
...YOU.

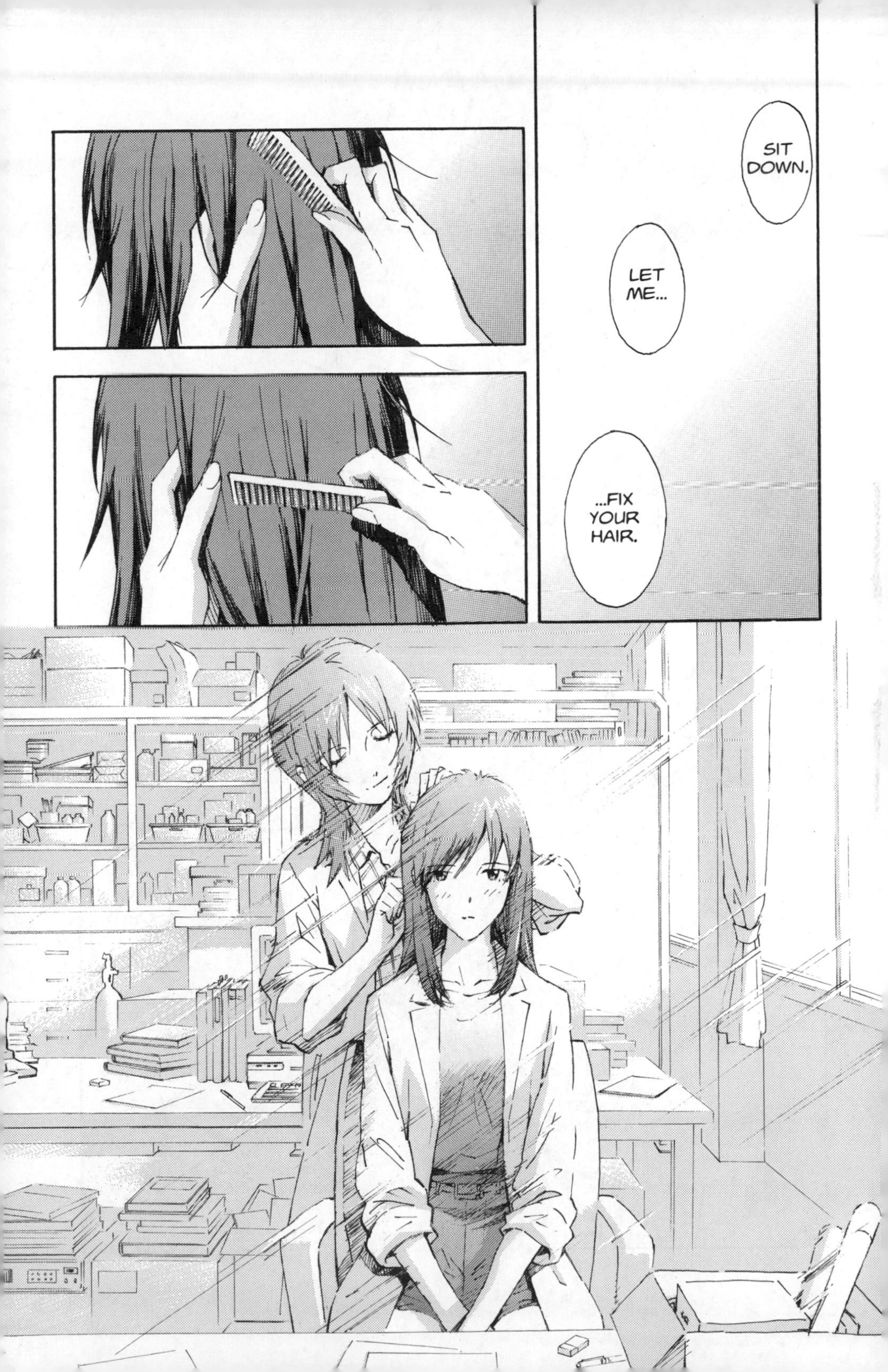
SIT DOWN.
LET ME...
...FIX YOUR HAIR.

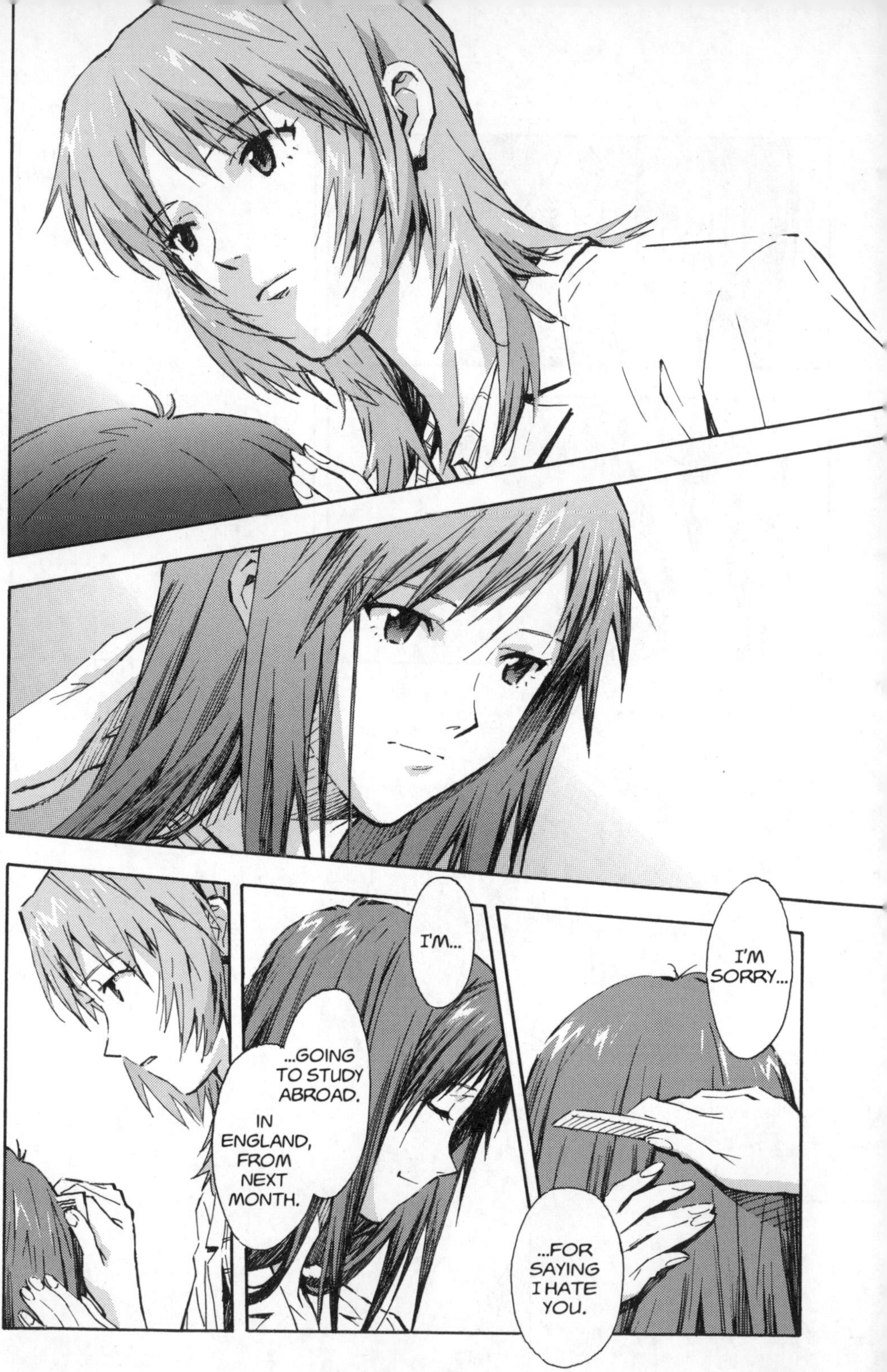
I'M SORRY...
...FOR SAYING I HATE YOU.
I'M...
...GOING TO STUDY ABROAD.
IN ENGLAND, FROM NEXT MONTH.

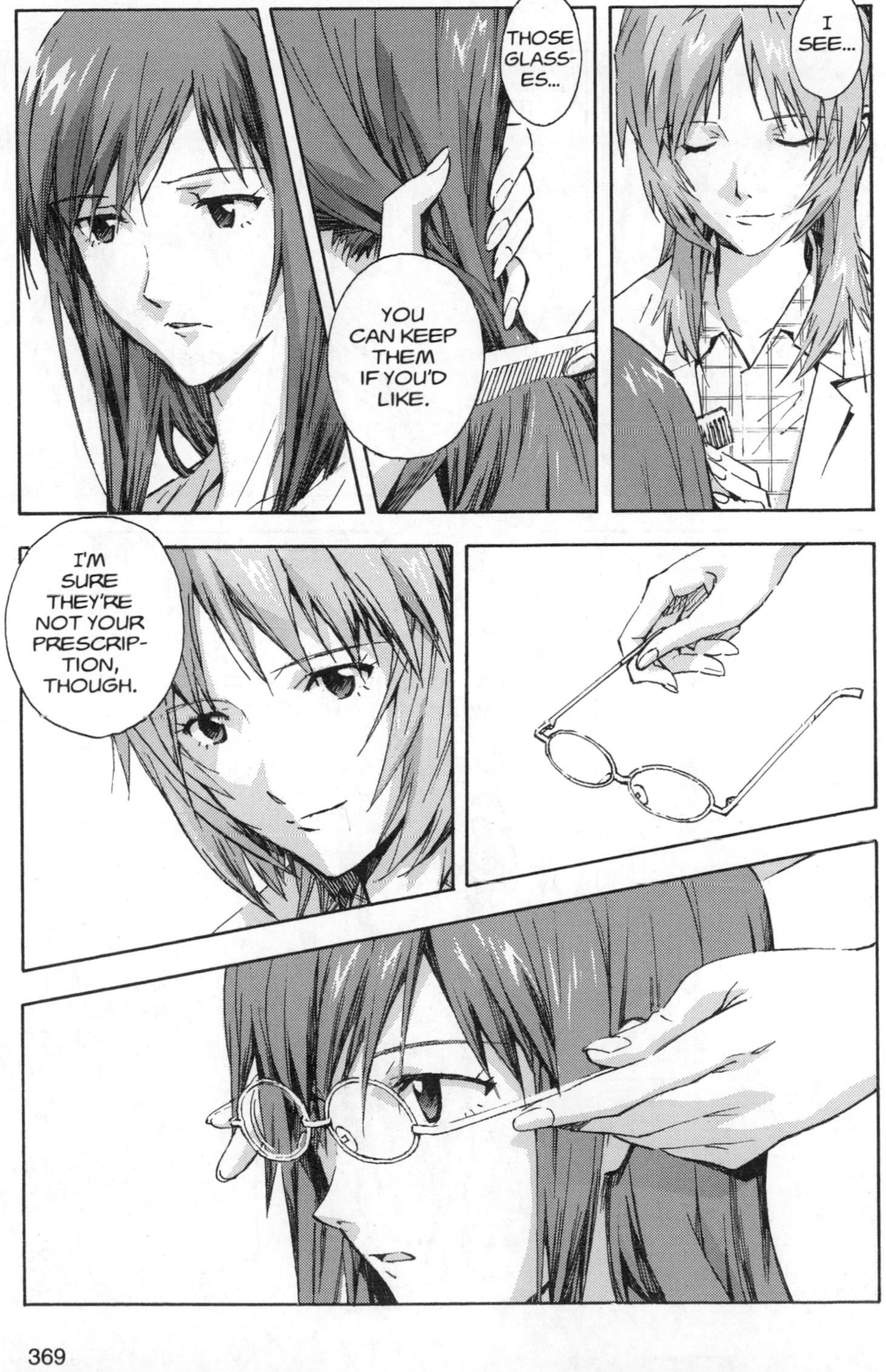
THOSE GLASS-ES...
YOU CAN KEEP THEM IF YOU'D LIKE.
I SEE...
I'M SURE THEY'RE NOT YOUR PRESCRIP-TION, THOUGH.

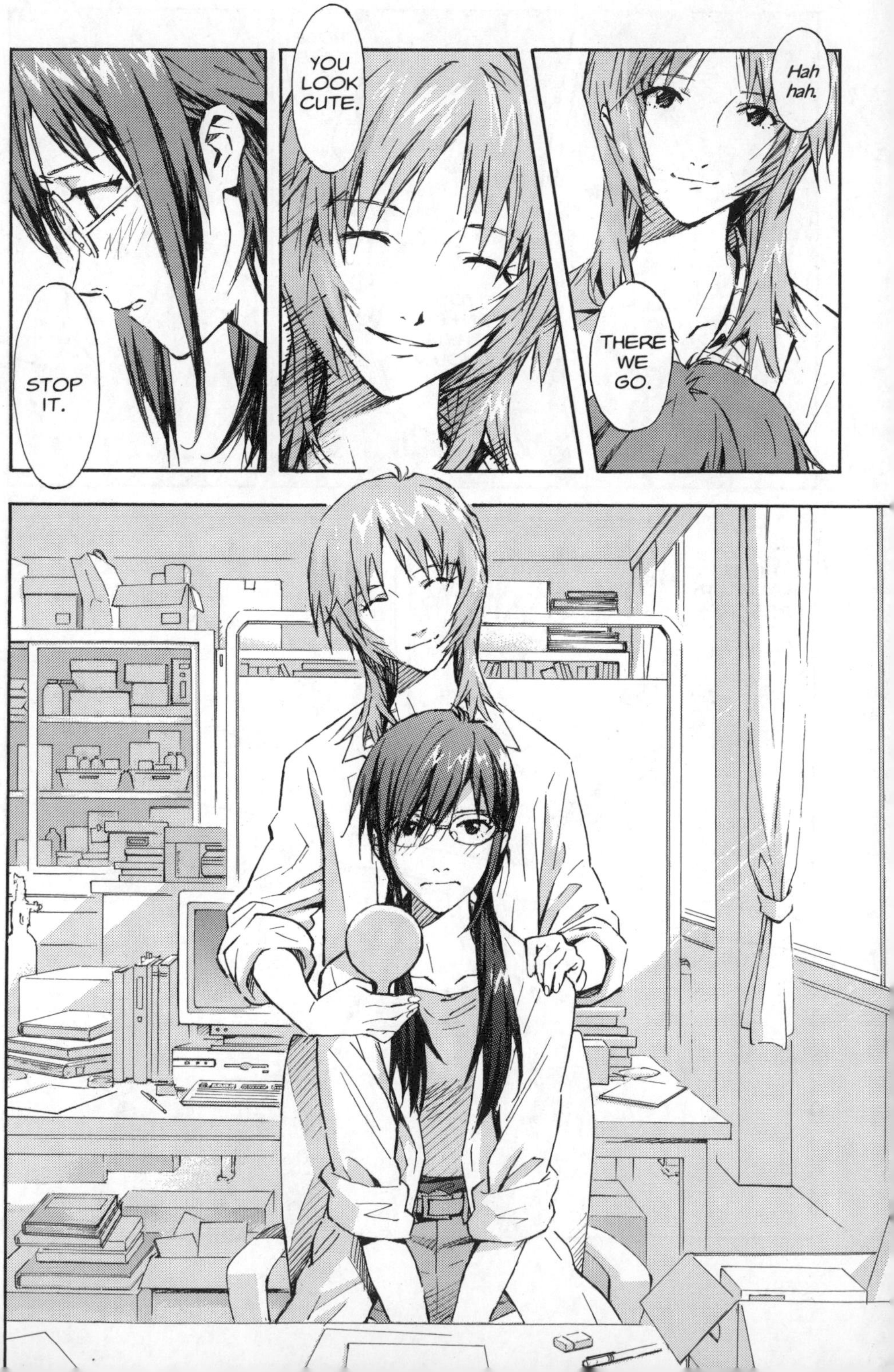
Hah hah.
THERE WE GO.
YOU LOOK CUTE.
STOP IT.

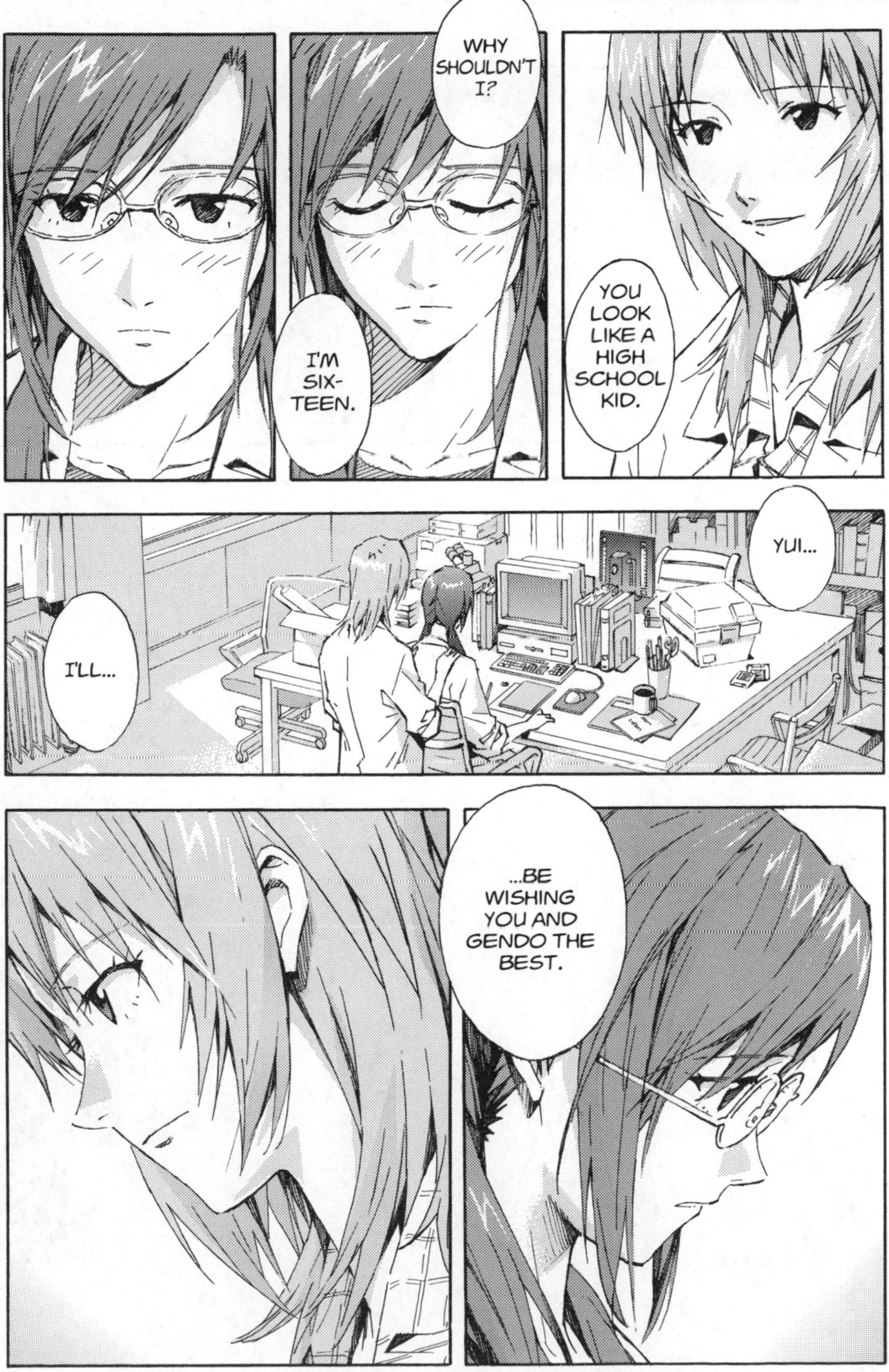
YOU LOOK LIKE A HIGH SCHOOL KID.
WHY SHOULDN'T I?
I'M SIX-TEEN.
YUI...
I'LL...
...BE WISHING YOU AND GENDO THE BEST.

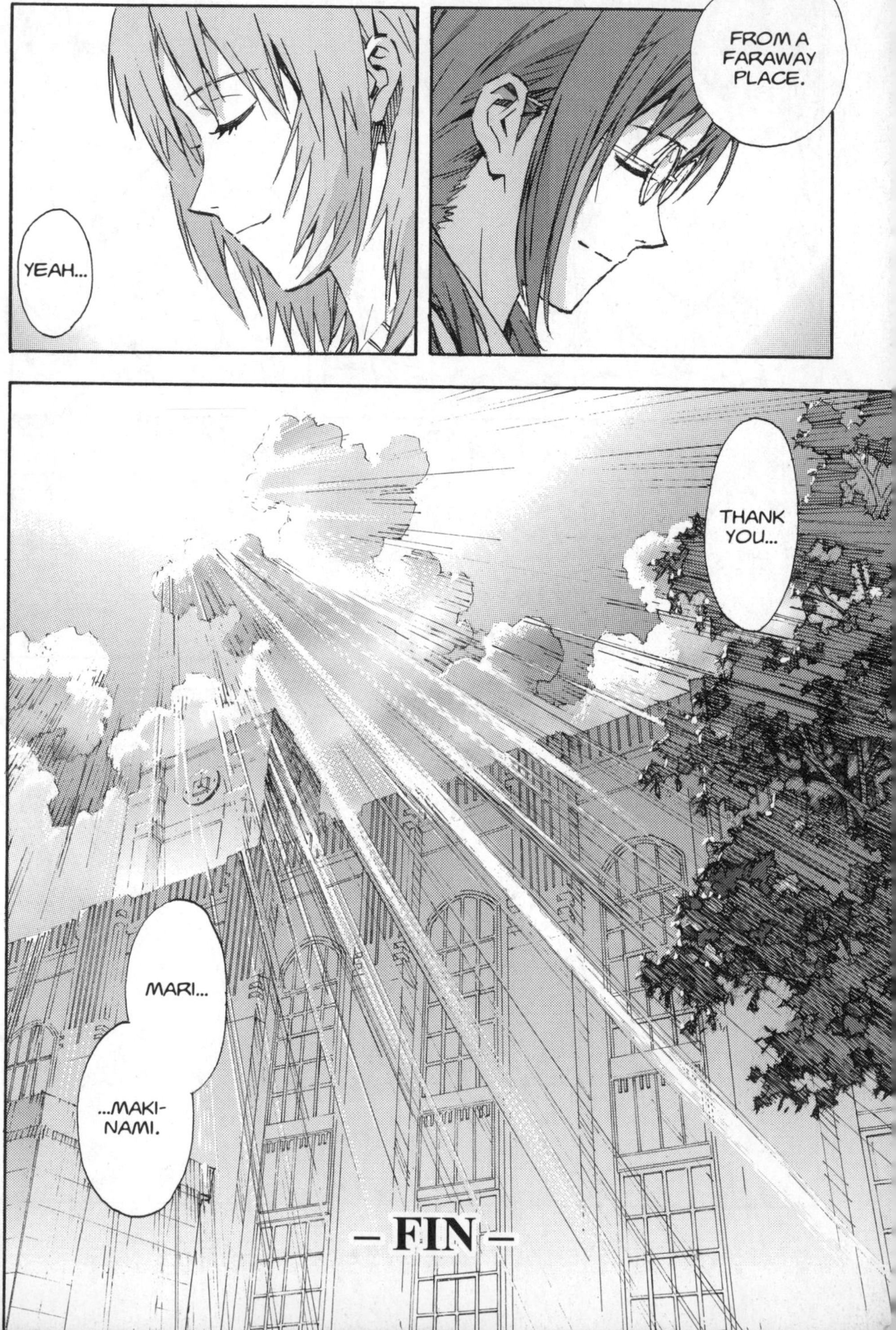
FROM A FARAWAY PLACE.
YEAH...
THANK YOU...
MARI...
...MAKI-NAMI.
– FIN –

NEON GENESIS EVANGELION

YOSHIYUKI SADAMOTO
PROFILE

Born January 29, 1962, in
Tokuyama city (now part
of Shūnan city), Yamaguchi
Prefecture. Blood type O.
He is known for his work
as a character designer
and animation director
on titles such as *Royal
Space Force: The Wings of
Honnêamise, Nadia: The Secret
of Blue Water, Neon Genesis
Evangelion, FLCL, Diebuster,
The Girl Who Leapt Through
Time, Summer Wars, Evangelion
(New Movie Series), Wolf
Children*, and more.

STAFF LIST

The Author — Yoshiyuki Sadamoto

Assistants — Mari Araki
Hidekazu Aburaya
Shiichi Kugura
Yasuhiro Henmi

Shigeto Koyama
Kumiko Sano

Special Thanks — GAINAX

Original Concept / khara

Thanks to MAKO

Thank you very much for waiting!
Here is the final volume.

I would like to say thank you to all my readers
for staying with me for such a long time.

I look forward to meeting you again
with my next work.

YOSHIYUKI SADAMOTO

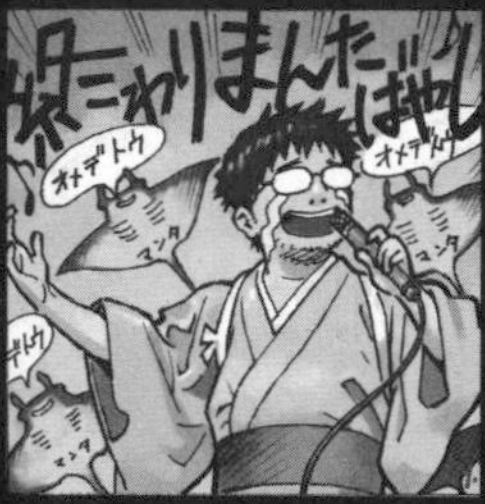
終わりまんたばやし
オメデトウ
オメデトウ
マンタ
マンタ
マンタ

*THE MANTAS SAY "CONGRATS" AS THE AUTHOR CELEBRATES THE CONCLUSION. IT'S THE FINAL VOLUME!

WRITER AND ARTIST

I'm filled with mixed emotions as I write this, but without a doubt I can say that it feels as if a huge weight has been lifted off my shoulders.

So many things have happened in the world over the last 20 years, yet by some sort of miraculous blessing, I'm able to sit in the same chair at the same desk and continue working.

Guess I've got my ancestors and some sort of god to thank for that.

I don't know how long I'll be able to keep on drawing, but I hope to keep at it and announce projects at my own pace.

To my readership, thank you so much for sticking with me all this time.

To my assistants, staff, and everyone involved that helped me along the way, I am incredibly grateful for you all.

See you again on my next project.

NERV

GOD'S IN HIS HEAVEN. ALL'S RIGHT WITH THE WORLD.

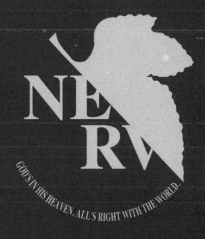

Shinji Ikari, Age 14

Shinji was the "Third Child" chosen to pilot the monstrous Evangelion series; biomechanical combat units developed by the secret UN paramilitary agency known as NERV. Resentful of his father and desperate for his approval, Shinji climbed into the entry plug of Eva Unit-01 to do battle with the enigmatic Angels.

Rei Ayanami, Age 14

Rei is the "First Child" to be chosen to pilot an Evangelion. While piloting Eva Unit-01, she was severely wounded fighting the Angel Sachiel during the same battle in which Shinji arrived at Tokyo-3.

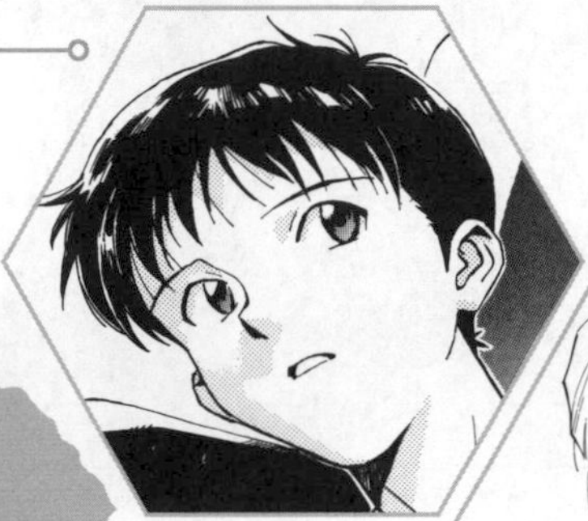

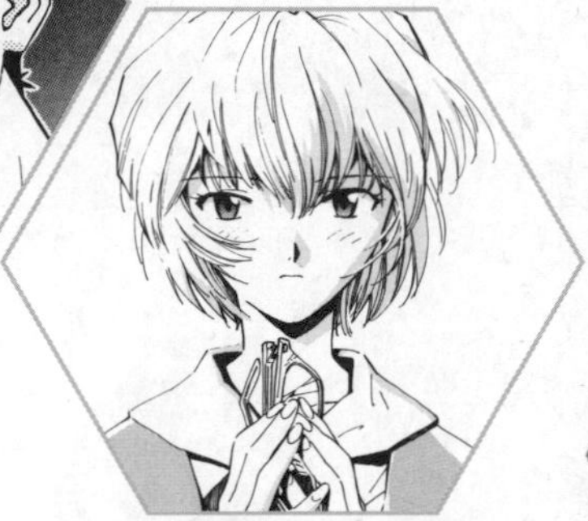

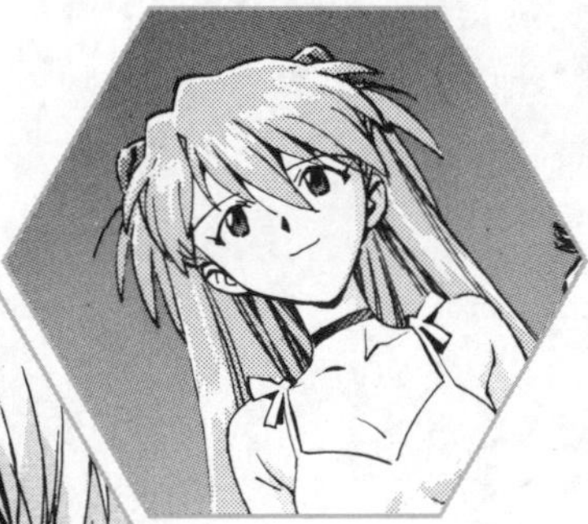

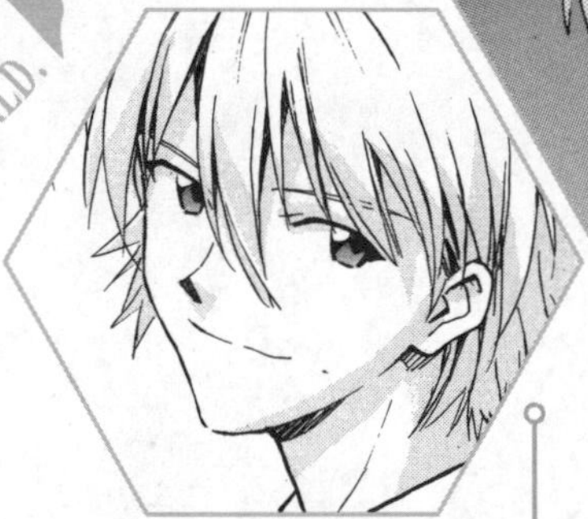

Asuka Langley Soryu, Age 14

A U.S. citizen of mixed Japanese and German ancestry, Asuka is a product of eugenic breeding. Selected to begin training as an Eva pilot from a very early age, Asuka is an excellent fighter, but she struggles with traumatic memories of her childhood.

Kaworu Nagisa, Age 14?

Kaworu introduces himself to NERV as the "Fifth Child." SEELE has sent him to NERV directly, not bothering to go through the Marduk Agency. But as NERV keeps the First Angel, Adam, so has SEELE kept the last, Tabris, the true name and identity of Kaworu Nagisa.

GENDO IKARI, AGE 48

Shinji's father. This ruthless and enigmatic man is the guiding force behind the development of NERV's Evangelion system. He is also the man entrusted to carry out the even more secret Instrumentality Project. Gendo was an absent father, leaving Shinji's upbringing to the boy's aunt and uncle.

MISATO KATSURAGI, AGE 29

Captain Katsuragi is the chief tactician for NERV, responsible for planning and guiding Evangelion missions against the Angels. She has forced Shinji to move into her apartment in an attempt to "fix" his "attitude"...

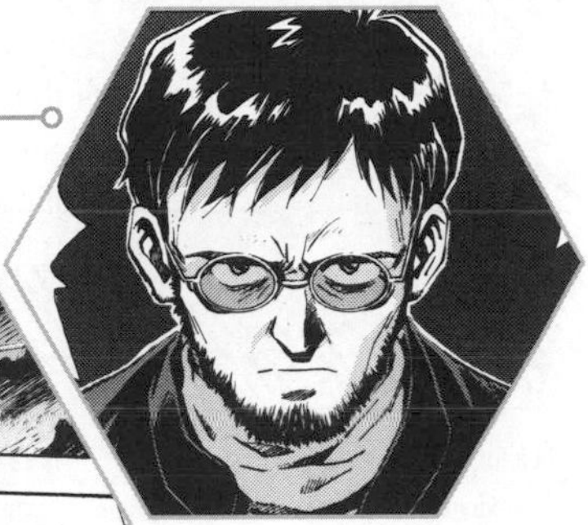

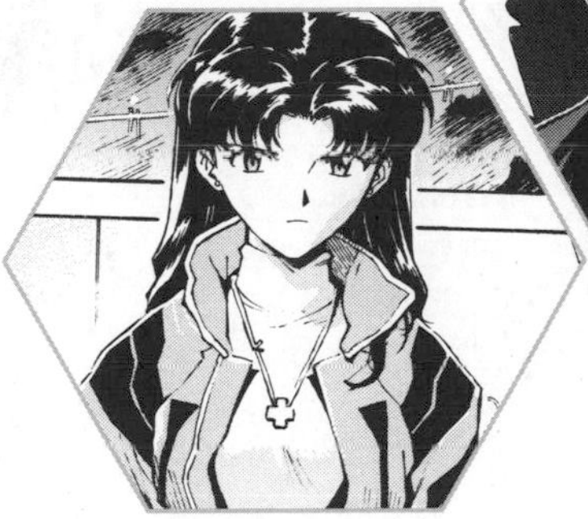

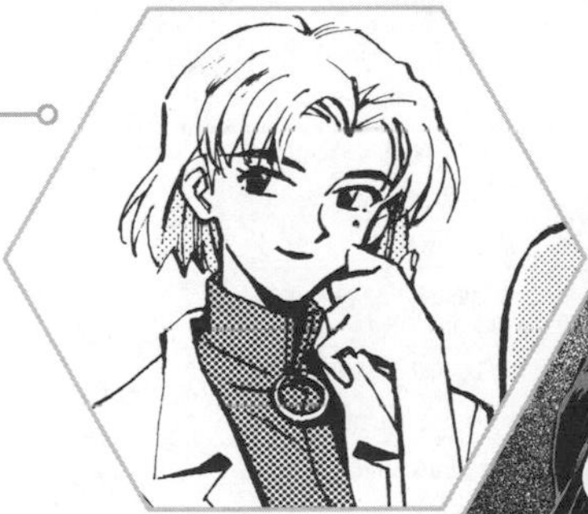

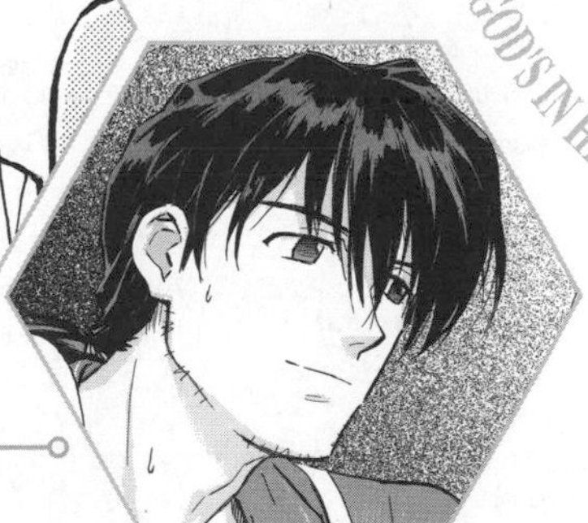

RITSUKO AKAGI, AGE 30

Technical supervisor for NERV's Project E (Evangelion). Dr. Akagi is a polymath genius who rode the wave of scientific revolution following the cracking of the human genetic code at the end of the twentieth century. Her disciplines include physics, biotechnology and computer science.

RYOJI KAJI, AGE 29

Intelligence agent working for NERV, although its senior personnel know that he is also spying for the Japanese Interior Ministry. It has also been suggested that Kaji is secretly working for a third party, SEELE. Despite his handsome, cool exterior, Kaji regards himself as weak, his life haunted by a youthful betrayal.

SOUND EFFECTS GLOSSARY

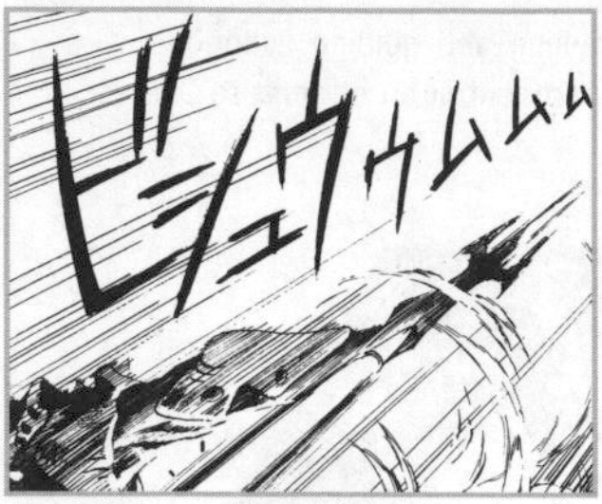
ビジュウウムムム

The sound effects in this 2-in-1 edition of *Neon Genesis Evangelion* have been preserved in their original Japanese format. To avoid additional lettering cluttering up the panels we have provided this list of sound effects (FX). Each FX is listed by page and panel number, so for example 6-5 would mean the FX is on page 6 in panel 5. If there is a third number, it means there is more than one FX in the panel—6-5-1 and 6-5-2 for example. The transliteration is given, followed by the English translation/approximation.

Part 1

6-1	gogogogogogo [rumbling]
6-2	dou [explosion]
7-1	doooooo [blast]
7-2	zuo [blast]
8/9	zuzuzu zuzuzu [rumbling]
10-2	gakiiiiii [blades clashing]
11-2	gakiiin [hitting away]
11-4	pipipipipipipi [beeps]
12-1	zuo [attacking]
12-2	do [stabbing]
14-1	ga [biting]
14-3	gugigi [pulling]
15-1	buchii [breaking]
15-3	bushuu [liquid spurting]
16-1	piii [beep]
17-1	gacha gacha [rattling]
19-4	dodoon [explosion]
20-1	ga [hitting]
20-2	do [hitting]
26-3	pipi [beeps]
26-4	gakooon [opening]
29-1	do [stabbing]
29-3	ga [clashing]
31-1	do [impaling]
32-1	zuzun [slamming down]
39-1	gugu [starting to get up]
39-2	gubyuru [getting up]
39-3	gigigi [menacing grunts]
39-4	shuuu [steam]
39-5	zaza [walking]
40-1	basa [wings appearing]
40-2	gigigigi [menacing grunts]
43-5	pii [beep]
44-5	pii [beep]
48-1	basa [wings flapping]
48-2	basasasa [wings flapping]
50-4	do [stabbing]
52-1	doshu [stabbing]
53-3	bashu [firing]
54-2	ba [fast movement]
54-3	ga [striking]
56-2	zun [stab]
62-2	gugu [pulling free]
63-3	dodon [falling]
68-1	baki bakin [breaking]
68-2	oooooo [roaring]
68/69-6	shuo [flying]
73-3	dokun [strong sensation striking]
76-2	byu [raising sword]
76-3	byuo [swinging]
77-1/2	dohyuru [spinning]
77-3	zun zun [striking]
78-1	zuvuvu [drilling]
78-2	zuzu [drilling]
78-3	basa basasa [wings flapping]
79-1	ga [biting]
79-2	ga ga [biting]
83-1	pasa [clothes falling]
84-3	zuru [arm separating]
84-4	dosun [arm falling]
90-4	pii [beep]
94-1	gubo [splattering]
95-2	zubyuru [arm reforming]
102-1/2	zuzuzuzuzu [rumbling]
102-2/3	gogogogogo [rumbling]
104-1/3	dooooooooo [blast]
105-1/2/3	dodododododododo [rumbling]
105-3	bii bii [beeps]
107-3	gogogogogogo [rumbling]
111-2	zuzozozozo [sliding]
111-2-2	zan [setting down]
119-3	pan [gunshot]
122-1	goho [coughing]
125-2	dokun [strong sensation striking]
125-3	dokun dokun [strong sensation striking]
125-4	dokun [strong sensation striking]
126-1	dokun [strong sensation striking]
132/133-2	vuwa [swoop of wings]
138-2	zushu [stabbing]
139-1/2/3	bushururu}ru [enveloping]
149-1/2	pipipipipipipipi [beeps]
149-4	gogogogogogogogo [rumbling]
155-3	zushuuuu [powerful burst]
160-1	miin miin miin miin [cicadas]
166-2	pan [smacking]
176-1	miin minminmin miin miin min [cicadas]

Part 2

185-1/2/3	gukyu gugyurugyu gyukyukyu [stabbing]
188-2	zububu [piercing]
188-3	zuzuzu [entering]
194-1	pasha [exploding]
198-3	pasha [exploding]

199-3	basha [exploding]
201-3	pasha [exploding]
215-2	pasha [exploding]
221-2	basha [exploding]
263-1/2/3/4	miin miin miin miin [cicadas]
275-1/2/3	bushuuuuuu [gushing]
280-1/2	guoooooo [rising]
293-1/2/3	gubyuru [untwisting]
320-1	za [footstep]
320-2	zaku [footstep]
322-1	za [footstep]
324-1	vuu [phone vibrating]
324-2	vuu [phone vibrating]
327-5	puan [train honking]
328-1	pushuu [doors opening]
328-4	gatan [doors closing]
333-1	zawa zawa zawa [people talking]
339-3	ban [slapping]
339-4	goho [coughing]
346-1/2/3	miin miin miin [cicadas]
352-3	byuu gakon [can falling out]
358-3	gaya gaya [hallway noise]
360-1	kana kana kana kana kana [bell ringing]
360-4/5/6	gatan don goton [crashing and banging noises]
361-2	chuu chuu chuu [rats squeaking]
362-1	chuu [rats squeaking]
364-2	gatan [slam]
364-3	dosa [bag flopping down]

NERV

GOD'S IN HIS HEAVEN. ALL'S RIGHT WITH THE WORLD.

Hey! You're Reading in the Wrong Direction!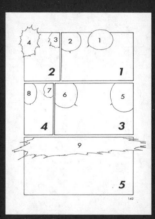

This is the **end** of this graphic novel!

To properly enjoy this VIZ graphic novel, please turn it around and begin reading from **right to left.** Unlike English, Japanese is read right to left, so Japanese comics are read in reverse order from the way English comics are typically read.

Follow the action this way

This book has been printed in the original Japanese format in order to preserve the orientation of the original artwork. Have fun with it!